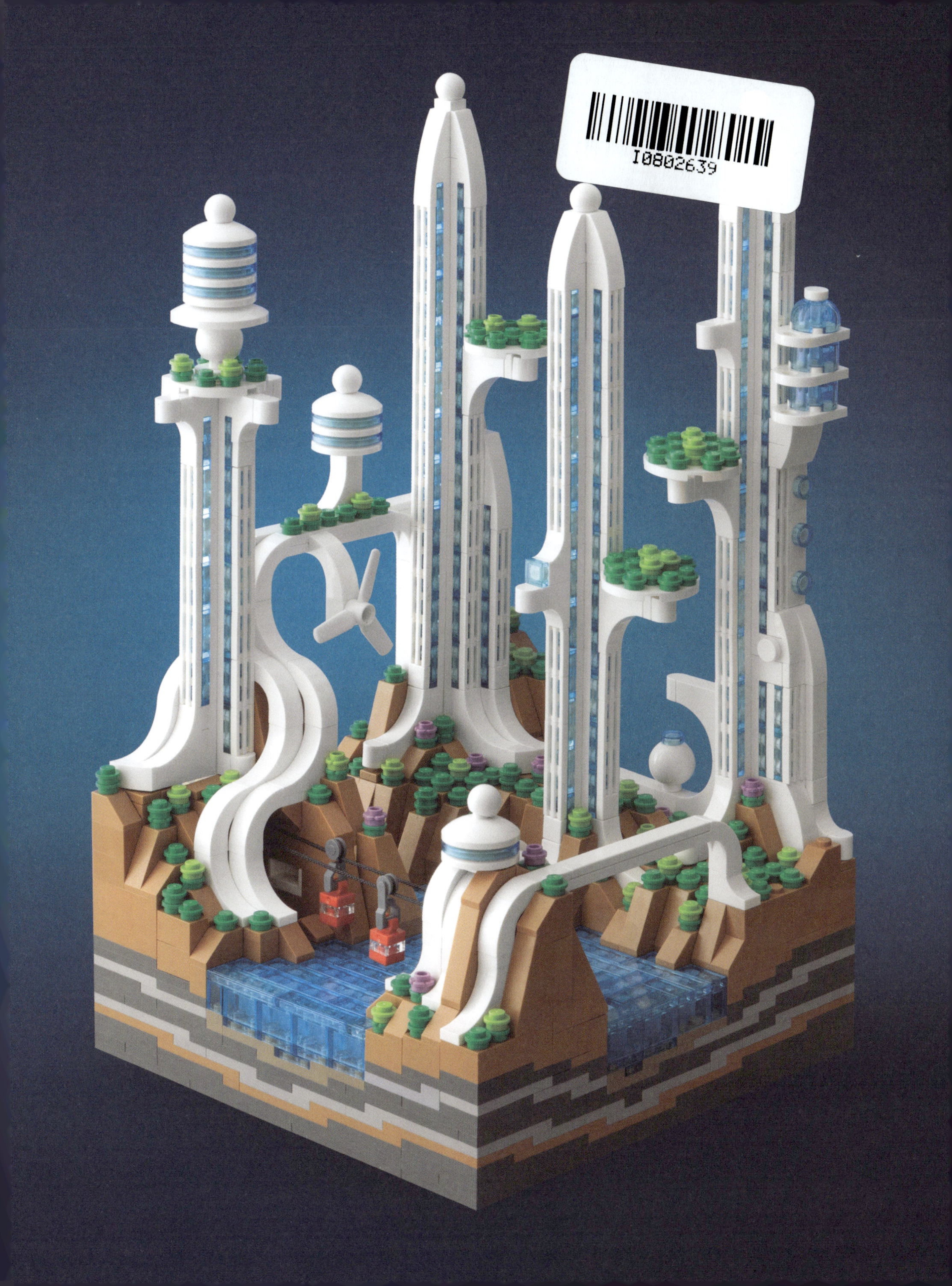

BUILDING LEGO® WORLDS

BUILDING LEGO® WORLDS

CREATE THE WORLDS YOU'VE ONLY IMAGINED

JEFF FRIESEN

no starch press®

SAN FRANCISCO

For Tetjana.

We played with LEGO the day we met. It wasn't exactly the coolest thing for people our age to be doing back then. Was it really more than 30 years ago?

And for June.

You arrived, and the world was painted in colors we had never imagined.

We don't play LEGO anymore, but this book exists only because you do.

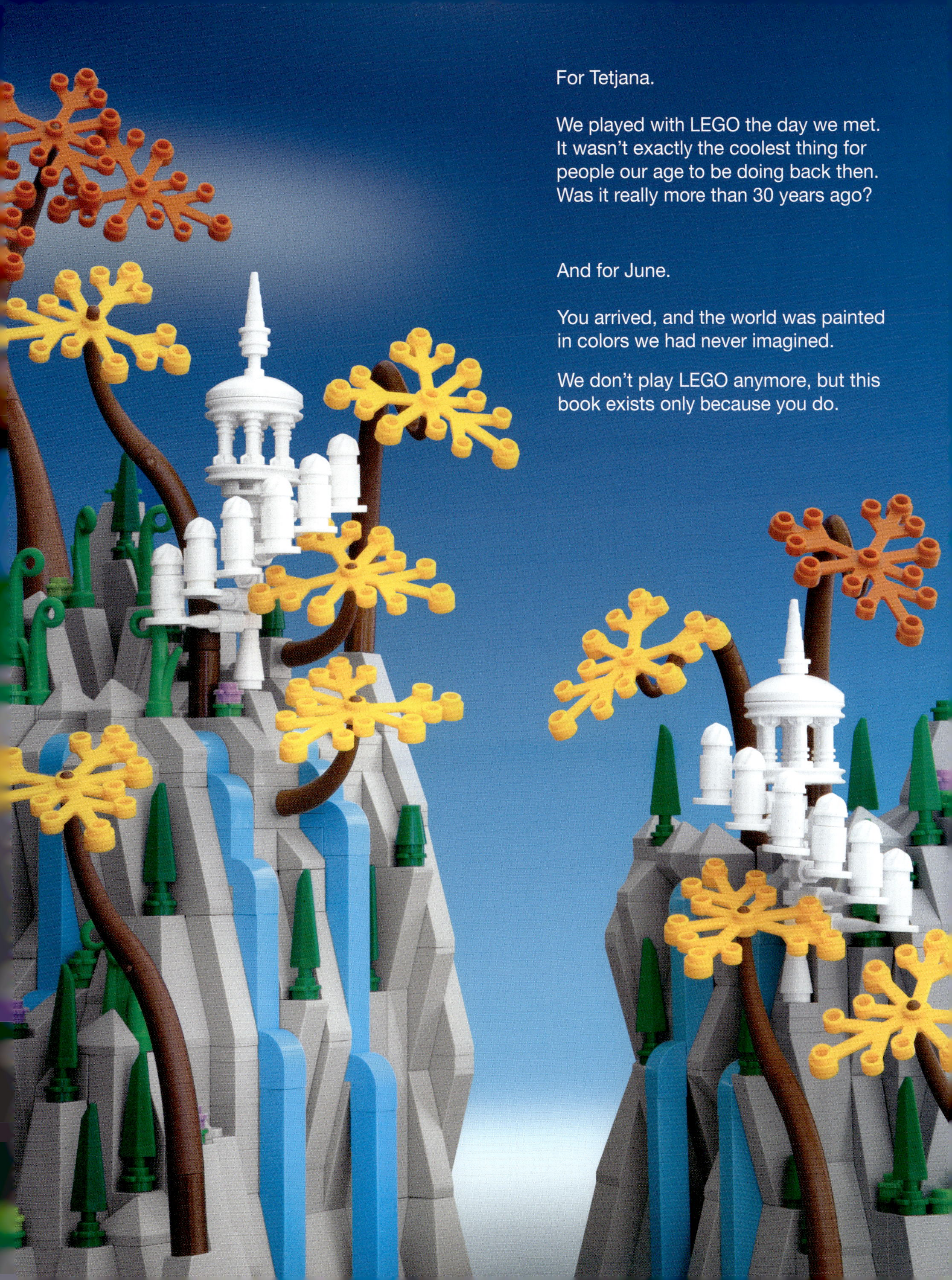

CONTENTS

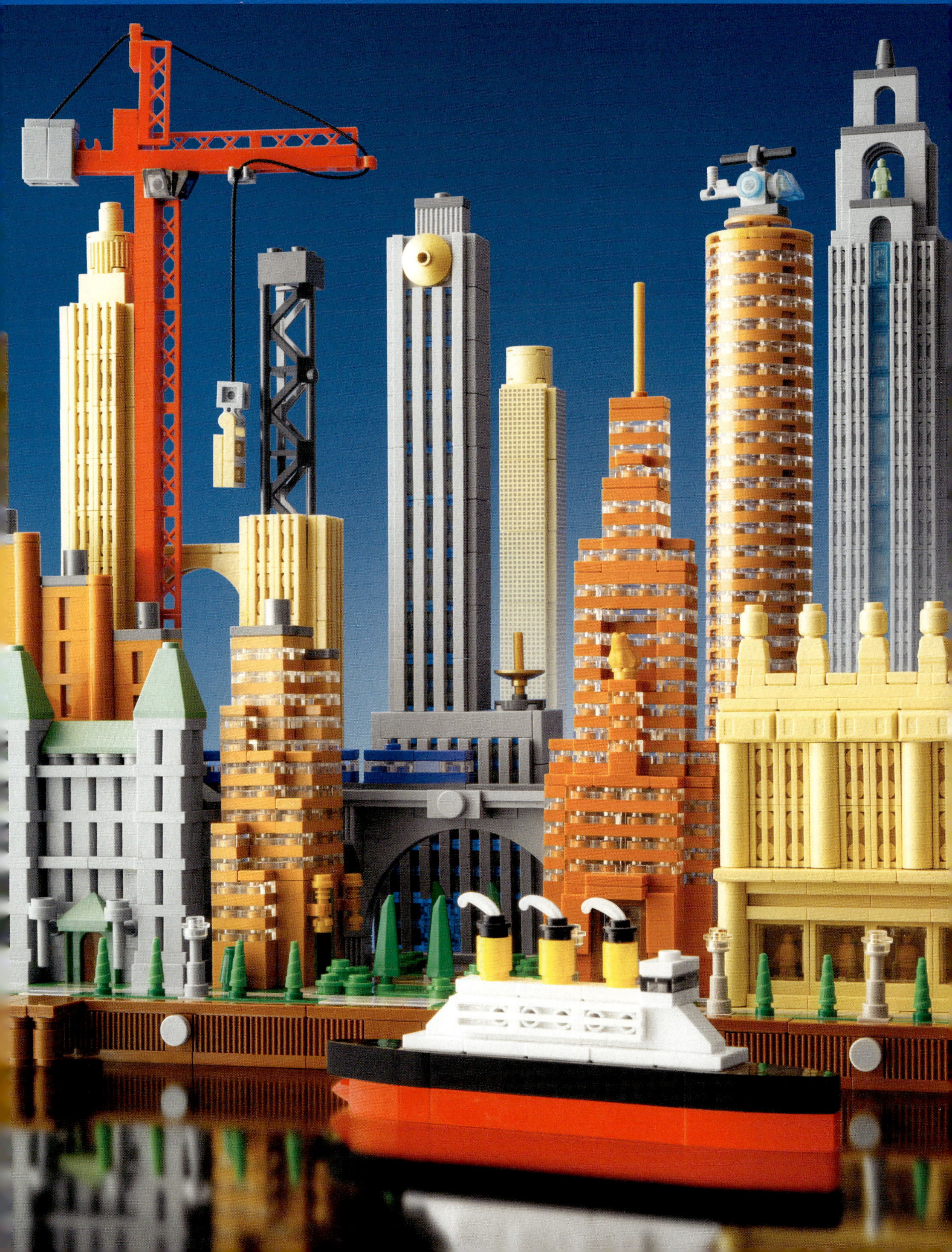

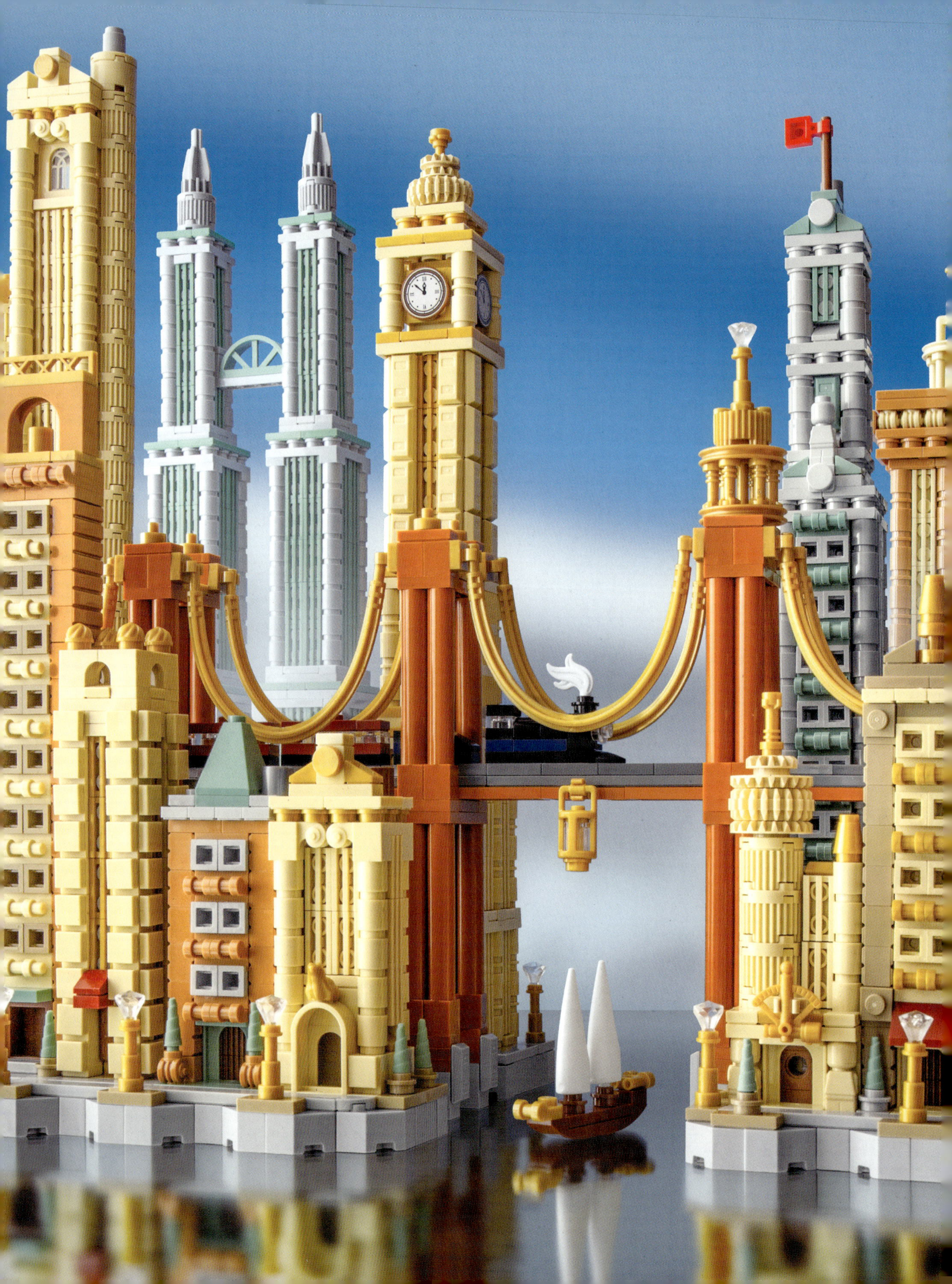

INTRODUCTION

WE ARE ALL WORLD-BUILDERS

As children, we love building worlds. We sculpt castles from sand, stack blocks into cities, and turn blankets into mountains. Without being taught, we effortlessly bring kingdoms, spaceports, and enchanted forests to life. If we're lucky, we have one of the best world-building tools of all: LEGO bricks.

As we grow up, LEGO gives us a way to keep building worlds—maybe no longer for play, but for creative expression and the tactile joy of just making something. Constructing a LEGO world offers the satisfying complexity of a puzzle game. It challenges your thinking but keeps you engaged every step of the way.

World-building is a powerful tool in storytelling. From the pages of literature to iconic movie moments, unforgettable settings draw us in and hold us there. Places like Gotham City or the dusty planet of Tatooine aren't just stages for characters—they become living characters themselves.

Now it's your turn to bring worlds to life. Gather your bricks, trust your imagination, and build the worlds that live in your mind. You've known how to do this since you were a kid.

HOW TO USE THIS BOOK

Think of this book as an extension of the LEGO building tradition. Its chapters are part of an ordered system, featuring modular elements you can combine in countless ways.

The first part lays the foundation for your world-building journey. You'll learn how to create a base and add natural features such as water, slopes, cliffs, and plant life. From there, the focus shifts to man-made structures, including streets, buildings, and modes of transportation.

The second part explores themed worlds, from pirate coves and elven havens to steampunk factories and cyberpunk dystopias. These chapters provide instructions for genre-specific builds and show how architecture shapes atmosphere.

Feel free to mix and match models from different chapters. If you want a stately airship soaring over a Roman temple, just build it! The possibilities are limitless.

Above all, this book is an invitation to create your own world. Read it in order, or pop in on a random page. Use the instructions as a guide or as a springboard for your own creations. The world is yours.

BUILDING TIPS

LEGO collections are as individual as fingerprints, and you may not have every brick needed to build a model in this book. Here are some tips for getting the parts you need.

BRICKLINK

The model on the right page uses loads of uncommon jumper arch elements—not to mention all the fancy sword hilt with dragon head blocks. If you tried to collect those pieces by buying complete LEGO sets, they'd cost as much as a used car. Luckily, we have BrickLink.

The BrickLink website is an indispensable resource for LEGO builders. It's a global marketplace for individual LEGO elements, where you can search by part name, number, or color. To keep shipping costs down, you can filter your search by country and order from shops closer to home. You can even add multiple items to a Wanted List and see which stores carry everything you need.

Most LEGO elements in this book are accompanied by part numbers, making them easy to find on *https://www.bricklink.com*.

MAKE BRICKS FROM BRICKS

Not every brick needs to be an exact match. A 2×4 brick can be replaced by two 2×2 bricks or four 1×2 bricks. It can also be made by stacking three 2×4 plates, and so on. LEGO building is flexible, and creativity often comes from problem-solving with the parts you already have.

COLOR SCHEMES

You can substitute any color in the instructions with one that fits your vision or that you simply have on hand. A waterfall doesn't have to be medium azure; it can be classic blue, dark blue, or even lavender, if that's your thing. Also, because interior bricks won't be visible from the outside, a cacophonous mismatch of colors is perfectly fine.

MAKE IT YOUR OWN

Just like with colors, you can tweak the instructions to make a model your own. Try new shapes and layouts—there's no wrong way to be creative!

A free, 160-page PDF of the complete build instructions for the Classic Skyscrapers city is available at *https://nostarch.com/building-lego-worlds*.

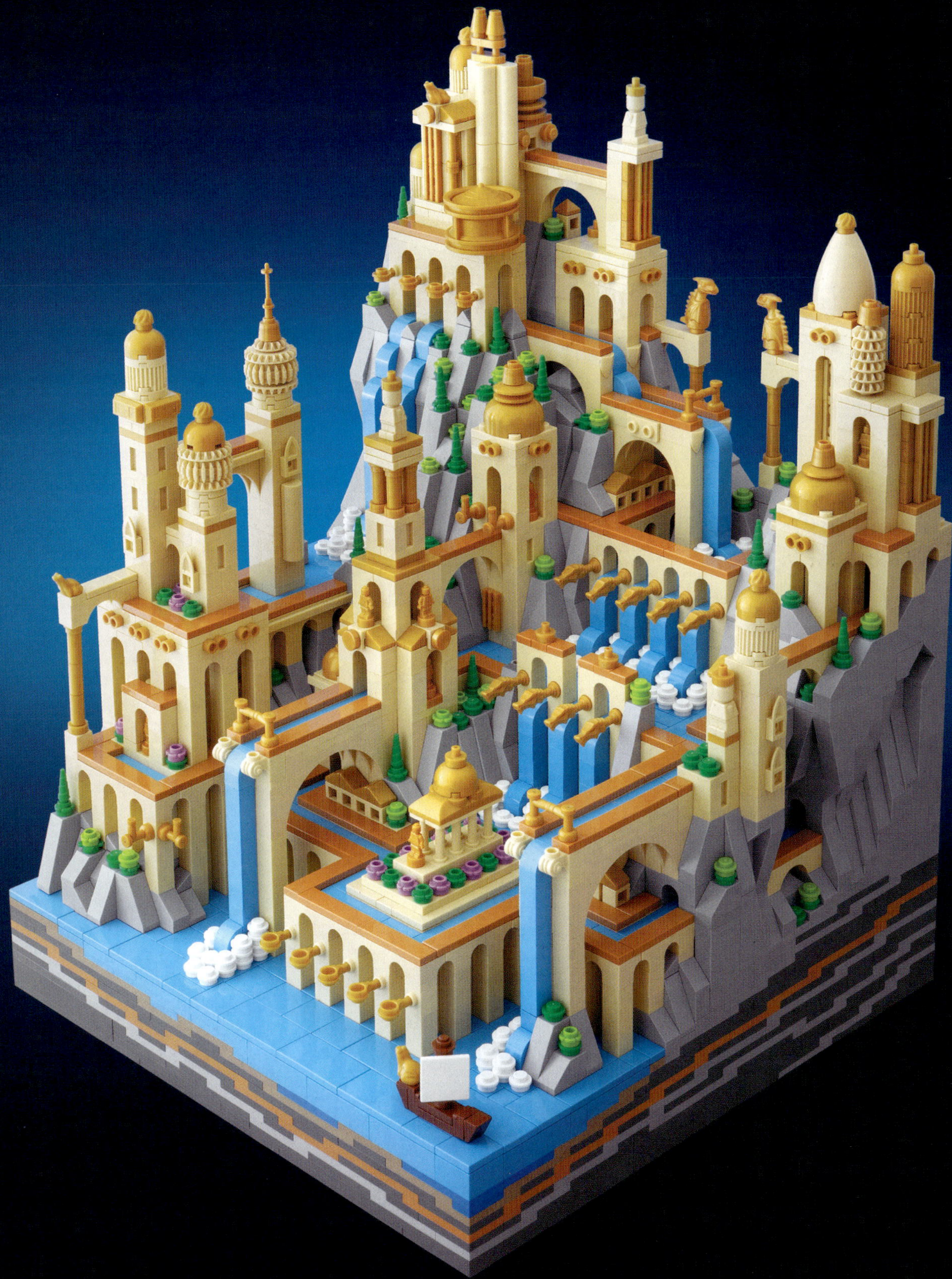

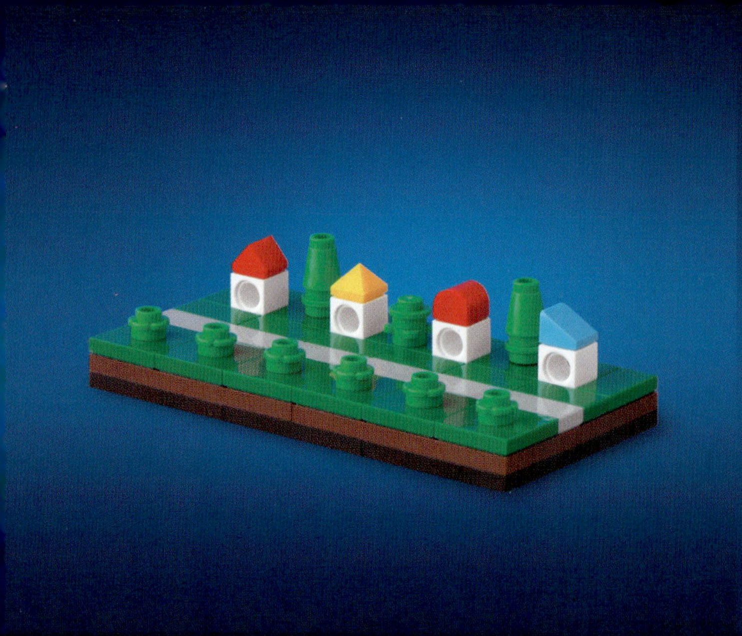
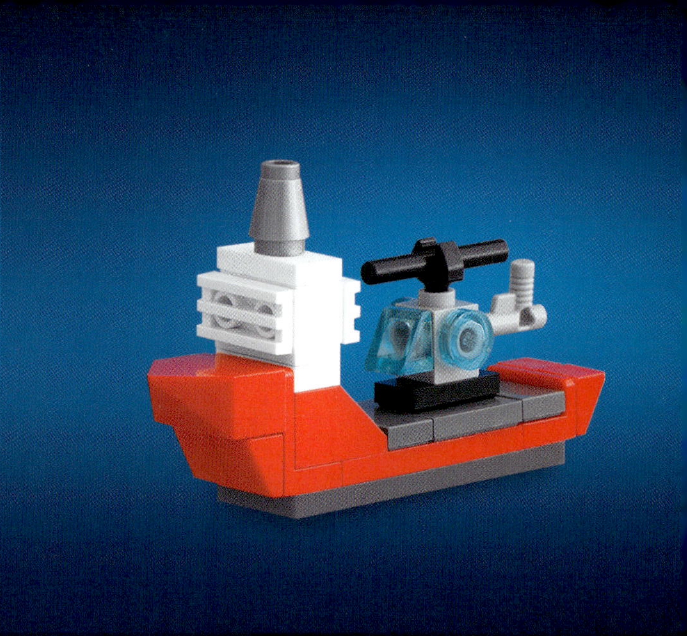
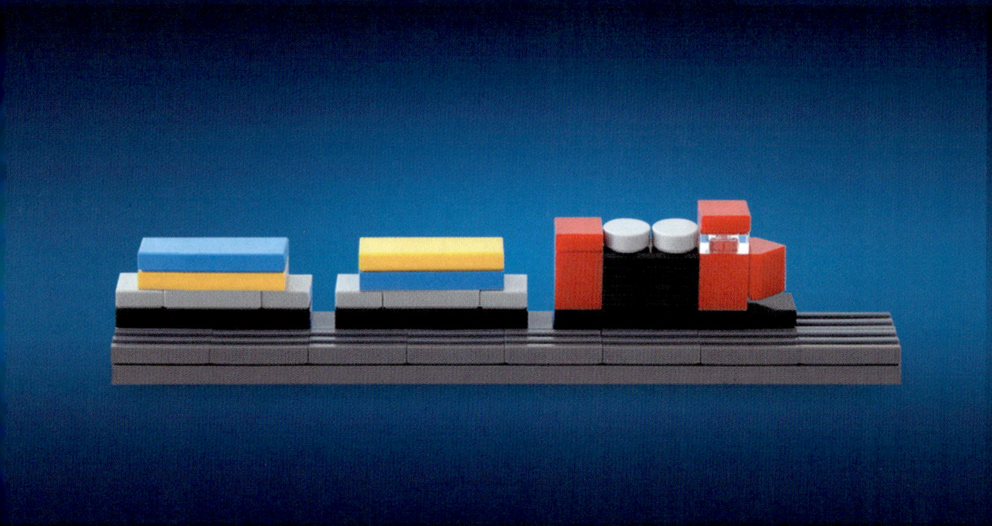
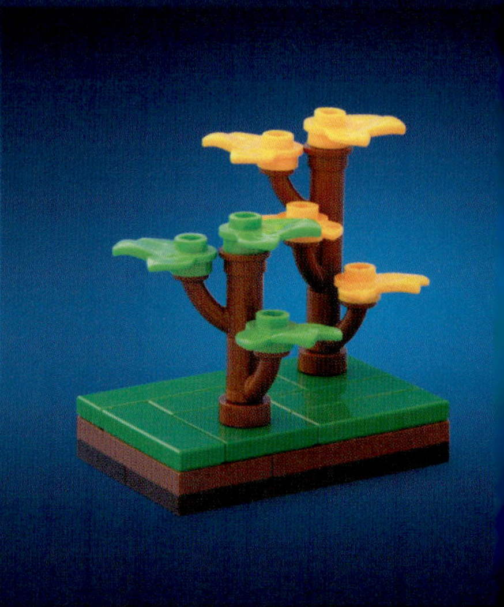
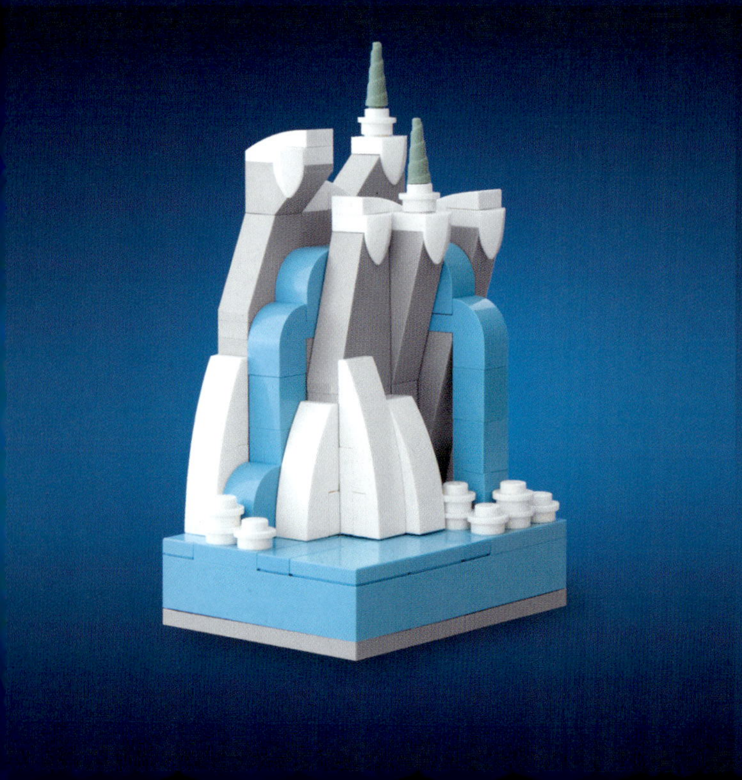
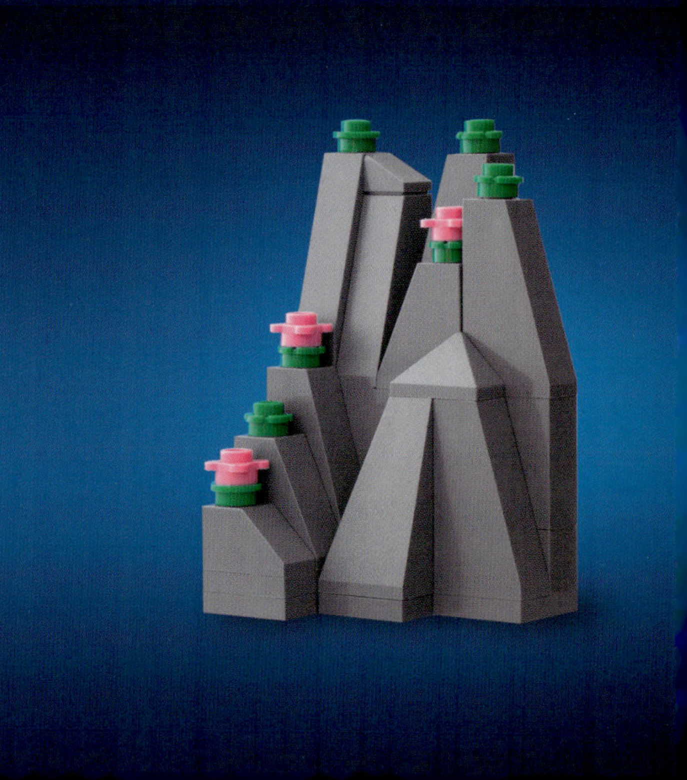

PART I: BUILDING BLOCKS

World-building begins with strong foundations. In this part of the book, you'll learn the essential techniques for building the landscapes, structures, and modes of transportation that bring LEGO bricks to life.

Pablo Picasso said, "Everything you can imagine is real." With LEGO, you can prove it.

TERRAFORMING

From solid bedrock to landscape and water features, this chapter shows how to create natural environments that form the foundation of your world.

BEDROCK

Plates are the bedrock of your LEGO world and define its size. They're available in sizes up to 16×16. If you want to build bigger, just join several plates together. Empty plates may not be much to look at, but imagine their boundless potential!

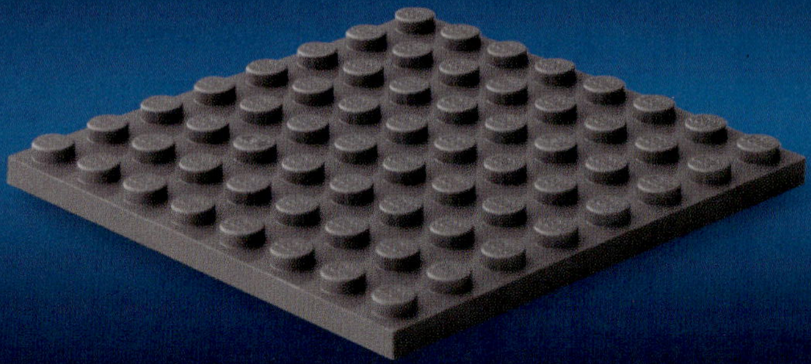

JOINING PLATES

In the real world, tectonic plates shift, causing earthquakes, volcanoes, and other natural disasters. In a LEGO world, you can avoid such calamities by firmly connecting your plates. Line them up carefully, then reinforce the seams from below using 2-stud-wide plates, as shown on the bottom right.

We use 2-stud-wide plates to join larger plates because it's best to avoid stacking larger LEGO plates directly on top of each other. Large plates tend to flex slightly, which is compounded when they're joined together. This may make your base slightly uneven. (If you're making a world of leaning towers, disregard this advice.)

The human eye is surprisingly good at spotting misalignment. Even a tilt as small as 1 degree can look "off," especially across a large build.

1

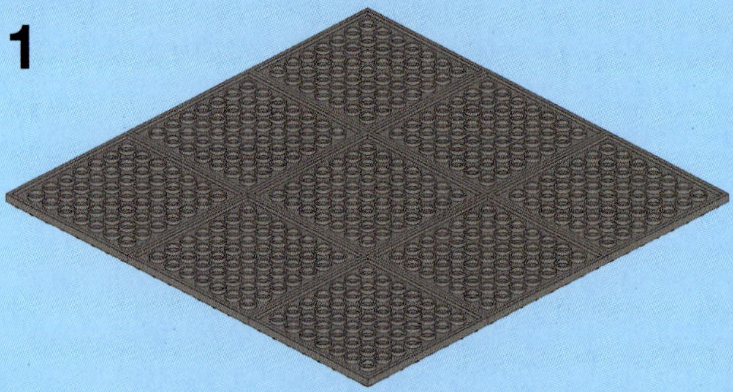

2

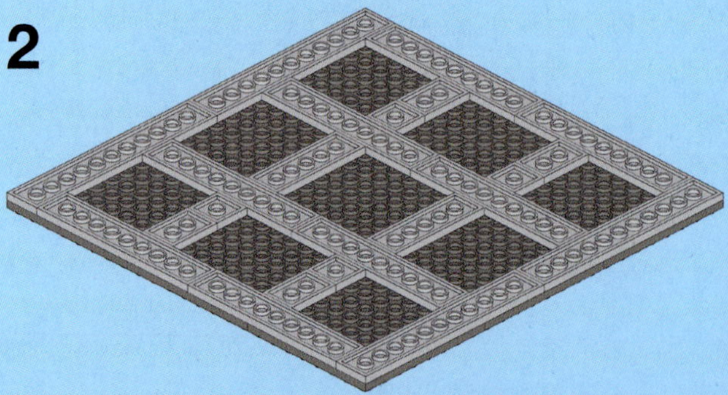

FLAT LANDSCAPES

Here's the simplest LEGO landscape: a flat surface made with tiles. You likely have loftier ambitions for your world, and growth requires studded elements. That said, refer to the tile type guide below for any flat sections you want to include.

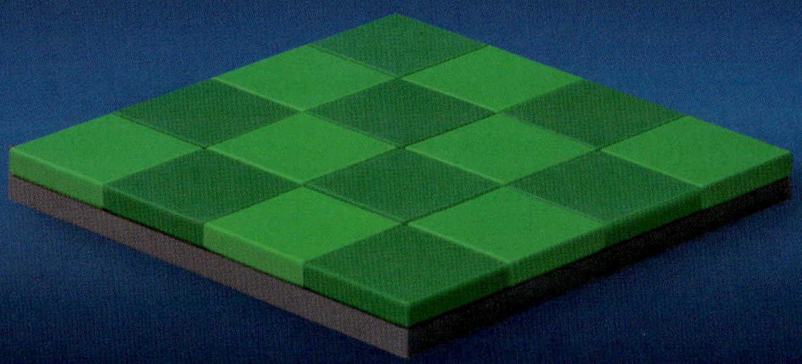

TILE TYPE GUIDE

Tiles come in a variety of sizes and colors, making them perfect for representing everything from smooth, flat earth to ice or man-made features like pavement. Later in this chapter, you'll discover how tiles can also bring water to life in your landscapes.

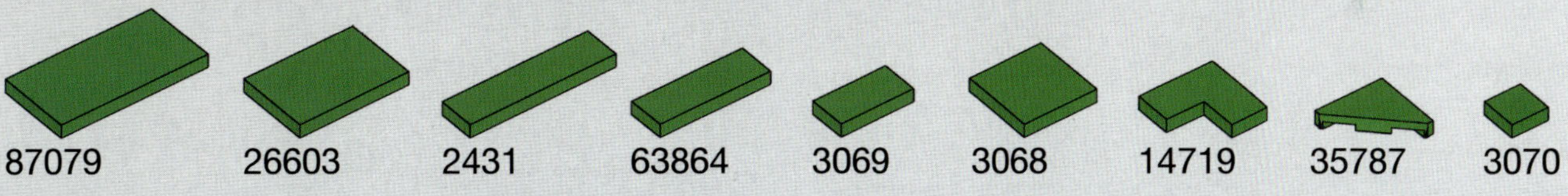

Tile colors can represent many types of landscapes. Here are some ideas to inspire your designs.

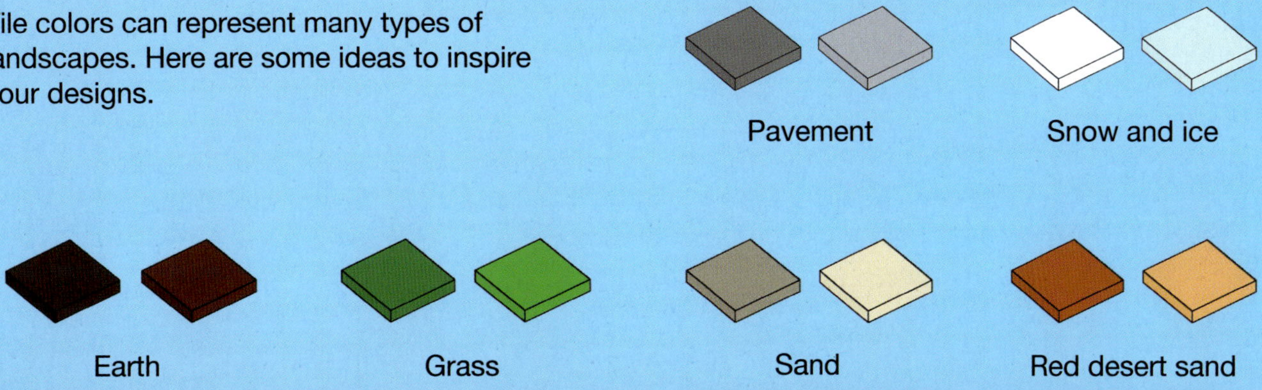

A BASE TO BUILD ON

You've learned how to create a bedrock base and a simple flat landscape to top it, but LEGO tiles are like barren plains from which nothing can grow. Your base will need studs wherever you want to place landscape features, buildings, or transportation. LEGO studs are like seeds—starting points from which your world can take shape and flourish.

There are builders who like to improvise as they go and builders who like to plan everything in advance. However you wish to proceed, the examples on these two pages show how bases looked before the world was built on top of them. As you can see, a world sprouts from studs!

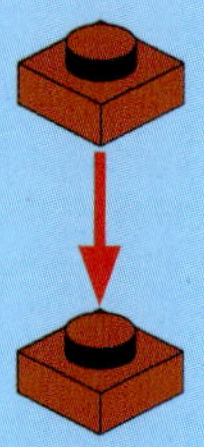

STUDS

The iconic cylindrical bumps on LEGO elements are called *studs*. They connect to other elements using clutch power.

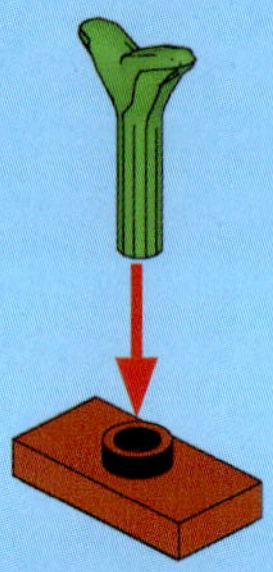

OPEN STUDS

Open studs have a hole in the center, allowing an additional connection point for bars or similar parts.

SMALL WORLDS

The themed worlds you'll discover later in this book are built on bases that are around 24×24 studs, but even an 8×8 plate (#41539) provides enough space to build a vibrant scene.

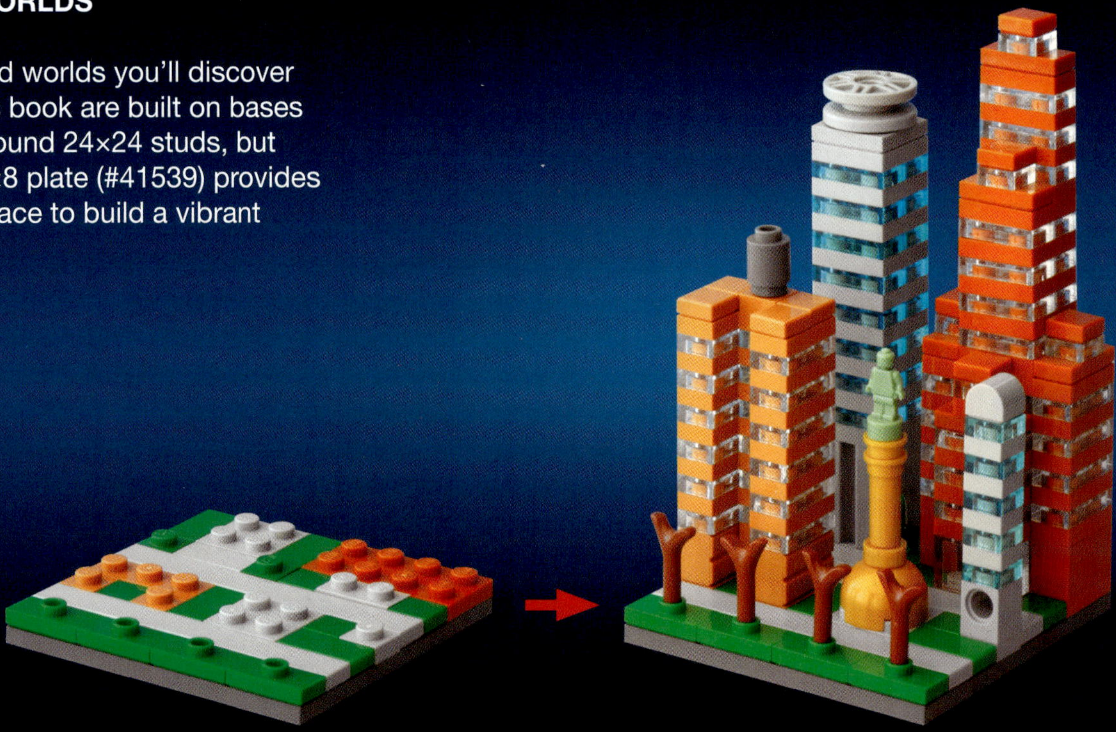

PANORAMIC WORLDS

You can create a panoramic world by starting with a base that's longer than it is deep. An 8×16 plate (#3865) is an ideal single-element foundation. It's compact enough for easy experimentation and can be expanded into a larger scene when you're ready to build a bigger world.

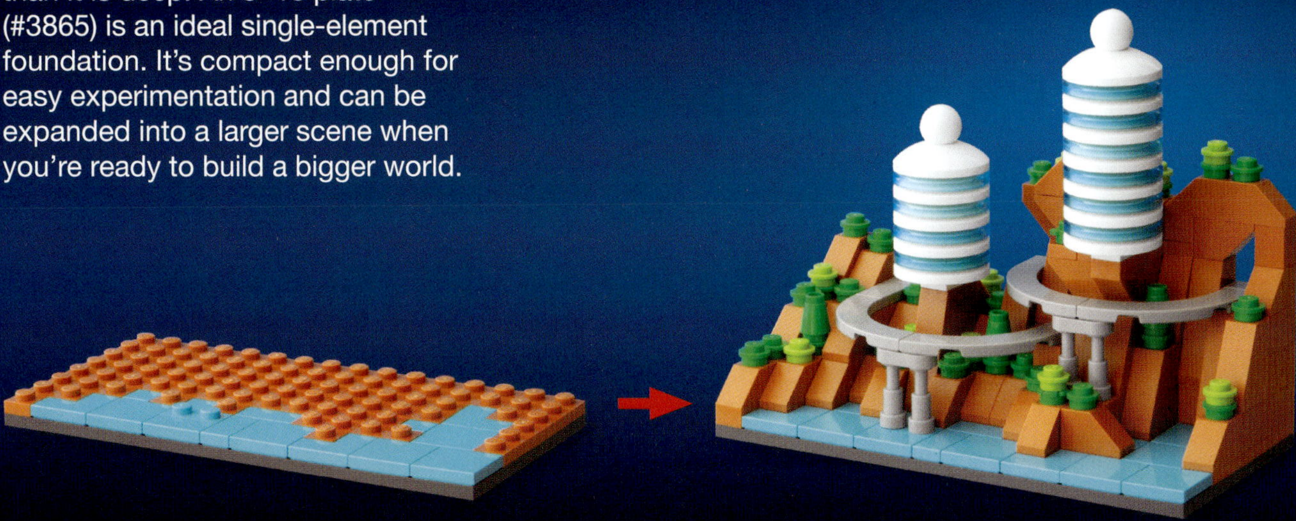

WIDE OR SQUARE?

People naturally see the world in a wide format, similar to the proportions of a movie screen. Building with a longer base captures that expansive feeling.

A square base, on the other hand, offers a balanced frame that encourages the eye to explore in all directions, not just left to right.

It's your choice!

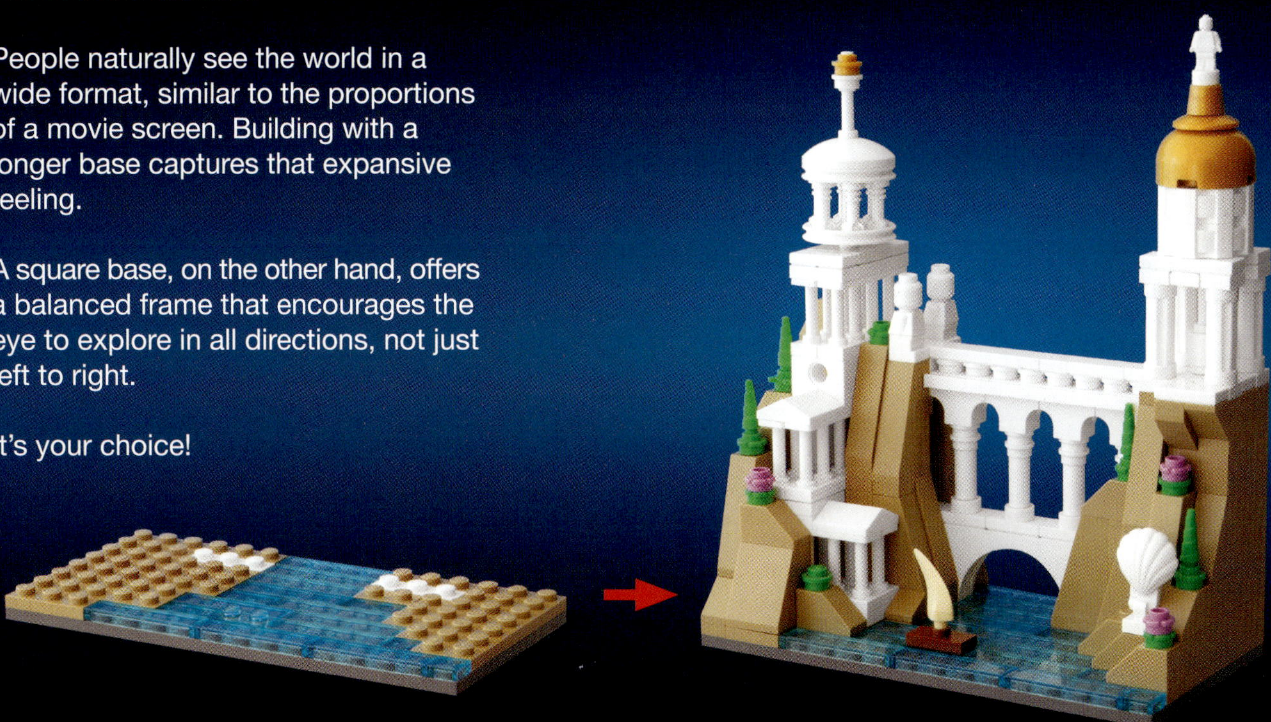

SLOPES

Slopes take your world to new heights. LEGO slope elements come in many shapes, sizes, and colors to shape your landscape, from gentle hills to towering mountains.

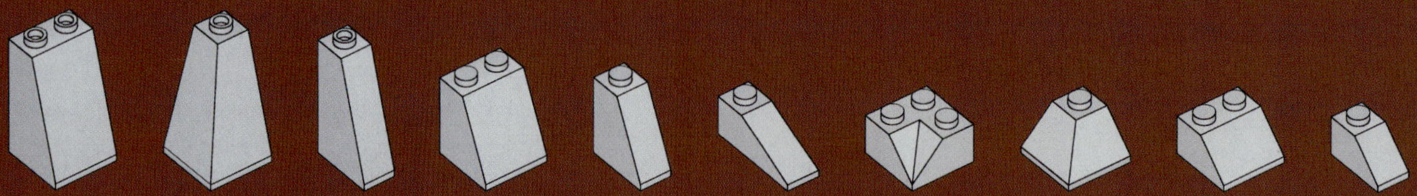

3684a 3685 4460b 3678b 60481 4286 3046 3045 3039 3040

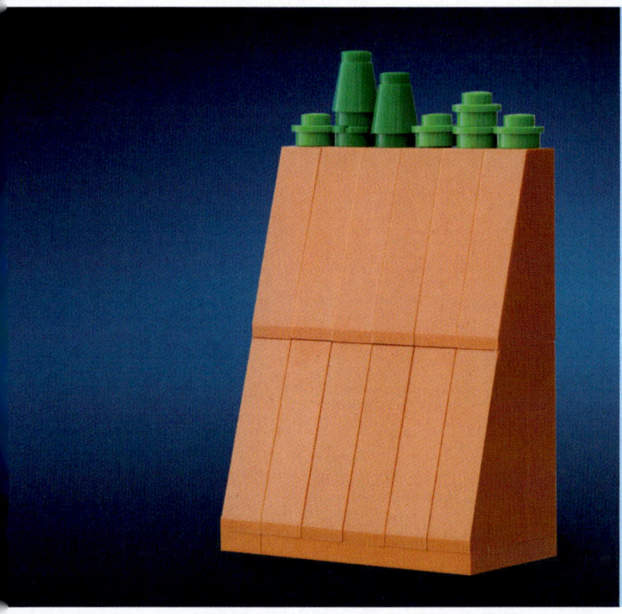

BASIC SLOPE

Simply stacking slopes, while supporting the non-sloped side with bricks, creates a uniform incline. While this kind of slope is uncommon in nature, it can represent man-made earthworks, such as the raised ground used for castle fortifications.

For a gentler rise, use slope bricks with shallower angles.

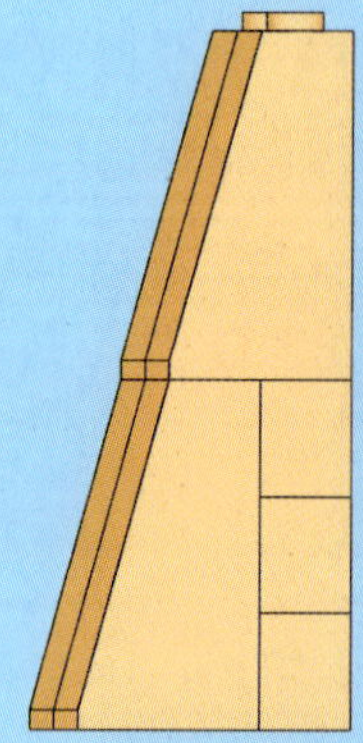

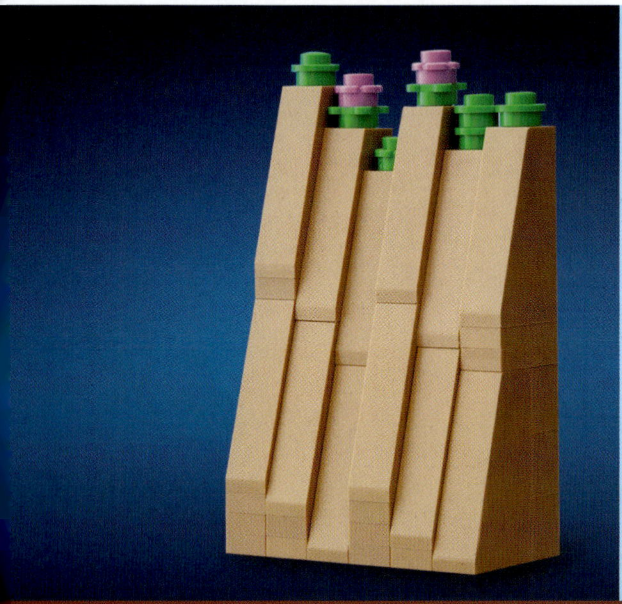

STAGGERED HEIGHTS

Staggering slope bricks by adding varying numbers of plates beneath them adds visual interest and creates a more natural-looking incline. This technique breaks up the uniformity of a straight slope and better mimics the uneven terrain found in real landscapes.

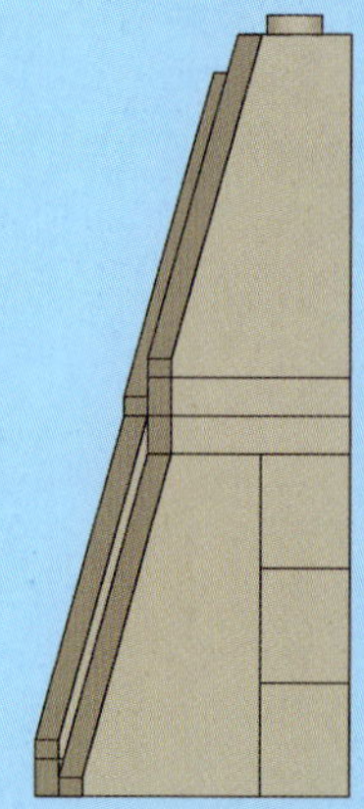

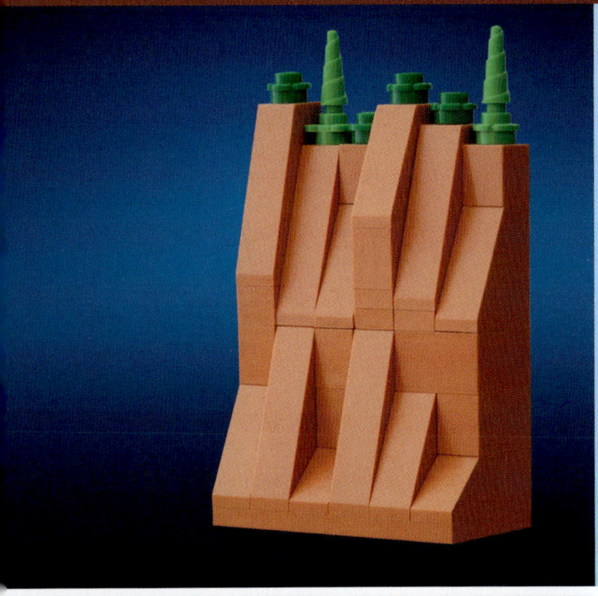

MIXED SLOPE TYPES

Mixed slopes combine staggered slope heights using bricks and plates with slope bricks of varying angles. The result is a more rugged appearance.

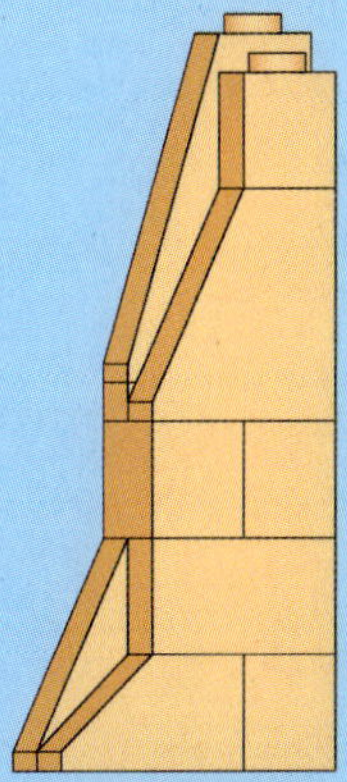

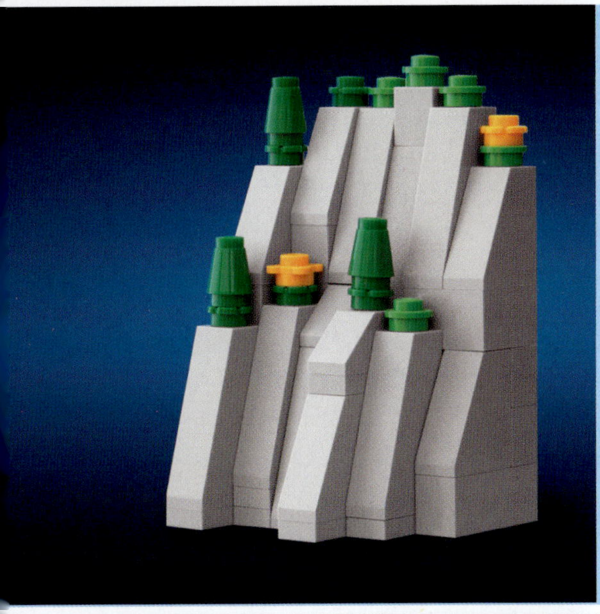

STAGGERED FOOTPRINT

In addition to staggering the height and angle of the slopes, you can also stagger the footprint, with some slope elements jutting out at the base. The result is a slope that's no longer uniform horizontally or vertically.

Exposed studs are left at varying heights, allowing for the placement of plants or small structures.

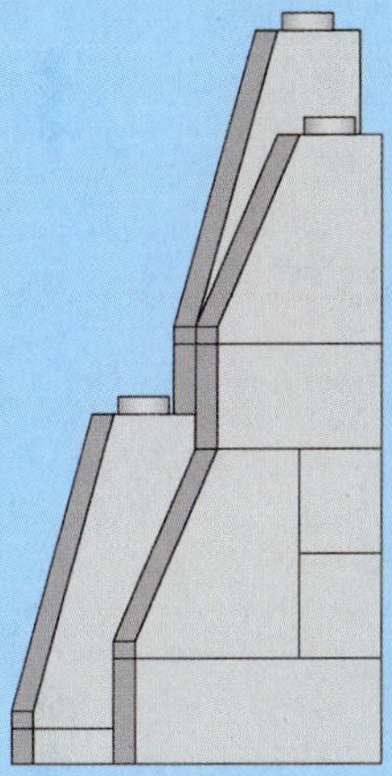

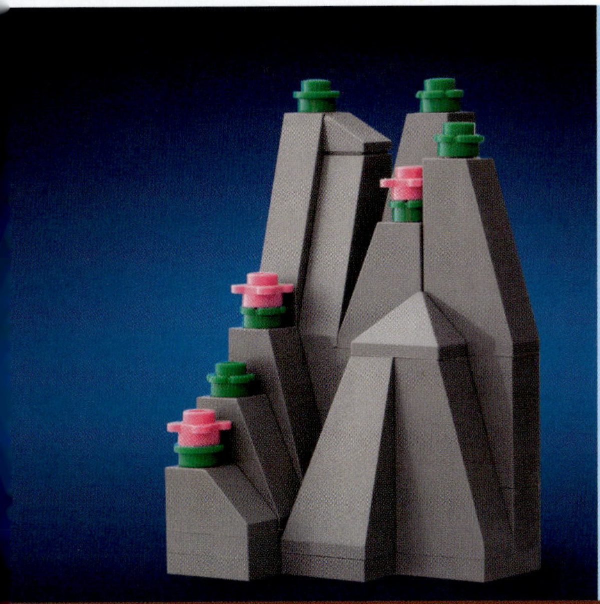

PERPENDICULAR SLOPES

This ultimate slope builds on all the previous stages and adds a new technique: placing slope elements perpendicular to one another.

Notice some of the exposed studs are topped with the studless slope pieces shown below.

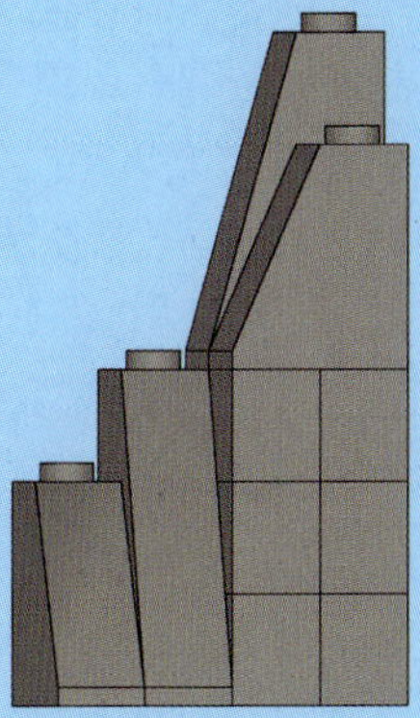

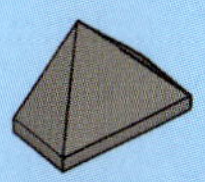

15571

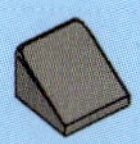

54200

CLIFFS

If you're dreaming of landscapes steeper than slopes, it's time to try some cliffs. Cliffs are built similarly to slopes but add LEGO's inverted slope elements, like the ones shown below, to create sheer drops and overhangs.

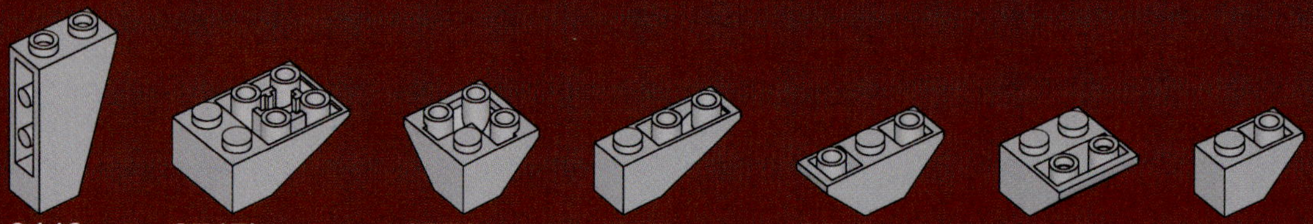

2449 3747b 3676 4287 2341 76959 3665

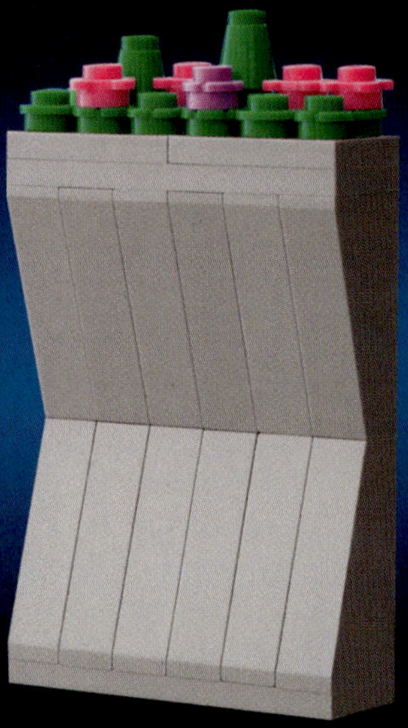

BASIC CLIFF

Capping regular slope elements with their inverted counterparts creates a sheer, 90-degree drop from top to bottom. This smooth, uniform cliff face looks like it was sculpted by man-made tools or machines. Perhaps it's part of a quarry or the walls of an ancient fortress carved into rock.

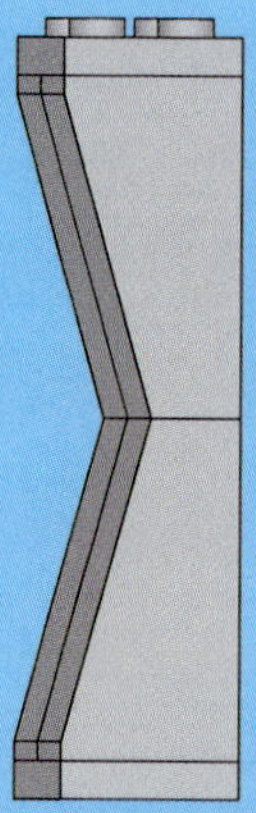

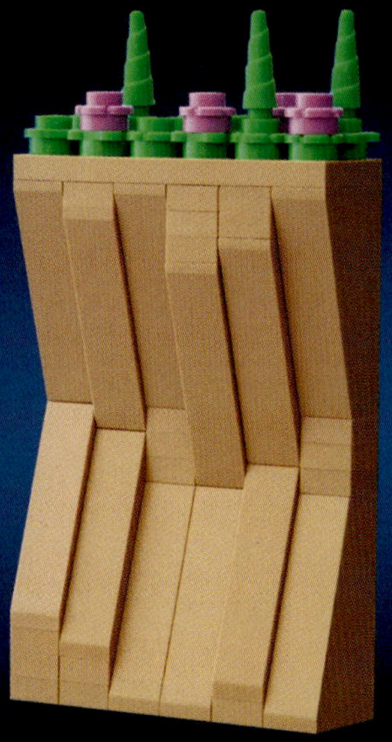

STAGGERED HEIGHTS

For more organic cliffs, stagger regular and inverted slope elements at different heights by stacking plates underneath. This uneven layering breaks up straight lines and echoes the rugged look of real rock formations.

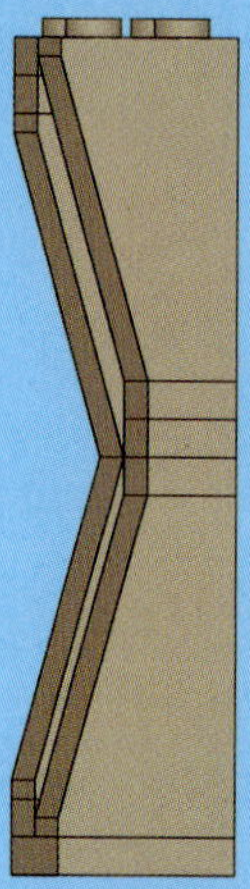

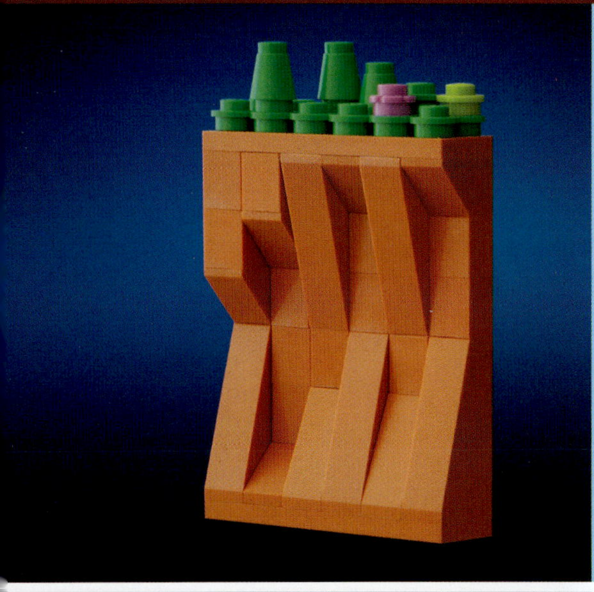

MIXED SLOPE TYPES

Combining both regular and inverted slope elements with different angles and heights adds visual complexity and depth. Rather than using plates to create height variation like the previous example, this type uses bricks. The result is more sheer vertical surfaces. Watch out for falling rocks!

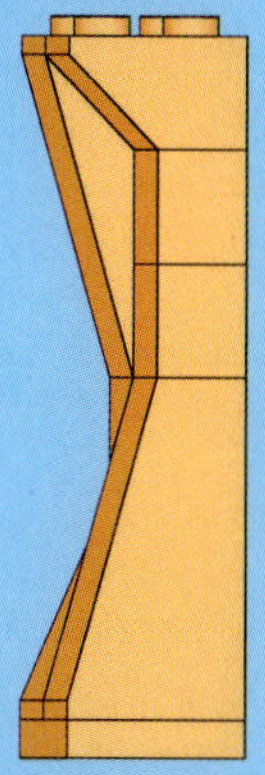

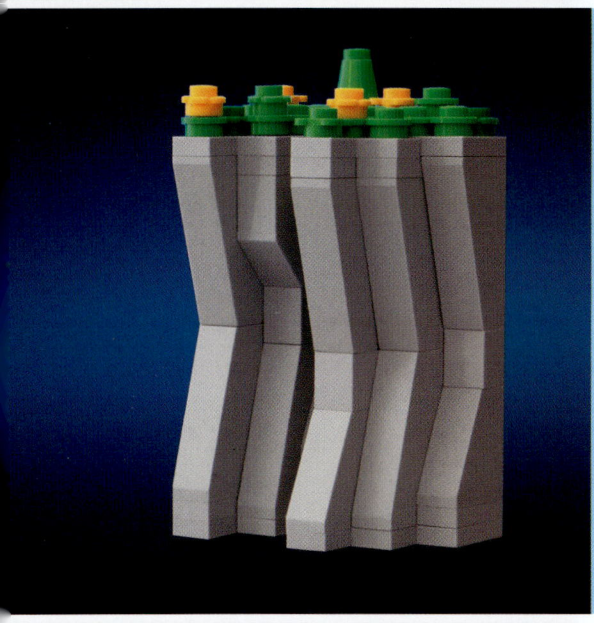

STAGGERED FOOTPRINT

Along with mixing brick heights and angles, as shown in the previous example, this cliff's bottom bricks extend out unevenly, creating an irregular footprint that looks as if it was carved by crashing waves.

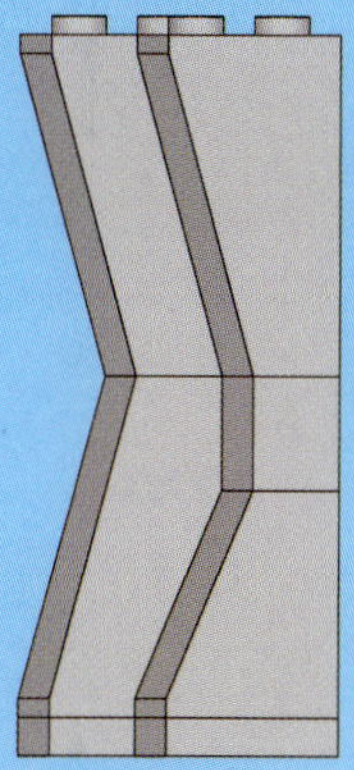

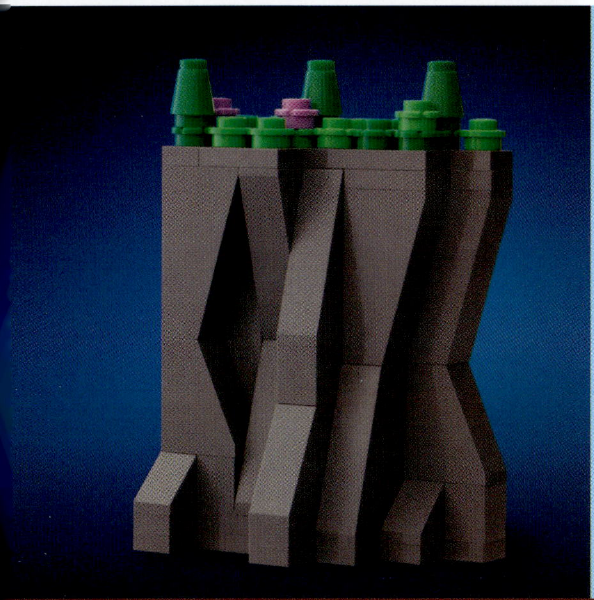

PERPENDICULAR SLOPES AND INVERTED SLOPES

As with the ultimate slope, this ultimate cliff builds on all the previous types and adds the technique of placing slope elements perpendicular to one another. This method creates complex angles that beguile viewers and stump climbers. You can also build cave entrances the same way.

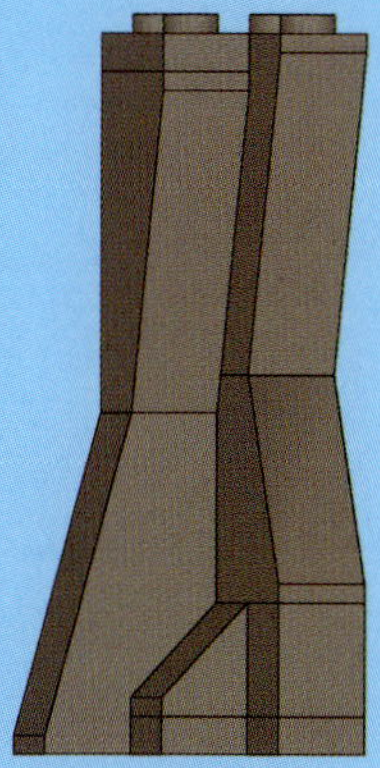

SOLID-COLORED WATER

Water brings life to a LEGO world and adds breathing room between landscape features.

ADVANTAGES

Using solid-colored tiles to represent water gives you access to a wide variety of tile shapes and shades of blue. To suggest depth, start with water-colored bricks and layer tiles on top. You can use darker shades of blue farther down to imply deeper water.

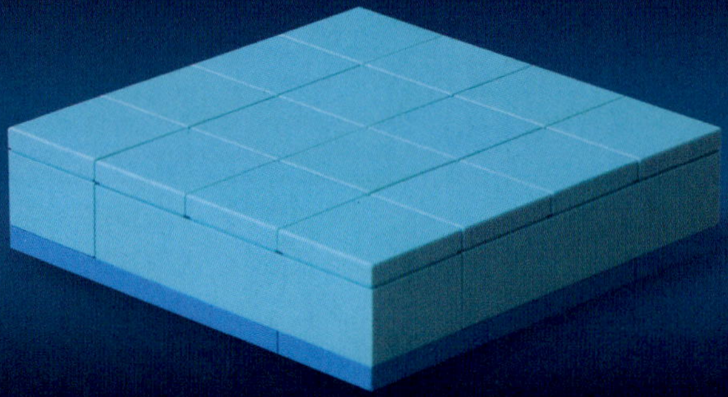

SOLID COLORS

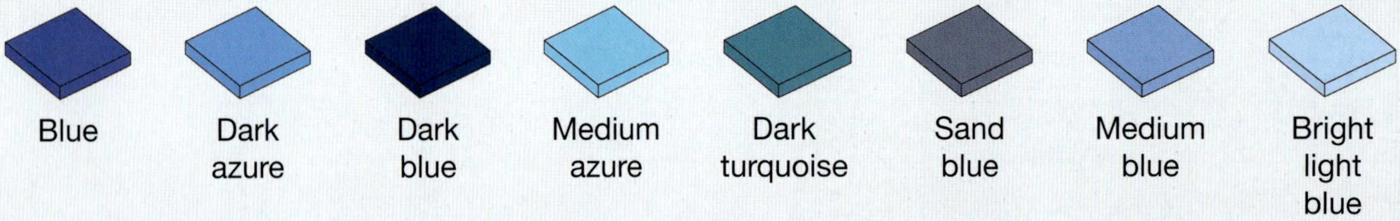

As always, use plates or other bricks with studs in areas where you plan to add features.

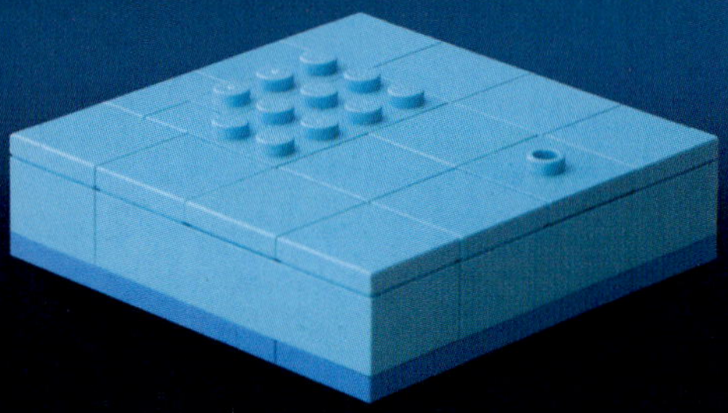

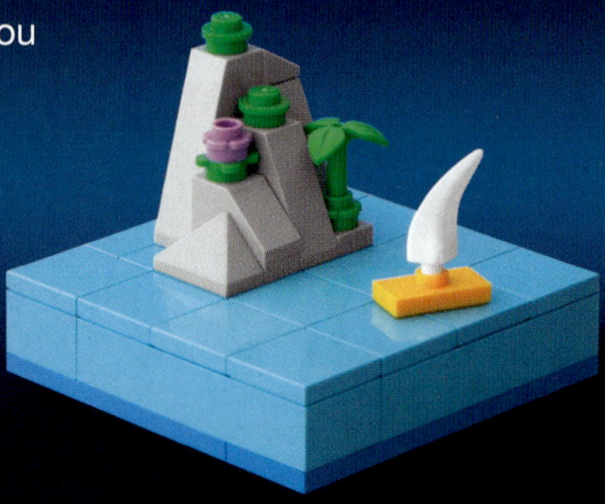

TRANSPARENT WATER

Transparent bricks create authentic water effects because they're more like the real thing.

ADVANTAGES

Using transparent tiles creates a shimmering, realistic surface that changes with lighting conditions. Though fewer shapes and colors are available compared to solid-colored tiles, the visual effect can be striking. Place transparent tiles over transparent bricks to suggest depth.

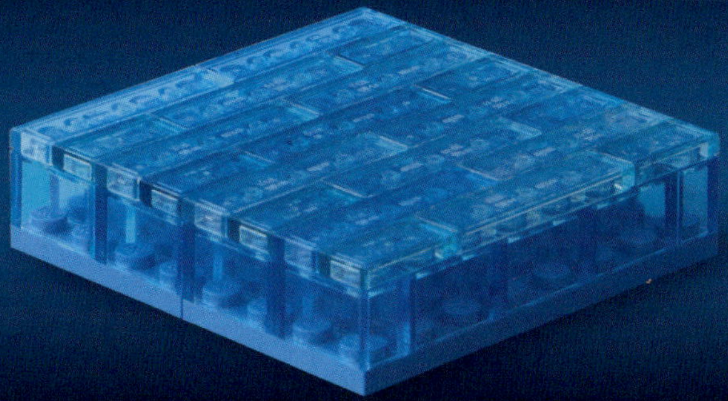

TRANSPARENT COLORS

While only two transparent blue colors are commonly available in tile elements, you can dramatically change their appearance by layering them over plates of different colors. Since plates come in nearly every LEGO color, this technique lets you create a wide range of depth effects.

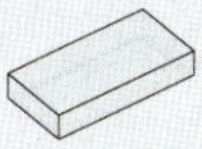

Trans-light blue

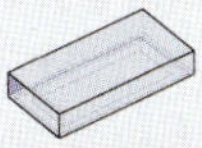

Trans-dark blue

1

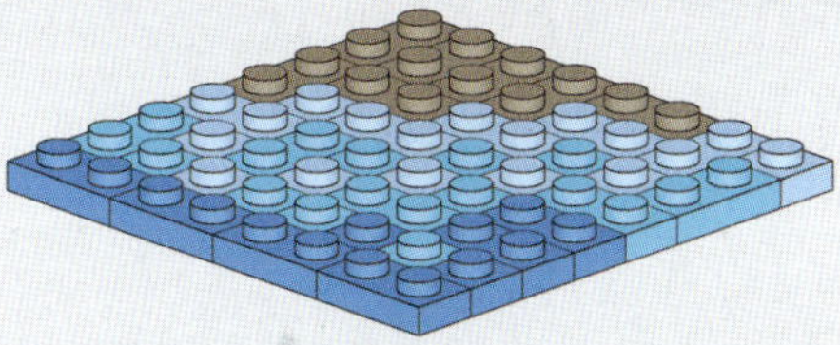

2

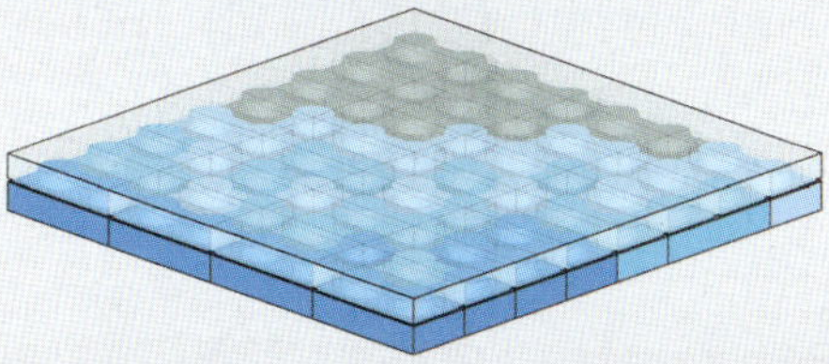

In addition to providing attachment points, studs can be used as ripples or waves.

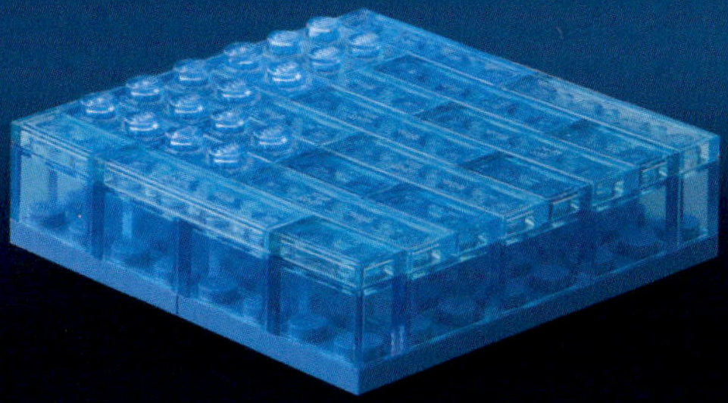

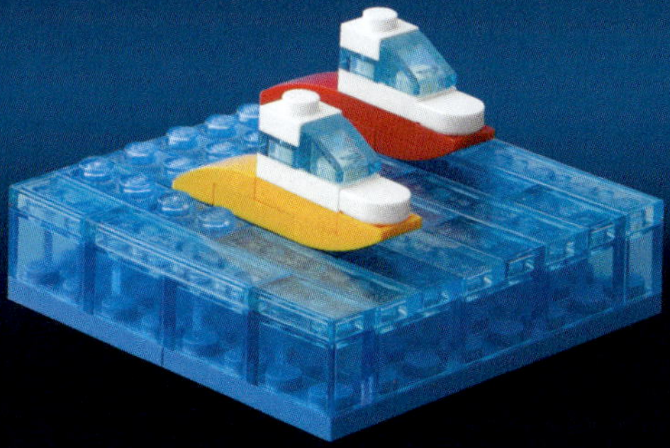

SOLID-COLORED WATERFALL

As with flat water, the advantage of using solid-colored bricks for waterfalls is that they come in a wider variety of element types than transparent ones, offering more options for shaping curves and flow.

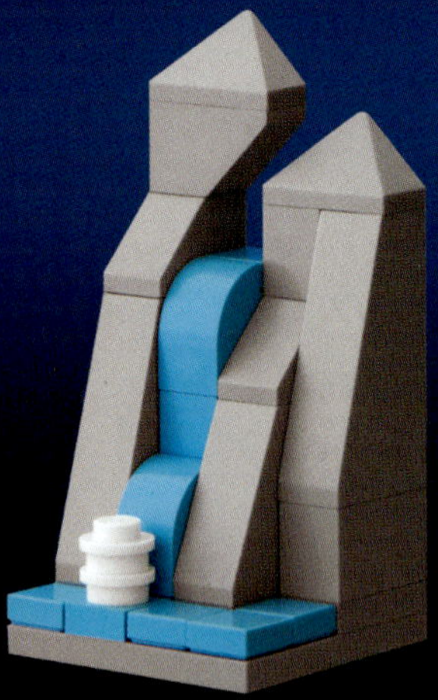

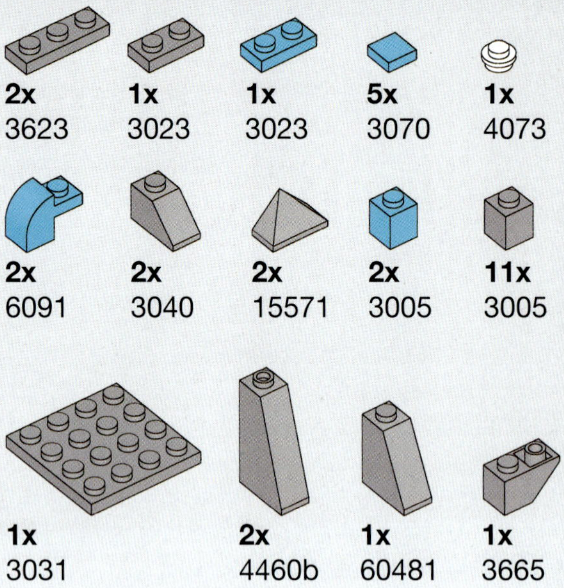

1

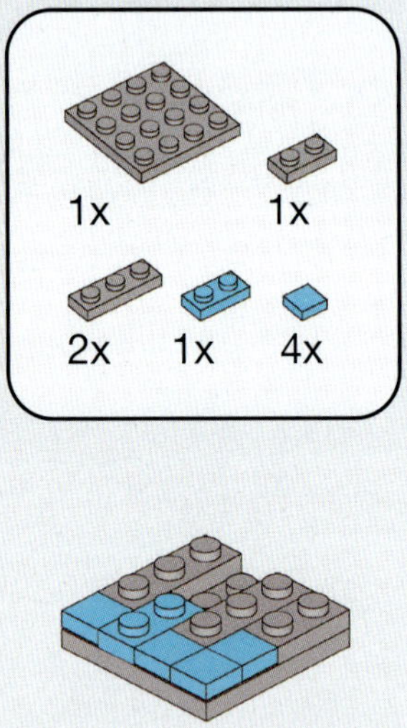

2

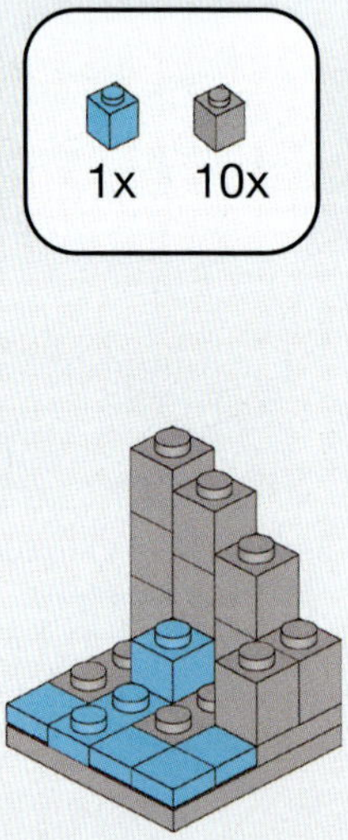

3

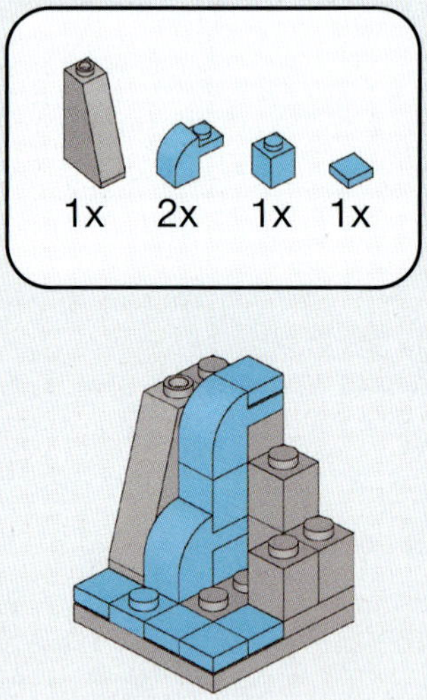

4

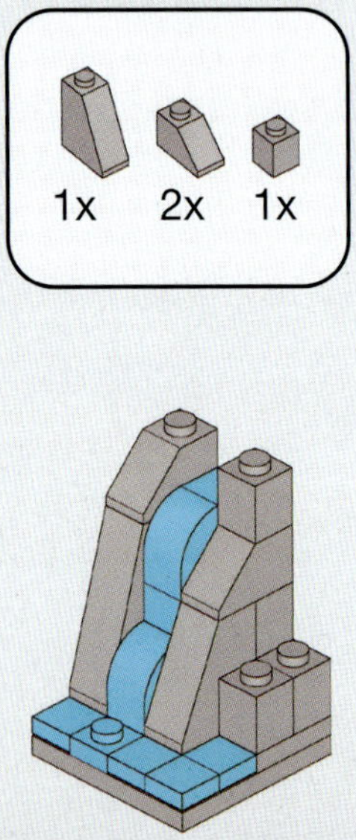

5

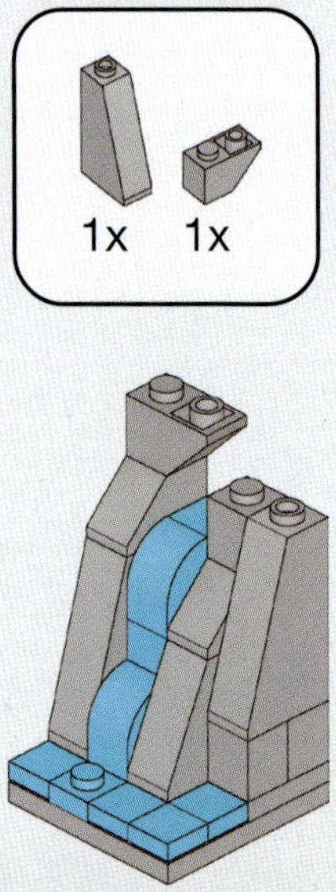

6

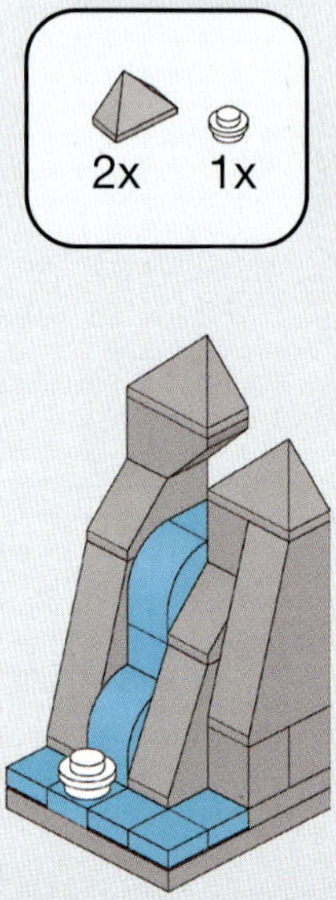

TRANSPARENT WATERFALL

Using transparent bricks to build LEGO waterfalls gives them a luminous quality similar to the real thing. While fewer element types are available compared to solid-colored bricks, the visual effect can make up for this limitation.

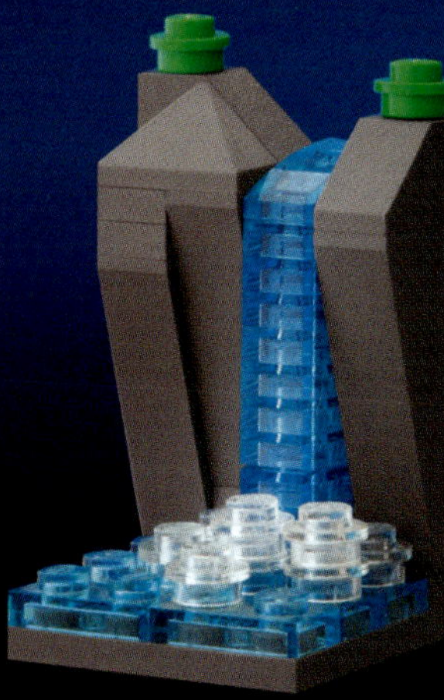

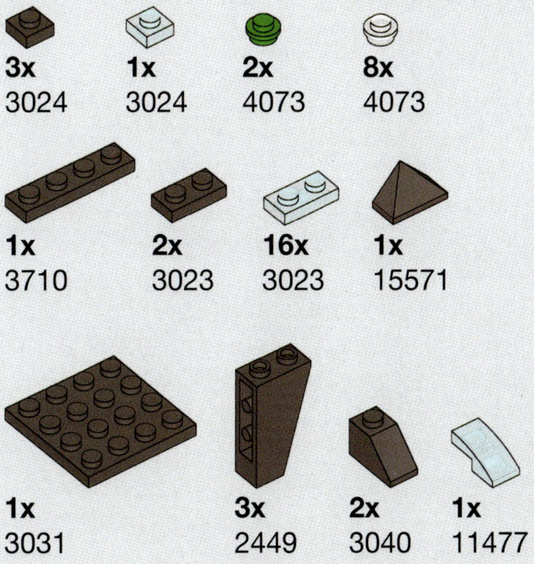

1

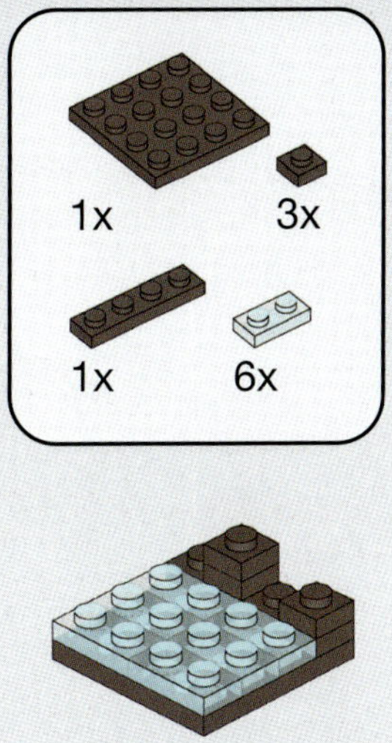

2

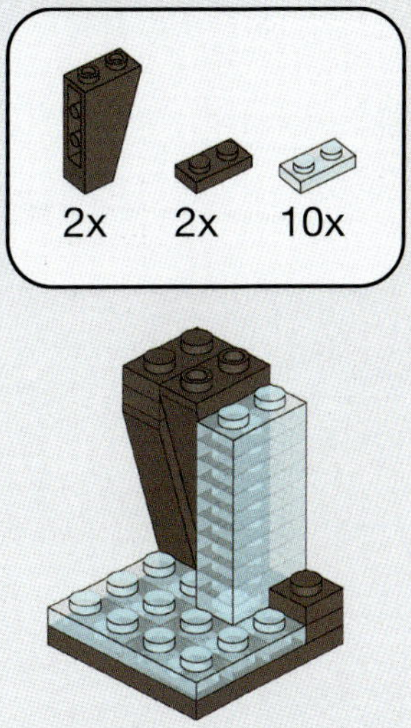

3

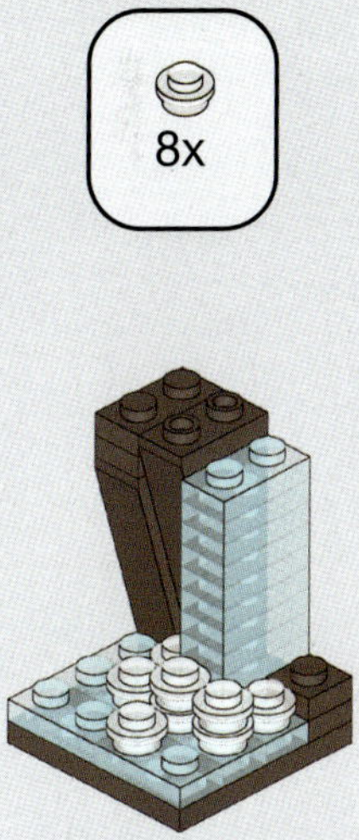

4

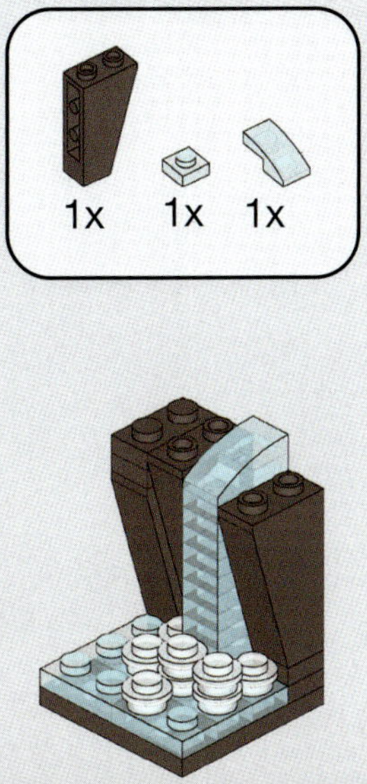

5

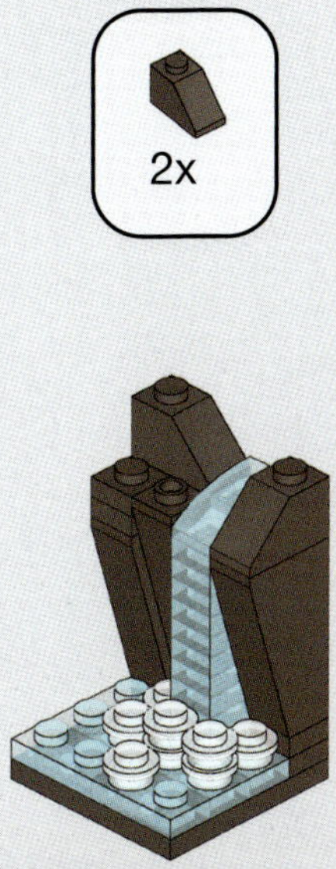

6

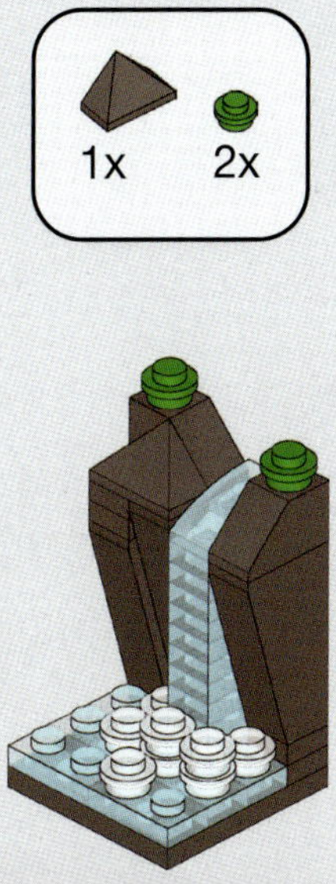

WINTER WATERFALL

Icy waterfalls are a magical feature of cold climates, where freezing spray and mist form towering sheets of ice along cliff faces.

This winter waterfall model uses sideways building techniques to create vertical ice walls. You can expand the techniques you learn in this build to create a massive waterfall landscape for a winter wonderland.

You'll explore more sideways building techniques for architecture in the "Building Sideways" chapter beginning on page 38.

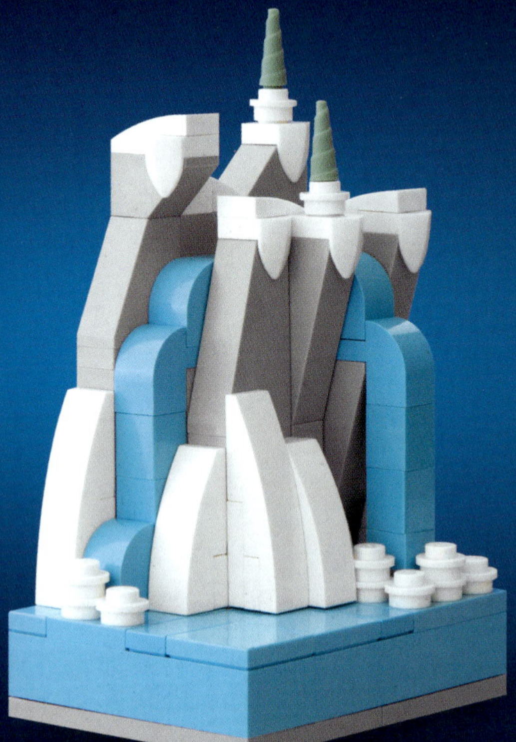

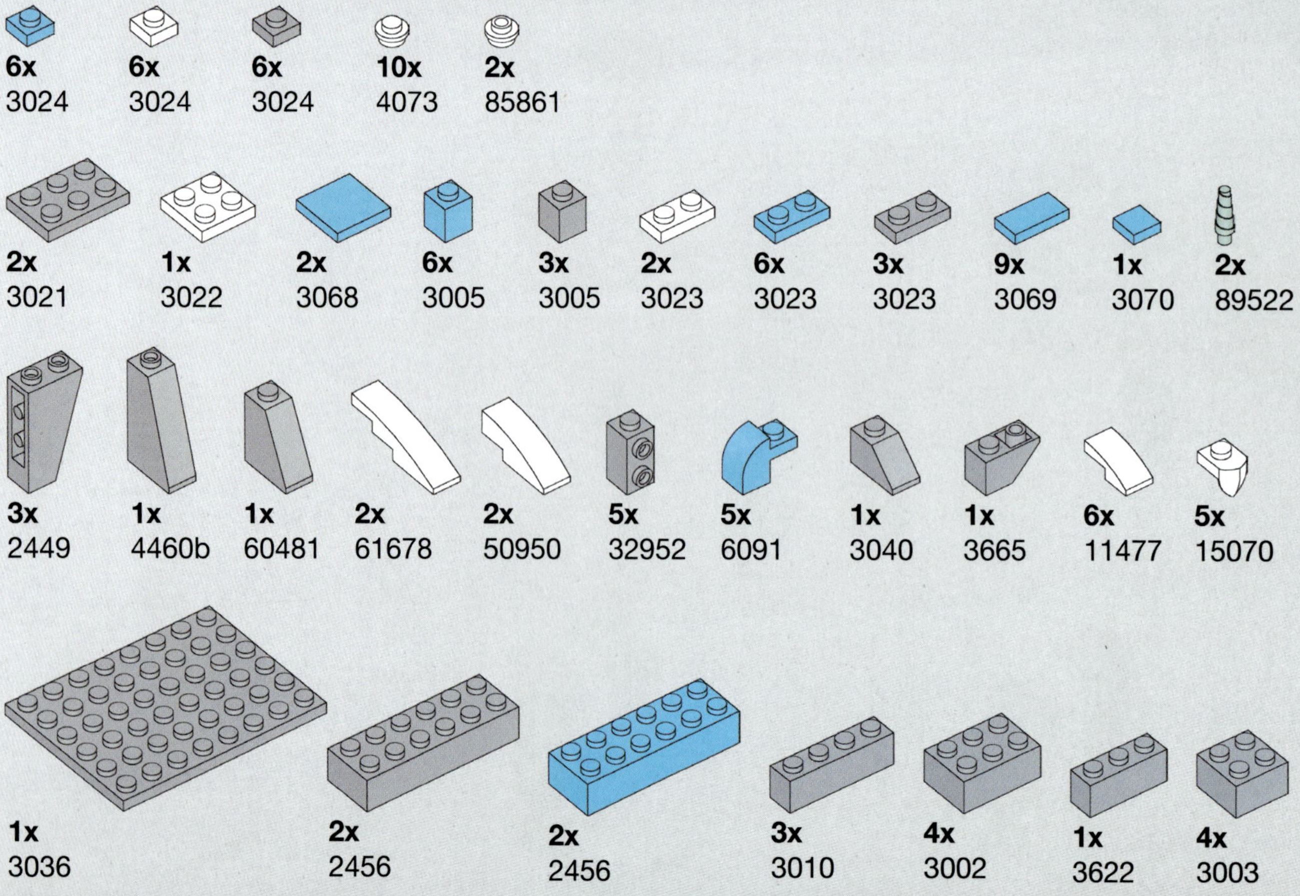

1

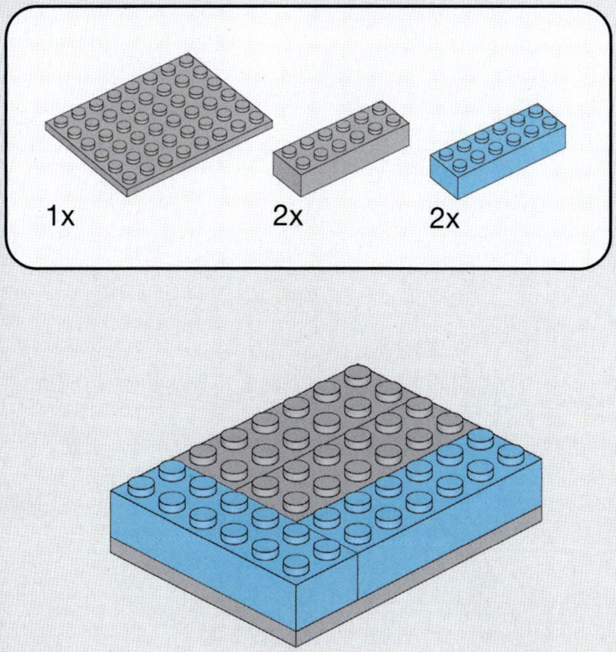

2

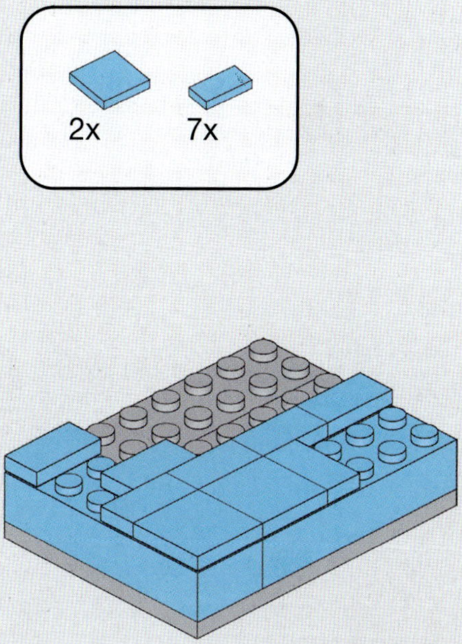

3

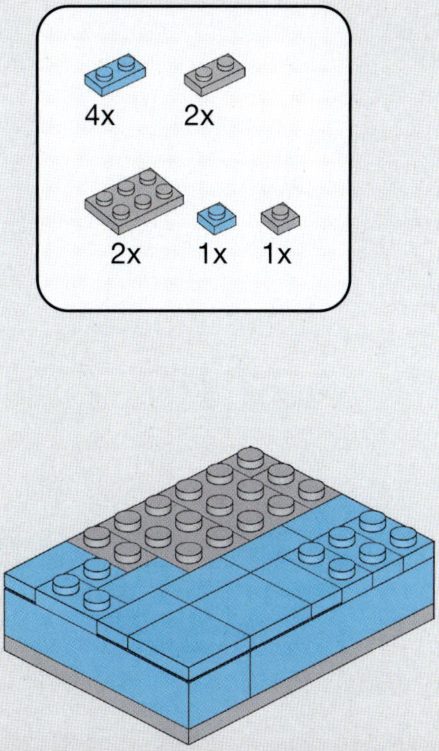

4

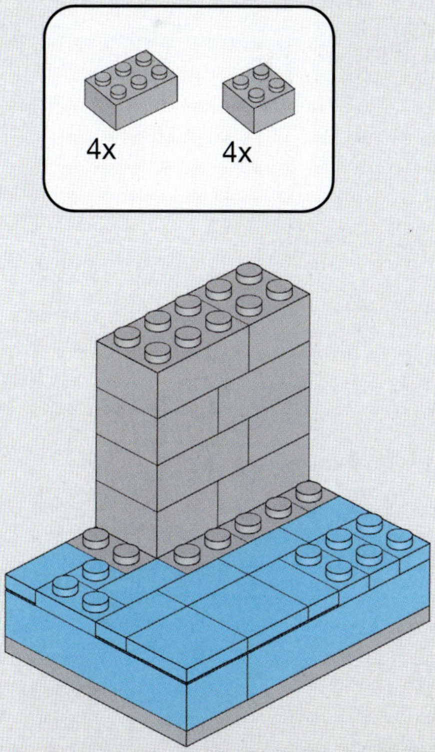

5

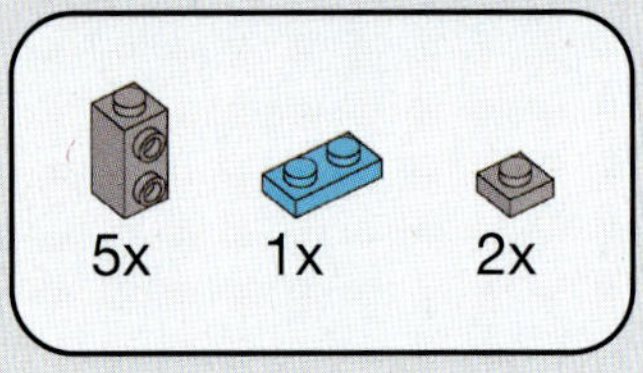

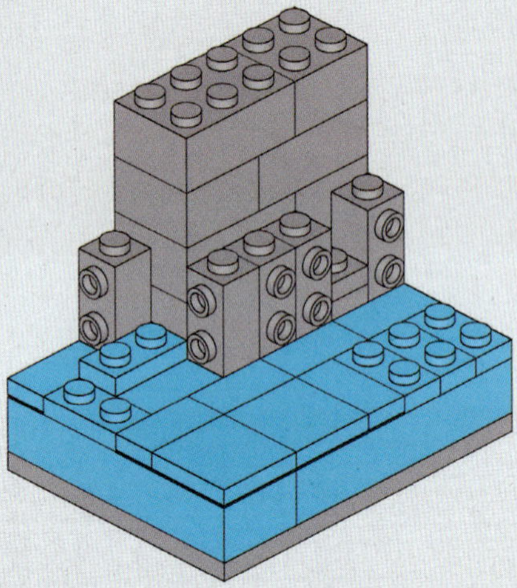

6

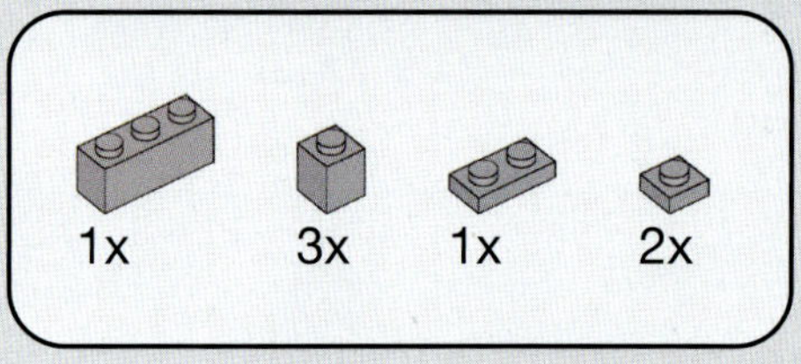

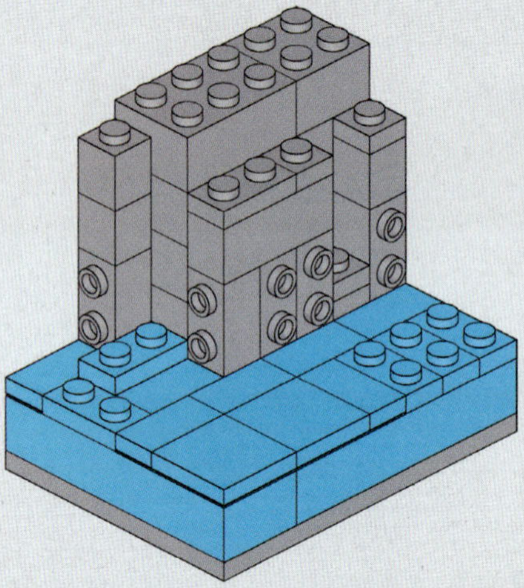

7

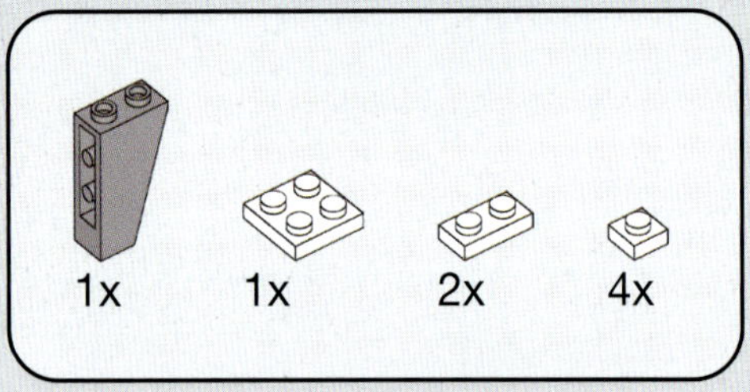

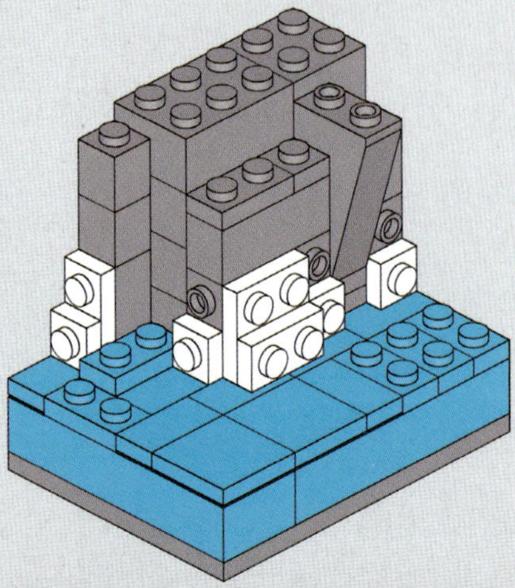

8

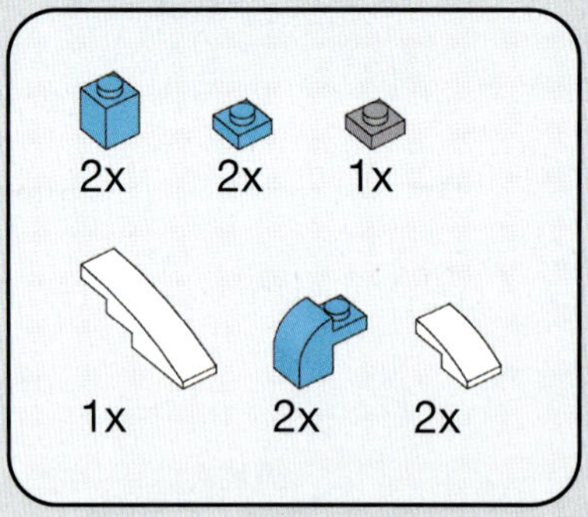

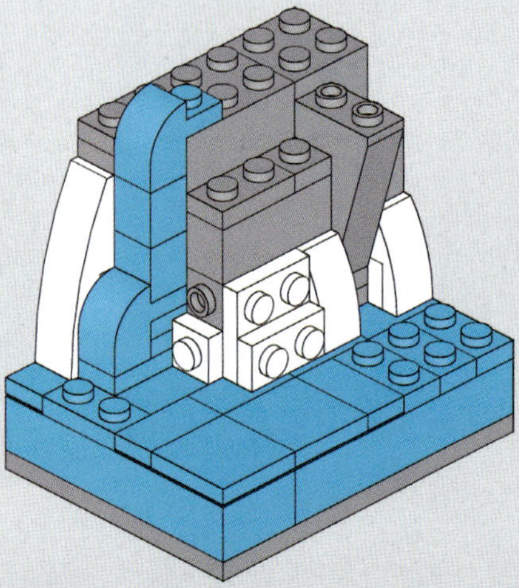

9

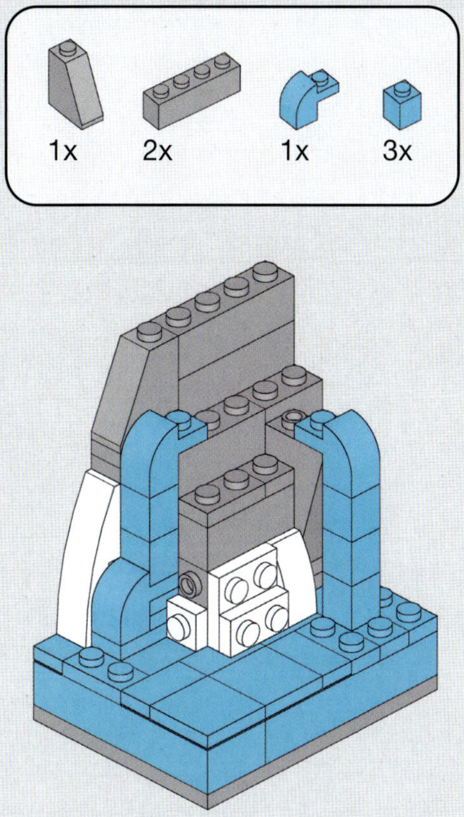

10

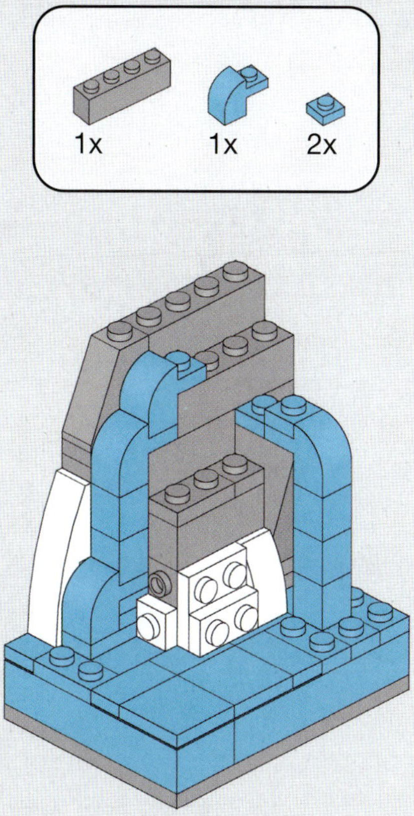

11

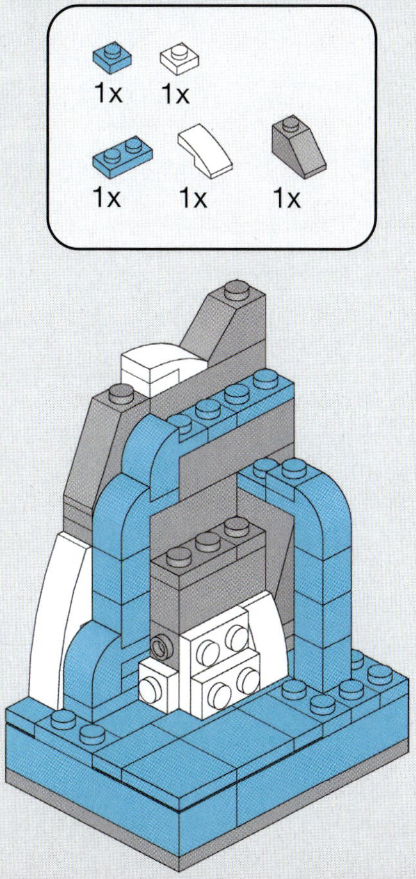

12

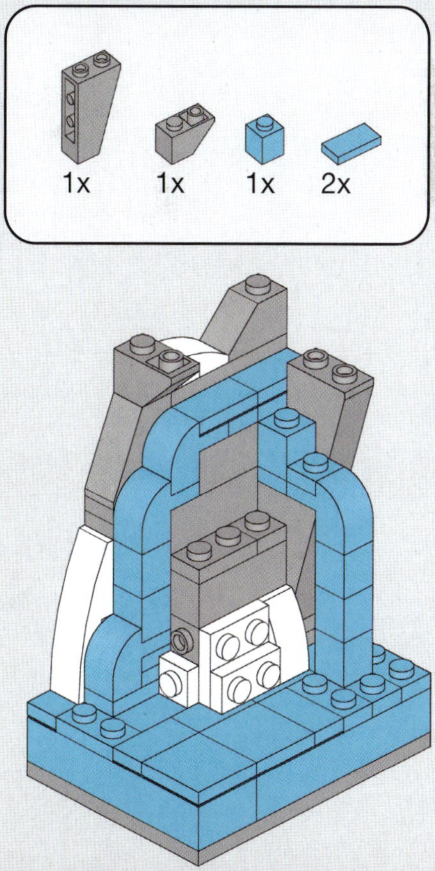

13

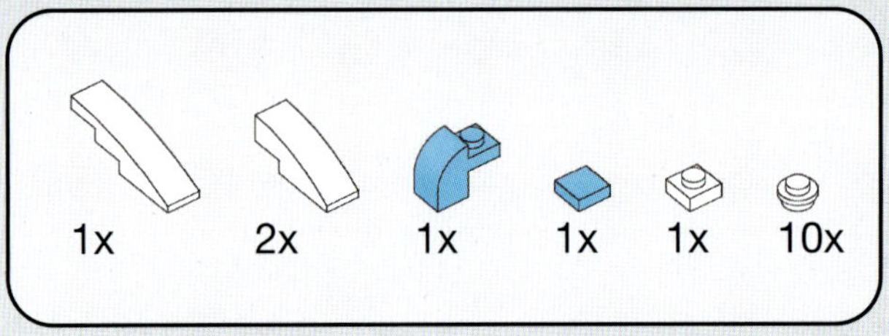

Before placing the 1×3 slope on the right, attach the 1×1 plate as shown.

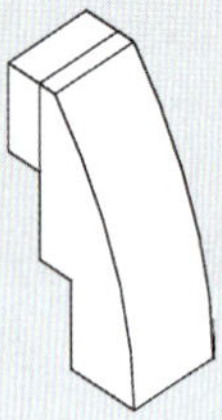

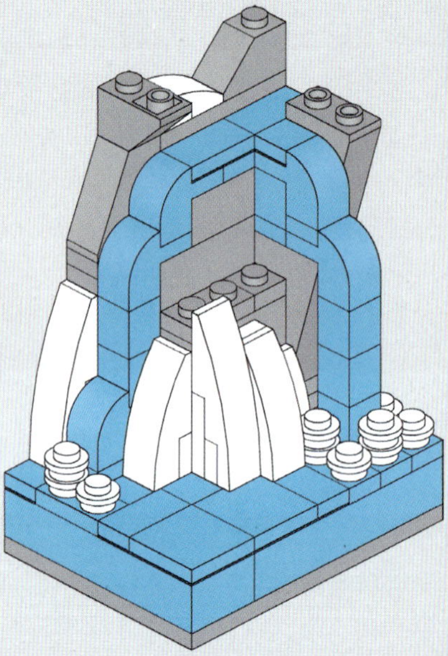

14

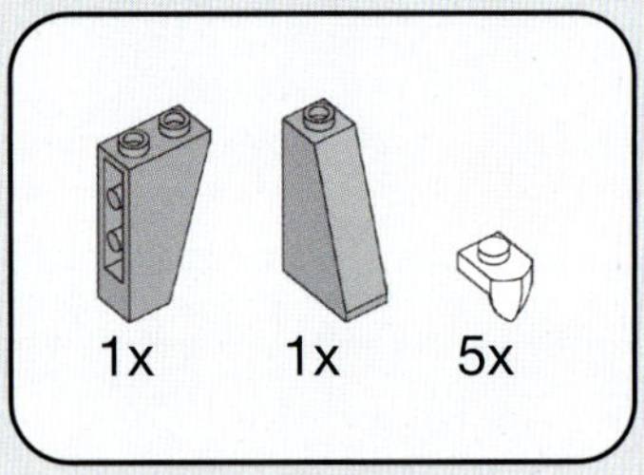

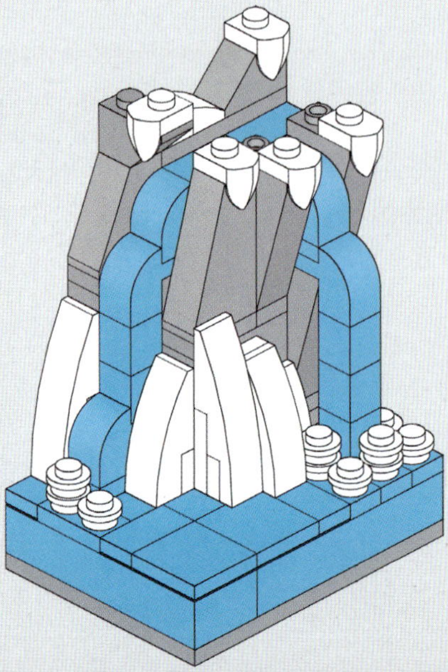

15

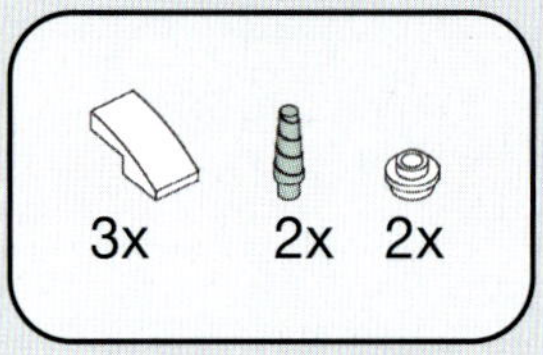

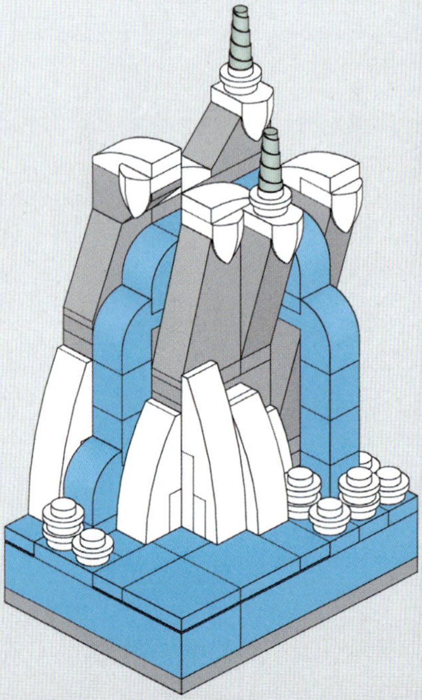

LANDSCAPE INSPIRATION

In Norse mythology, a cosmic cow named Audhumla played an important role in creating the Viking world—yes, it's complicated. You'll only need your imagination and some LEGO bricks to expand your winter waterfall into a mythical Viking landscape.

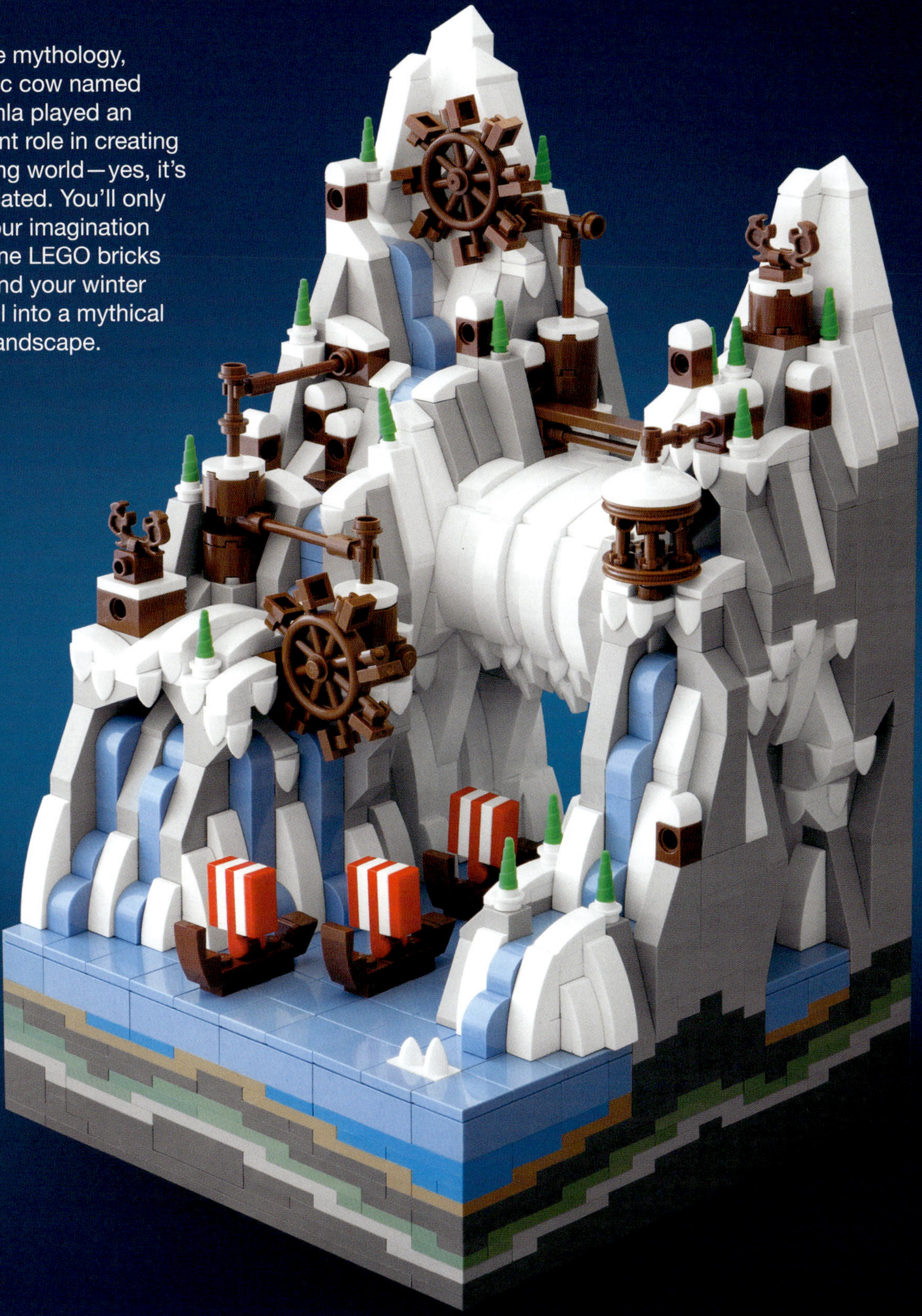

PLANT KINGDOM

Plants bring vibrance to a LEGO world, adding bursts of color like earthbound fireworks. They can serve as subtle accents or take center stage in a lush garden scene. LEGO plants need no watering and can be rearranged at will—though they may need the occasional dusting.

BUSHES AND SHRUBS

Humble 1×1 round plates transform into verdant plant growth. A single stud is enough space to add some color with a bush or shrub.

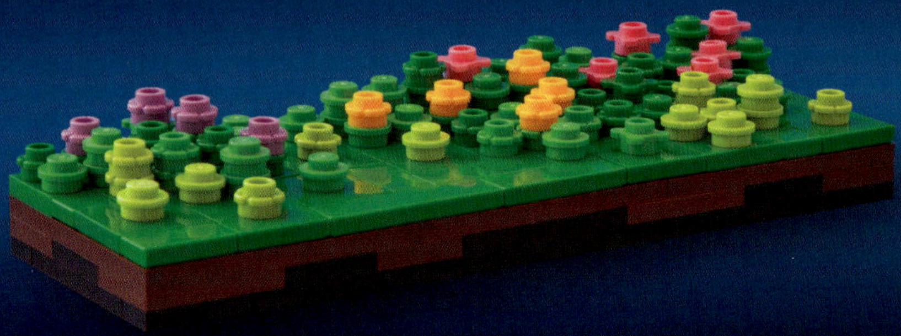

Shrubs and bushes are made using basic 1×1 round plates (#4073) and 1×1 round plates with flower edges, available in four-petal (#33291) and five-petal (#24866) varieties.

These elements come in a wide range of colors for green, flowering, and autumnal foliage. Use them individually or stack them for natural variations in height.

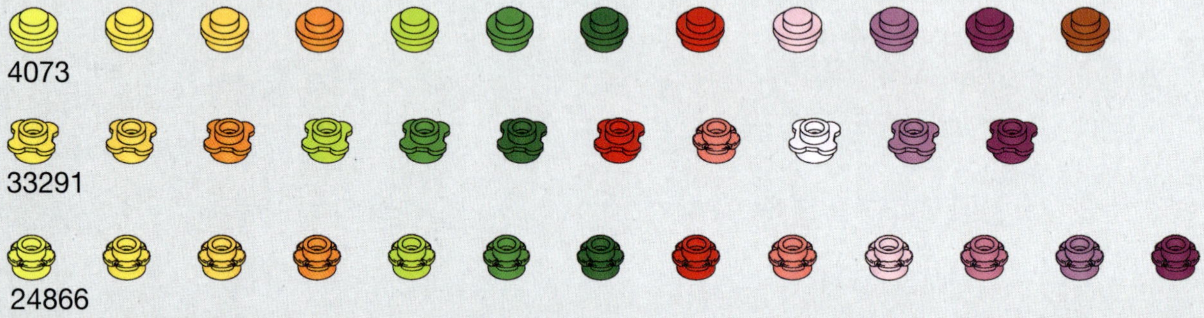

SIMPLE TREES

You can create a forest using simple trees made from just two elements: a 1×1 round plate with an open stud as the base and a vertical piece for the trunk or foliage.

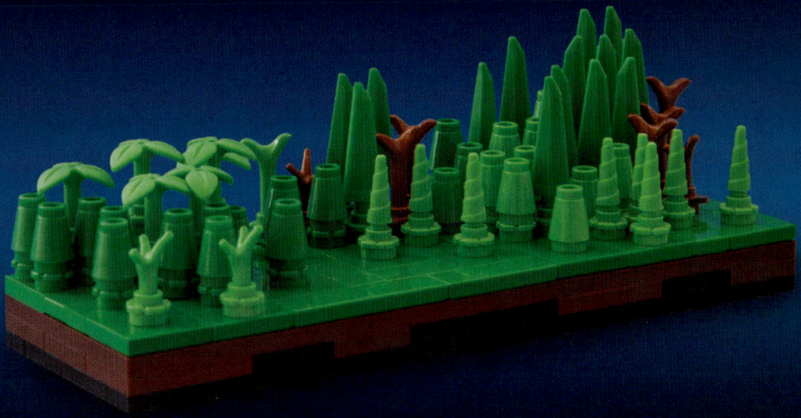

The 1×1 round plates with open studs below serve as bases for the vertical elements on the right. Combine them to create a wide variety of trees.

A 1×1 cone (#4589b) can stand on its own. Using a base element provides extra detail.

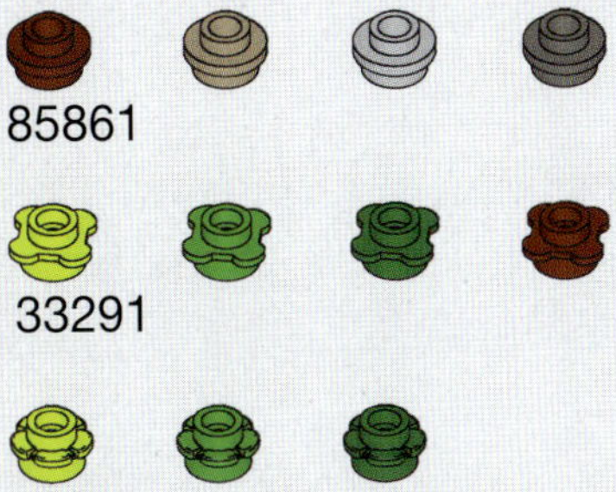

+

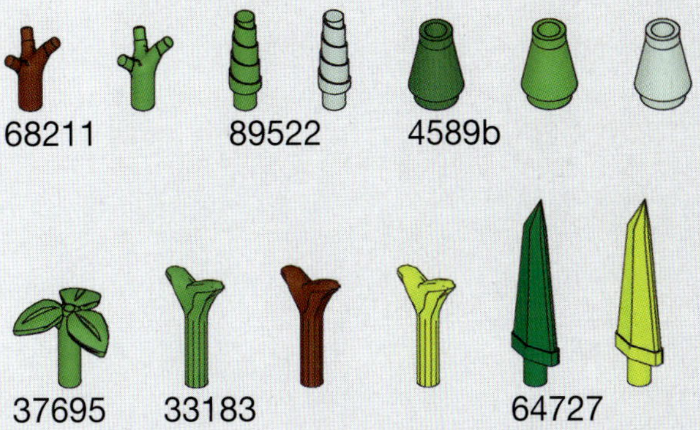

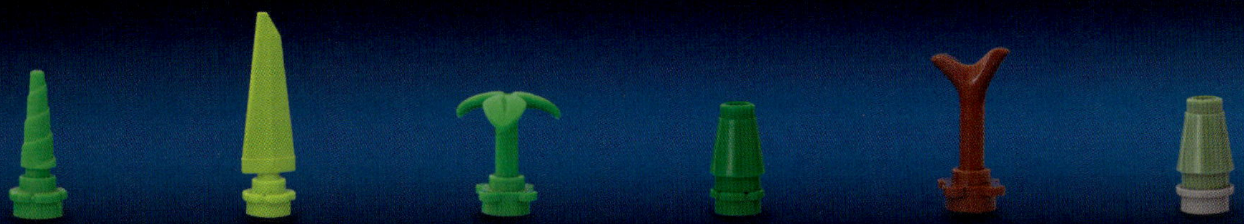

REDWOOD TREE

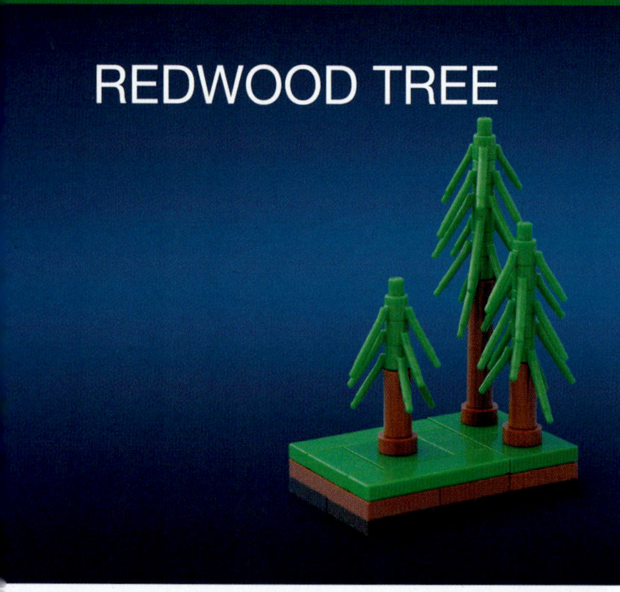

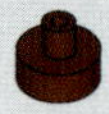

1x
20482

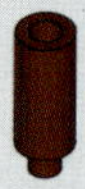

1x
37762

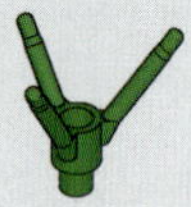

4x
24855

Add extra trunk or leaf elements—or both—to adjust your tree's height.

1

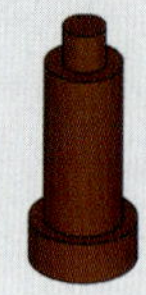

2

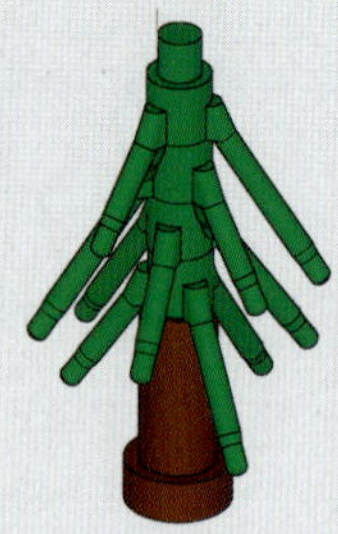

FLOWERING TREE

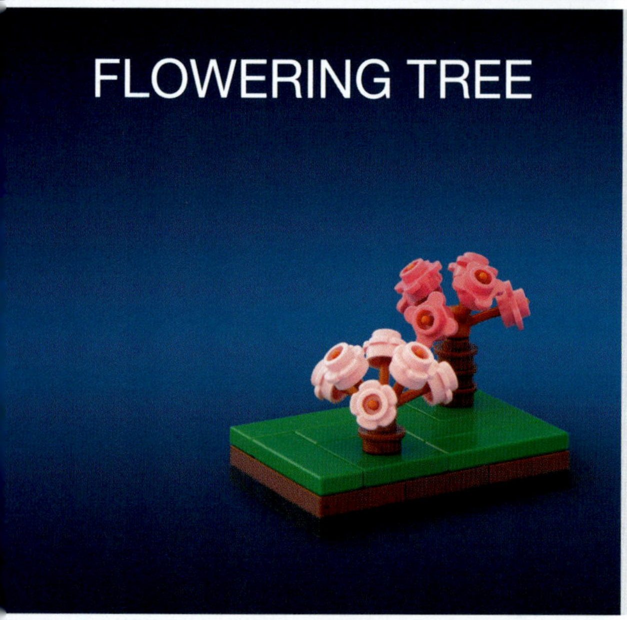

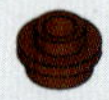

2x
85861

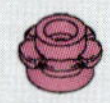

6x
24866

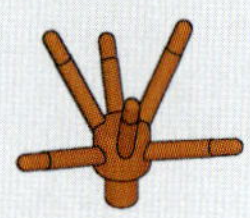

1x
19119

Add extra trunk elements to make your tree taller. Customize the stem and flower colors to your preference.

1

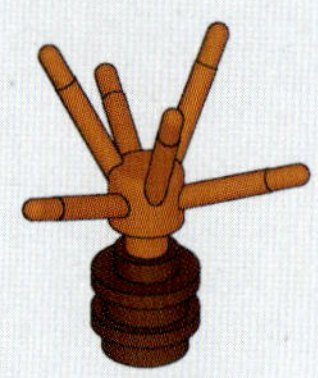

2

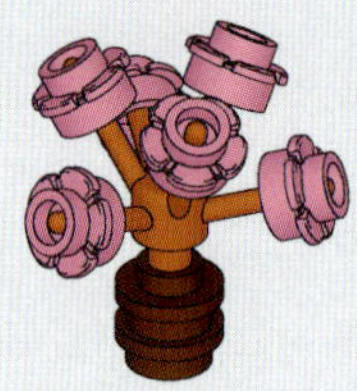

BIG-LEAF MAPLE

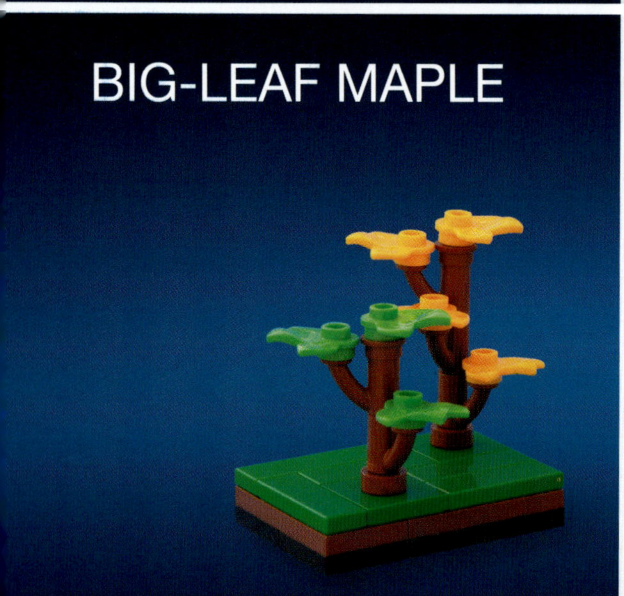

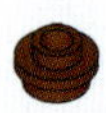

1x
85861

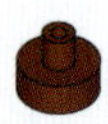

1x
20482

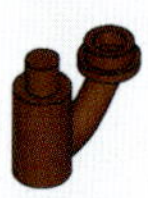

2x
1566

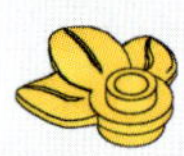

3x
32607

Add extra trunk elements to change the height. Customize the leaf colors as you prefer.

1

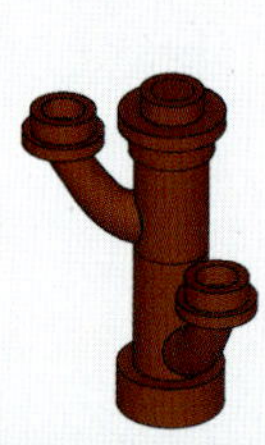

2

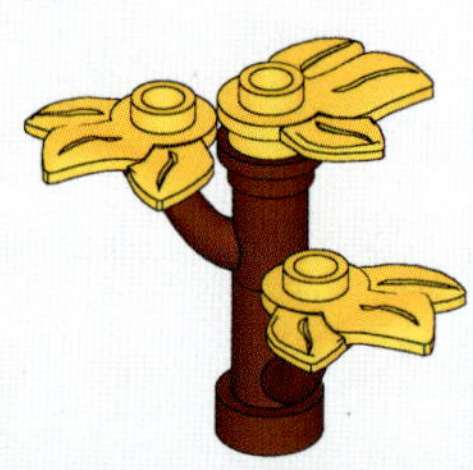

GARDEN OF SIMPLE PLEASURES

In your world, plants can be wild or tamed. These plants form a manicured garden, deliberately shaped by landscape architects. Below, you'll find simple instructions to re-create each of the plants pictured.

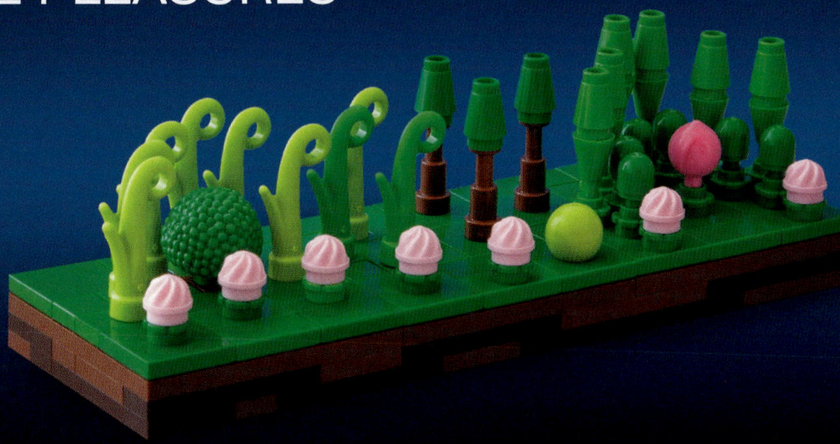

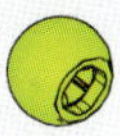

1x
32474

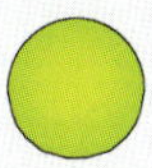

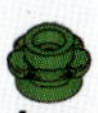

1x
24866

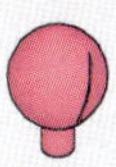

1x
5234

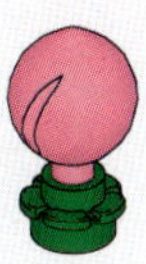

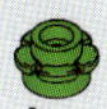

1x
24866

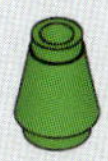

1x
4589b

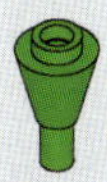

1x
11610

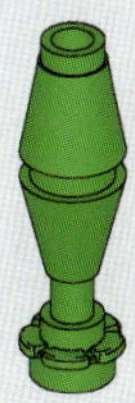

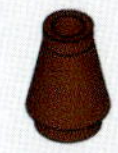

1x
4589b

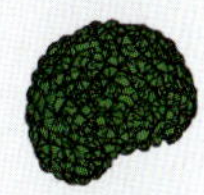

1x
87995

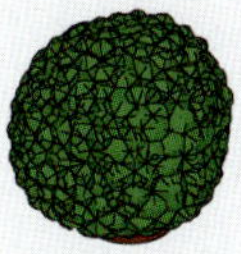

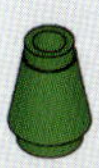

1x
4589b

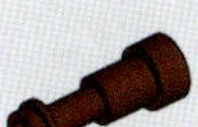

1x
64644

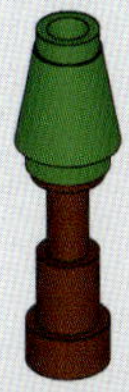

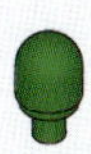

1x
58176

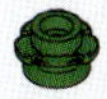

1x
24866

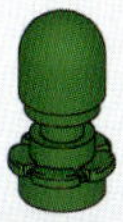

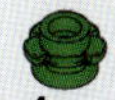

1x
24866

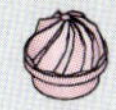

1x
15470

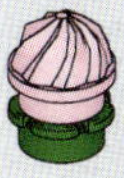

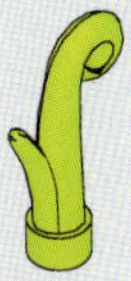

1x
15279

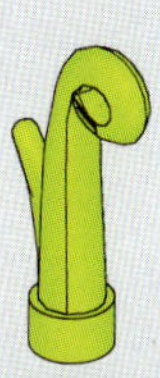

UMBRELLA TREE

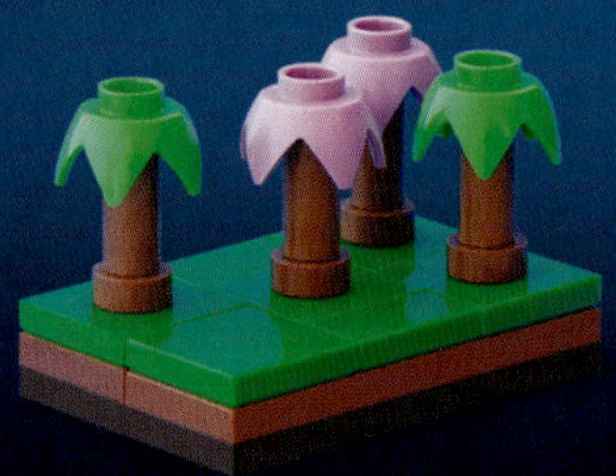

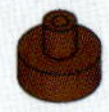

1x
20482

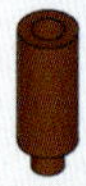

1x
37762

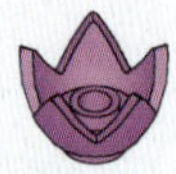

1x
39262

The inverted crown used to make this tree is available in seasonal colors, from spring lavender to summer green to autumn yellow.

1

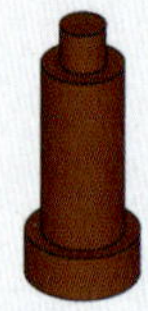

2

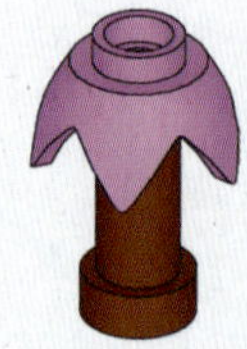

CEDAR HEDGE

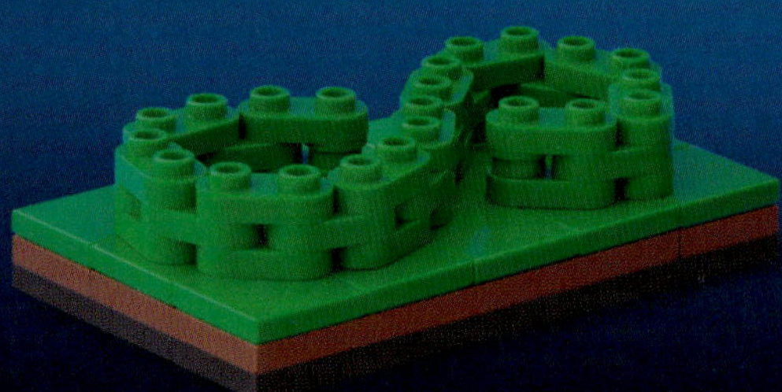

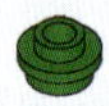

2x
85861

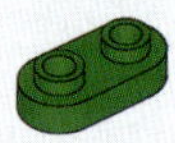

11x
35480

Shape the round plates used for the cedar hedge to form curves or sharp angles. Use this building technique to create hedges of any length.

1

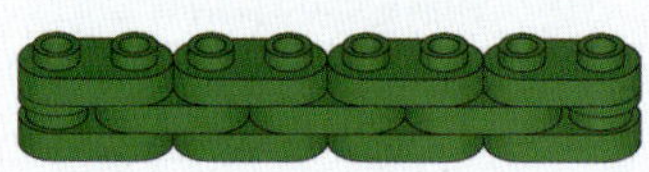

2

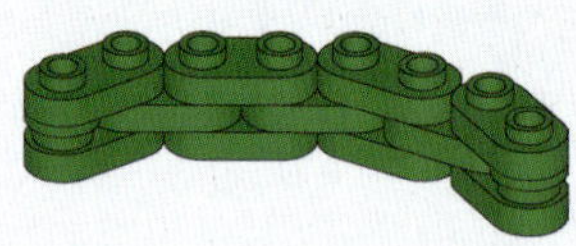

TOPIARY

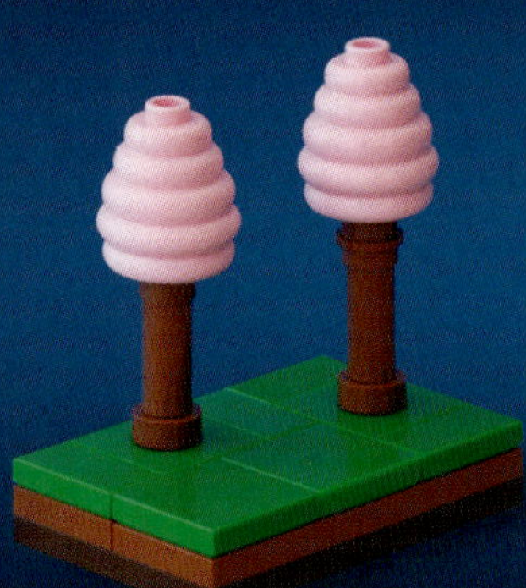

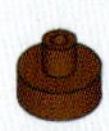

1x
20482

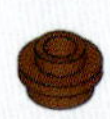

1x
85861

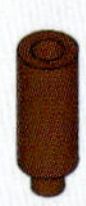

1x
37762

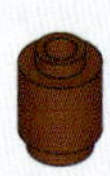

1x
3062

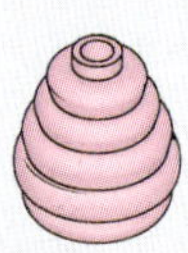

1x
35574

Add extra 1×1 round plates to adjust your topiary tree's height.

1

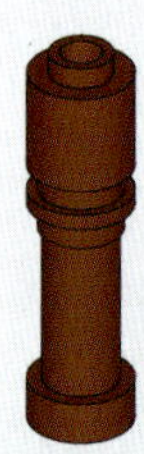

2

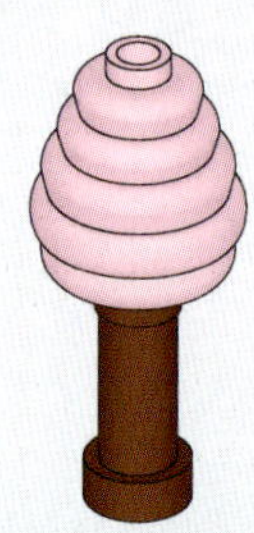

GARDEN INSPIRATION

Formally arranged garden plants contrast with the tall conifers that grew here naturally before the castle's construction.

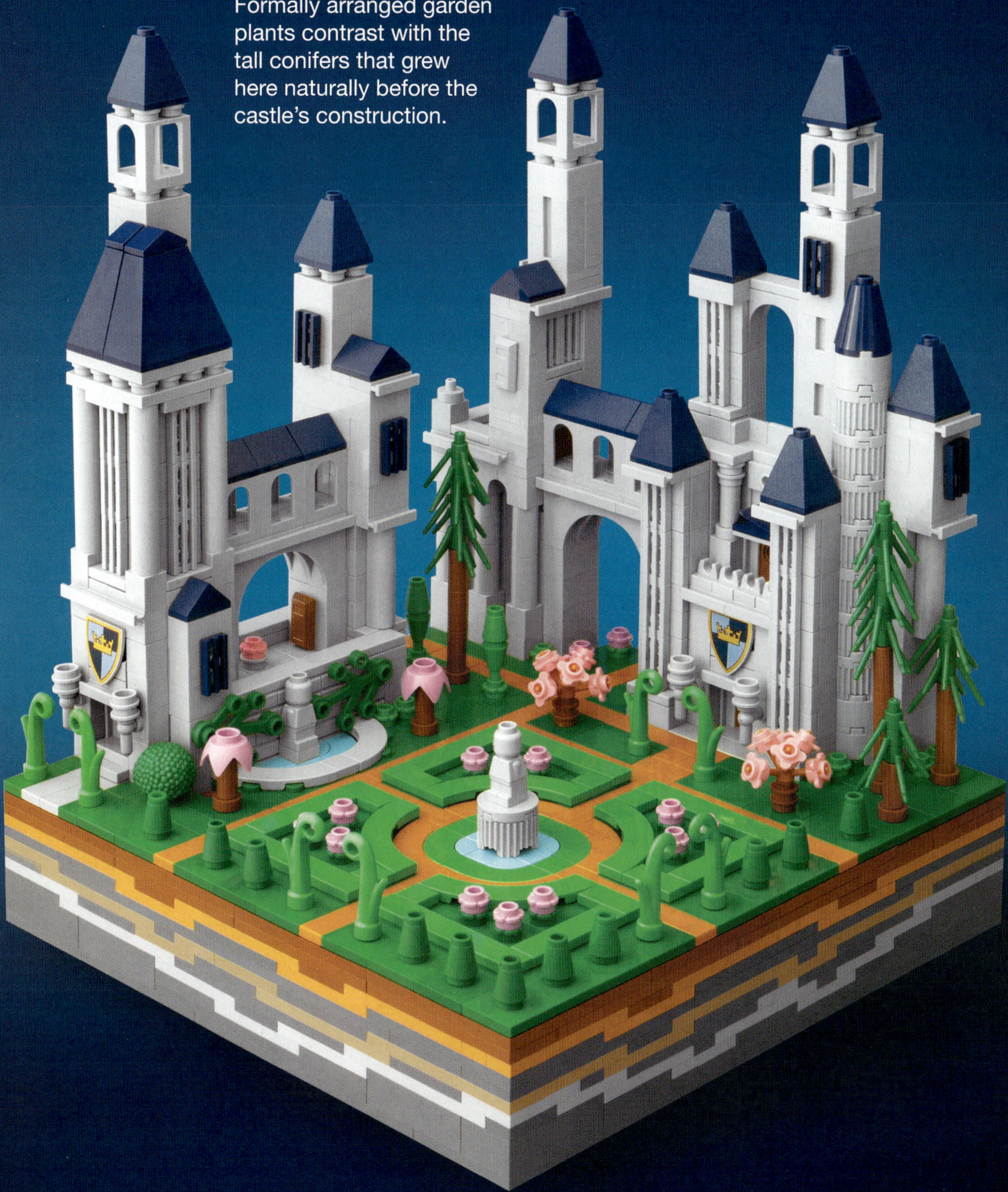

TINY HOMES

Homes are the heart of any civilization, whether built from straw, stone, wood, or brick. Houses make a world feel lived-in and alive. With just two bricks, you can create a cozy dwelling in your world.

These houses follow a simple formula: one element for the walls and door, and another for the roof. With different color and element choices, these two ingredients create a wide array of architectural styles.

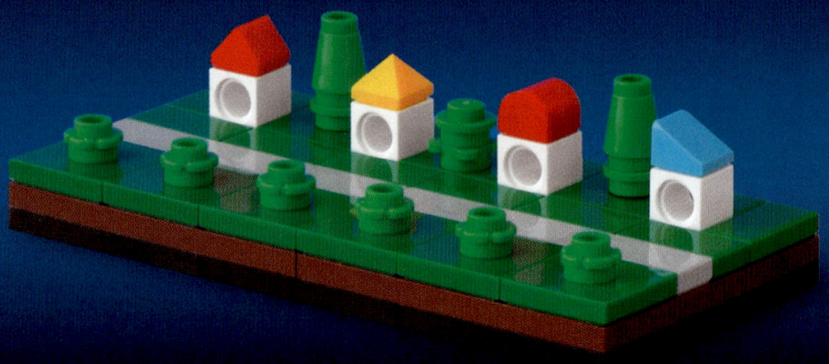

HOUSE

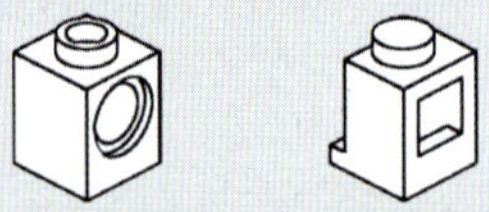

6541 4070

BASE ELEMENTS

+

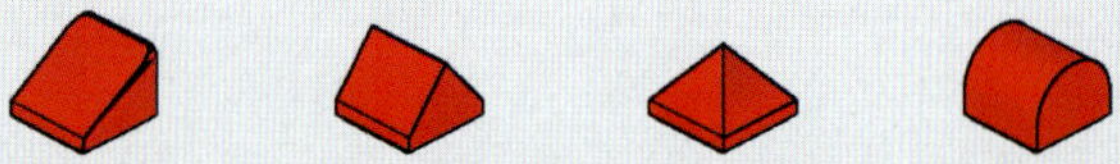

54200 35464 22388 49307

ROOF ELEMENTS

Roof colors can represent different materials, from the warm tones of terra-cotta tiles to the cool grays of slate. Here are some roof ideas for your homes.

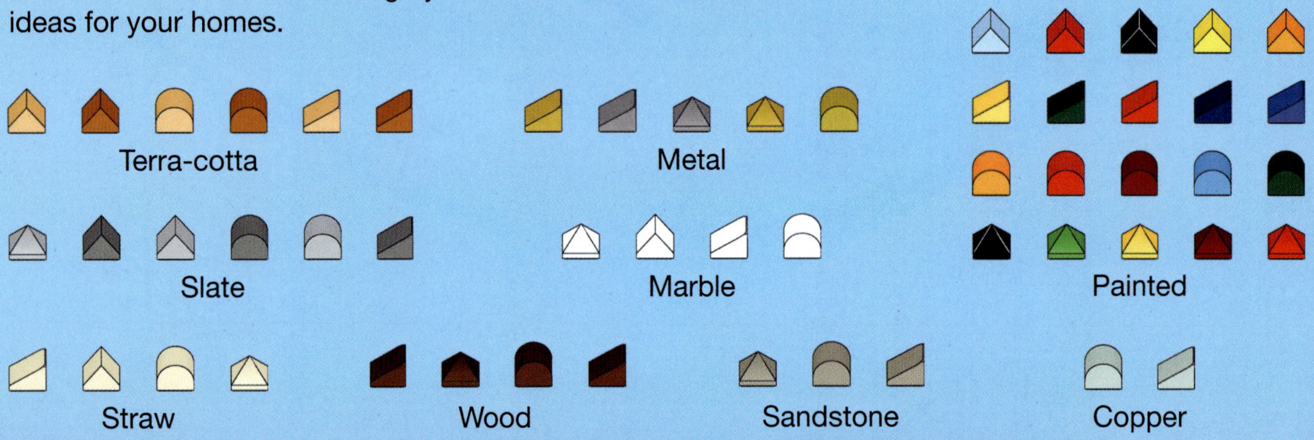

STREETSCAPING

Streetscaping is the art of designing the spaces between buildings. A well-planned street isn't just a way to get from place to place—it's a journey enhanced by safety features and interesting things to see.

Streetscaping defines your world as a thriving metropolis or a cozy country hollow. Experiment with infrastructure and rebuild as you please—most LEGO projects don't require city council approval.

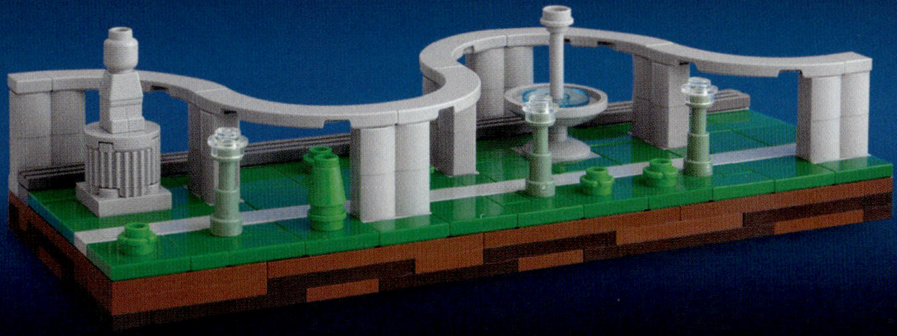

BASIC ROADS

Roads are represented by tile elements that come in an array of shapes, allowing them to fit into any build.

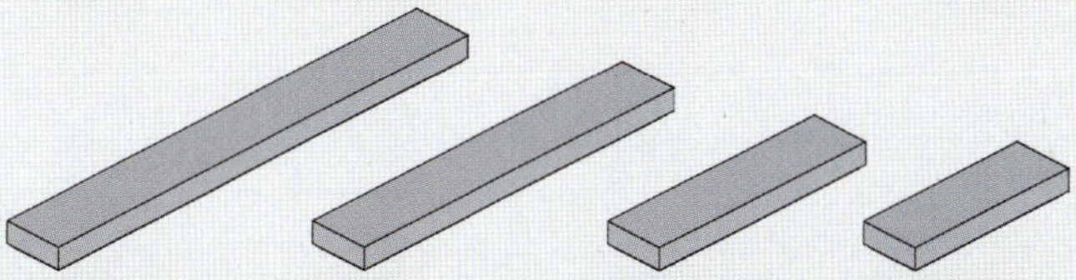

4162 6636 2431 63864

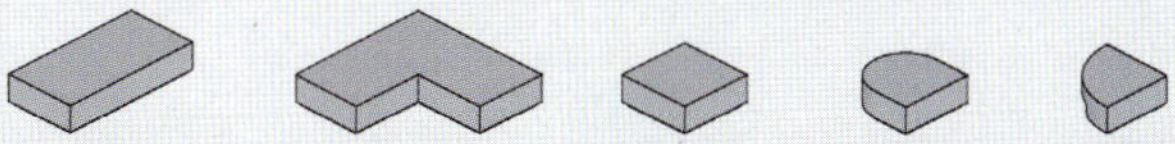

3069 14719 3070 24246 25269

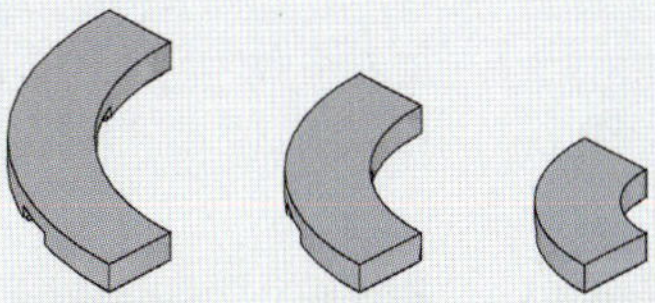

27507 79393 27925

RAILROADS

Make railroads with grille tiles, currently available in only one size.

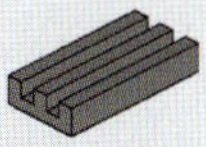

2412b

Use different tile colors to represent various road surfaces. These suggestions cover common options, but if a yellow brick road is more your style, so be it!

Pavement Asphalt

Gravel Dirt

ELEVATED HIGHWAY

Zoom above the fray on an elevated highway. Keep your highways simple, or make them squiggly like a spilled bowl of spaghetti.

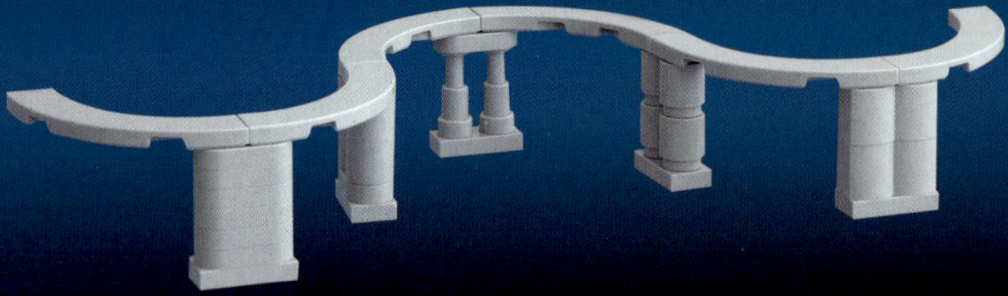

Elevated highways rest on supports called *piers*. Here are some ideas for LEGO concrete piers. You can increase their height by adding 1×2 plates to the bottom.

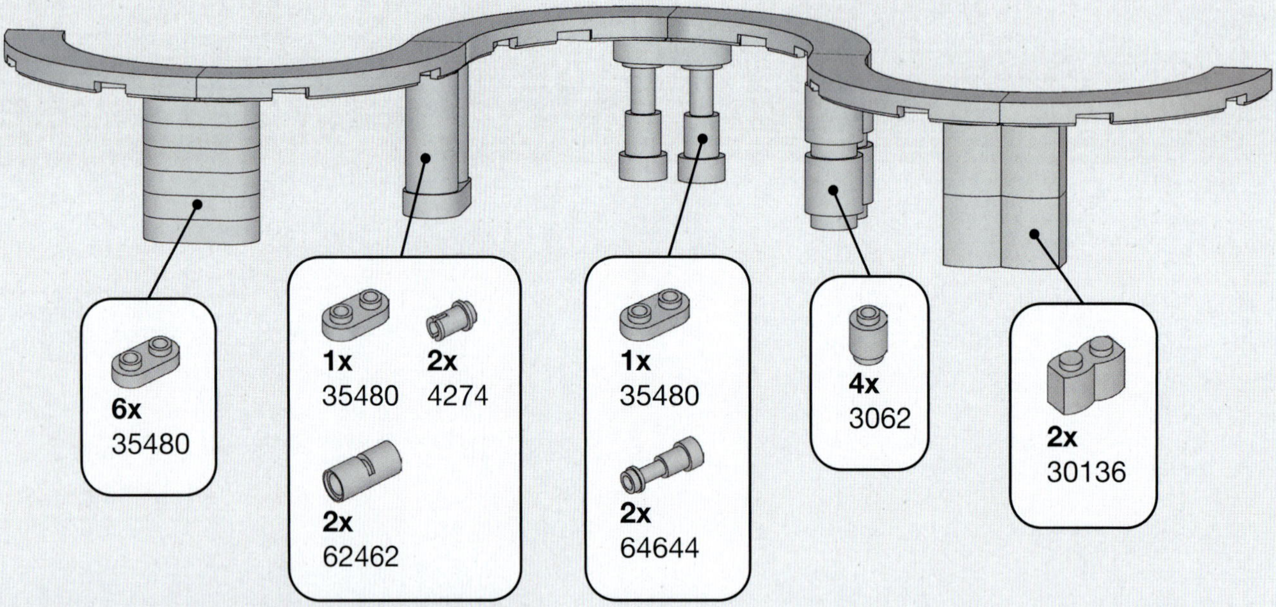

STREETLAMPS

Light the way with practicality or style.

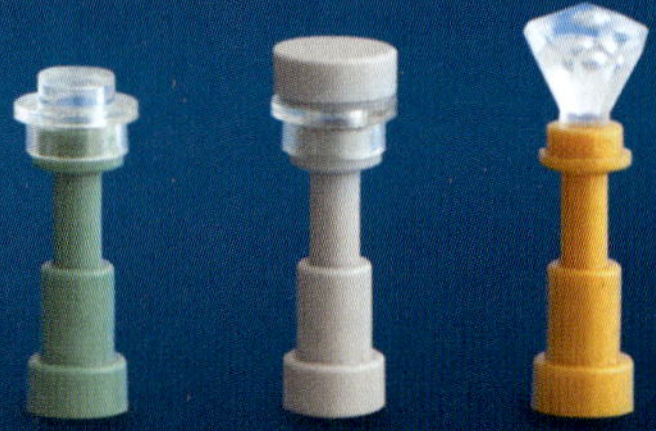

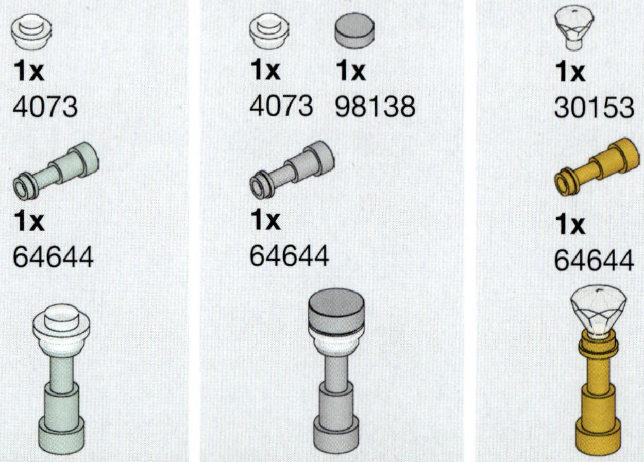

TRUSS BRIDGE

Where there are obstacles to overcome, a sturdy truss bridge gets it done.

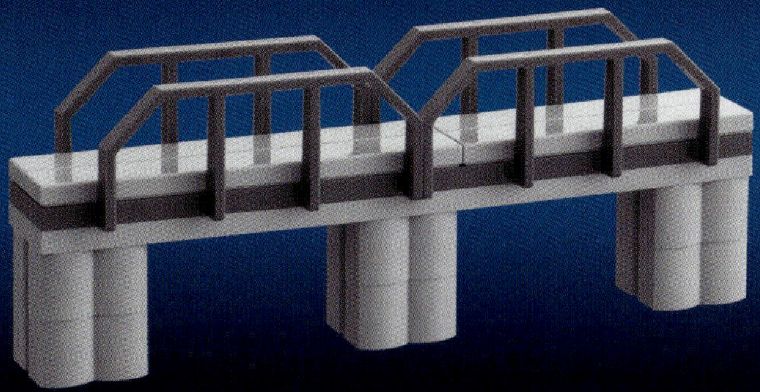

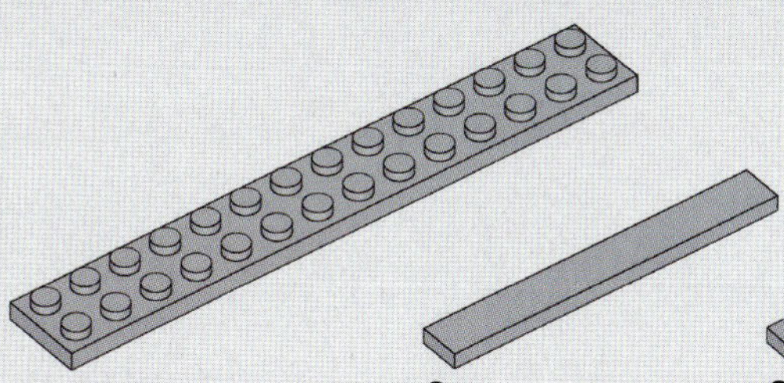

1x
91988

2x
4162

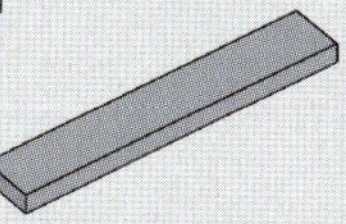

2x
6636

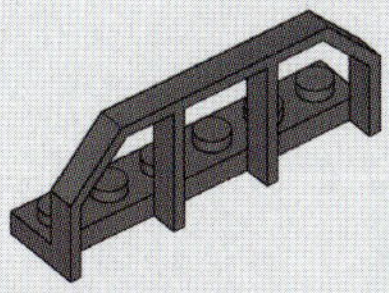

4x
6583

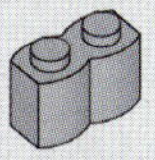

12x
30136

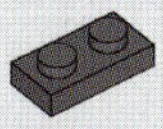

2x
3023

1

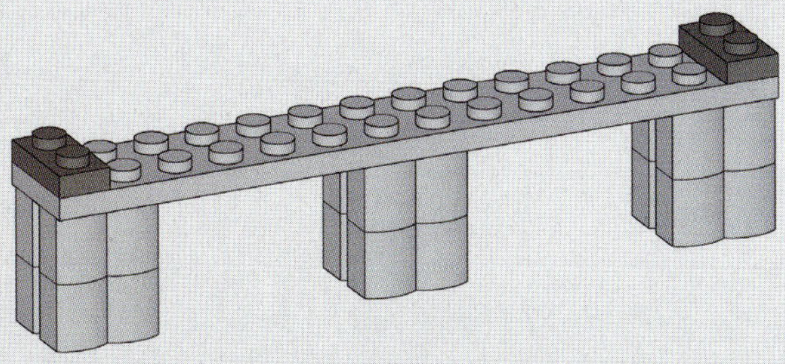

2

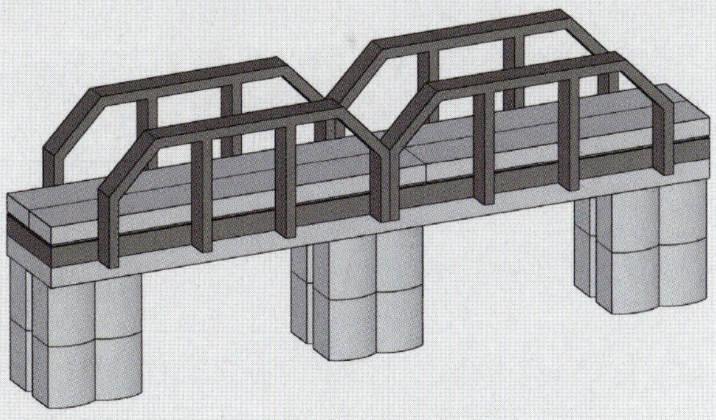

ARCH BRIDGE

The arch bridge is an ancient design still used today.

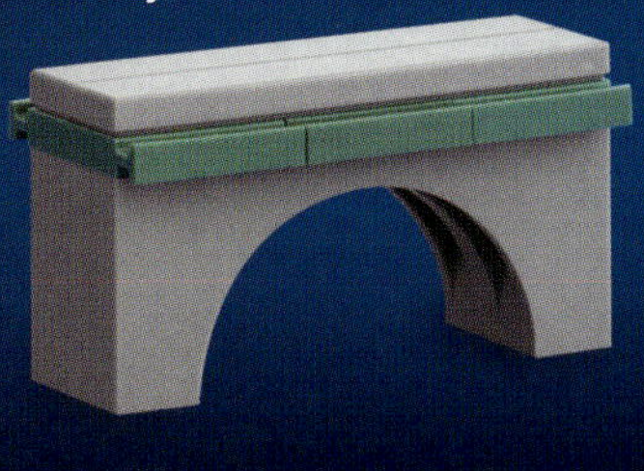

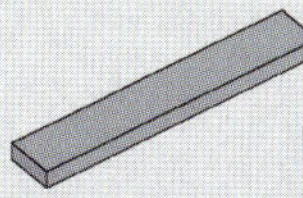

2x
6636

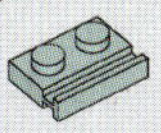

6x
32028

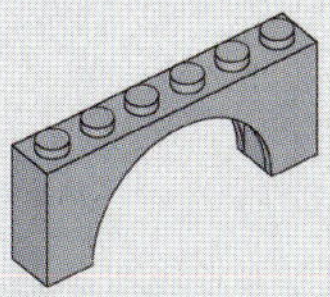

2x
15254

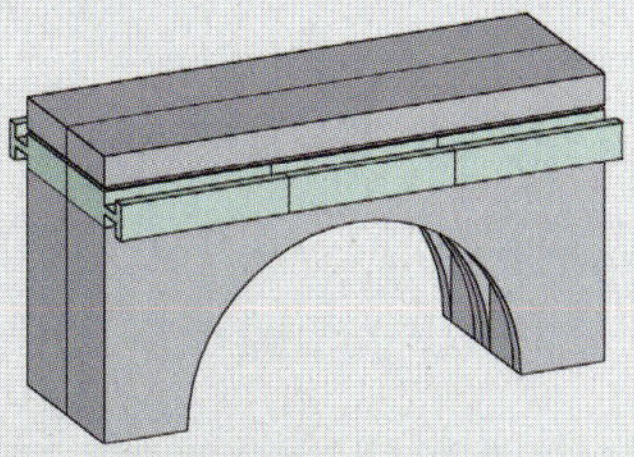

HERO PILLAR

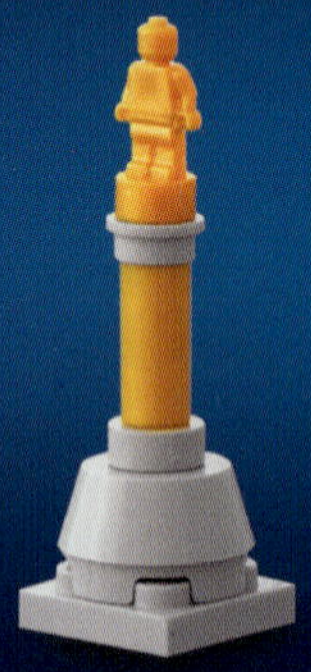

1x 90398 | 1x 4073 | 1x 20482

1x 3022 | 1x 98100 | 1x 37762

1

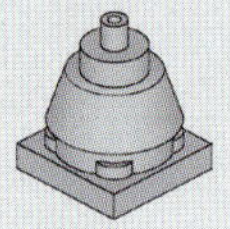

2

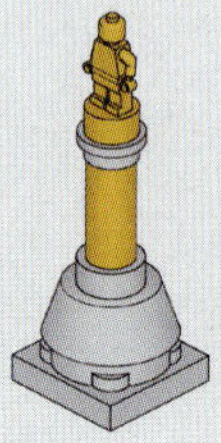

PLAZA STATUE

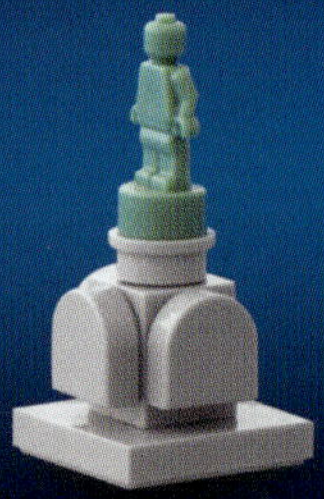

4x 24246 | 1x 4073

1x 87580 | 1x 90398 | 1x 4733

1

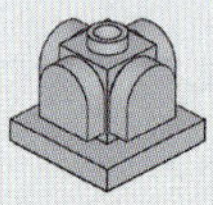

2

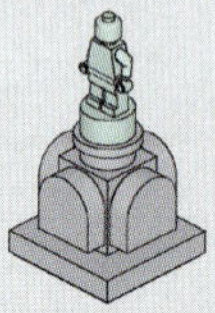

MONUMENT

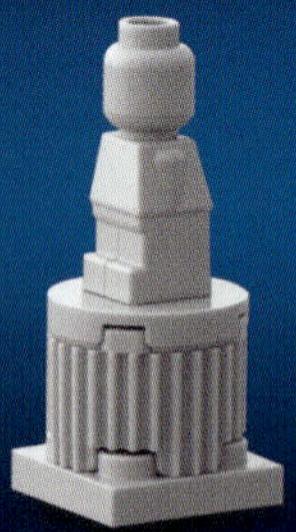

1x 3022 | 1x 18674

1x 85863 | 1x 92947

1

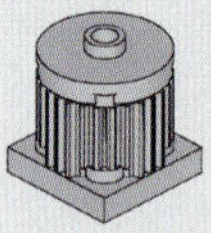

2

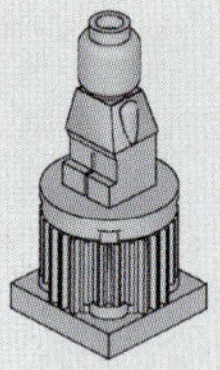

COIN FOUNTAIN

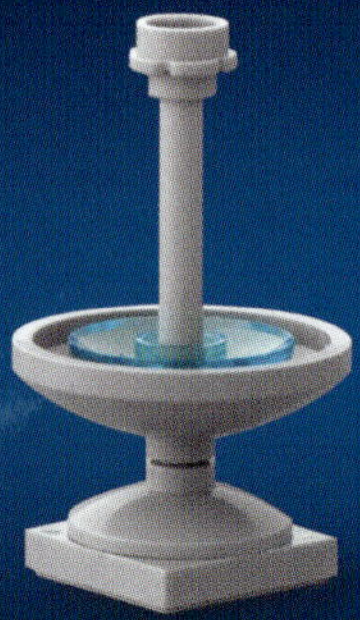

1x 4740 | 1x 4740 | 1x 24866

1x 43898 | 1x 30374 | 1x 87580

1

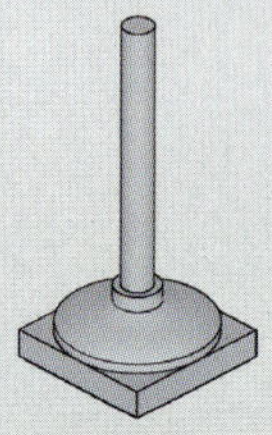

2

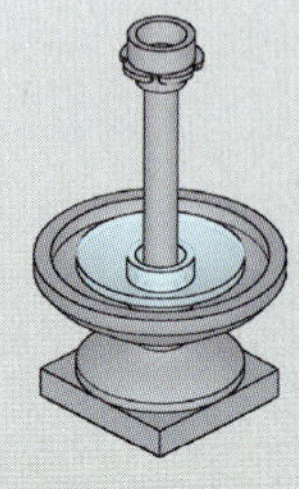

RINGWAY

In a futuristic world, streets might be a thing of the past. Magnetic ring transport is theoretical today, but it works perfectly in a science fiction setting.

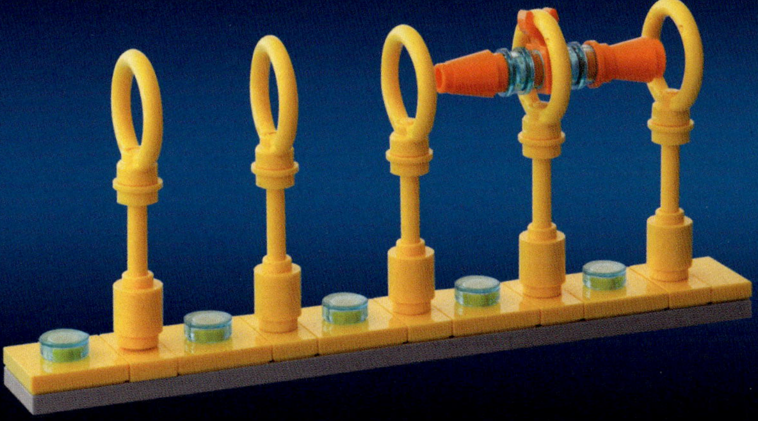

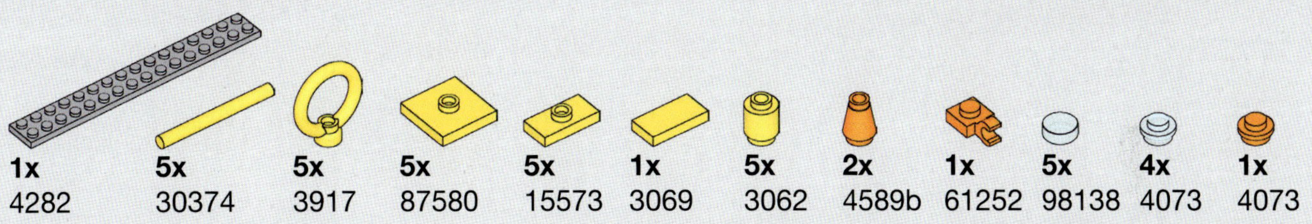

1

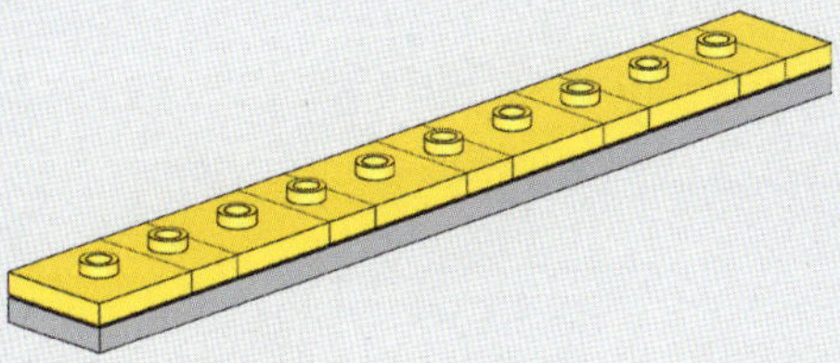

2

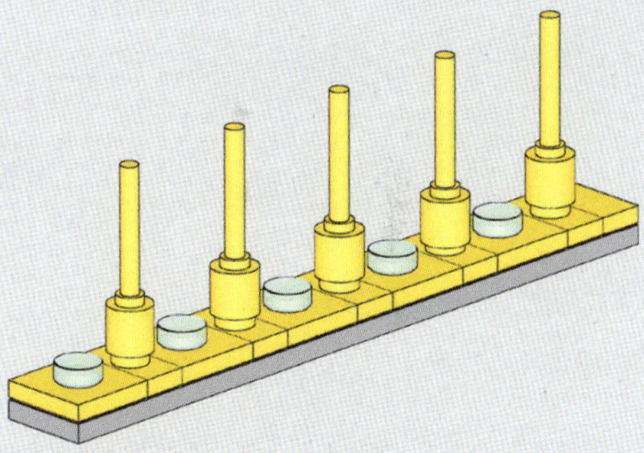

3

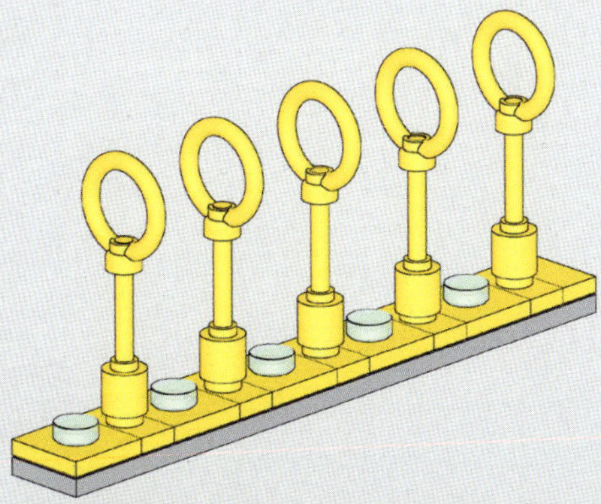

4

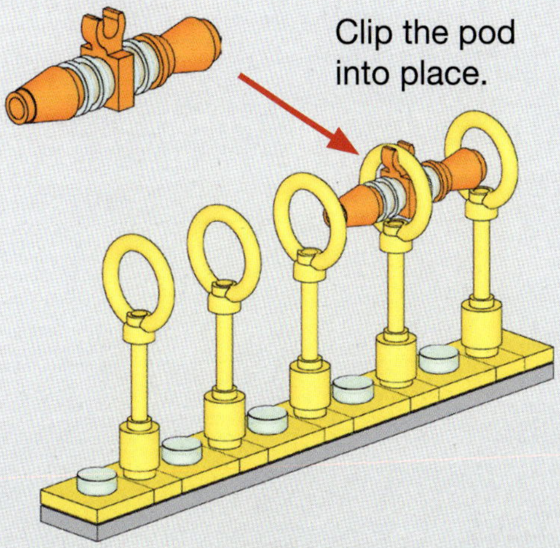

STACKING SKYLINES

Civilizations almost always feel the urge to build skyward. As children, we stack wooden blocks, the simple toy that evolved into the modular system of bricks we know and love. Now, stacking LEGO bricks into skyscrapers scratches that innate human itch in miniature.

To construct basic high-rises, we can go back to the 1950s and combine some of LEGO's oldest elements—plates—with the original LEGO building technique: stacking pieces on top of one another.

This tried-and-true method has stood the test of time across millions of LEGO creations.

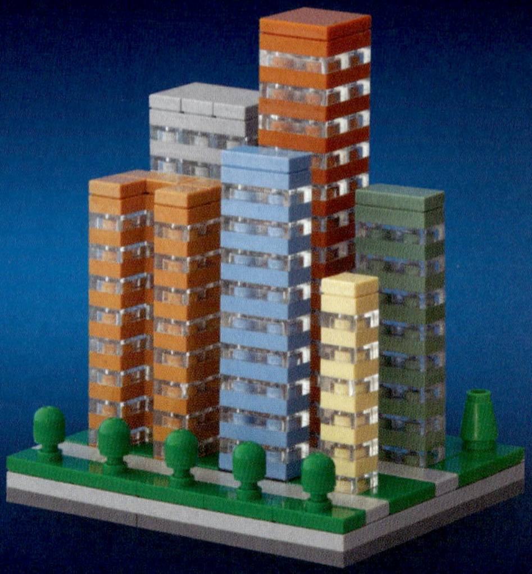

SIMPLE STACKED SKYSCRAPER

The essential formula for a stacked building is to alternate solid-colored bricks with transparent bricks, representing windows. Topping the building with a tile completes the simple structure. You can apply this formula to any plate size. Build as high as you dare.

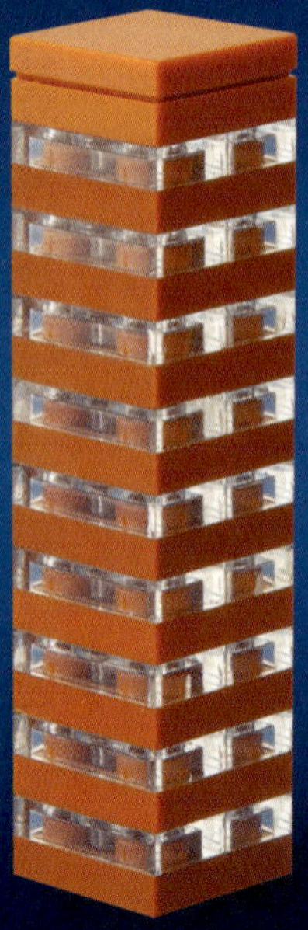

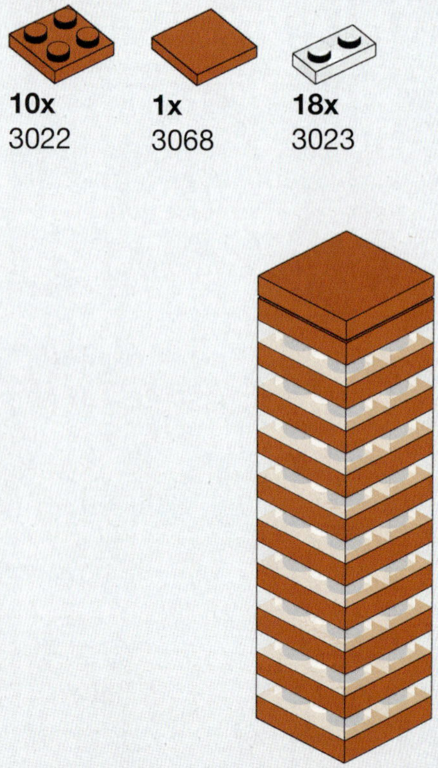

STACKING TIPS

Solid-colored plates come in many shapes, while the selection of transparent plates is more limited. Match the footprint of solid-colored layers by combining 1×1 (#3024) and 1×2 (#3023) transparent plates as needed.

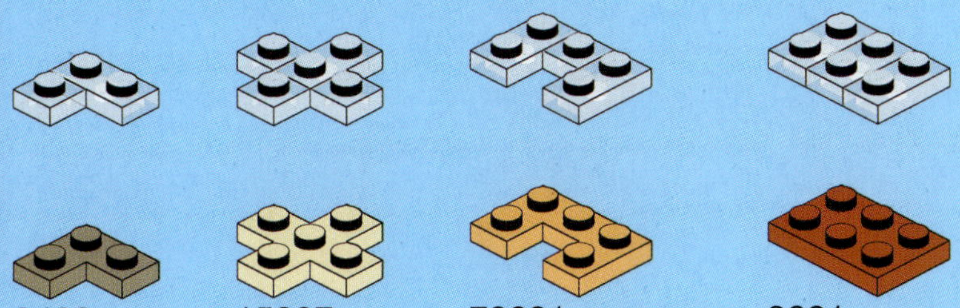

2420 15397 73831 3021

Stack rounded plates to create buildings with curved shapes. 1×1 round plates (#4073) are widely available in transparent colors, and they can stack with all solid-colored round plates.

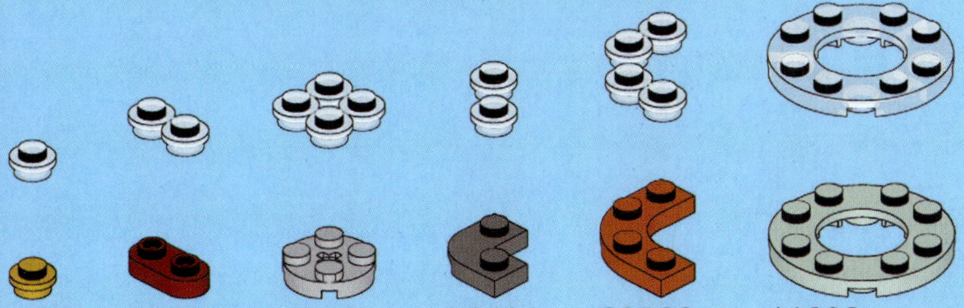

4073 35480 4032 79491 68568 11833

Top your models with tiles that match your building's footprint.

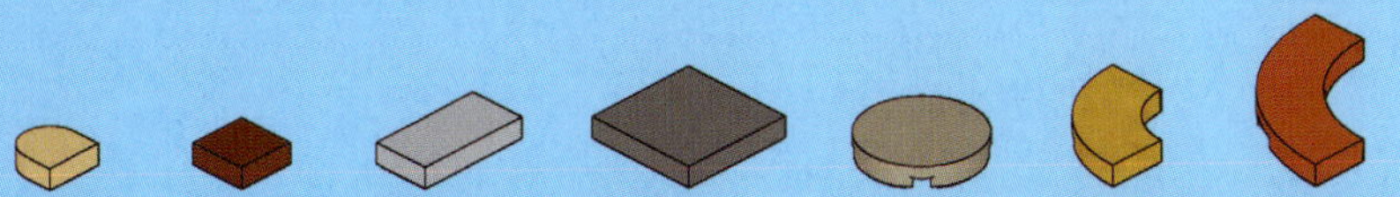

24246 3070 3069 3068 4150 27925 79393

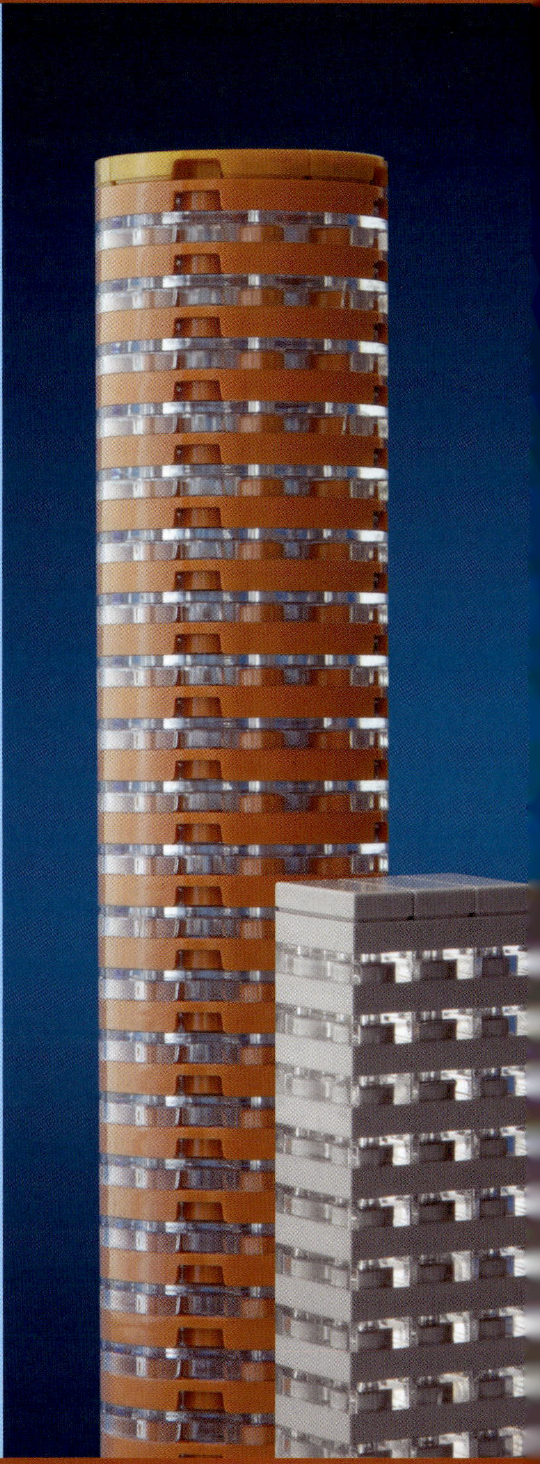

BASES AND ROOFTOPS

Simple plate stacks make convincing buildings, but if you want to take them a step further, customizing the bases and rooftops adds detail, interest, and realism to your models. Buildings often follow the same form as ancient Greek columns: They have a base, a repeating vertical section, and a distinctive top. Use the examples on these two pages for inspiration.

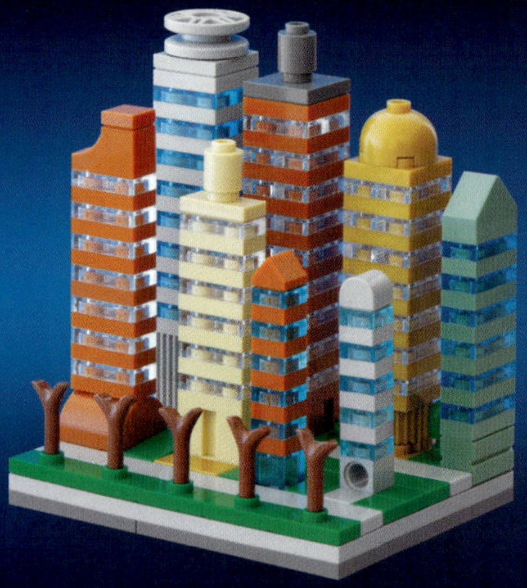

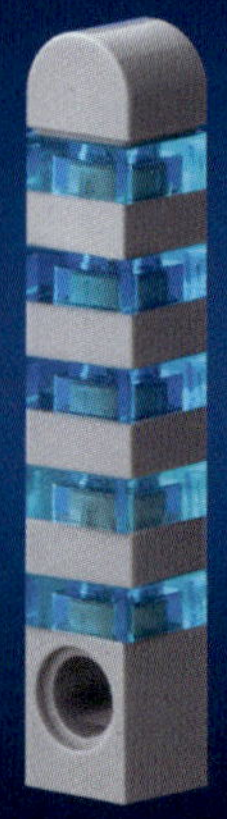

4x 3024
5x 3024
1x 6541
1x 49307

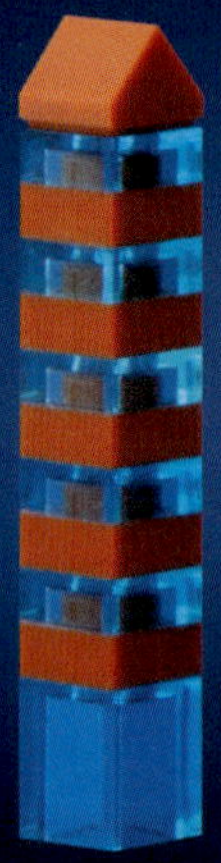

5x 3024
5x 3024
1x 3005
1x 35464

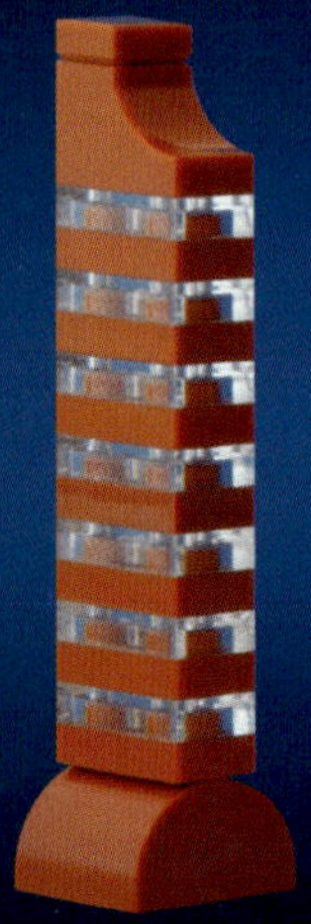

1x 3070
7x 3023
7x 3023
1x 30165
1x 78666

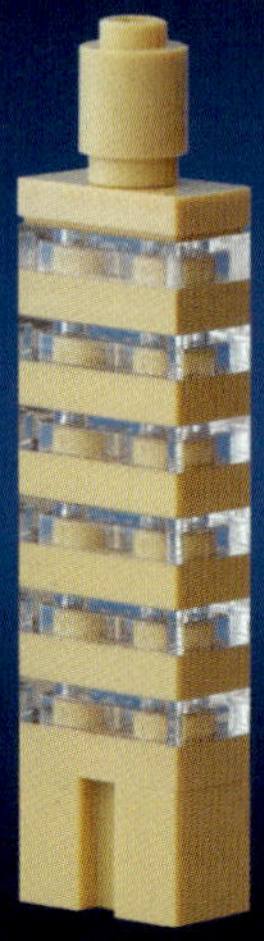

1x 15573
6x 3023
6x 3023
1x 4216
1x 3062

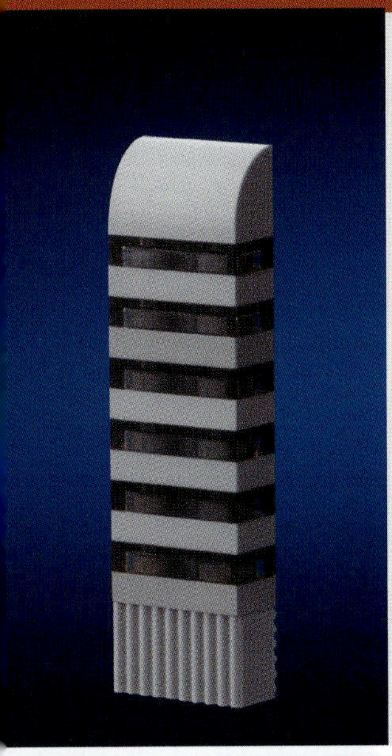

6x 3023 | 6x 3023 | 1x 37352 | 1x 2877

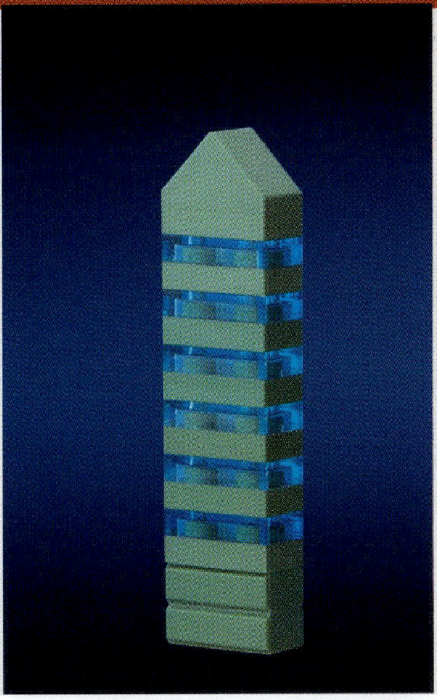

7x 3023 | 6x 3023 | 1x 98283 | 1x 3044c

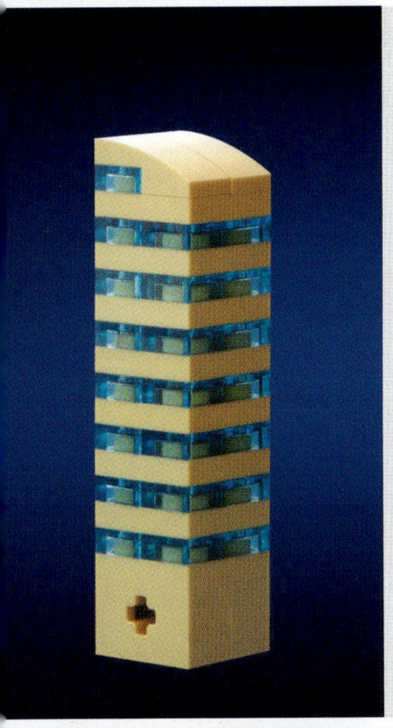

2x 32064 | 8x 3022 | 2x 11477 | 15x 3023

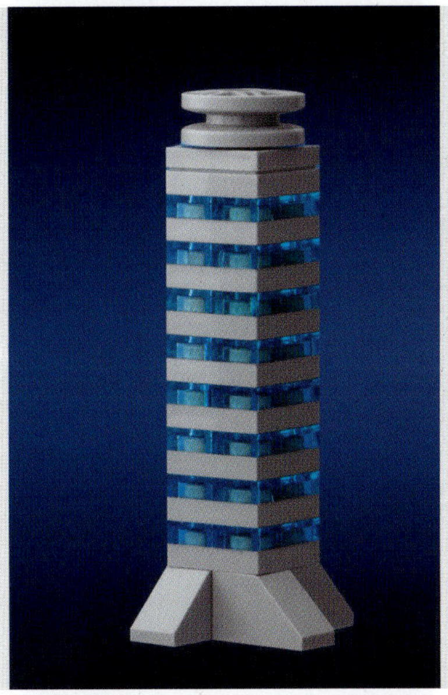

16x 3023 | 9x 3022 | 1x 87580 | 4x 3040 | 1x 56902

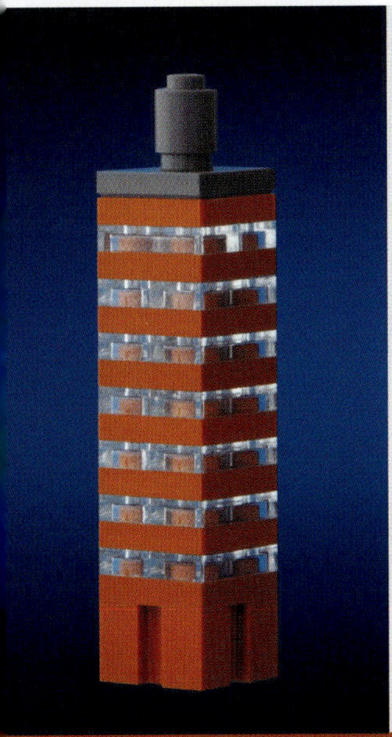

14x 3023 | 1x 87580 | 1x 3062 | 1x 90258 | 8x 3022

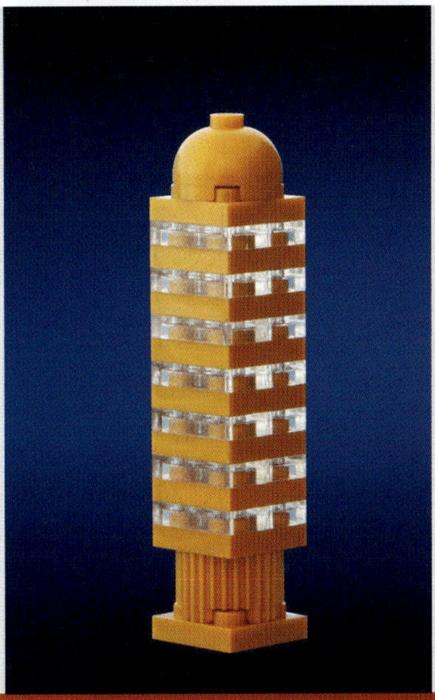

1x 92947 | 1x 553 | 9x 3022 | 14x 3023

TIERED BUILDING TECHNIQUES

Another way to add architectural interest and realism to your stacked LEGO buildings is to vary the footprint of floors as you build upward. This technique breaks up the monolithic form of simple stacks and gives your structures an eye-catching silhouette.

Whether you want to replicate the iconic step-back skyscrapers of New York City or experiment with unique shapes, varying the size of floors opens up infinite possibilities.

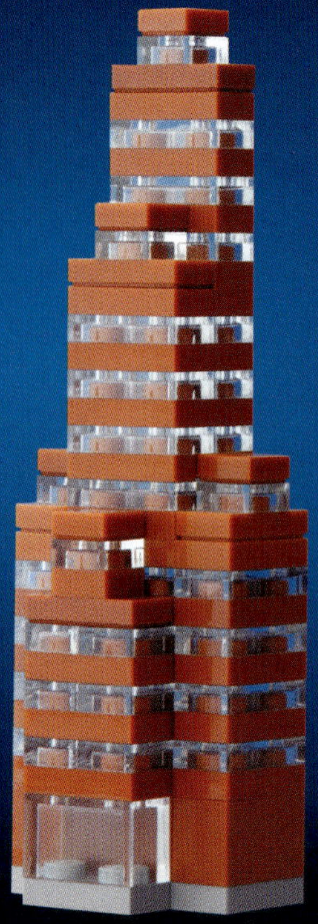

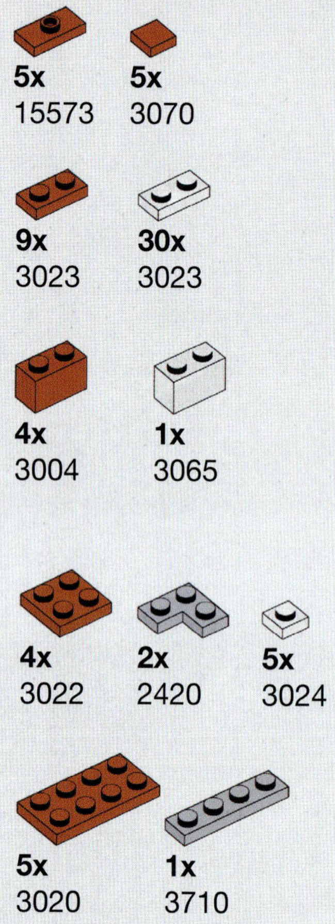

1

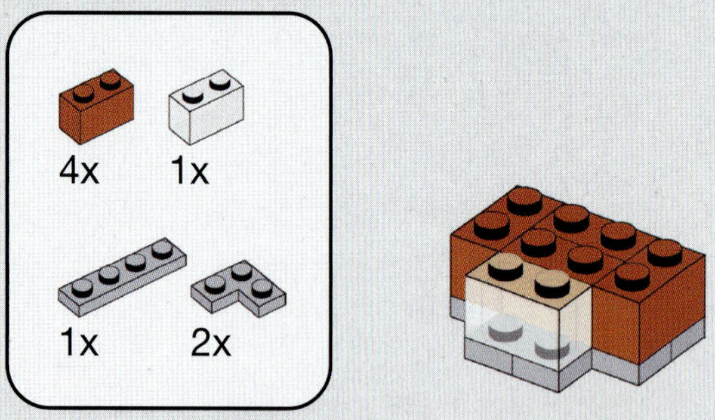

2

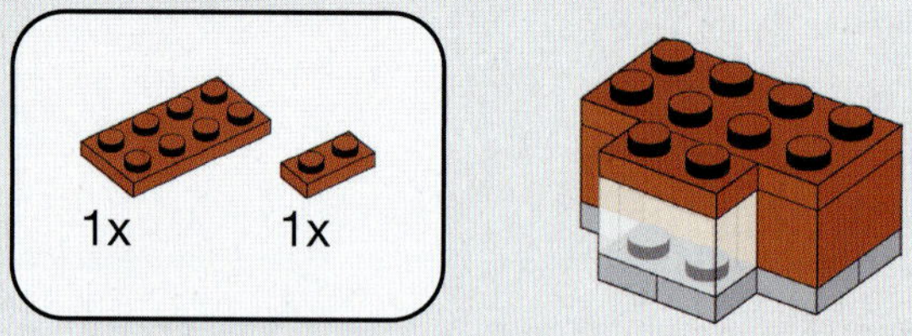

3

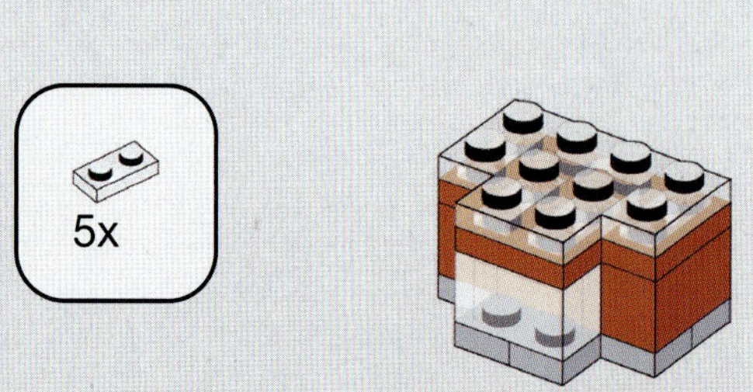

4

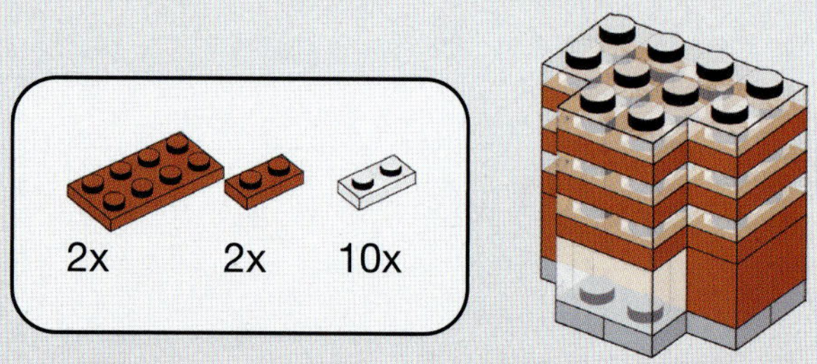

5

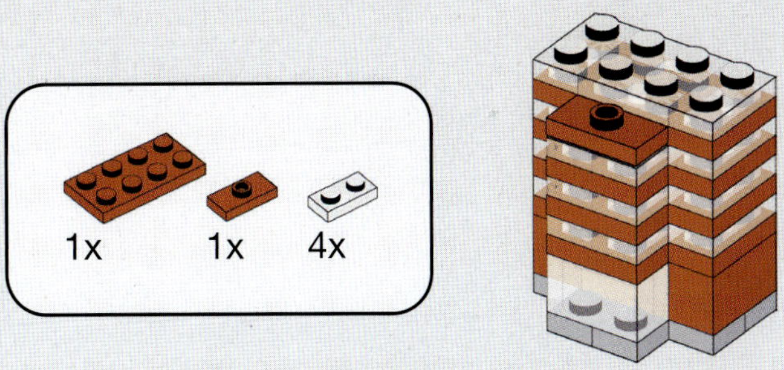

6

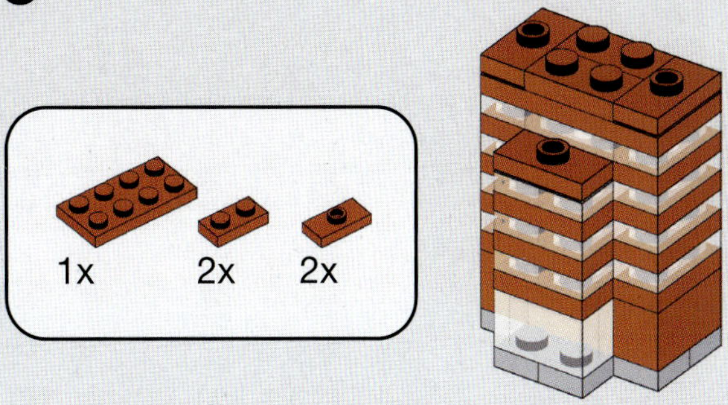

7

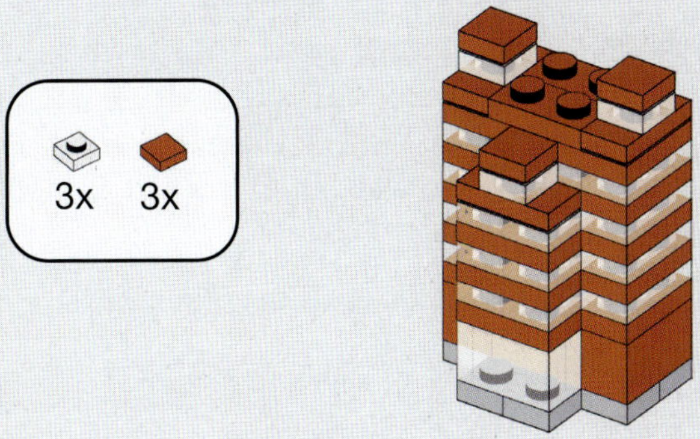

8

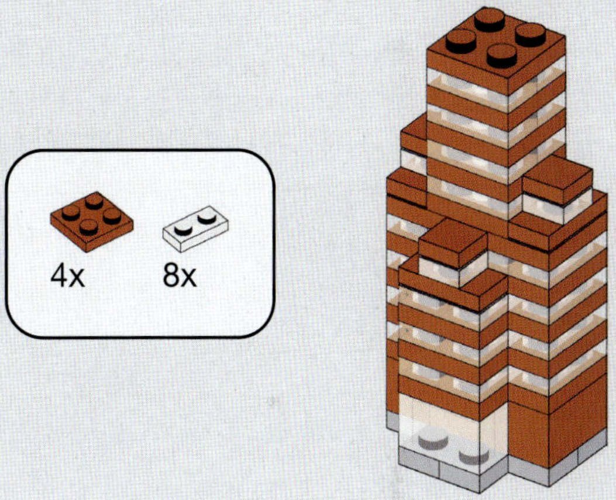

9

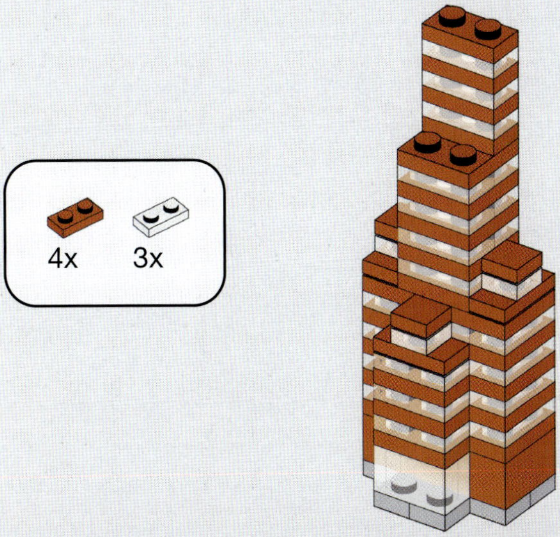

10

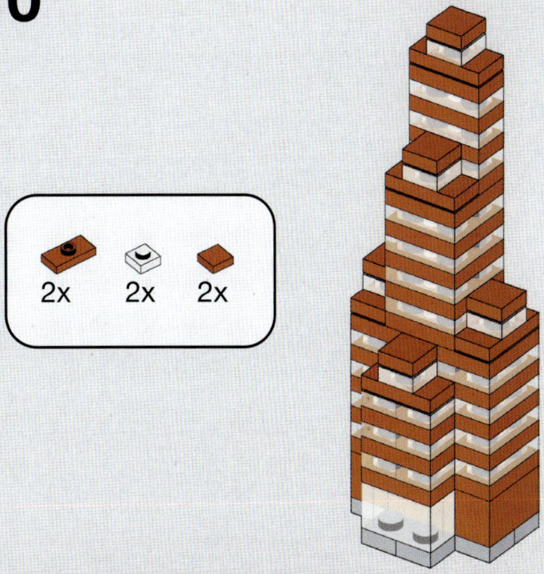

BUILDING SIDEWAYS

Sideways building is great for adding architectural details to your structures. It lets you include more features in a smaller space than simple stacking techniques allow.

Most sideways building techniques use "SNOT" (Studs Not On Top) bricks. Earlier versions match the dimensions of standard 1×1 and 1×2 bricks, with studs on at least one side as well as the top. LEGO has recently expanded the SNOT inventory with bricks that are five plates high, which align perfectly with elements placed sideways.

Turned on their side, transparent flat tiles can be used as glass curtain walls, and grille tiles can become columns or window frames. SNOT construction is also useful in creating landscapes, as seen in the Winter Waterfall on page 14. Study the basics here, then watch for more SNOT techniques in the coming pages.

ELEMENTS FOR SIDEWAYS BUILDING

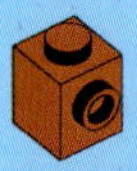
87087

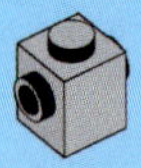
47905

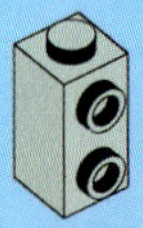
32952

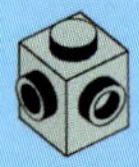
26604

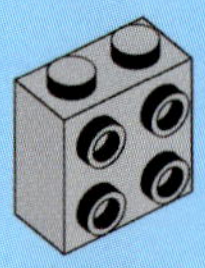
22885

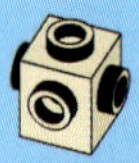
4733

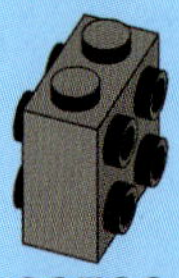
80796

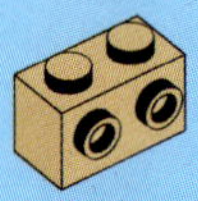
11211

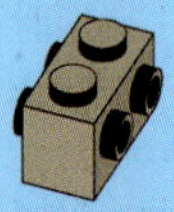
52107

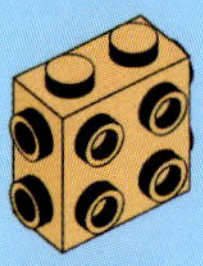
67329

TIPS FOR SIDEWAYS BUILDING GEOMETRY

When stacking traditional one-brick-high SNOT elements, stagger them with two plates in between to maintain proper LEGO geometry for attaching elements sideways.

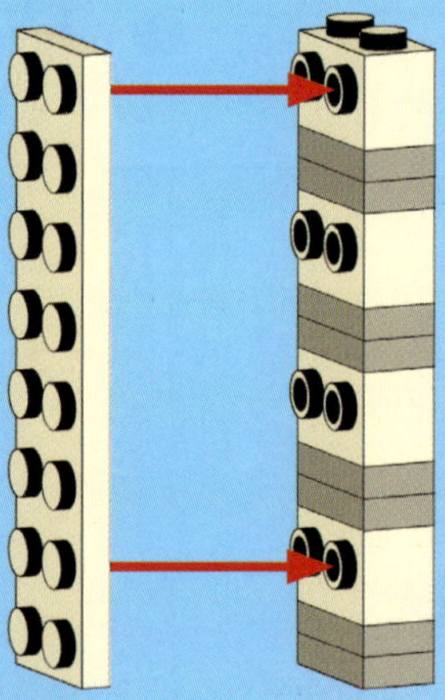

The newer five-plate-high SNOT bricks align with sideways-attached LEGO elements as is.

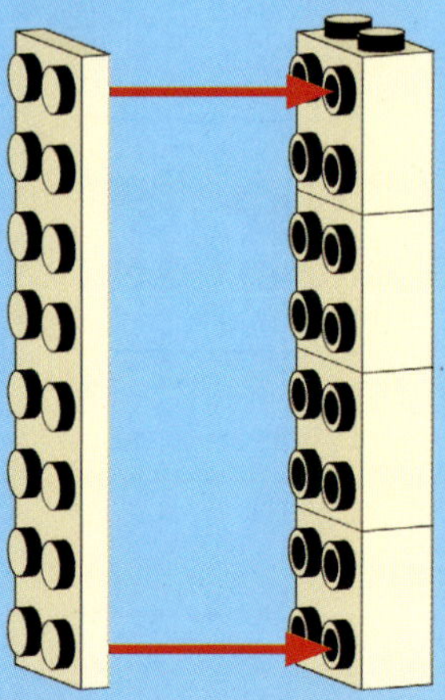

SIDEWAYS STYLING

This small model puts sideways building techniques into practice, using SNOT bricks to create a variety of architectural features in a compact space. This level of detail would be difficult to achieve with a traditionally stacked building of similar size.

Once you've built this model, try experimenting with other sideways-placed elements!

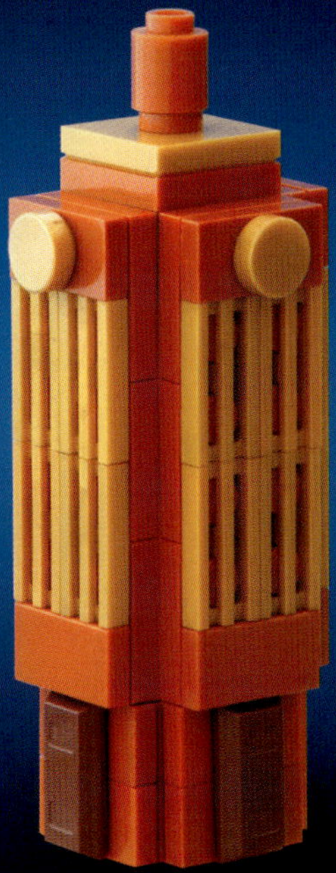

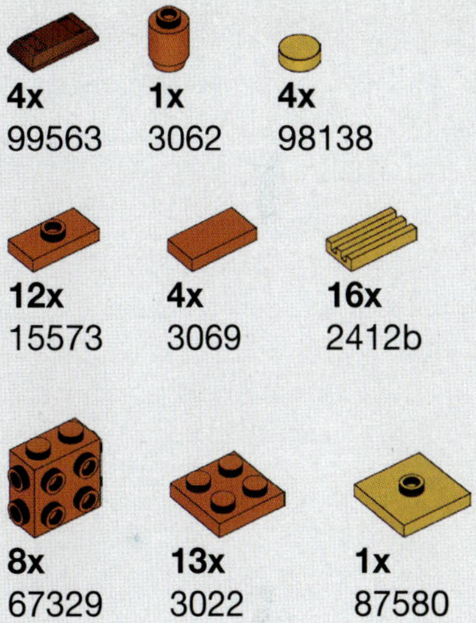

1

All four sides are identical.

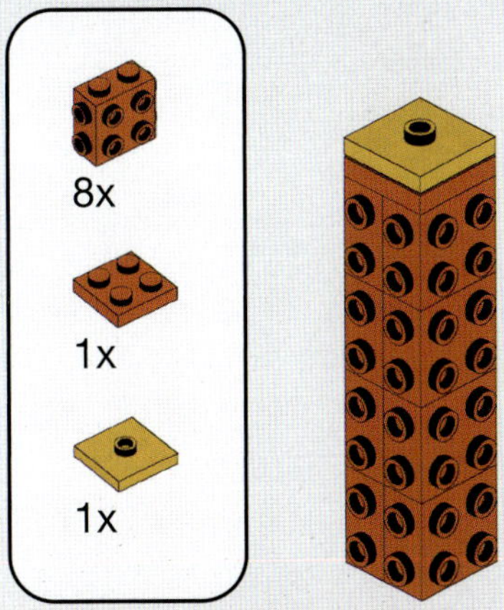

2

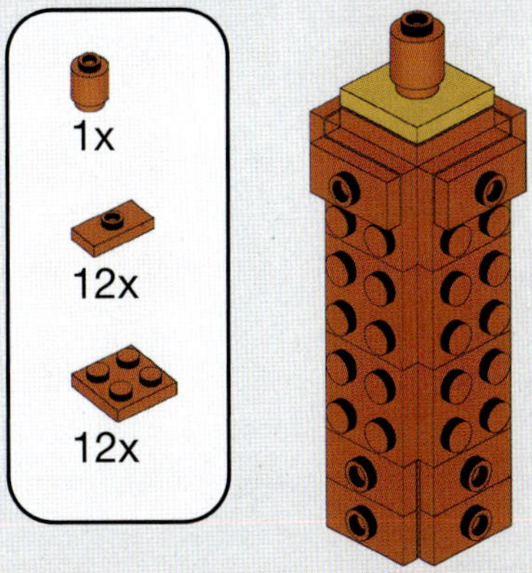

3

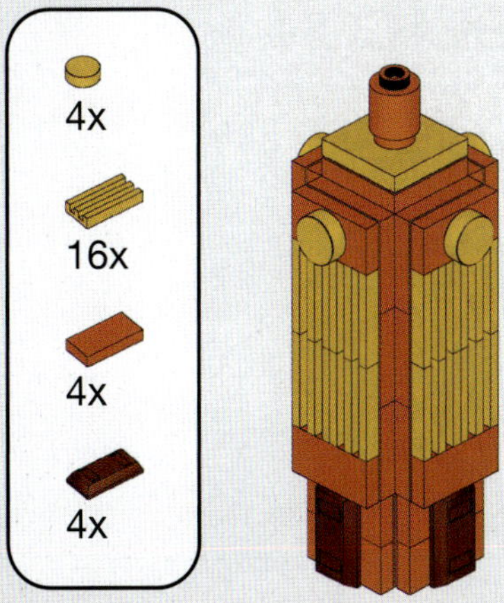

THREE-BRICK BUILDINGS

You've learned about stacking, and you've learned about building sideways. Now it's time to channel your inner sushi chef and create amazing designs using minimal ingredients. Every building in this chapter is constructed using just three brick types, and the rules are strict: Identical bricks in different colors count as separate elements.

These limitations might seem burdensome at first, but every hero's journey includes challenges essential for growth. Creating a world brick by brick is an epic task! Each build can be customized by adjusting its height: Stack bricks higher to create towering skyscrapers, or remove bricks to form cozy dwellings. Let these designs serve as inspiration for your own creations.

ARCOLOGY

4073

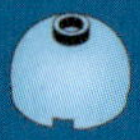
553

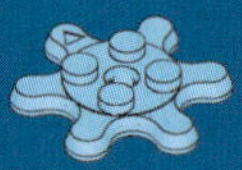
35442

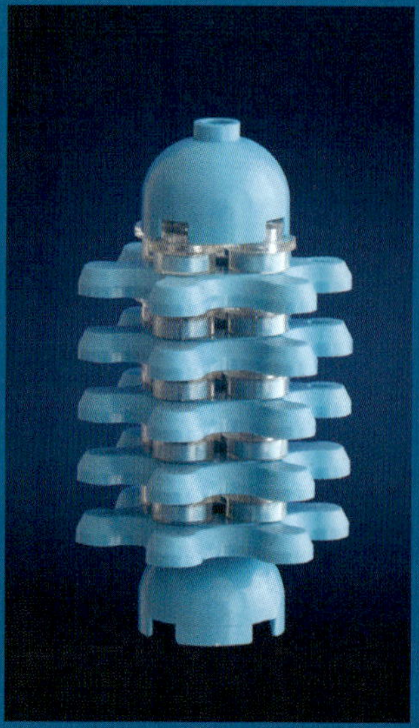

CURVING CONDO

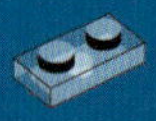
3023

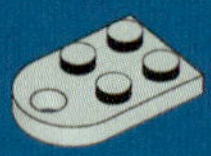
3176

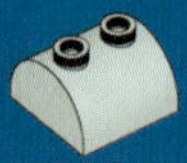
30165

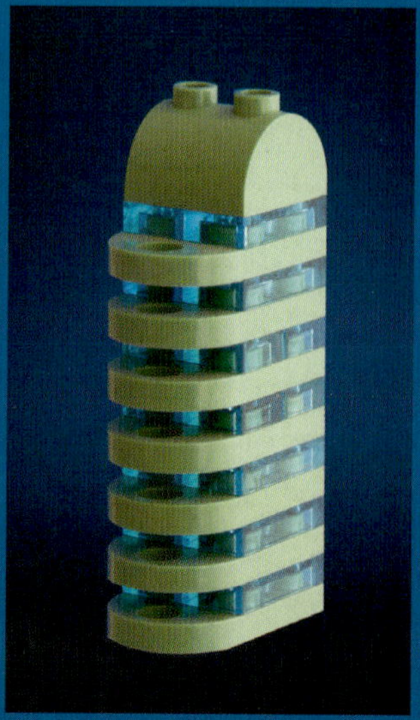

BRUTAL BEACON

98138

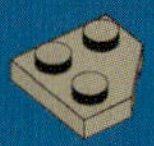
26601

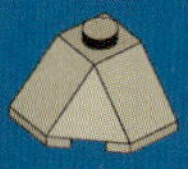
13548

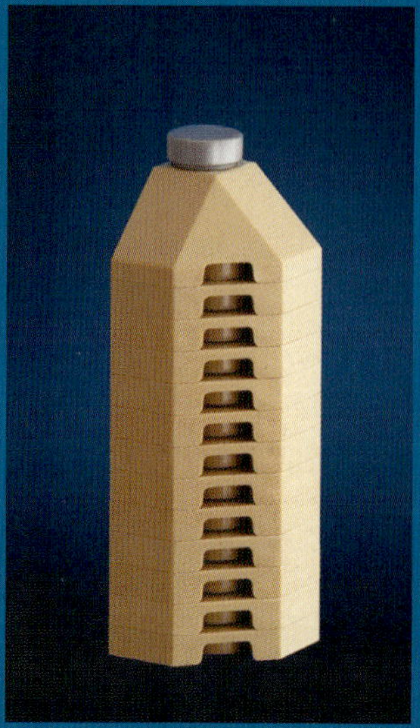

FOUNDRY LOFTS

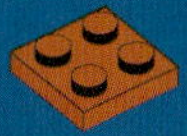
3022

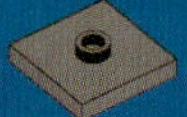
87580

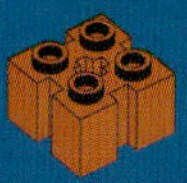
90258

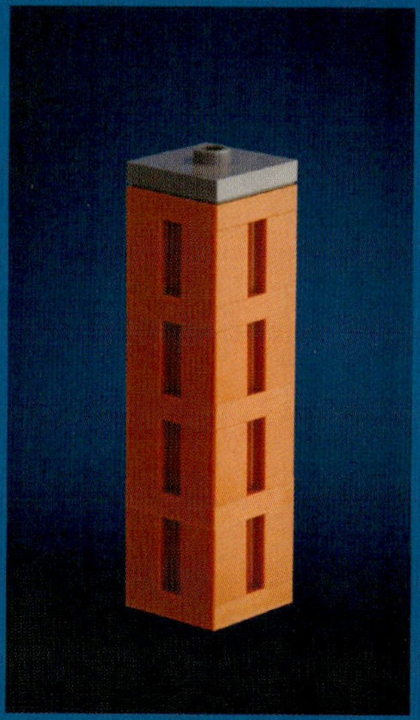

ZIGZAG

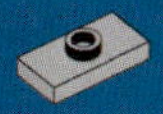
15573

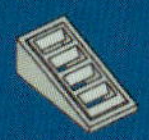
61409

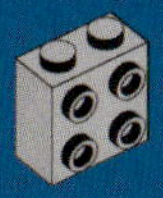
22885

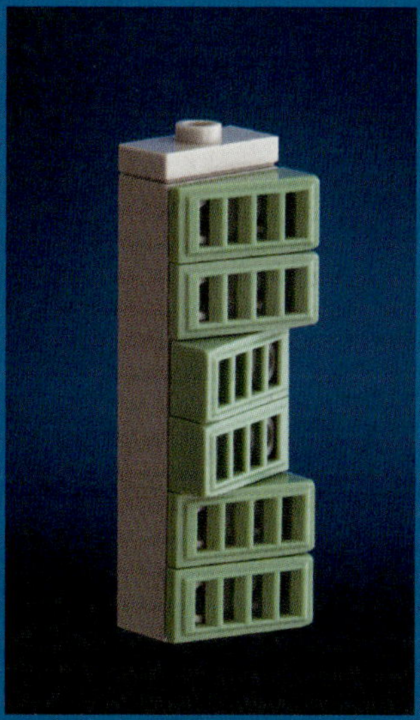

TERRACES

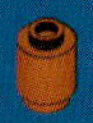
3062

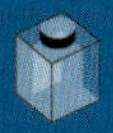
3005

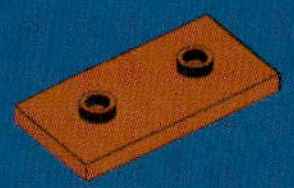
65509

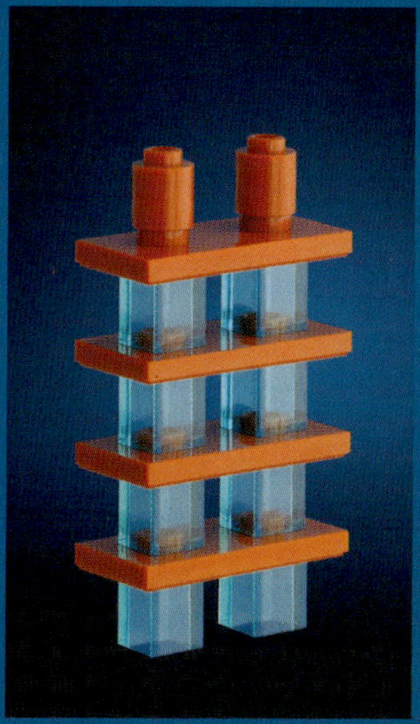

LOOKING GLASS

98138

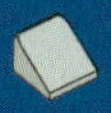
54200

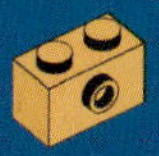
86876

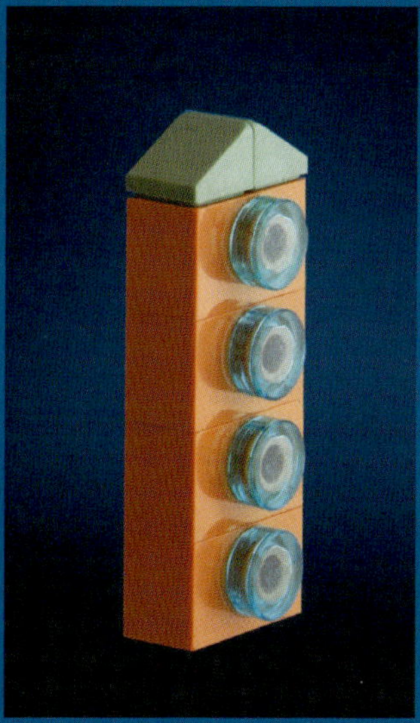

TWISTER

98138

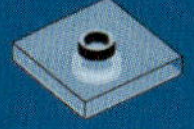
87580

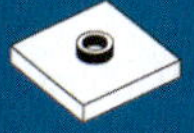
87580

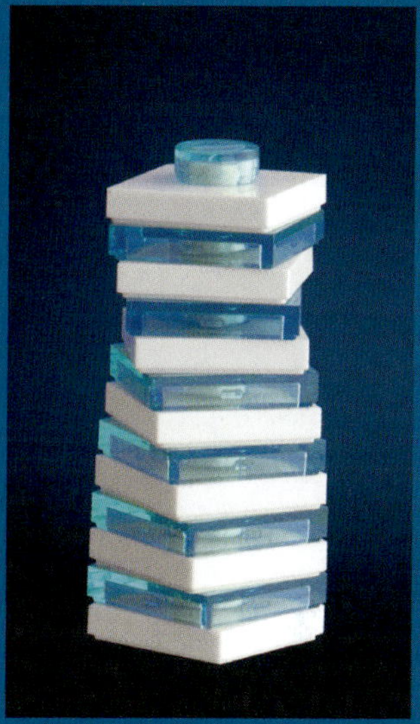

STAINLESS CITADEL

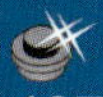
4073

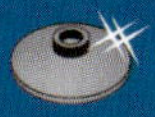
4740

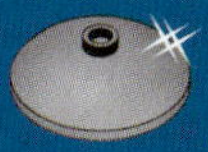
43898

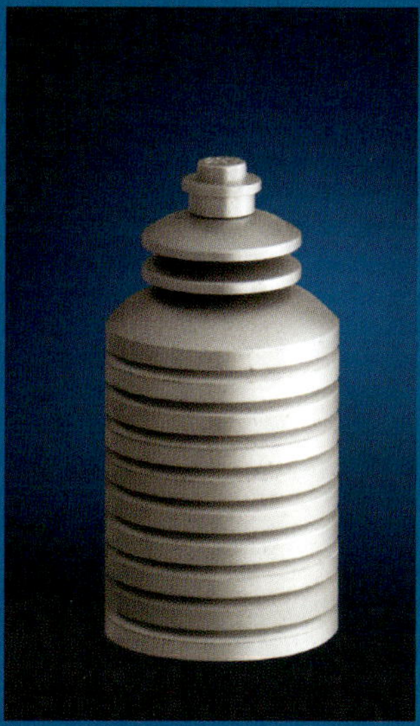

STERLING MANOR

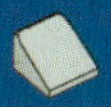
54200

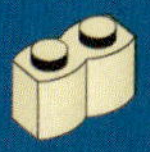
30136

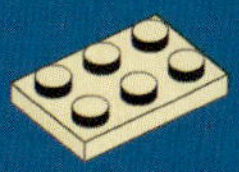
3021

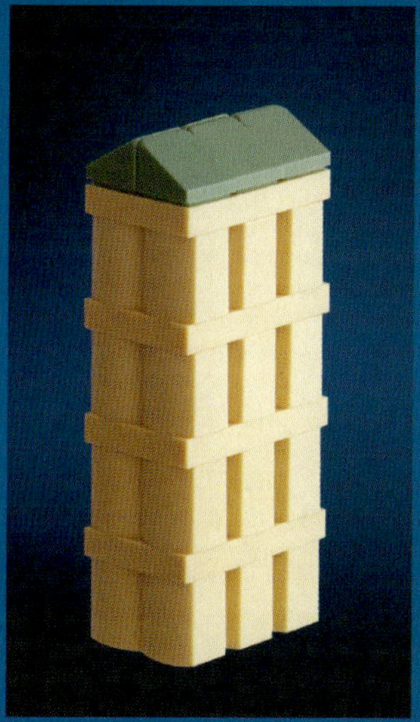

SKY GARDEN

24866

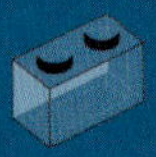
3065

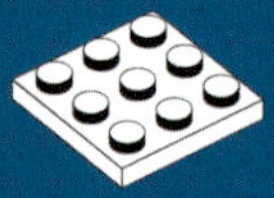
11212

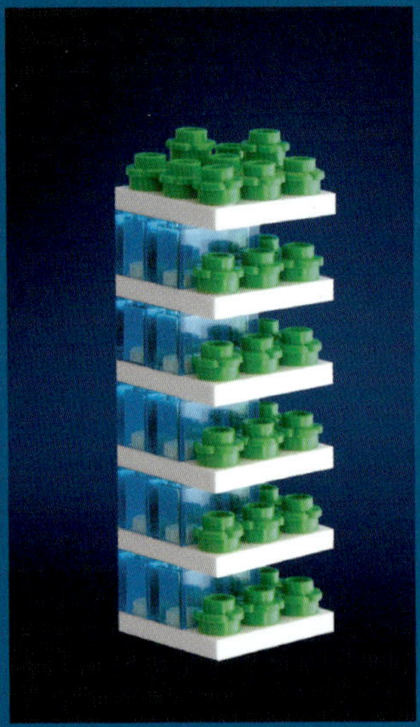

ZIGGURAT

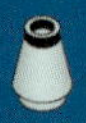
4589

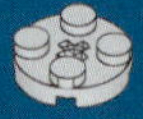
4032

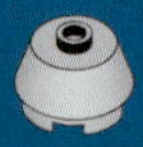
98100

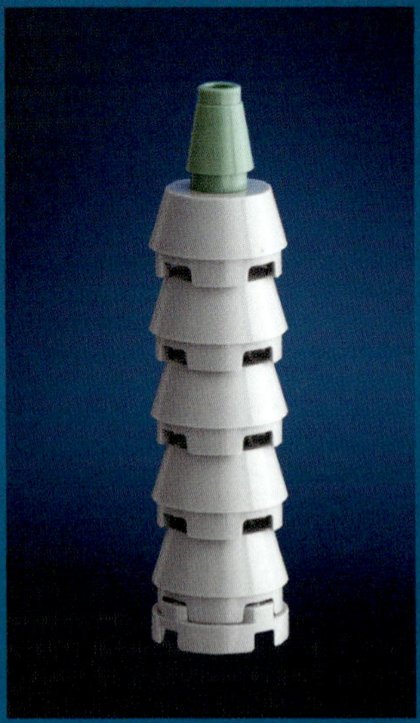

RIGHT ROUND

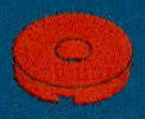
15535

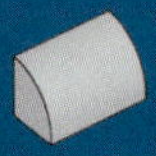
37352

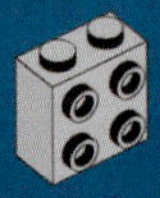
22885

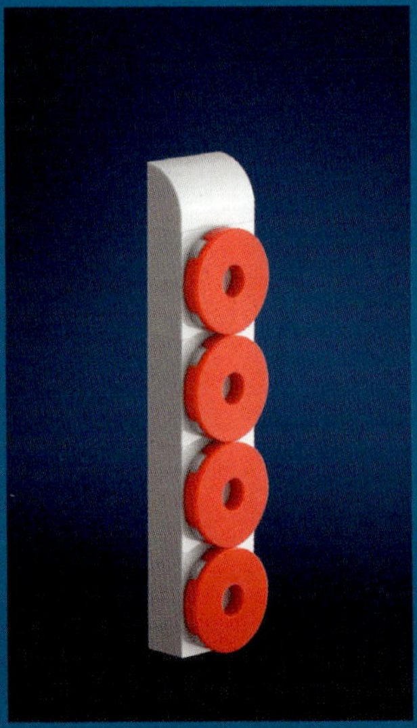

JETSON'S JUNCTION

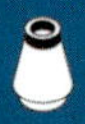
4589

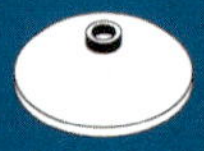
43898

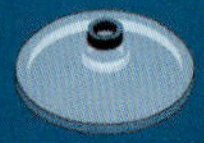
43898

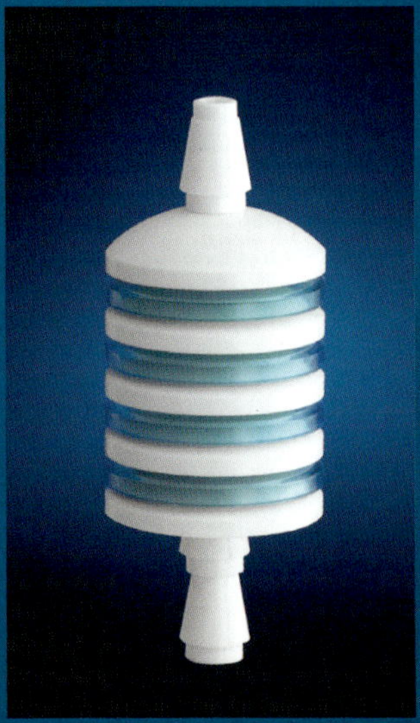

GLASS HOUSES

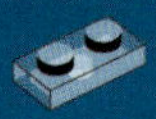
3023

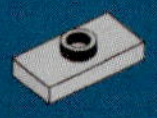
15573

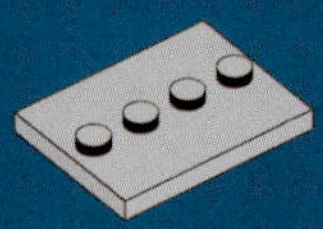
88646

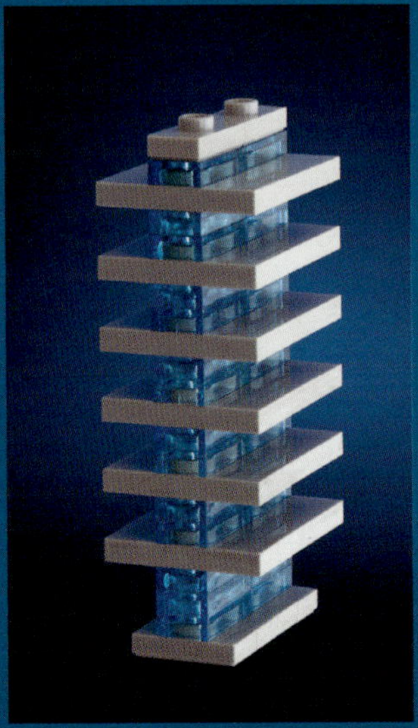

GOLDEN GRILLE

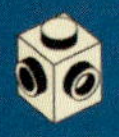
26604

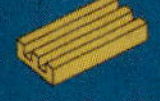
2412b

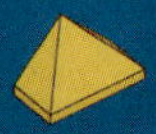
15571

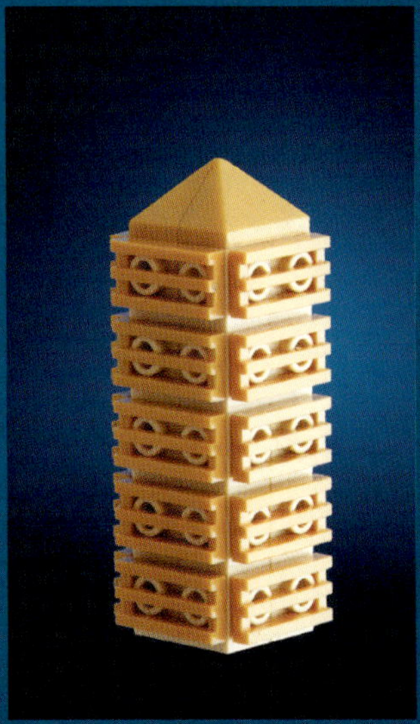

FLOWER TOWER

98138

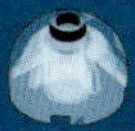
553

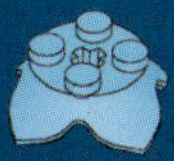
15469

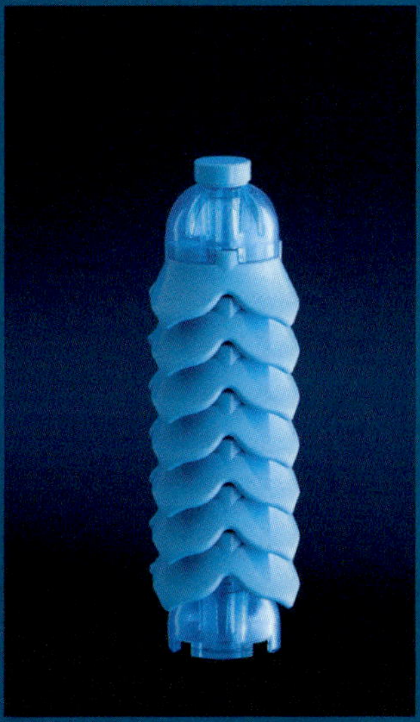

RED SHIFT

3070

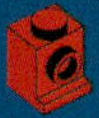
4070

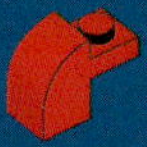
6091

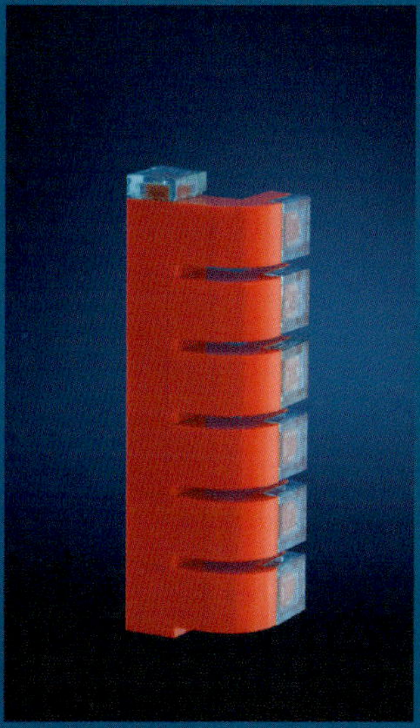

ADOBE ABODE

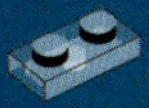
3023

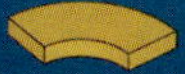
27925

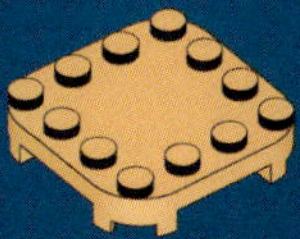
66792

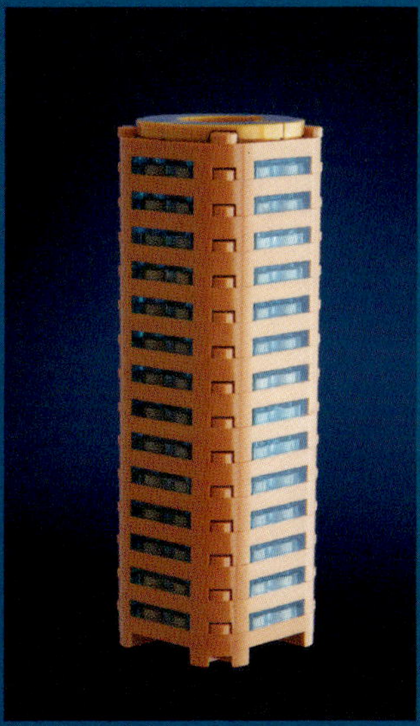

MOSAIC

3070

3070

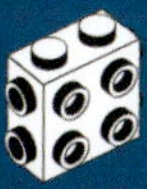
67329

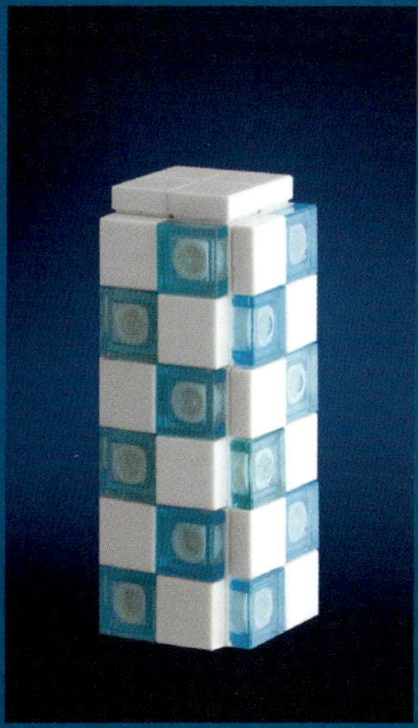

MARTELLO

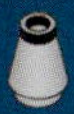
4589

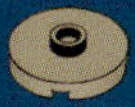
18674

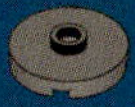
18674

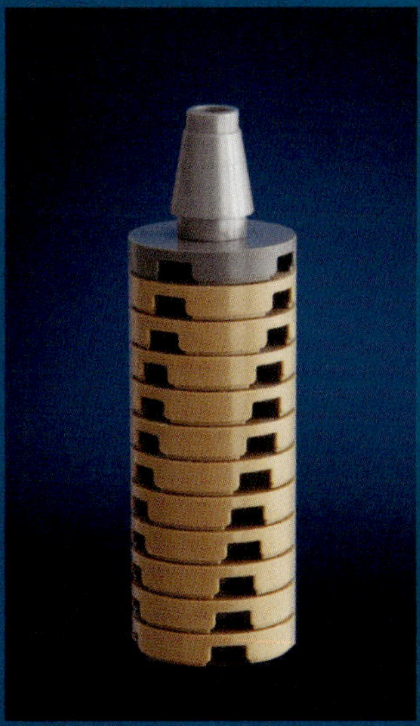

CONCRETE CRIBS

3044c

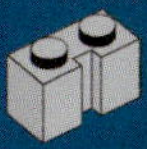
4216

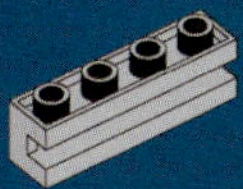
2653

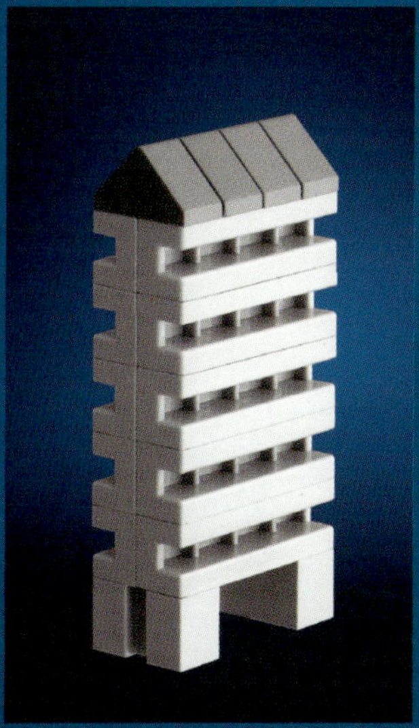

MODUHAUS

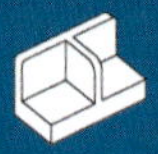
93095

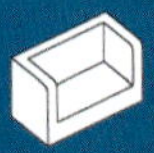
23969

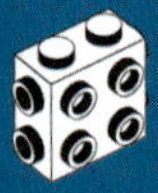
67329

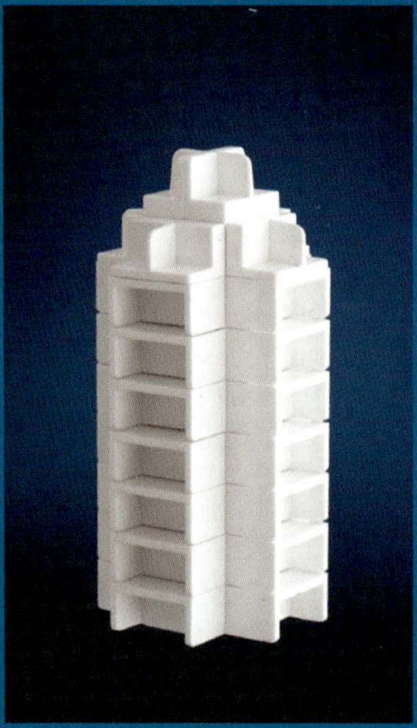

WIZARD'S KEEP

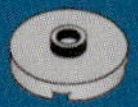
18674

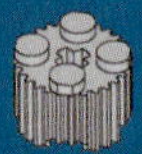
92947

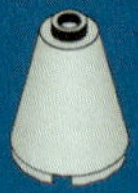
3942c

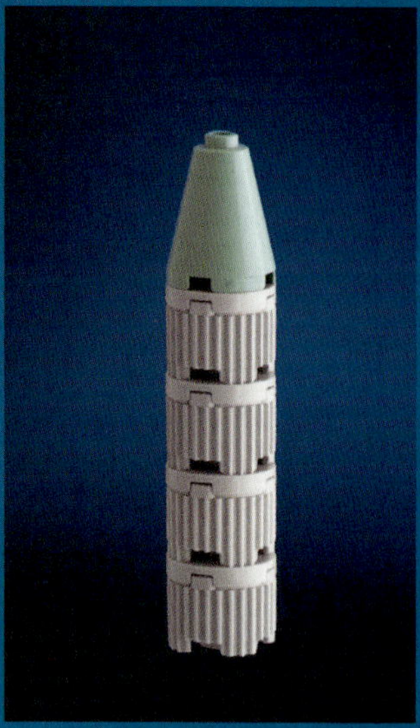

AZURE GLOW

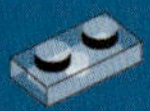
3023

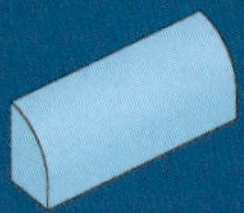
6191

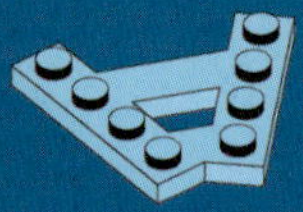
15706

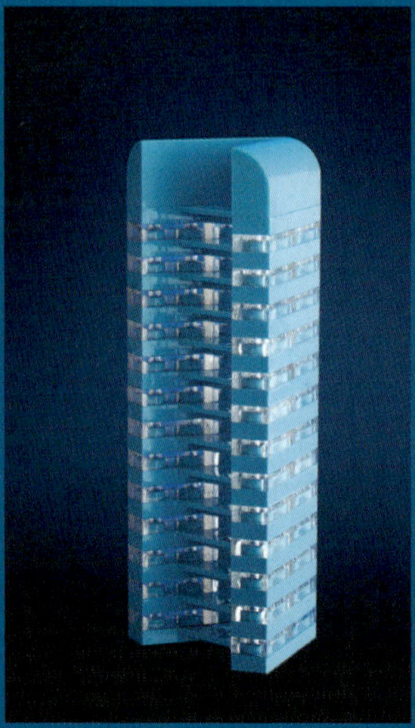

THE GILDED SUMMIT

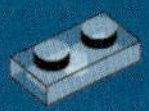
3023

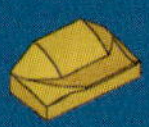
47458

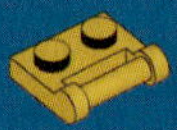
48336

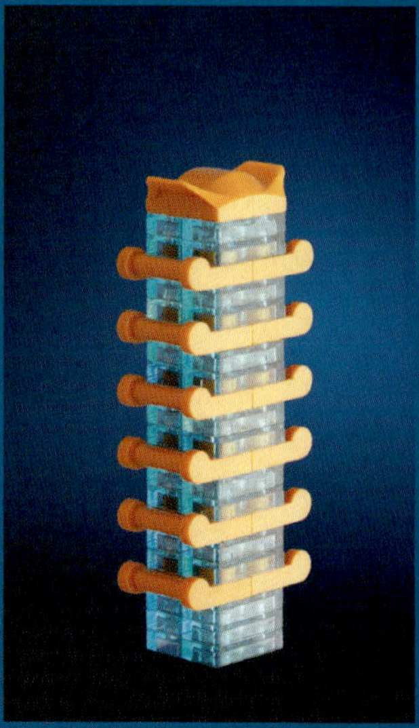

ROTUNDA

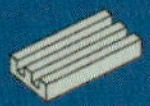
2412b

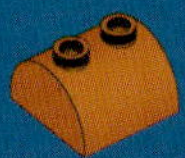
30165

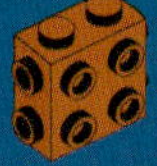
67329

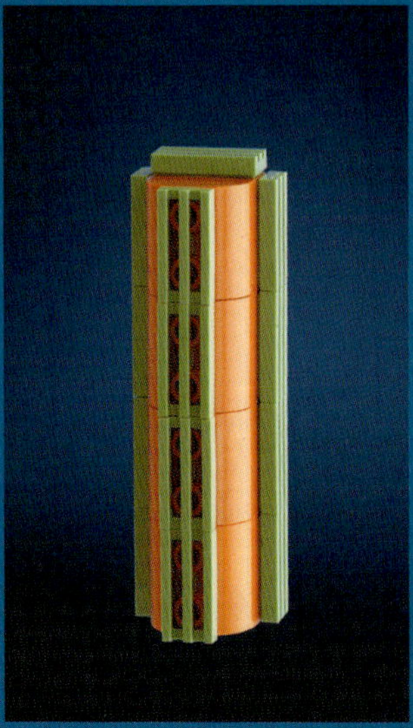

URBAN TREE

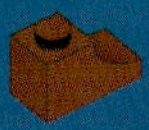
78666

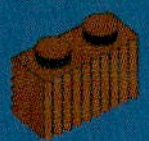
2877

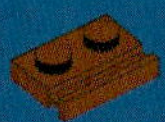
32028

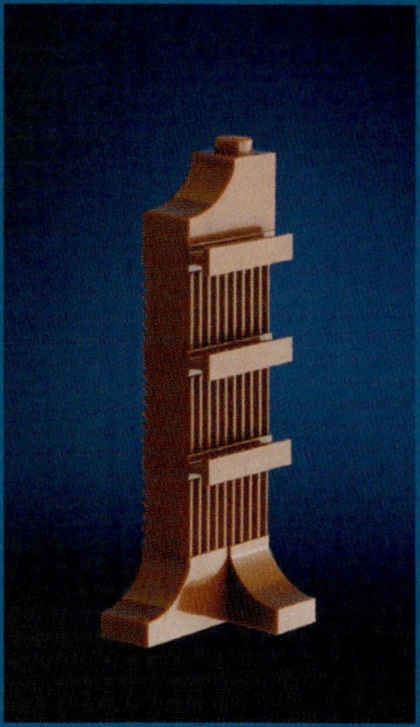

SUITE STACK

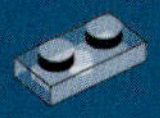
3023

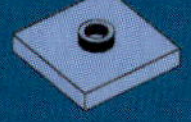
87580

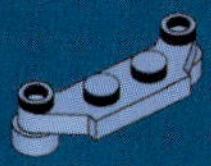
4590

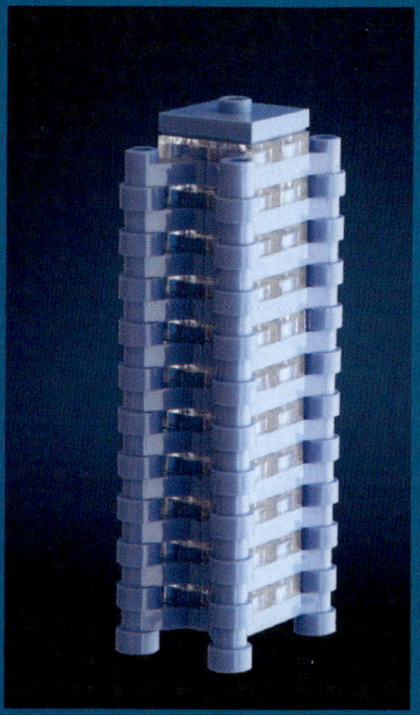

THE HIVE

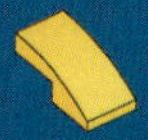
11477

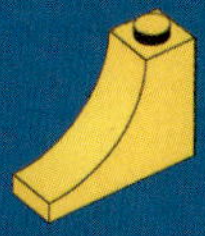
18653

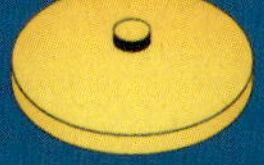
3960

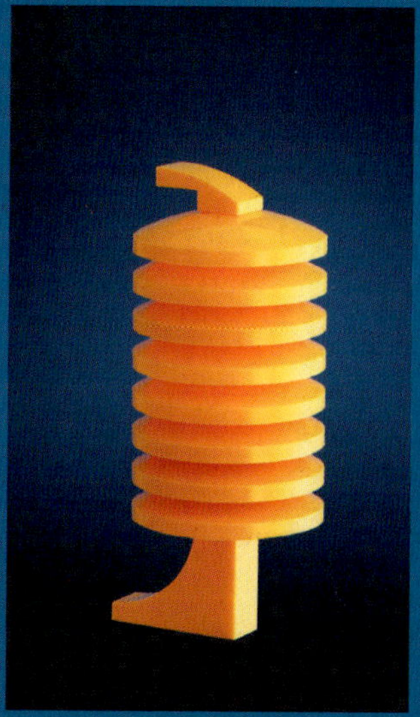

WOVEN SANDSTONE

4073

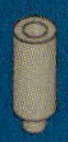
37762

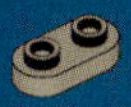
35480

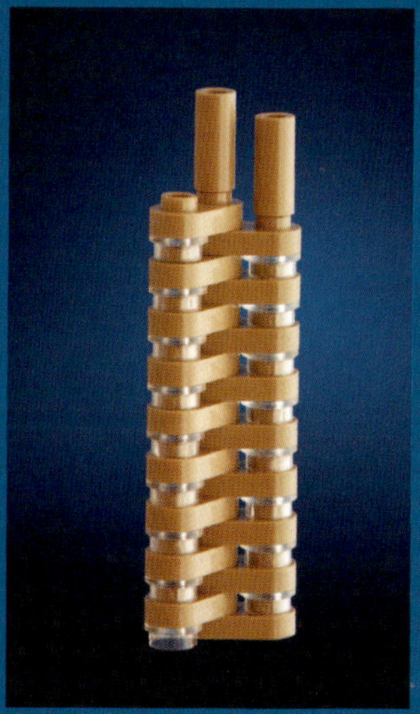

CLOUD BANK

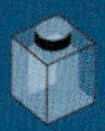
3005

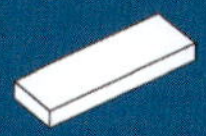
63864

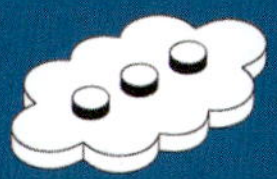
35470

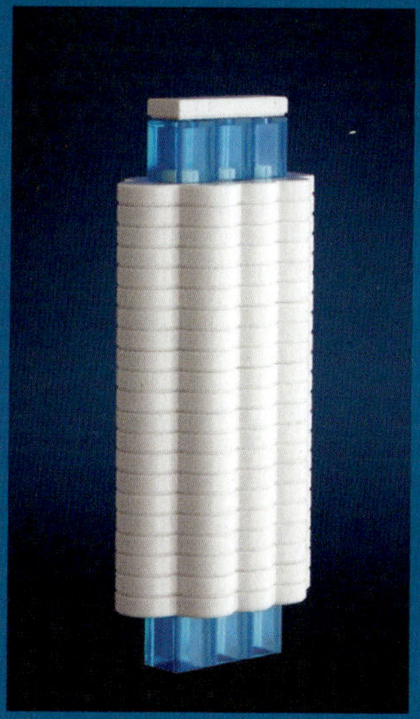

SURF'S UP

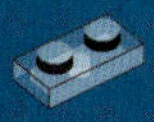
3023

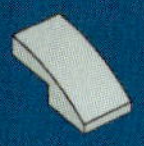
11477

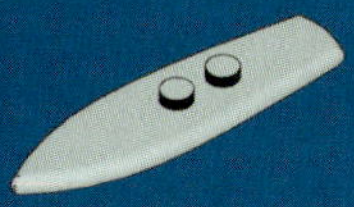
90397

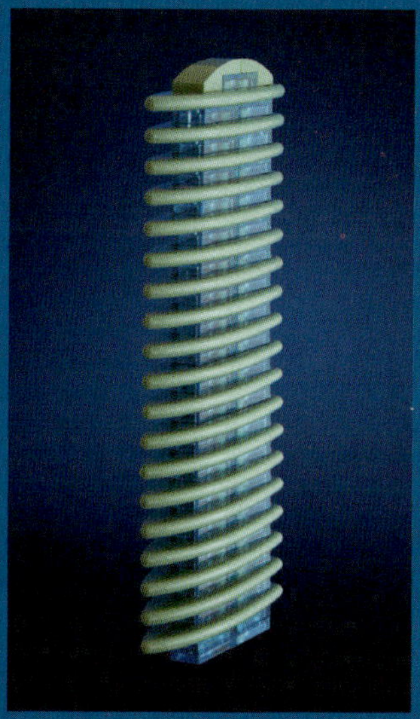

REGENCY HEIGHTS

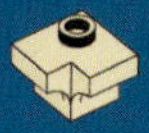
38585

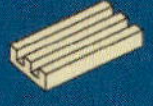
2412b

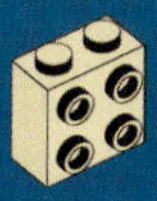
22885

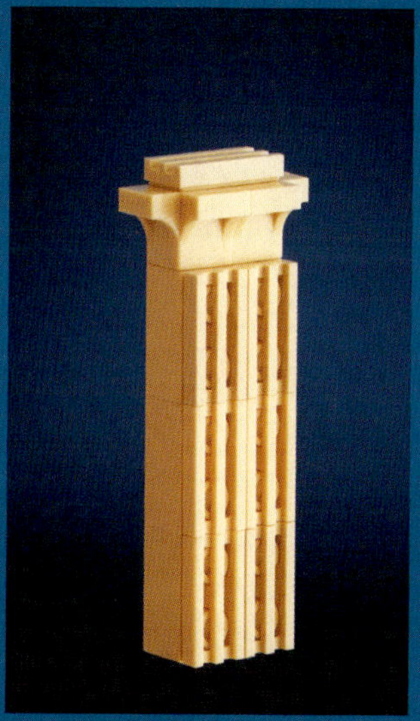

WATERCRAFT

Add exploration, trade, drama, and fun to your world's waterways with watercraft. From wooden boats to towering container ships, these vessels shape the stories unfolding across your rivers, seas, and lakes.

SIMPLE SAILBOAT

Simple sailboats are an ancient technology that never goes out of style. They're at home in both historical and modern settings.

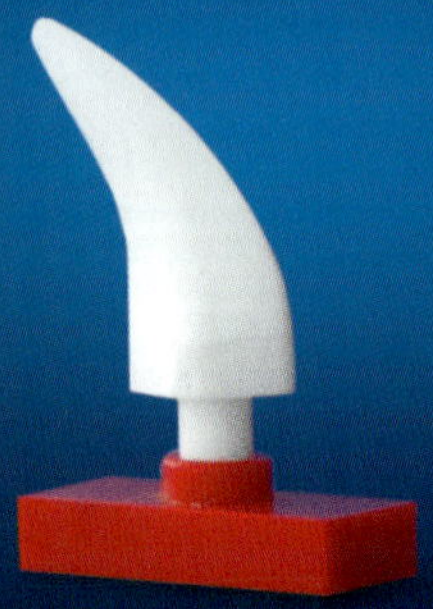

Use any color of 1×2 jumper plate to represent a wooden or painted fiberglass hull.

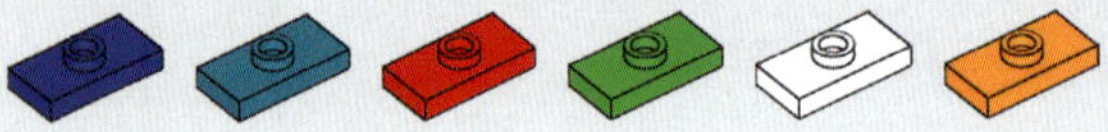

15573

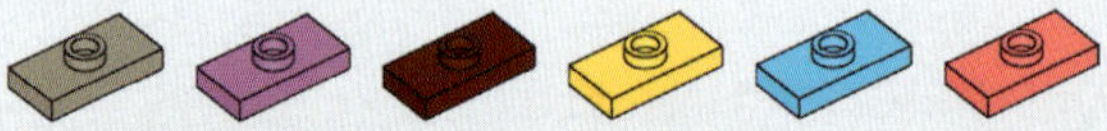

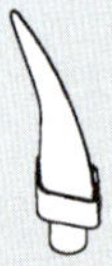

1x
87747

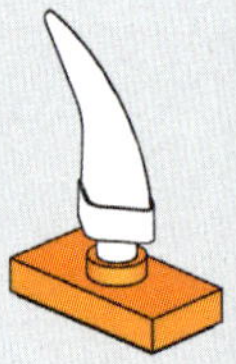

SCHOONER

With streamlined hulls and lofty sails, schooners bring majesty and motion to your coastal scenes.

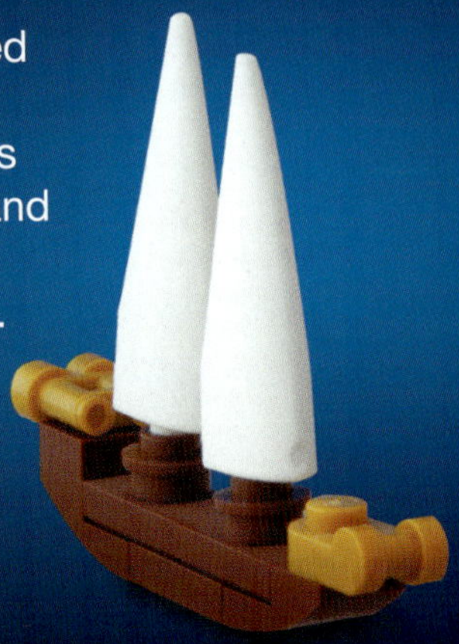

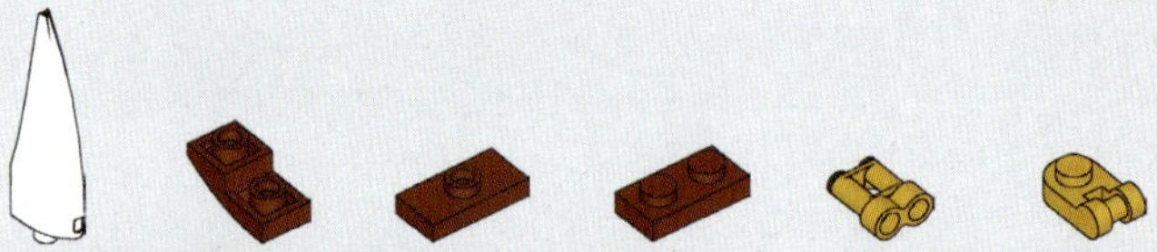

2x 11089 **2x** 24201 **2x** 15573 **1x** 3023 **1x** 30162 **1x** 26047

2x
85861

1

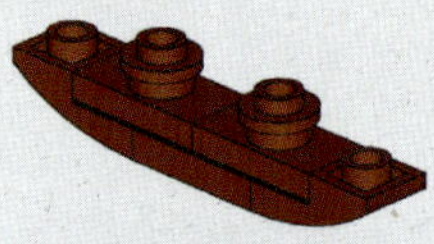

2

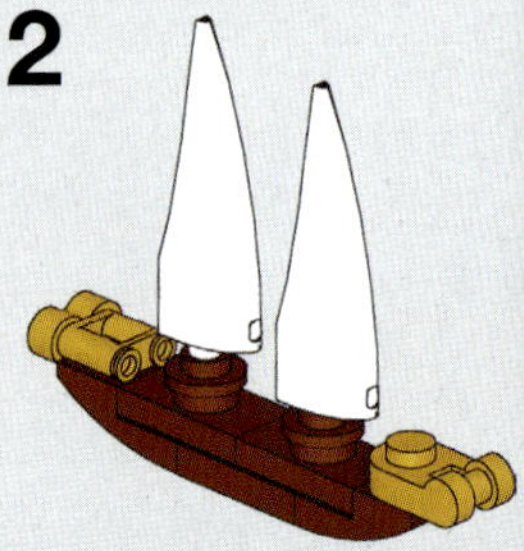

FISHING BOAT

Build a sturdy craft that keeps your seaside settlements flush with fish.

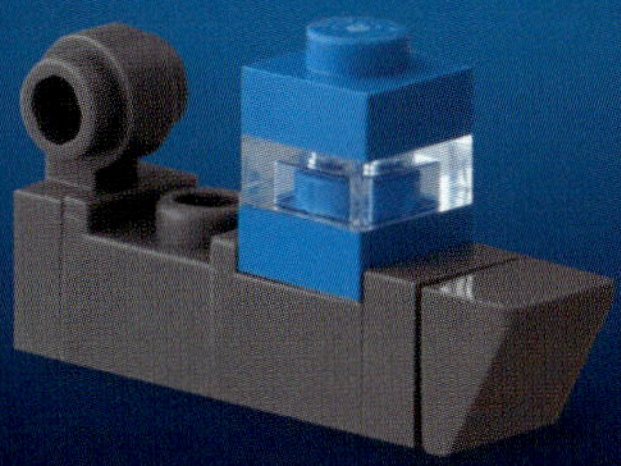

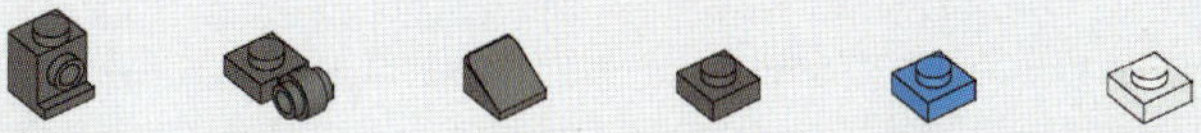

2x	1x	1x	1x	2x	1x
4070	4081b	54200	3024	3024	3024

1

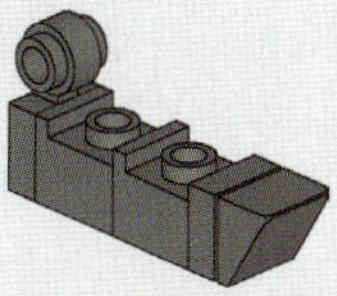

2

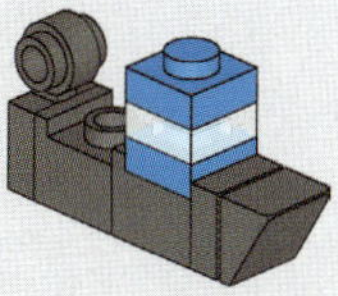

POWERBOAT

Vibrant powerboats add speed and pops of color that complement blue water perfectly.

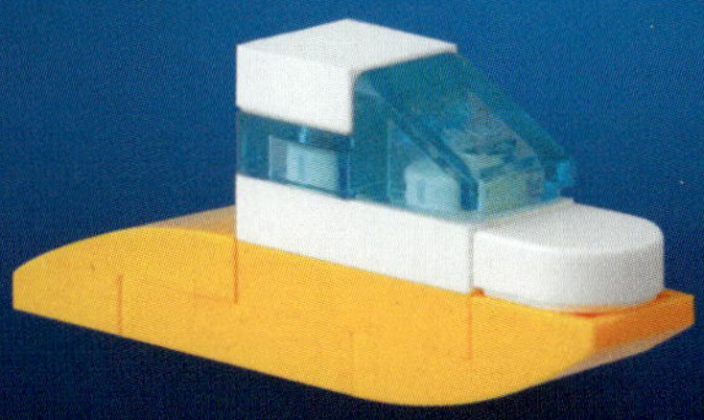

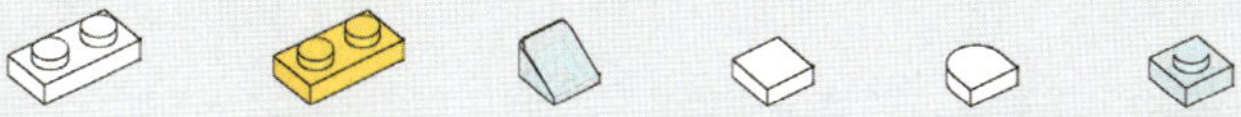

1x	2x	1x	1x	1x	1x
3023	3023	54200	3070	24246	3024

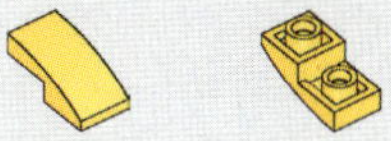

1x	1x
11477	24201

1

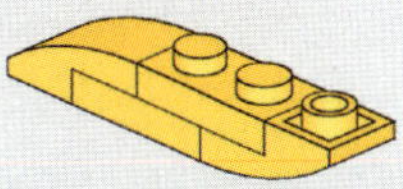

2

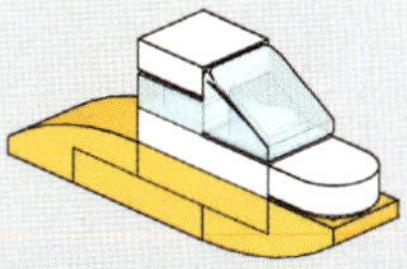

RESCUE SHIP

Rescues at sea have great storytelling potential. Set the stage for drama with a rescue ship.

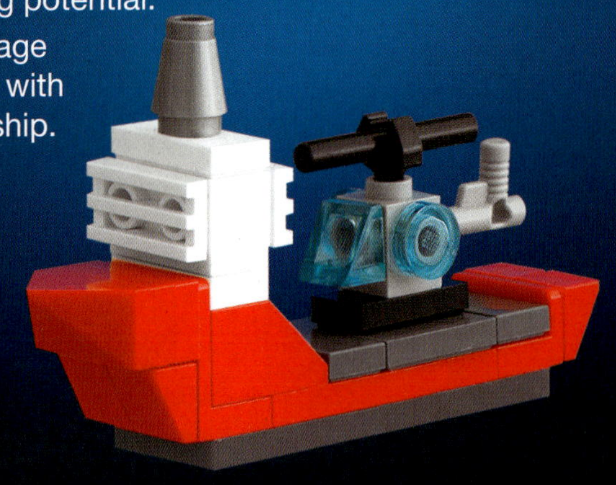

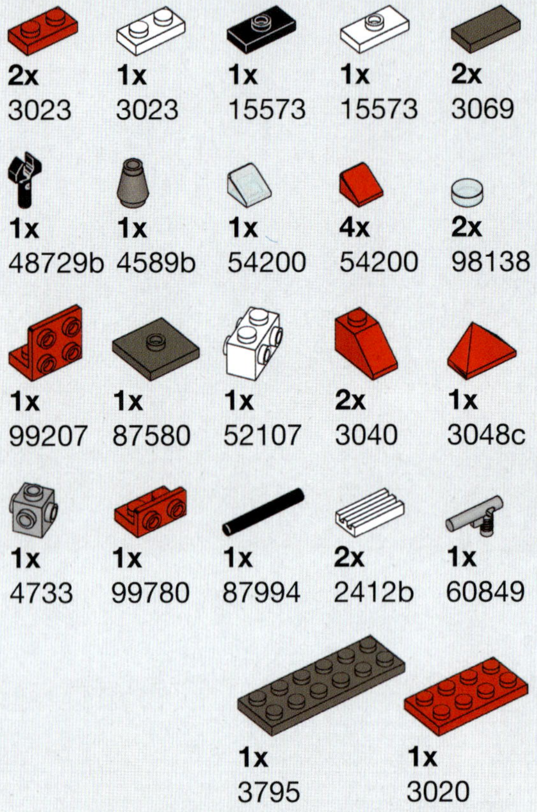

1

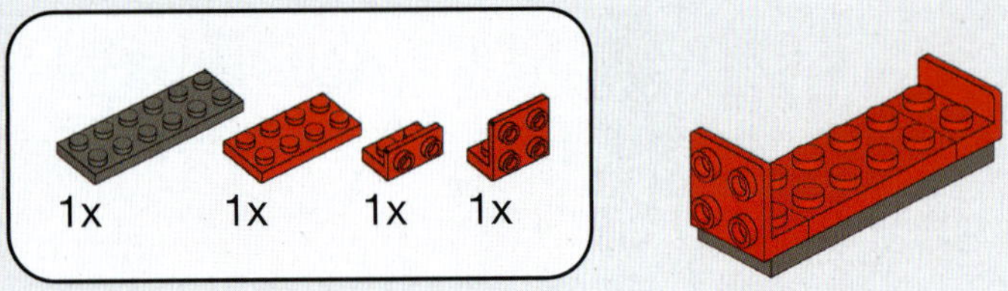

2

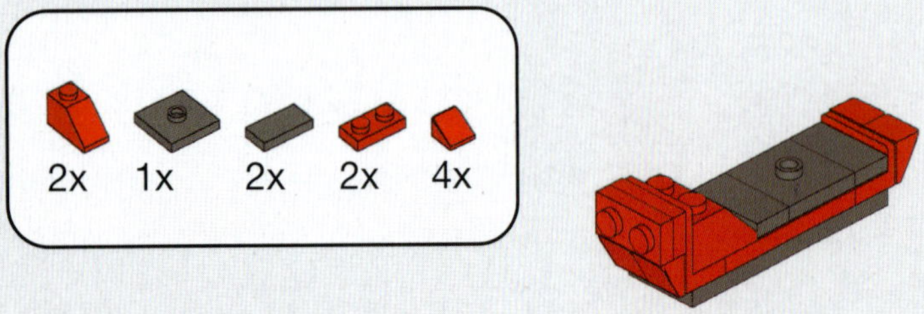

3

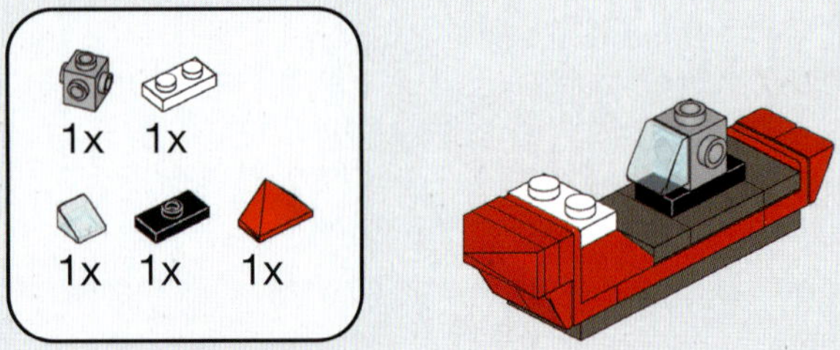

4

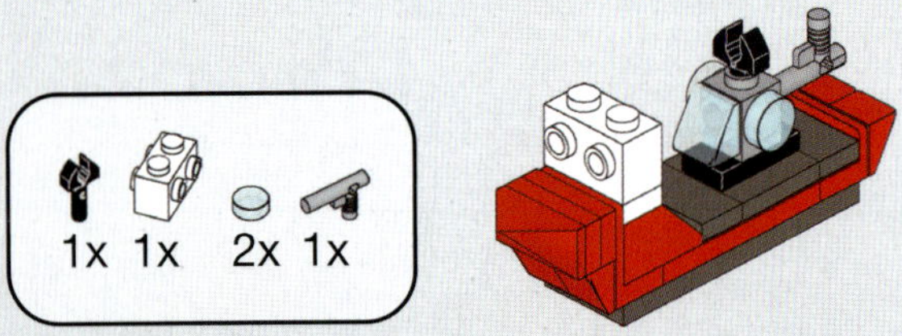

5

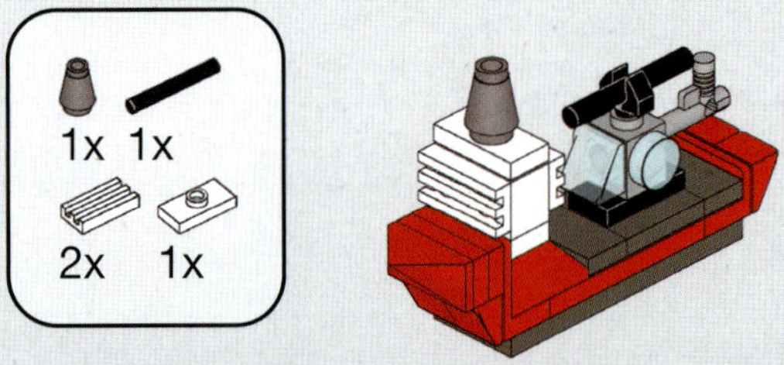

CONTAINER SHIP

Shipping containers are like giant LEGO bricks. A deep-sea container ship adds colorful commerce to your world.

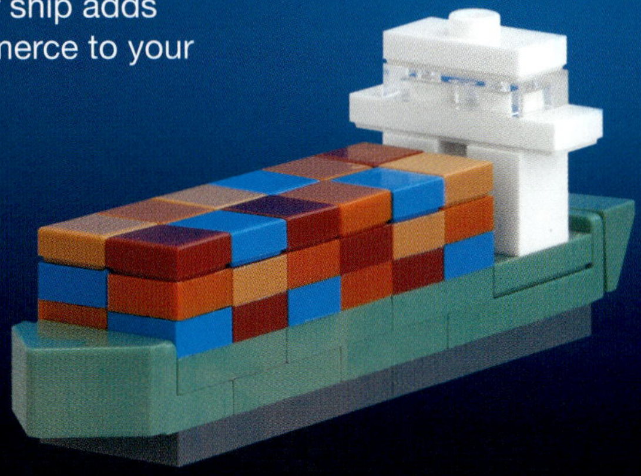

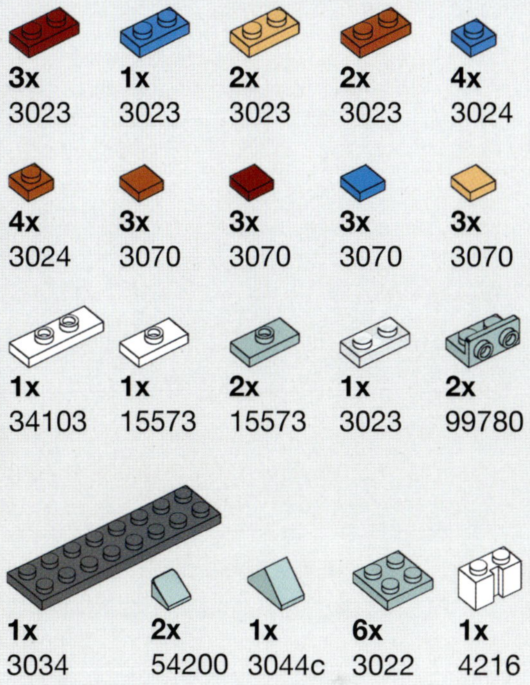

1

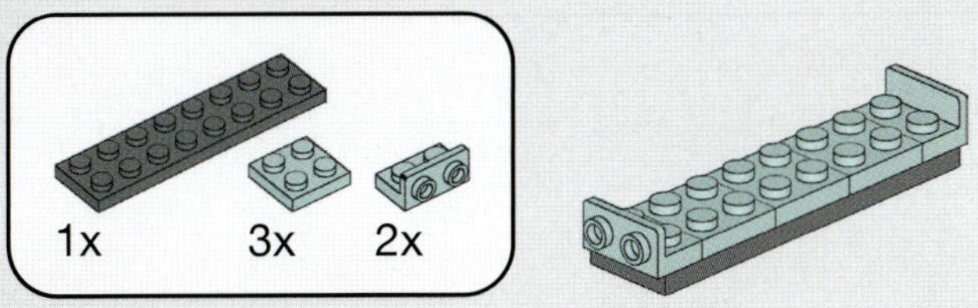

2

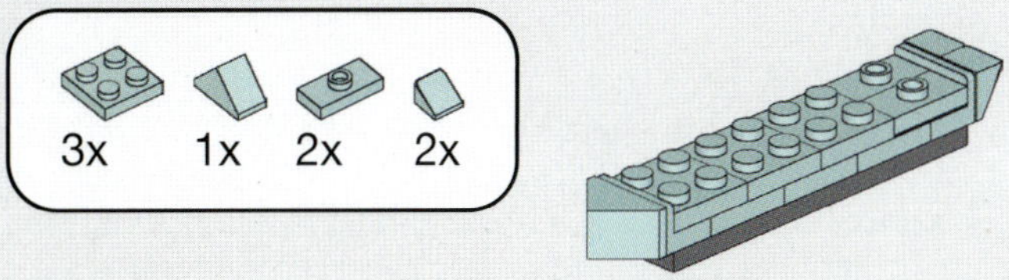

3

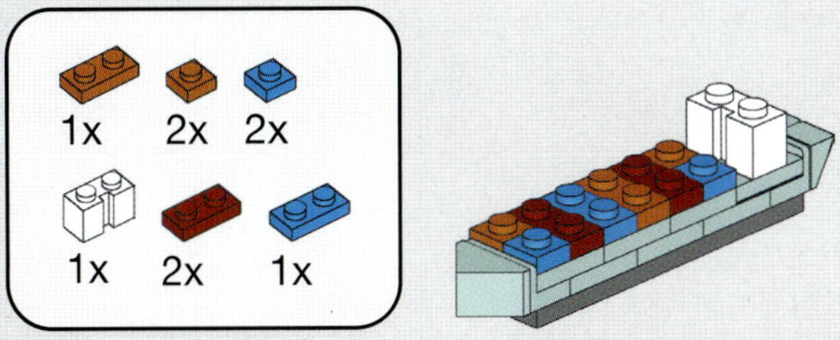

4

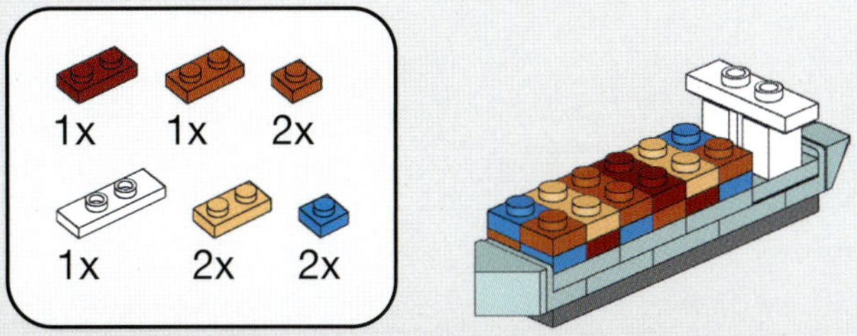

5

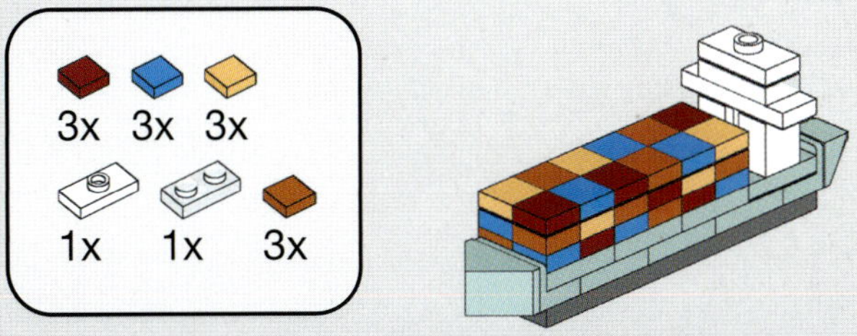

MAKE IT YOUR OWN

Container ships can serve as floating paint-swatch displays. Choose your own palette!

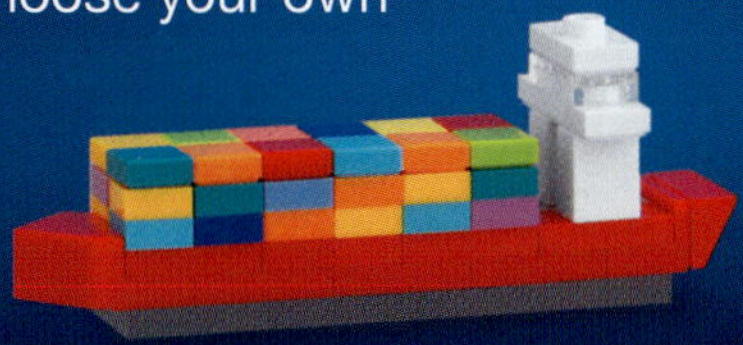

CRANE SHIP

This ship helps build the offshore structures in your world, from towering rigs to secret laboratories.

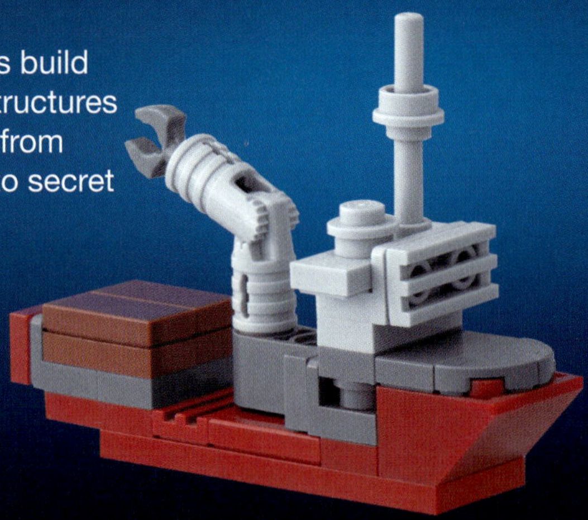

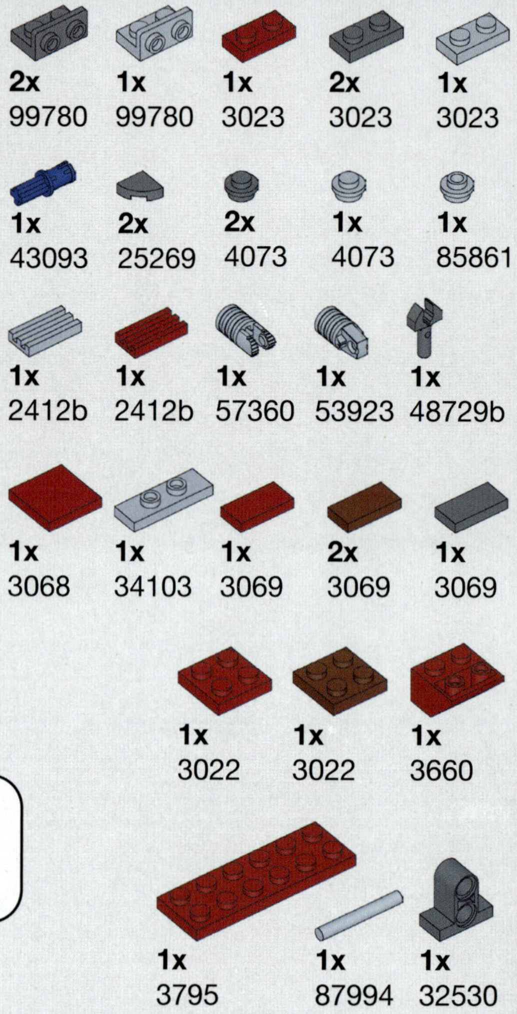

1

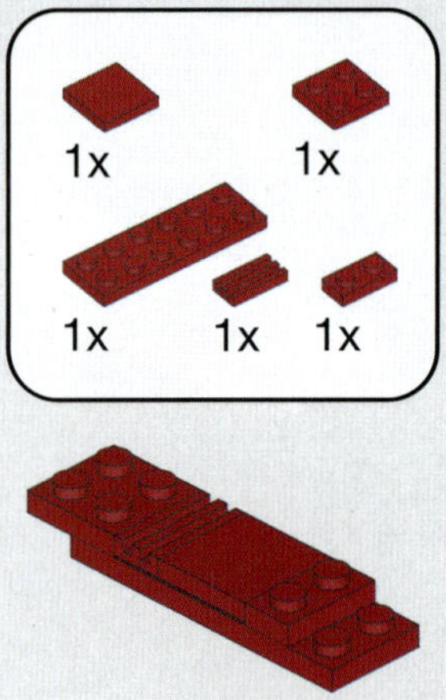

2

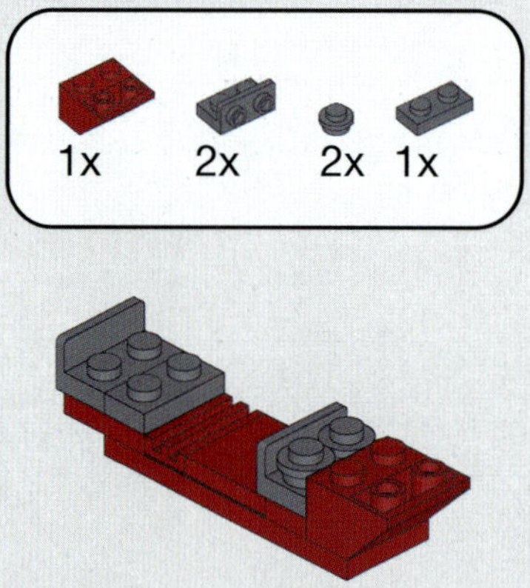

3

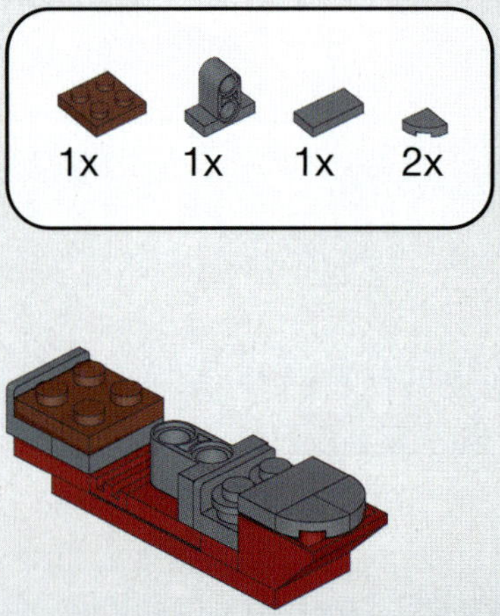

4

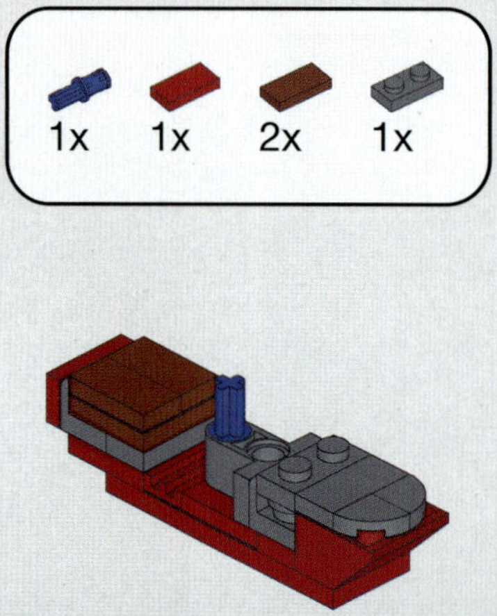

5

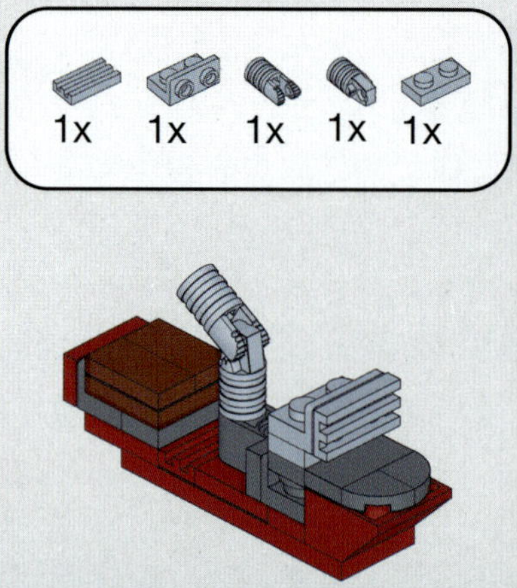

6

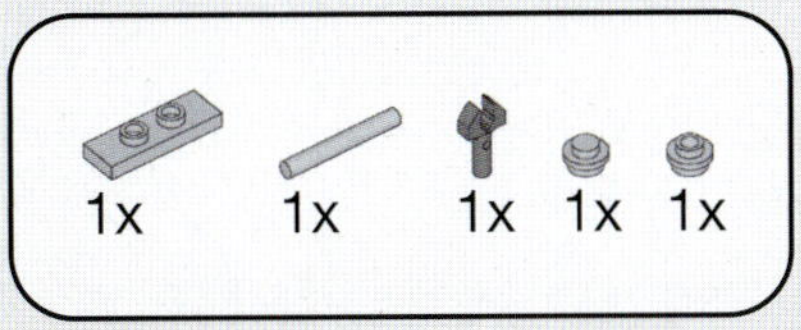

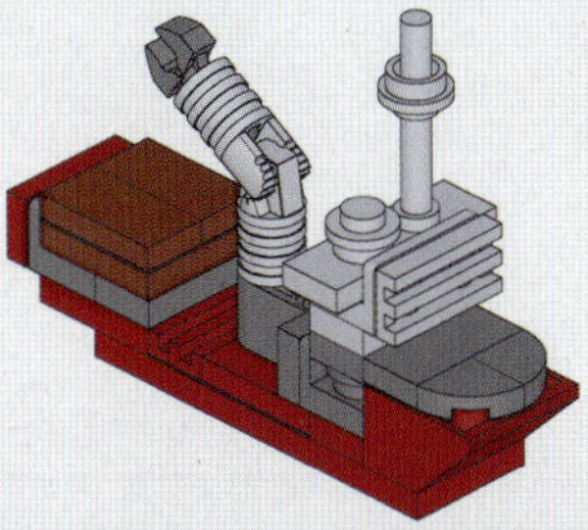

NAUTICAL INSPIRATION

As the saying goes, "A ship is safe at shore, but that's not what it's built for." Once you've made a ship, create some destinations for it!

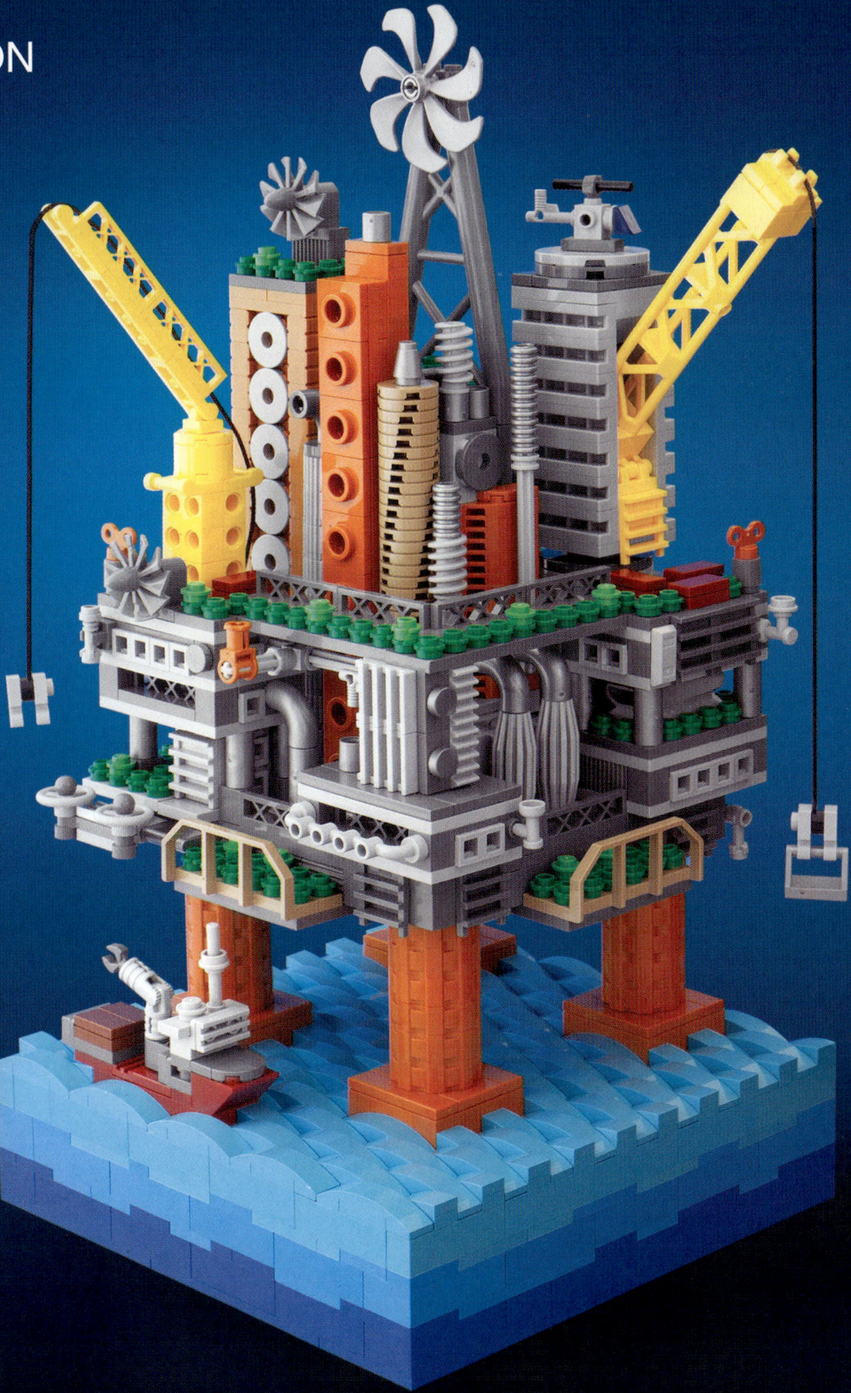

Make waves using 1×4 curved slopes, staggering them by two studs in each row. You can use 1×2 curved slopes at the base's edges.

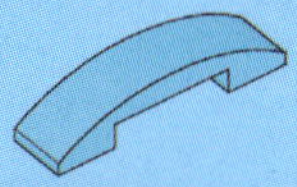

93273

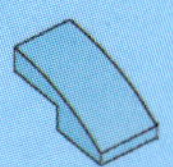

11477

TRAINS

Bring adventure, activity, and industriousness to your world with the addition of a train. From the whooshing speed of bullet trains to the sooty charm of steam locomotives, you set the pace at which your world moves.

LIGHT-RAIL TRANSIT

Light-rail transit offers a blend of efficiency and style perfect for modern urban transportation.

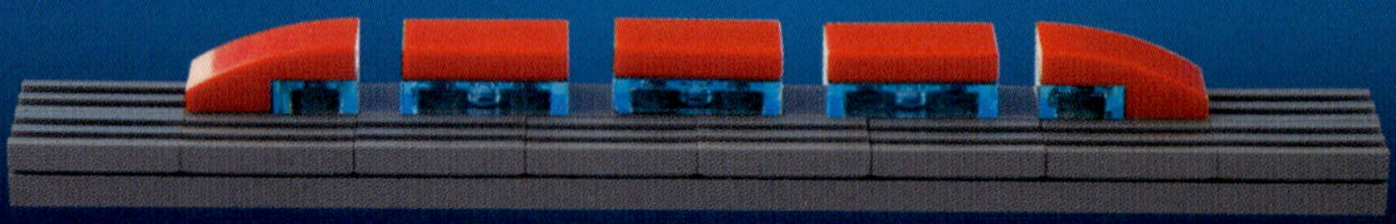

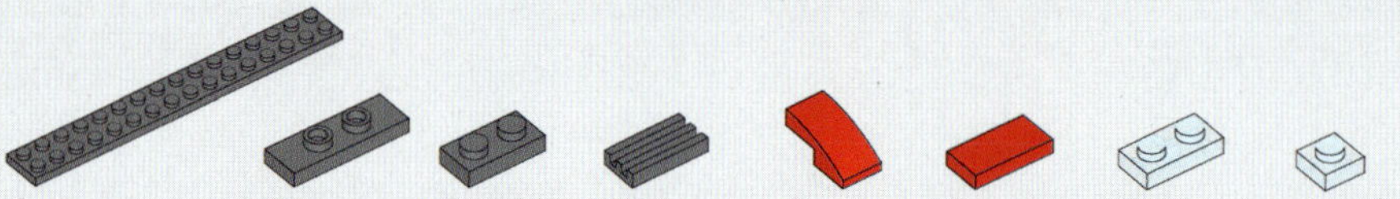

1x	**2x**	**3x**	**10x**	**2x**	**3x**	**3x**	**2x**
4282	34103	3023	2412b	11477	3069	3023	3024

1

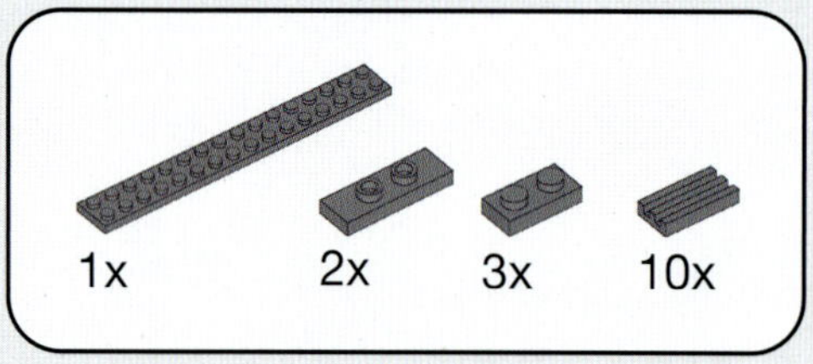

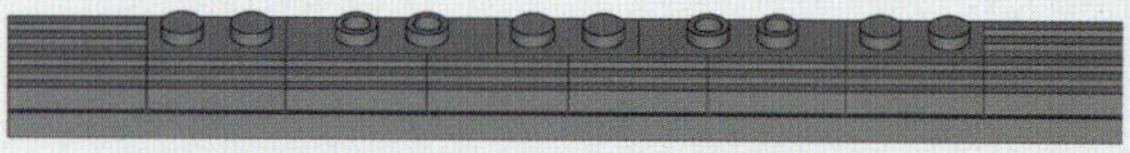

2

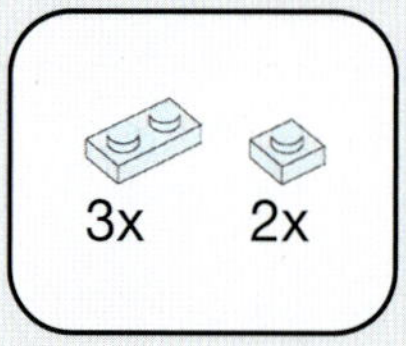

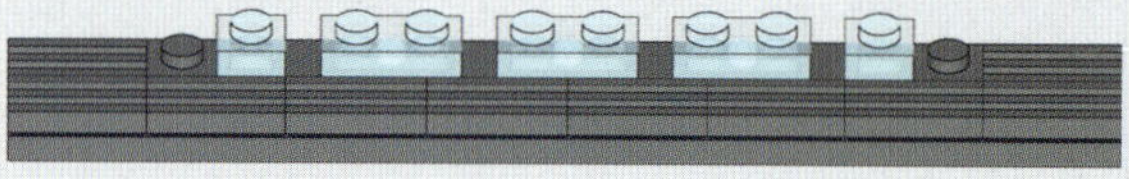

3

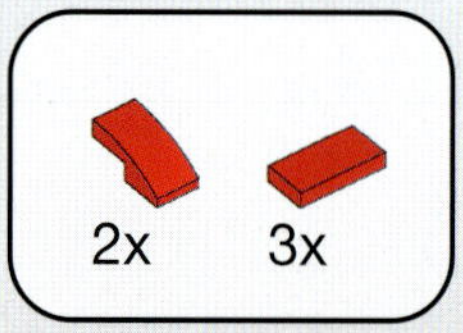

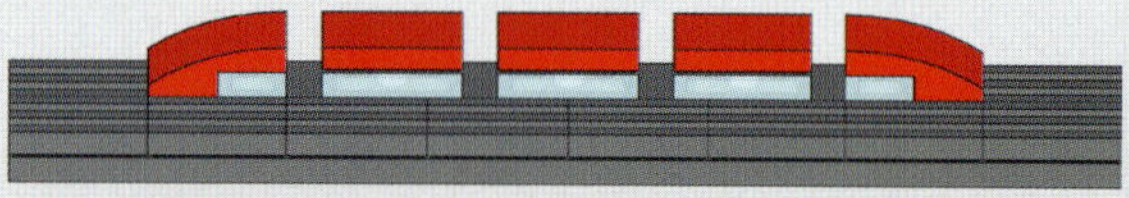

BULLET TRAIN

If your world moves at high speed, consider expressing that velocity with a bullet train, known as a *Shinkansen* in its birthplace of Japan.

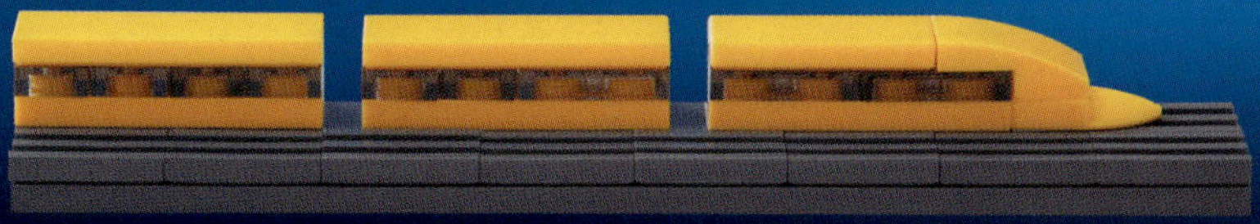

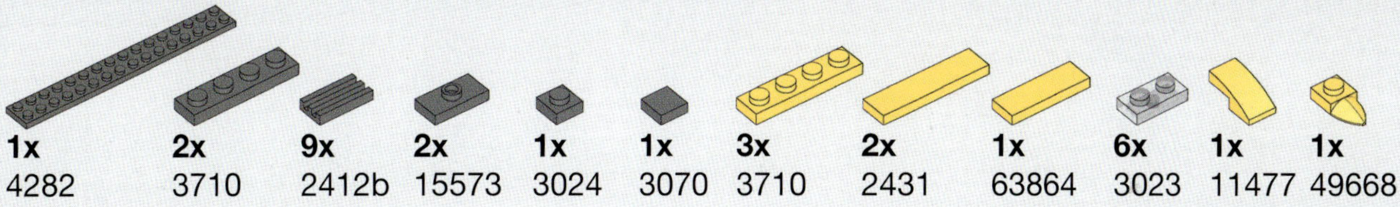

1

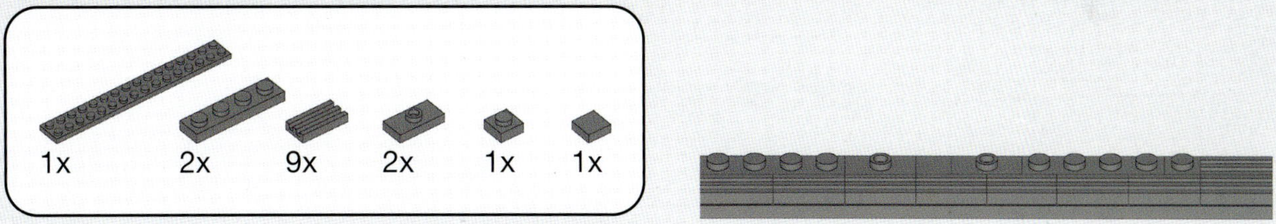

2

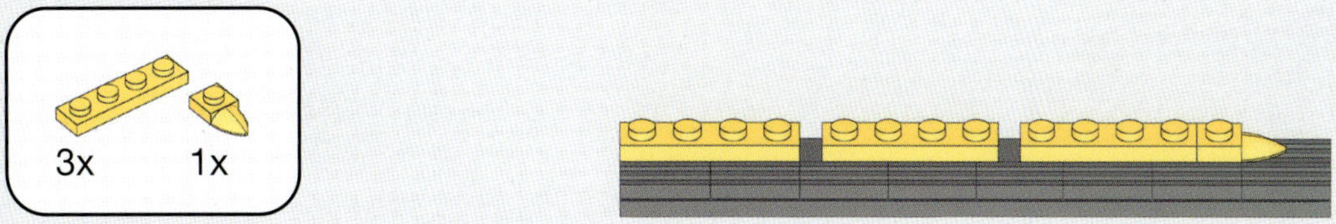

3

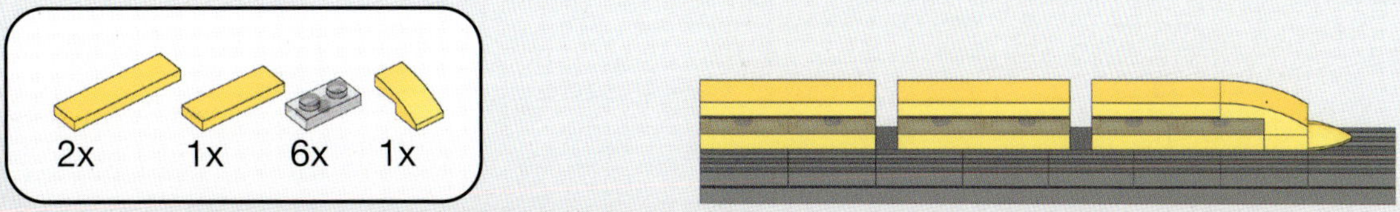

STEAM TRAIN

Steam trains are the fire-breathing dragons of transportation. They add history and drama in any place they appear.

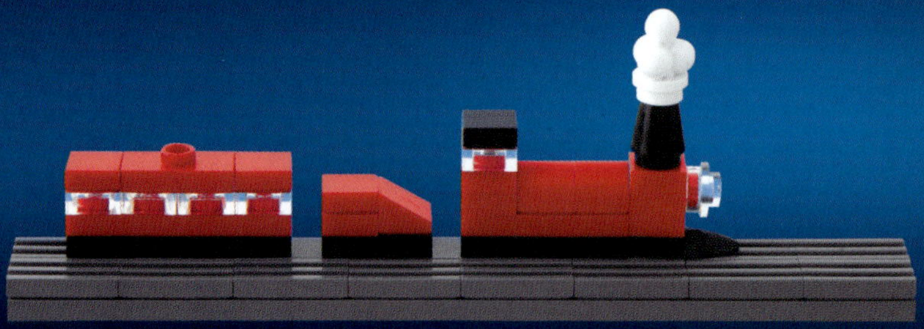

Qty	Part
1x	4282
1x	3710
1x	3623
1x	34103
11x	2412b
1x	3710
1x	3710
1x	3623
1x	3623
1x	3023
1x	3070
1x	4070
2x	3023
1x	54200
2x	49307
3x	3024
1x	4073
1x	4589b
1x	6254
1x	15573
1x	49668
1x	3024
3x	3070

1

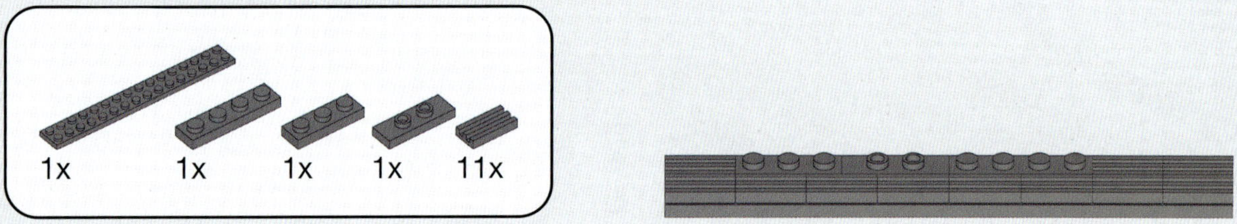

2

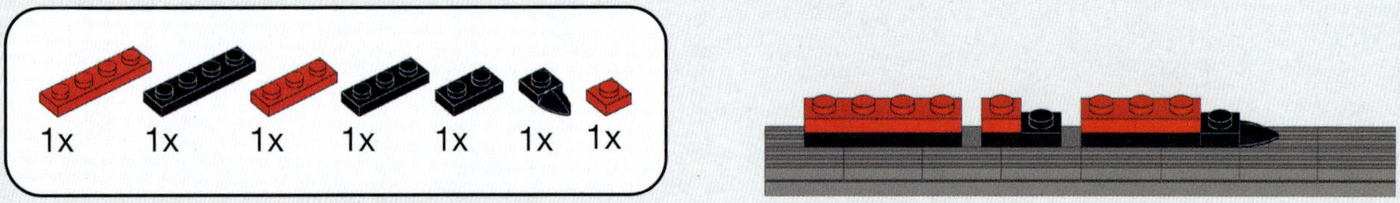

3

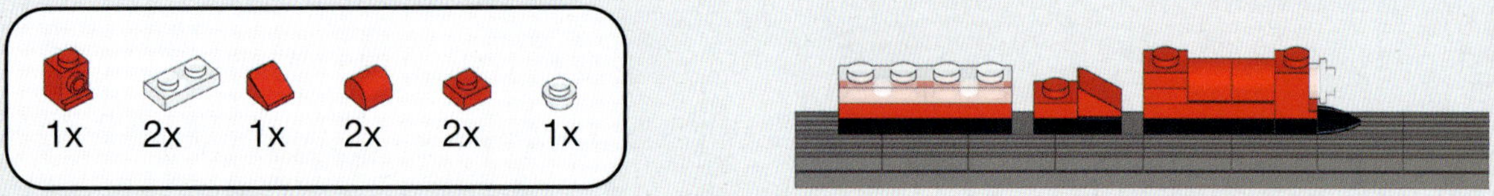

4

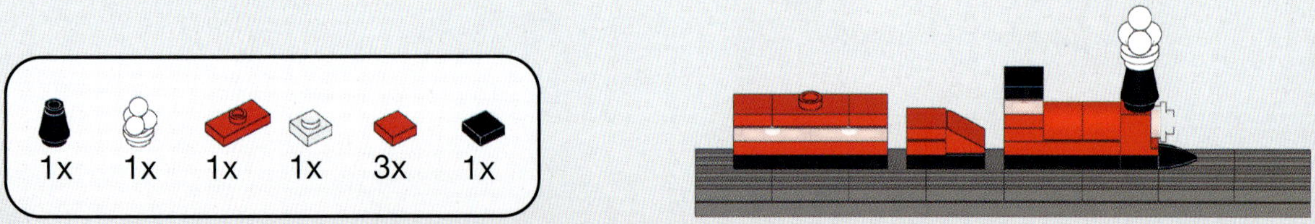

FREIGHT TRAIN

Shipping containers aren't just for ships. Freight trains pull them like colorful ribbons across the landscape.

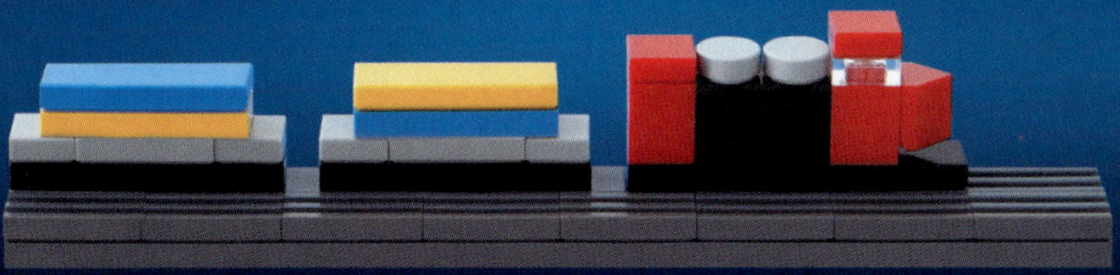

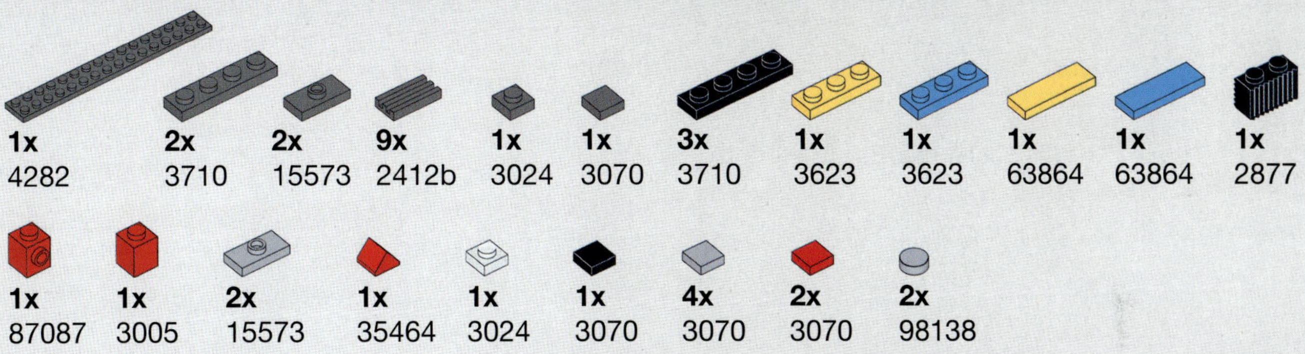

1

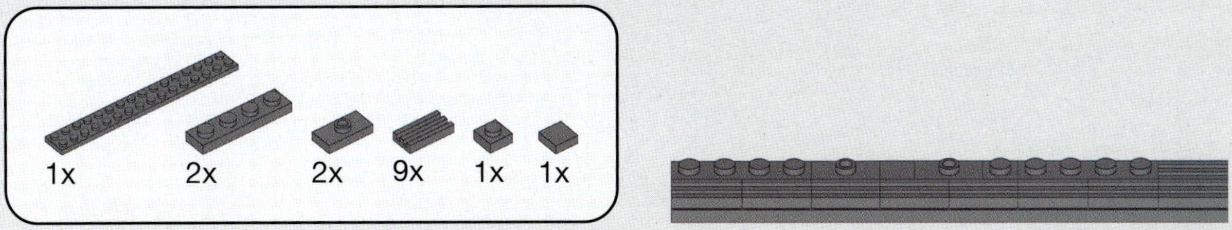

2

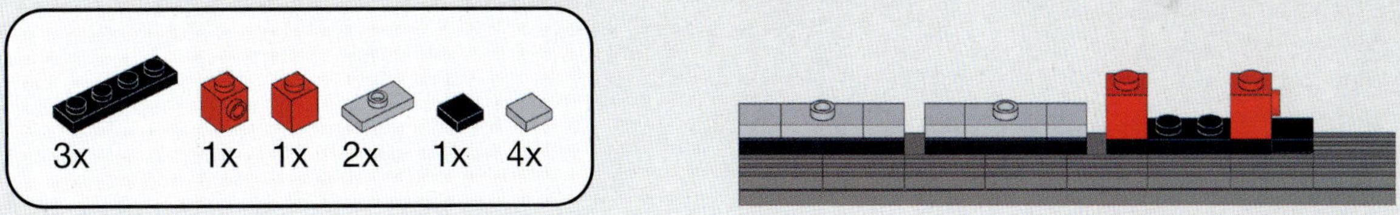

3

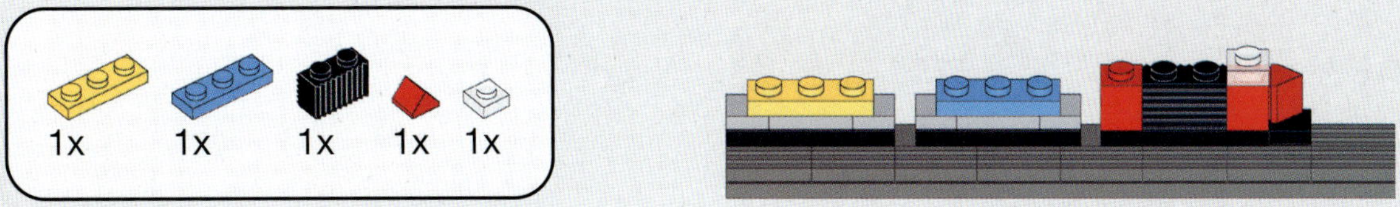

4

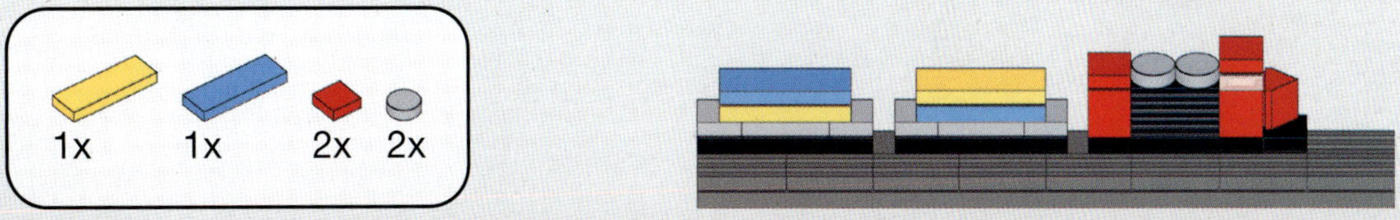

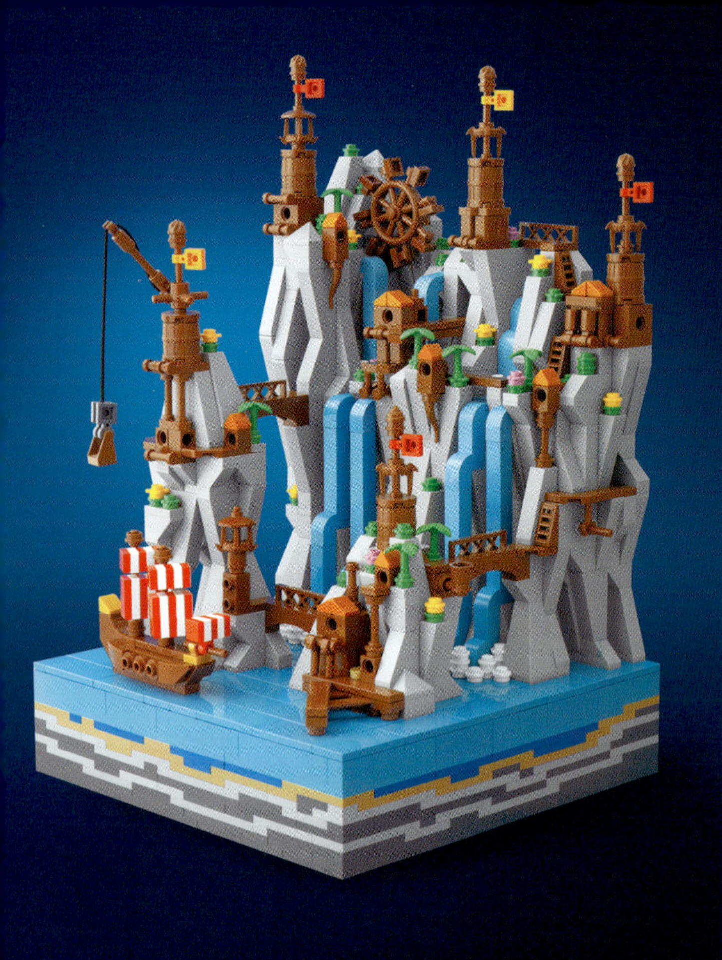
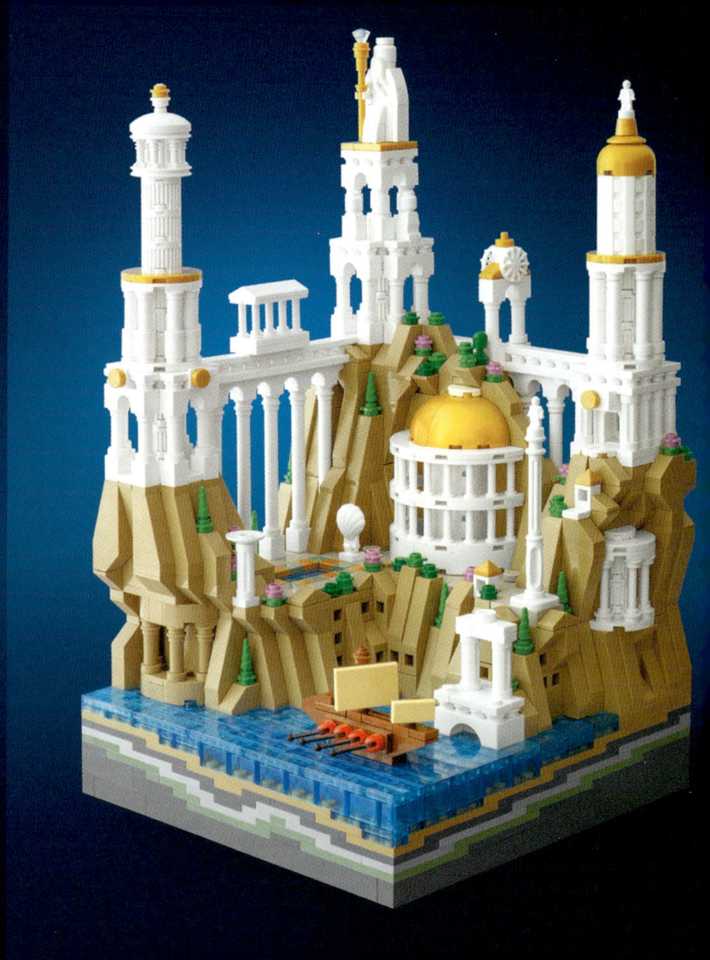
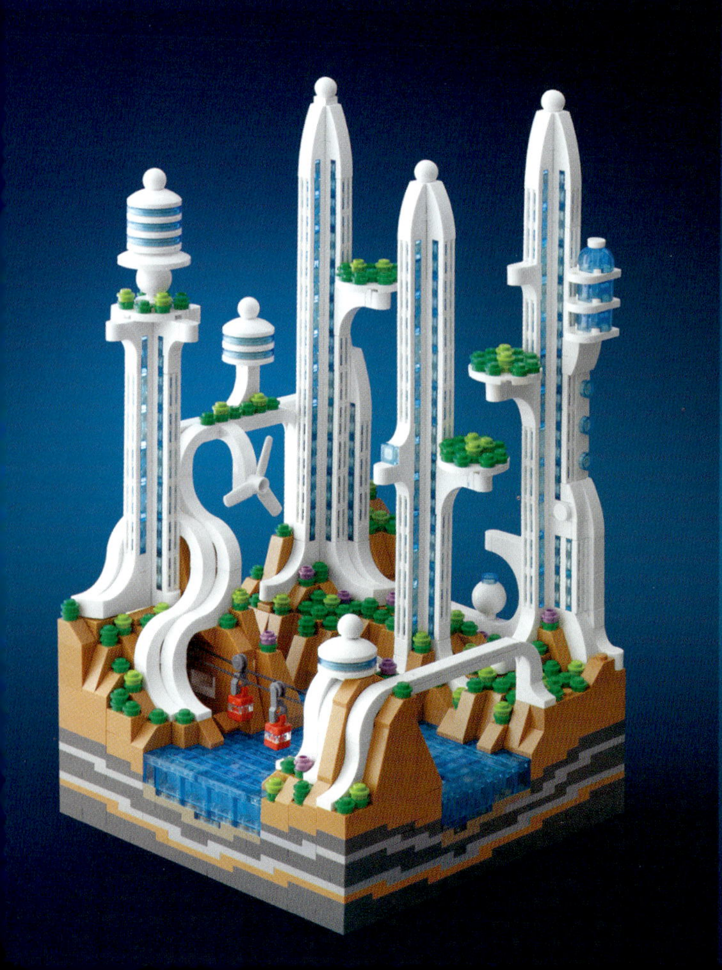
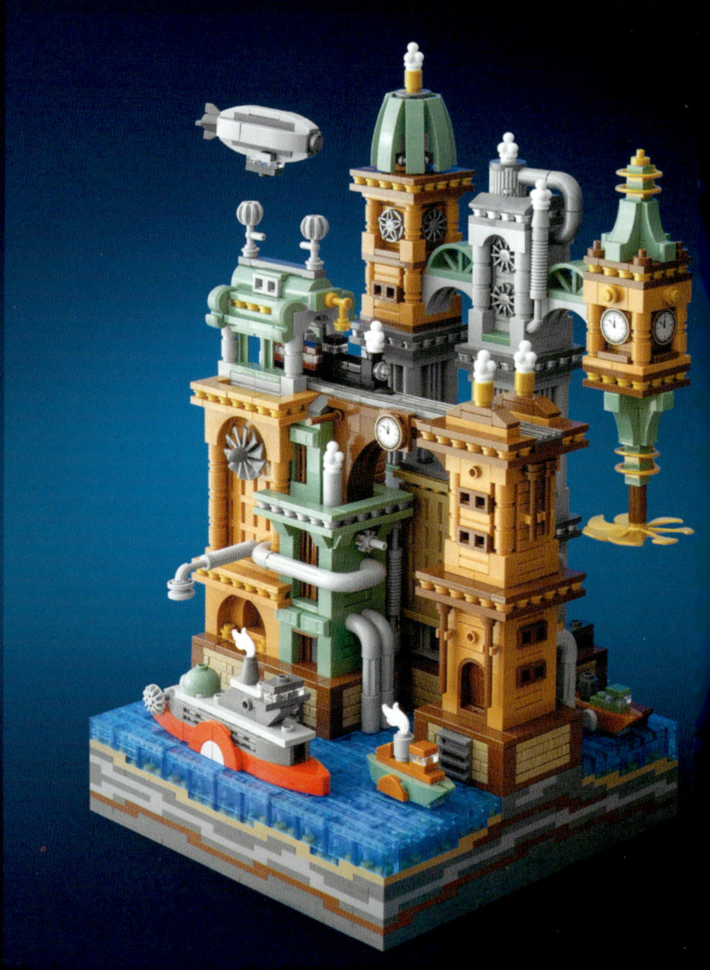

PART II: THEMED WORLDS

In this part of the book, you'll explore themed worlds that show how architecture, transportation, and scenery work together to create a cohesive setting. World-building with LEGO tells a story that uses thoughtful design in place of words.

ELVEN HAVEN

"Form follows function" is a principle that shaped modern architecture, favoring practicality over ornamentation. Among elven architects, however, form *is* function. Beauty is never superfluous, but a necessity that lifts the spirit.

Elven architecture features organic curves, soaring spires, and intricate latticework, appearing as though shaped by nature itself. Their structures reflect a reverence for harmony, lightness, and craftsmanship.

It's no coincidence that many LEGO elements used for elven architecture were originally designed for use as foliage. By using these organic shapes in unexpected ways, you can bring the wonder of elven design to life in your own worlds.

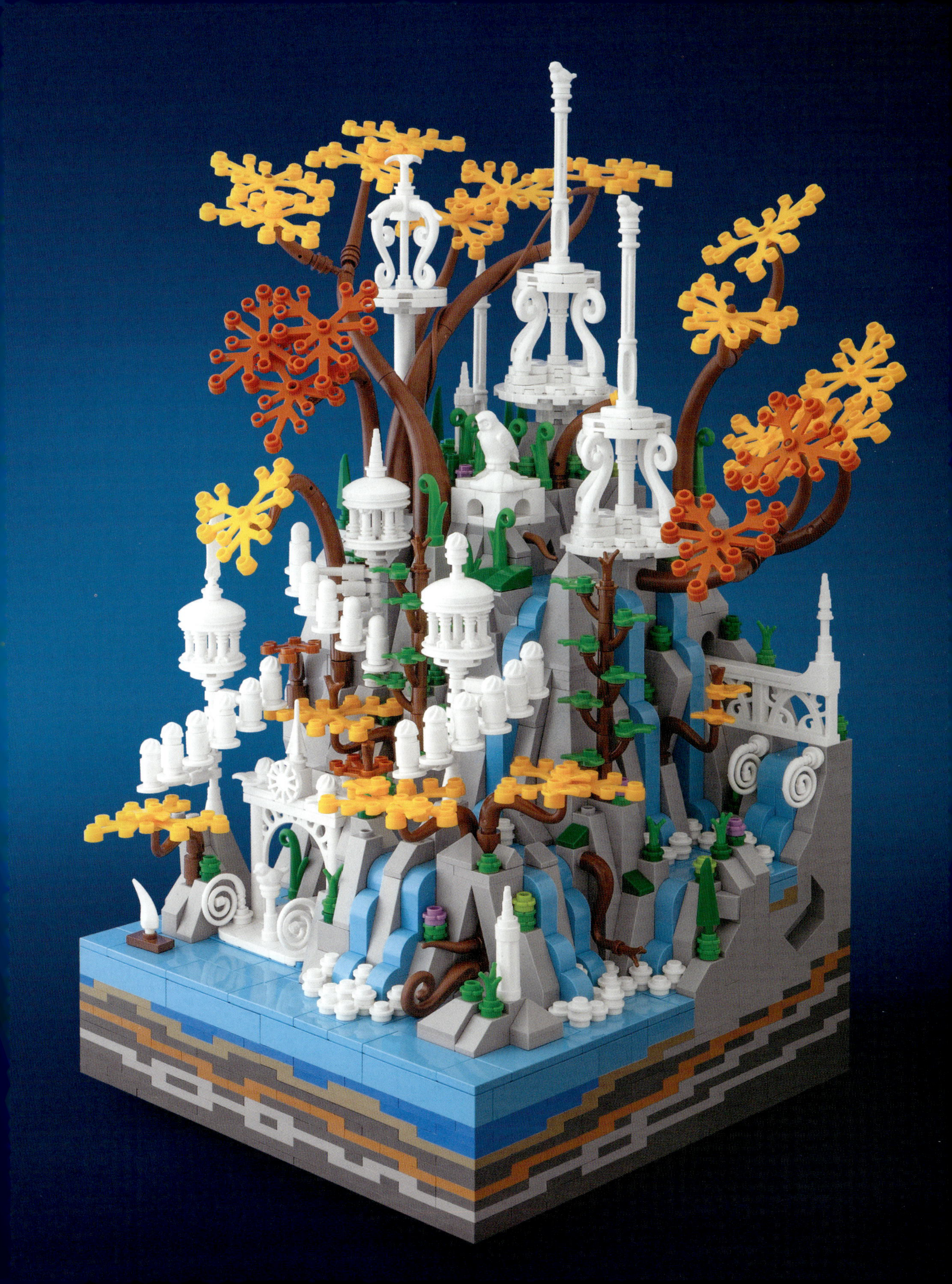

STARGAZER'S TOWER

The Stargazer's Tower rises above the forest canopy like a fantastical tree made of white marble. Architecture that emphasizes verticality draws the eye upward to connect with the sky.

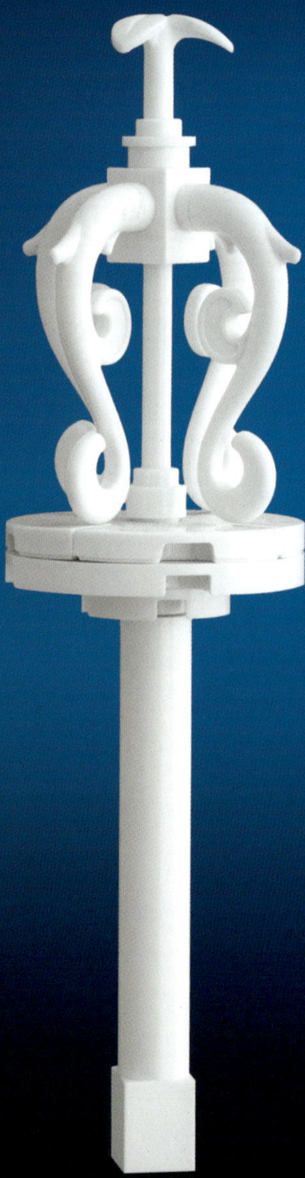

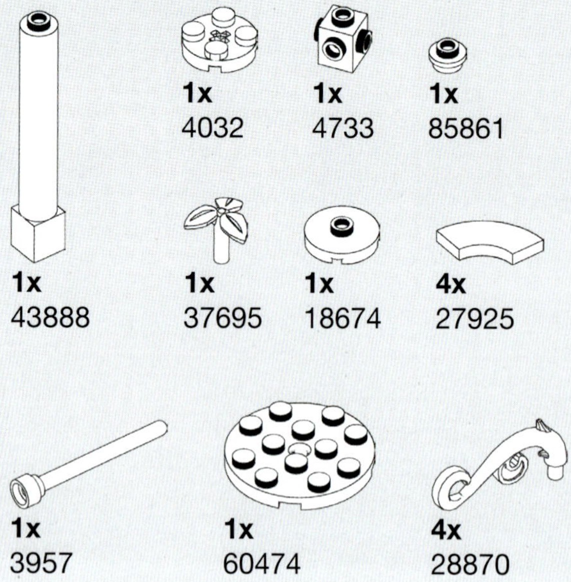

1

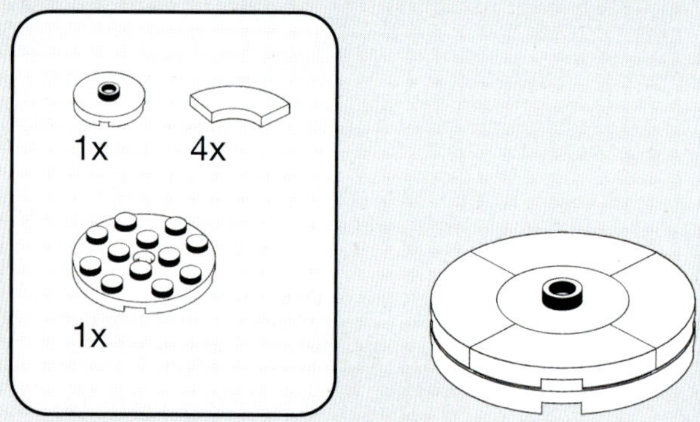

2

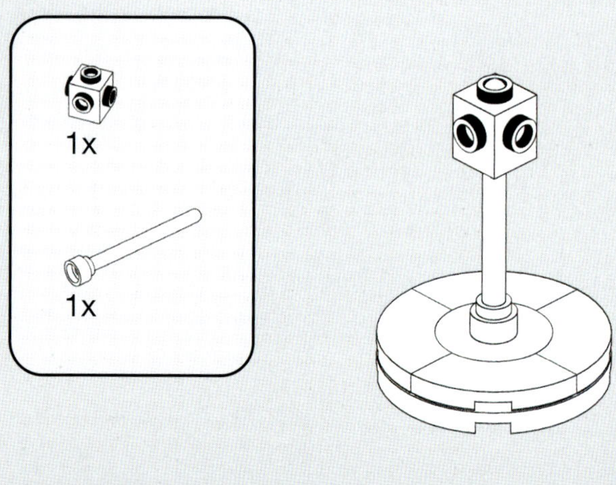

3

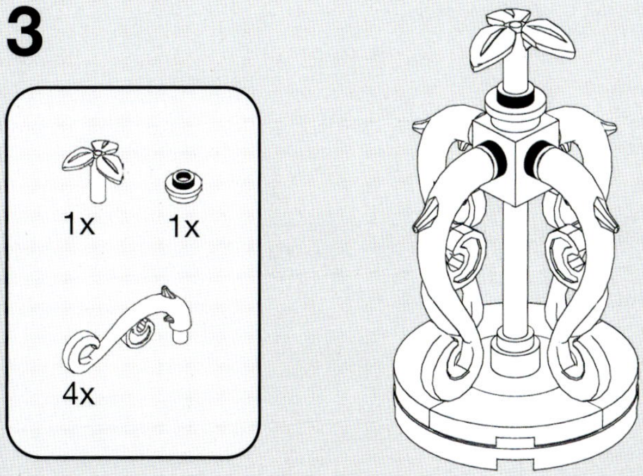

4

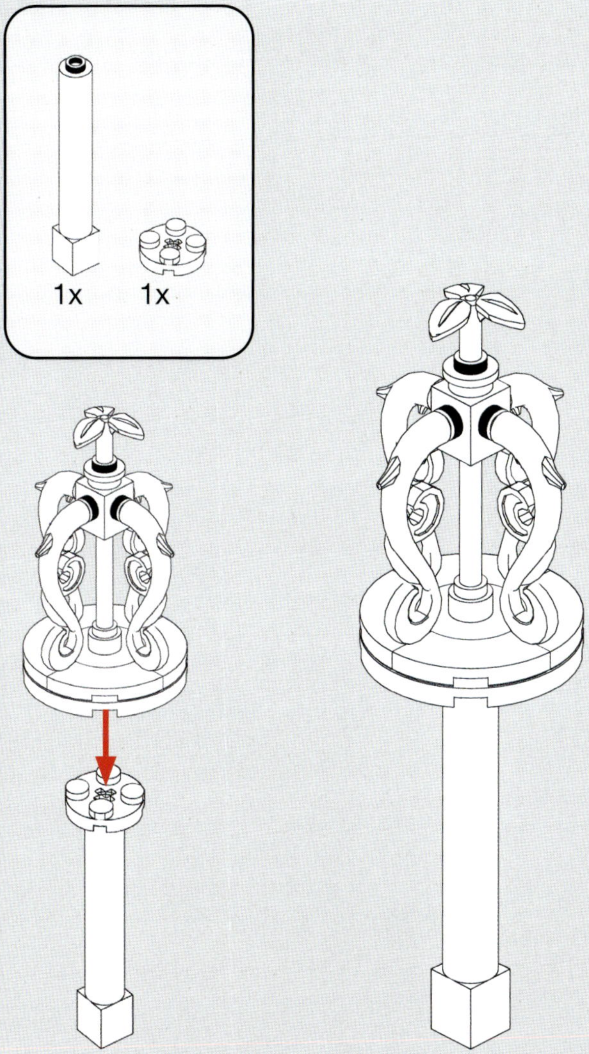

MAKE IT YOUR OWN

Add a roof to your tower with a 3×3 dish (#43898), as shown below. Top the dish with a 1×1 cone (#4589) or any 1×1 element you prefer.

Add height to your tower by stacking 1×1 round bricks (#3062) onto the supporting pillar. Your tolerance for wobbliness is the only limit to how high you can go!

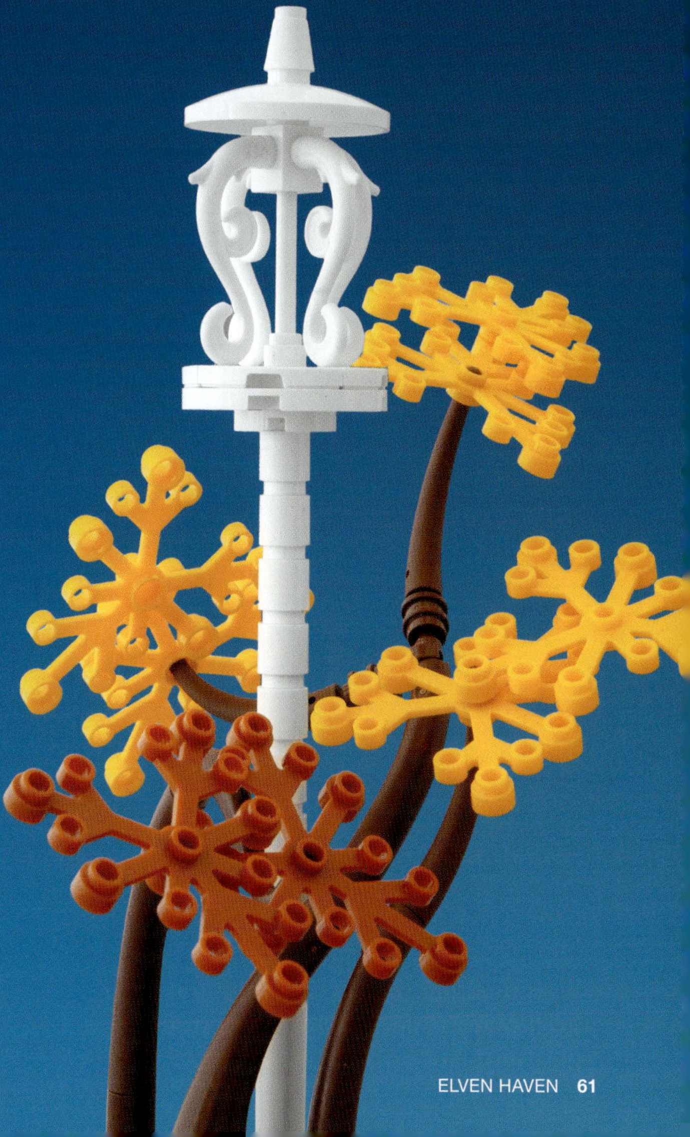

SPIRAL TREEHOUSE

The Spiral Treehouse climbs into the forest like a whirlwind flowing between branches. In elven design, spirals echo the forms of plants, flowing water, and even the structure of galaxies. They suggest motion or fluidity in solid structures.

Builders, be warned: It takes patience to level the different floors of the Spiral Treehouse, but don't spiral into despair! The result is a beautiful structure that captures the magic of elven craftsmanship.

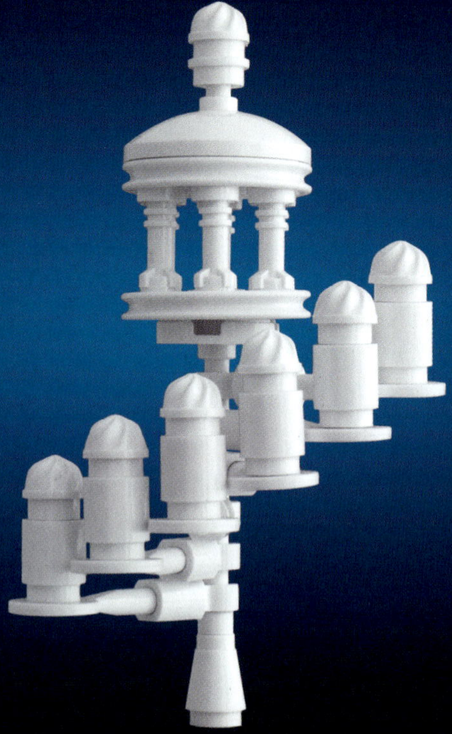

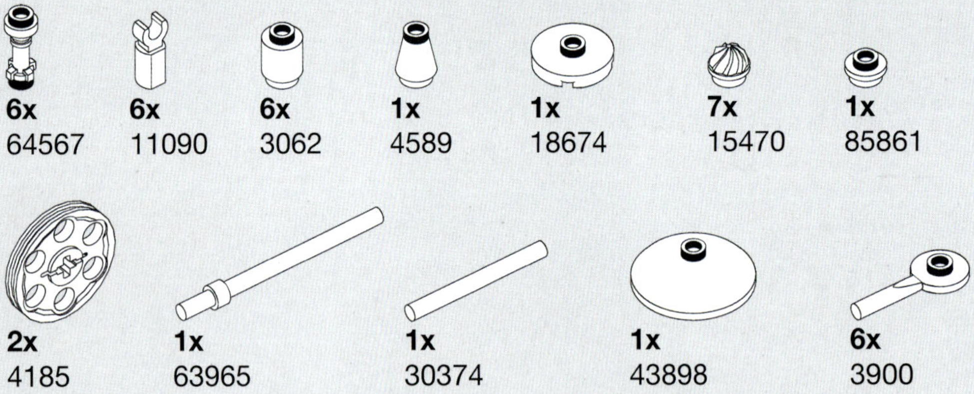

1

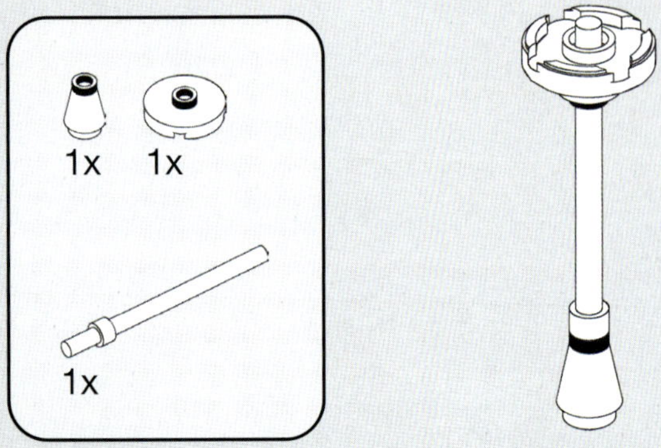

2

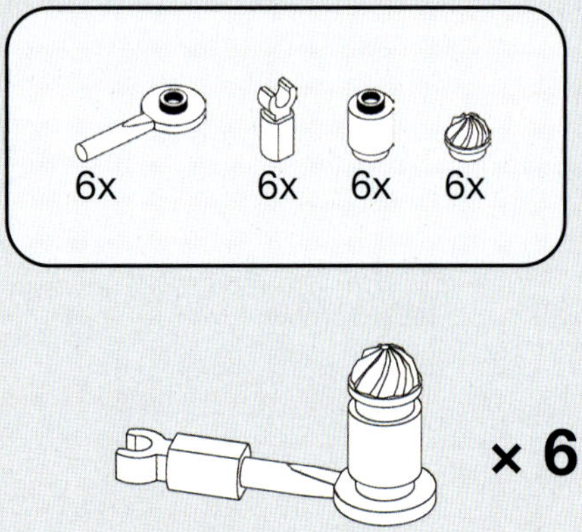

3

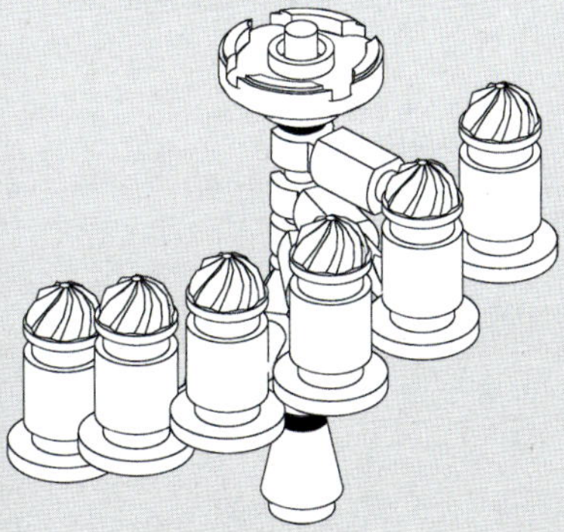

Clip the assemblies from step 2 onto the bar from step 1, arranged as illustrated.

4

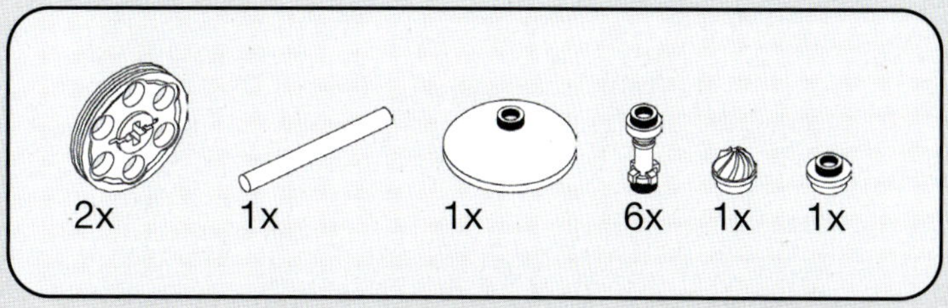

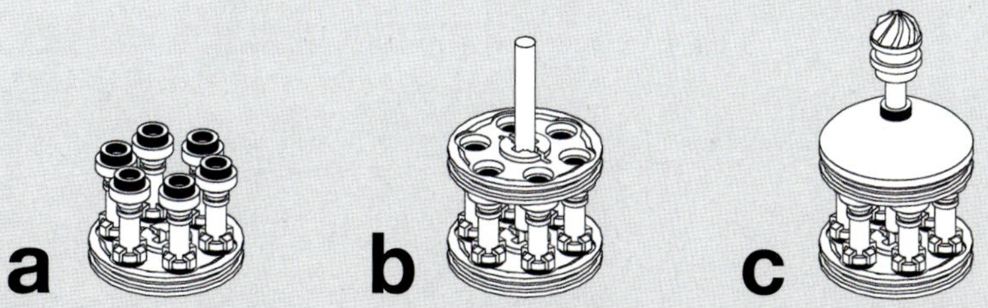

Don't push the bar into the bottom pulley.

5

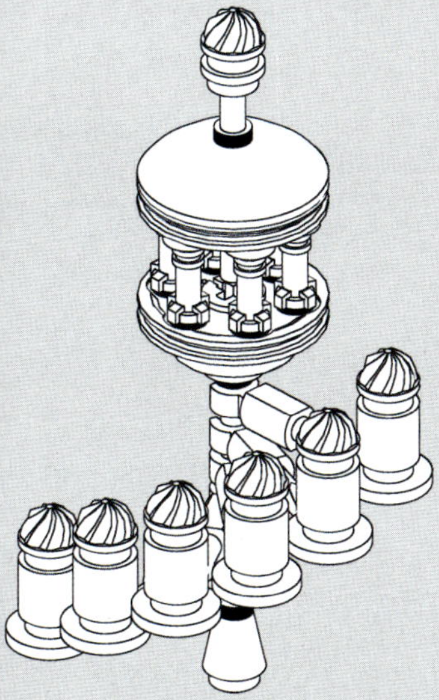

Attach the assembly from step 4 onto the assembly from step 3.

MAKE IT YOUR OWN

Replace the vertical swirl round plates—originally designed as soft-serve ice cream for minifigures—with other 1×1 elements. Unicorn horns (#89522) maintain the swirling aesthetic, while Bionicle Barraki eyes (#58176) create smooth, rounded roofs.

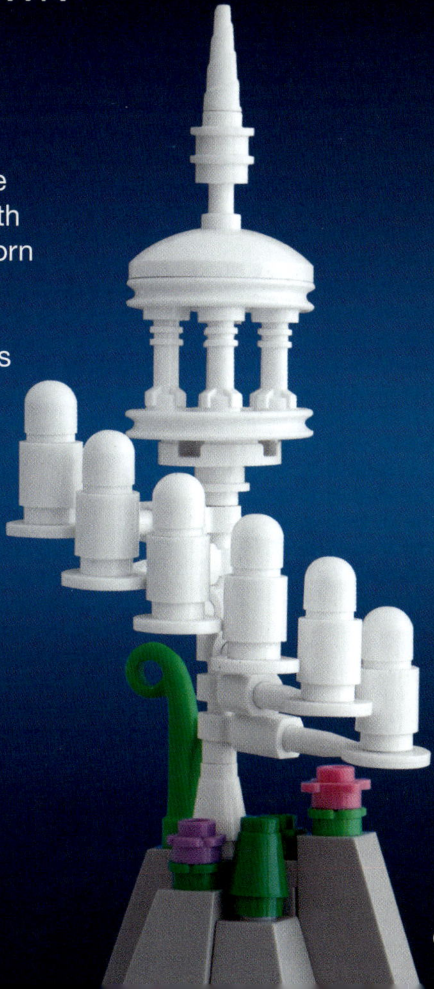

SYLVAN SANCTUARY

The Sylvan Sanctuary is an open-air structure designed for quiet reflection, communion with nature, and debating whether the squirrels are plotting a rebellion. Its roof provides just enough shelter to shield one from the elements while still allowing the surrounding forest to be fully embraced.

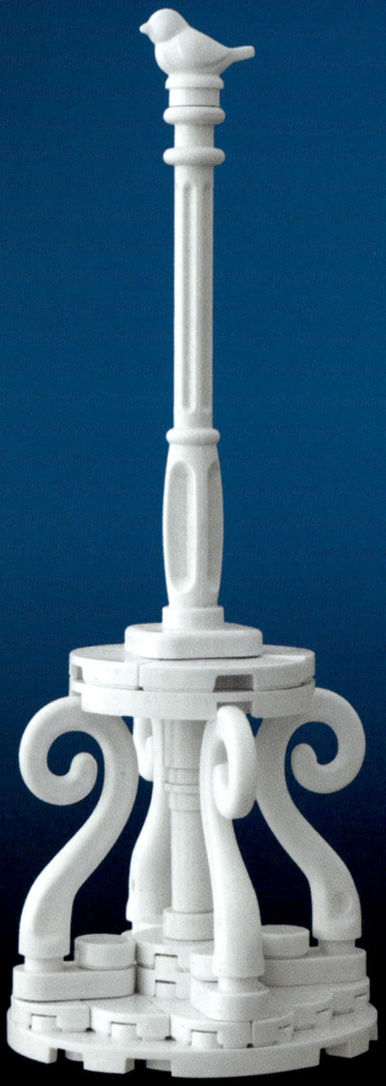

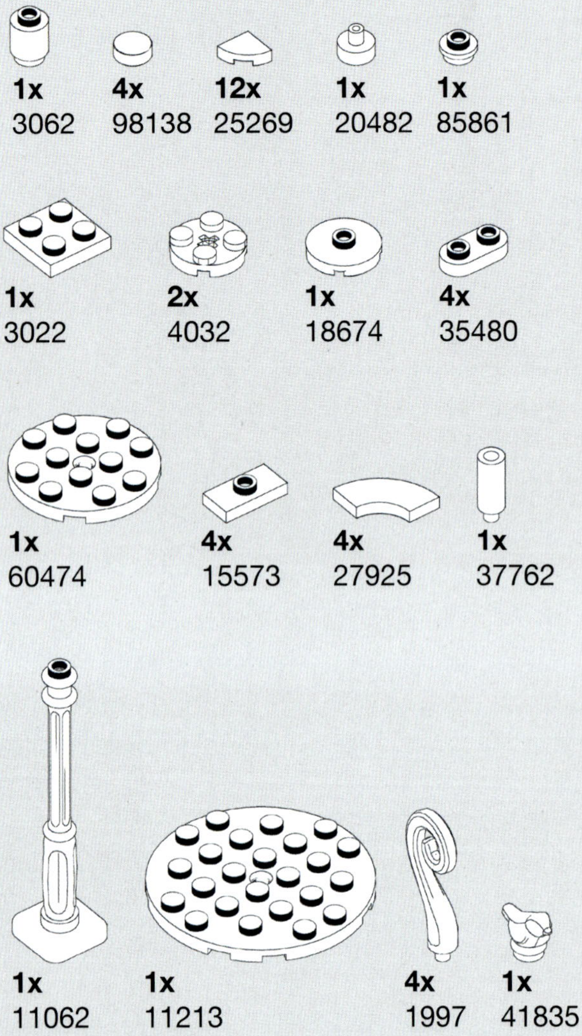

1

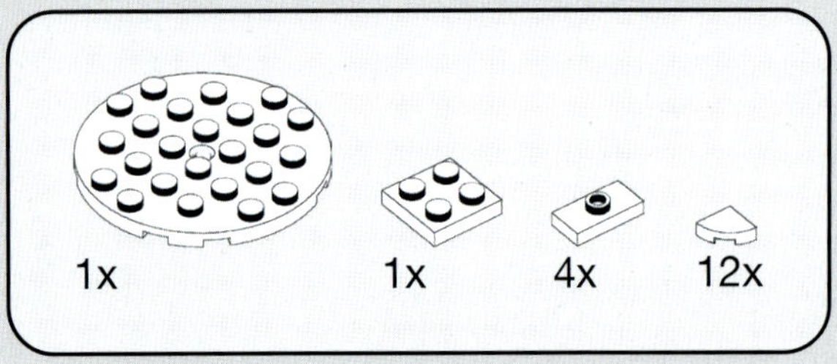

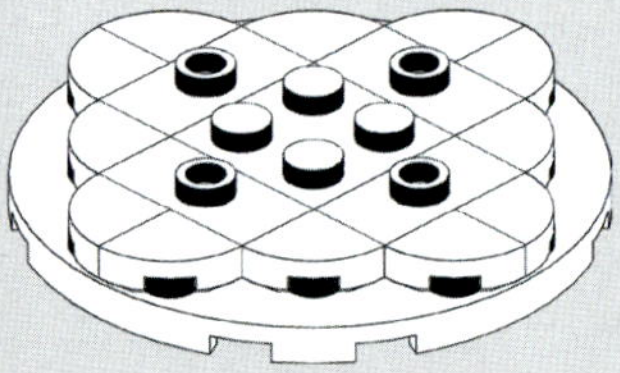

2

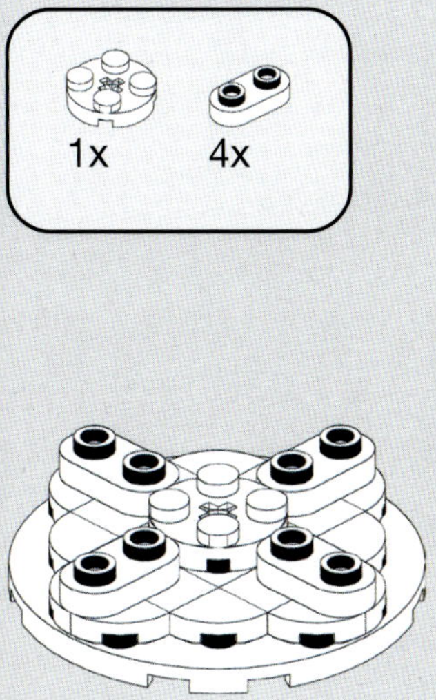

3

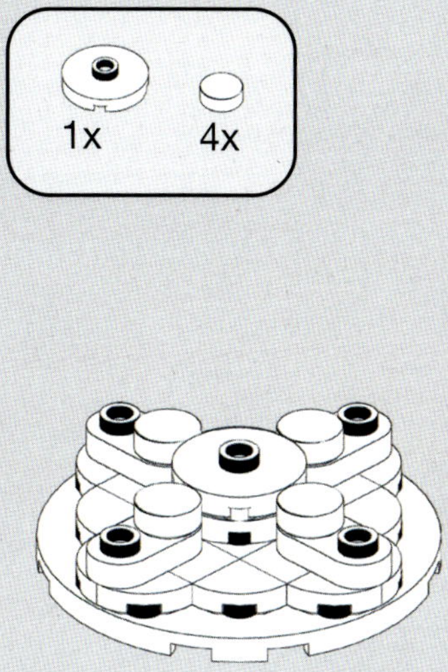

4

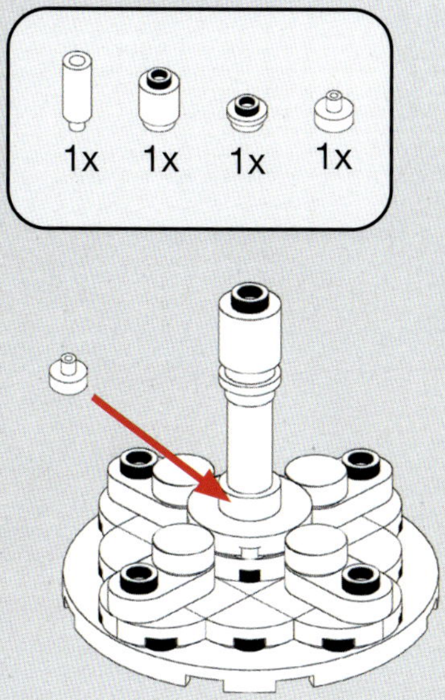

5

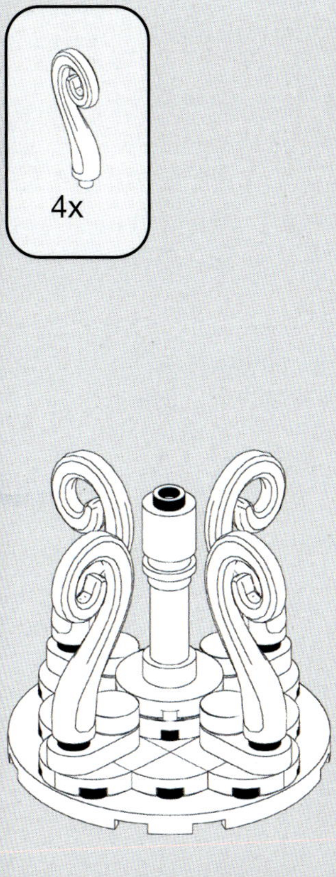

6

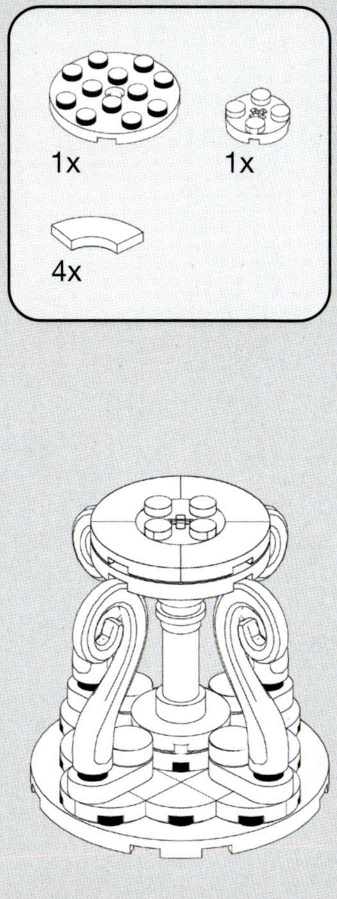

7

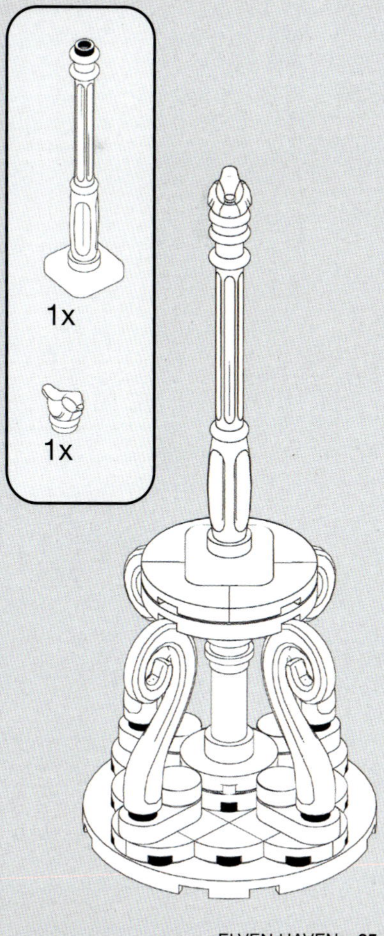

The Sylvan Sanctuary rooftop offers many options for customization, as removing the top pillar provides four studs to build on. Here, the upper model has its pillar replaced with a 2×2 dome (#553) topped with a unicorn horn (#89522).

Raise your structure above the forest canopy by adding an elegant supporting column. The column shown here is made by alternating 2×2 fluted round bricks (#92947) with 2×2 round plates (#4032).

The lower model replaces the 2×2 round plate used on top with a 2×2 round tile with open stud (#18674). A 1×1 round cone (#4589) and unicorn horn (#89522) are placed on the open stud to create a graceful spire.

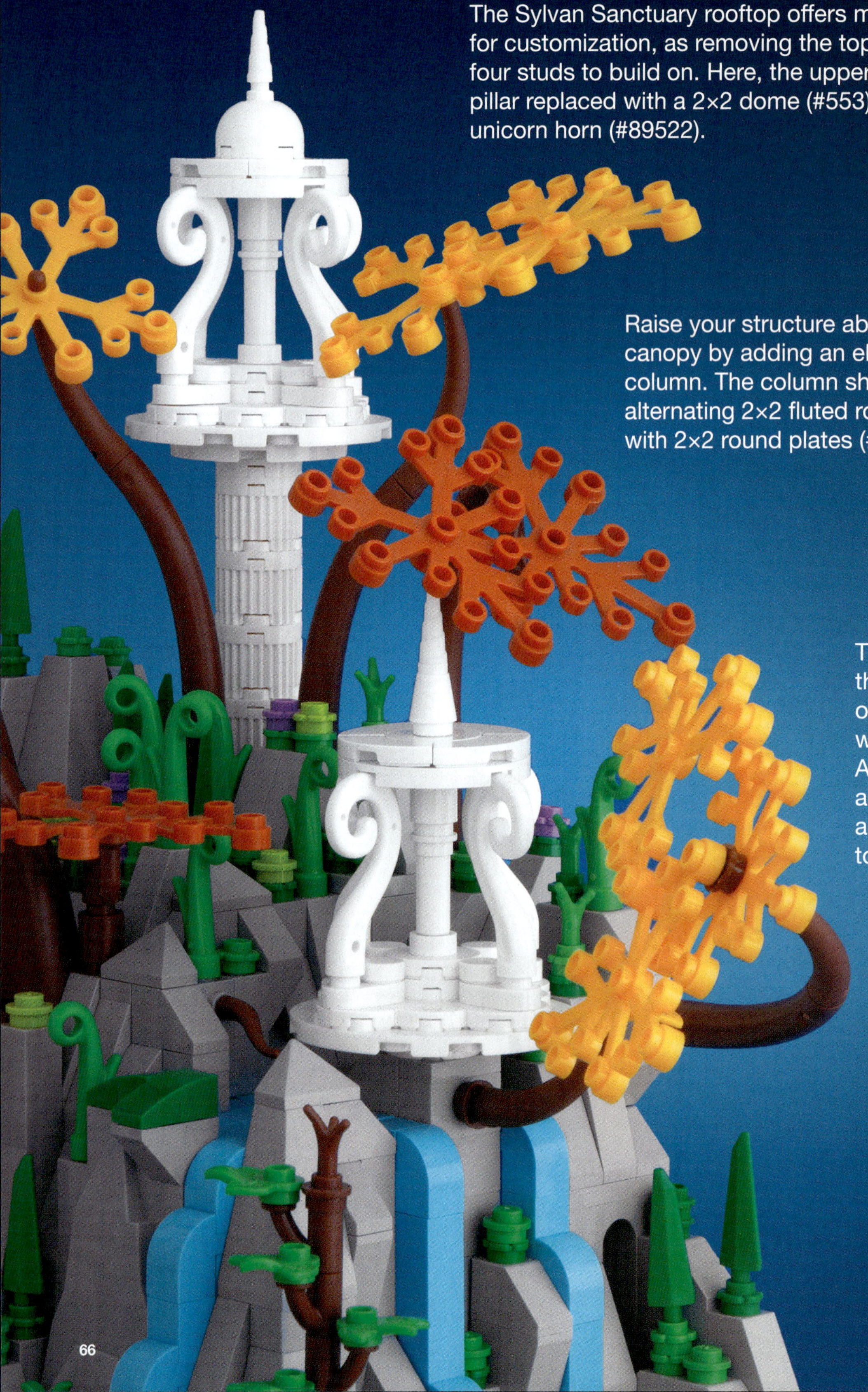

EVENTIDE LANDING

The Eventide Landing is a serene dockside structure where the elves welcome visitors with style—whether it's dignitaries from distant lands or hobbits looking for a third breakfast.

Its lacy, open-air design gives the impression of weightlessness, allowing heavy carved stone to feel airy and ethereal.

Coiled whip elements (#61975) are great for whipping your elven architecture into shape. The swirling form mimics snail shells and pea shoots.

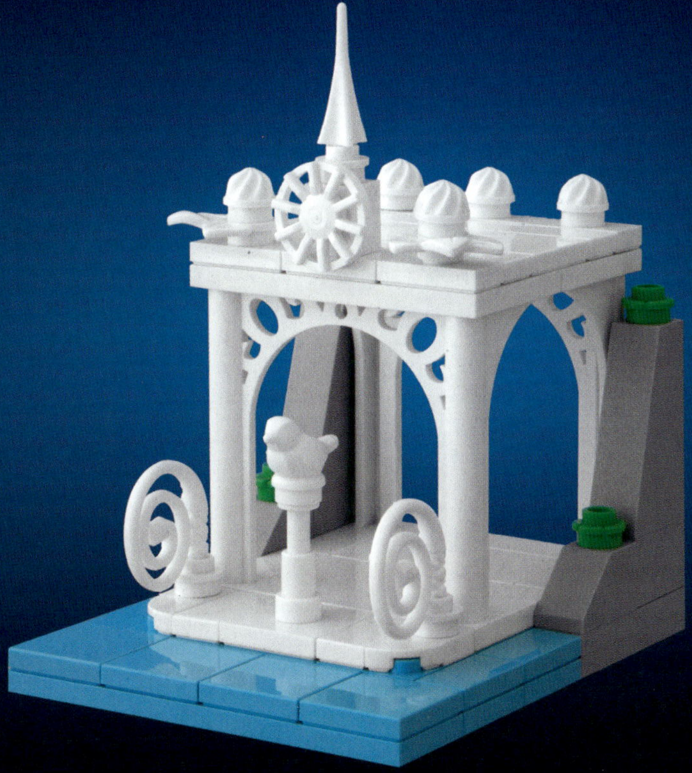

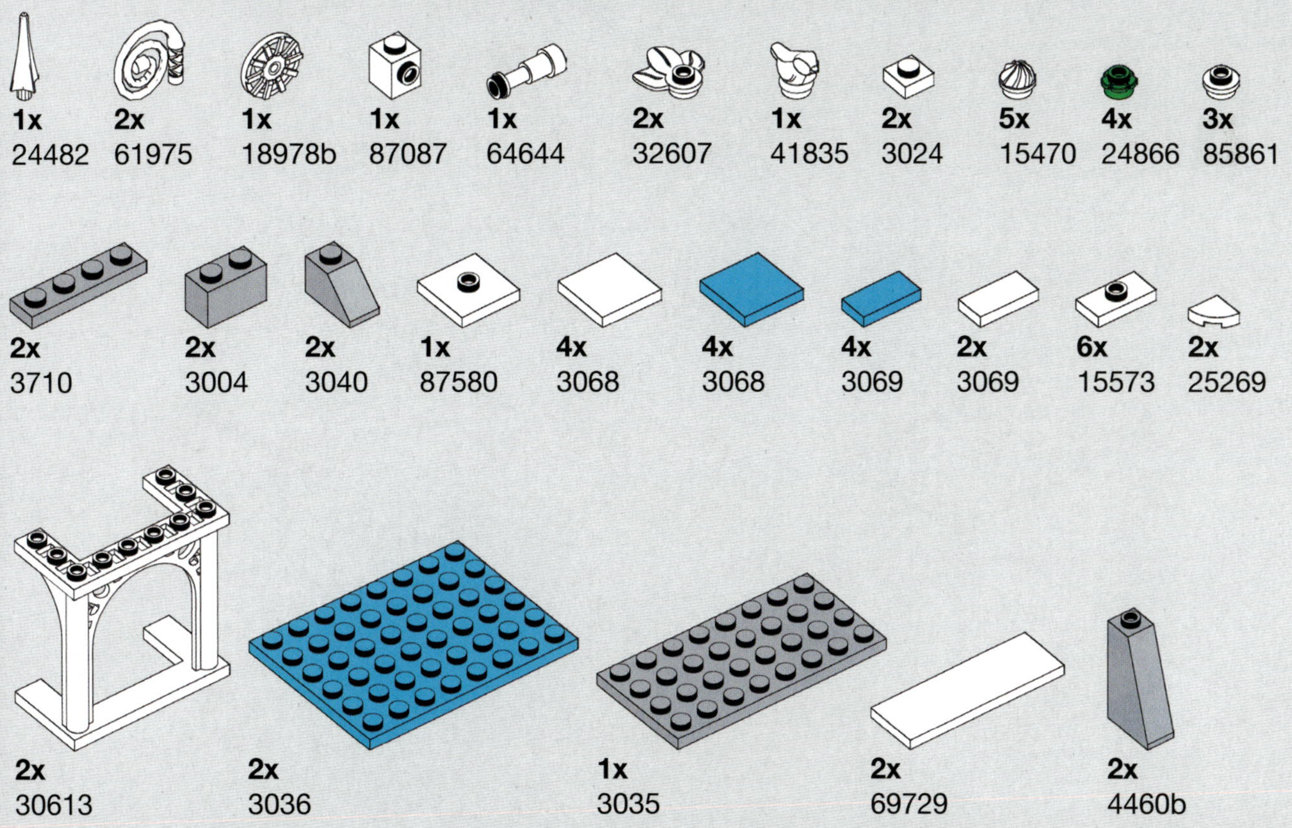

1

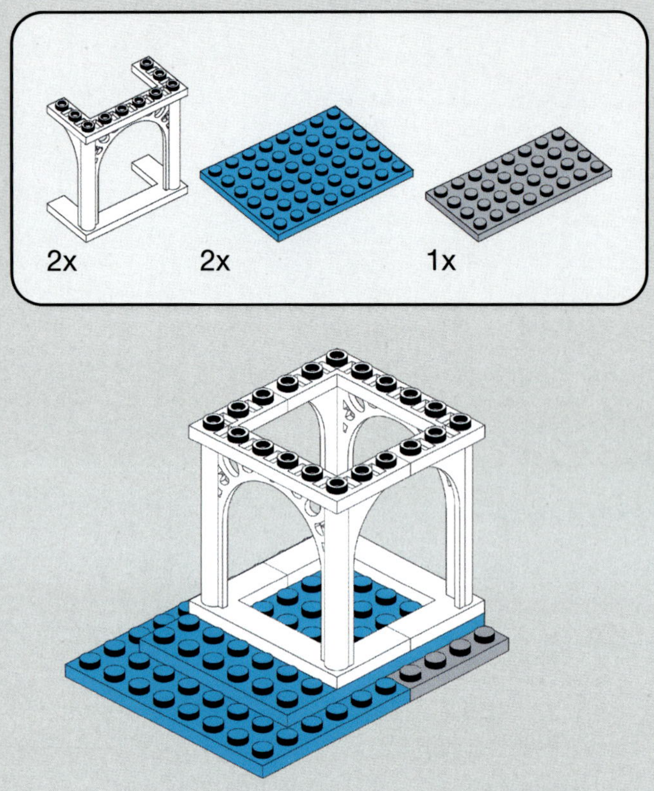

2

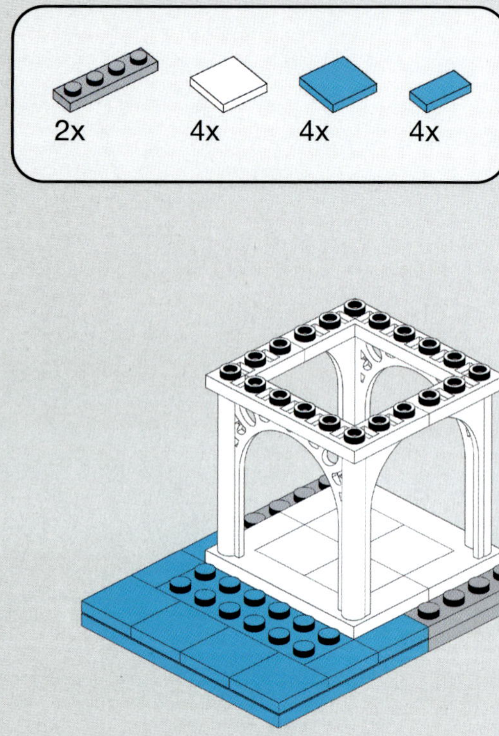

3

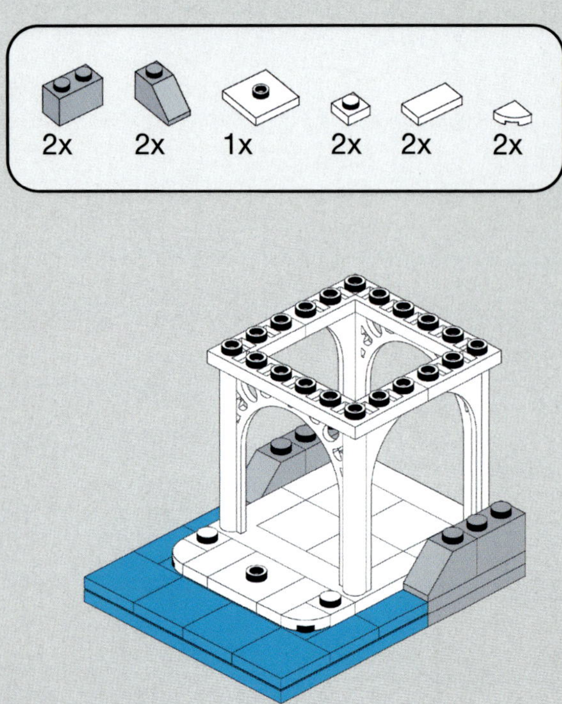

4

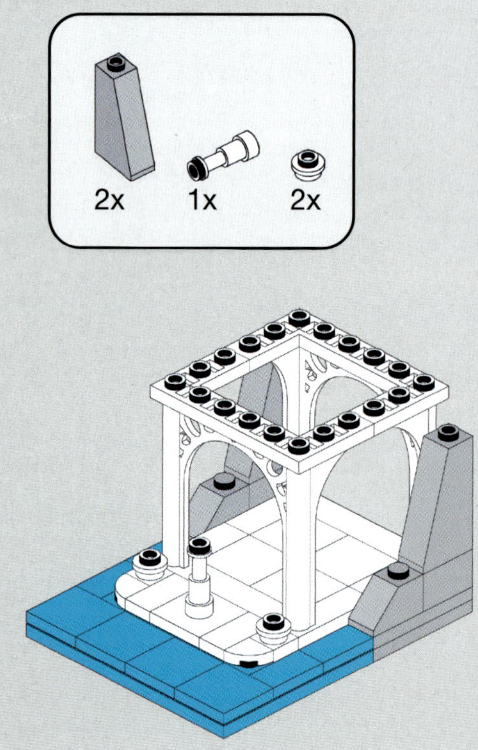

5

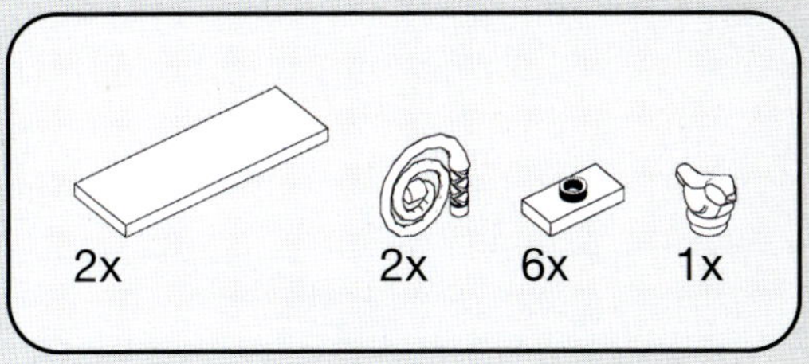

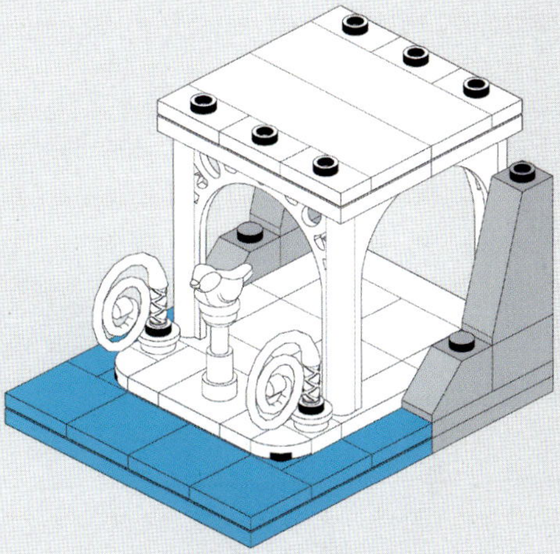

6

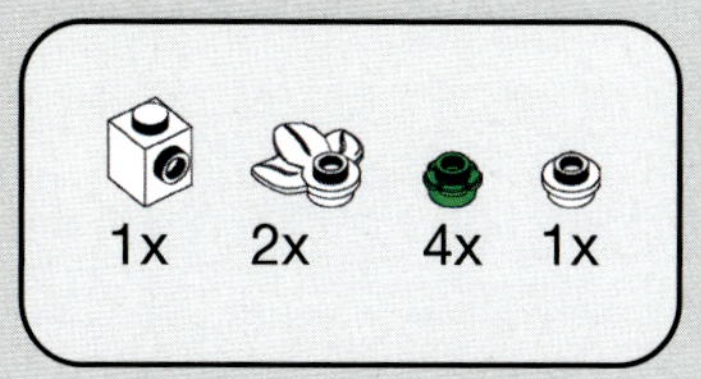

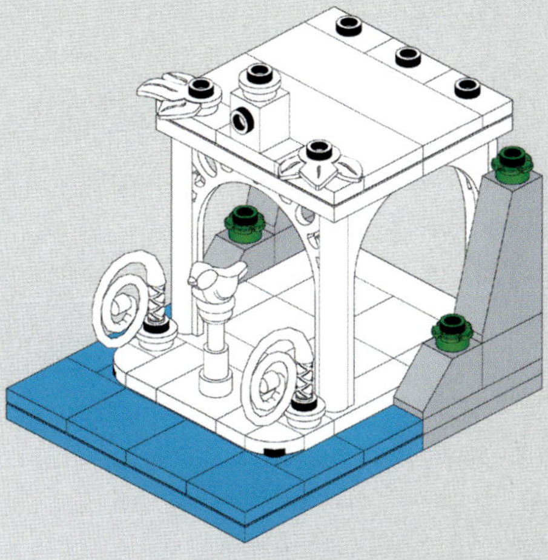

7

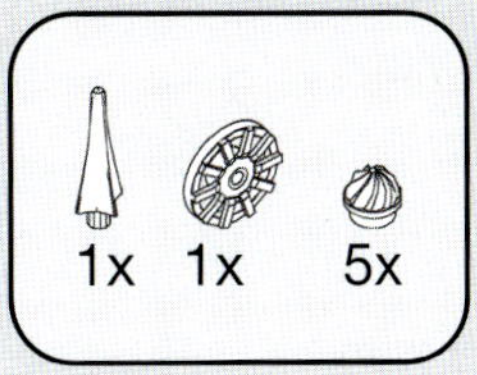

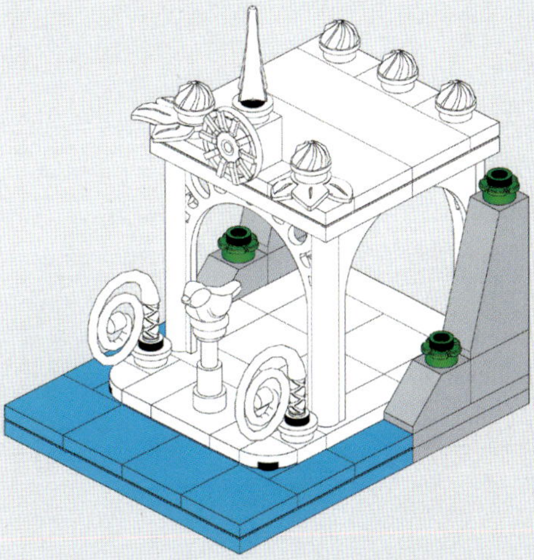

MAKE IT YOUR OWN

Give your Eventide Landing an oceanic theme by replacing the bird statue with a folding clam shell (#18866), attached to a modified 1×1 with open O clip tile (#15712).

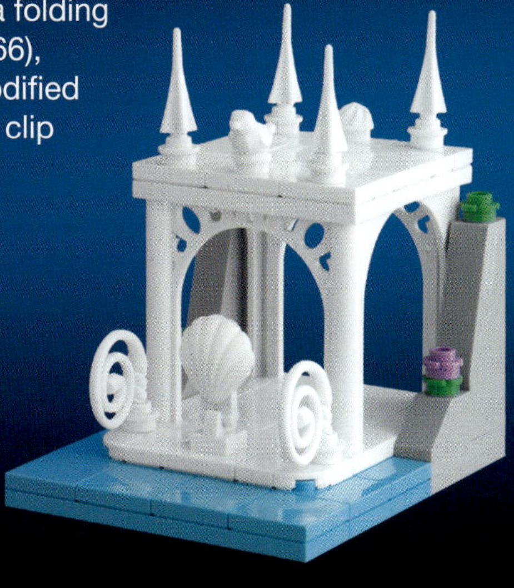

ELDER TREE

These centuries-old trees are revered by the elves and add gravitas to forest landscapes.

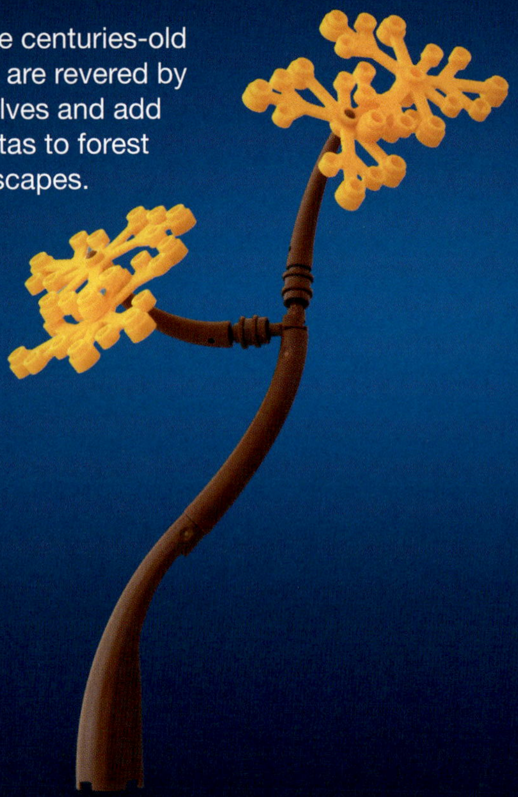

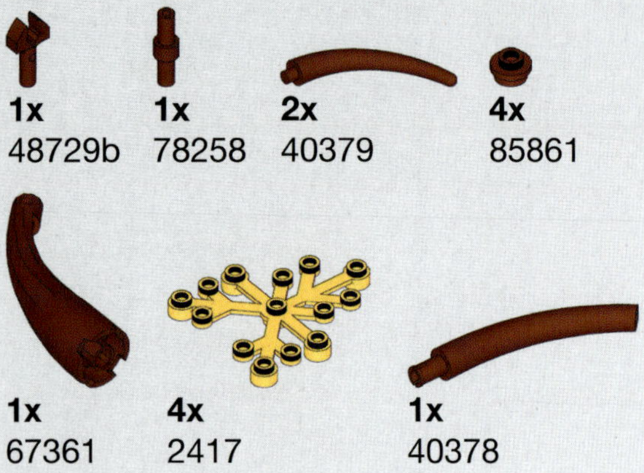

1

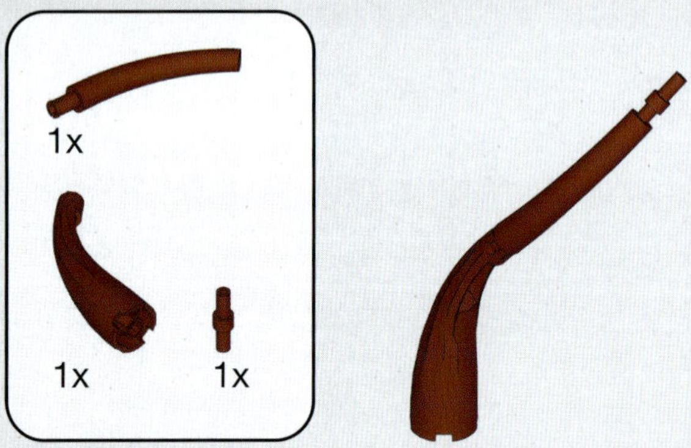

BENT OAK

The Bent Oak appears to bow toward forest visitors.

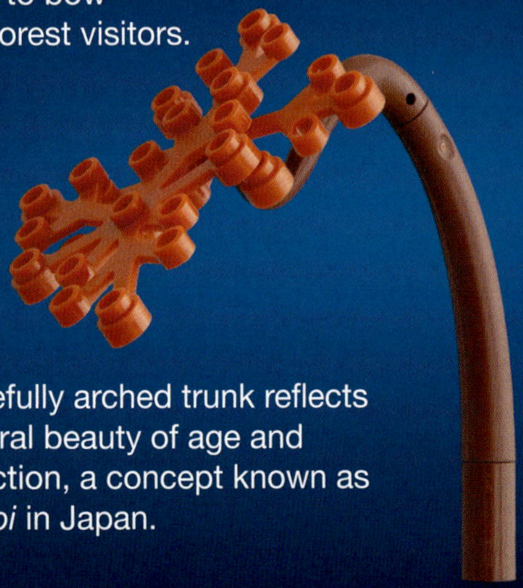

Its gracefully arched trunk reflects the natural beauty of age and imperfection, a concept known as *wabi sabi* in Japan.

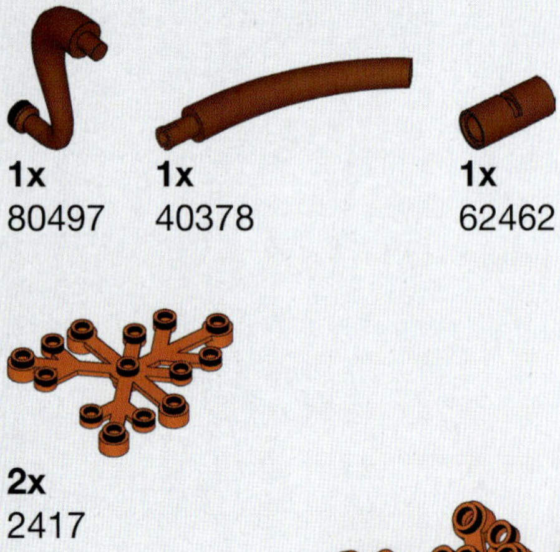

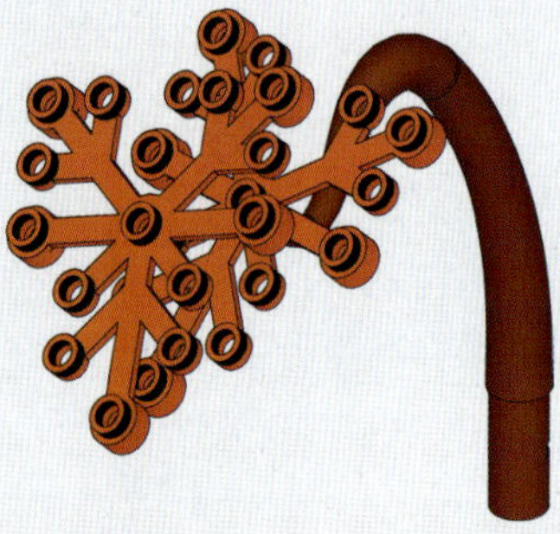

2

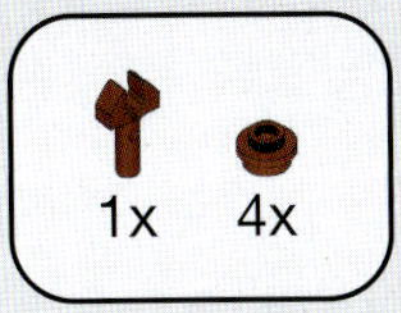

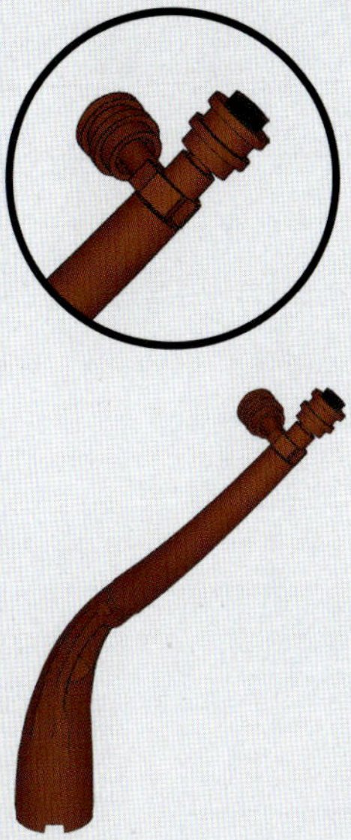

3

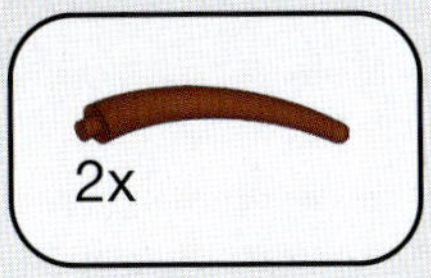

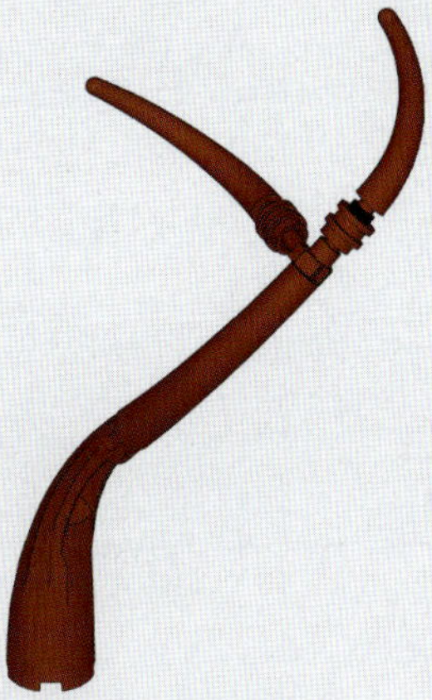

4

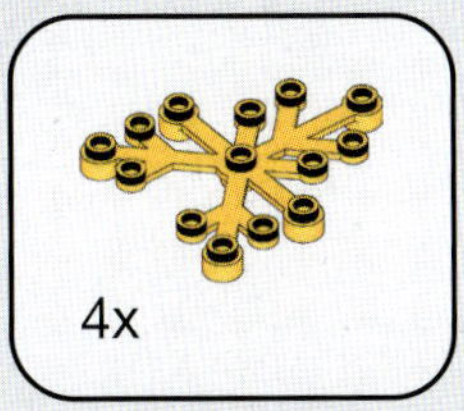

Rotate the branches to give your tree a custom shape.

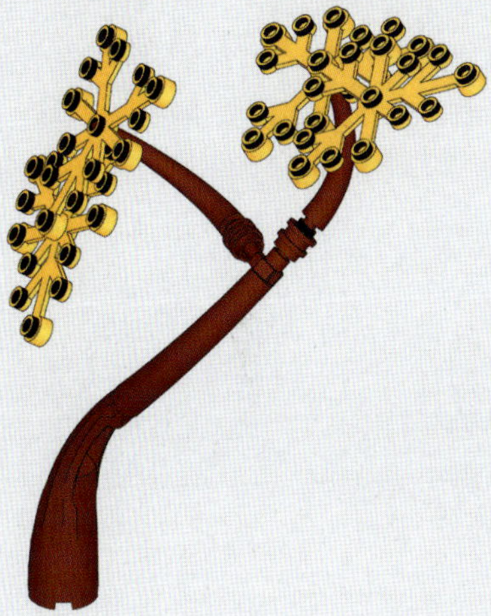

WIND DANCER

The Wind Dancer's curving trunk sways gently in the breeze.

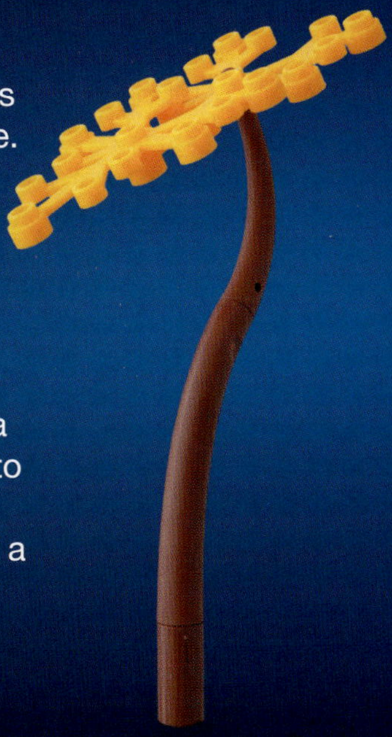

Gentle curves are a welcome addition to LEGO landscapes, taking the edge off a traditionally blocky medium.

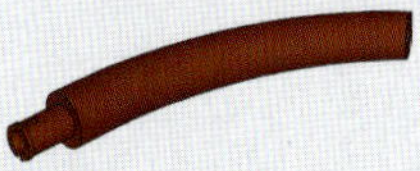

1x
40378

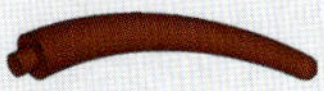

1x
40379

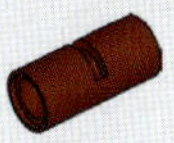

1x
62462

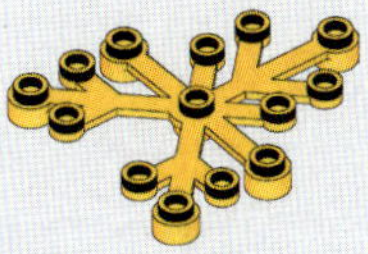

2x
2417

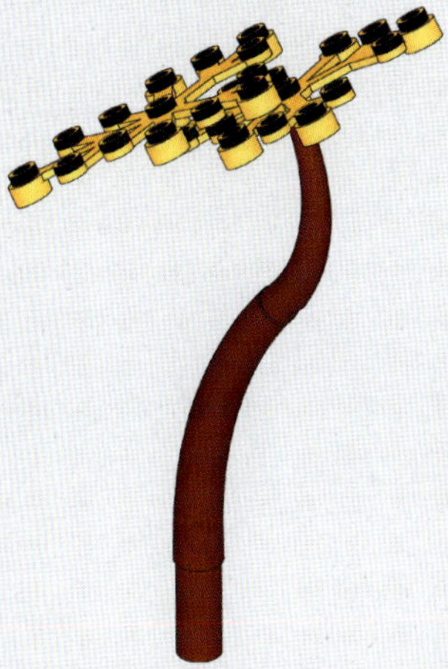

PIRATE COVE

This bustling pirate cove is so industrious that its denizens could be making an honest living—but then they'd lose the freedom of bringing excitable parrots to work.

Ramshackle pirate buildings, crafted from flotsam, wrecked ships, and beachcombed treasures, are what formally trained architects call *vernacular architecture*, the art of creating functional buildings from everyday, salvaged materials. It's a folk style that captures the resourcefulness and rebellious spirit of a pirate world.

You can channel this same spirit by sifting through your LEGO collection. Use the pieces you have on hand to create a unique style!

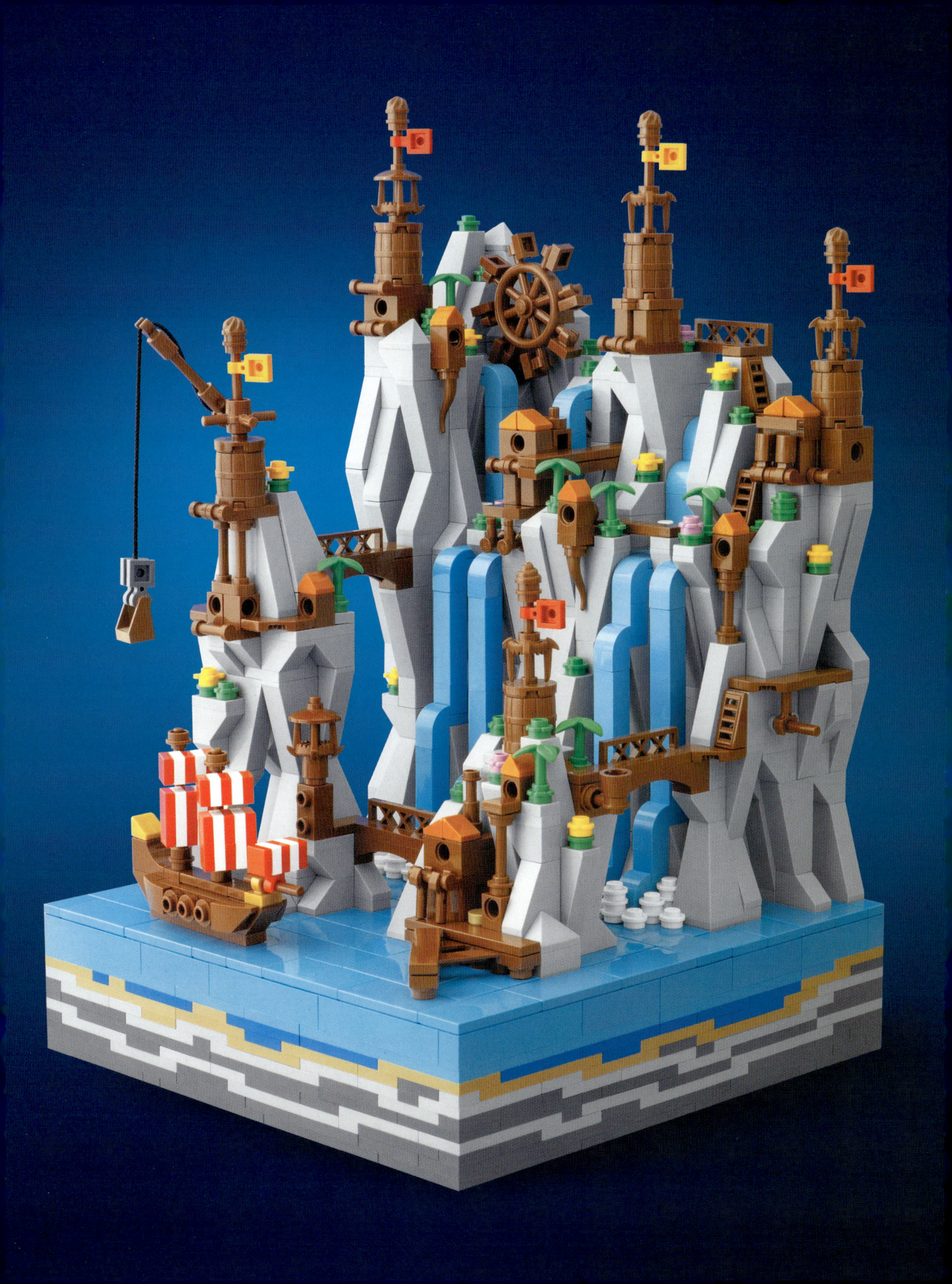

SHIP OF THE LINE

A *ship of the line* is a large, heavily armed warship designed to take part in the "line of battle," where opposing navies arrange their ships in a line to exchange broadsides in a well-mannered fashion. This ship of the line was recently liberated from the Imperial Navy by pirates and now serves as their flagship and floating rum storage unit.

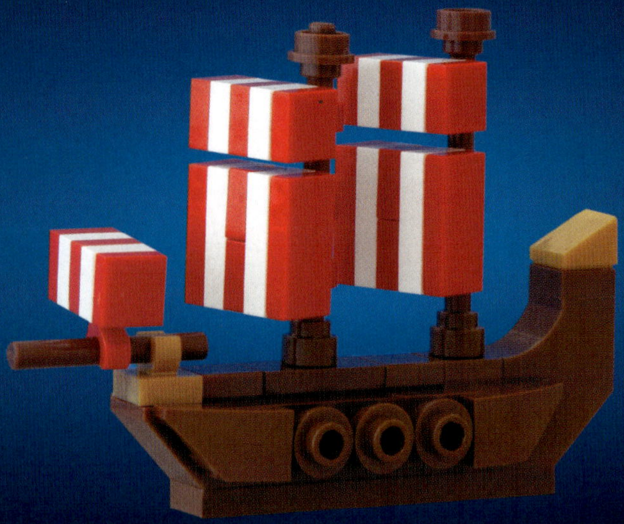

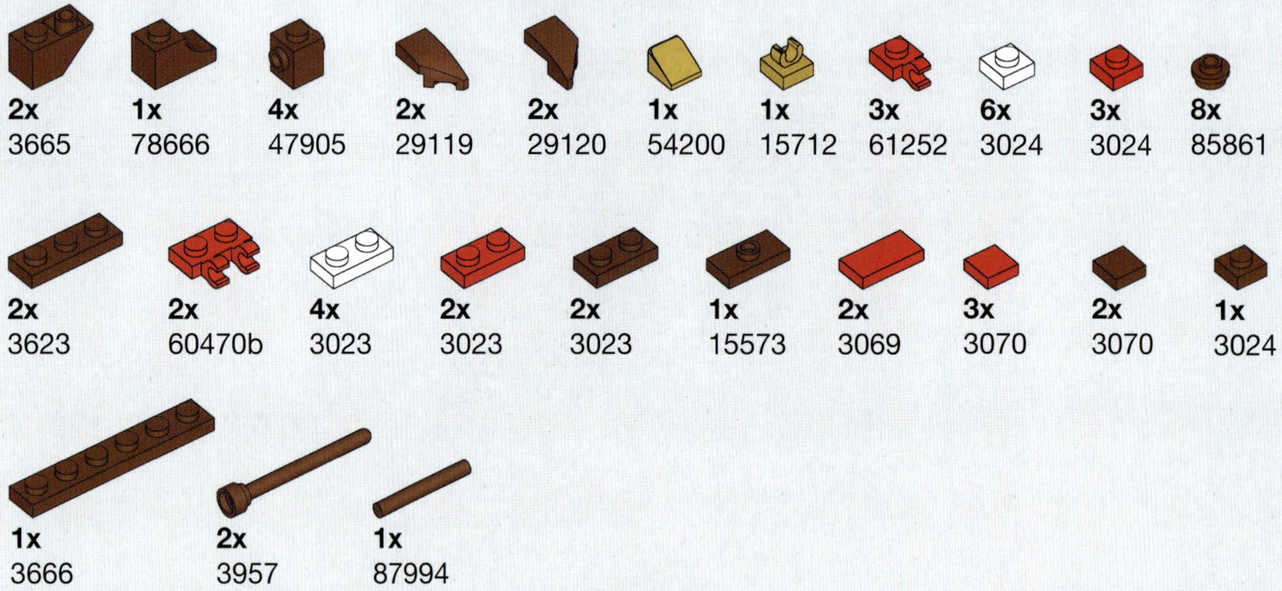

1

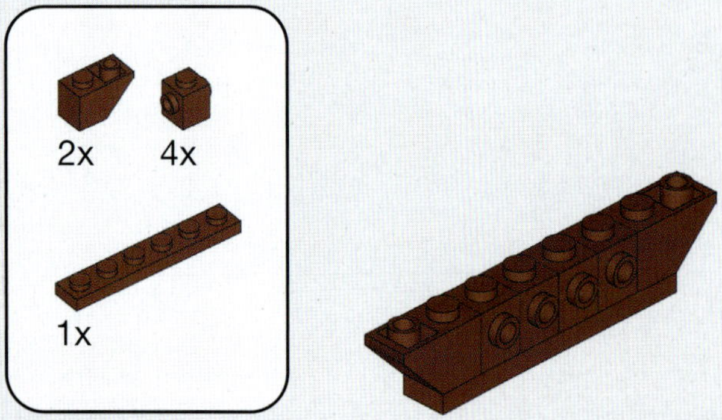

2

The ship's sides are identical.

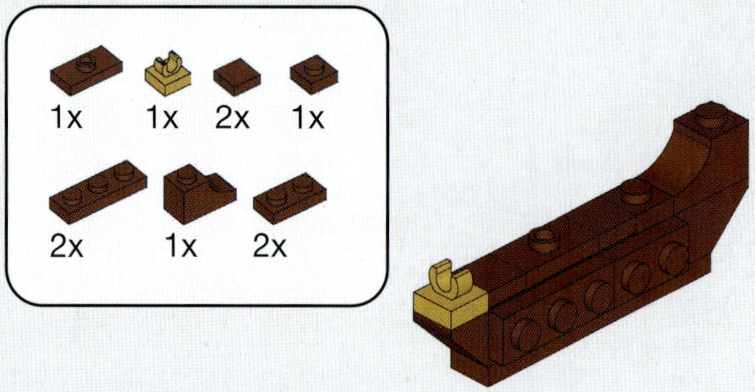

3

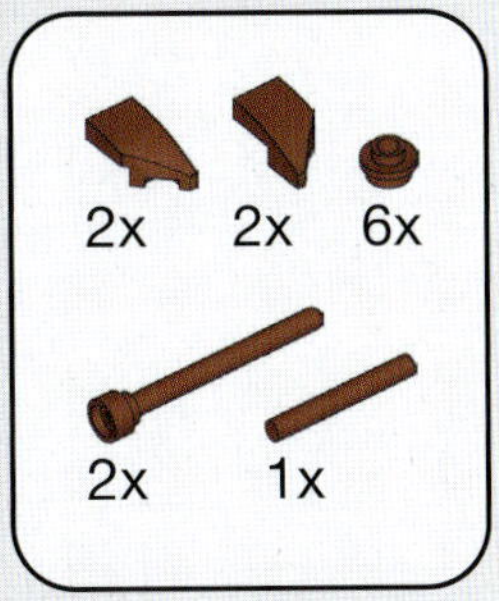

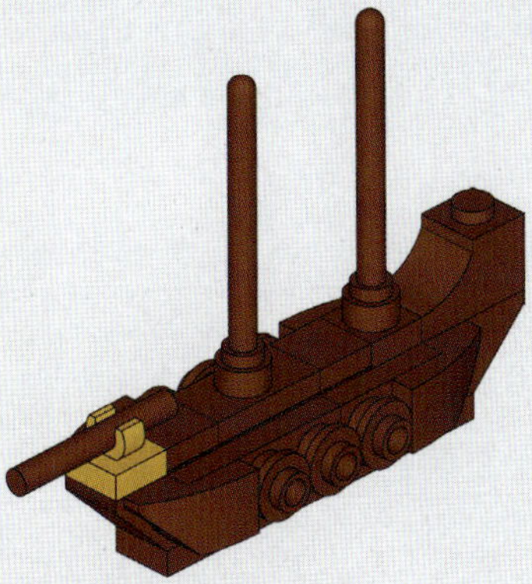

4

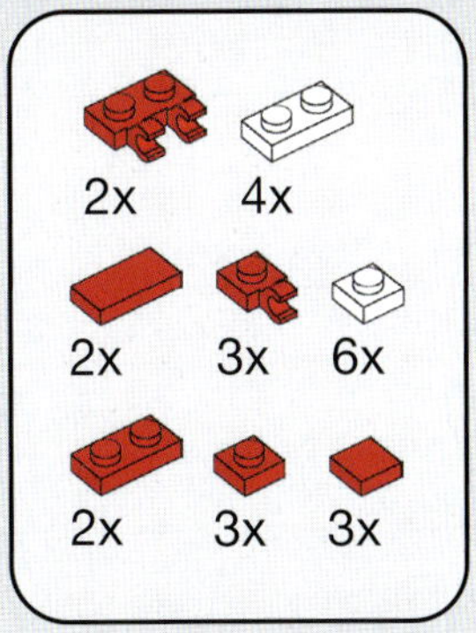

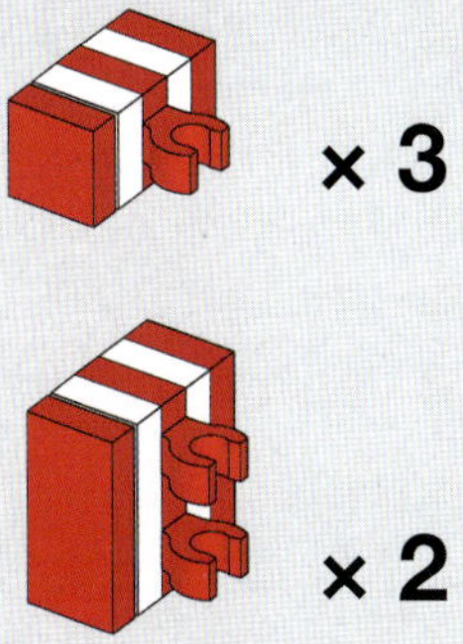

5

Clip the sails from step 4 to the ship as illustrated.

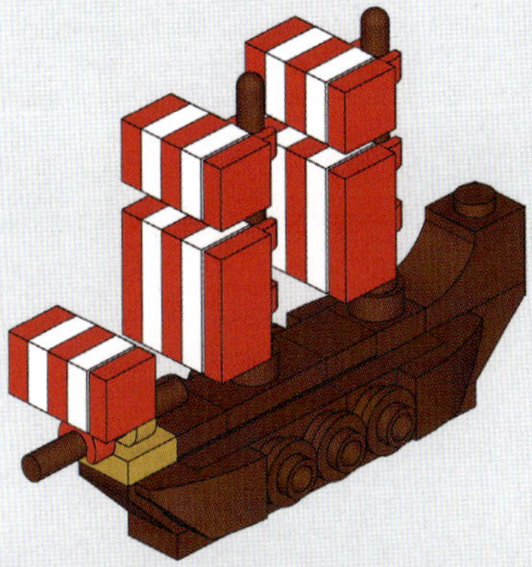

6

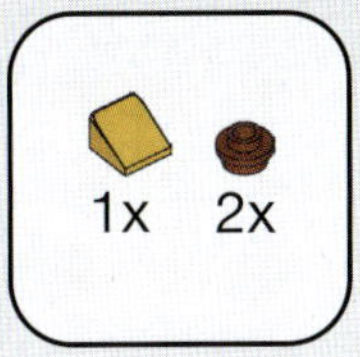

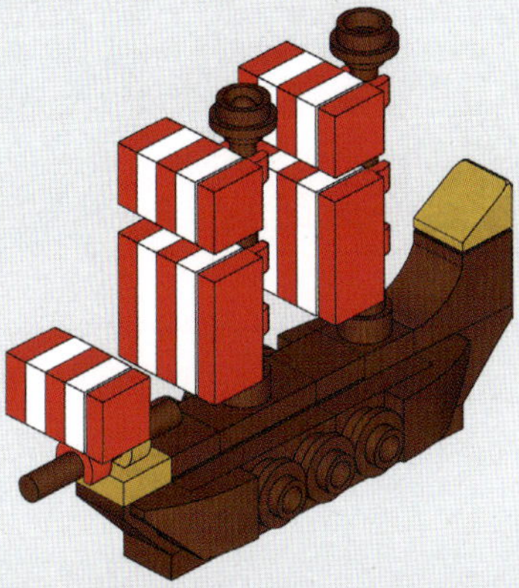

MAKE IT YOUR OWN

Keeping your powder dry? Why not bring your cannons to life with a repurposed ice cream scoop element (#6254)? Restyle the stern with a pearl gold frog (#x223) and a modified 1×1 brick with scroll with hollow stud (#20310).

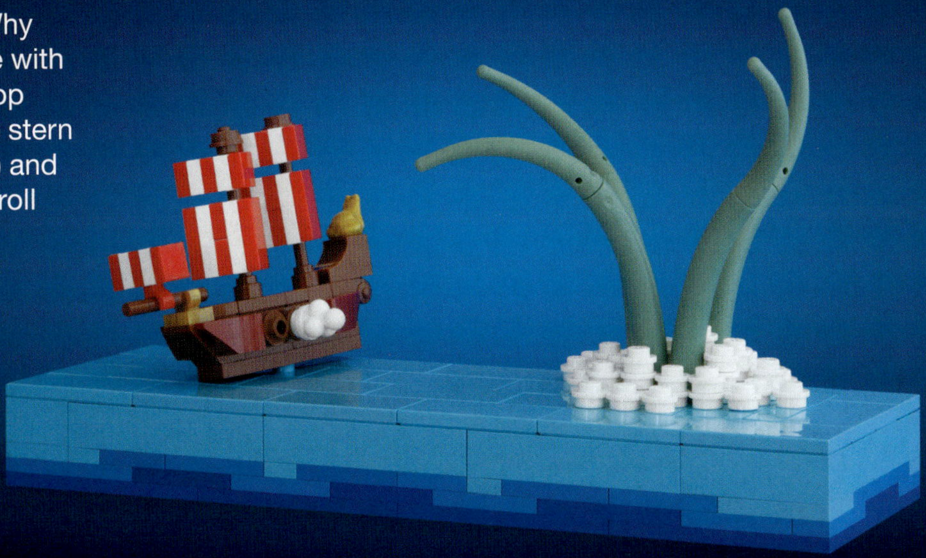

SCALLYWAG WHARF

Every pirate needs a place to tie up their ship, share tall tales, polish their peg leg, and brush up on pirate grammar among friends. The Scallywag Wharf offers all this and more for just half a pocket of doubloons. Parrots are welcome at no extra charge.

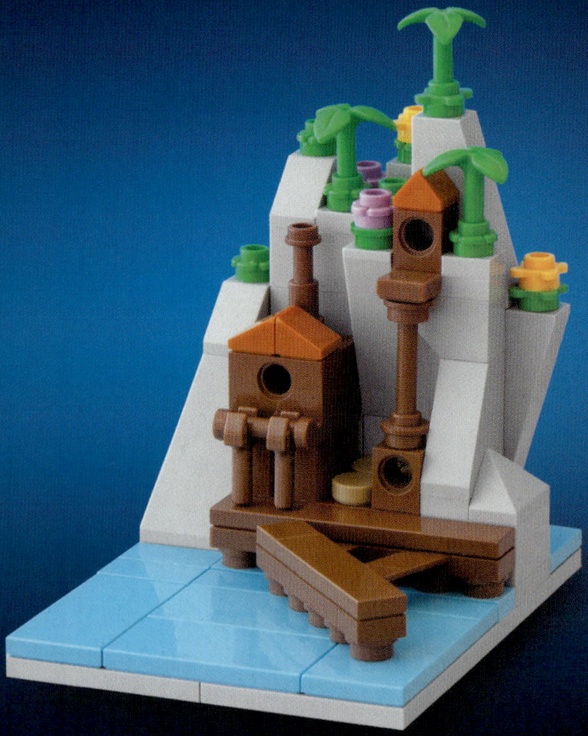

Qty	Part
1x	64644
1x	15573
1x	3023
2x	54200
1x	35464
1x	3024
2x	3070
3x	98138
10x	24866
2x	24866
2x	24866
2x	85861
11x	4073
2x	2357
1x	3004
1x	3665
4x	3040
1x	15571
1x	3004
1x	3700
2x	30136
1x	48336
2x	6541
6x	3069
4x	3023
2x	2449
2x	3685
1x	4460b
1x	60481
1x	15706
1x	6636
4x	87079
1x	2431
1x	87994
3x	37695
2x	48729b
2x	3030
1x	3034
1x	3795
1x	3666
2x	3001
1x	3001
4x	3003

1

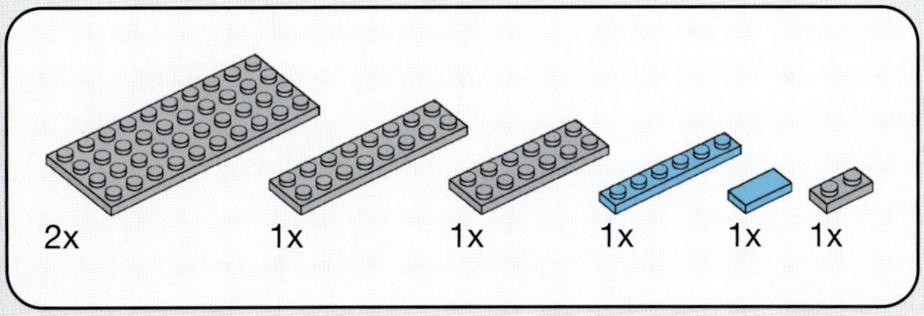

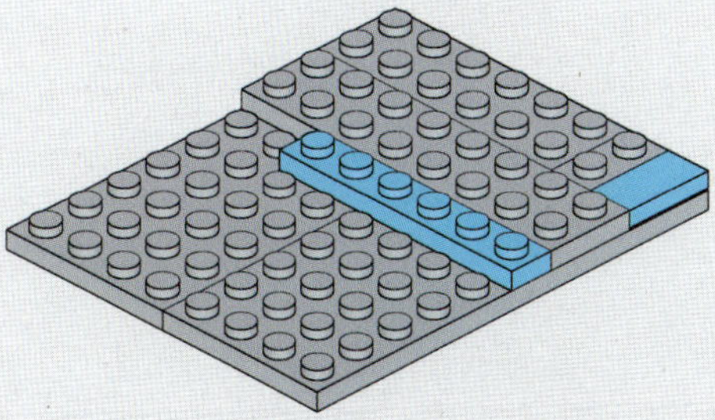

2

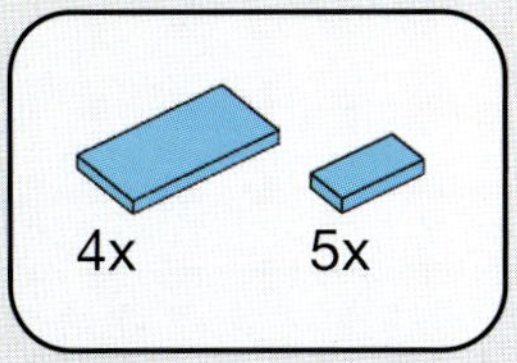

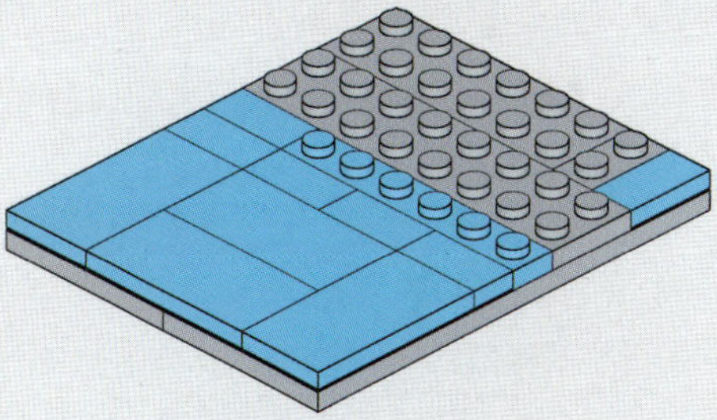

3

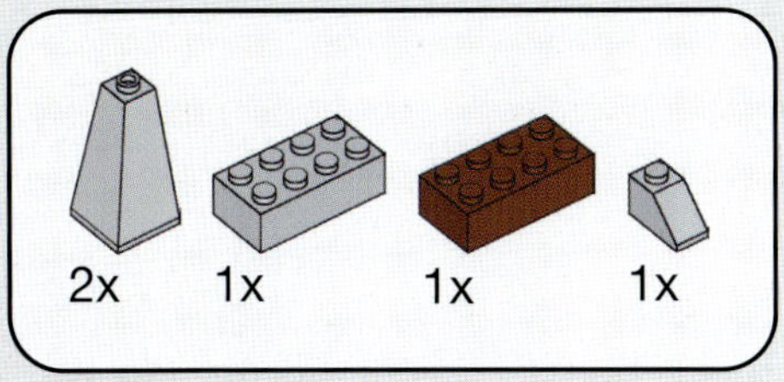

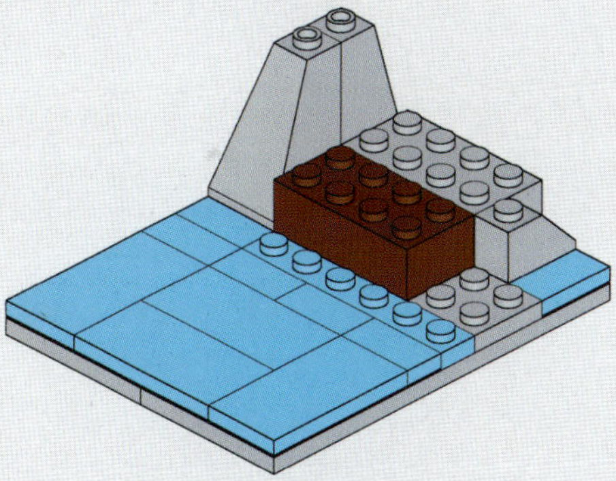

4

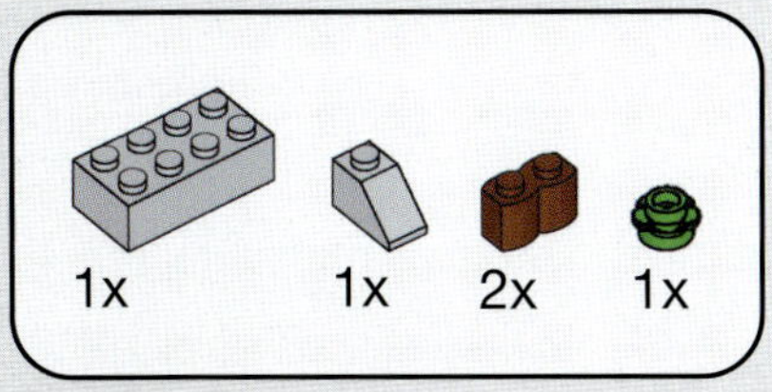

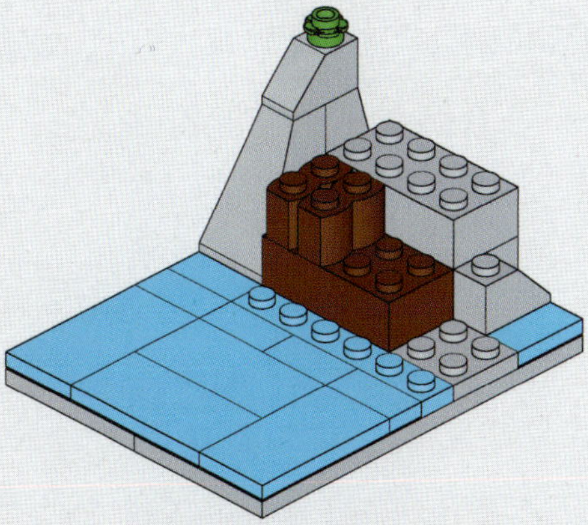

5

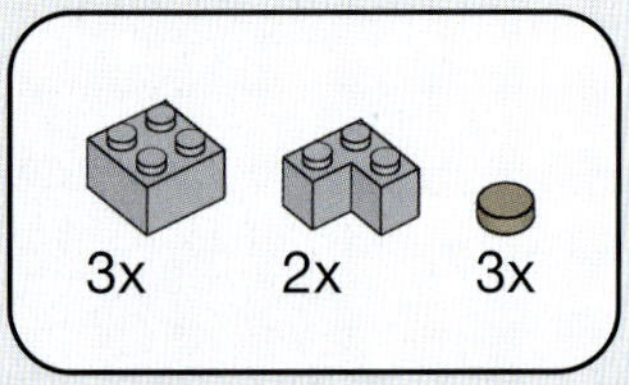

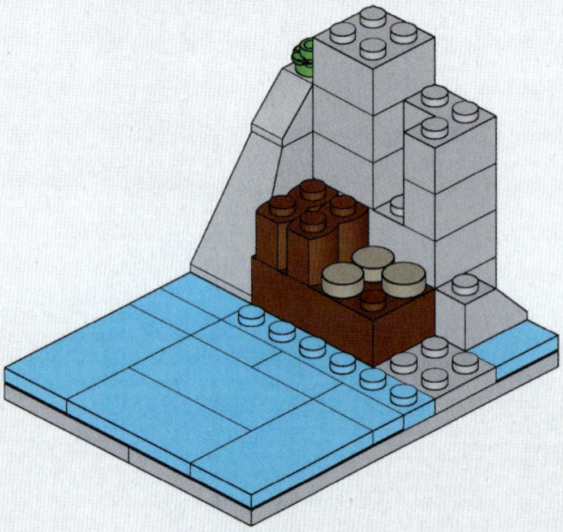

6

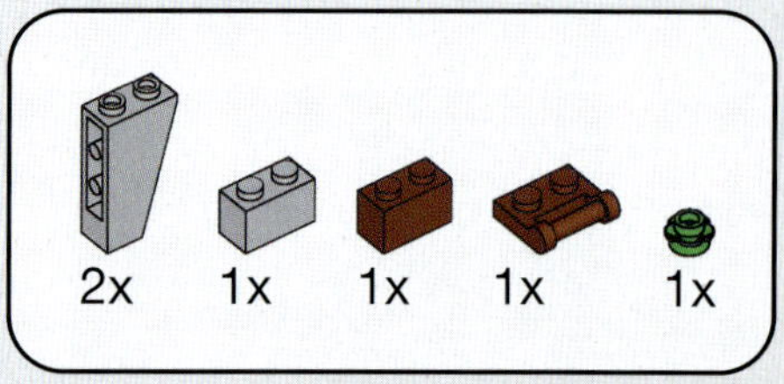

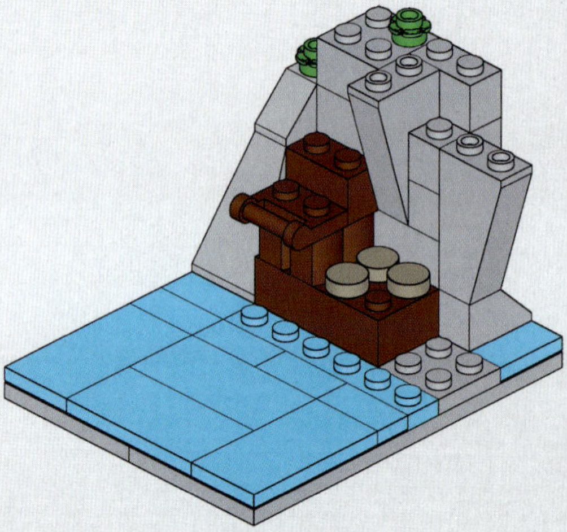

7

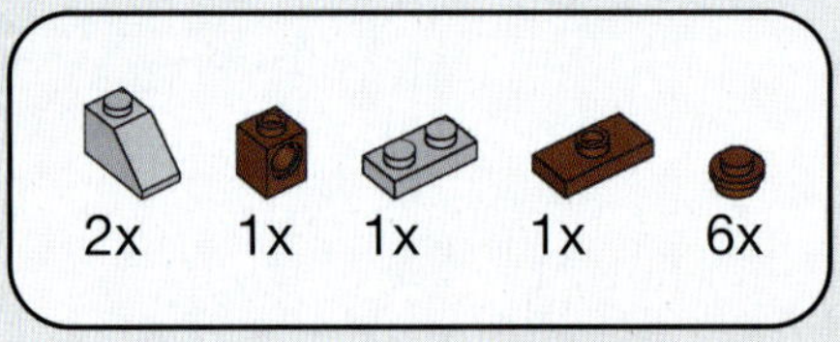

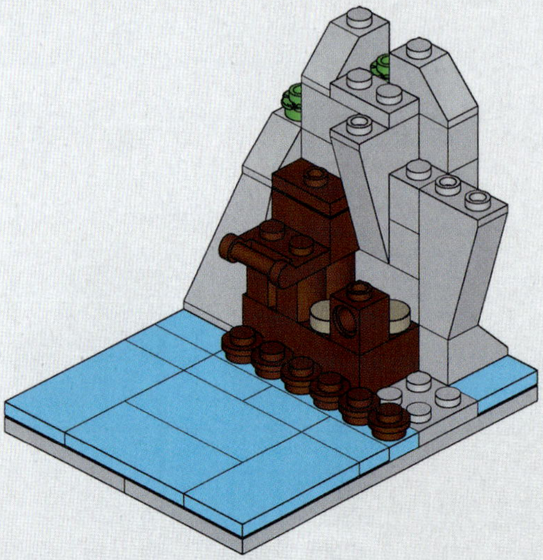

8

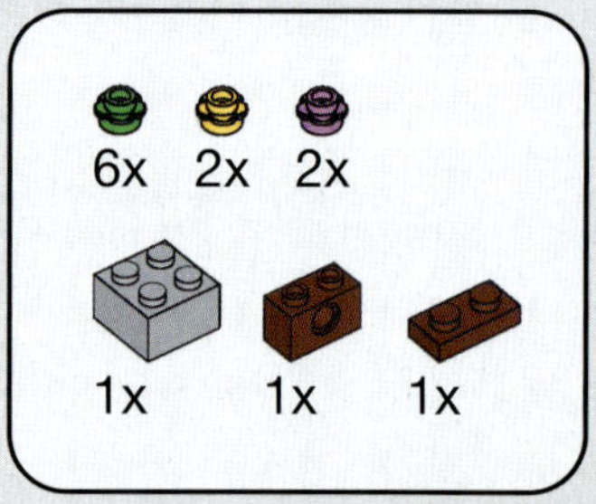

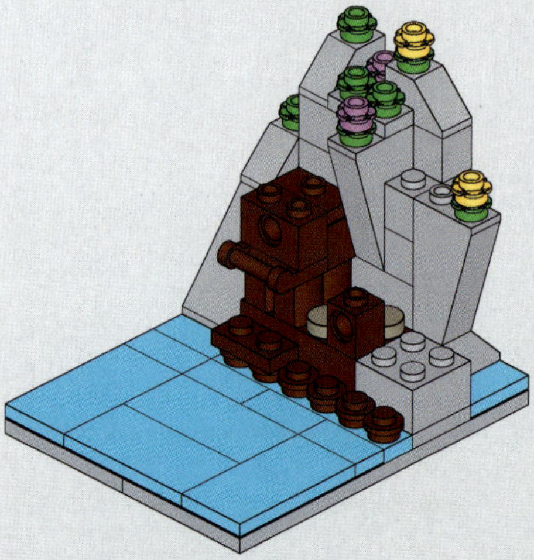

9

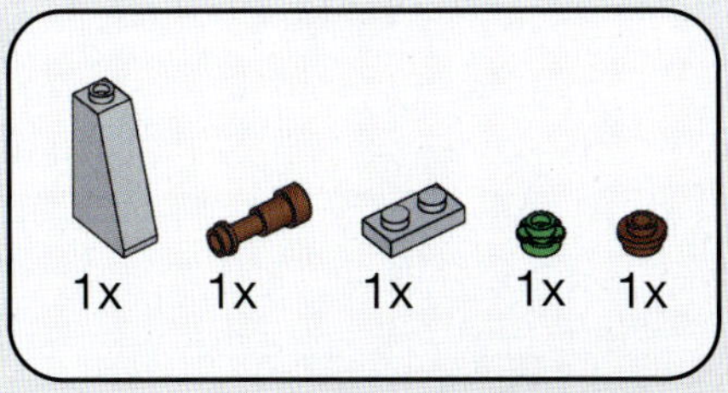

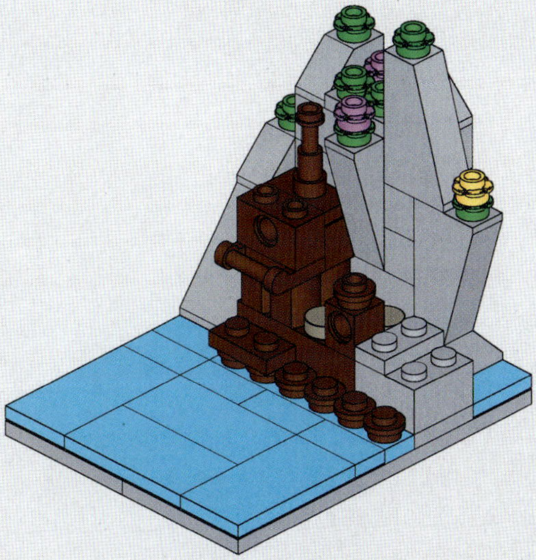

10

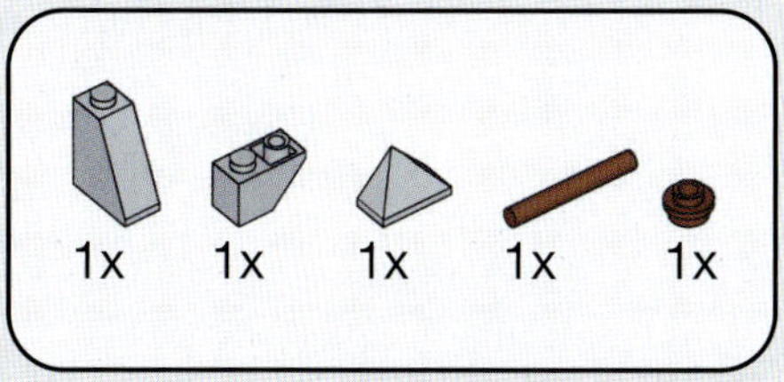

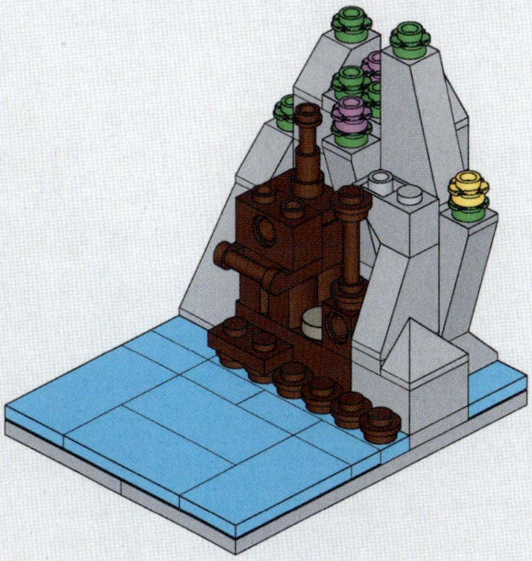

11

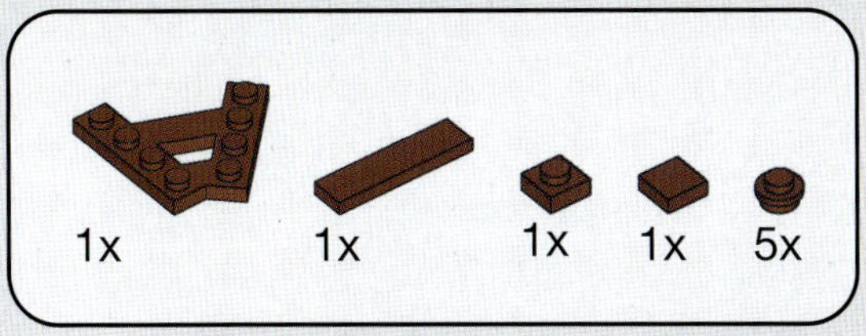

a

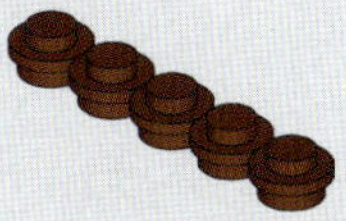

b

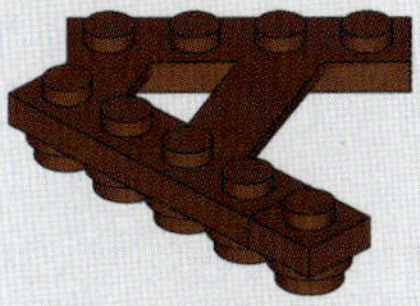

c

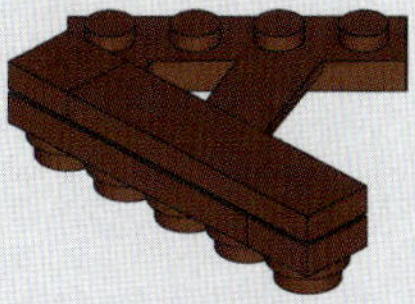

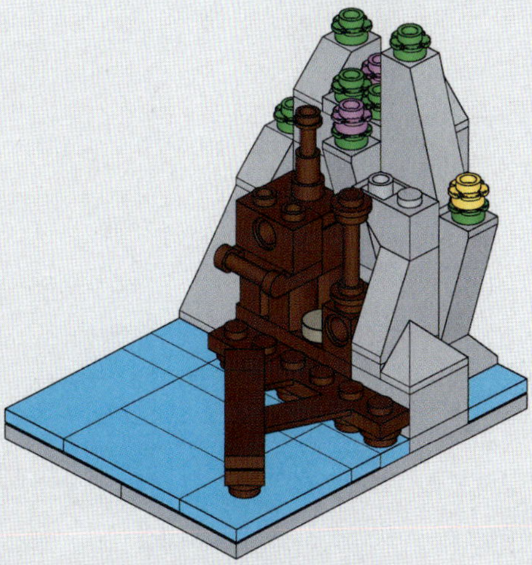

12

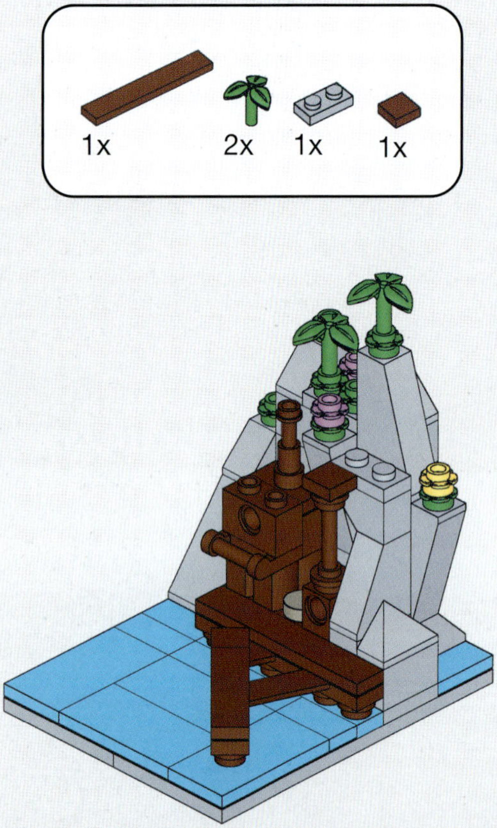

13

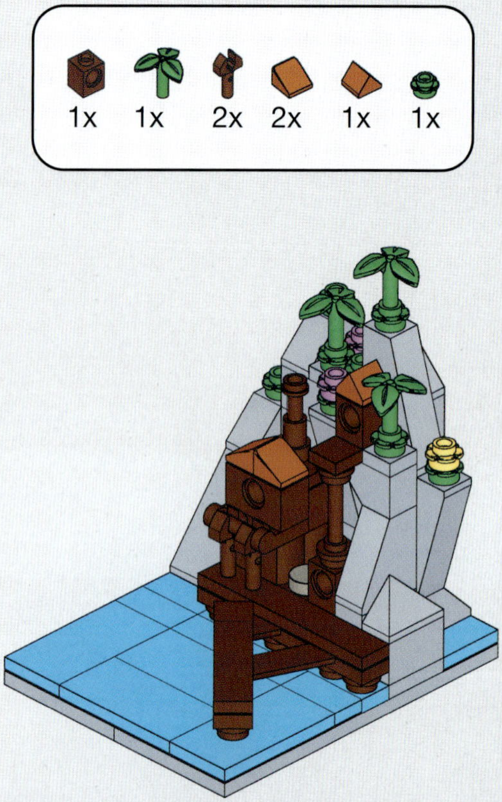

MAKE IT YOUR OWN

Combine the builds in this chapter to create a pocket-sized pirate world, complete with all the essential elements.

The bridge is made with a 1×6 arch (#3455) topped with a 1×4×1 fence lattice (#3633).

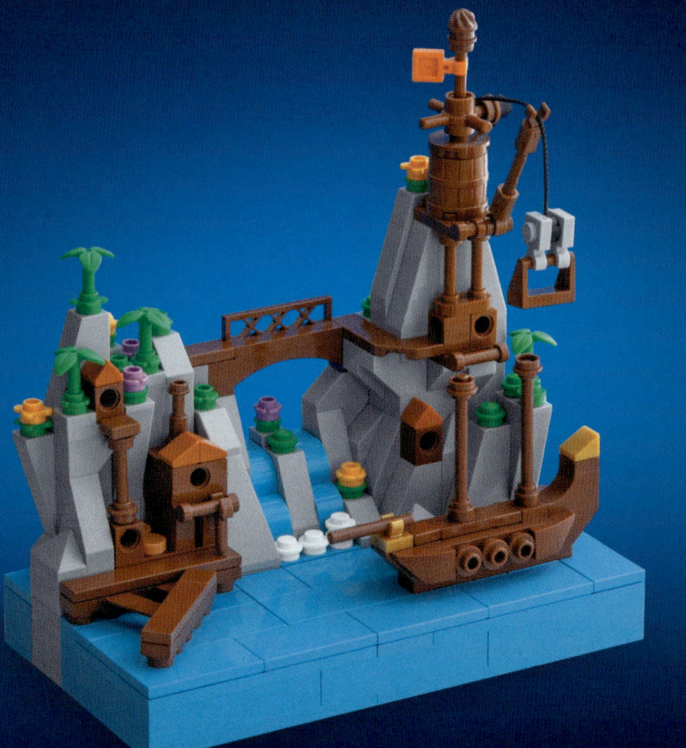

DOCKSIDE CRANE

Keep your treasures high and dry with a handy crane.

You can adjust the crane arm's angle to line up perfectly with docked ships.

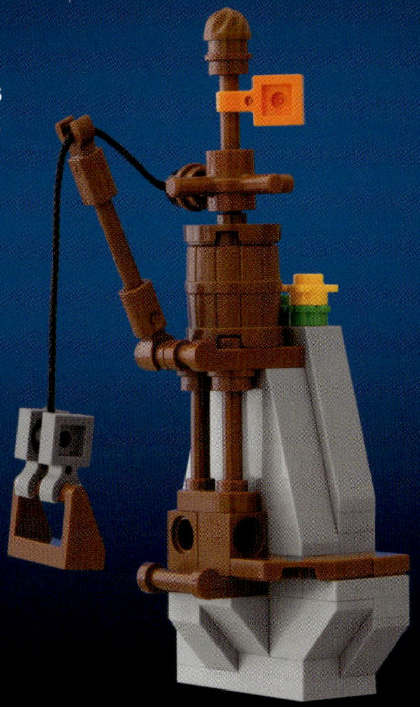

1x 61252	2x 4085d	1x 3070	5x 85861	1x 33291	2x 33291
1x 48336	2x 60478	1x 18674	2x 6541	1x 27263	
4x 4460b	1x 2489	1x 2432	1x 30374	3x 87994	1x 48723
2x 3004	4x 3665	6x 3023	1x 35480	1x 15470	2x 11090
1x 3010	1x 3020	3x 3710	1x x127c10pb01		

1

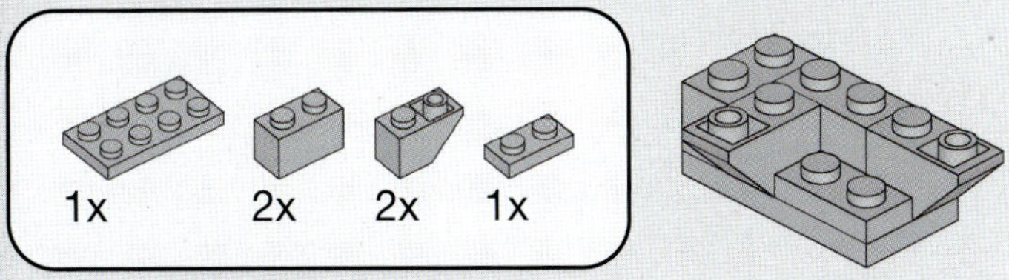

2

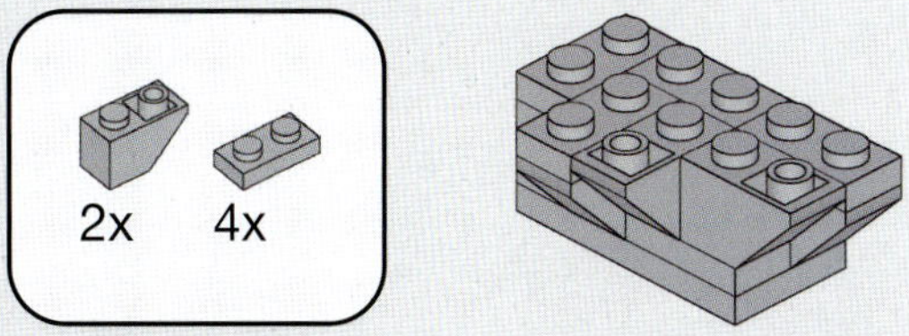

3

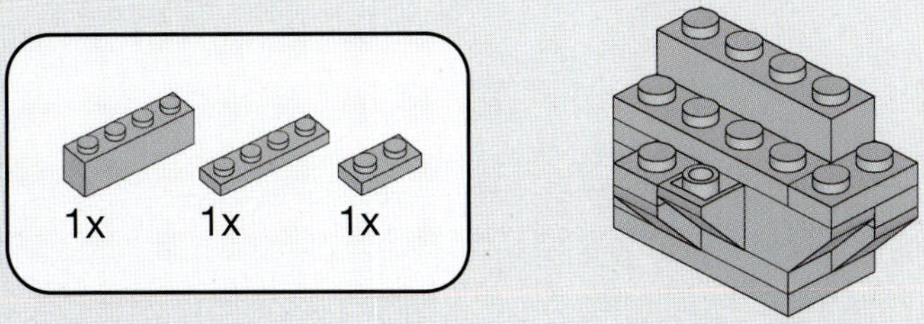

4

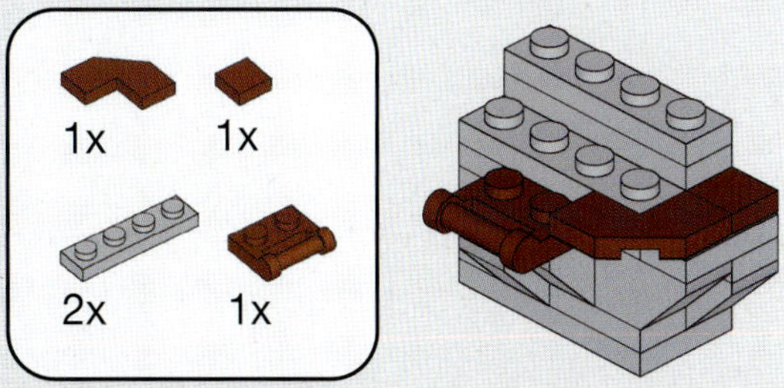

5

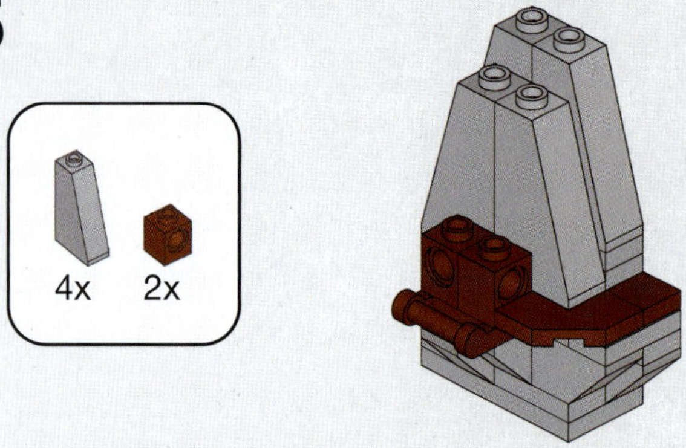

6

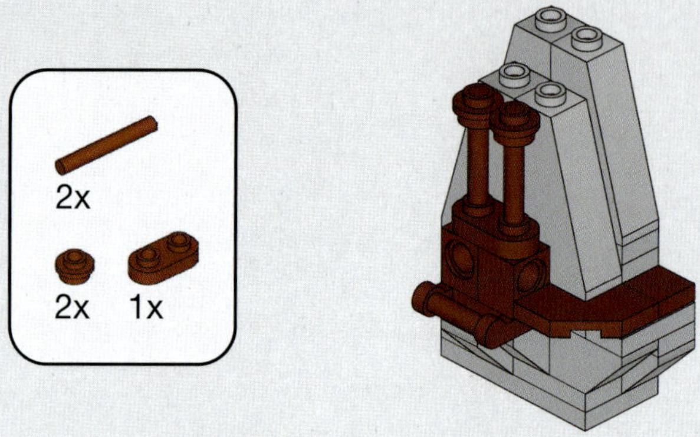

7

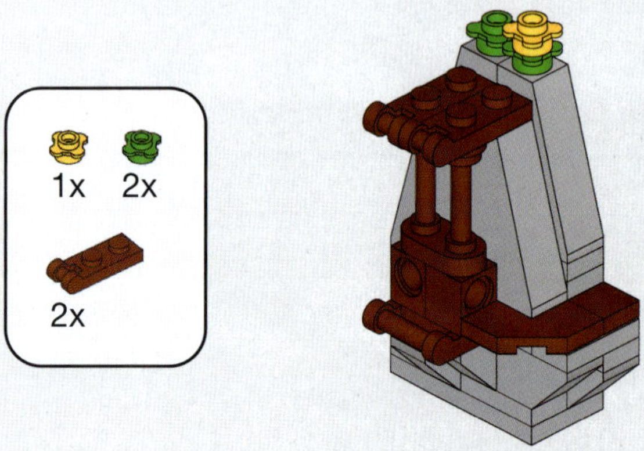

8

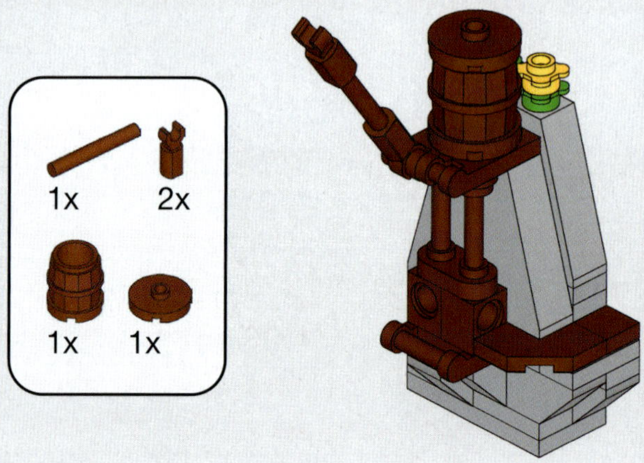

9

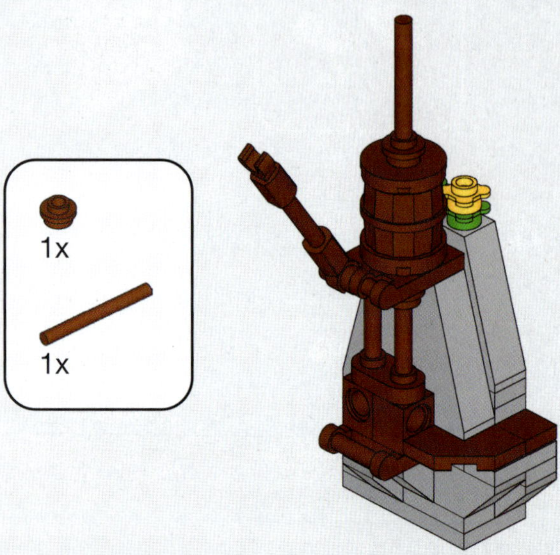

10

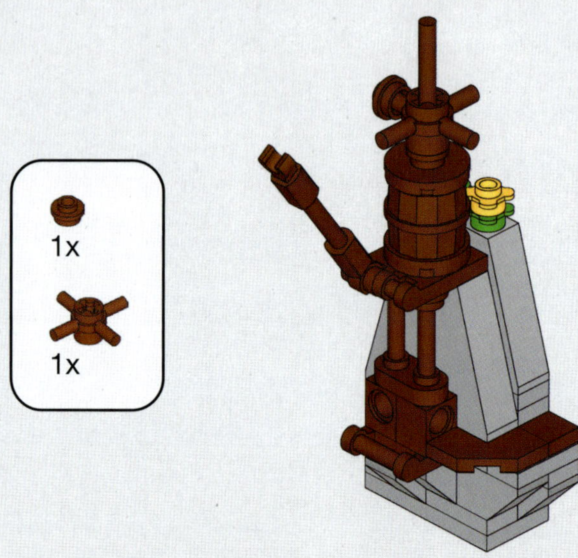

11

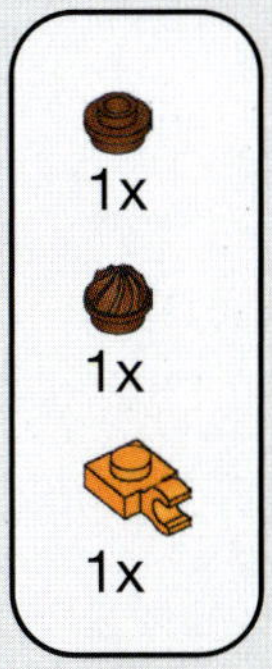

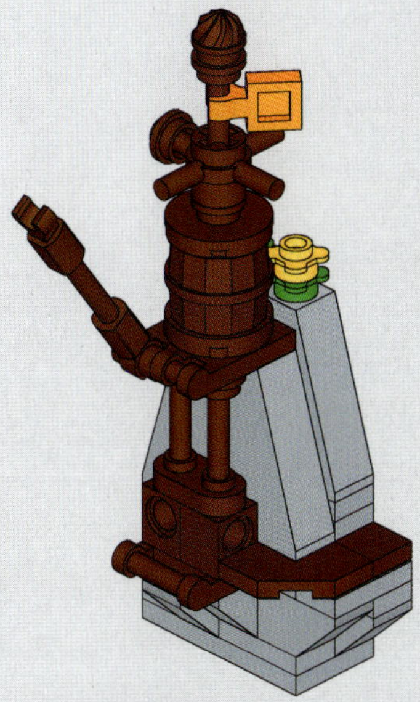

12

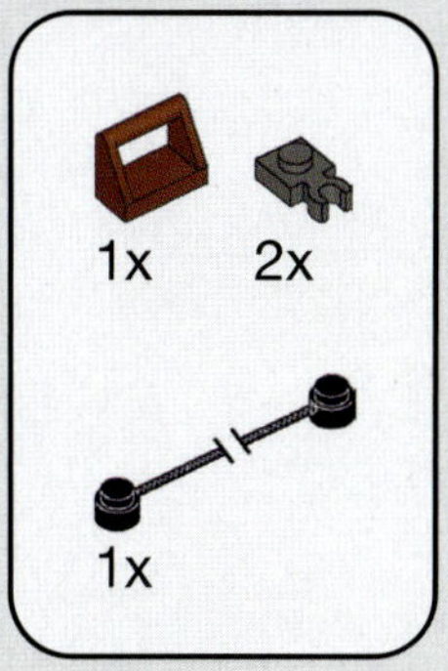

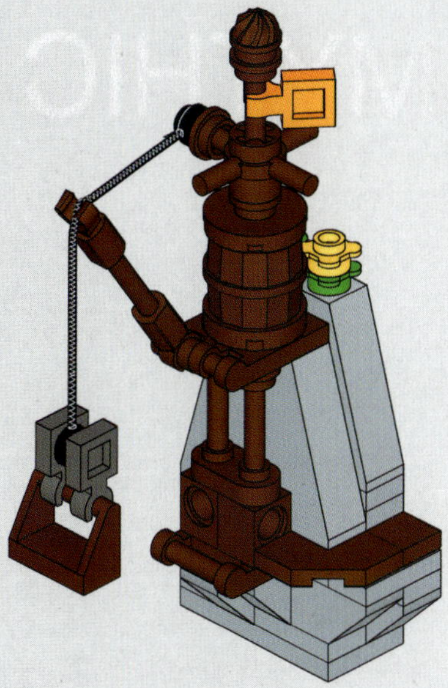

ROGUE'S ROOST

A watchtower stands guard against those who would take back stolen treasures.

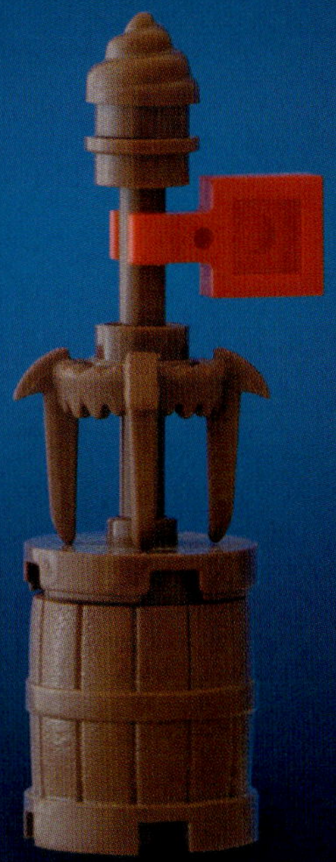

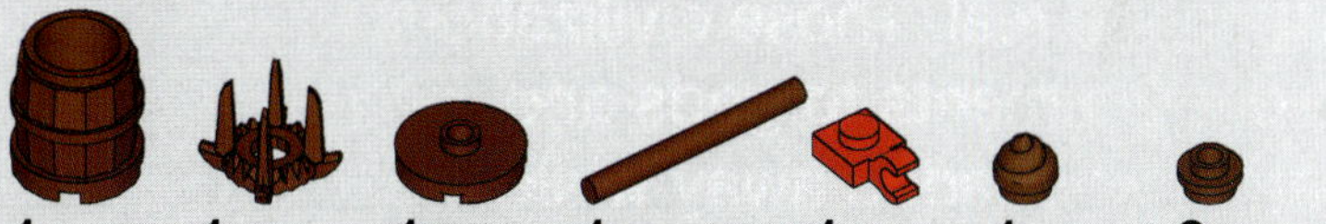

1x	**1x**	**1x**	**1x**	**1x**	**1x**	**2x**
2489	18165	18674	30374	61252	53119	85861

1

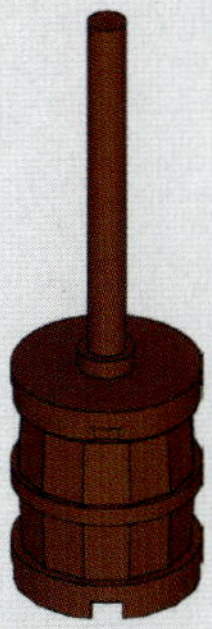

2

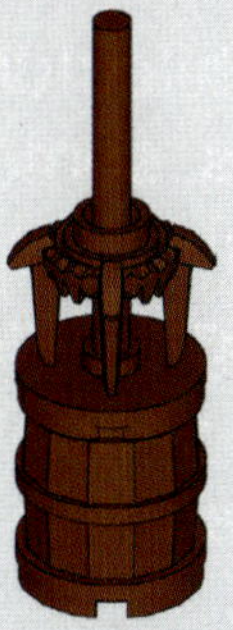

3

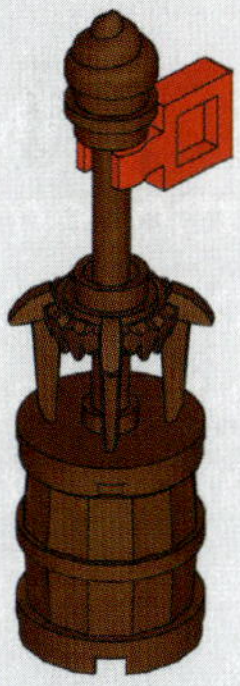

Element #18165 is available on BrickLink, but it's a pricey piece. You can leave it out or replace it with a more common element.

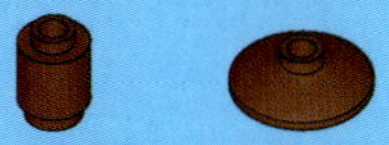

3062 4740

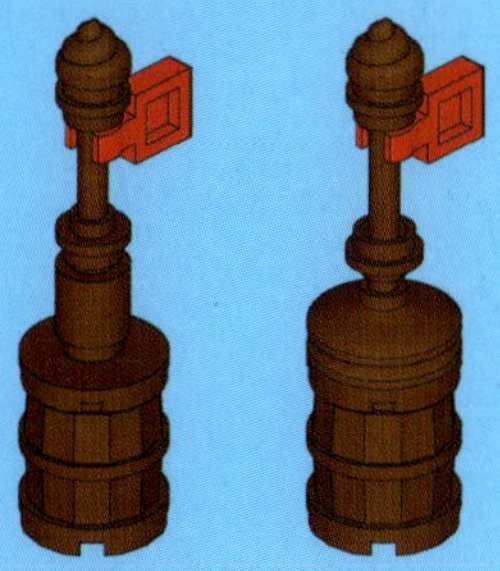

MYTHIC EMPIRE

The architecture of Ancient Greece and Rome has endured for centuries, like a myth made real. These civilizations crafted monuments to gods and emperors who faded away while the buildings remained standing. In the end, it may have been the architects and engineers who were the true heroes of the age.

Greek and Roman architecture lives on in modern buildings, sometimes in appearance and sometimes in the geometry underpinning the design. Its influence continues to shape how we define beauty and balance in design today.

You can create your own legendary architecture, even without access to marble quarries or gold mines. LEGO's precisely engineered and durable bricks let you build timeless monuments right on your kitchen table—just be careful the dog doesn't eat them.

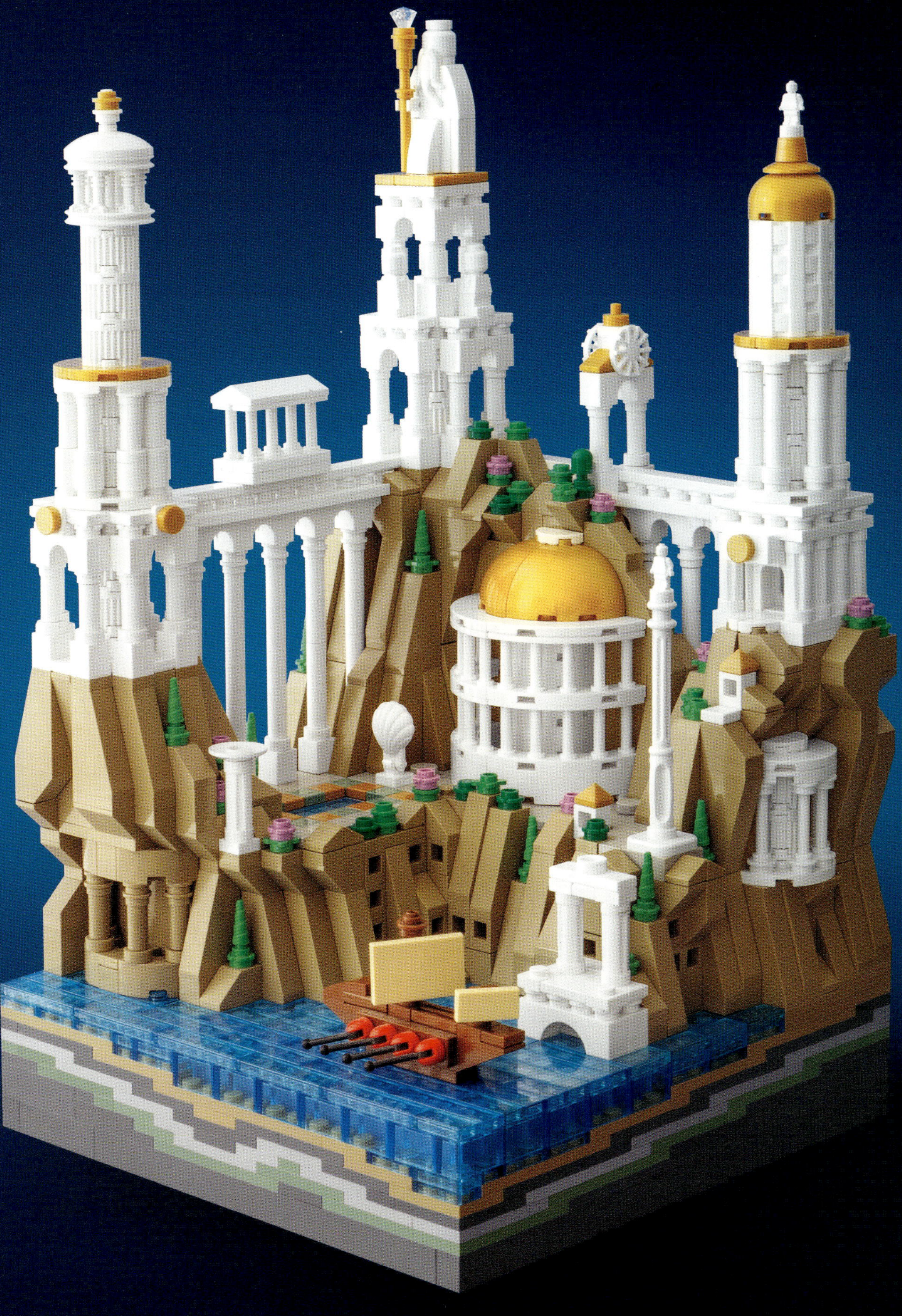

GRAND STATUE

Colossal statues are symbols of divine power, human ambition, or a combination of the two. They impress the masses and try to remind everyone of who's really in charge. Customize your statue using other minifigure beards and hairpieces from your collection.

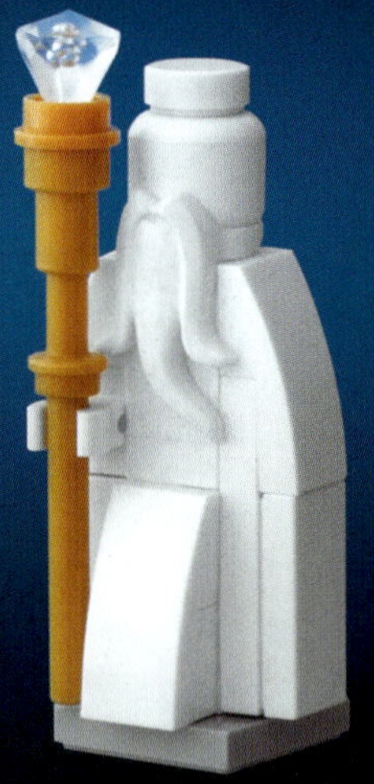

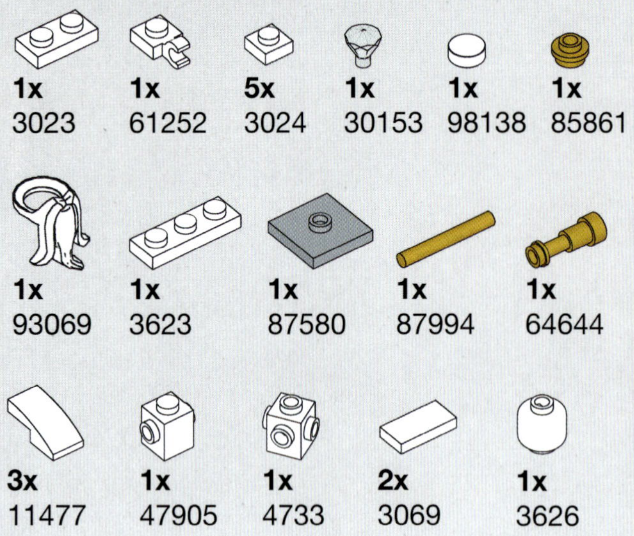

1

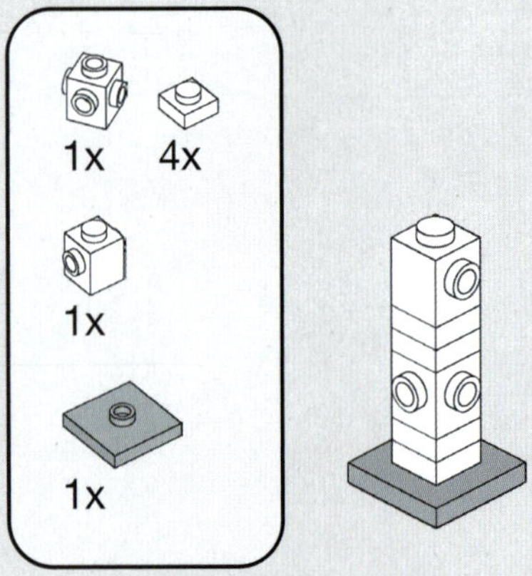

2

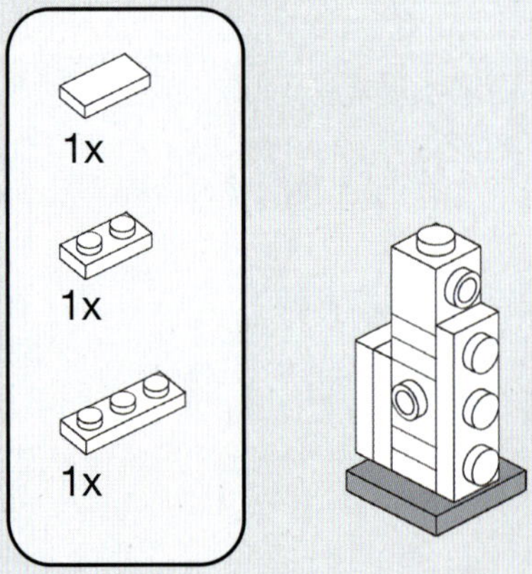

3

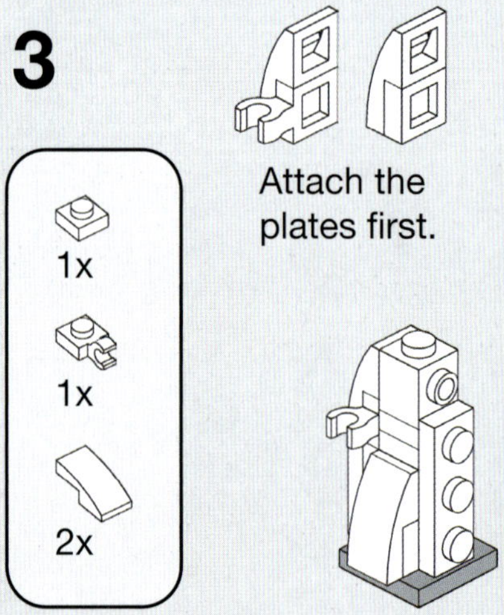

4

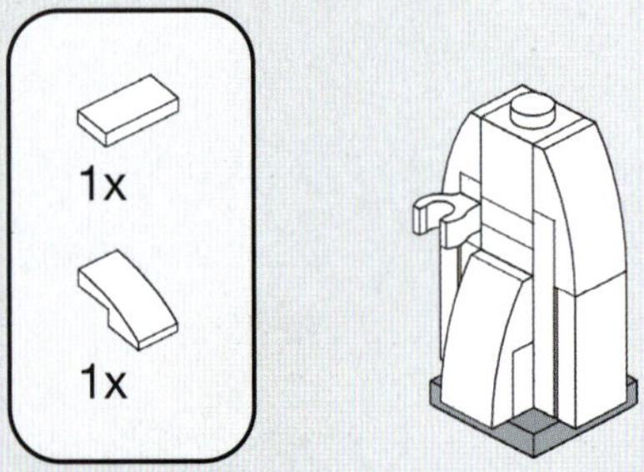

5

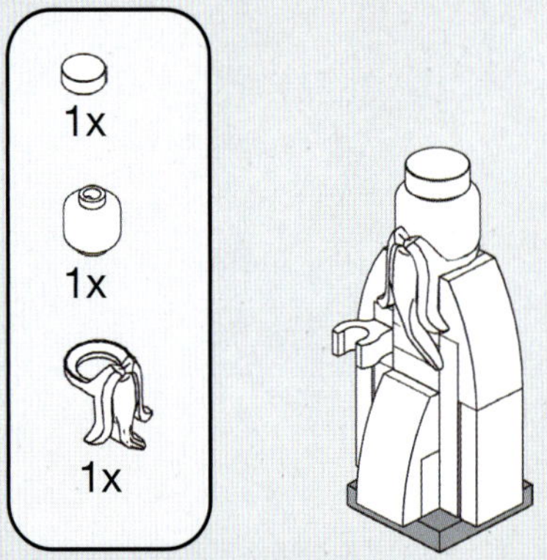

6

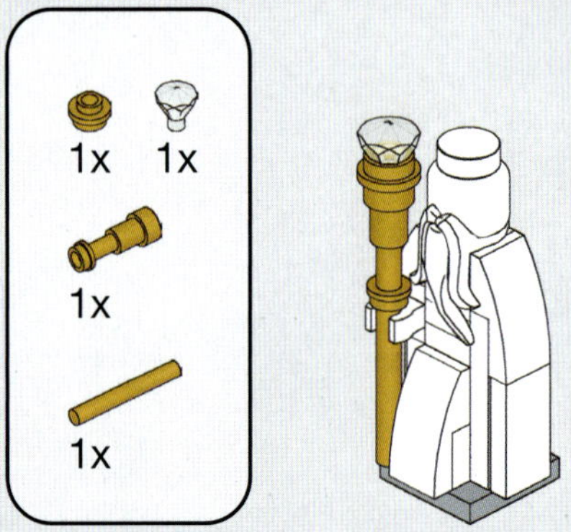

AQUEDUCT

The Roman aqueduct is one of history's great feats of engineering, combining form and function through the power of the arch. Aqueducts transport water from wilderness springs to thirsty cities. Expand yours as needed.

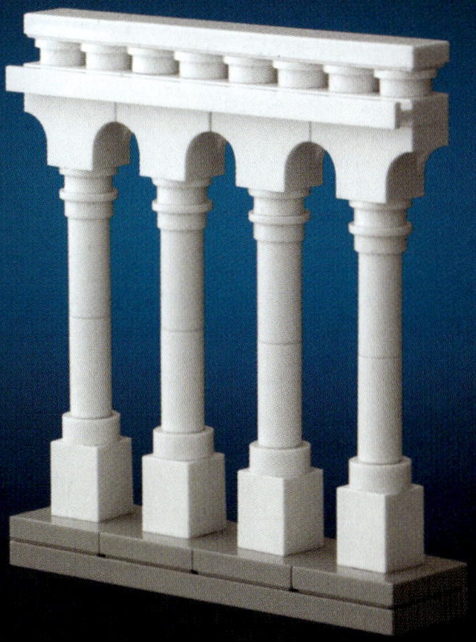

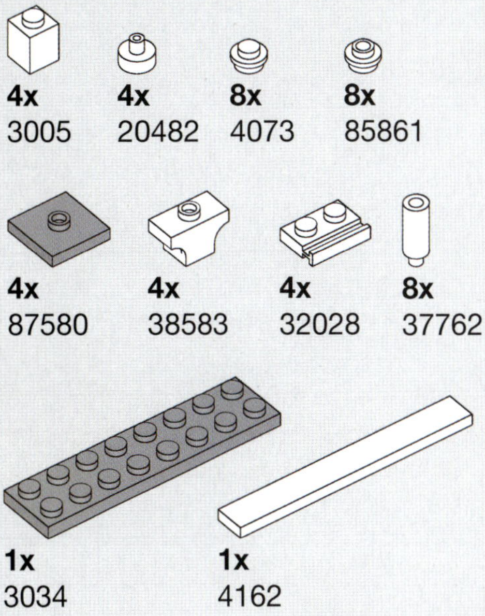

1

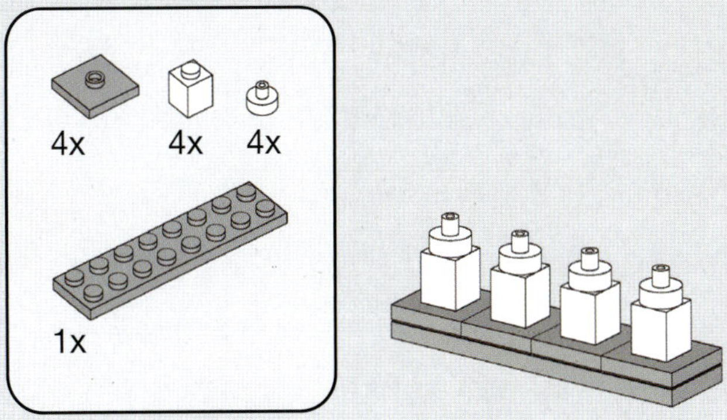

2

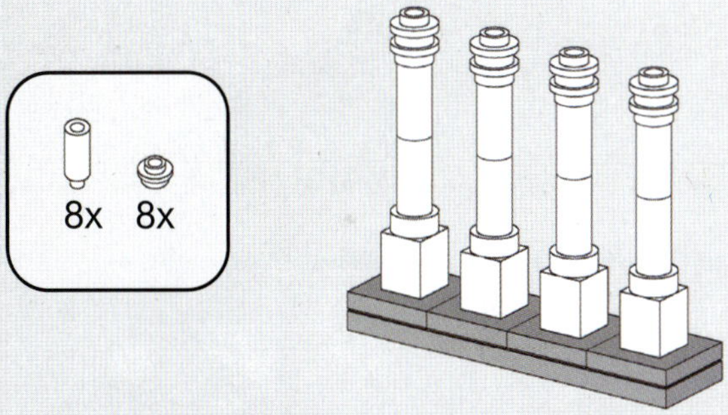

3

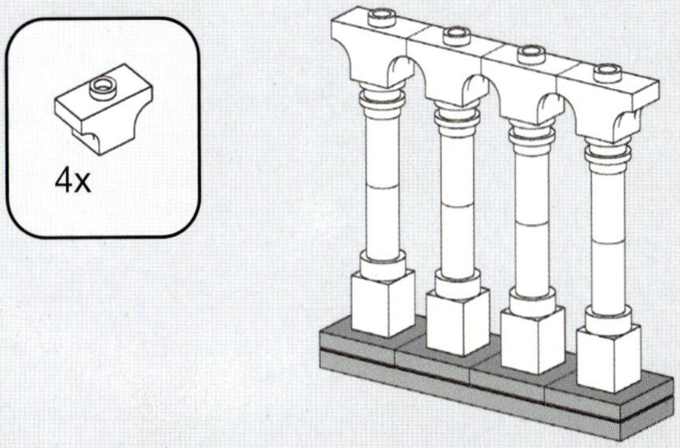

4

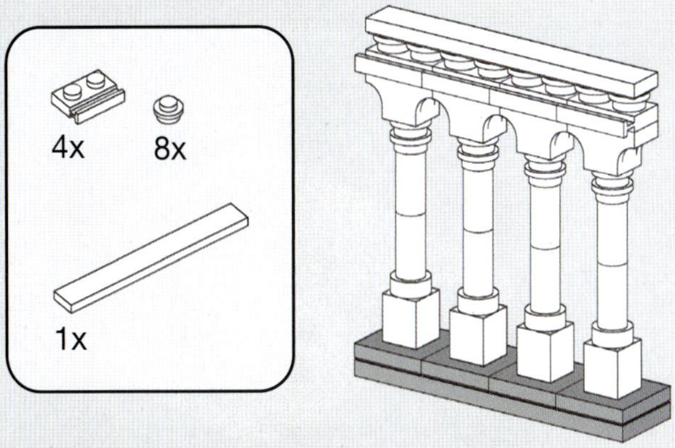

CIRCLE TEMPLE

This temple blends Greek and Roman styles, drawing inspiration from the round, column-ringed Tholos at Delphi and the domed Pantheon in Rome. It exudes a sense of cosmic scale, even when held in your hand.

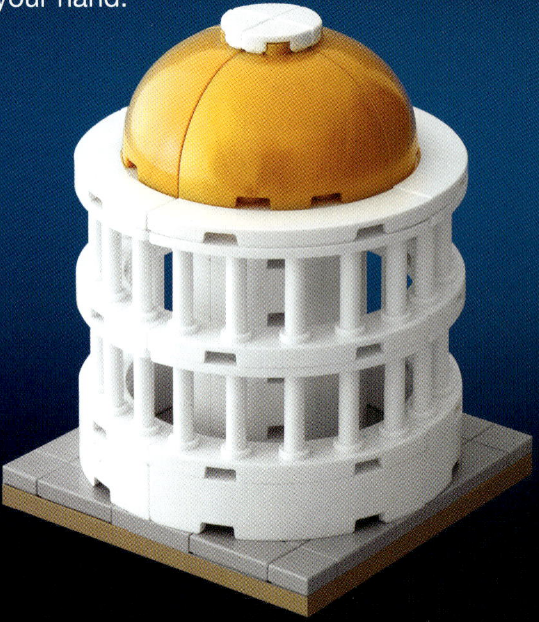

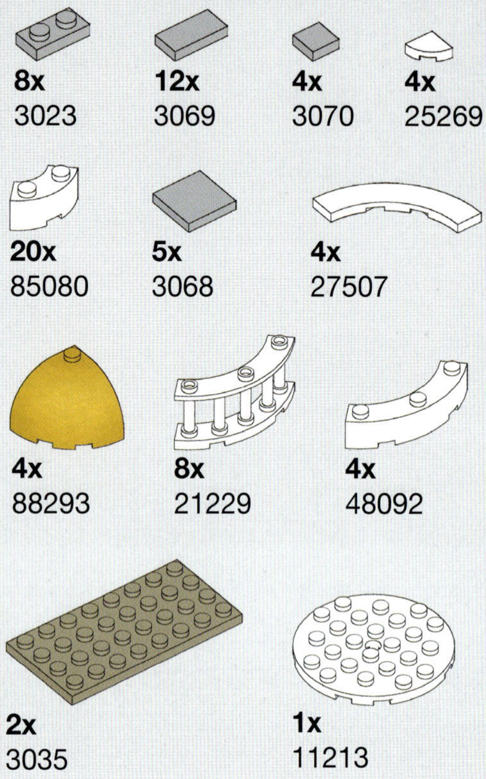

1

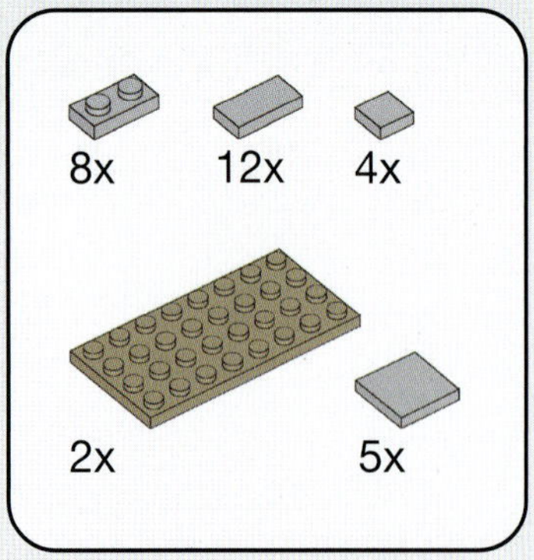

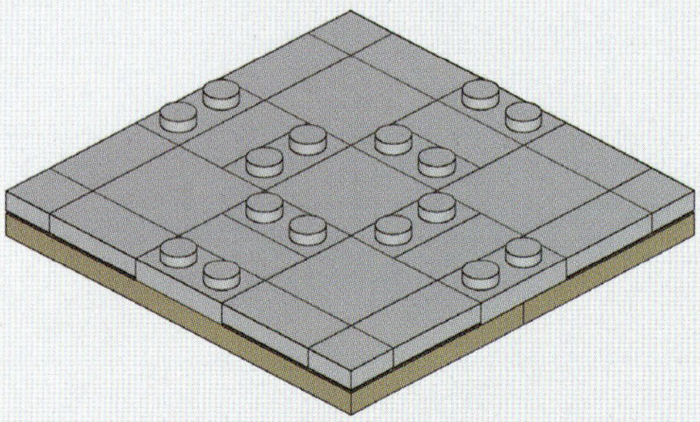

2

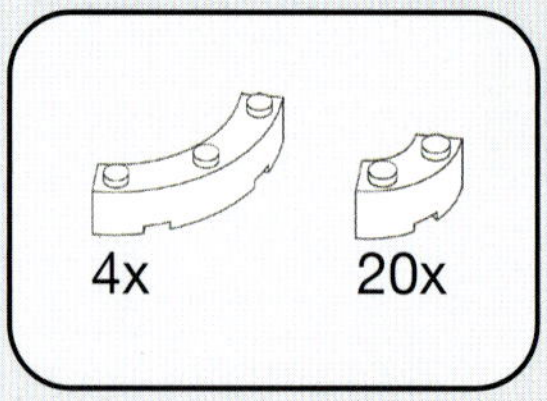

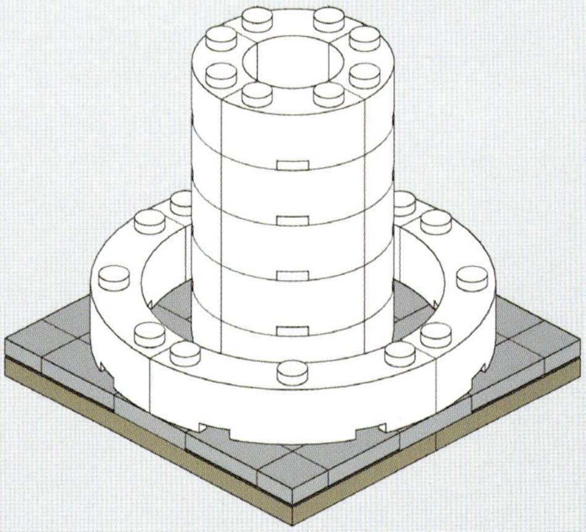

3

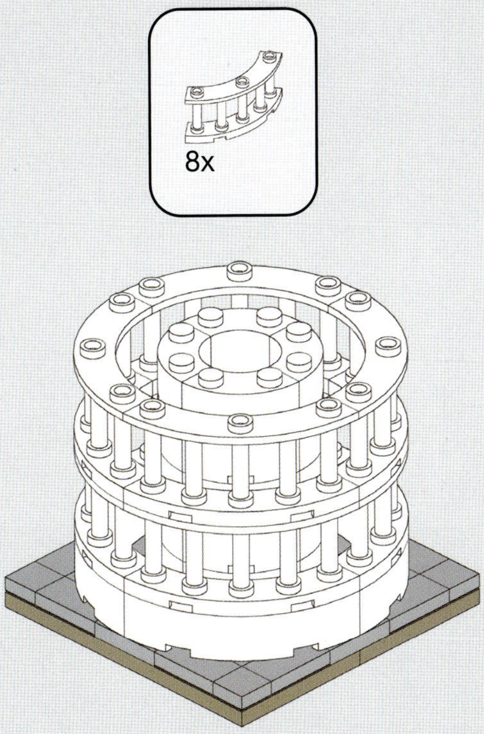

4

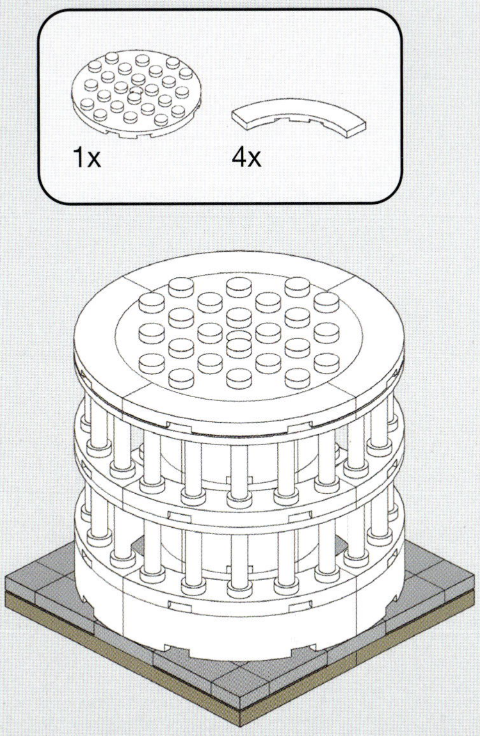

5

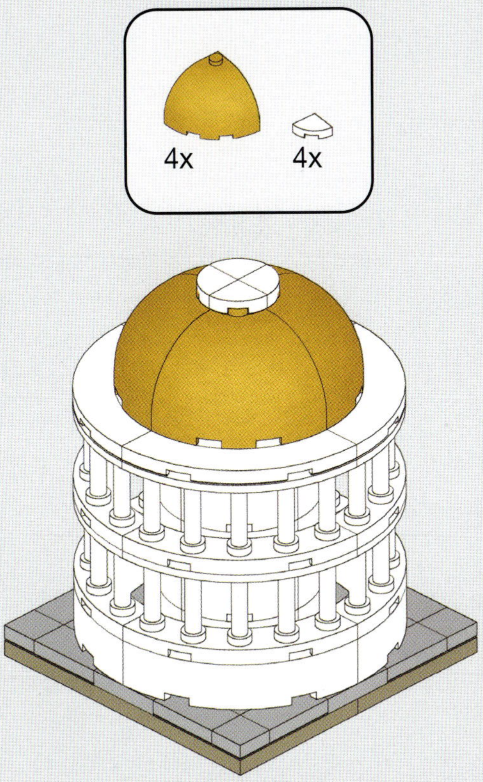

MAKE IT YOUR OWN

By removing the dome and expanding the circular shape into an ellipse, you can transform a peaceful temple into a gladiatorial arena.

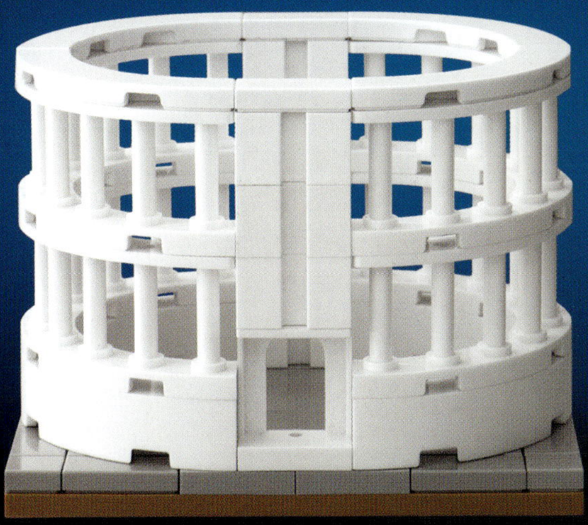

TRIREME

With rows of oars on each side, this sleek warship doesn't wait for the wind. It can outmaneuver larger vessels with ease. Just don't inquire about the working conditions on board.

Line up the oars perfectly to suggest a disciplined crew, or arrange them haphazardly to suggest a brewing mutiny.

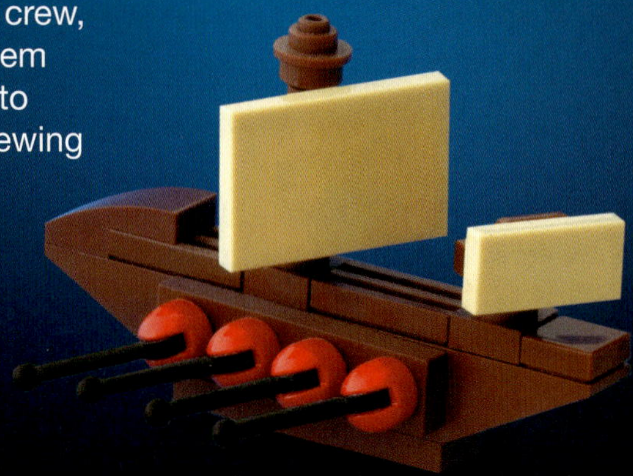

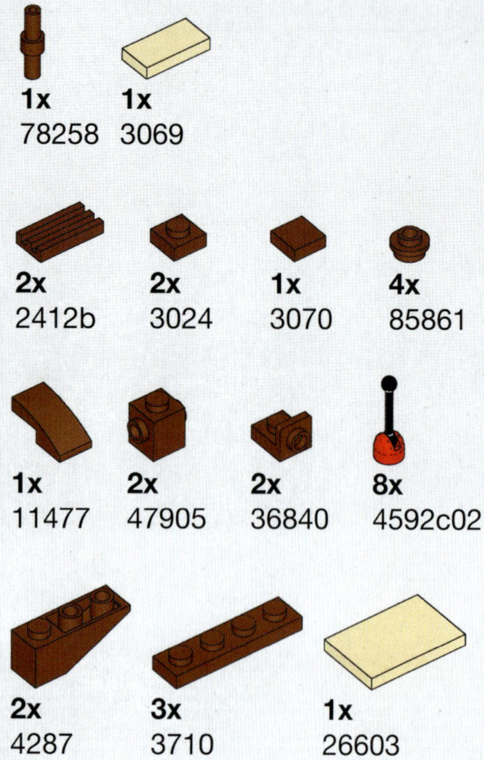

1

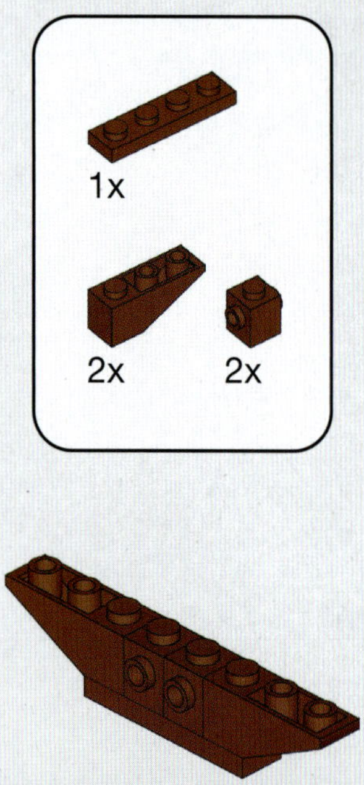

2

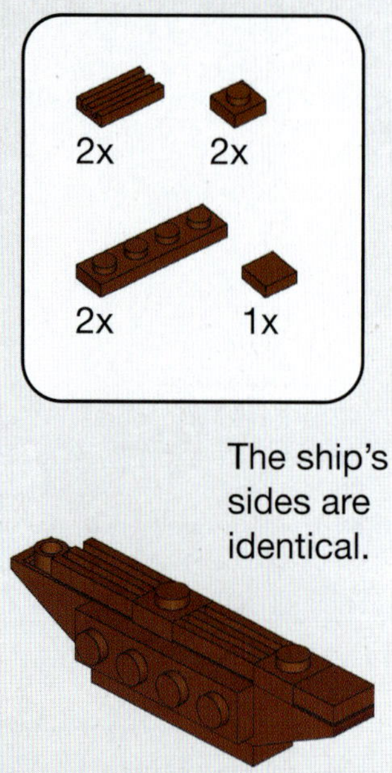

3

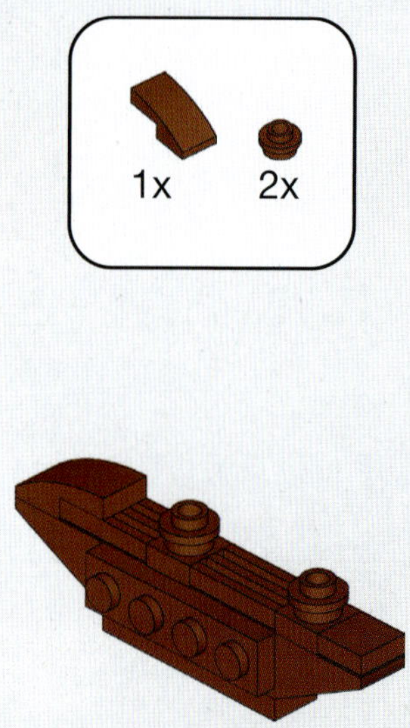

4

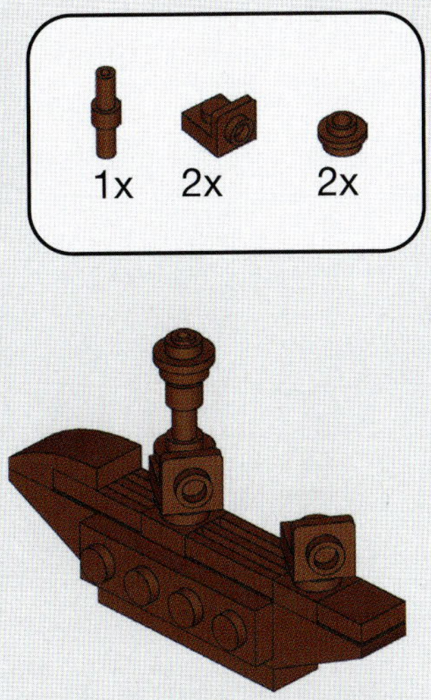

5

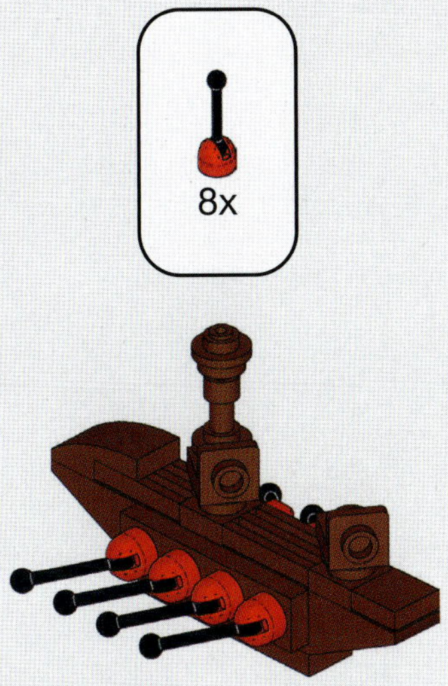

6

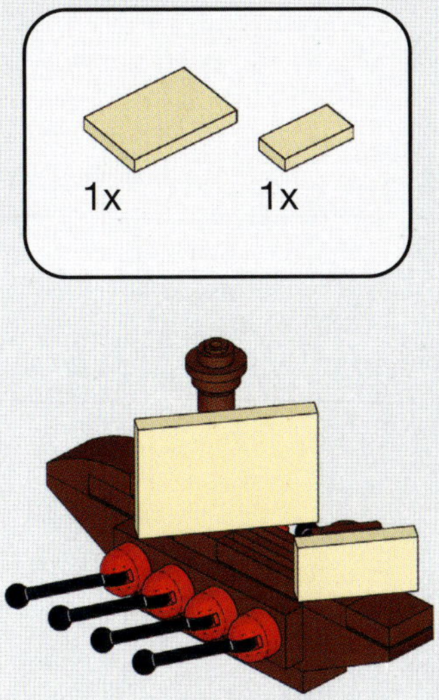

MARBLE GATE

An imposing entrance carved from marble welcomes travelers but subtly reminds them to stay in line.

LEGO's inverted modified 1×3 tile (a tile with studs on the bottom) is used to span the fluted columns.

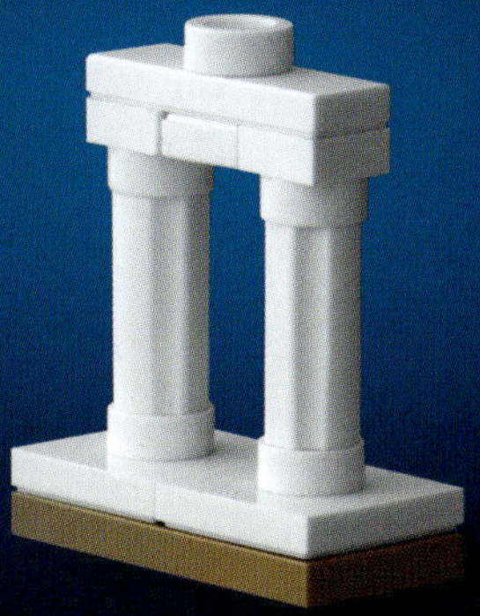

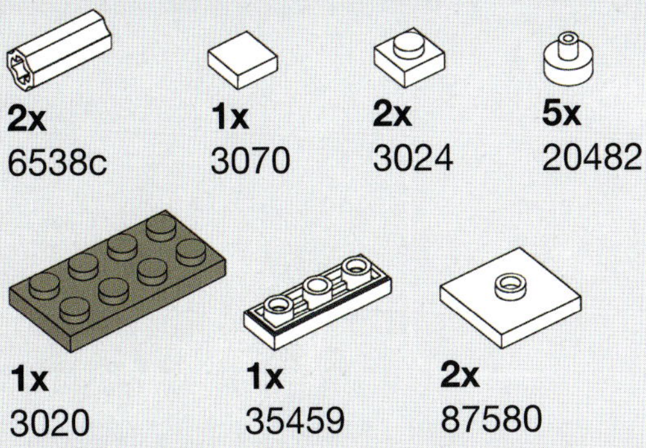

1

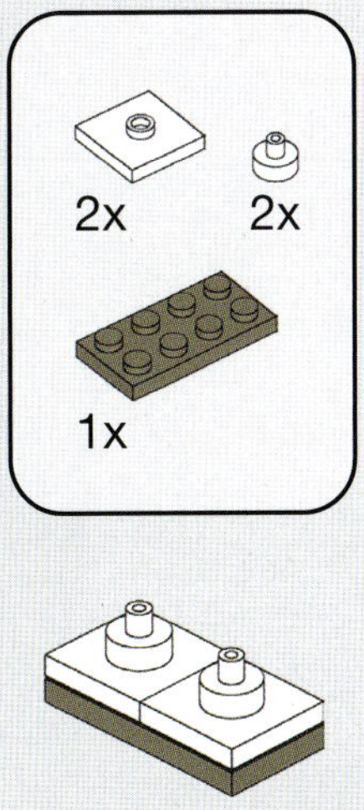

2

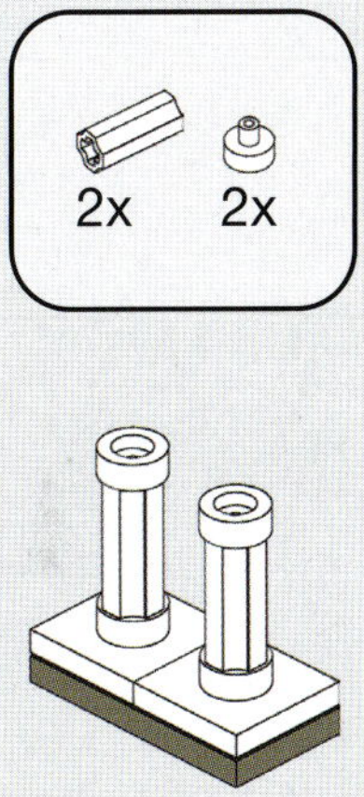

3

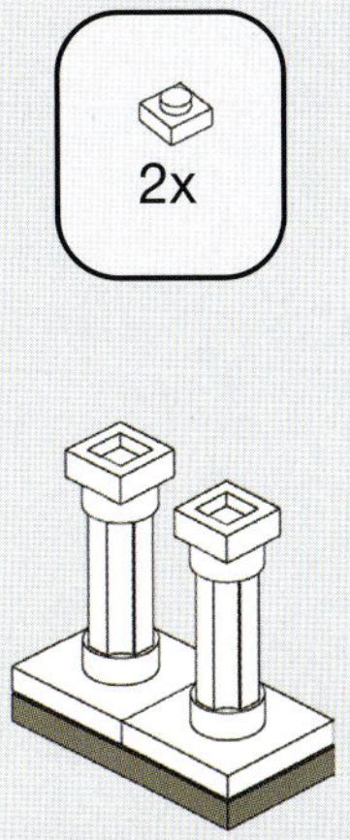

4

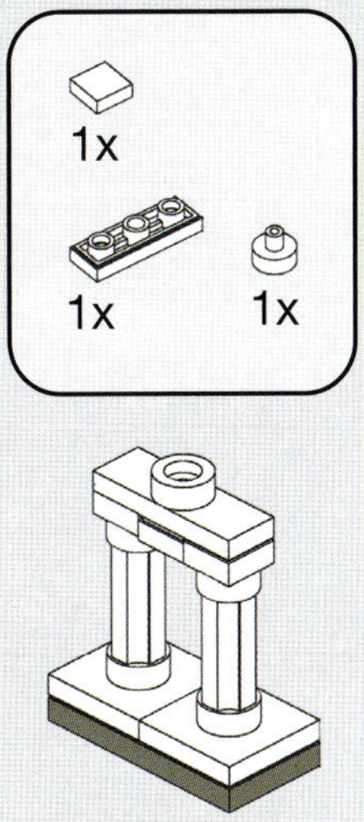

LIGHTHOUSE

Inspired by the legendary Lighthouse of Alexandria, this beacon guides sailors through treacherous seas and into safe harbors. It's the original GPS.

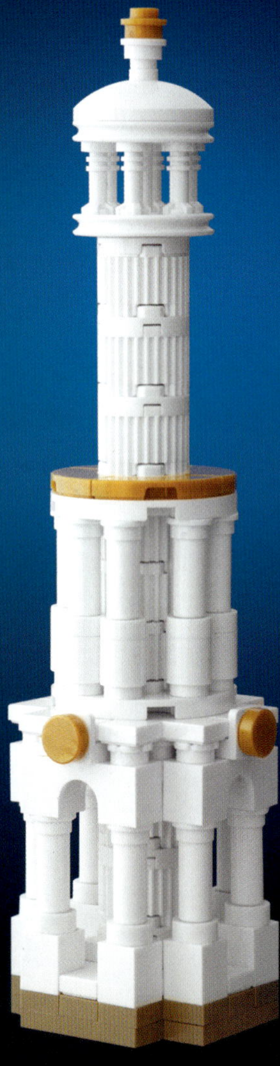

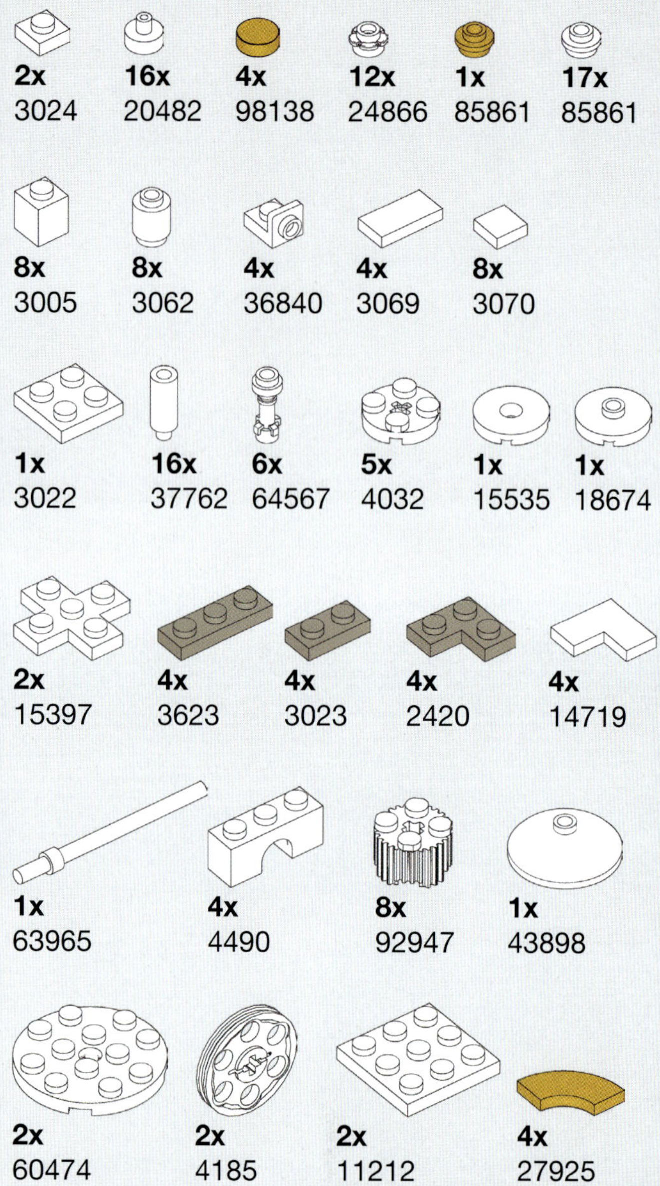

1

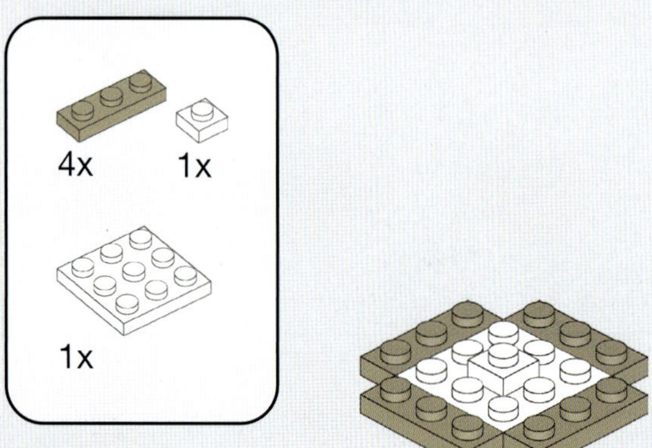

2

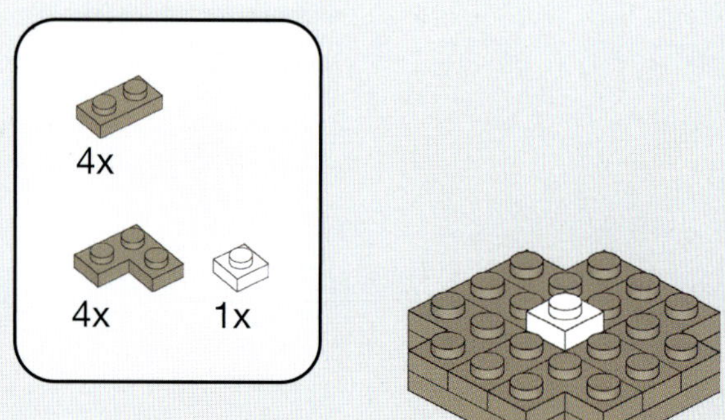

3

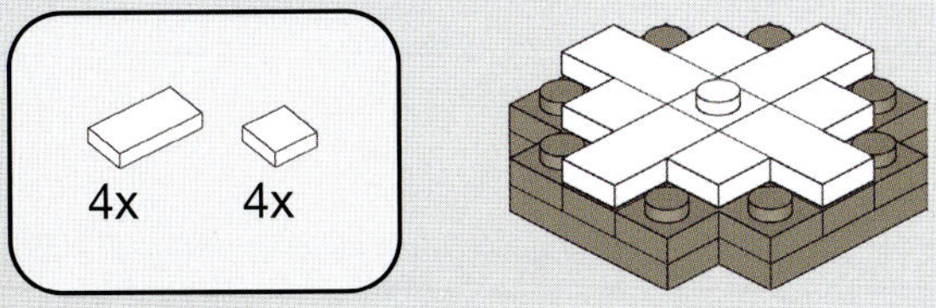

4

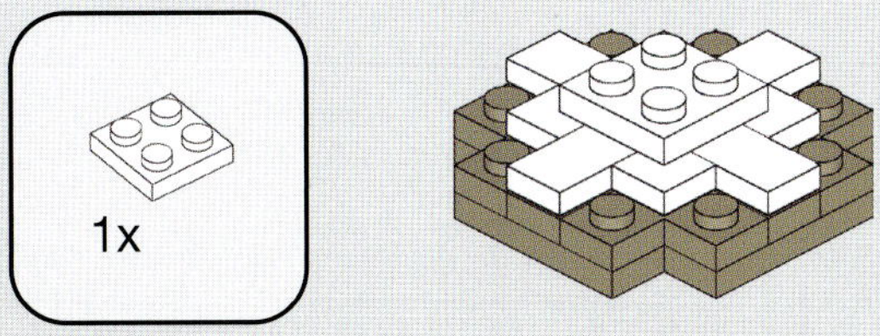

5

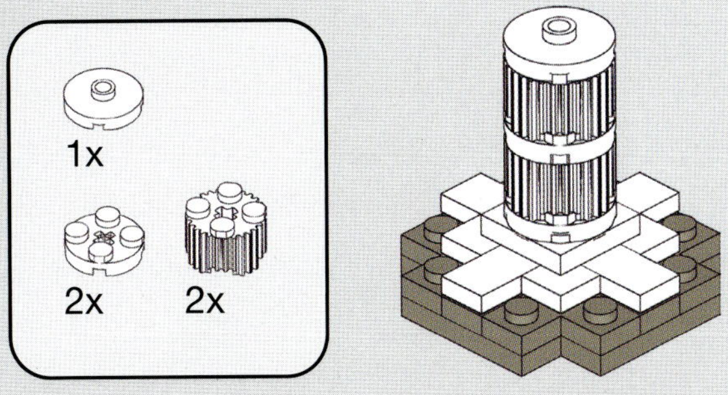

6

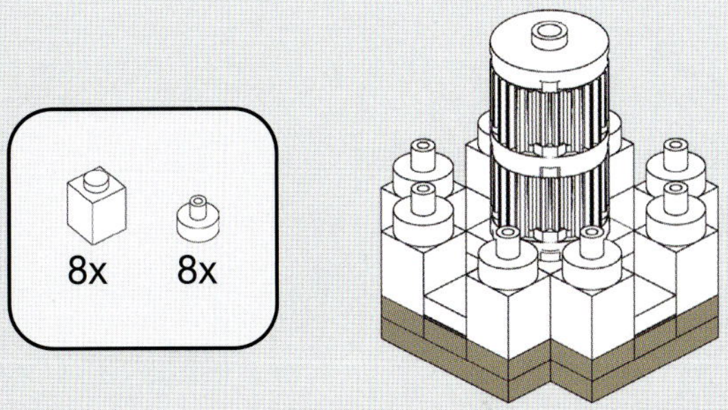

7

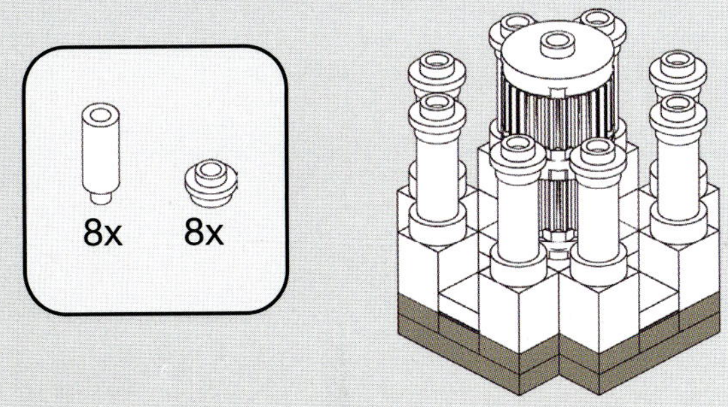

8

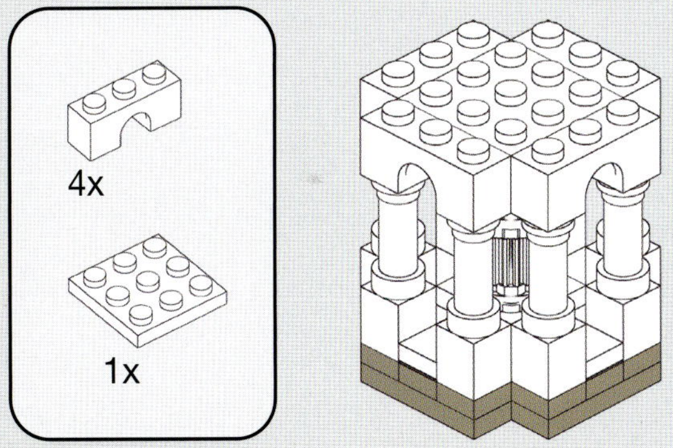

9

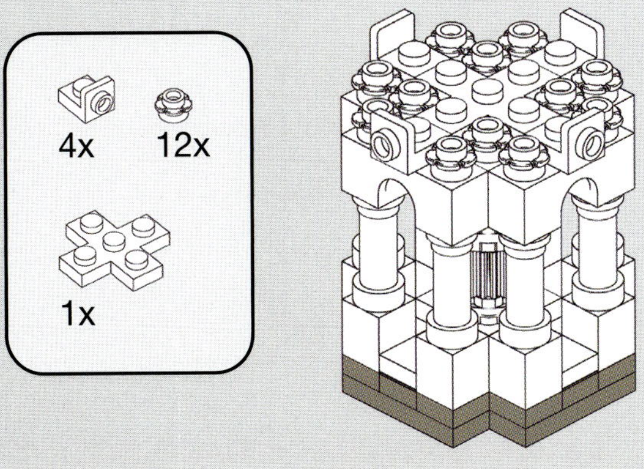

10

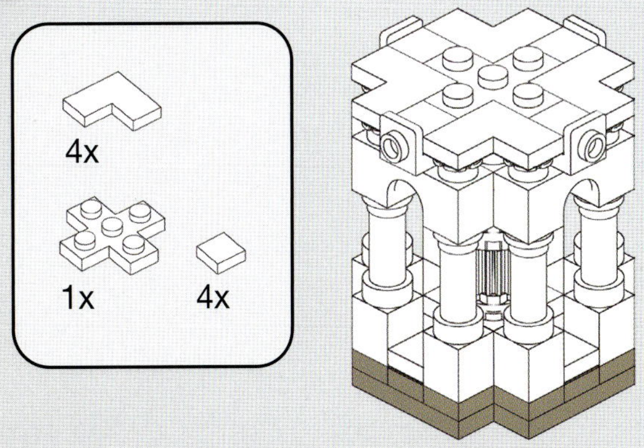

11

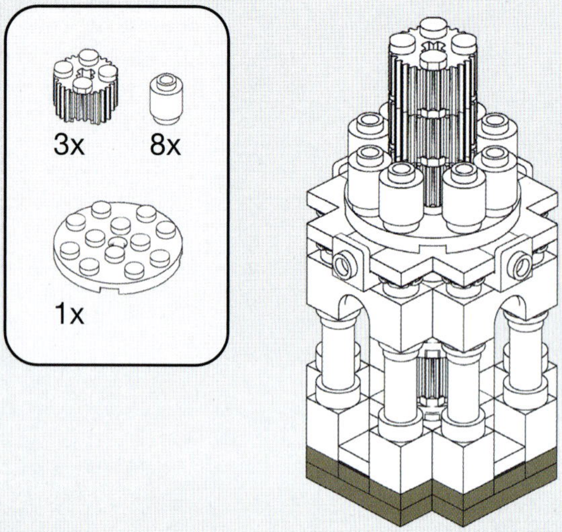

12

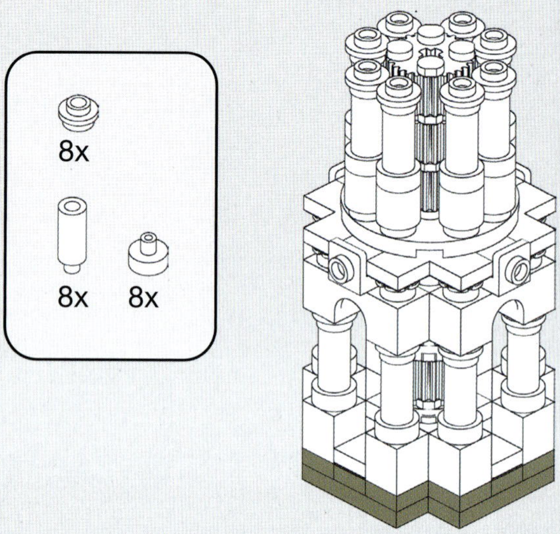

13

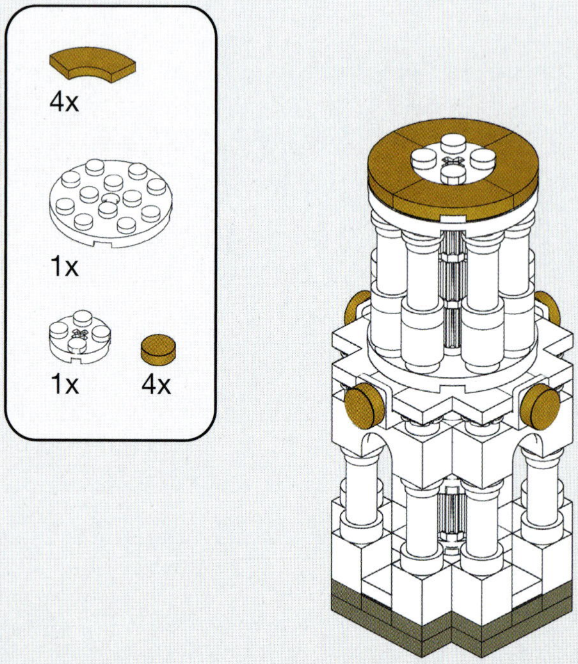

14

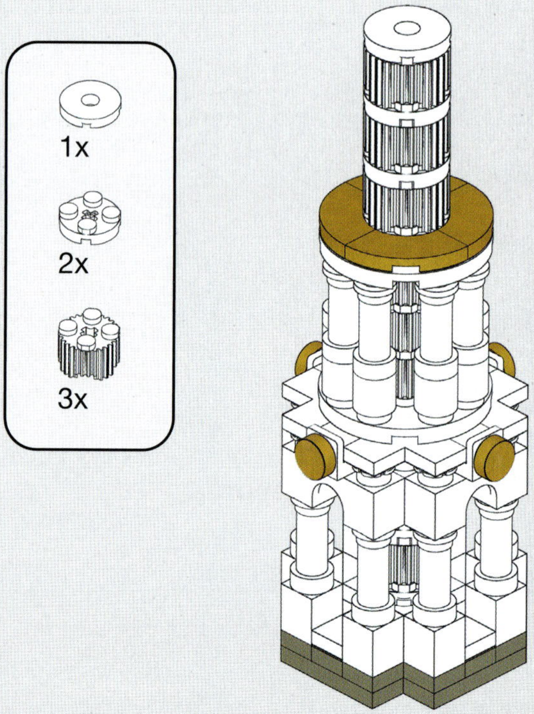

15

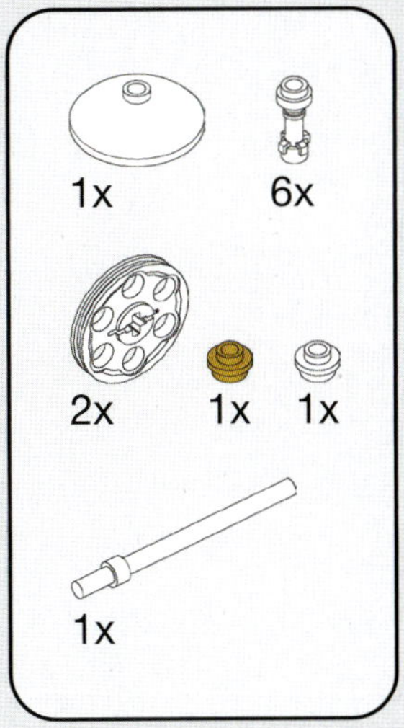

a

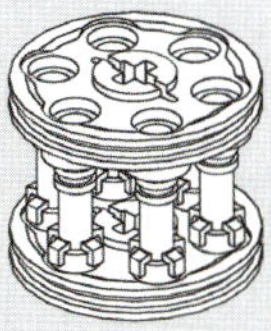

b

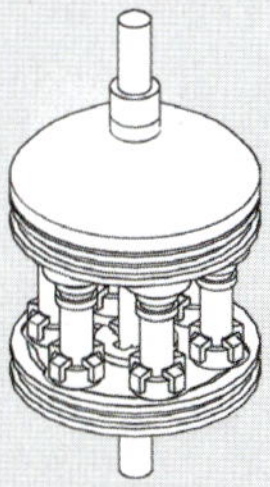

c

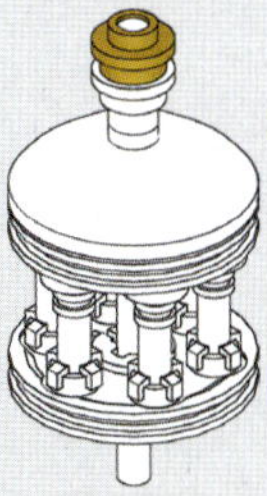

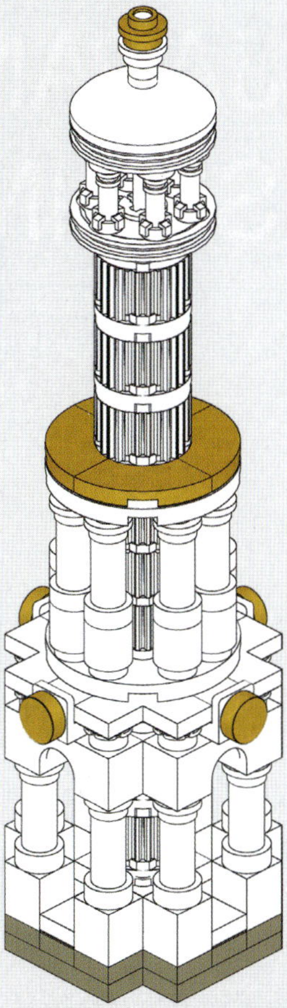

MAKE IT YOUR OWN

Light the beacon fire by adding some trans-orange candle flames. If your world is based on Middle-earth, the Riders of Rohan should soon be on their way.

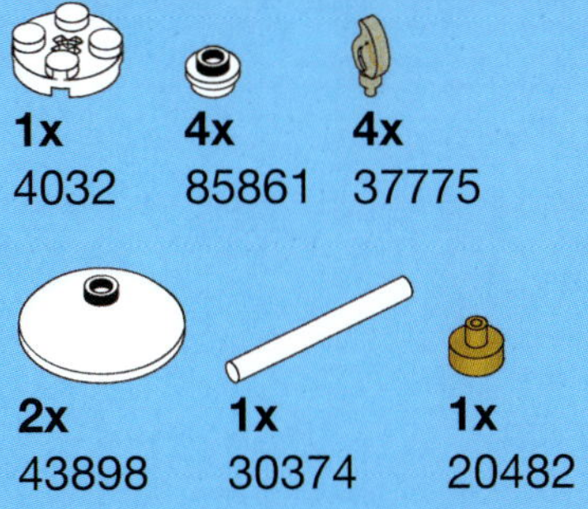

1

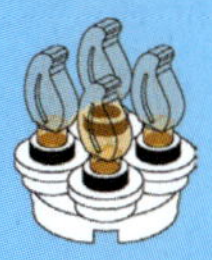

2

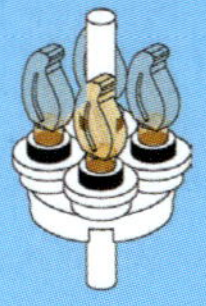

3

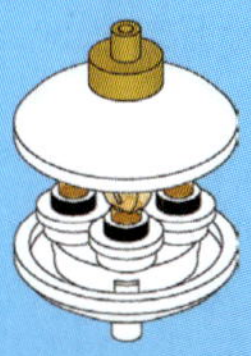

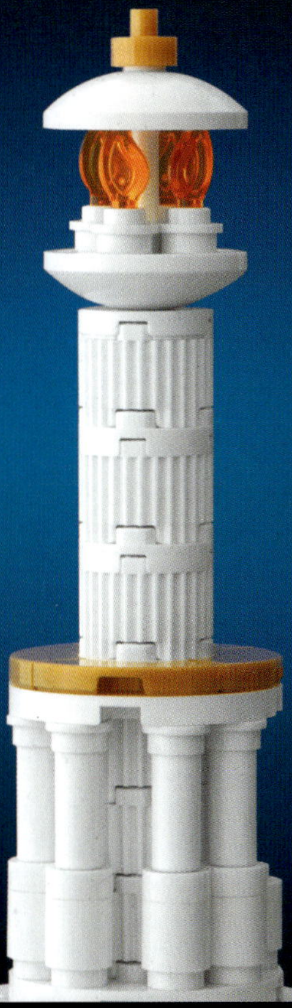

JAPANESE HOT SPRINGS VILLAGE

You emerge from the tunnel into a world transformed. The industrial cityscape has vanished, replaced by a landscape seemingly caught between reality and dreams. Pagodas rise from ancient woodlands, and steam rises like a spirit above a hot-spring bathhouse. There's no map to this place.

This world is inspired by the atmosphere of Studio Ghibli films, which have settings that feel both familiar and fantastical. Traditional Japanese architecture is blended with a touch of whimsy, and pockets of wilderness invite you to relive a child's sense of discovery.

LEGO, which gives us a bridge to the wonder and curiosity of childhood, is the perfect medium for crafting a place where imagination is made real.

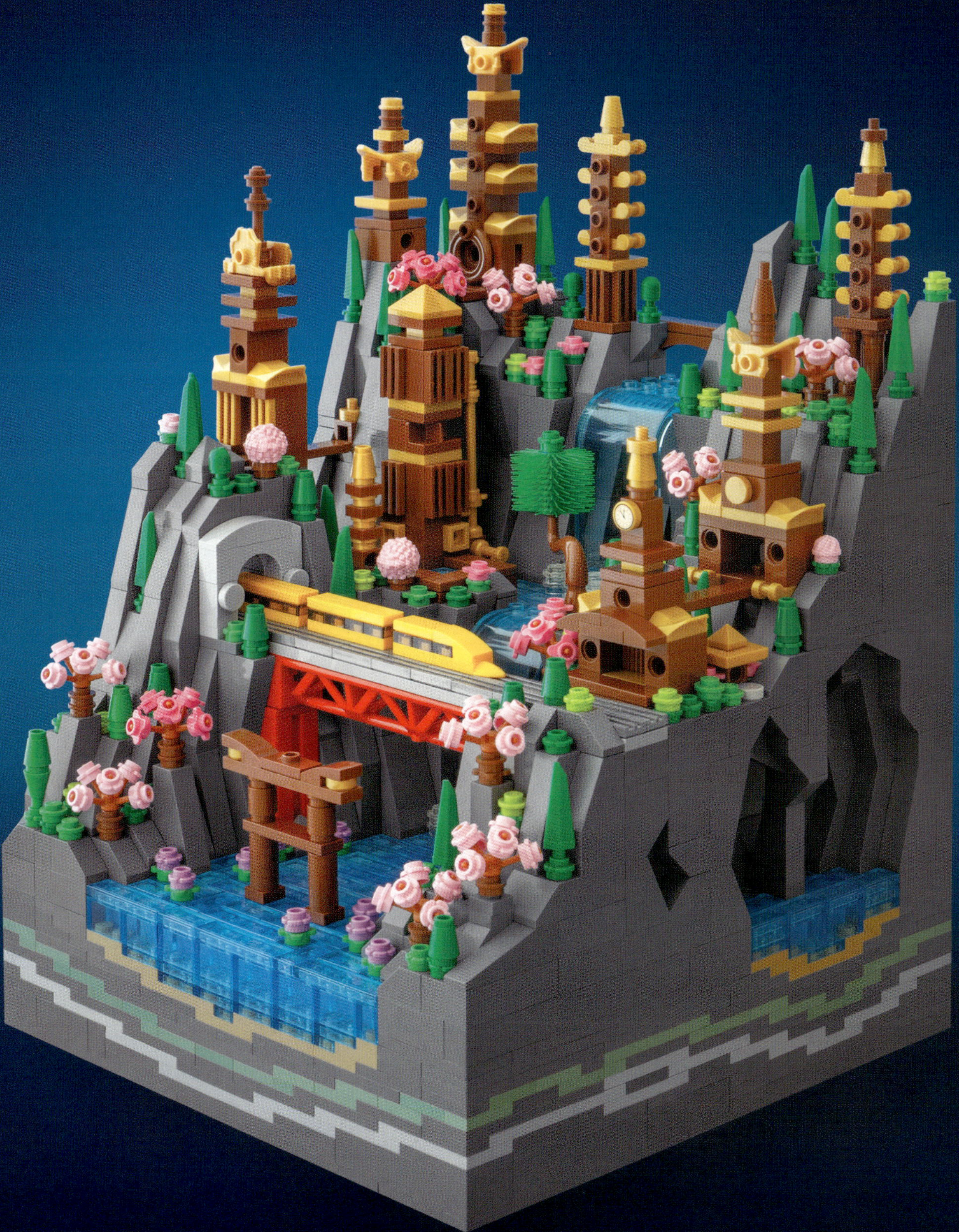

TORII GATE

Passing through a torii gate symbolizes the transition from the mundane to the sacred—a perfect build to start this chapter!

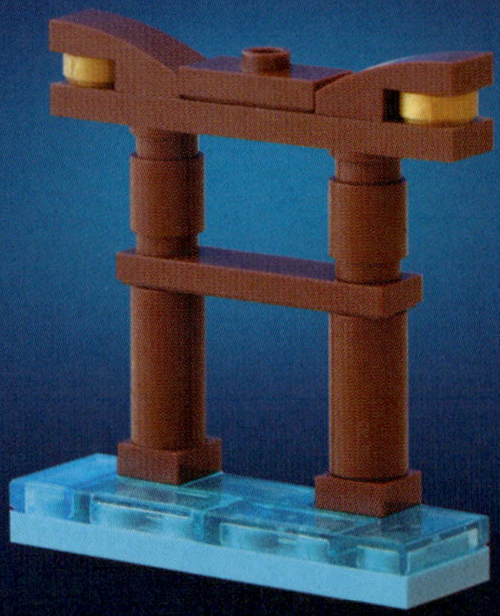

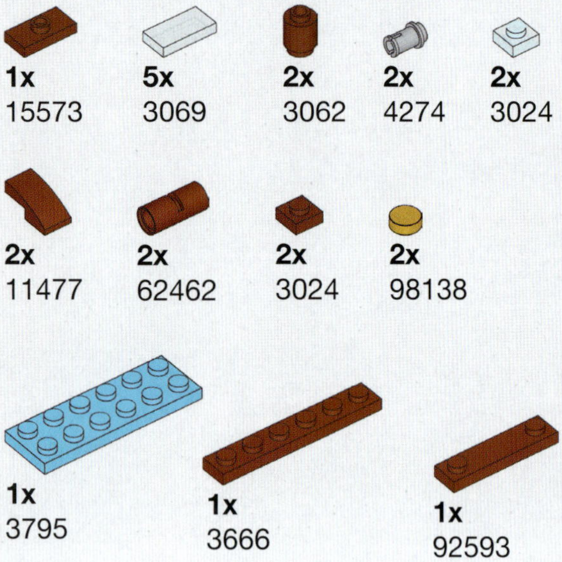

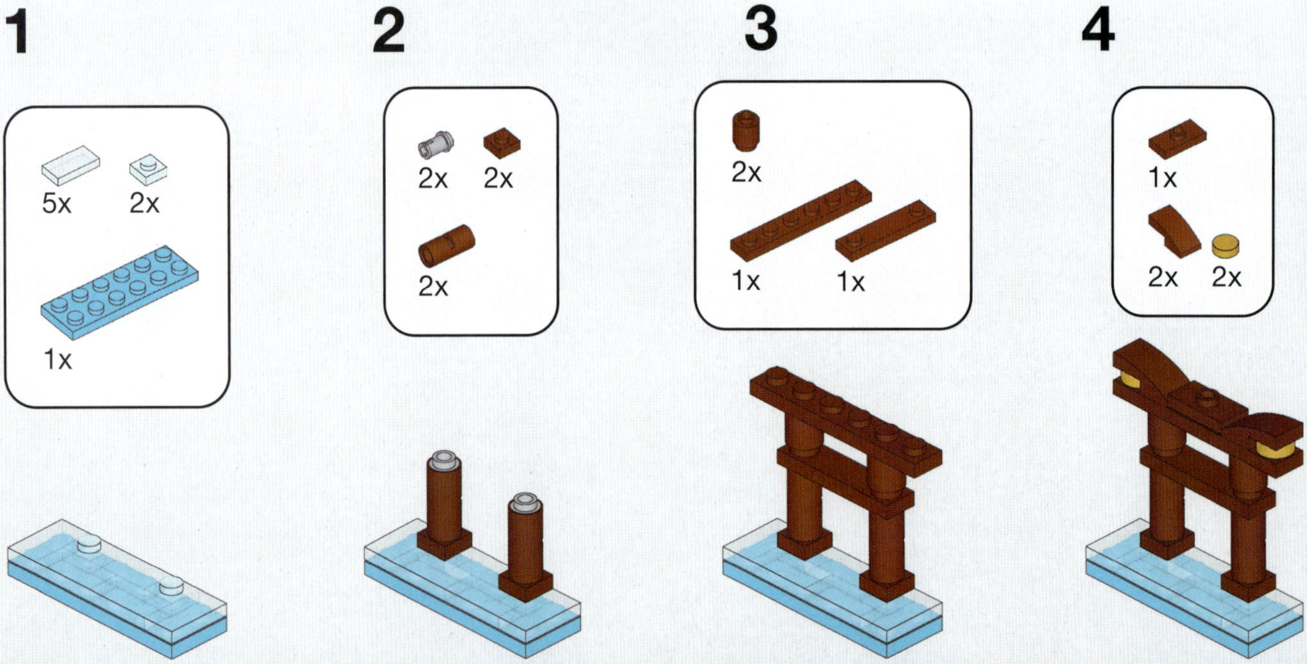

MAKE IT YOUR OWN

Torii gates are often painted red, but you can use gray to create a stone version. Swap any of the reddish-brown parts for a variety of colors. The open stud on top can be customized with any 1×1 element or bar element.

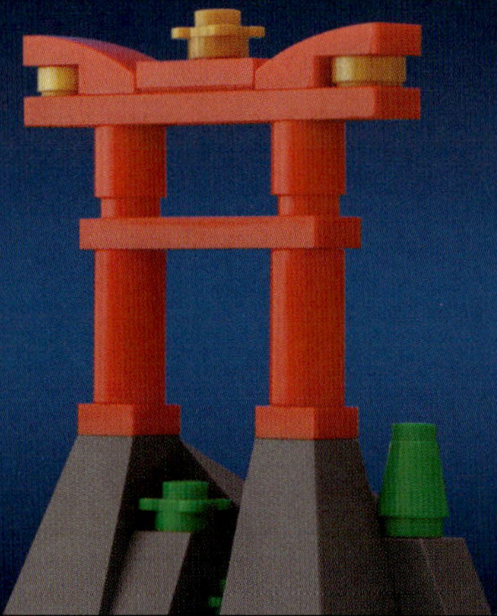

FOREST SHRINE

This small shrine packs a lot of detail into a 2×2 build by using armored shoulder plates, typically found on adventurous medieval minifigures.

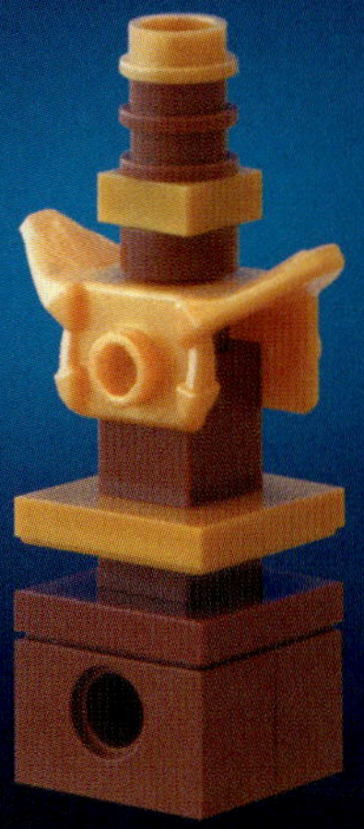

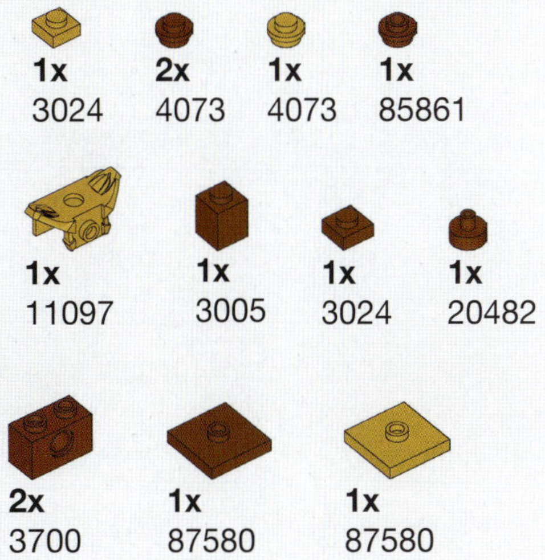

1

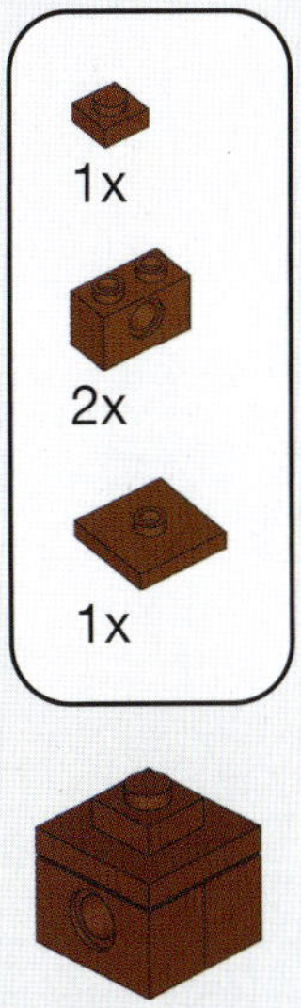

2

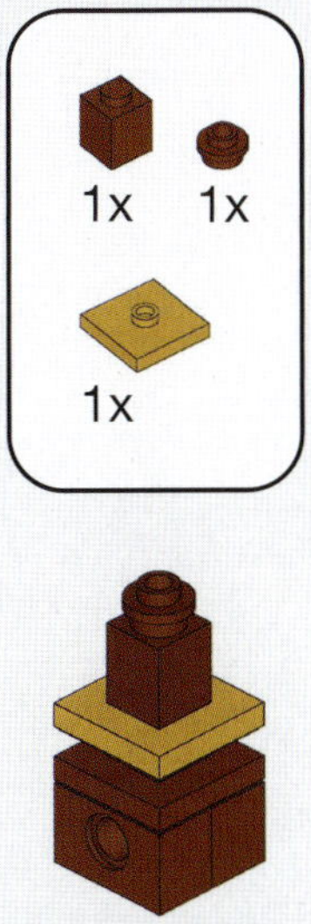

3

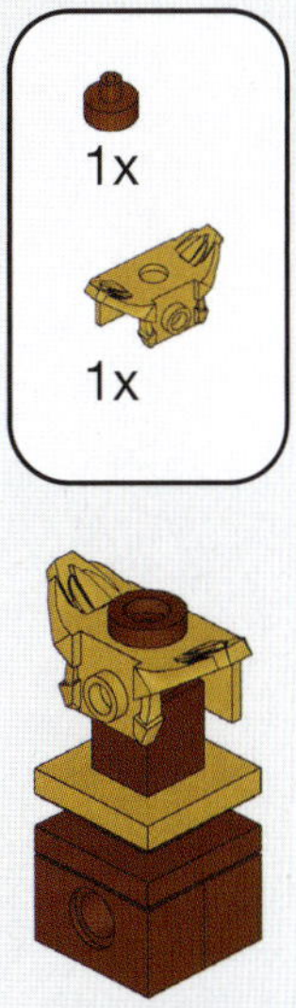

4

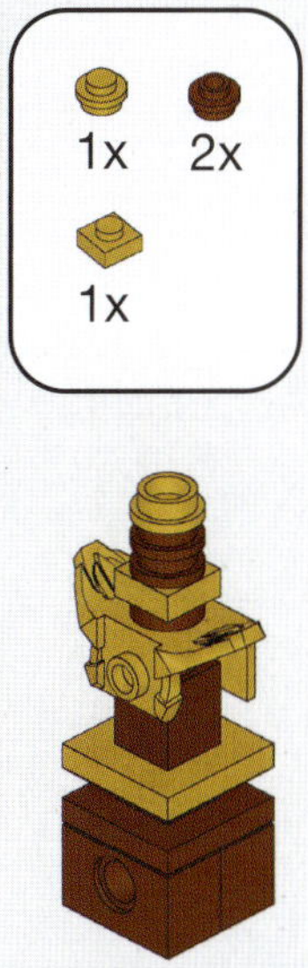

MAKE IT YOUR OWN

Experiment with other minifigure shoulder accessories to create distinctive rooflines. The shrine on the left uses fringed epaulettes (#2526), and the right-side shrine uses a minifigure armored breastplate with shoulder pads (#11098). Both are placed upside down.

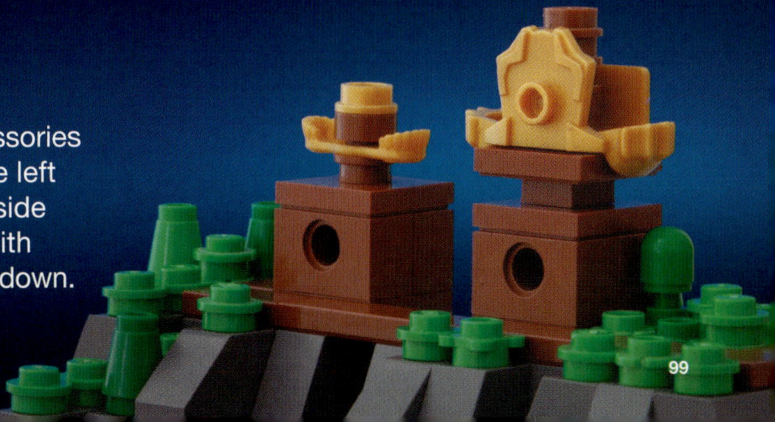

TRAIN STATION

This whimsical train station provides a passage from the familiar into a world of alluring mysteries. Will you find your way back?

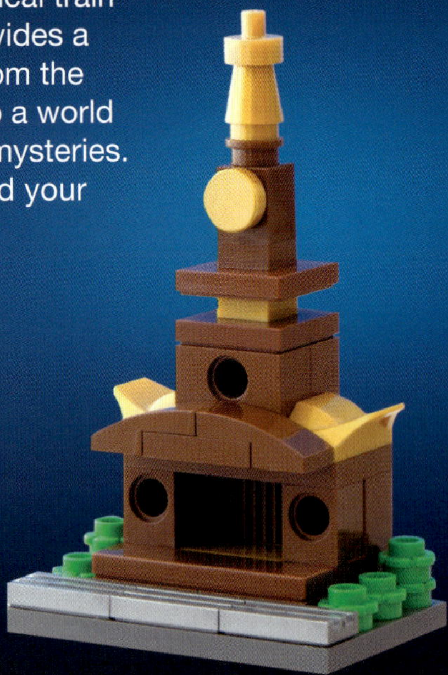

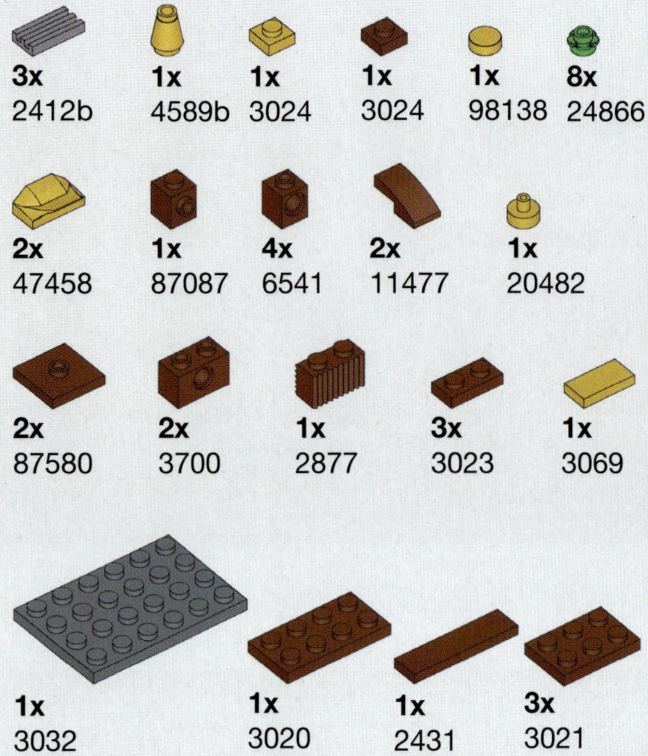

1

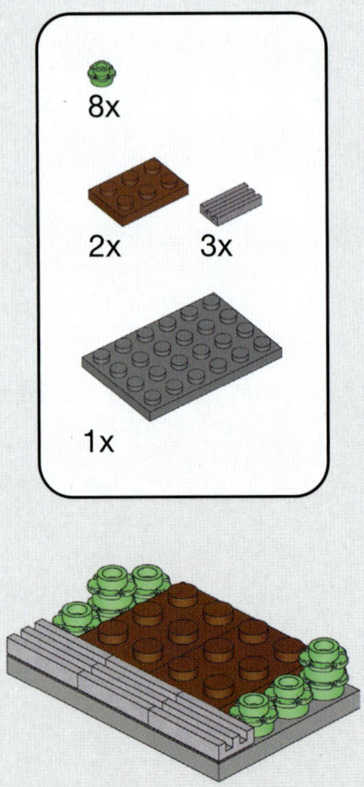

2

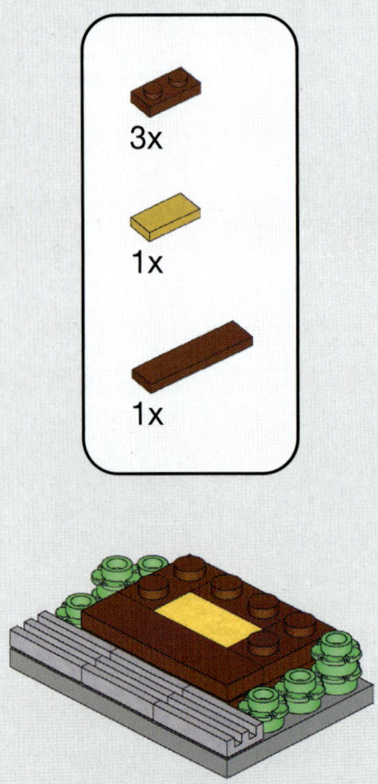

3

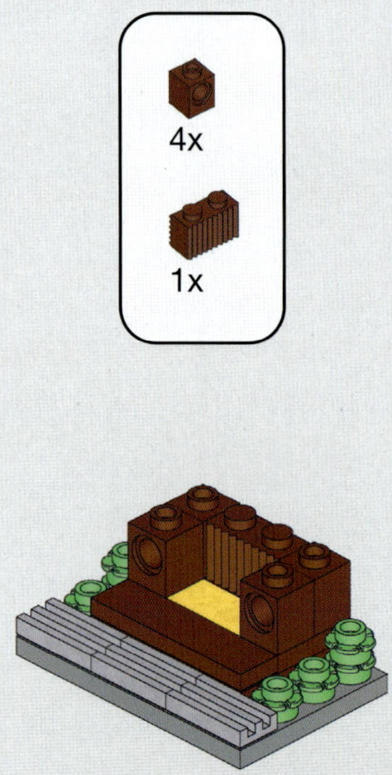

4

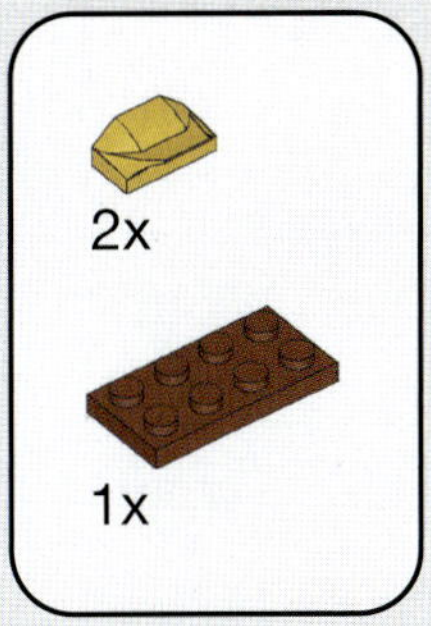

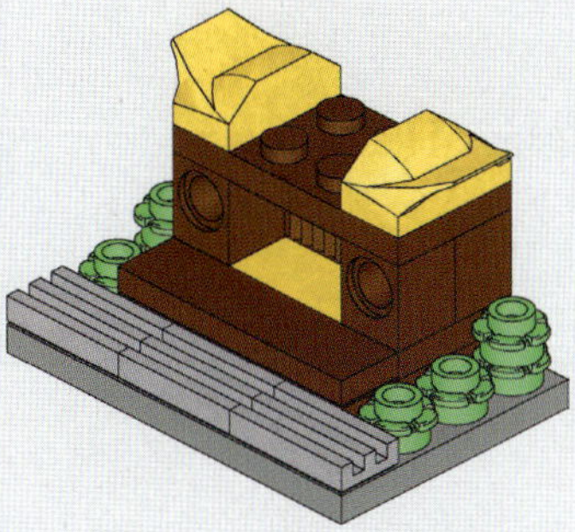

5

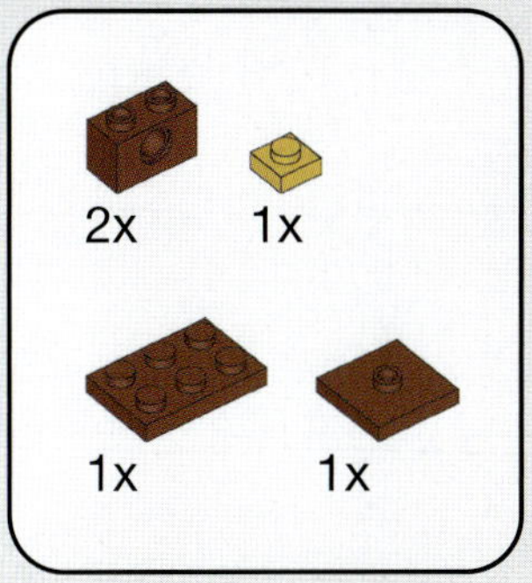

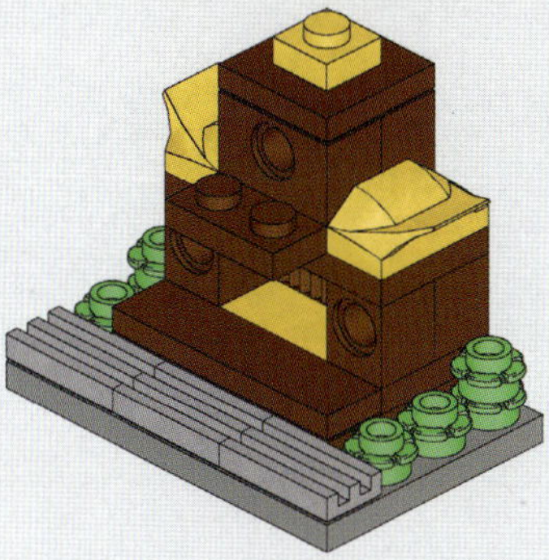

6

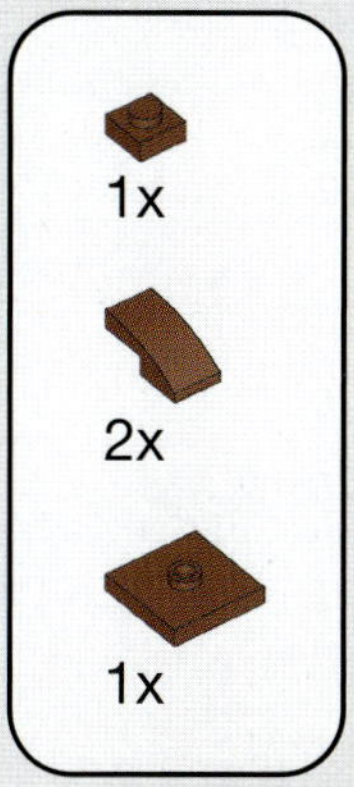

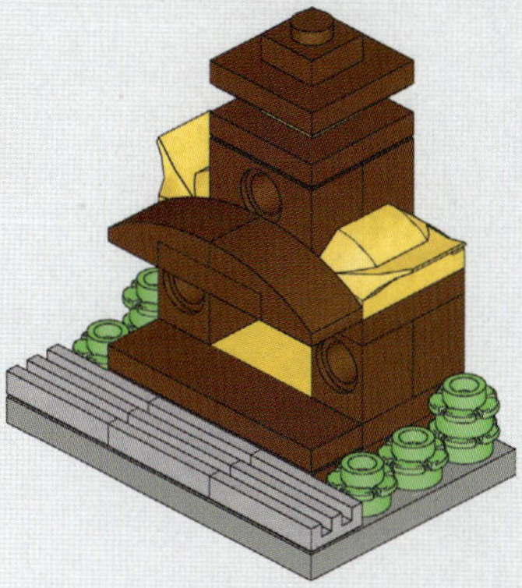

7

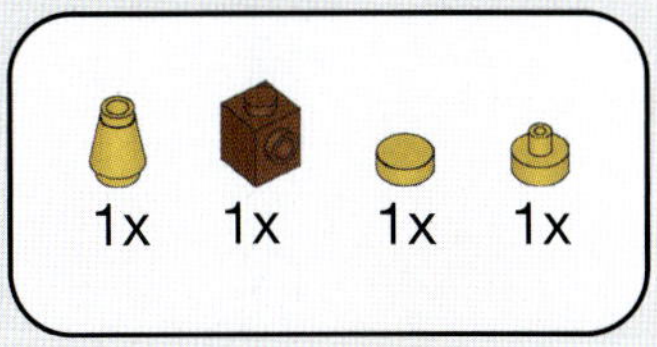

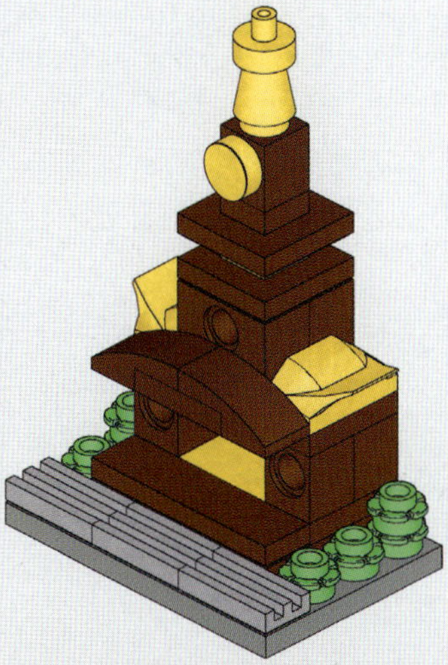

MAKE IT YOUR OWN

Take your train station to the next level by adding a 1×1 round tile with tan clock face pattern (#98138pb259).

Add a train from the "Trains" chapter beginning on page 52. A modern bullet train contrasts perfectly with the rustic station.

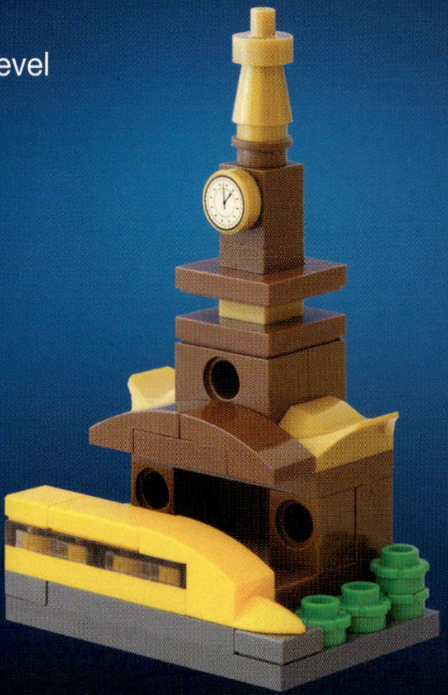

ONSEN PALACE

In this enchanted hot-spring retreat, travelers find solace in warm, mineral-rich waters—provided the local snow monkeys make room.

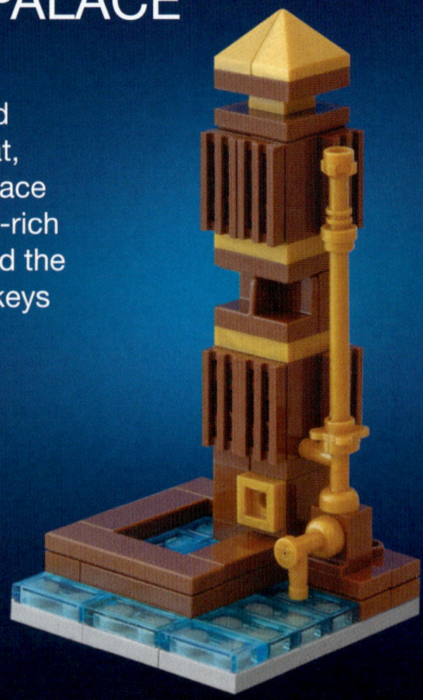

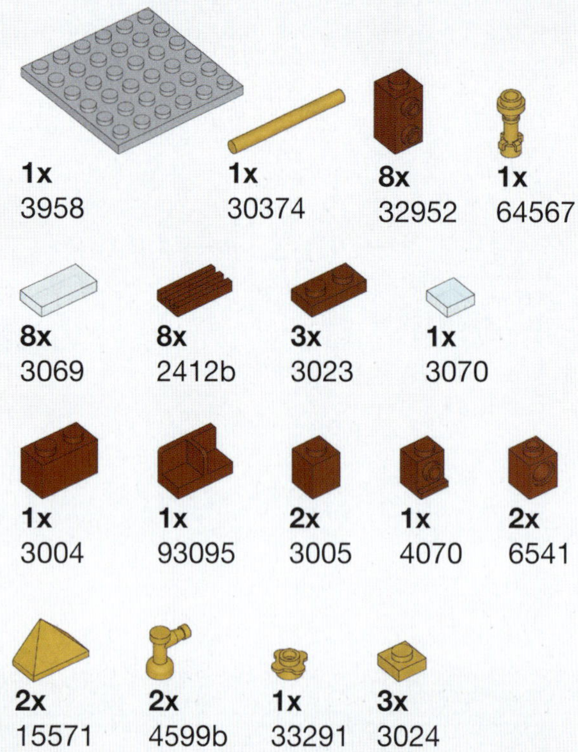

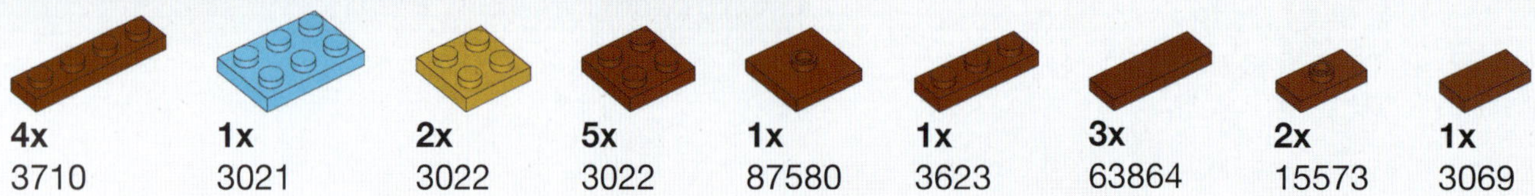

1

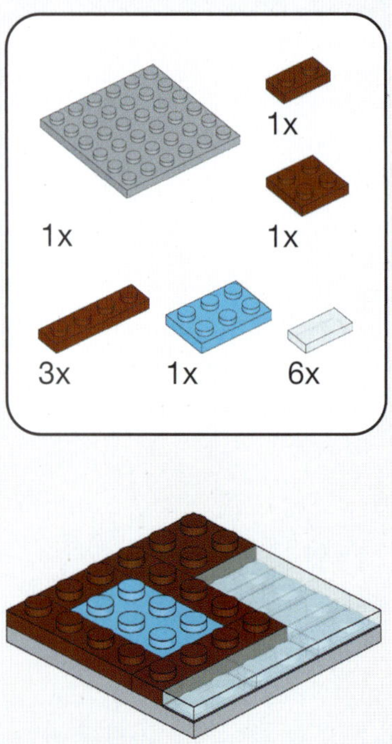

2

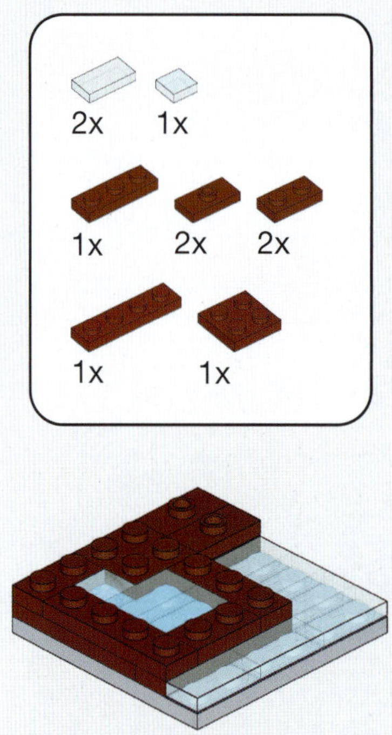

3

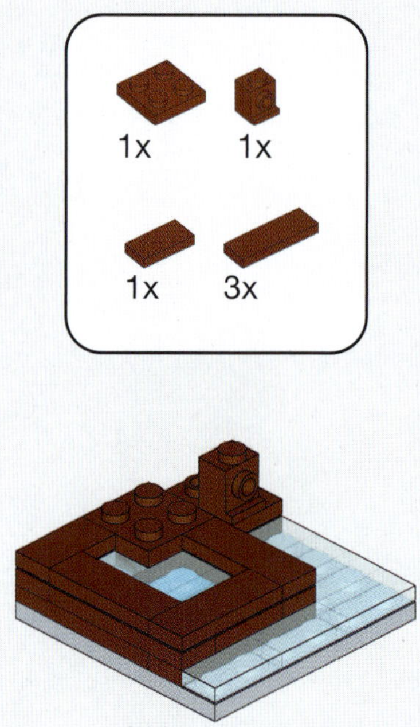

4

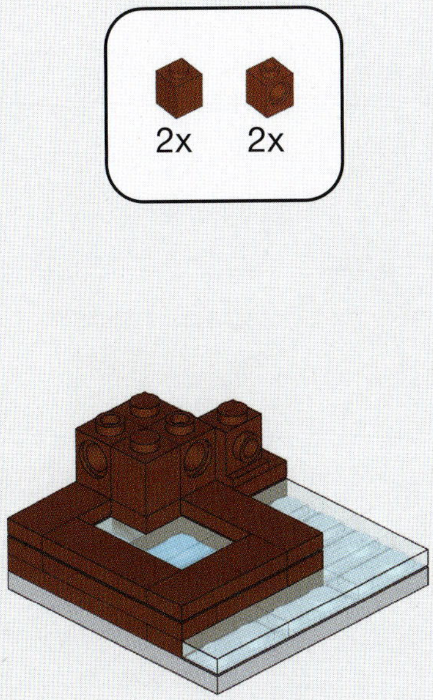

5

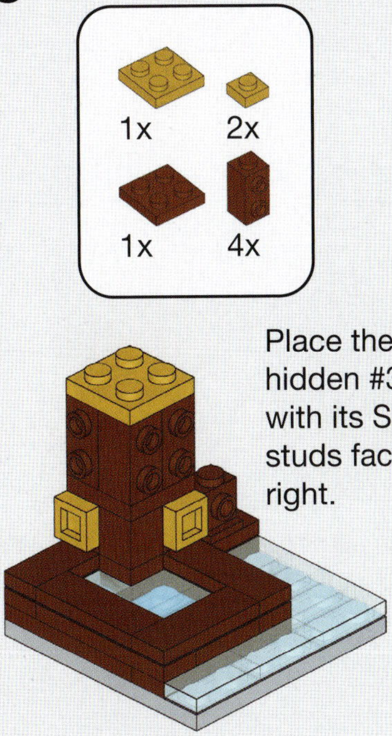

Place the hidden #32952 with its SNOT studs facing right.

6

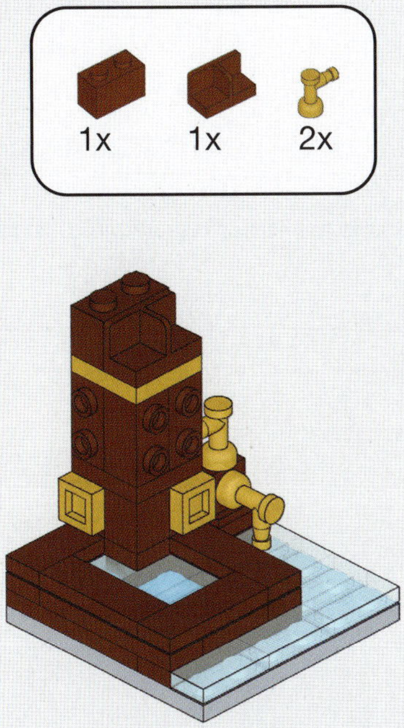

7

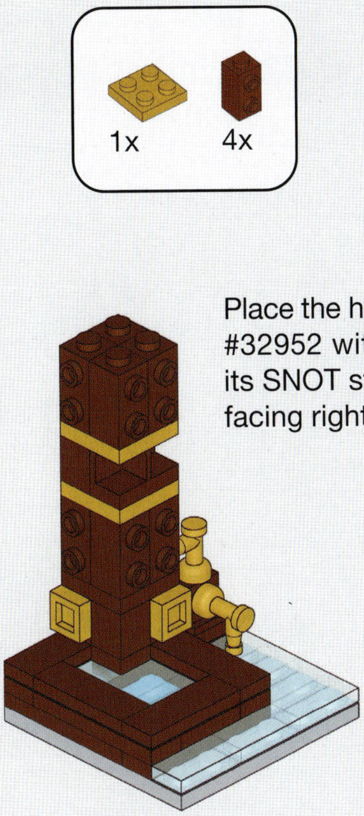

Place the hidden #32952 with its SNOT studs facing right.

8

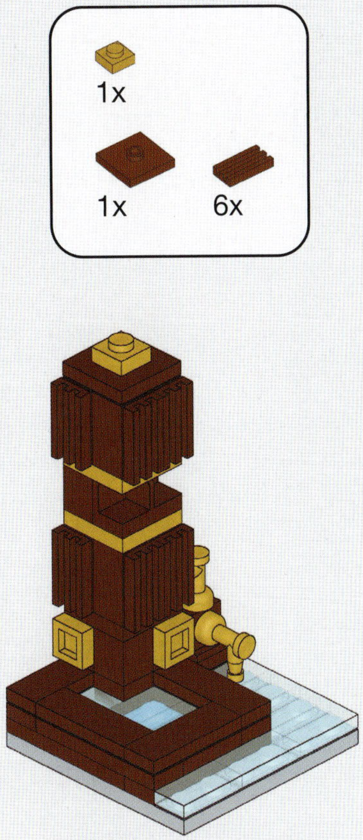

9

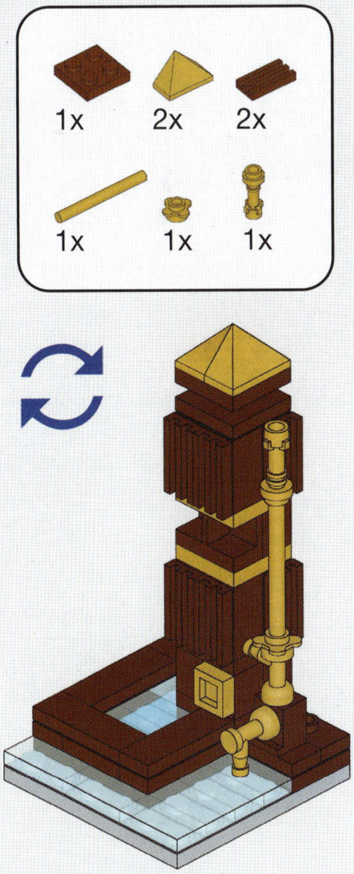

PINE PAGODA

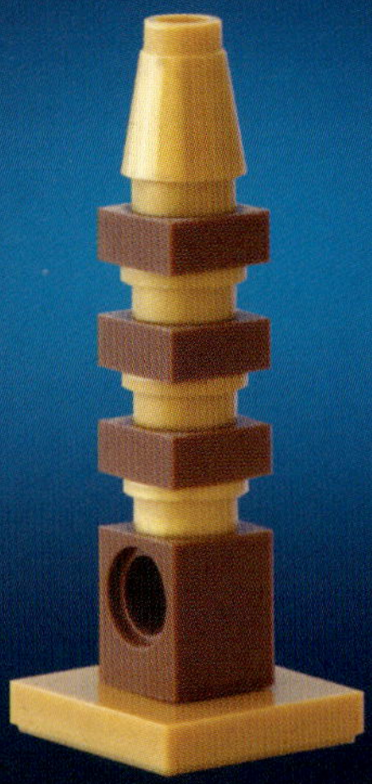

3x
4073

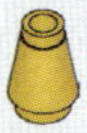
1x
4589b

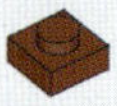
3x
3024

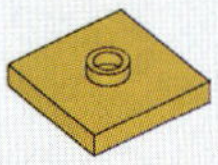
1x
87580

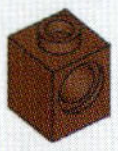
1x
6541

Change your Pine Pagoda's height by adding or removing plates.

1

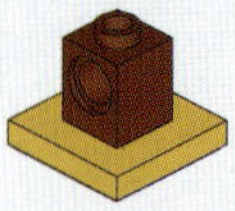

2

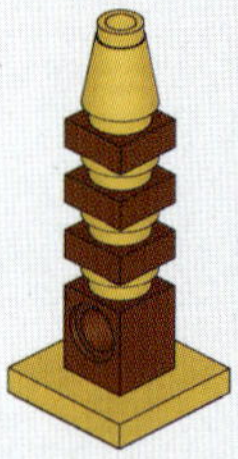

TEAHOUSE

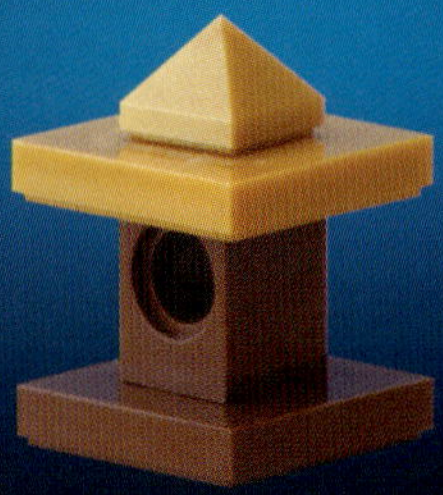

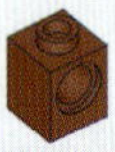
1x
6541

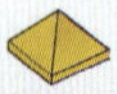
1x
22388

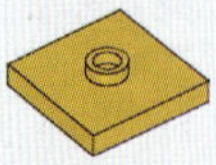
1x
87580

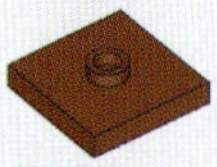
1x
87580

1

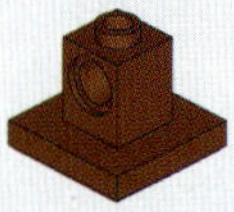

2

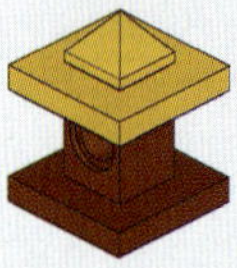

BRISTLECONE PINE

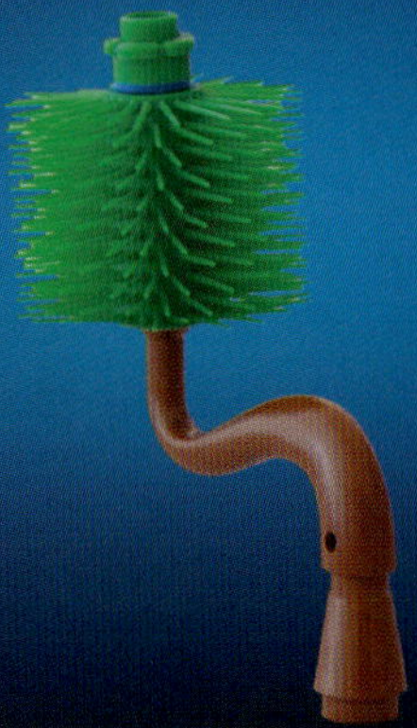

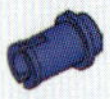
1x
4274

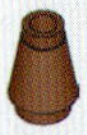
1x
4589b

1x
24866

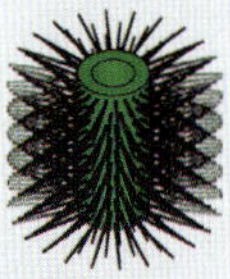
1x
2498

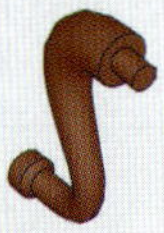
1x
80497

This build is for those who enjoy both unusual-looking trees and tracking down rare LEGO parts. The green vehicle brush is harder to find than a 1×1 plate in shag carpet!

1

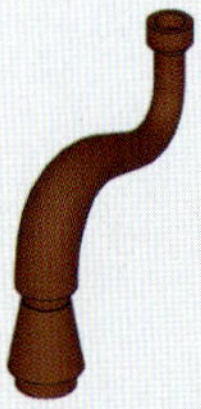

2

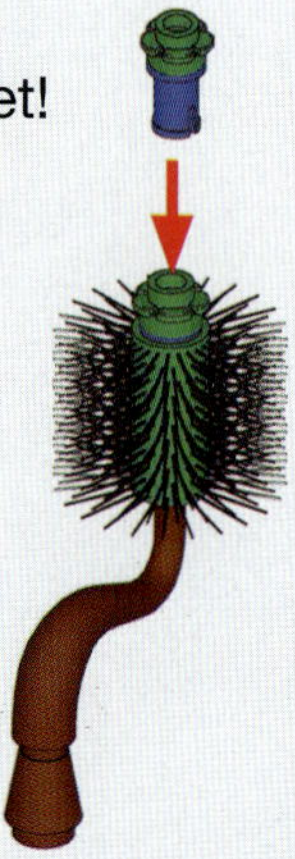

GOLDEN PAGODA

This radiant pagoda brings the sun to Earth with its golden accents. Its tiered eaves and fine details reflect centuries of craftsmanship.

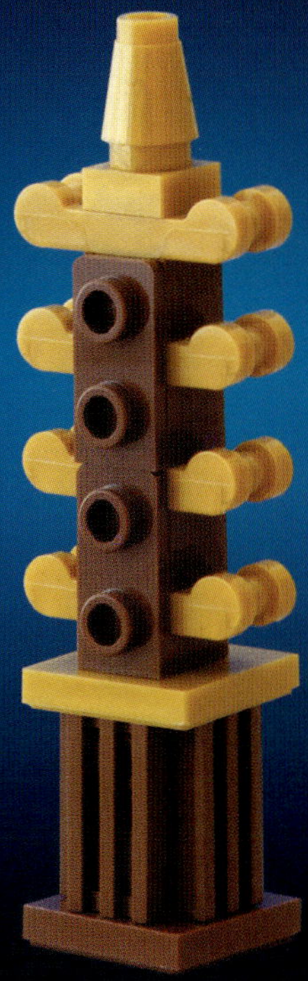

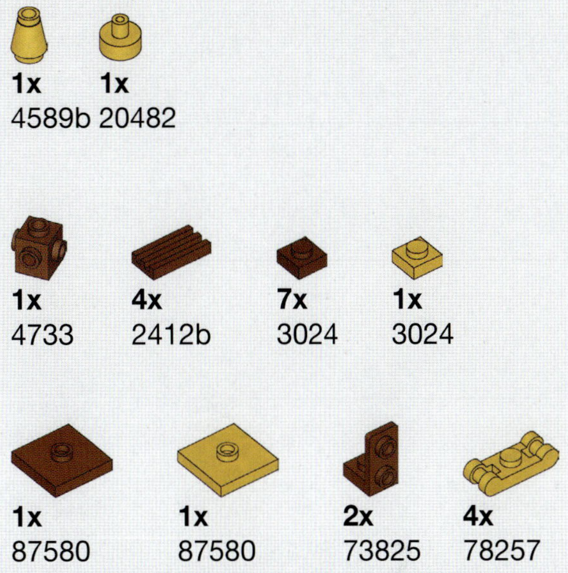

1

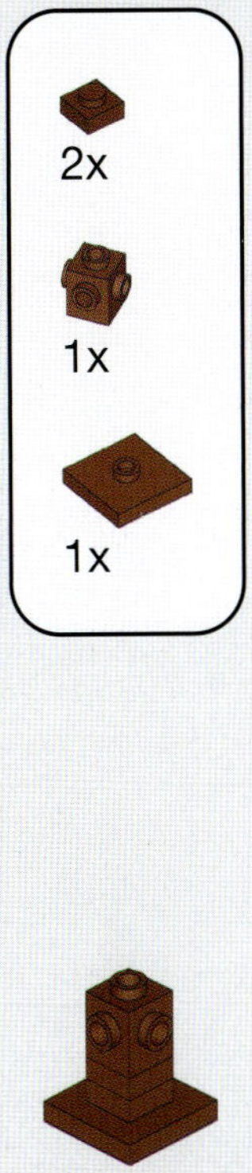

2

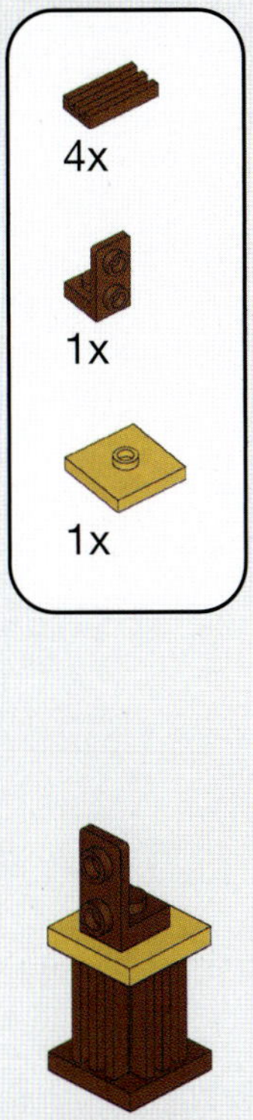

3

4

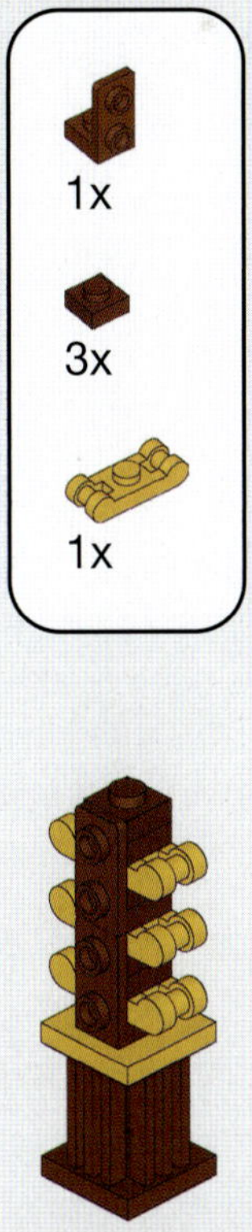

5

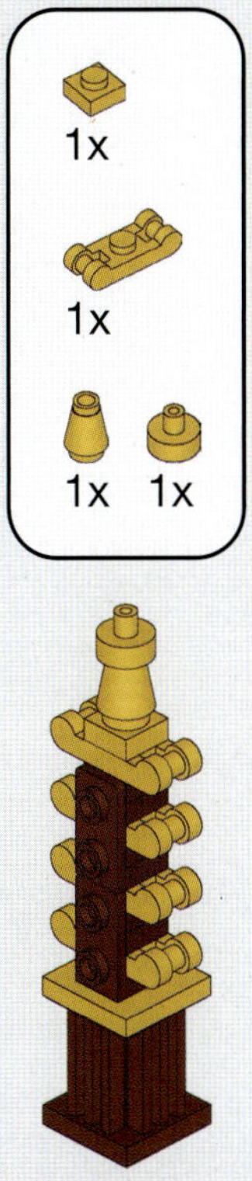

CLASSIC SKYSCRAPERS

Around the turn of the 20th century, something new appeared on the horizon in the booming cities of New York and Chicago. Engineering innovations like steel-frame construction and elevators combined with the majesty of Gothic and Baroque styles to create towering "castles in the sky." These early skyscrapers remain global landmarks, standing proudly among their modern counterparts.

Both Gothic and Baroque architecture emphasize grandeur and intricate detailing. Sideways building techniques and creative use of pieces bring the ornate facades of early skyscrapers into your own Gilded Age world—small in size, but big in ambition!

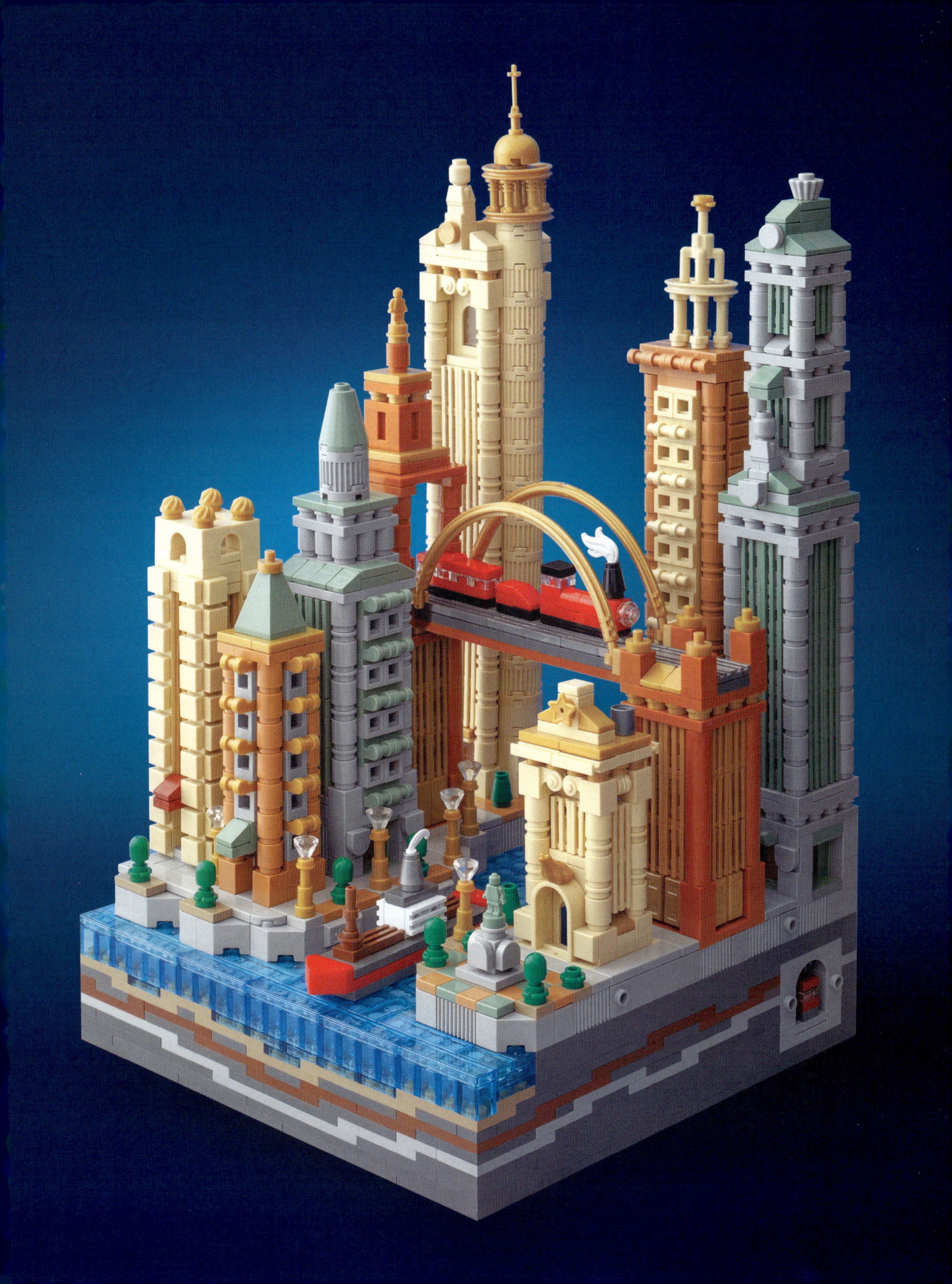

CORNERSTONE COMMONS

Cornerstone Commons is a striking structure that showcases classic masonry craftsmanship with pronounced quoins.

Quoins are the prominent stone or brick blocks that reinforce the corners of a building. *Quoin* is also a useful word to learn for any Scrabble players out there.

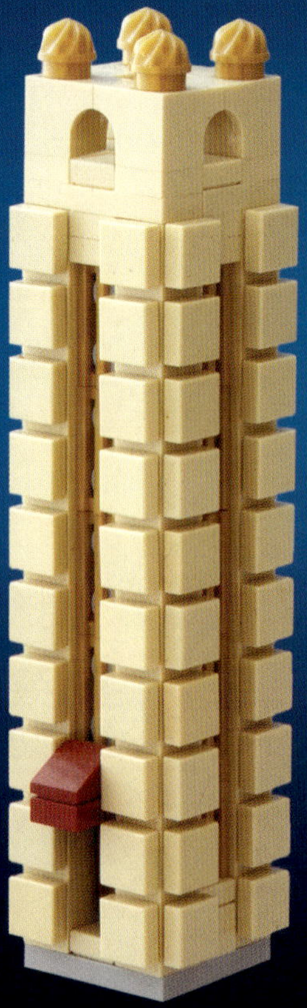

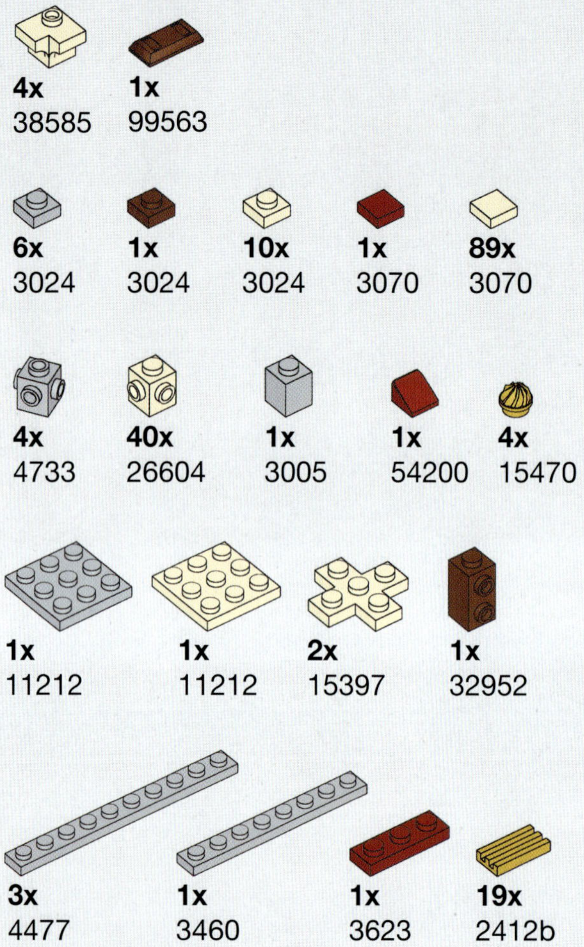

1

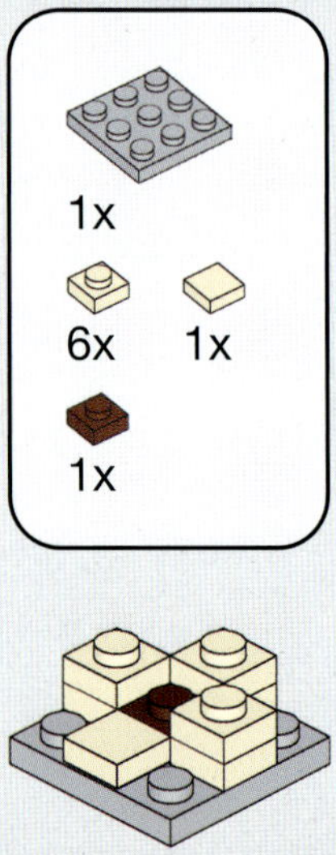

2

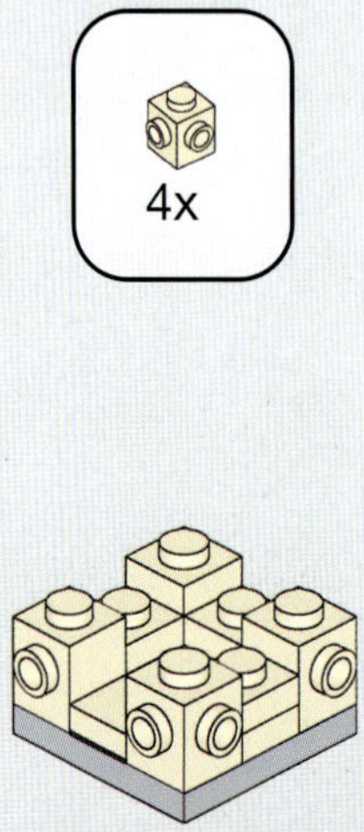

3

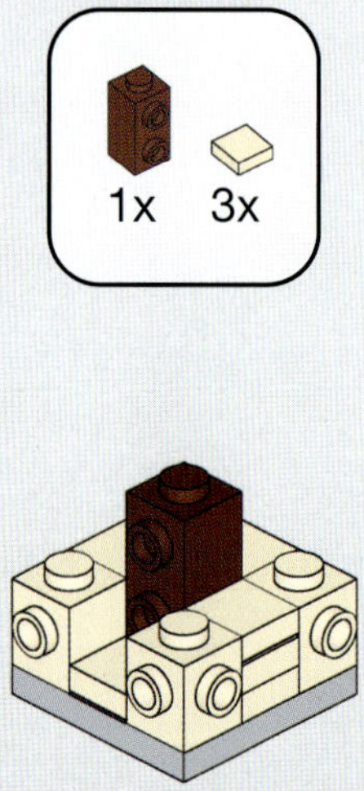

4

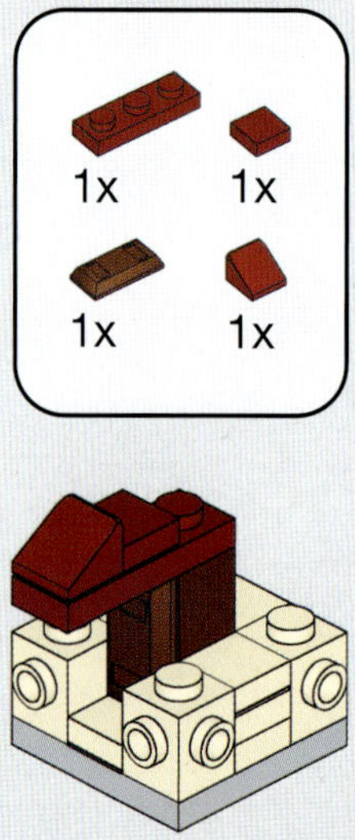

5

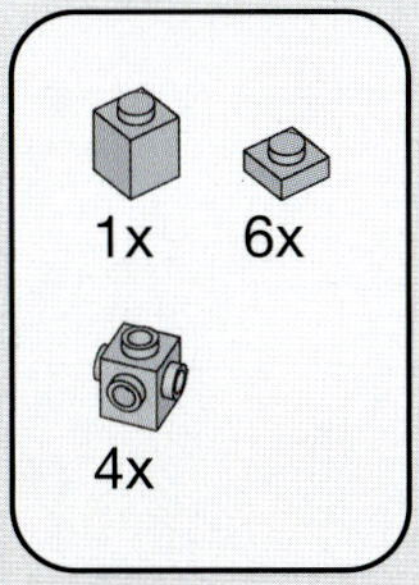

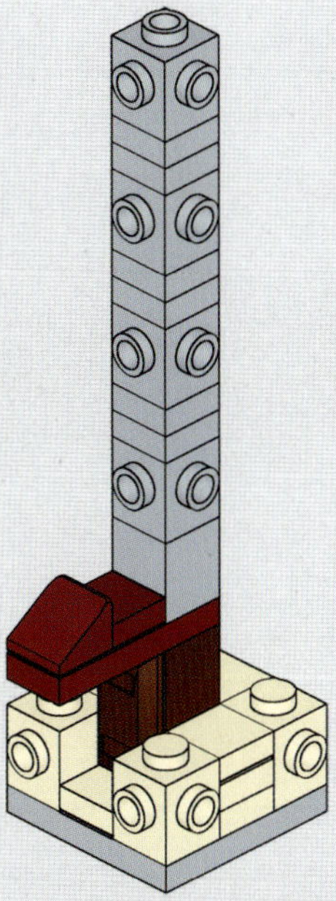

6

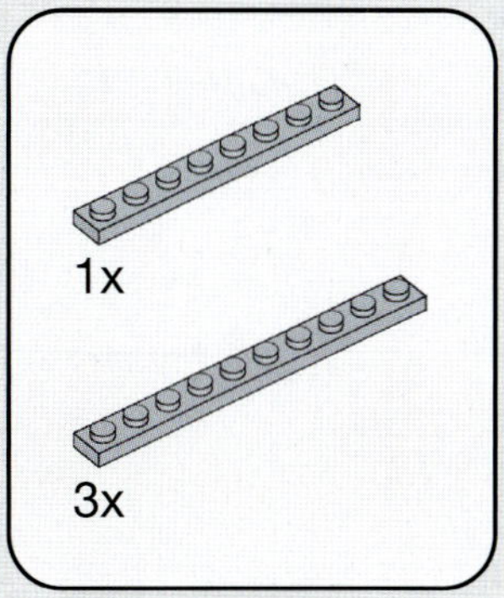

The three sides without a doorway are identical in this model.

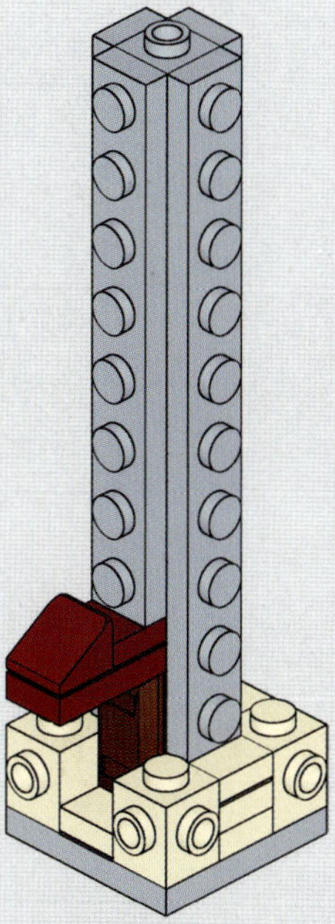

7

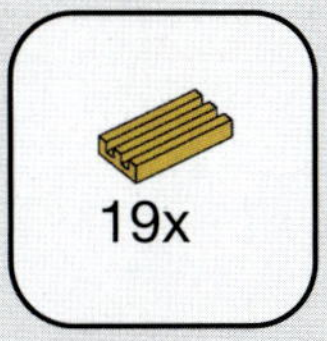

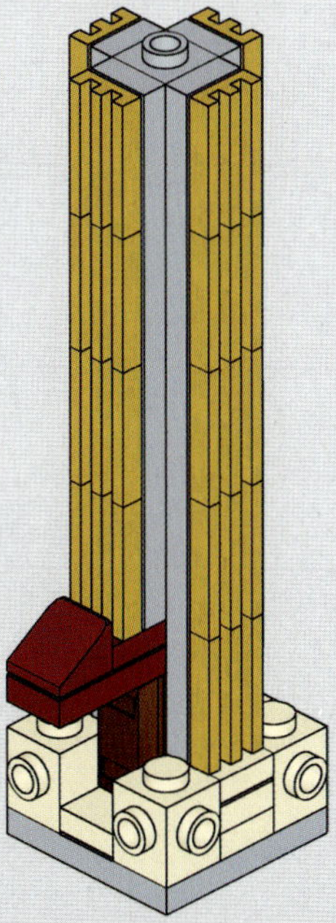

8

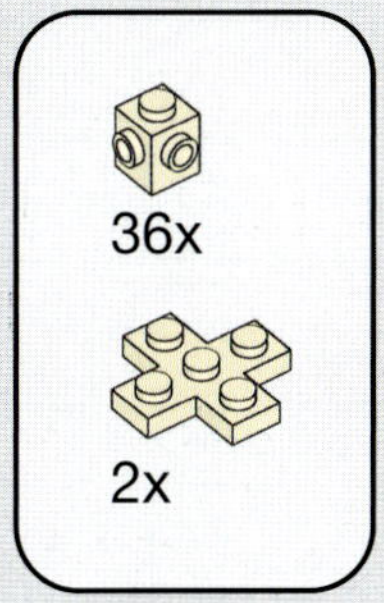

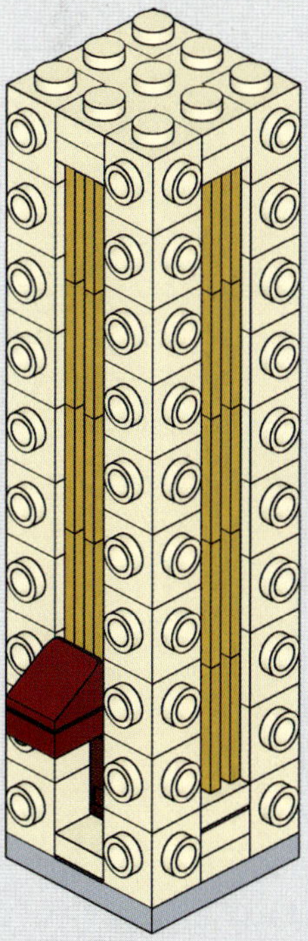

9

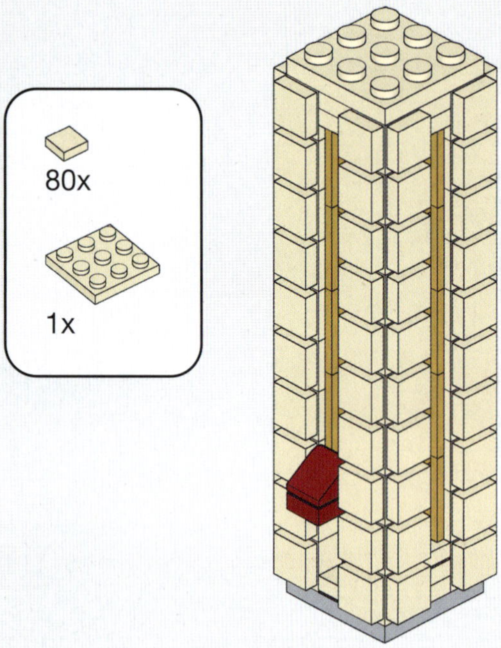

10

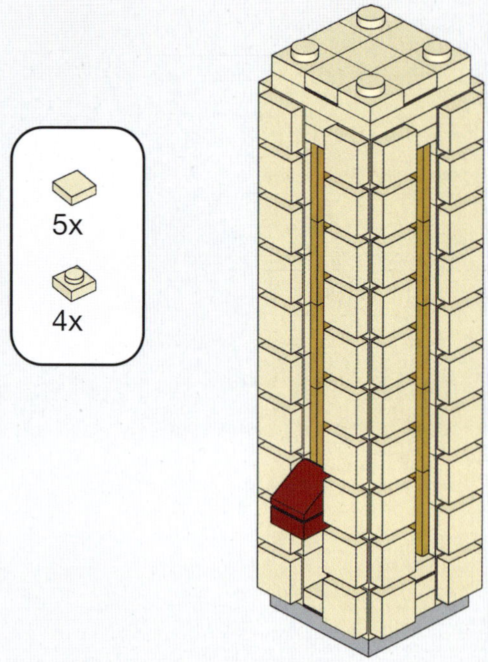

11

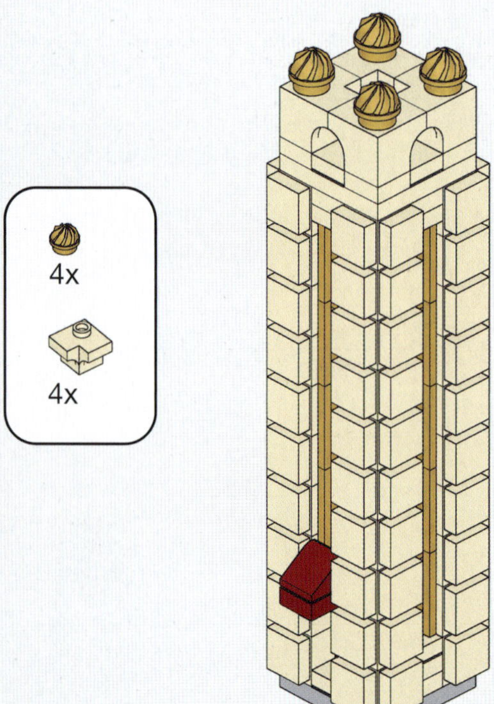

MAKE IT YOUR OWN

You can give Cornerstone Commons a more modern look by swapping grille tiles for trans-blue ones. Add a touch of whimsy to the rooftop with a large golden ornament. LEGO bricks are made for experimentation. Invent your own architectural style!

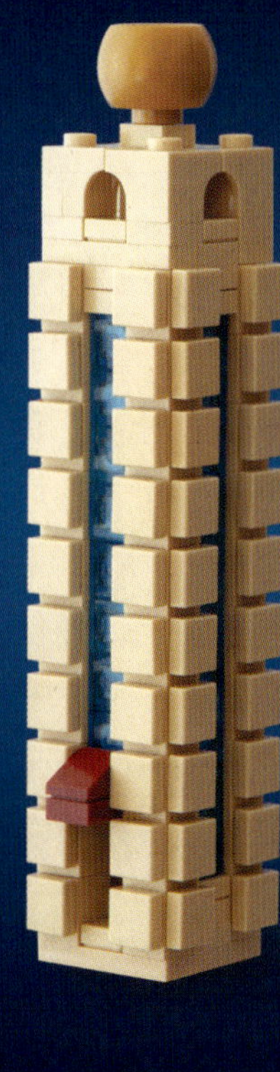

GOTHIC HEIGHTS

Neo-Gothic architecture brings a medieval touch to modern buildings. vertical lines emphasize height, ornate detailing echoes medieval cathedrals, and the tower adds a castle-like presence to the skyline. It's a perfect residential building for bat-costumed crime fighters.

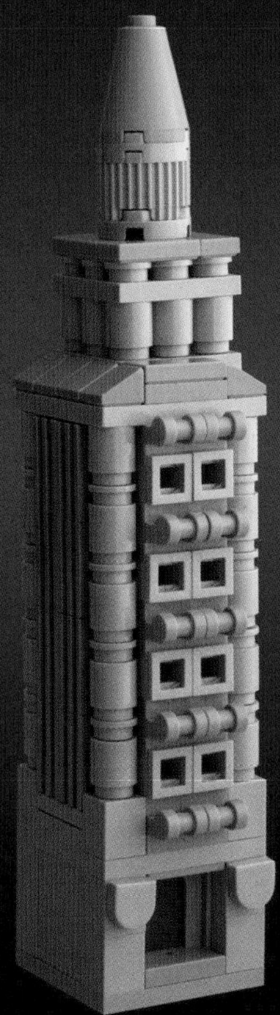

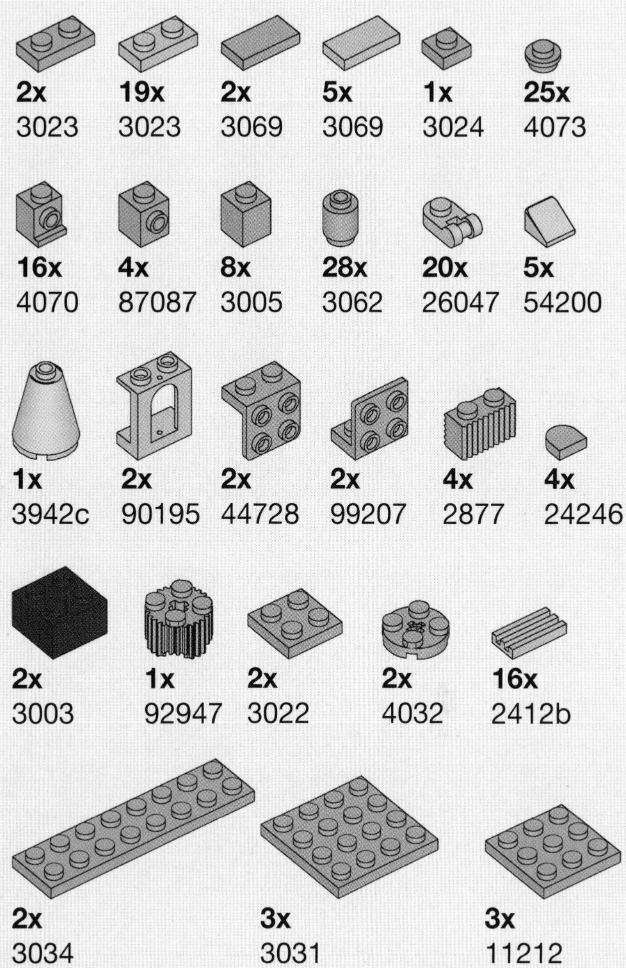

In steps 1 to 8, the model's front and back are identical, as are its left and right sides.

1

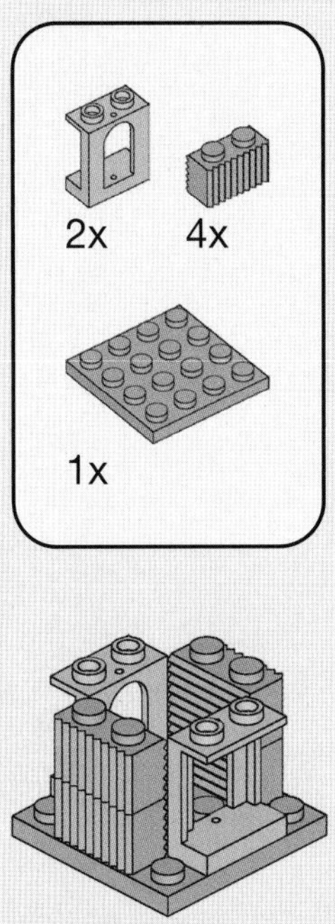

2

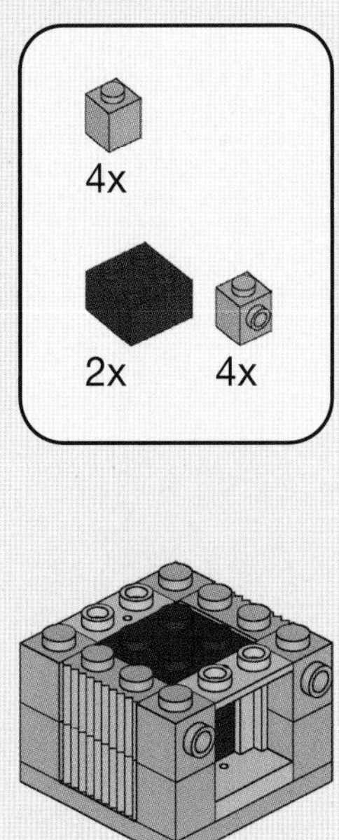

3

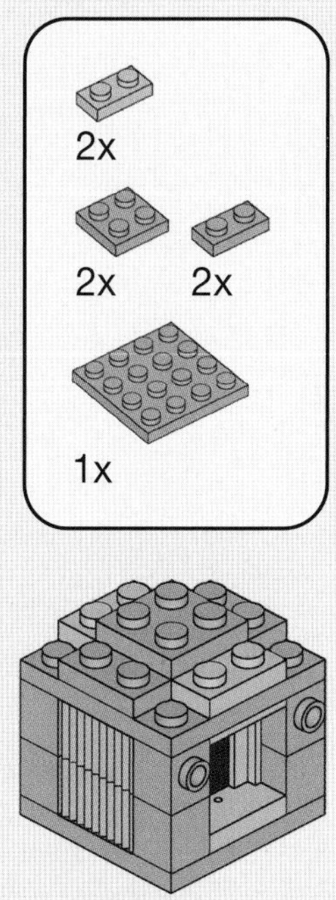

4

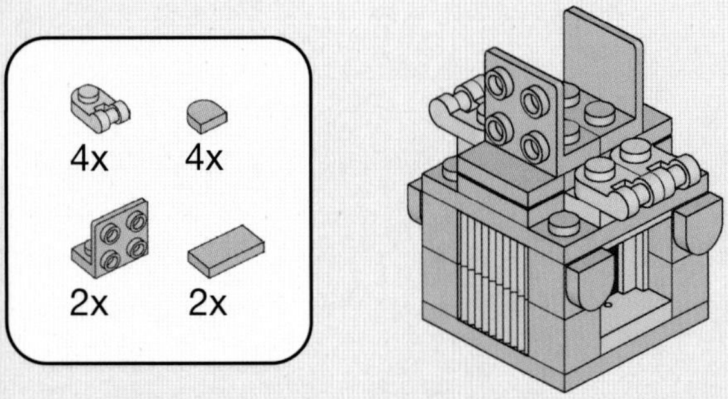

5

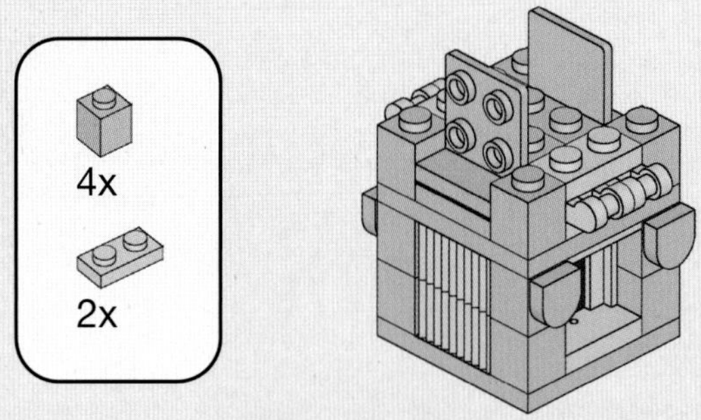

6

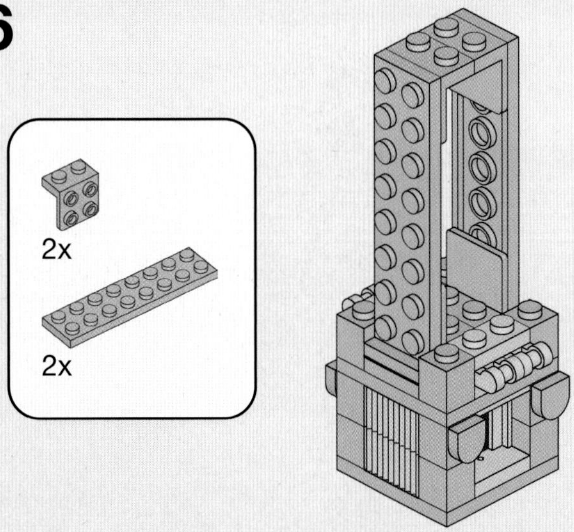

7

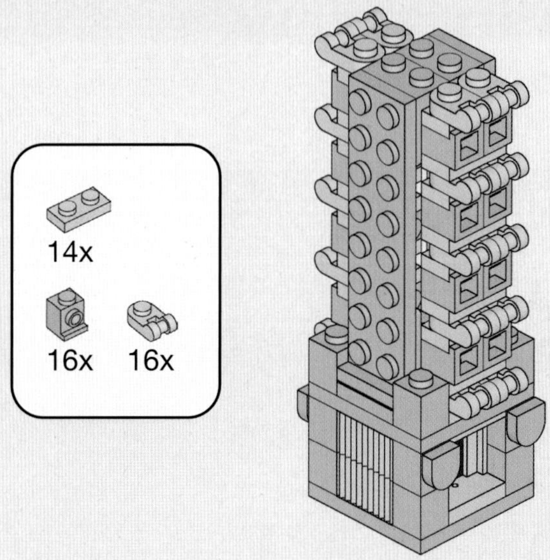

8

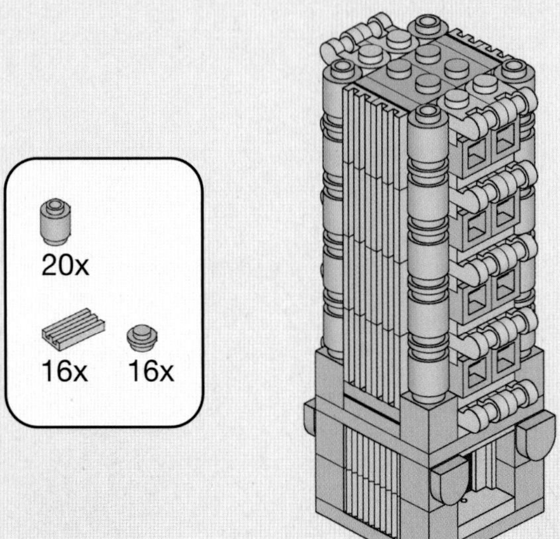

9

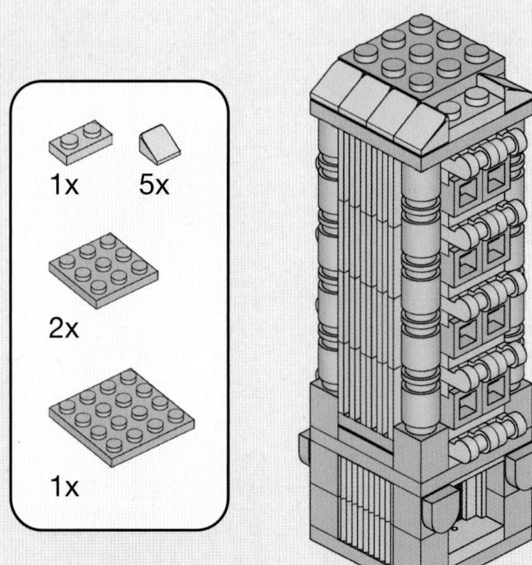

10

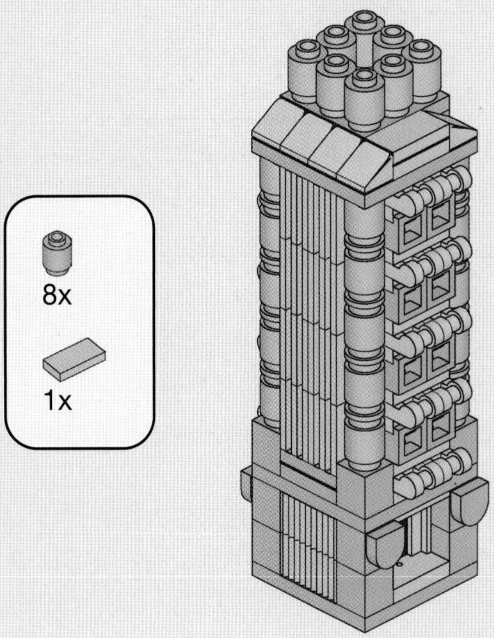

11

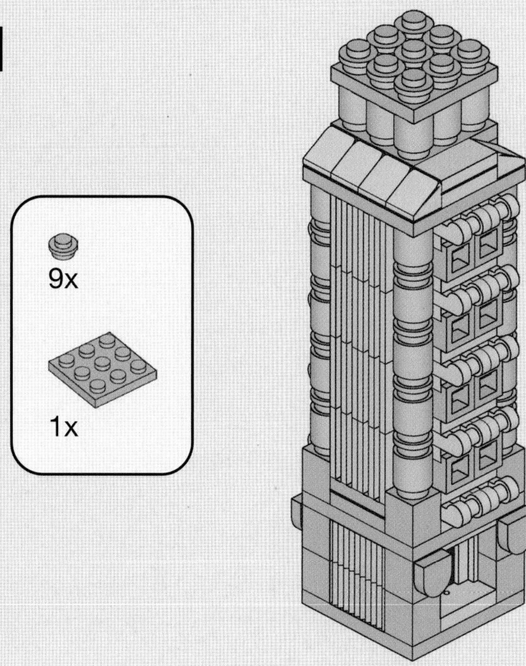

12

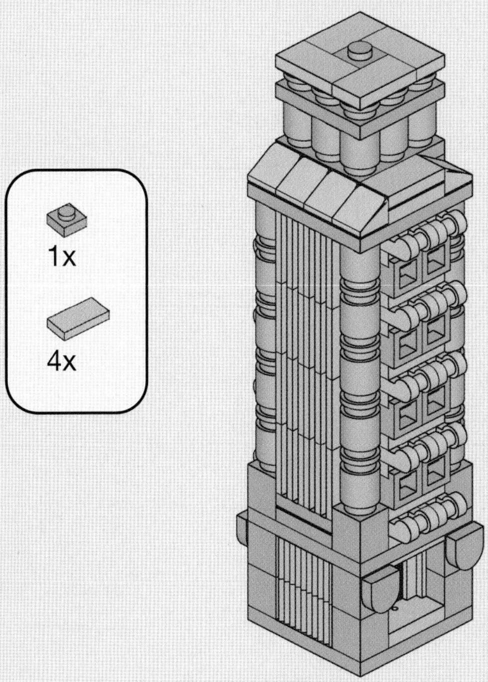

13

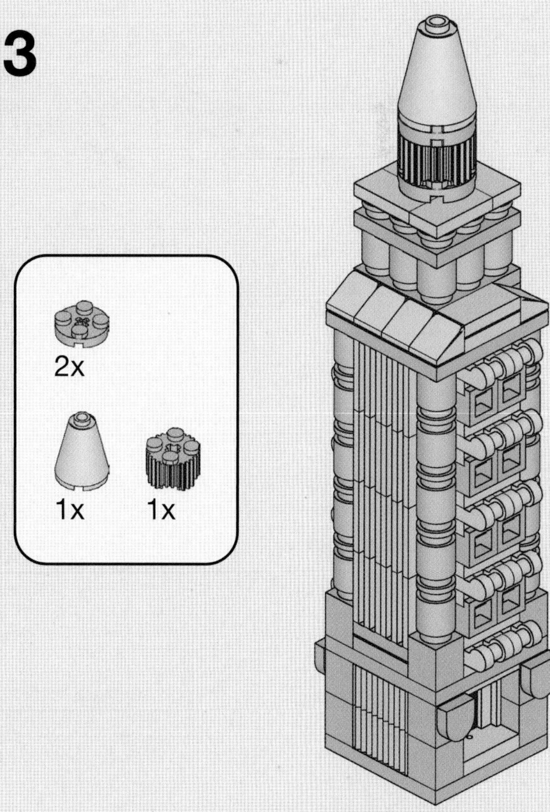

THE SHINING GATE

The Shining Gate is a radiant tied-arch bridge that provides passage into your LEGO world. A landmark bridge is more than just infrastructure; it's a symbol of transition and triumph over obstacles.

The bridge rests on massive piers that also double as apartments for those who don't mind the thunderous noise of passing trains.

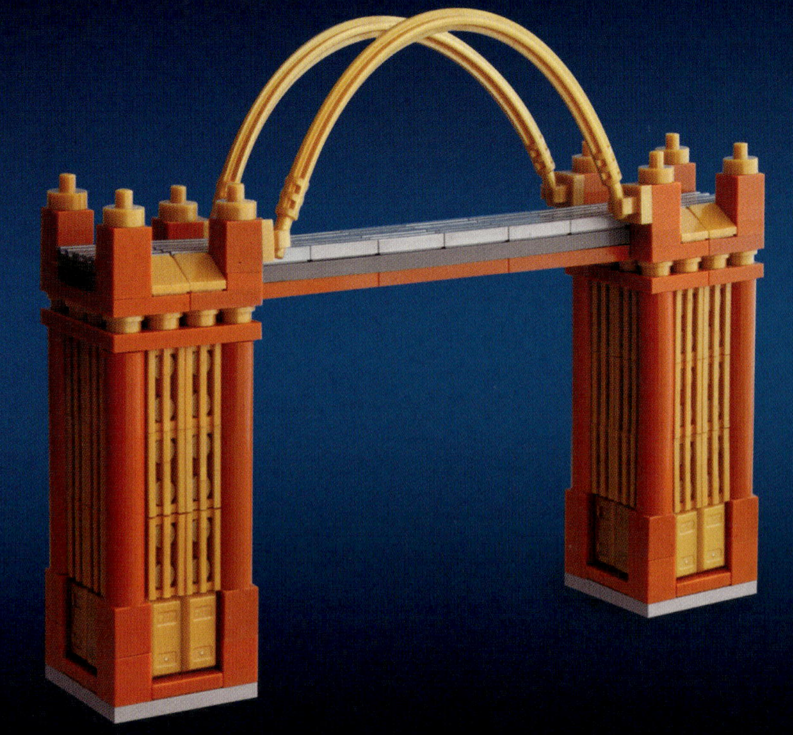

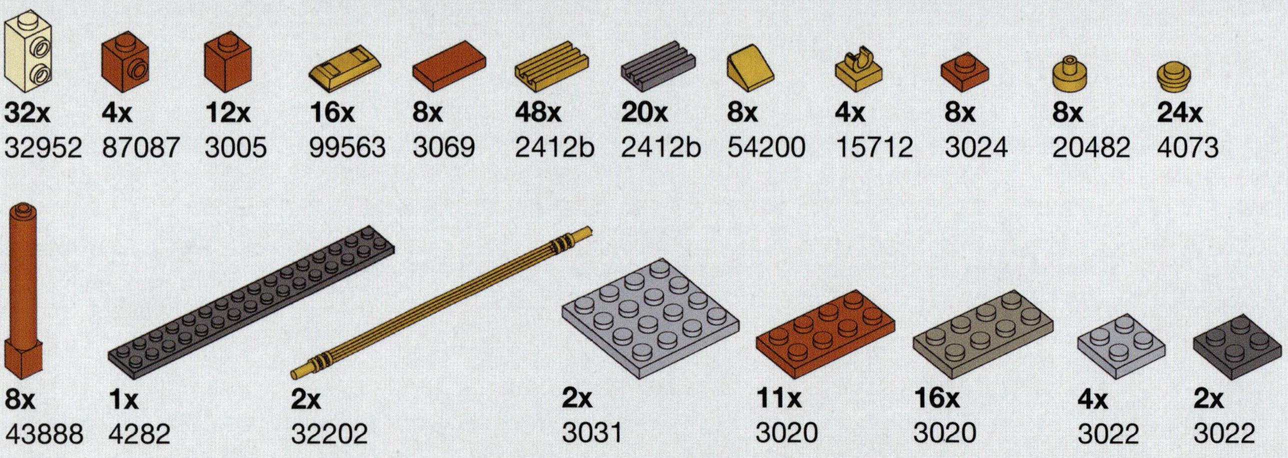

1

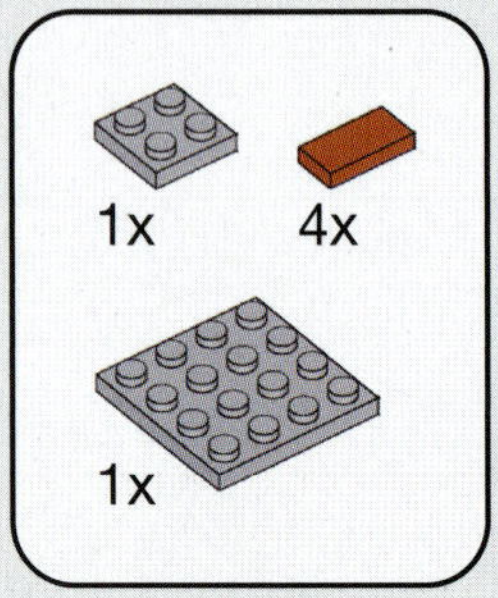

From steps 1 to 6, the model is identical on all sides.

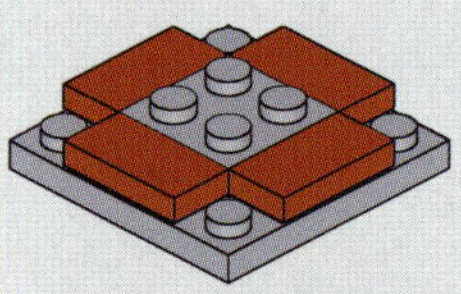

2

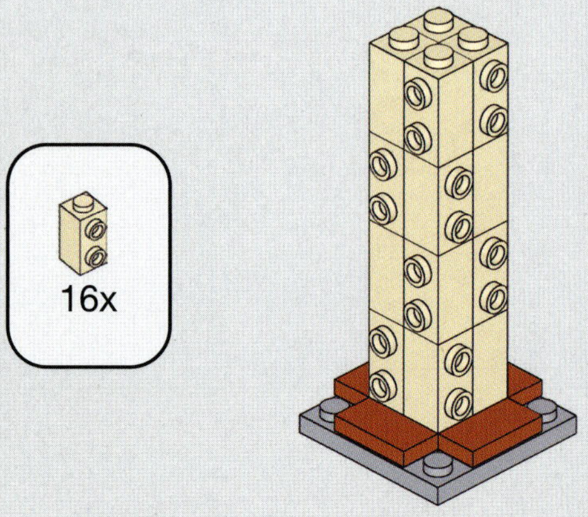

3

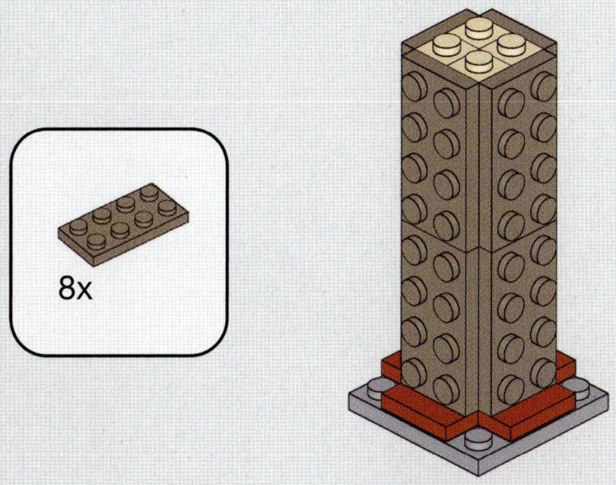

4

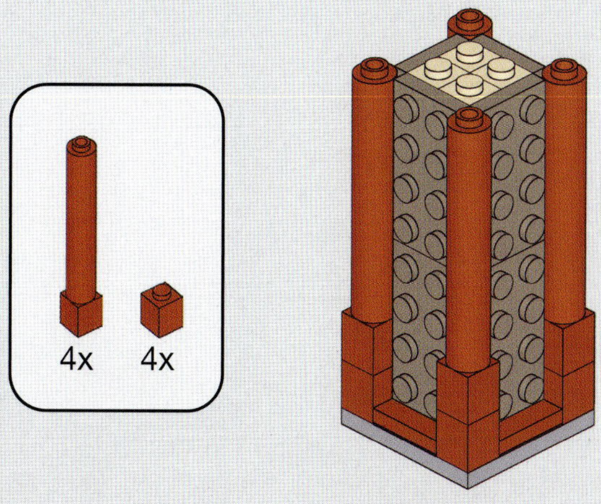

5

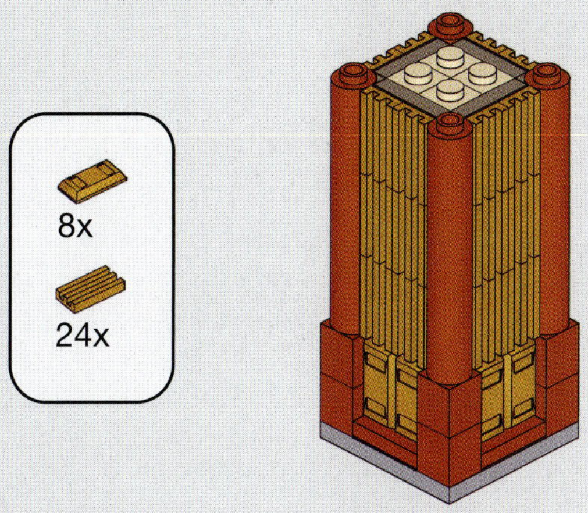

6

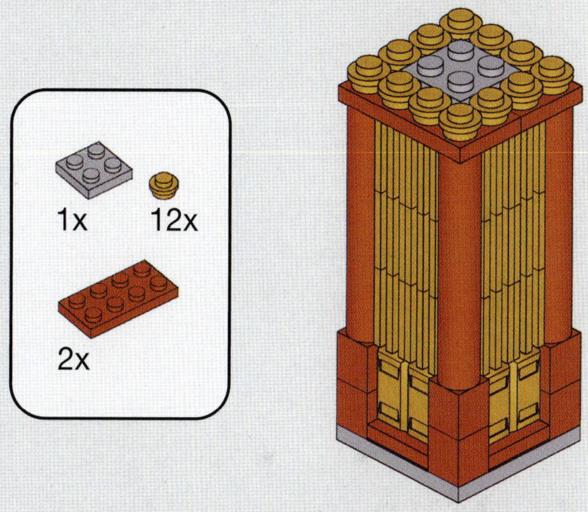

7

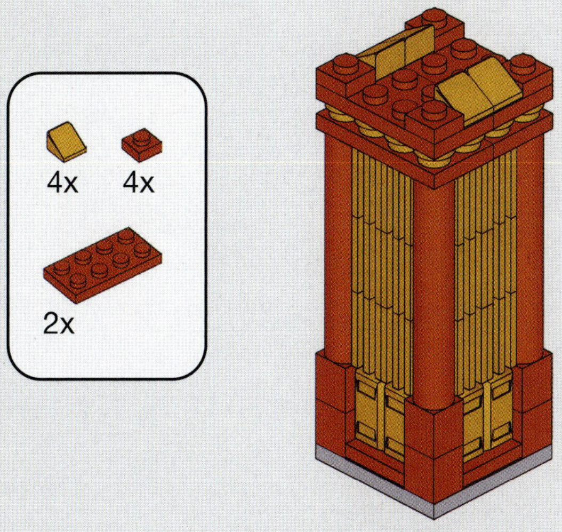

8

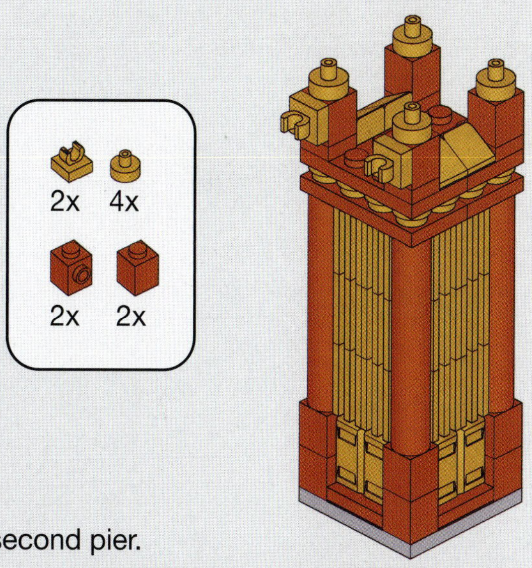

Repeat steps 1 to 8 to build a second pier.

9

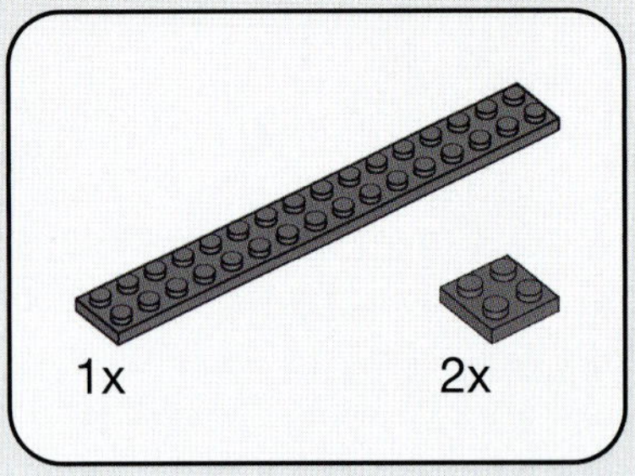

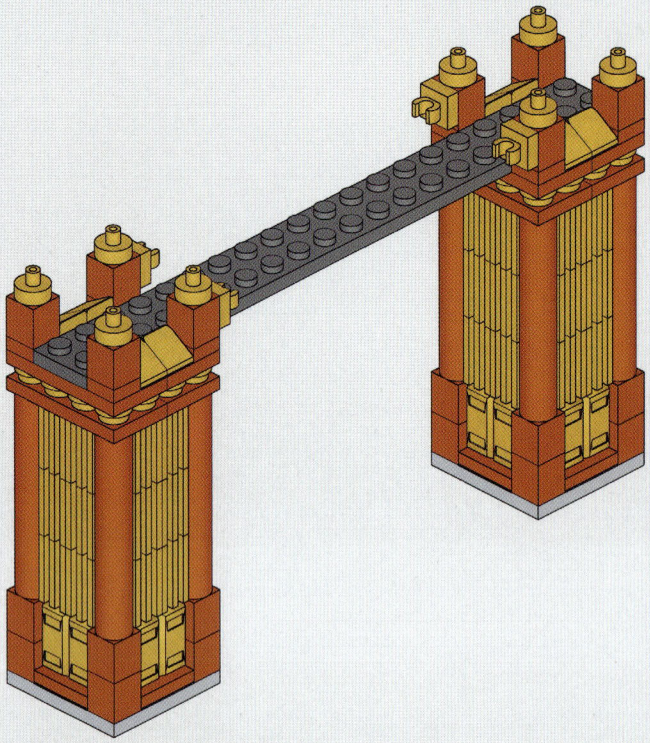

10

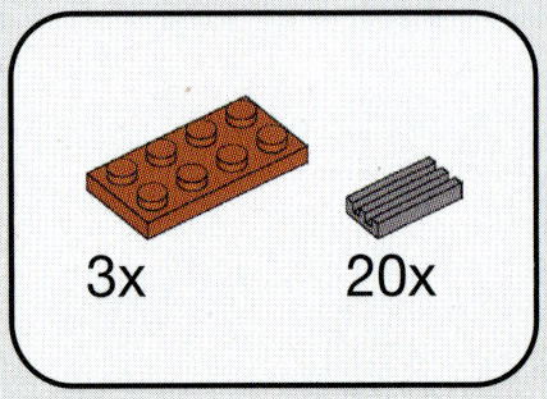

Attach the 2×4 plates from below.

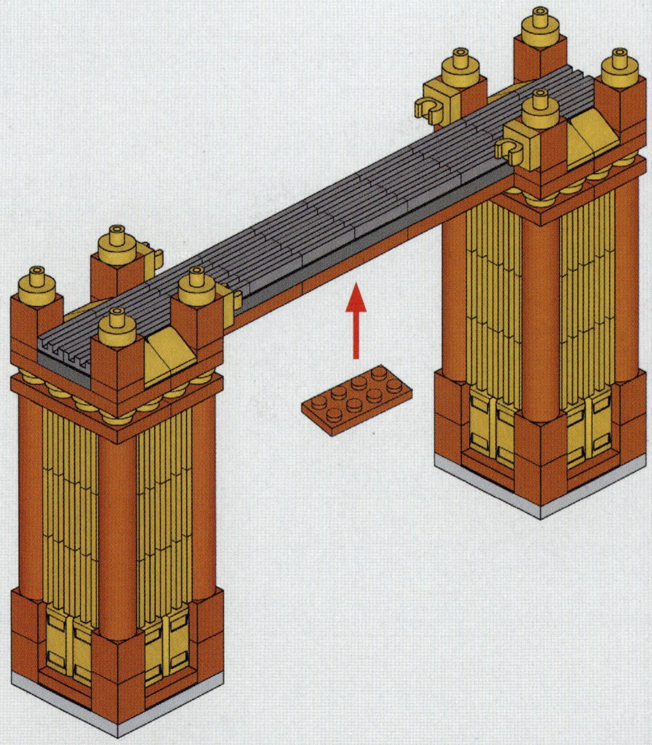

11

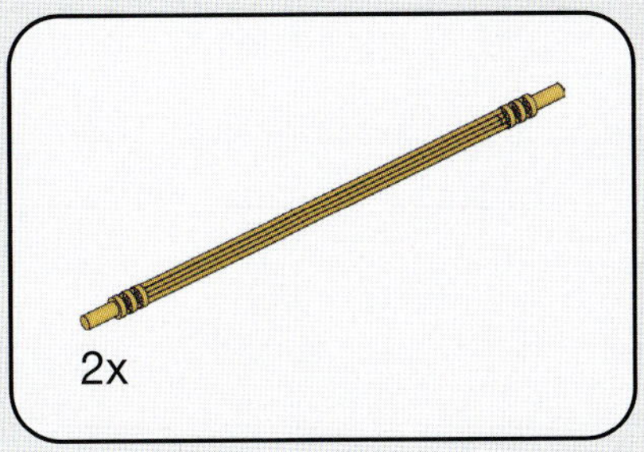

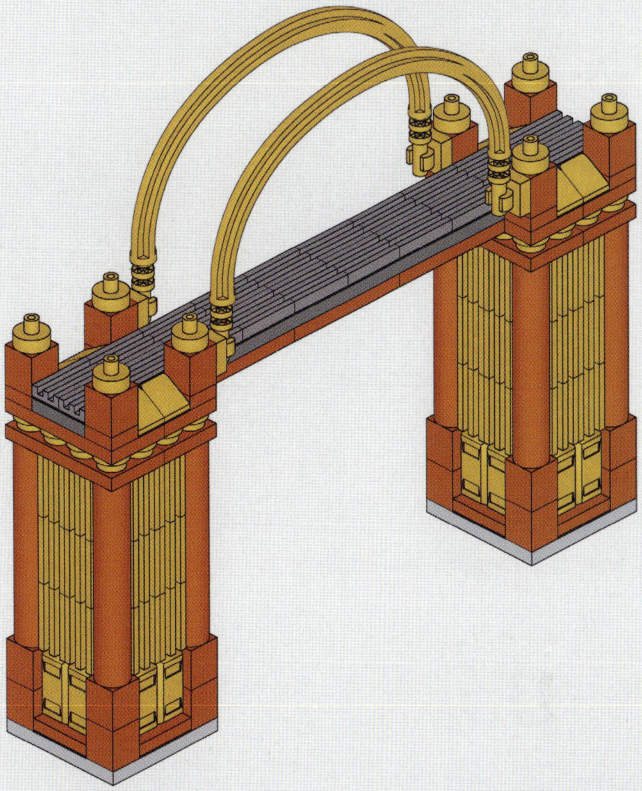

MAKE IT YOUR OWN

If you don't have soft axle pieces to create arches, no problem! You'll still end up with a monumental beam bridge. Add towers on either side for extra architectural flair.

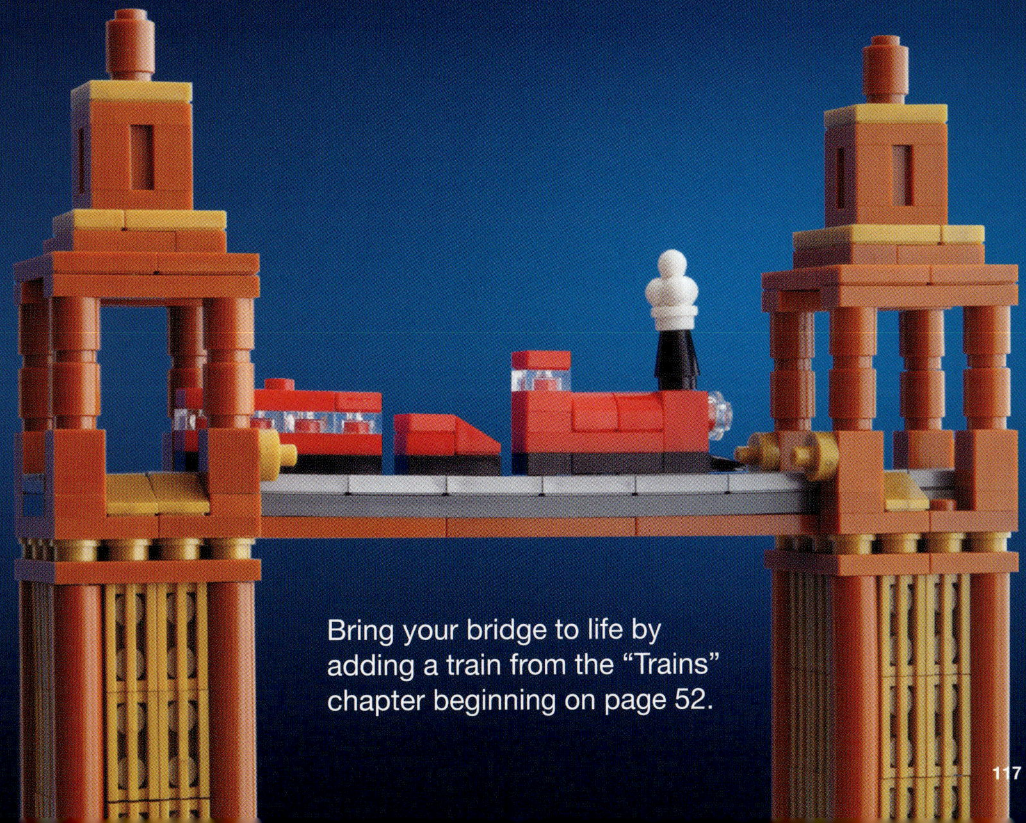

Bring your bridge to life by adding a train from the "Trains" chapter beginning on page 52.

CLOUD CASTLE

Are you searching for the crown jewel of your LEGO skyline? Cloud Castle is a Baroque skyscraper that takes opulence to the stratosphere.

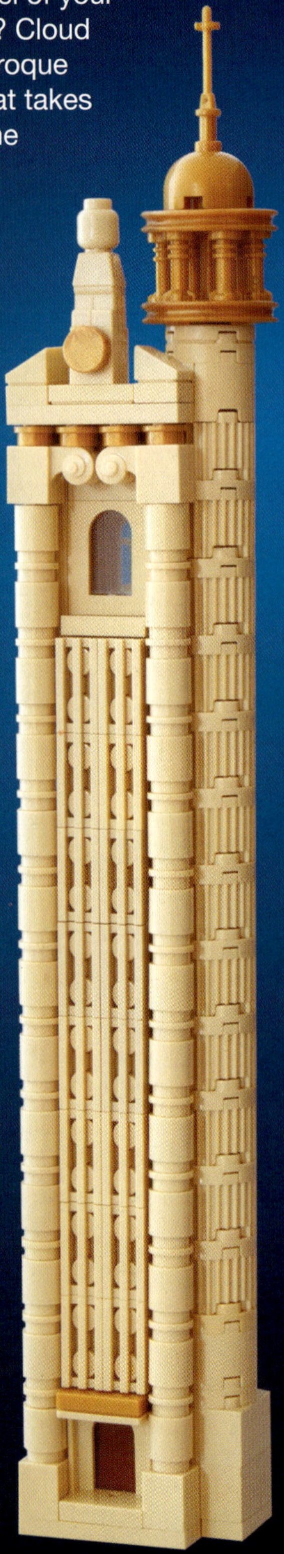

Quantity	Part
2x	87087
4x	3005
52x	3062
48x	4073
10x	4073
2x	98138
1x	90540
1x	85863
6x	64567
1x	553
32x	2412b
6x	54200
2x	4185
4x	90195
12x	3003
2x	3003
12x	92947
1x	3941
1x	68013
8x	11211
19x	4216
4x	20310
1x	15535
14x	4032
2x	60601
2x	3710
2x	32028
1x	3023
1x	3023
2x	15573
1x	3031
1x	3031
1x	30374
3x	3022
2x	4282
4x	3069

1

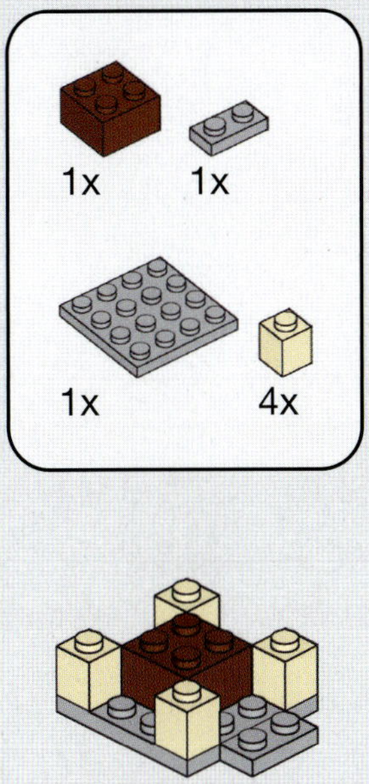

2

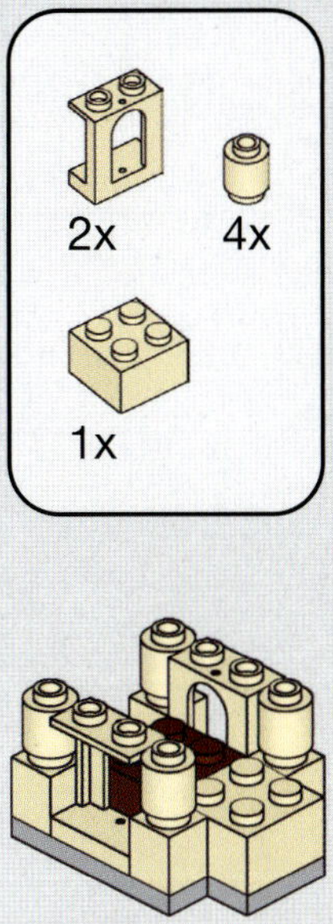

3

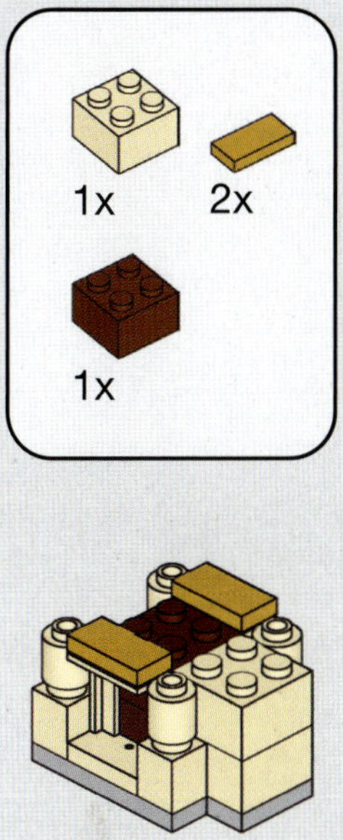

4

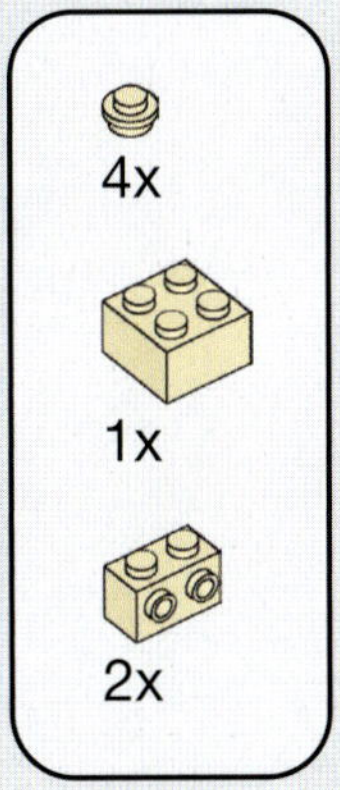

The front and back are identical in this step.

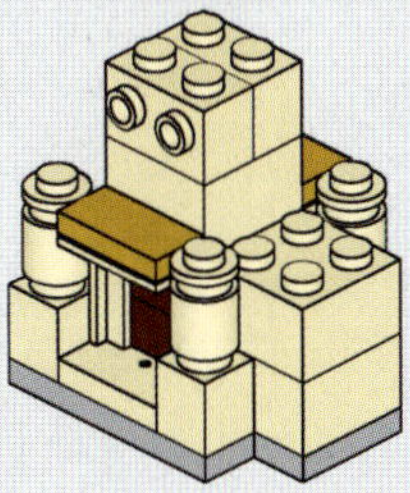

5

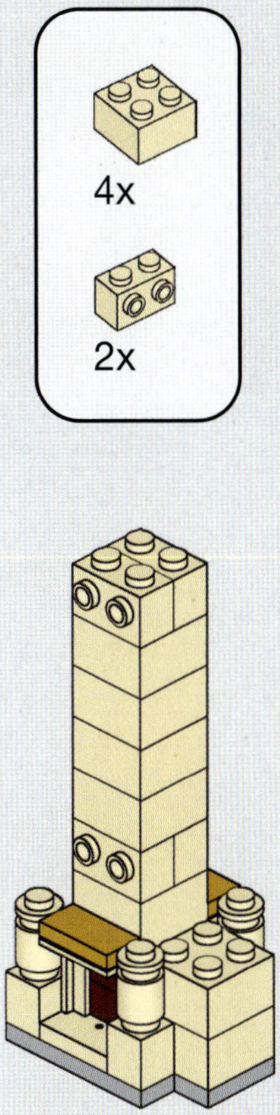

6

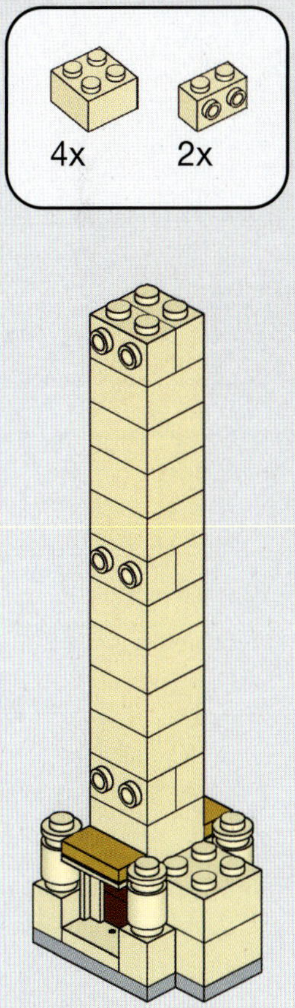

7

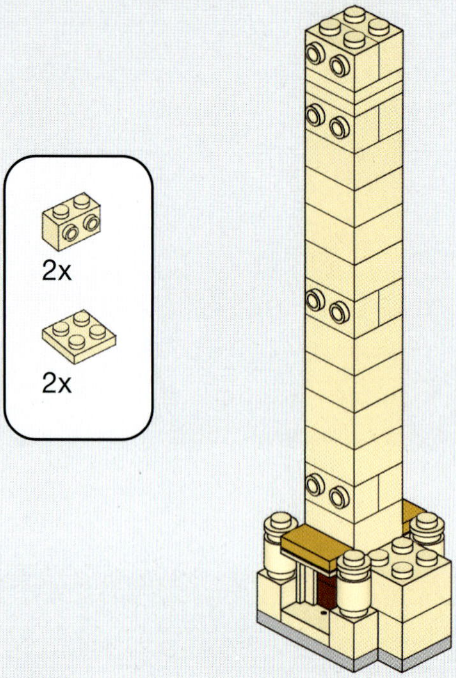

8

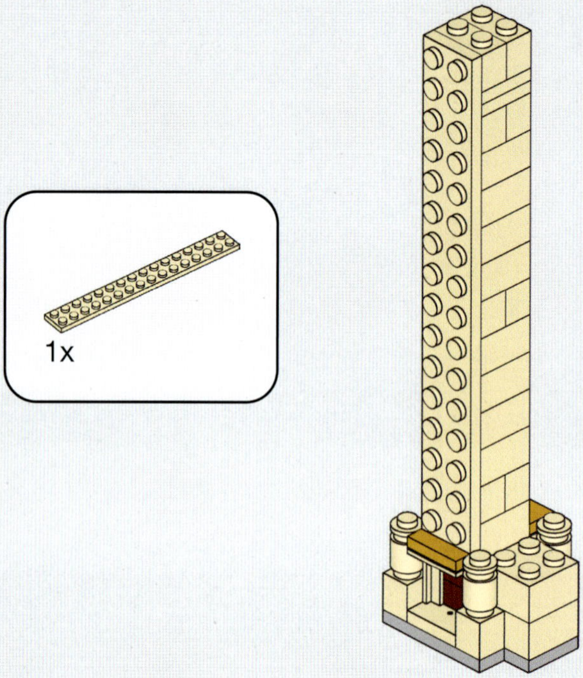

9

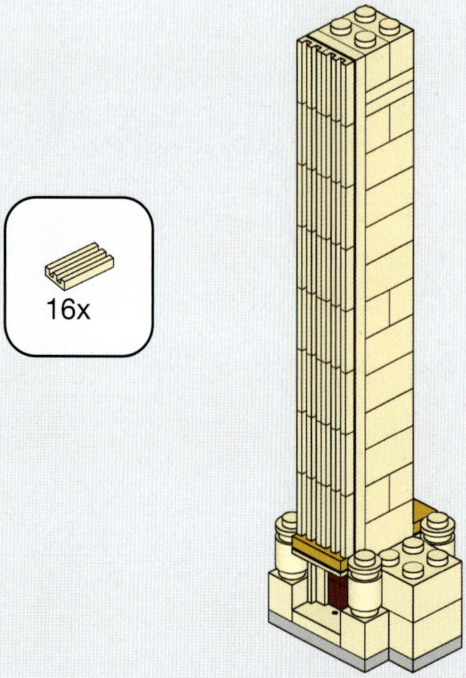

10

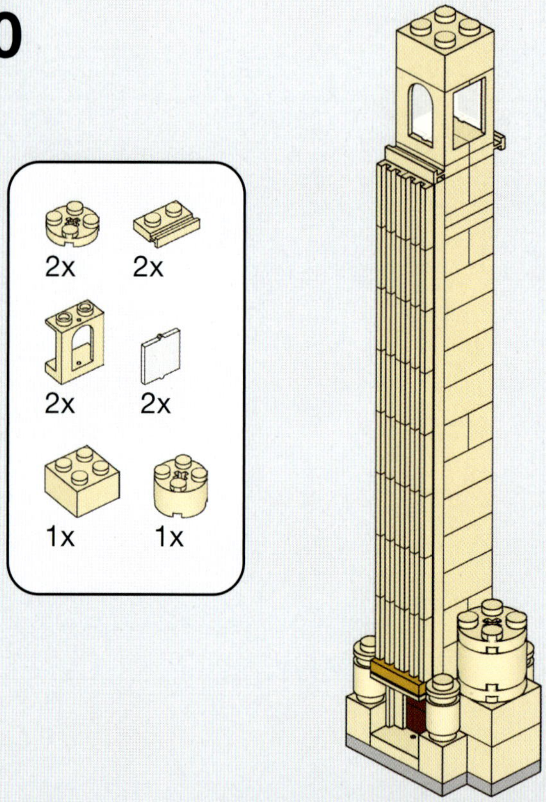

11

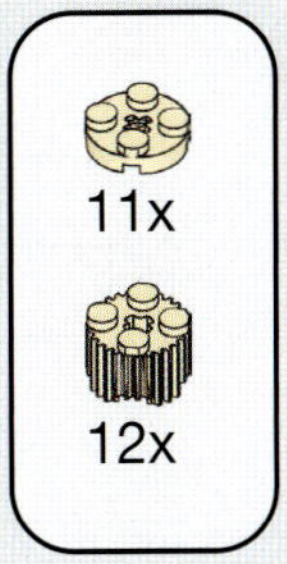

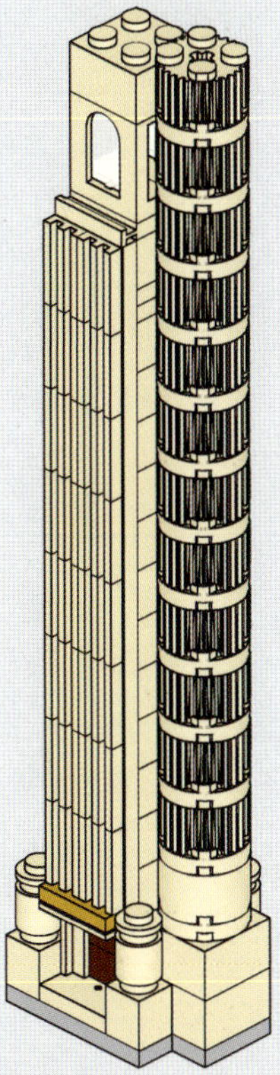

12

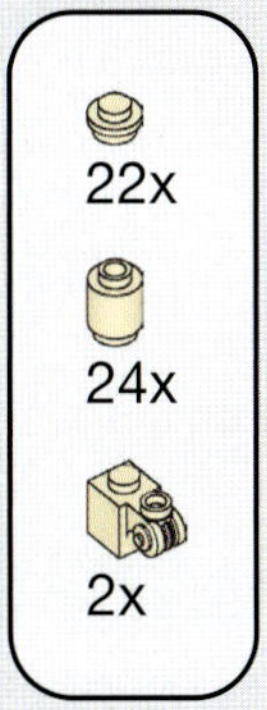

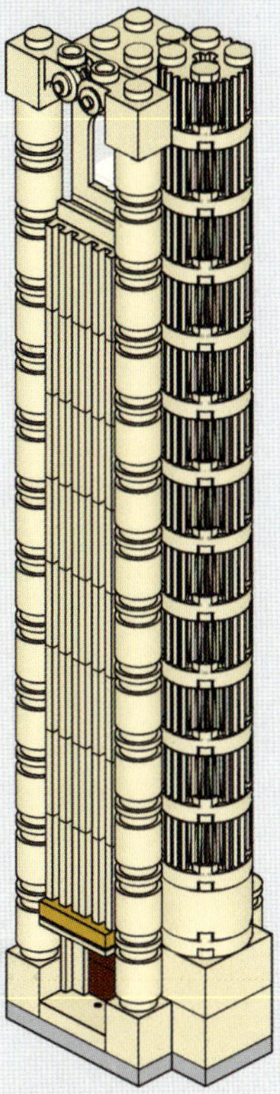

13

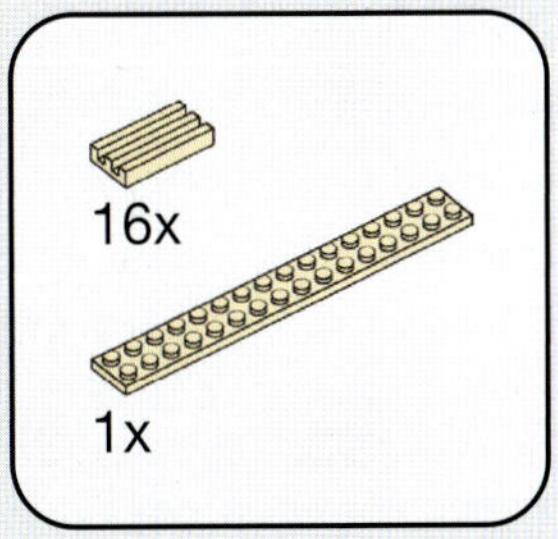

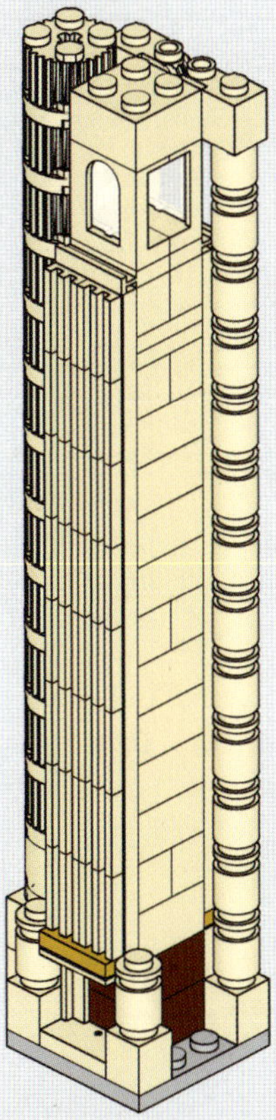

14

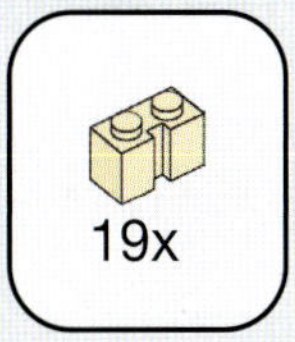

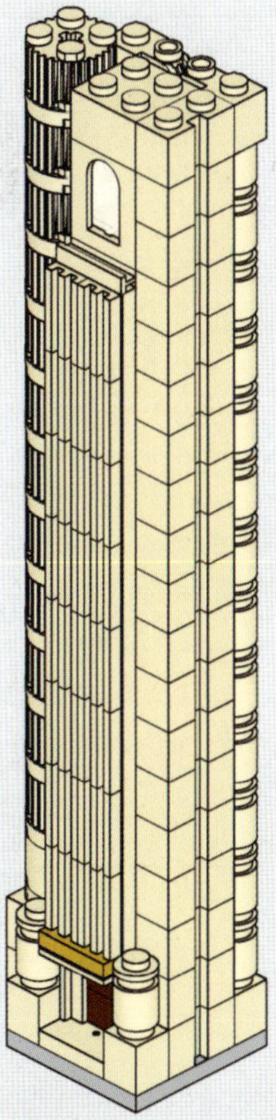

15

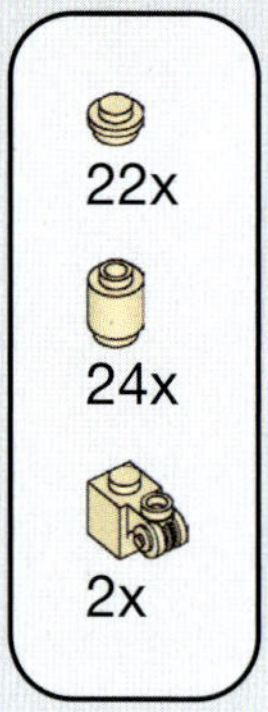

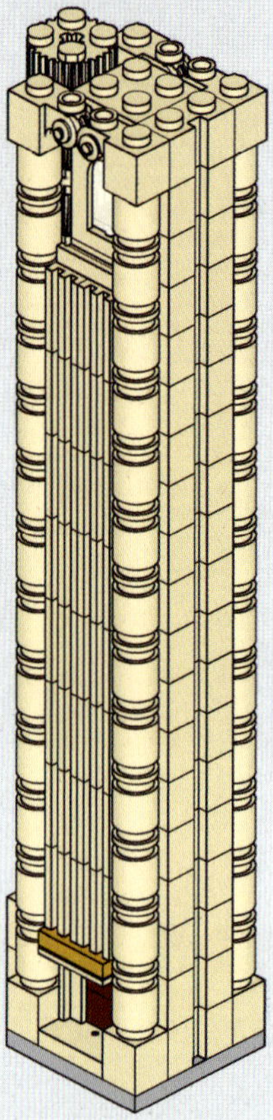

16

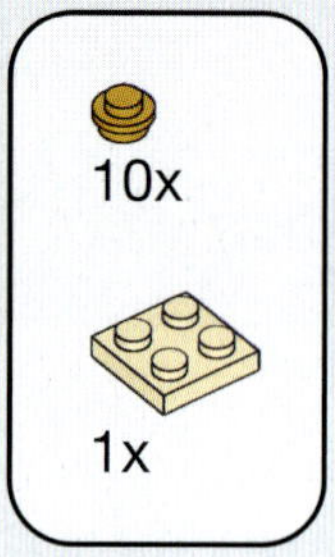

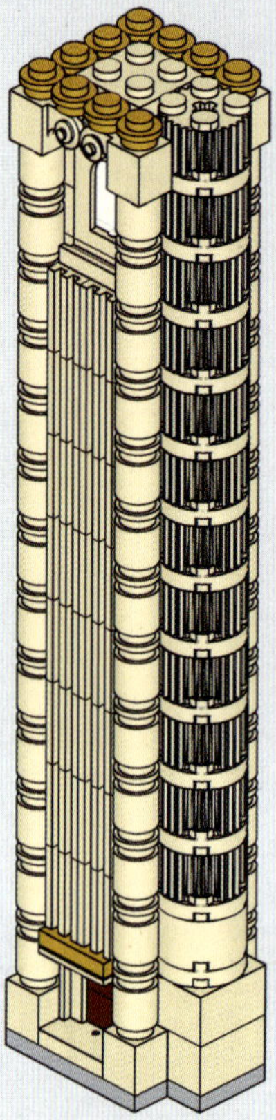

17

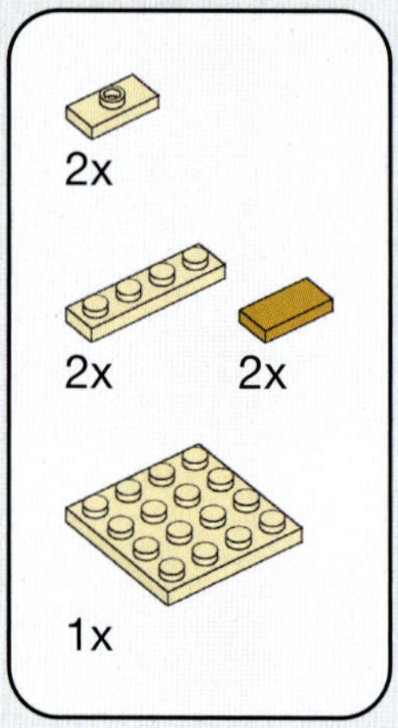

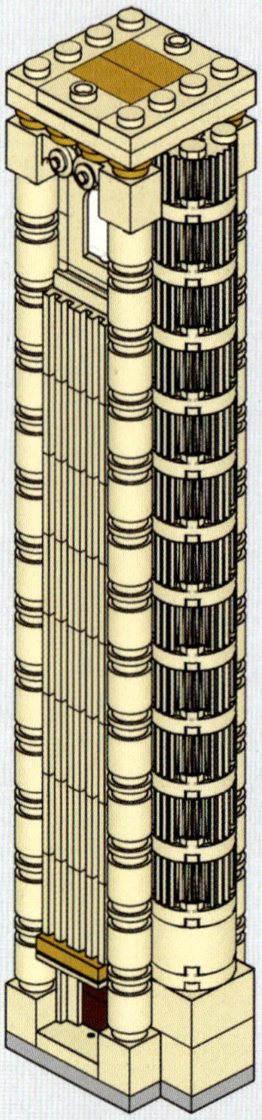

18

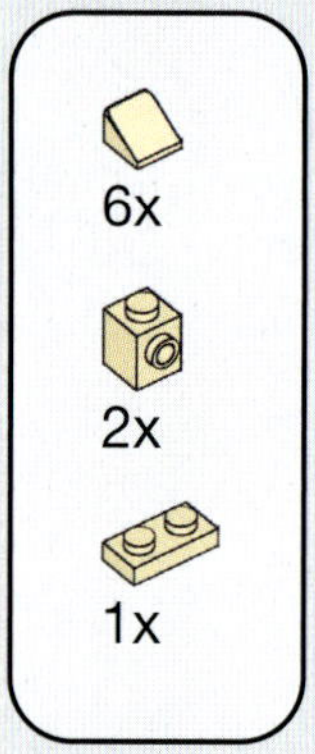

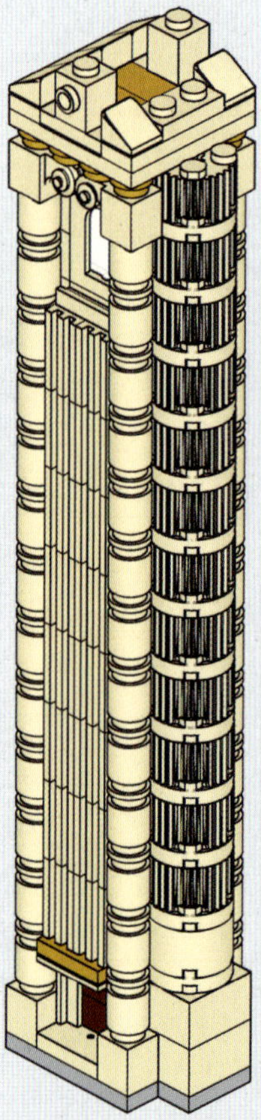

19

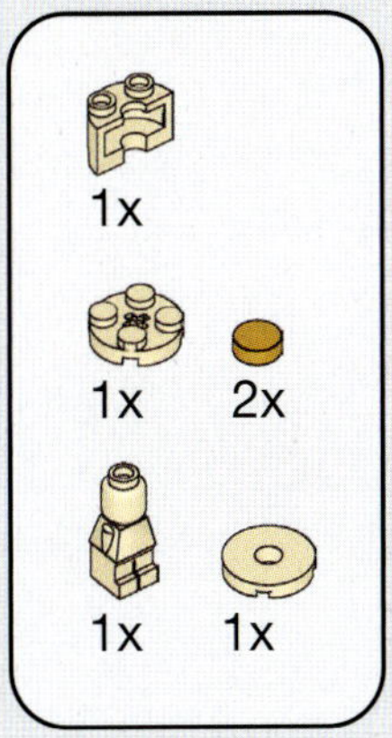

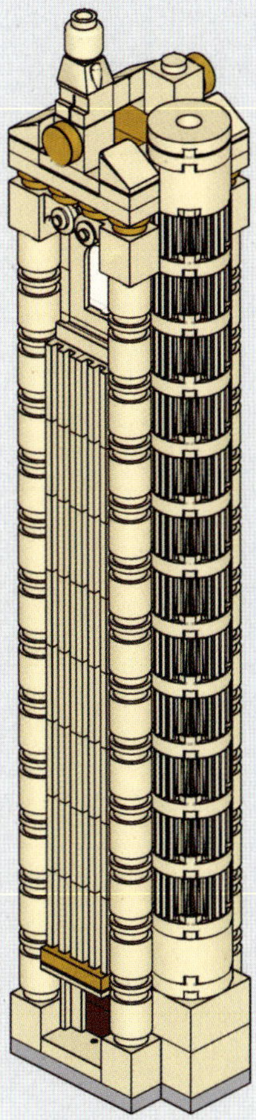

20

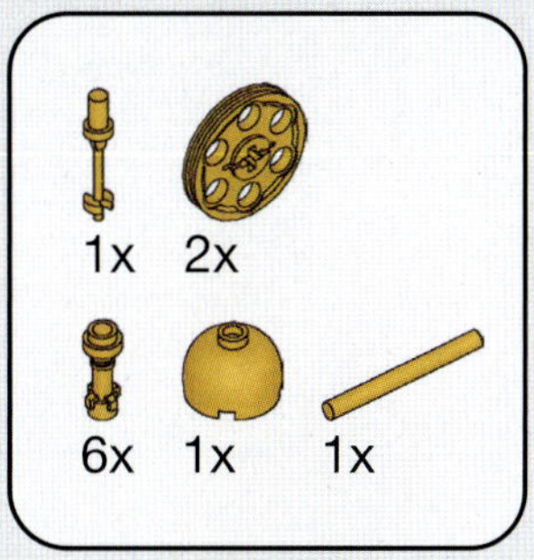

a

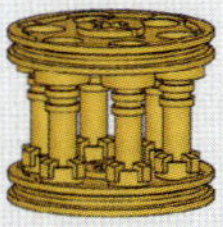

b

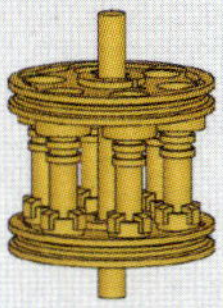

c

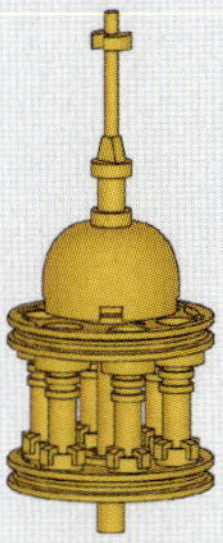

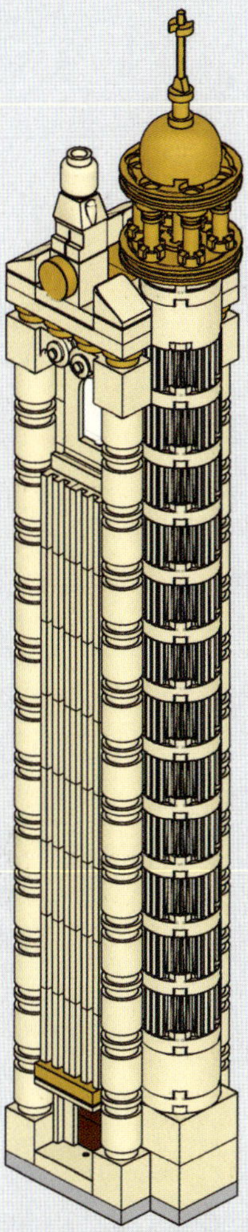

MAKE IT YOUR OWN

The Cloud Castle's roof defines its presence in the sky, and it's easy to personalize. Add a narrow-base chicken (#95342) to keep a watchful eye on the city below.

Replace the golden rotunda with a detailed castle turret. Instructions are provided on the right.

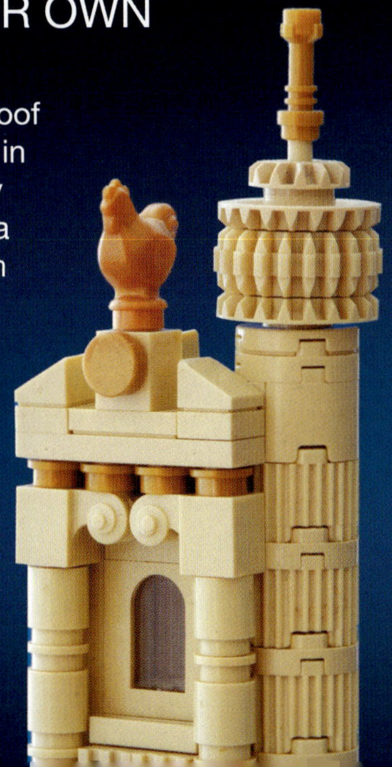

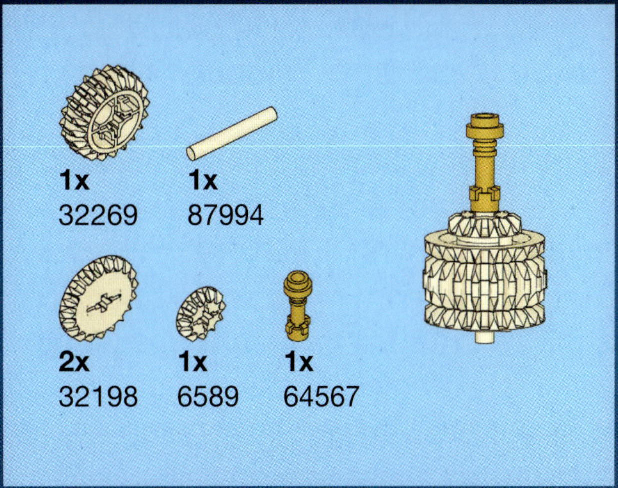

MODERN METROPOLIS

LEGO's clean, modular essence makes it naturally suited to building a modern world of high-tech structures and efficient transportation. Like any great design, a great LEGO model balances aesthetic appeal with practical function. Every LEGO element holds both artistic and engineering potential, some immediately apparent and others revealed through creative experimentation.

LEGO lets you think like a designer, engineer, and architect all at once. In this chapter, you'll explore techniques that might seem impossible at first, such as creating curved forms using only right-angled bricks. Build a world where creativity and innovation shape the future.

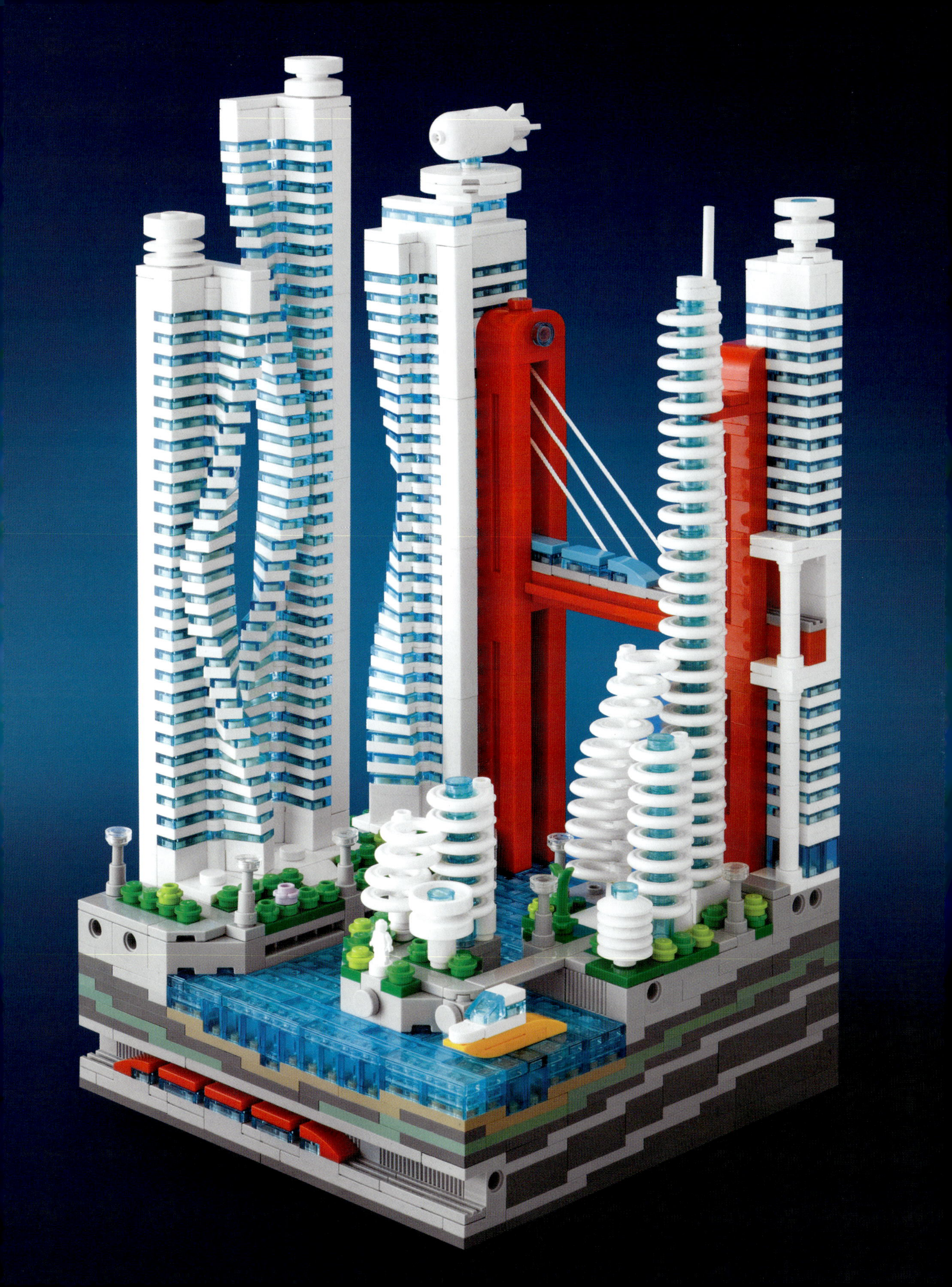

SKYWAVE

The Skywave is a skyscraper designed for endless transformation. Thanks to hinge elements, its parabolic curves can be reshaped at will, allowing you to customize its silhouette as often as you like.

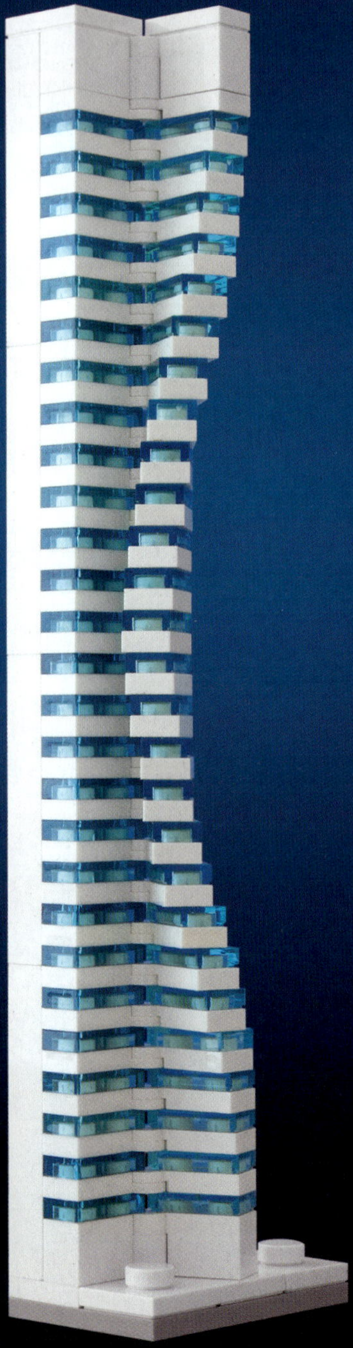

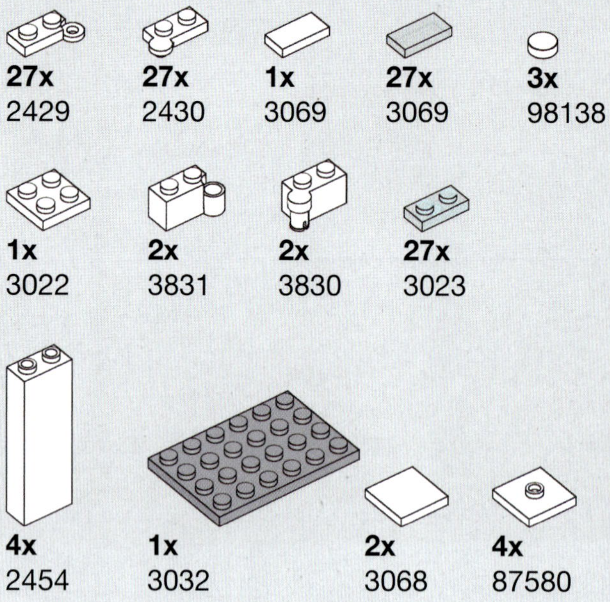

1

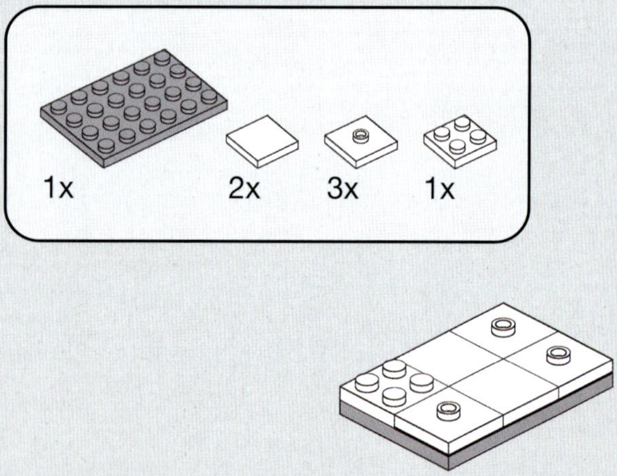

2

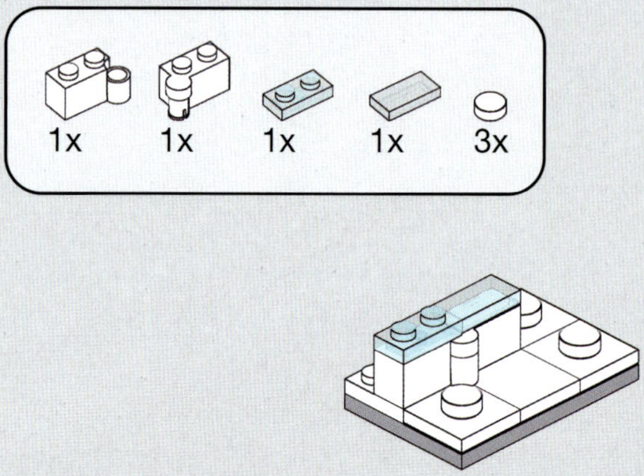

3

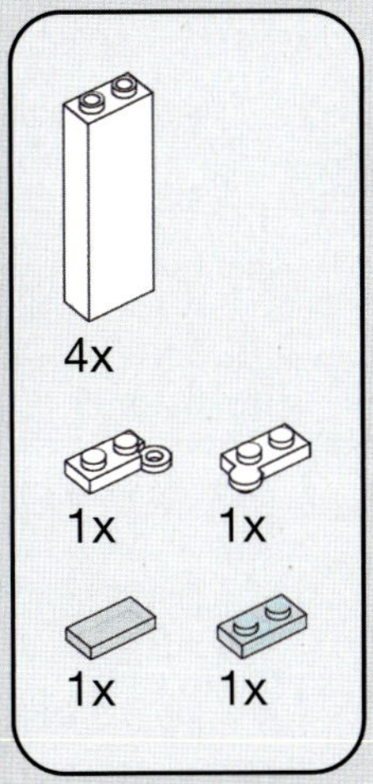

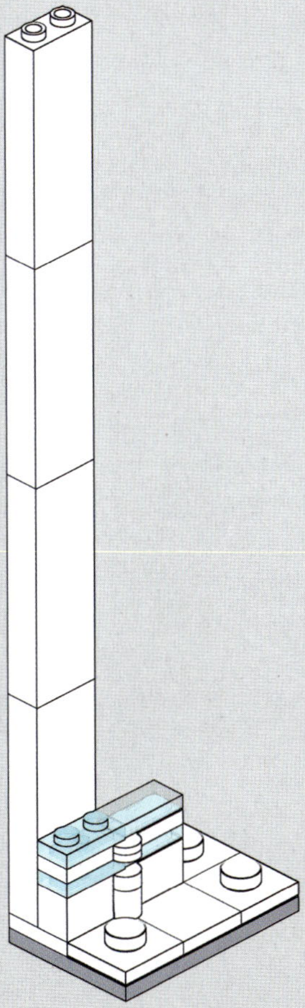

4

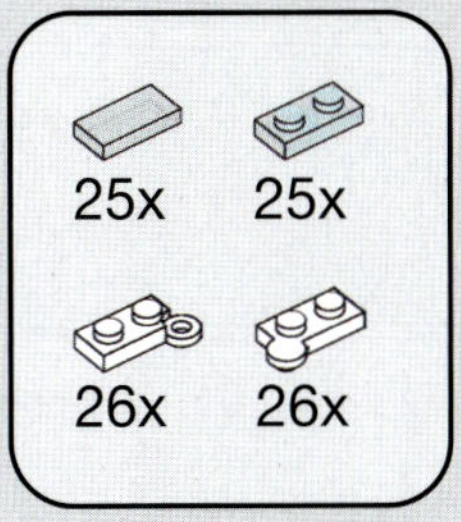

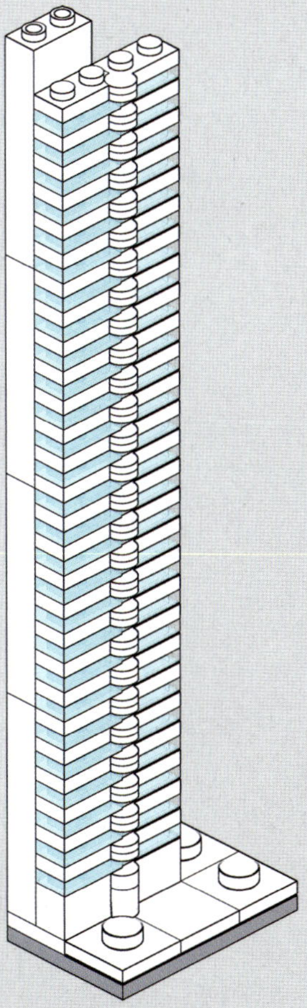

5

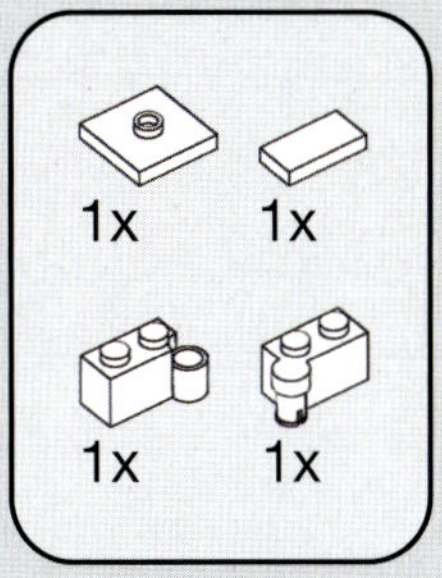

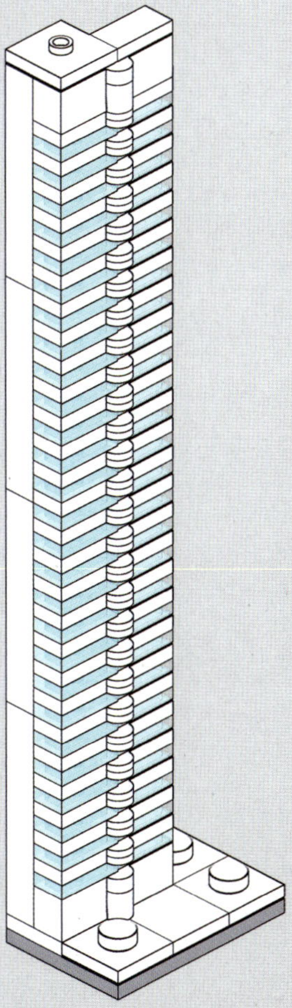

6

Shape the model as shown below, or create your own unique design. The next page has more ideas for shaping your Skywave building.

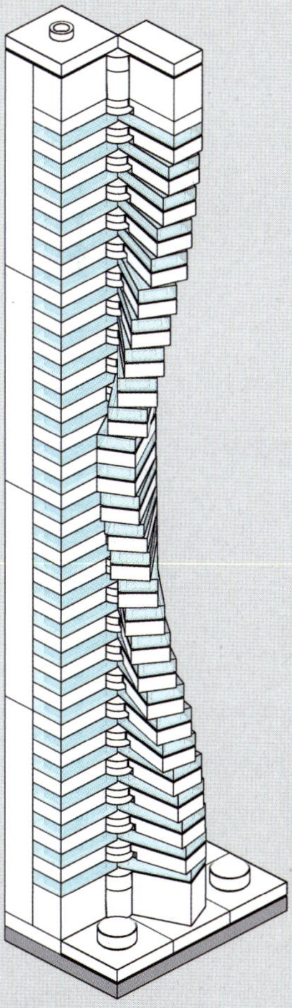

MAKE IT YOUR OWN

Here are some examples of Skywave shaping. Using only the Skywave instructions, you can create an entire city of unique skyscrapers. To add a transportation feature, include the Blimp Landing Pad shown on the facing page.

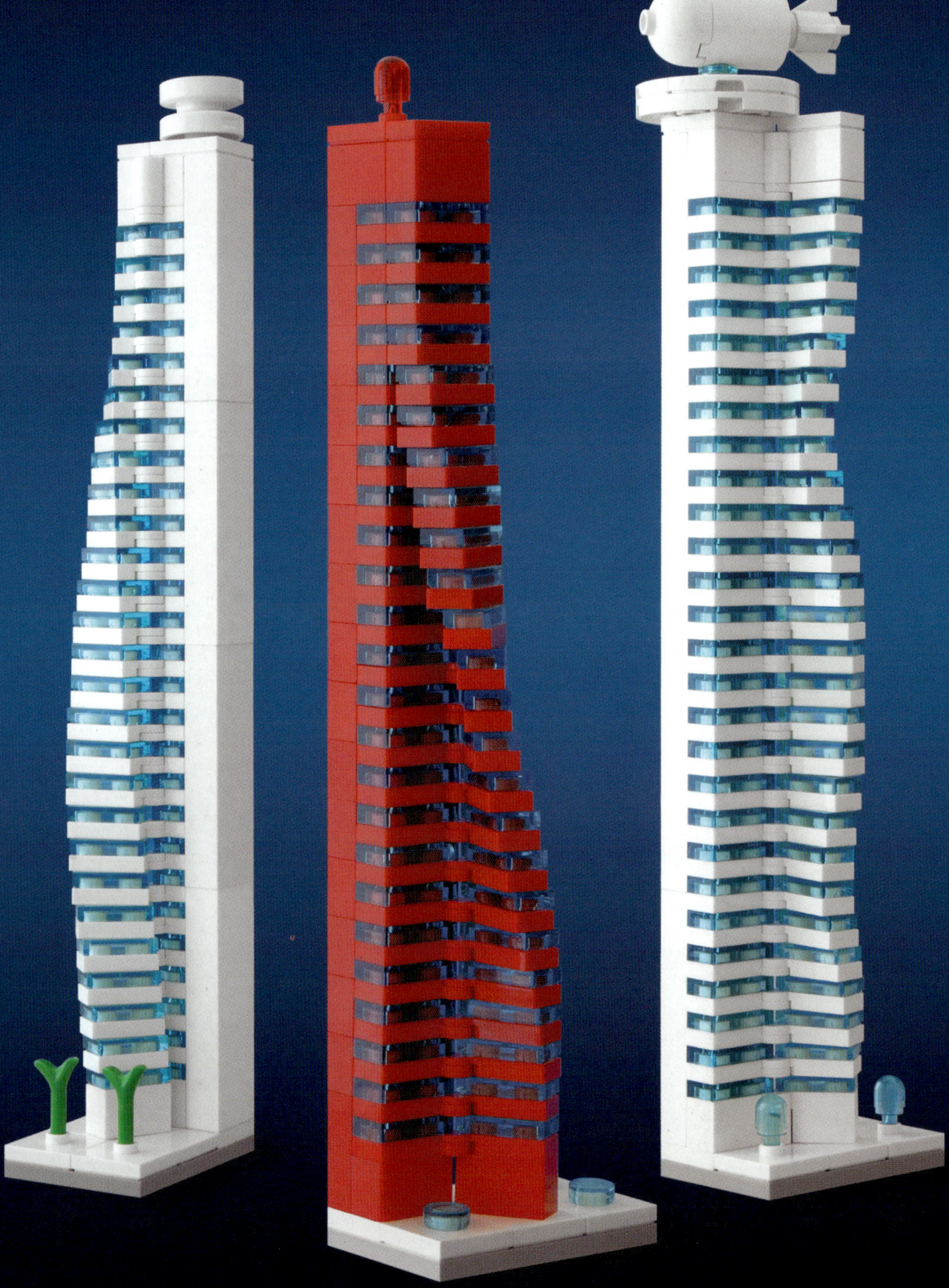

BLIMP LANDING PAD

Use the Blimp Landing Pad on its own, or attach it to the top of a skyscraper above city streets.

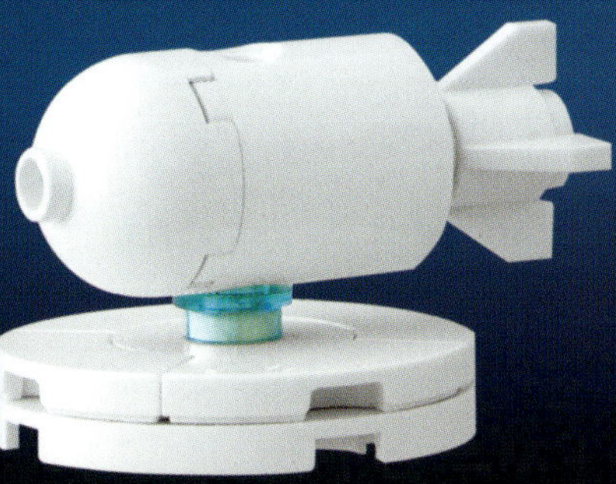

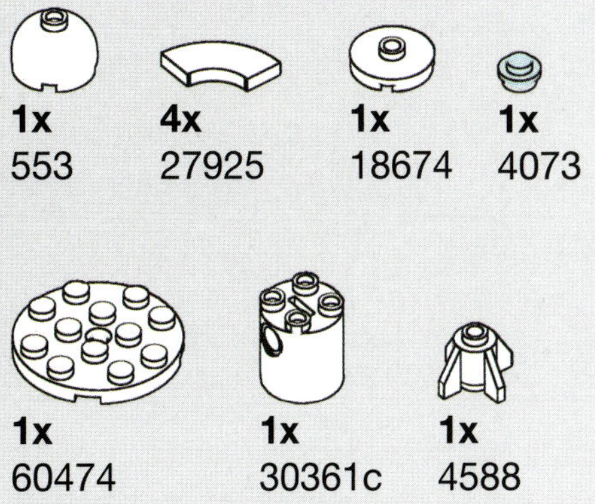

1

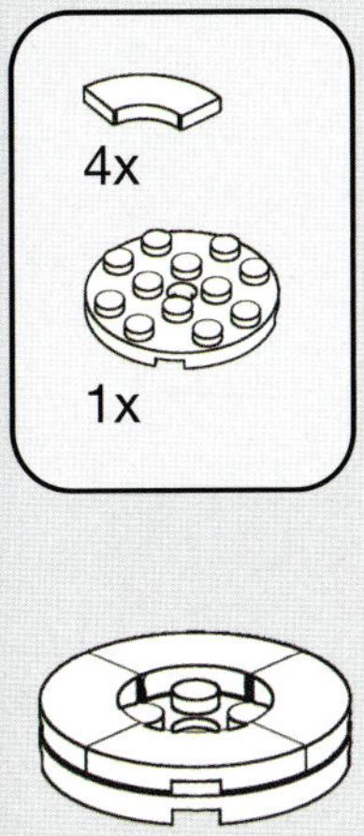

2

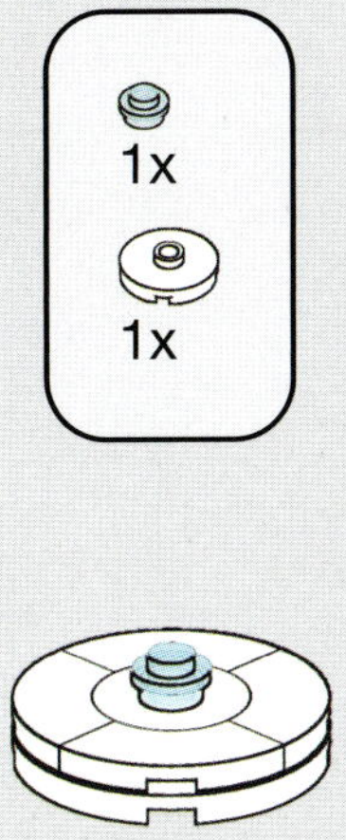

3

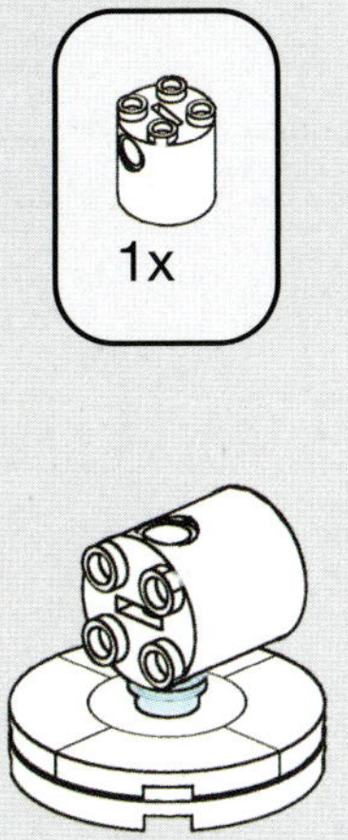

4

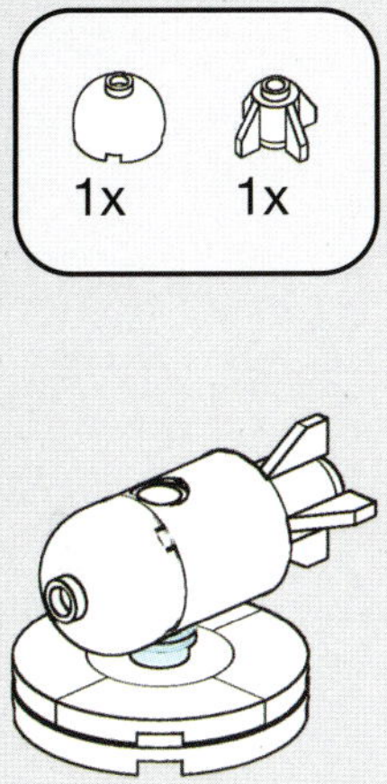

MAKE IT YOUR OWN

Raise your landing pad into the sky with a pedestal. From left to right, these landing pads rest on a 2×2 cone (#3942b), two 2×2 fluted round bricks (#92947), and a stack of 2×2 dishes (#4740).

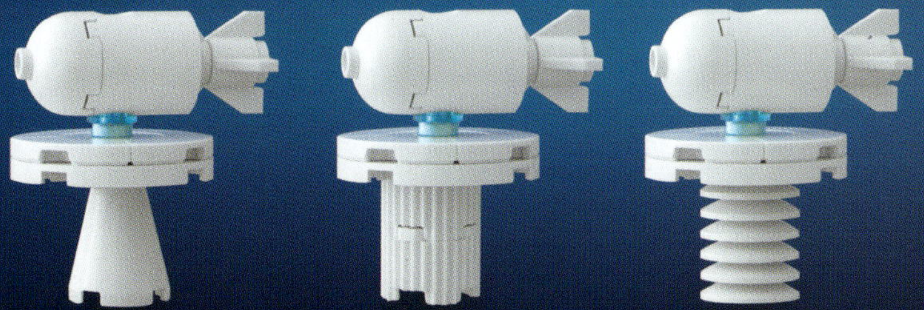

RING RISE

This modern tower blurs the line between structure and sculpture. It's made with elements usually used as minifigure life preservers. Just be sure your minifigures aren't planning a beach day!

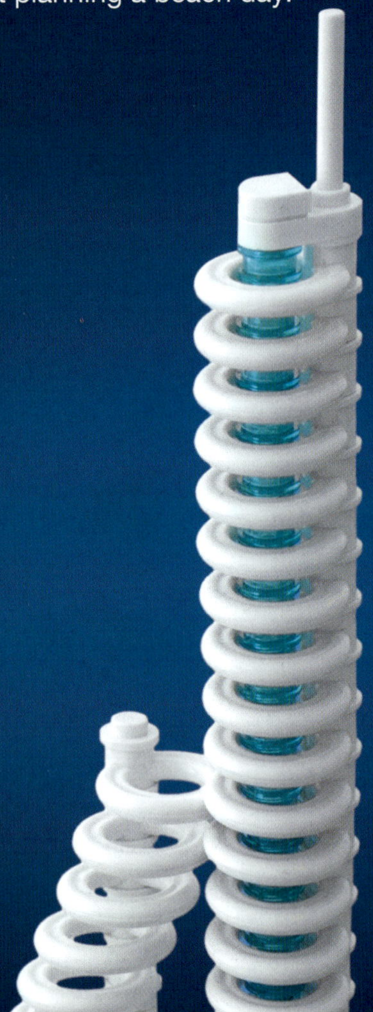

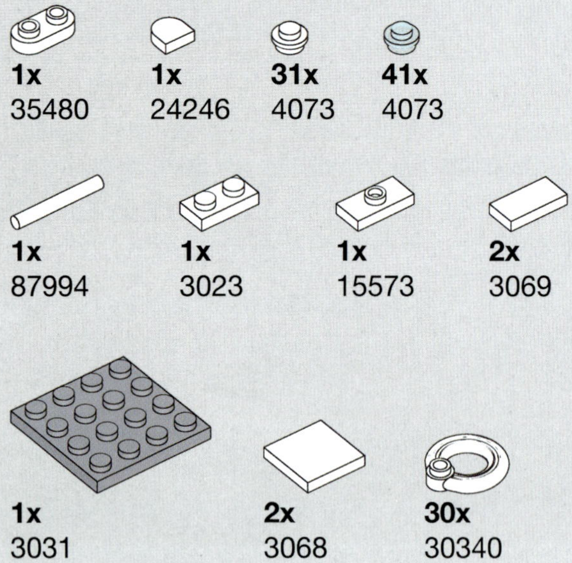

1

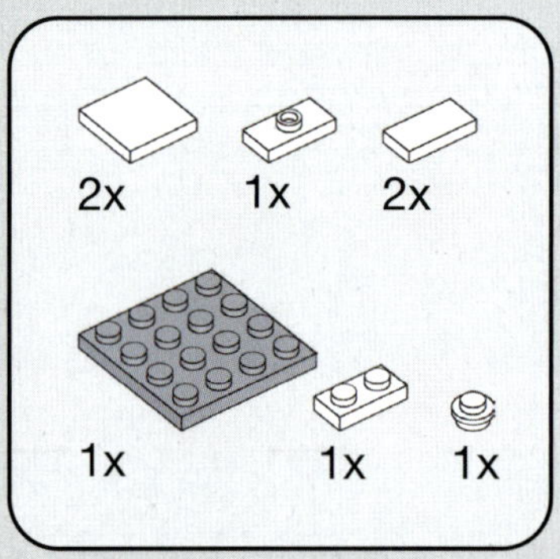

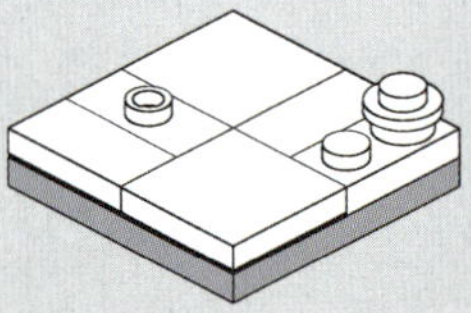

2

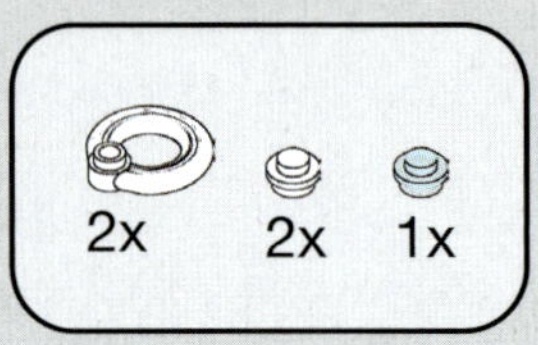

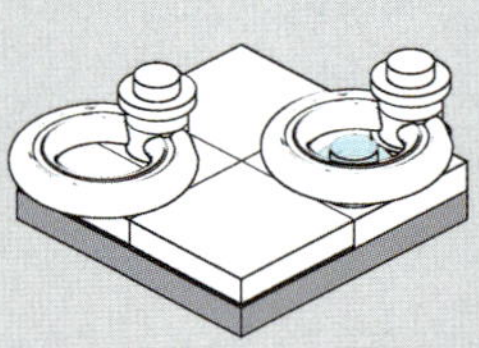

3

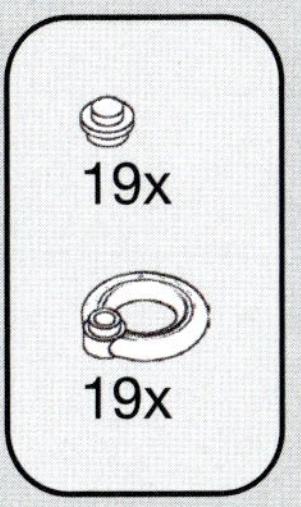

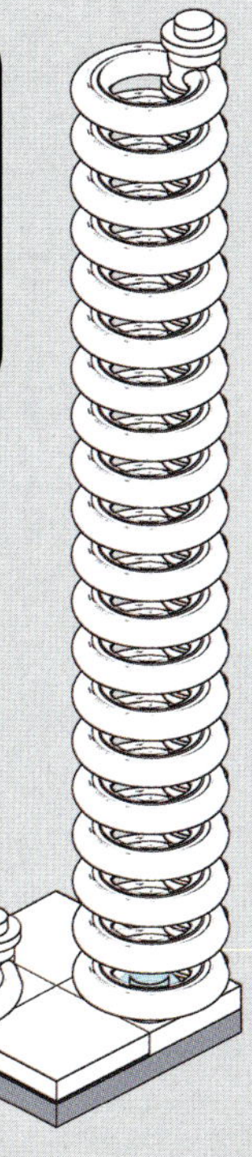

4

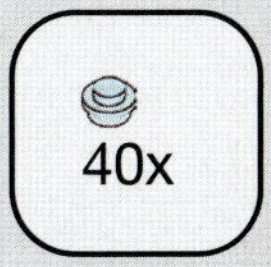

Stack the 1×1 round plates before attaching to the model.

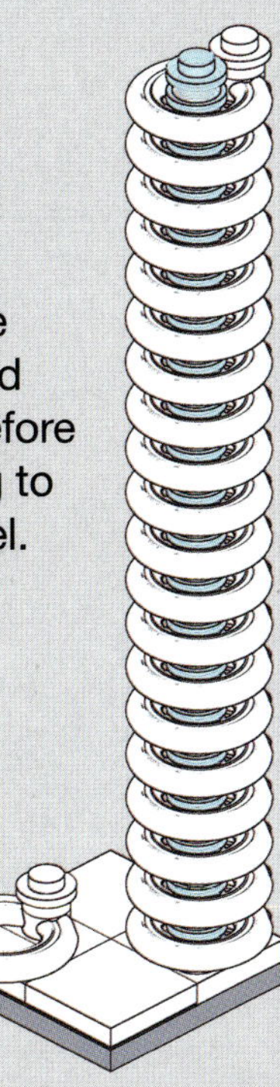

5

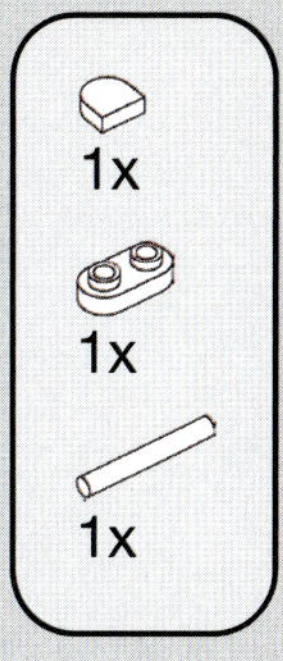

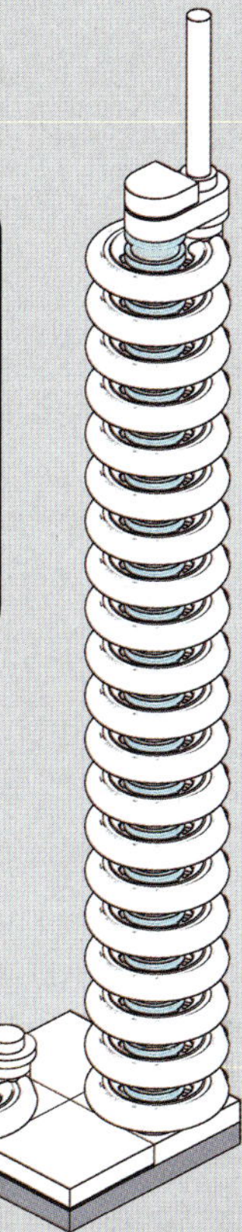

6

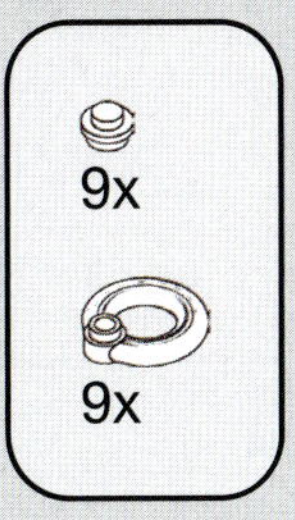

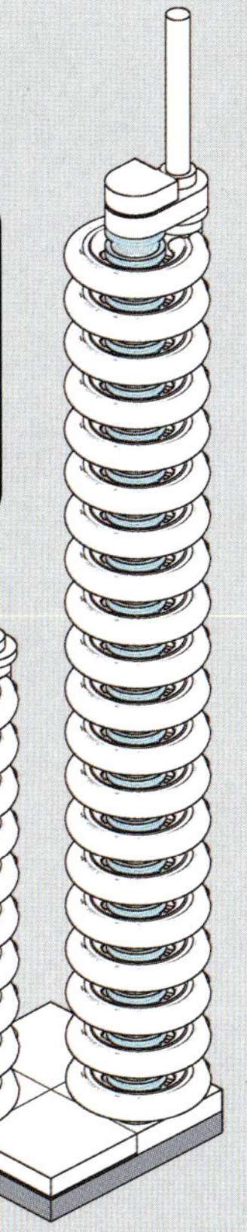

7

Twist the shorter ring column as illustrated.

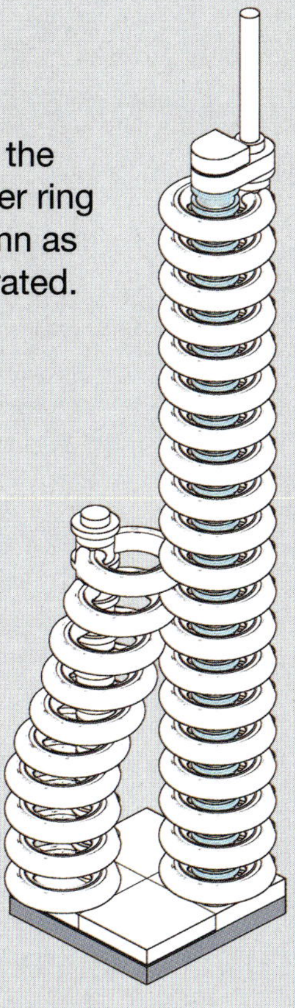

MAKE IT YOUR OWN

Forgo any semblance of practicality altogether and create a skyscraper-sized art installation.

Remove the transparent stud core from the center to freely rotate the rings.

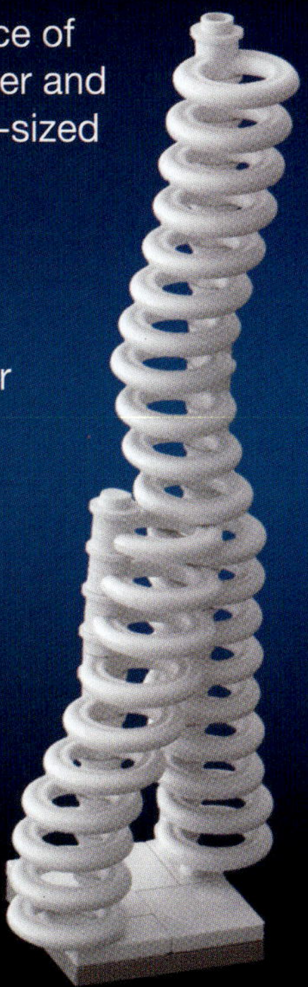

BOARDWALK

Fairgrounds and carnivals are fantastic world-building tools because they mix celebration with a hint of darkness and risk. Combining voluntary dizziness with a stomach full of mini-donuts doesn't seem like a recipe for success, yet somehow, a boardwalk's blend of nostalgia, thrill-seeking, and deep-fried food melts human willpower. Maybe there's something freeing about abandoning caution and good sense once in a while. We can laugh at mortality, with our seat belts firmly fastened.

LEGO's Friends series has introduced a rainbow of bright colors that are perfect for building fairground attractions. Structural integrity is highly encouraged—but not strictly enforced.

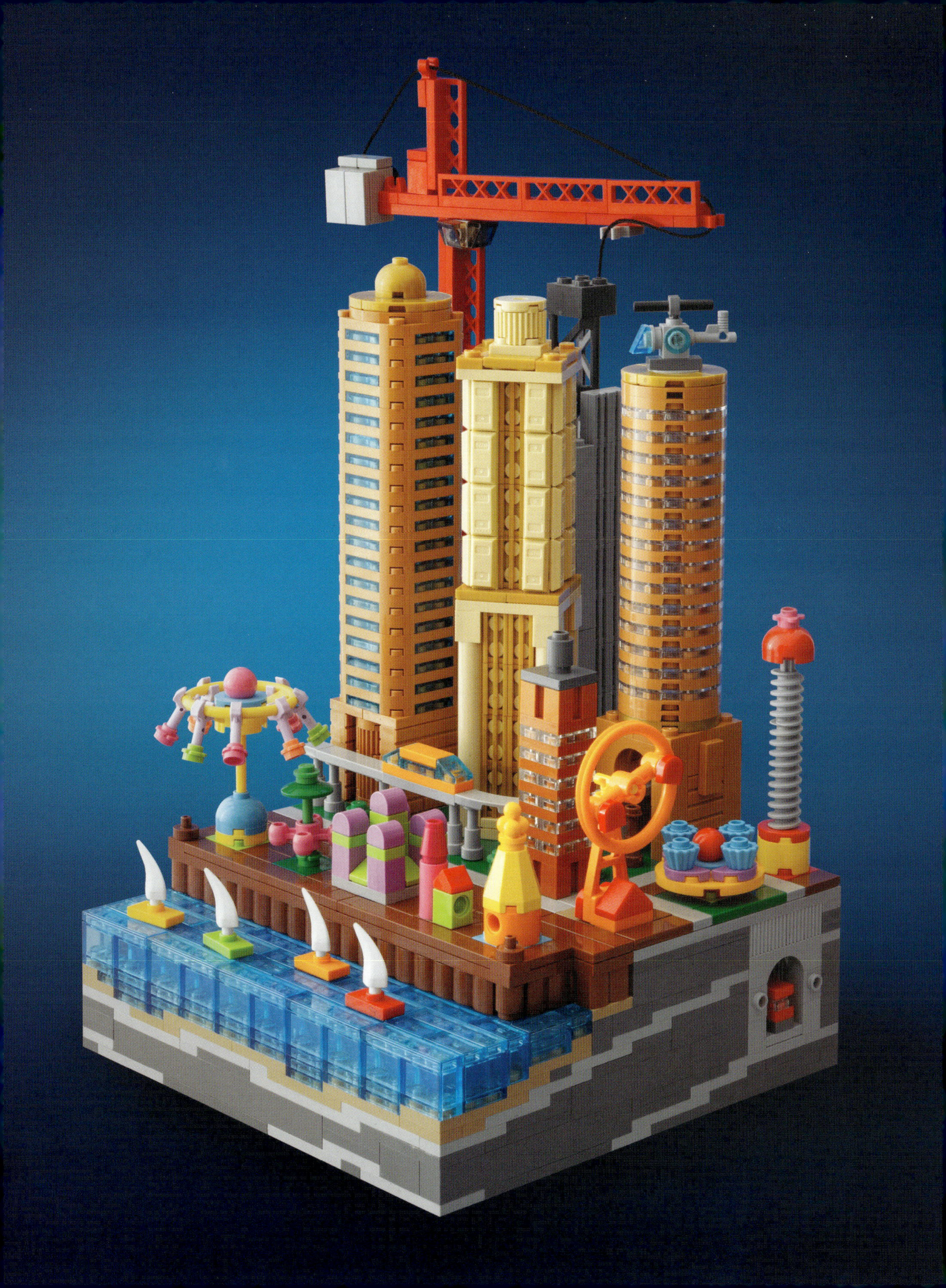

SIMPLE BOARDWALK

This boardwalk model fits all the fairground amusements in this chapter, as shown. It's easy to customize for your own layout. Just leave exposed studs wherever you want to add a ride or building.

No shoreline in your setting? No problem. Amusement park rides can be added à la carte to any scene. Try placing a spinning swing ride on a skyscraper rooftop for maximum thrills!

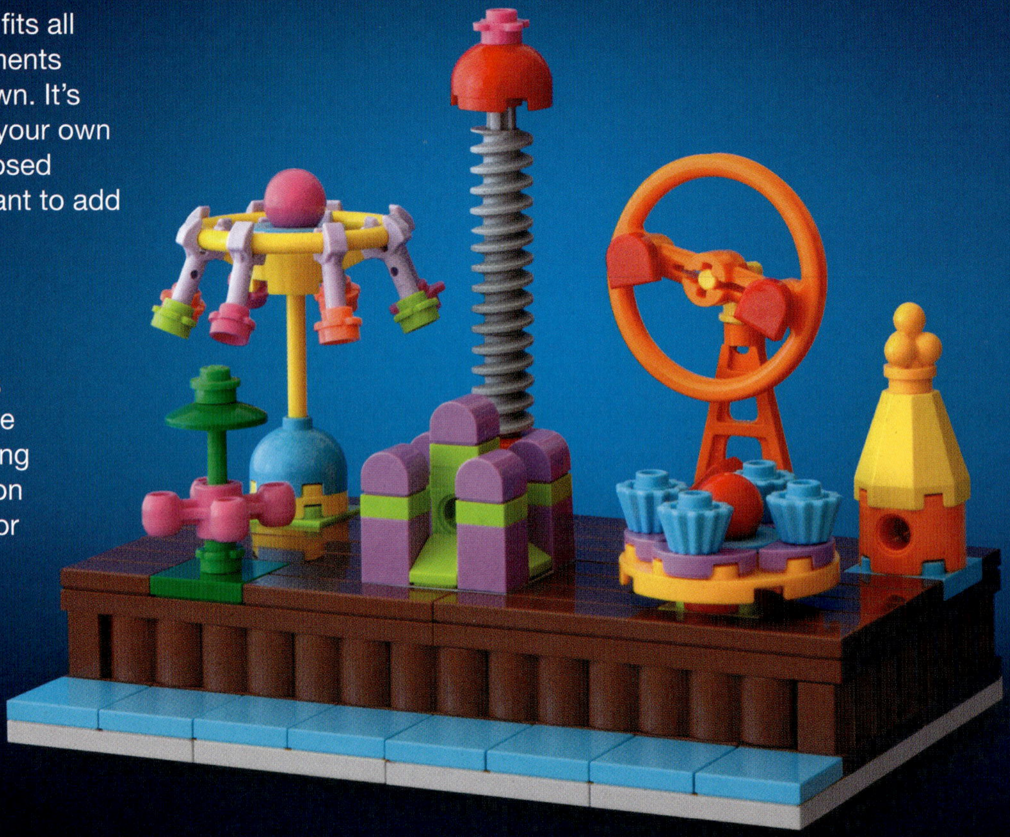

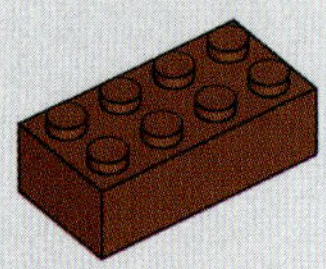

6x
3001

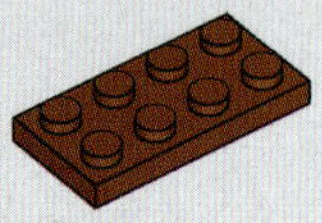

13x
3020

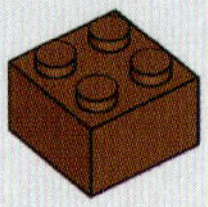

2x
3003

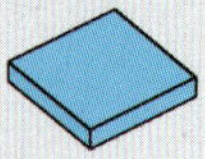

8x
3068

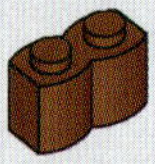

15x
30136

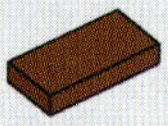

9x
3069

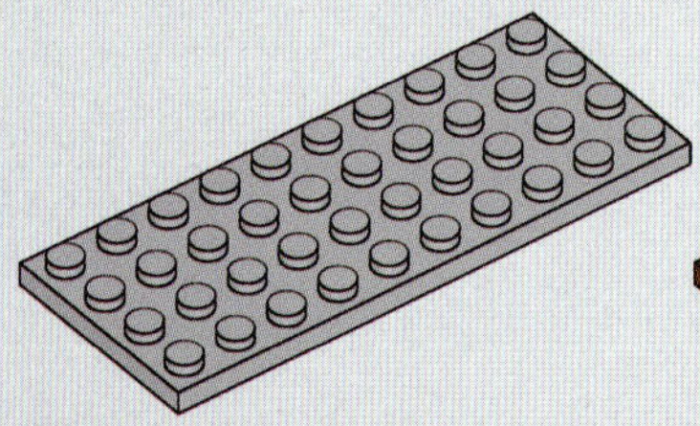

4x
3030

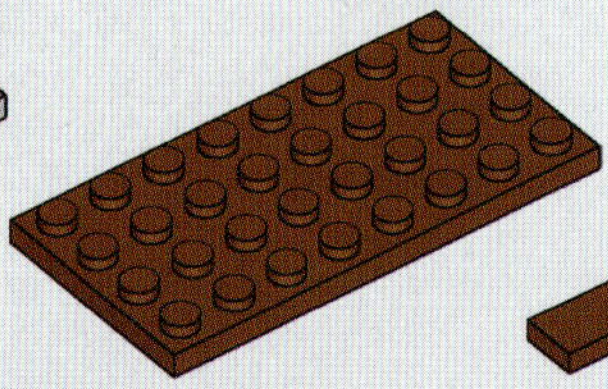

4x
3035

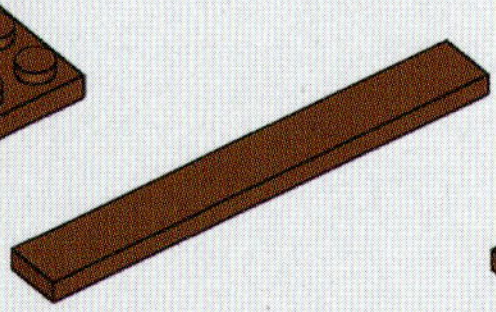

4x
4162

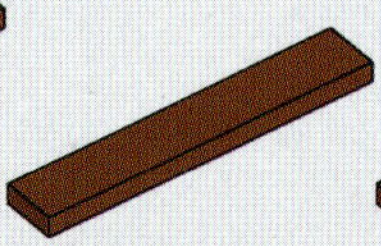

2x
6636

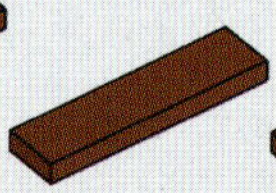

3x
2431

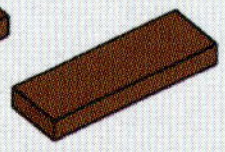

7x
63864

1

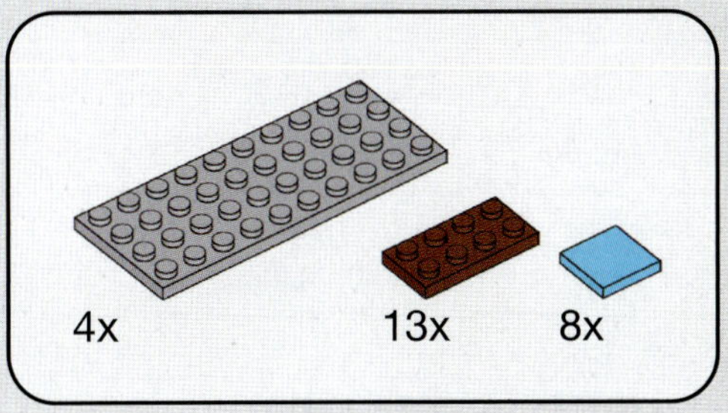

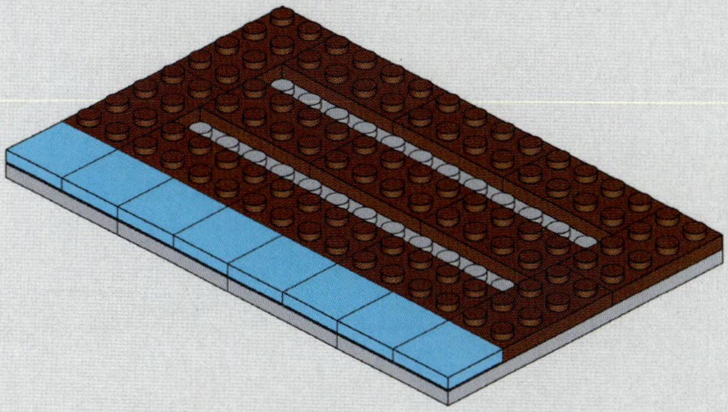

2

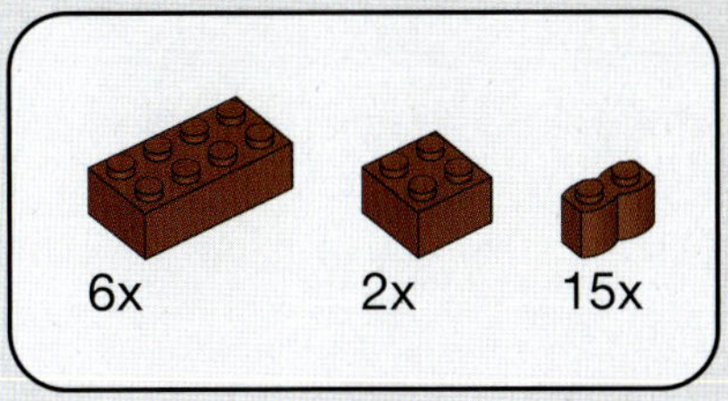

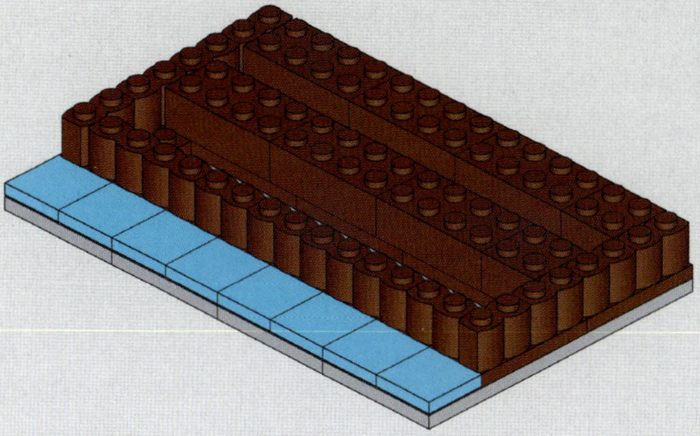

3

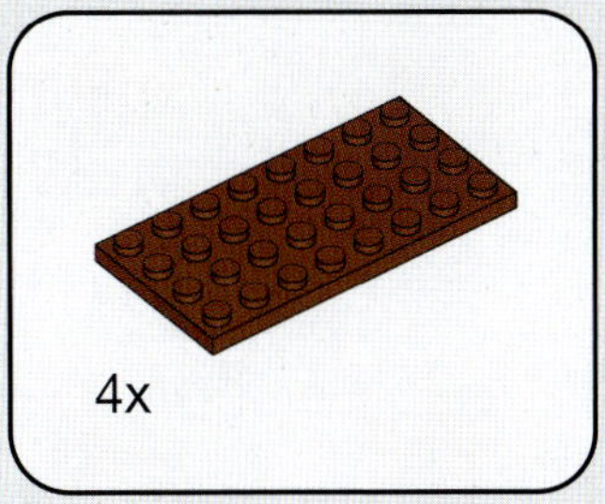

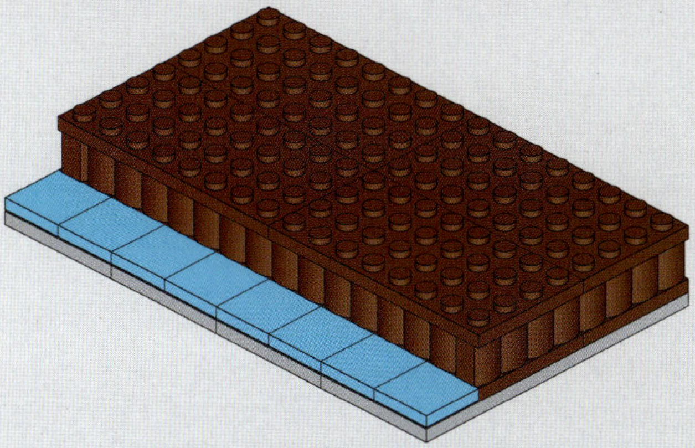

4

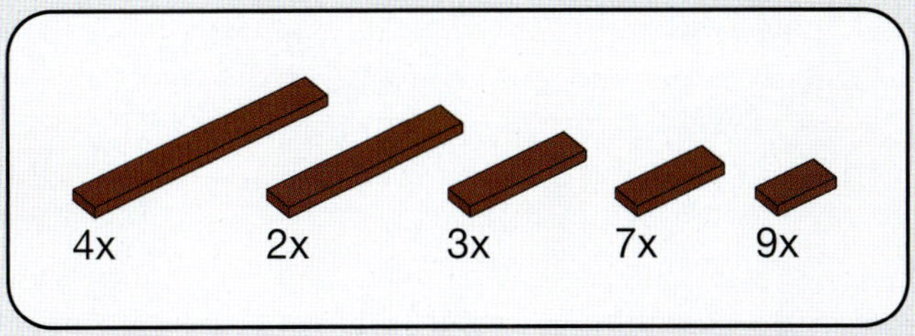

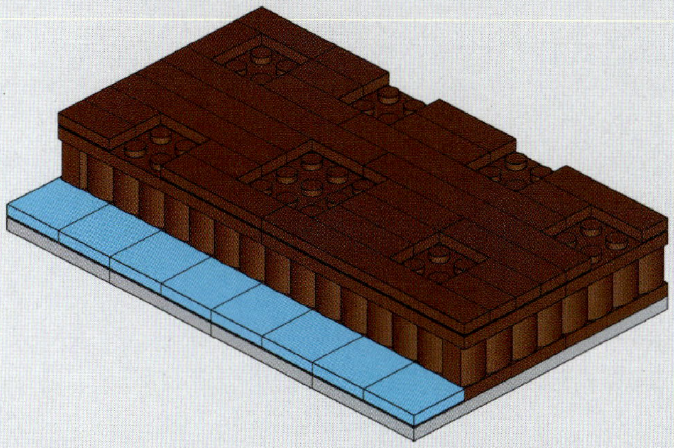

FLYING SWINGS

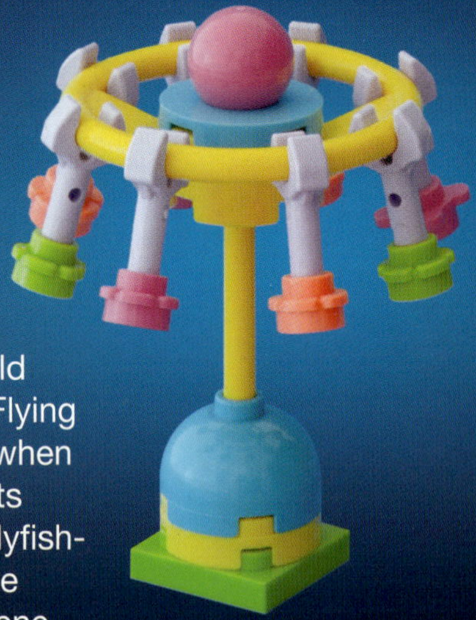

Send your world spinning with Flying Swings. Even when standing still, its technicolor, jellyfish-like appearance dazzles the scene.

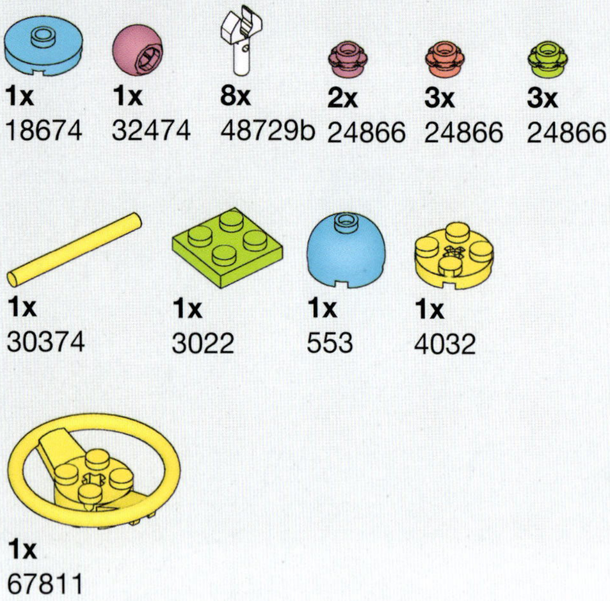

1

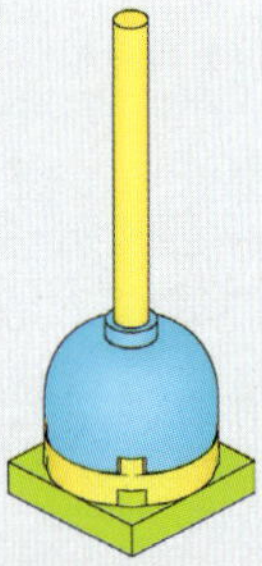

2

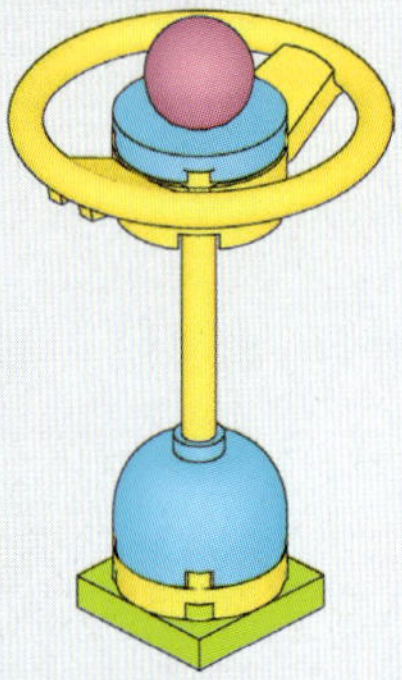

3

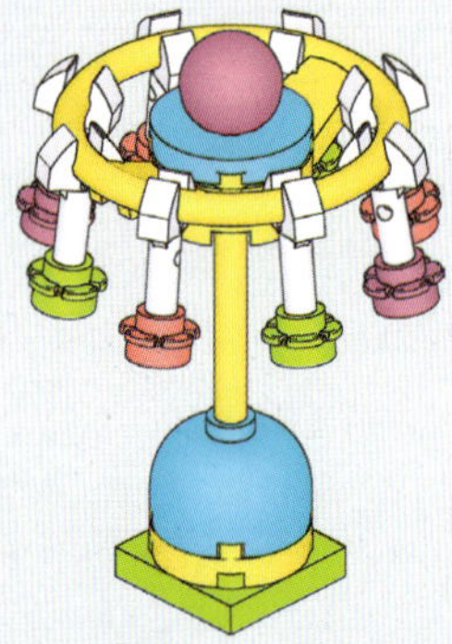

GARDEN TEACUPS

The Garden Teacups design works in a fair, a park, or an enchanted garden where the plants come to life.

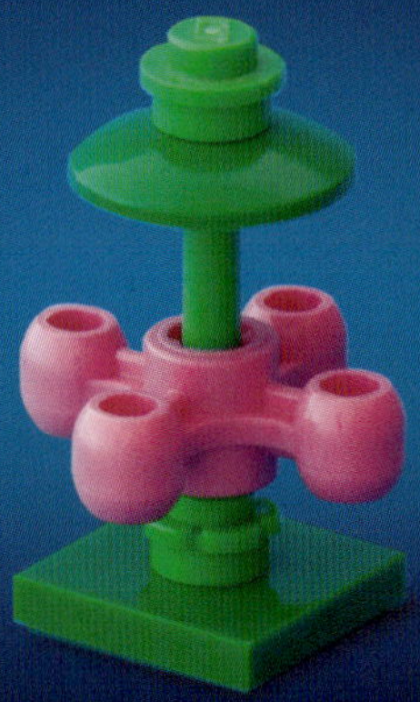

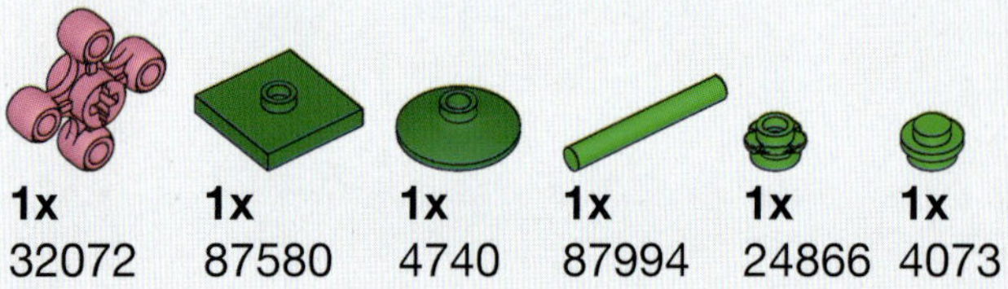

1

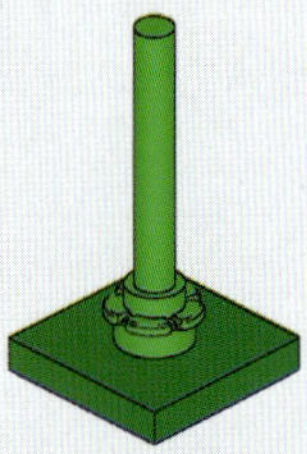

2

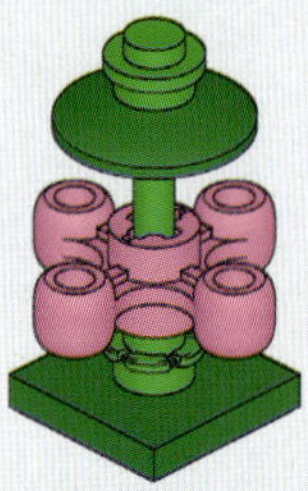

LOOPER

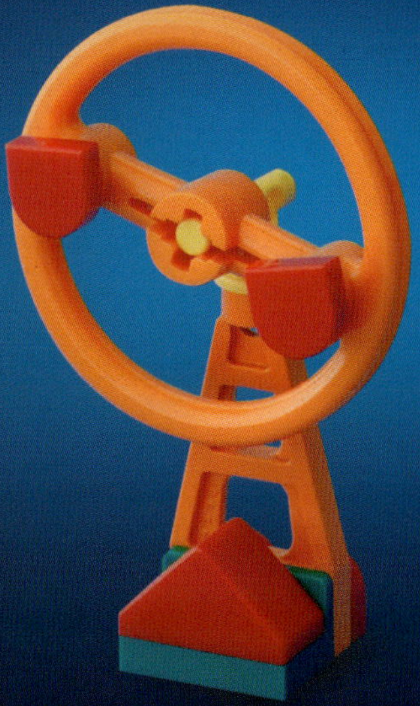

Sometimes the citizens of your world need a new perspective—like a completely inverted one.

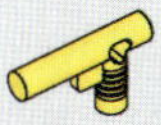
1x
60849

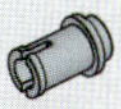
2x
4274

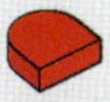
4x
24246

1x
85861

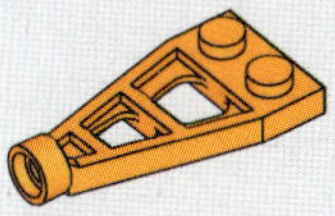
1x
4596

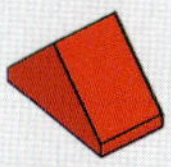
1x
3044c

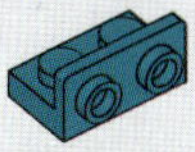
1x
99780

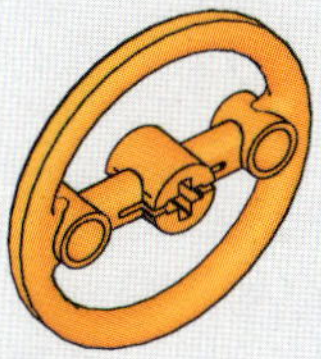
1x
3736

1

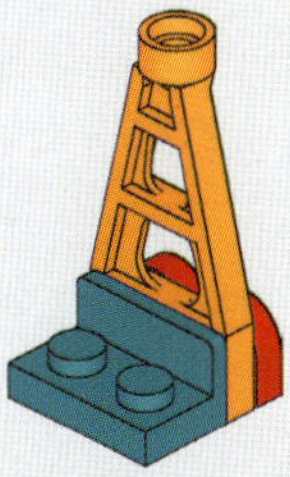

2

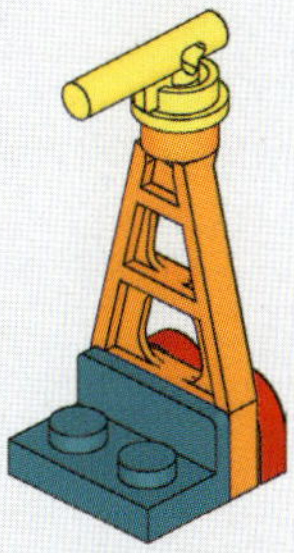

3

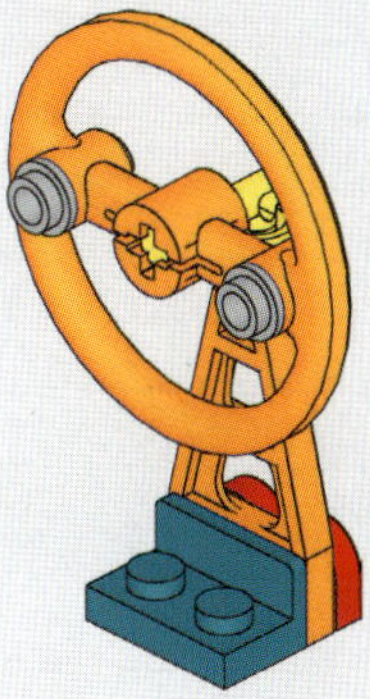

4

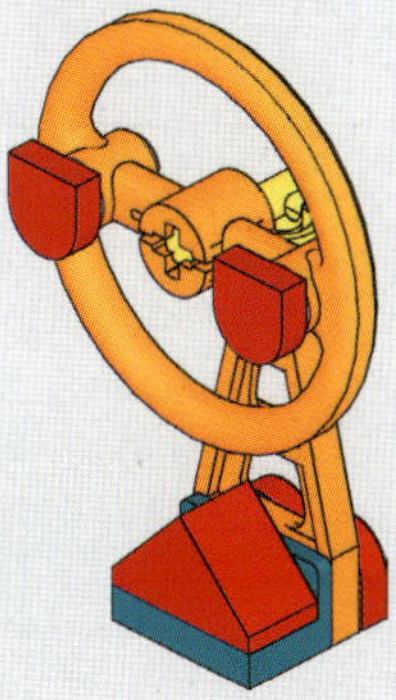

ICE CREAM HUT

Ice cream is a welcome addition to almost any setting. The Ice Cream Hut may not be a ride, but choosing between 200 flavors can still leave you dizzy.

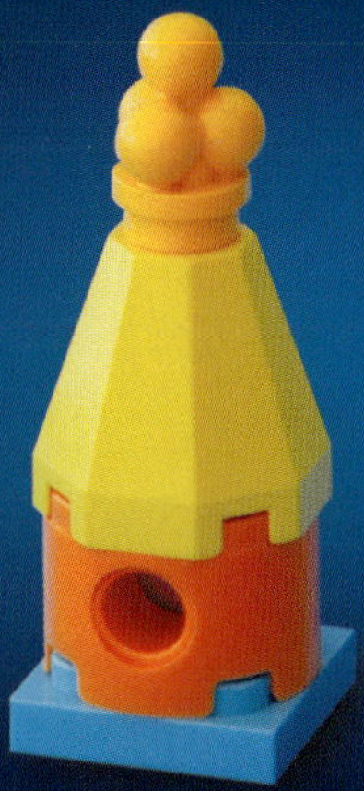

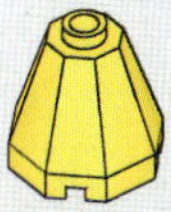
1x
6039

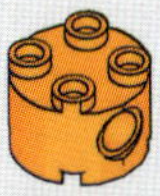
1x
17485

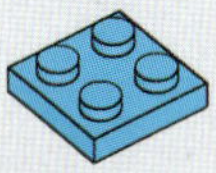
1x
3022

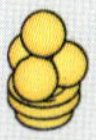
1x
6254

1

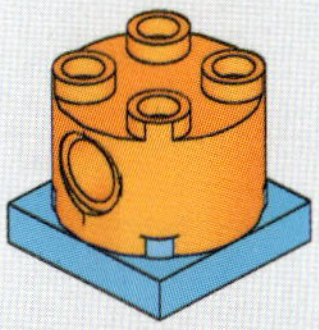

2

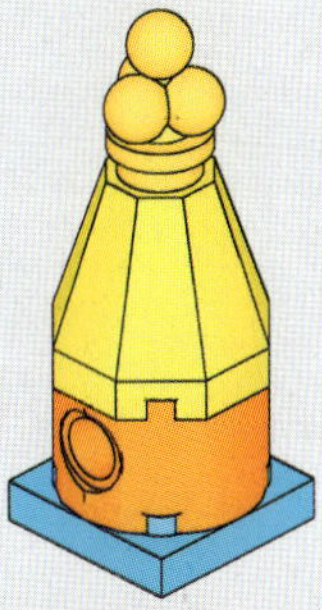

BOUNCY CASTLE

The Bouncy Castle instantly signals a playful environment, or a surreal structure in a world of blow-up buildings.

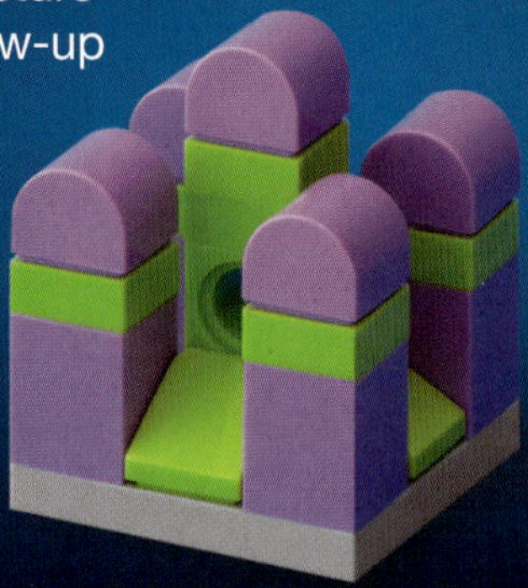

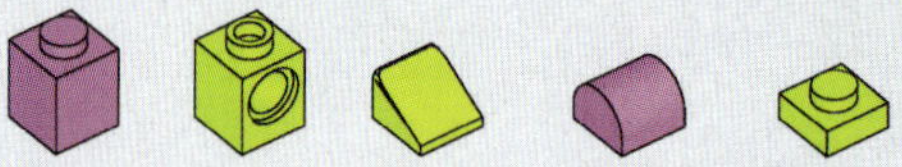

4x 3005 | 1x 6541 | 4x 54200 | 5x 49307 | 7x 3024

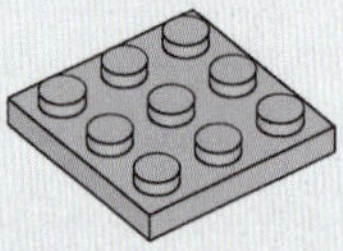

1x 11212

1

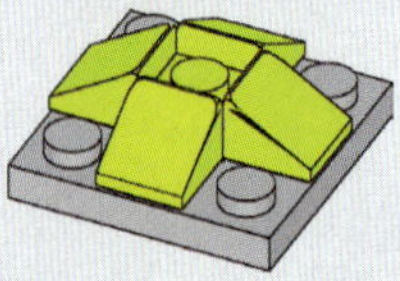

2

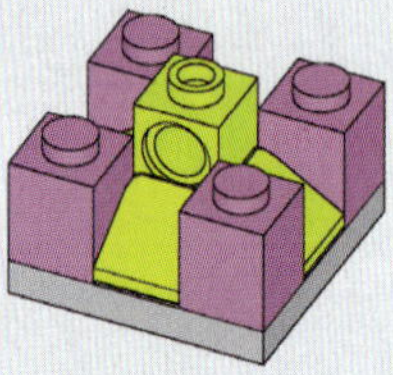

3

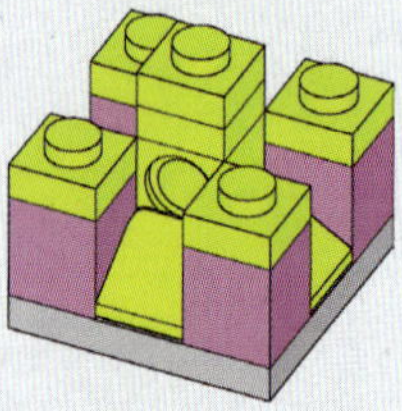

4

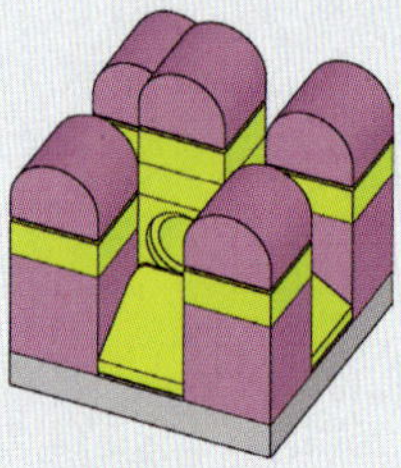

SPINNER

Muted tones have their charms, but bright, clashing colors attract all the attention.

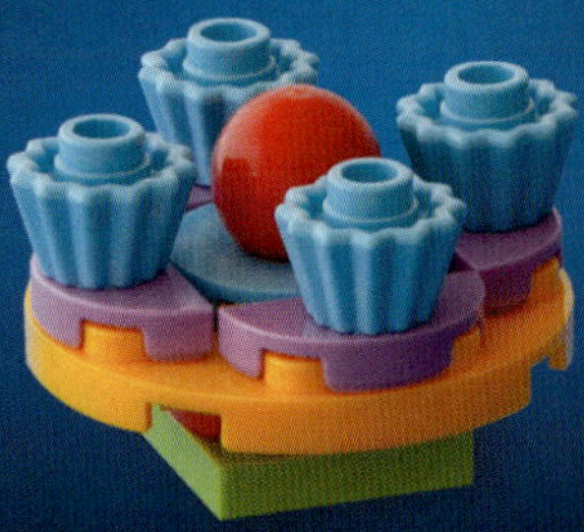

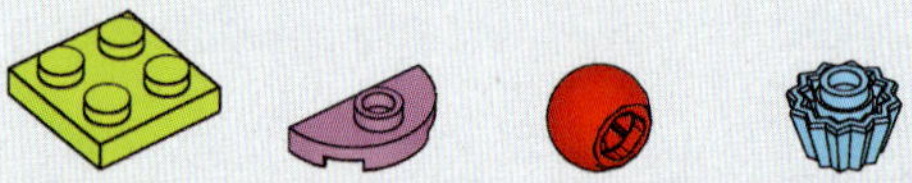

1x 3022 | 4x 1745 | 1x 32474 | 4x 65468d

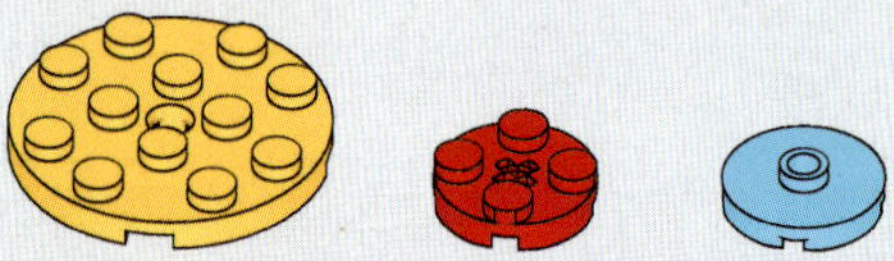

1x 60474 | 1x 4032 | 1x 18674

TWISTY SLIDE

Archimedes' screw design, dating from the 3rd century BCE, reaches its pinnacle with the twisty slide.

This tall attraction adds curving forms to blocky city skylines.

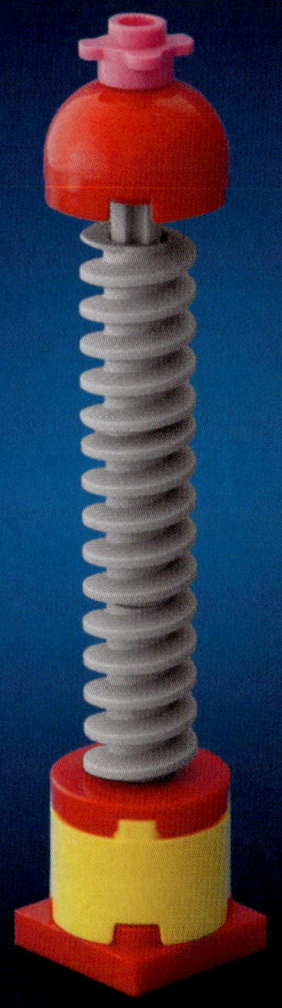

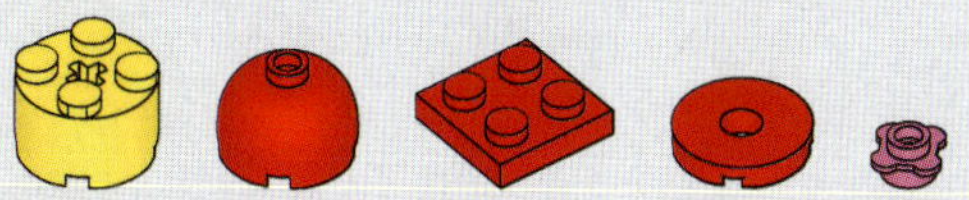

1x 3941 | 1x 553 | 1x 3022 | 1x 15535 | 1x 33291

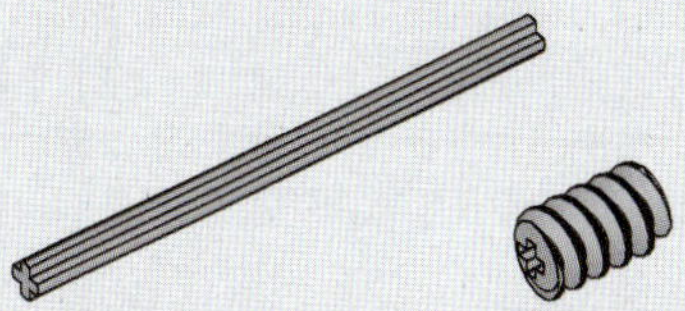

1x 60485 | 3x 4716

1

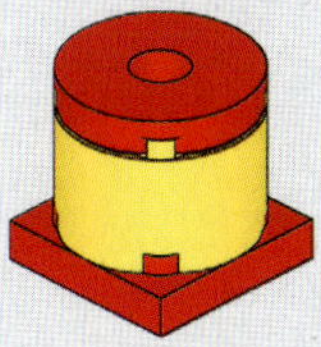

2

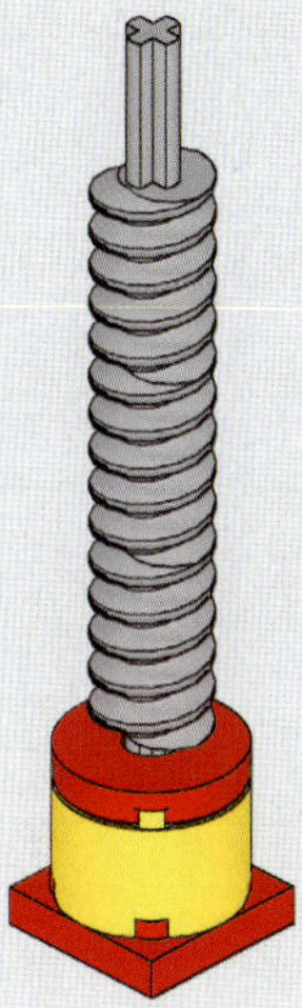

3

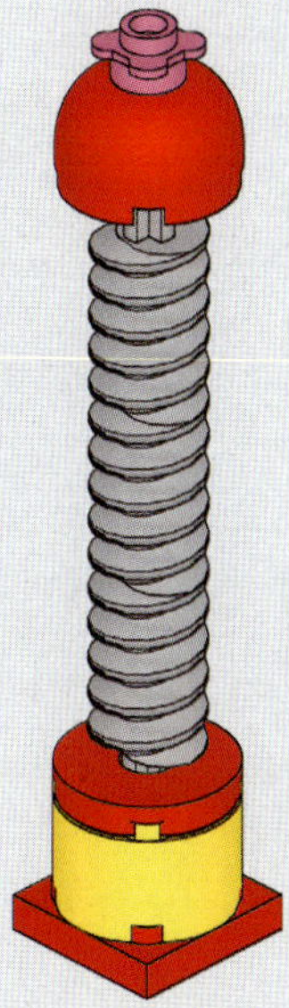

1

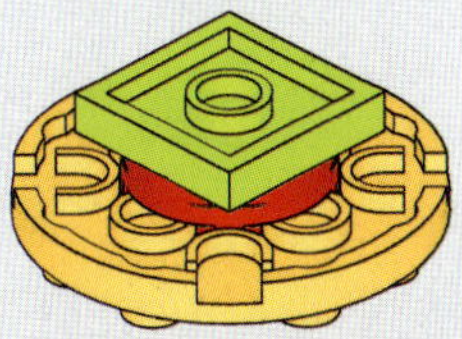

2

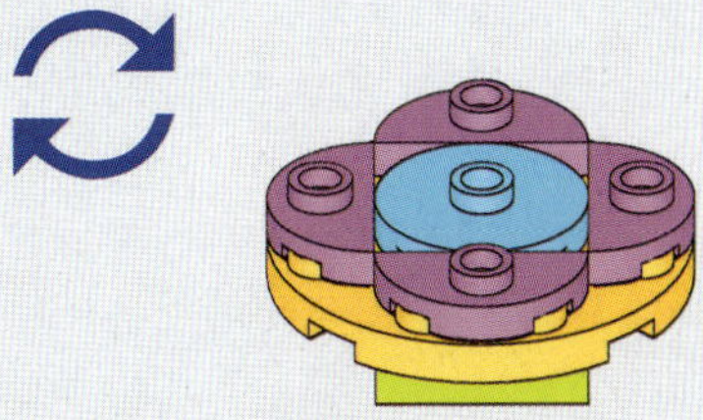

3

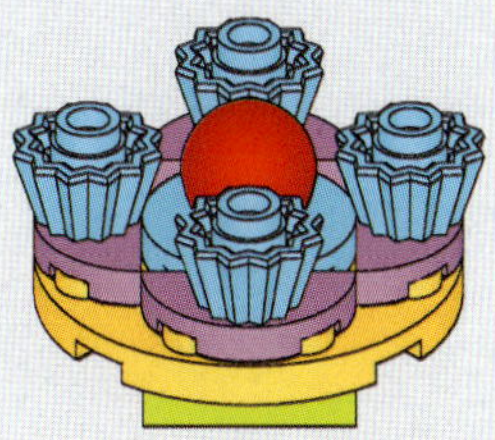

ART DECO FUTURISM

We think of Art Deco as a historical style, but during its heyday it was a vision of the future. Bold geometry, streamlined forms, and metallic finishes imagined cities of tomorrow. It's no wonder the style became the visual language for world-building in some of the earliest science fiction films, such as 1927's *Metropolis*.

Both Art Deco and LEGO still feel modern today, generations after they first appeared. Both exemplify fine craftsmanship and invite creativity within a structured system. It only makes sense to build the promise of tomorrow using the bold designs of history.

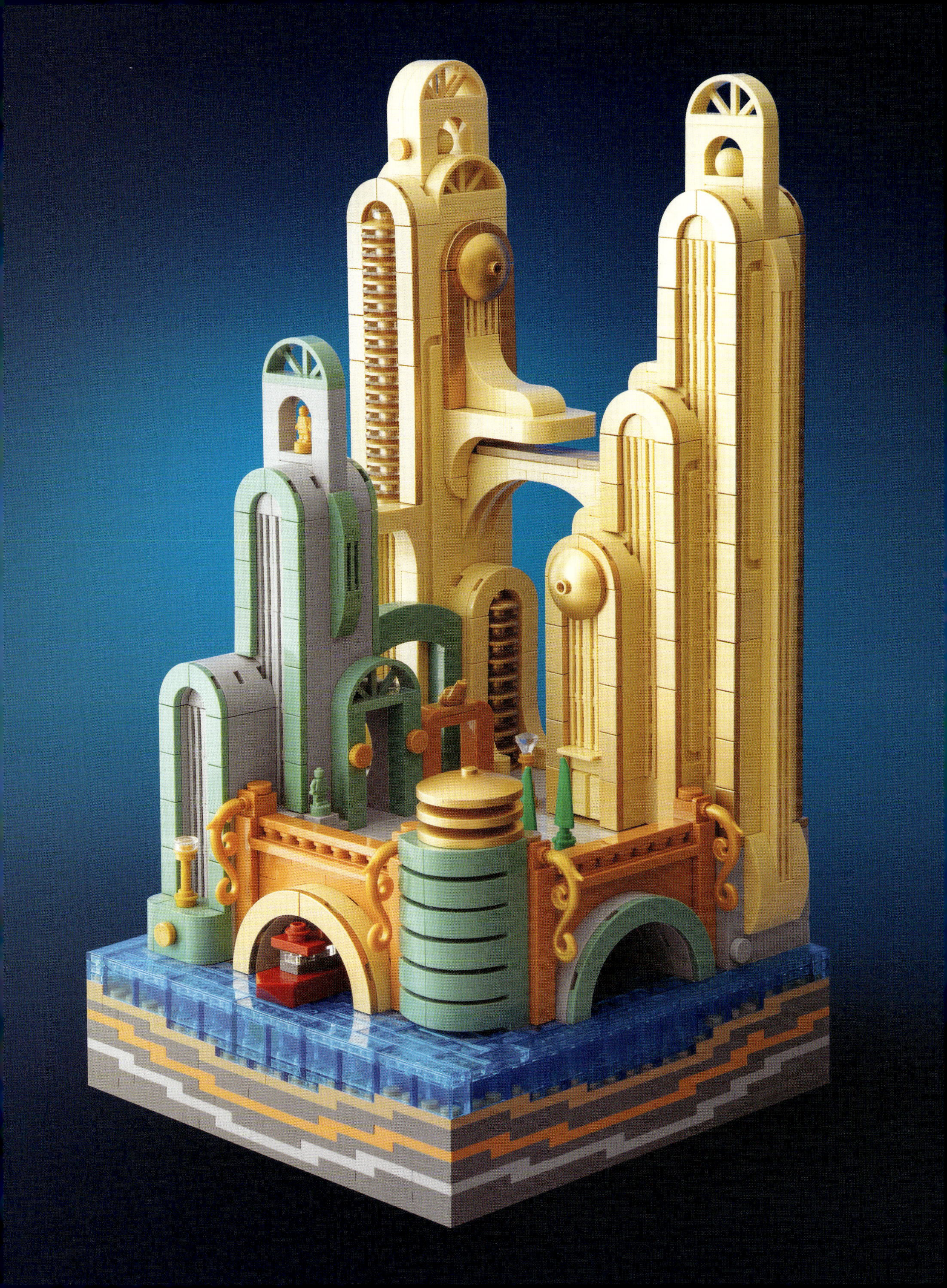

THE SUNBURST

The Sunburst is a showstopping fusion of Art Deco elegance and futuristic design. You can't quite place which era it belongs to, which is exactly why it looks at home in many different worlds.

Once you learn the building techniques, the Sunburst is easy to customize. Create a smaller, single-arched structure that won't break the bank, or expand the cascading forms across the horizon.

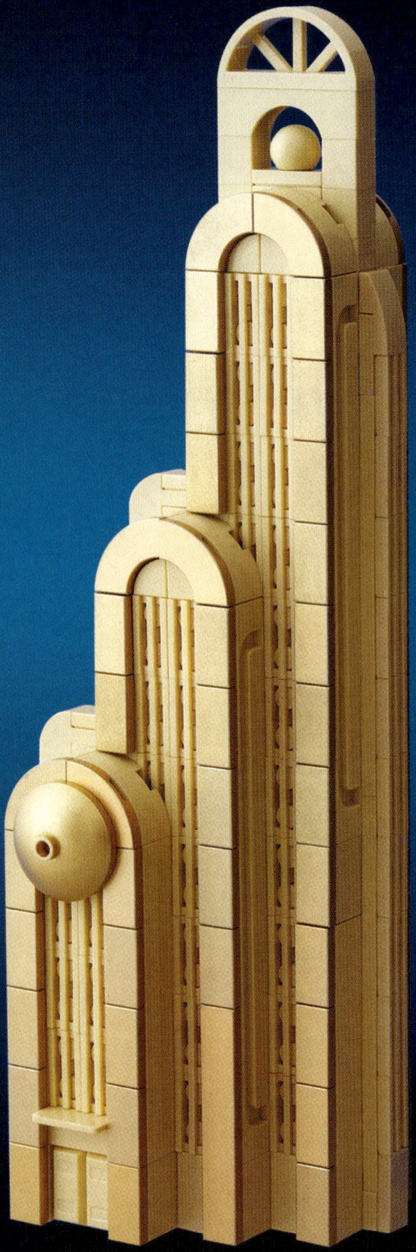

2x 3004	**1x** 4865b	**24x** 26604	**2x** 47905	**4x** 3005	**6x** 4032	**1x** 18674	**1x** 32474	**2x** 3070	**6x** 25269	**1x** 4073
26x 3710	**2x** 3623	**2x** 3023	**73x** 2412b	**2x** 99563	**1x** 15573	**6x** 3069	**59x** 3069	**8x** 27925		

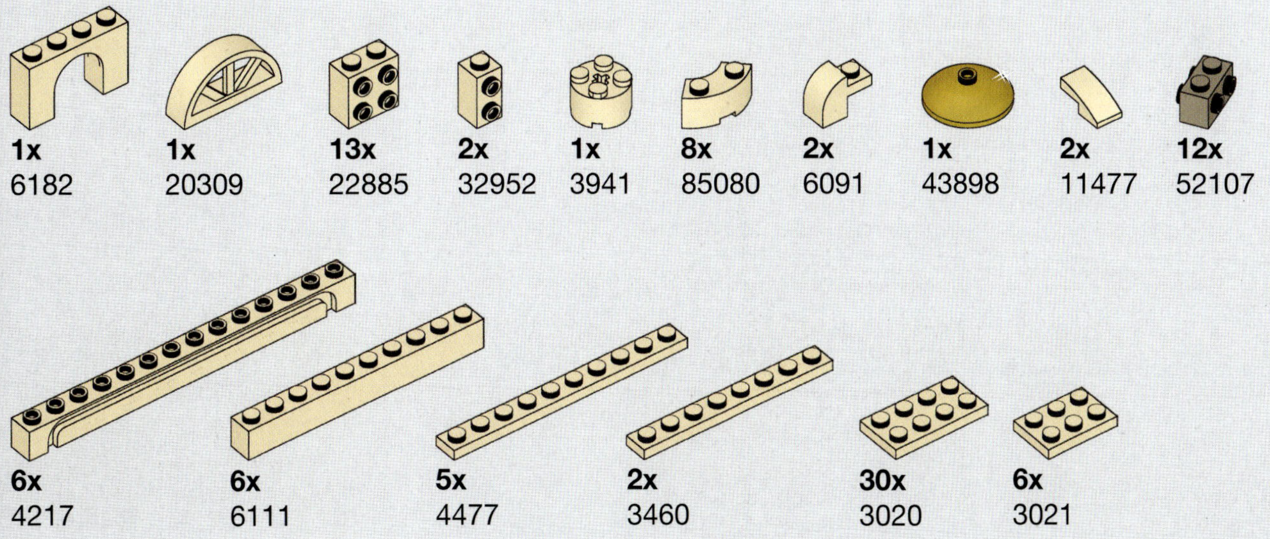
1x
6182
1x
20309
13x
22885
2x
32952
1x
3941
8x
85080
2x
6091
1x
43898
2x
11477
12x
52107
6x
4217
6x
6111
5x
4477
2x
3460
30x
3020
6x
3021

1

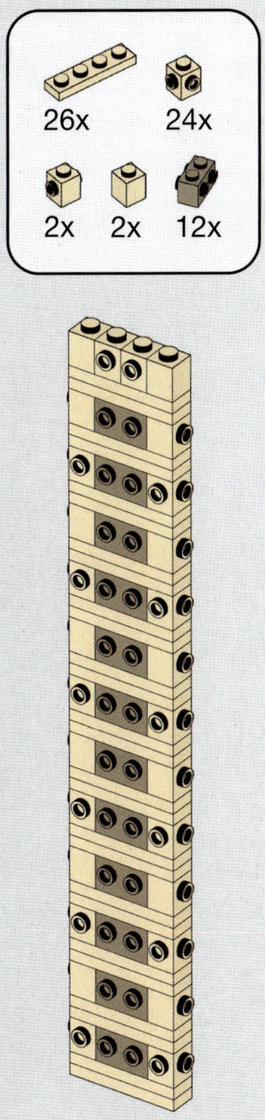
26x
24x
2x
2x
12x

2

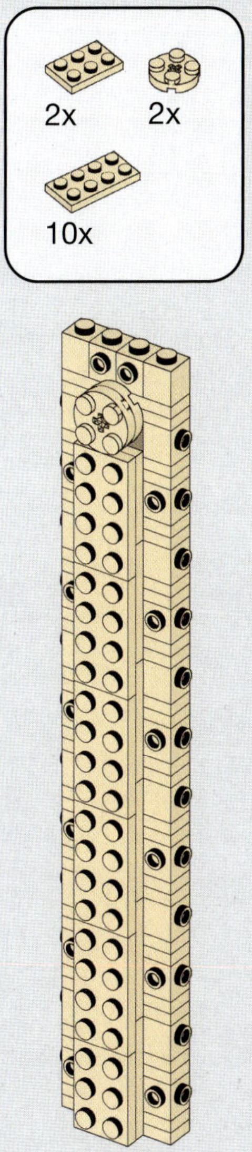
2x
2x
10x

3

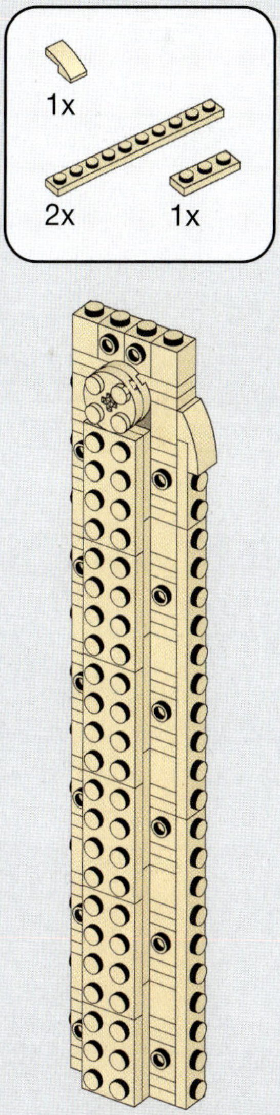
1x
2x
1x

4

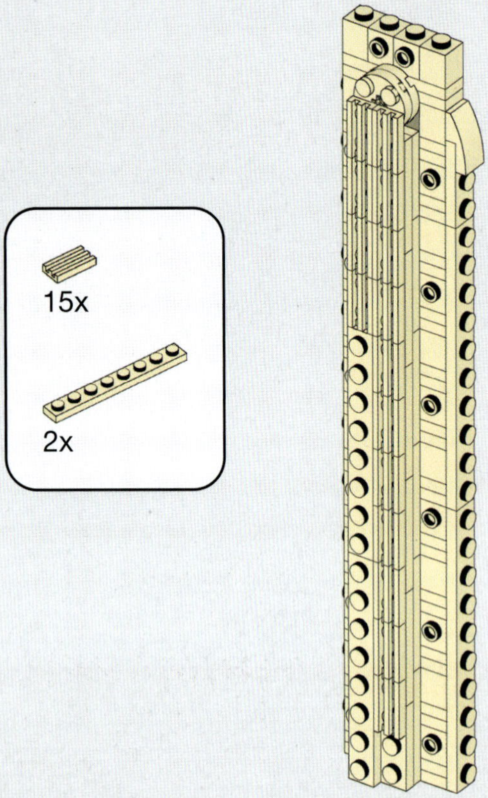

5

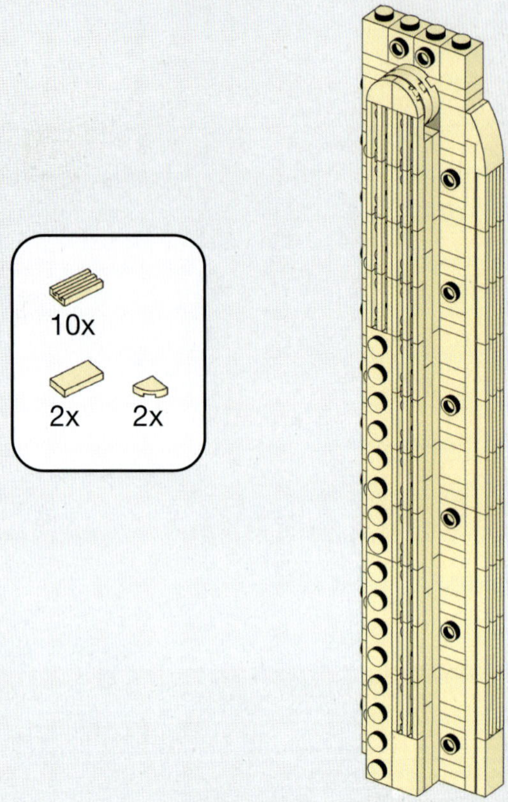

6

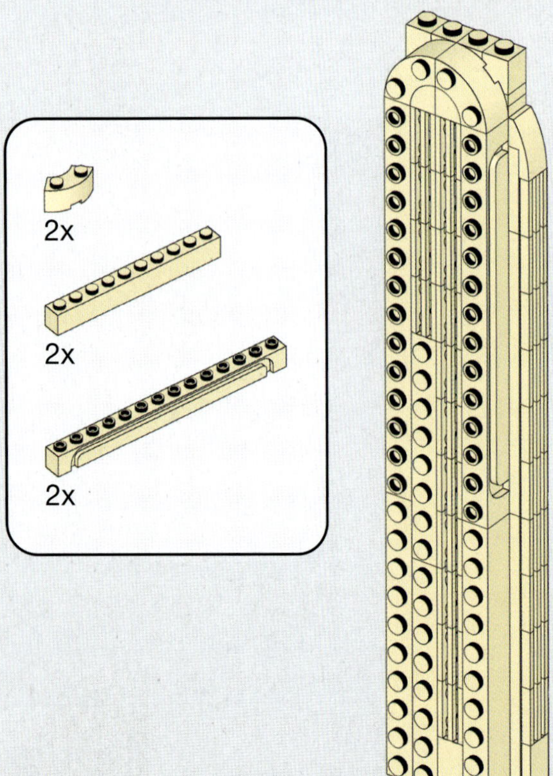

7

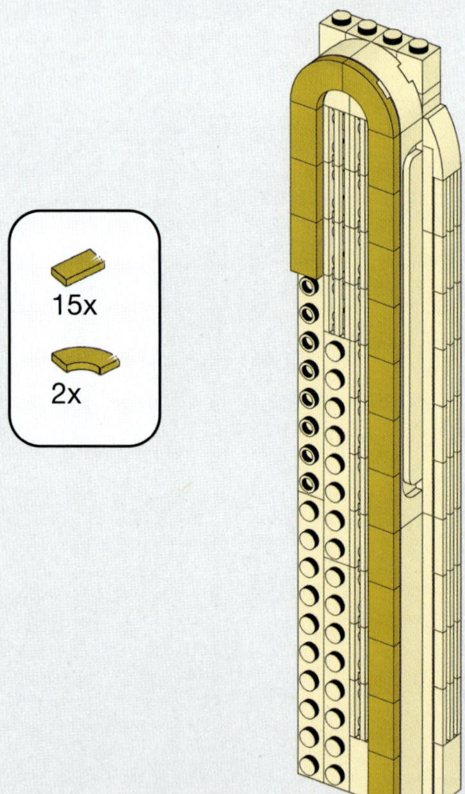

8

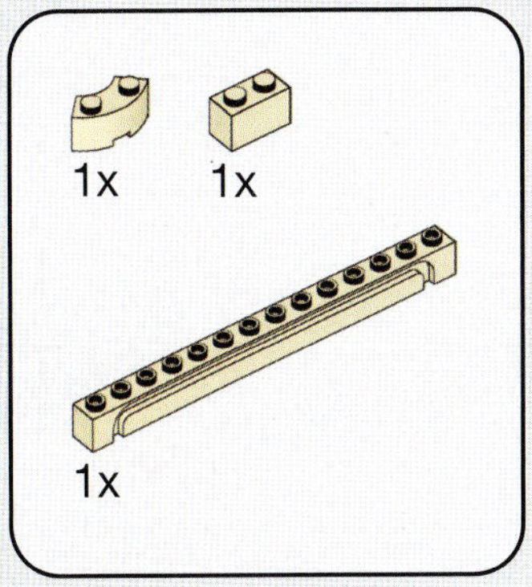

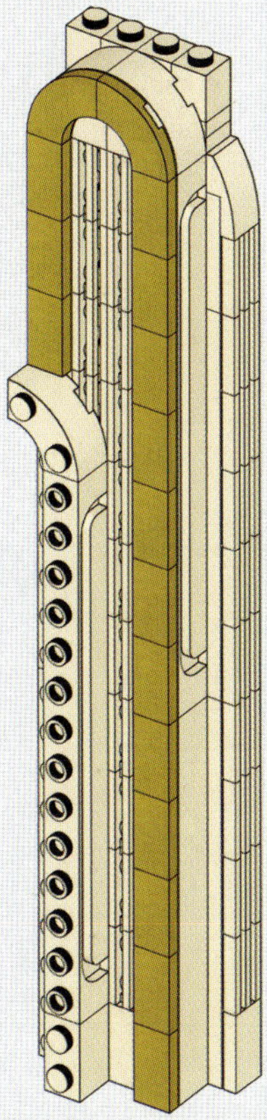

9

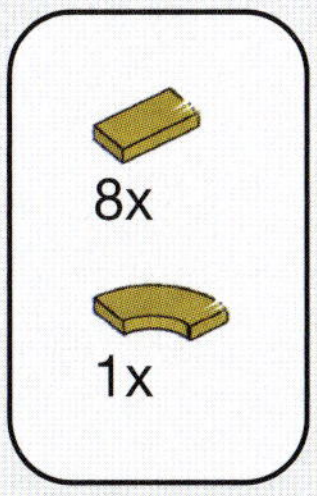

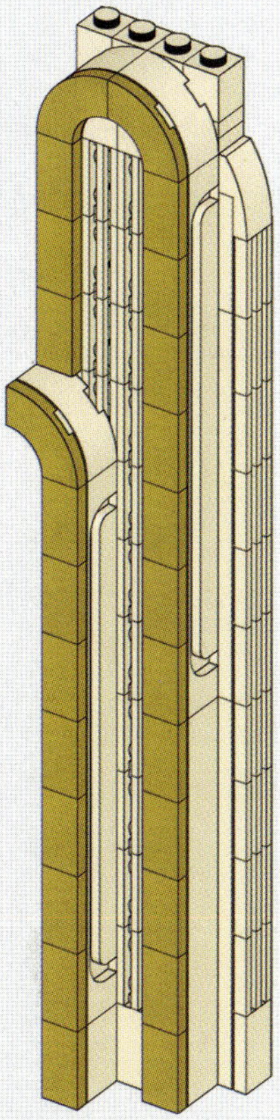

10

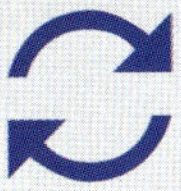

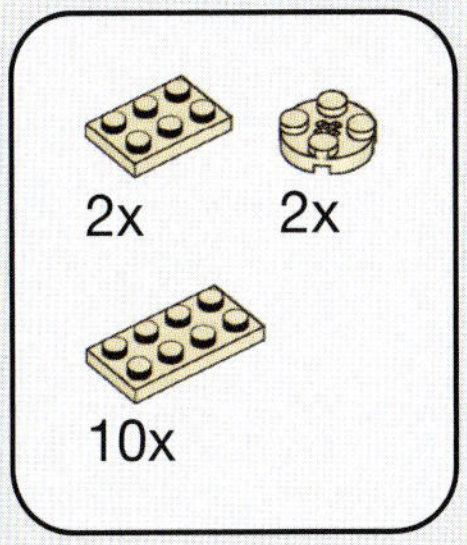

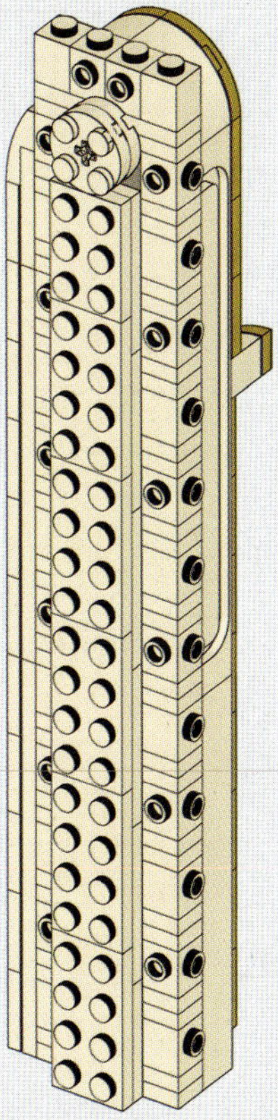

11

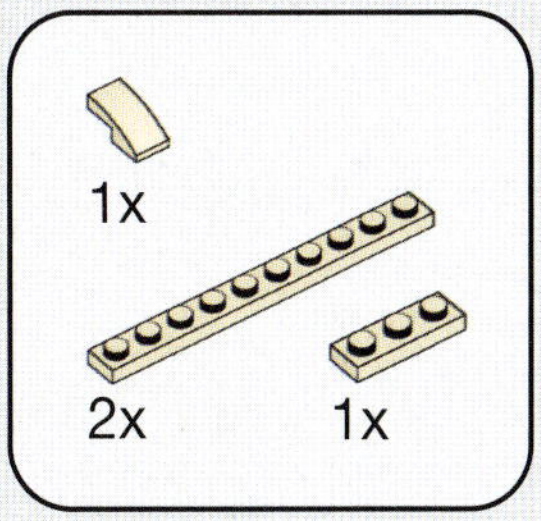

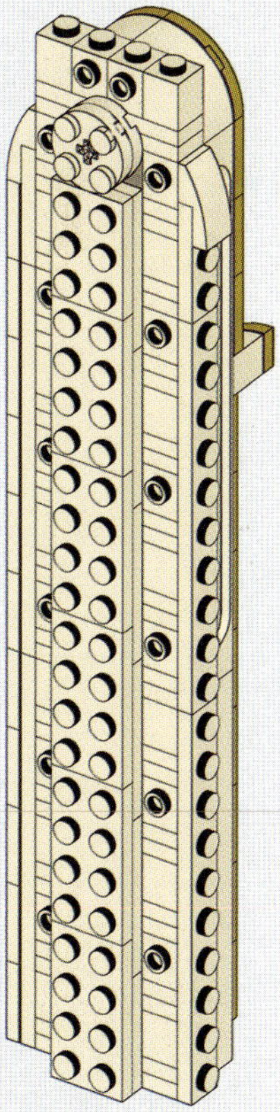

12

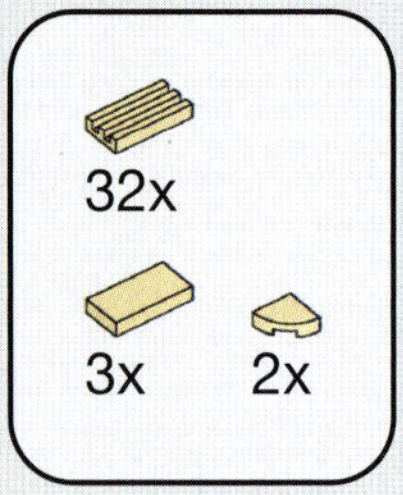

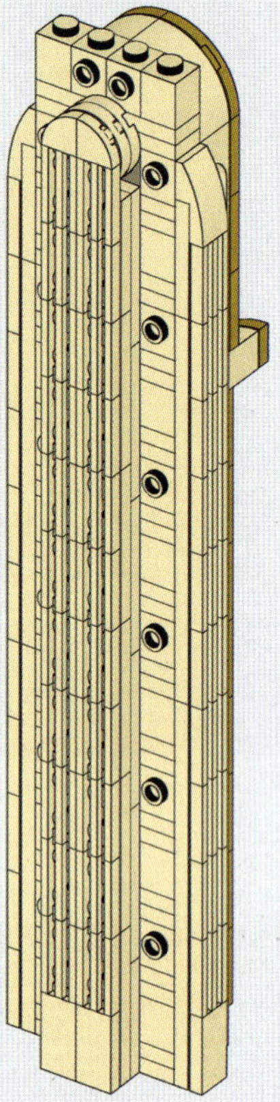

13

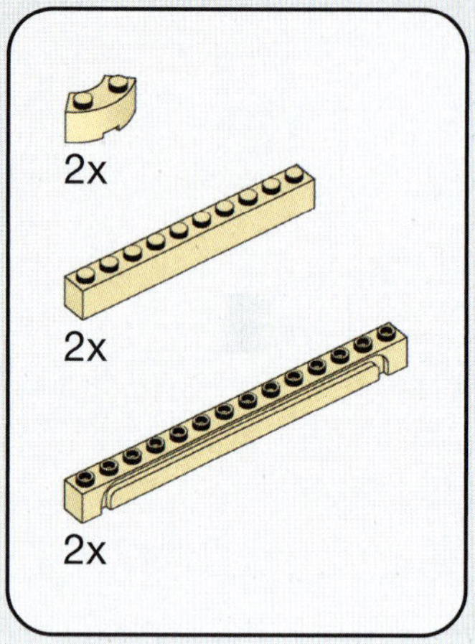

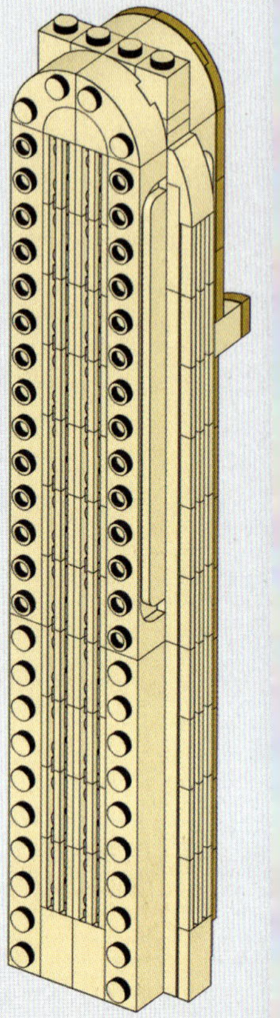

14

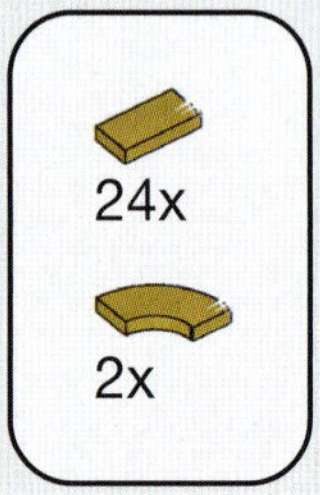

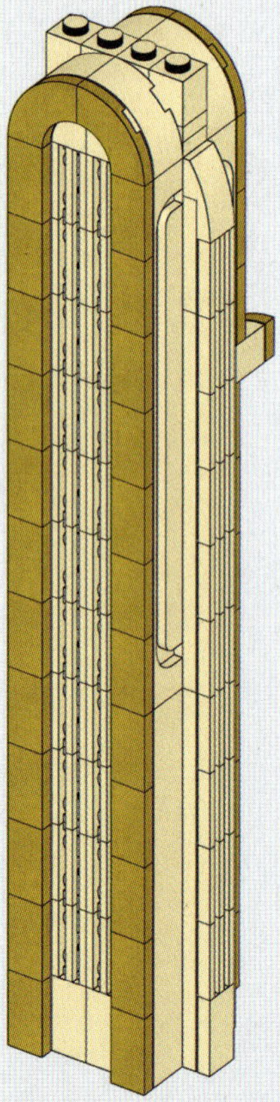

15

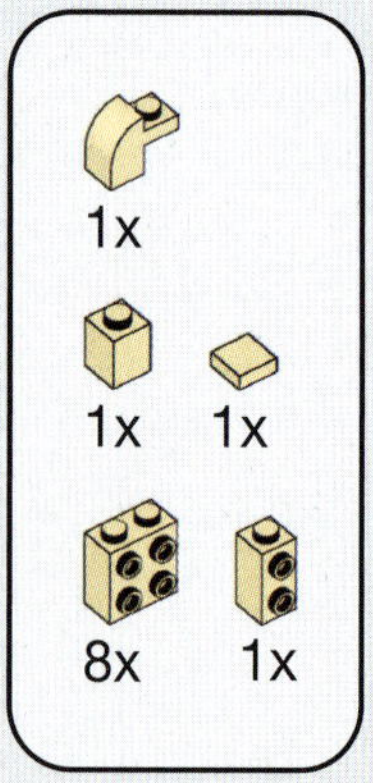

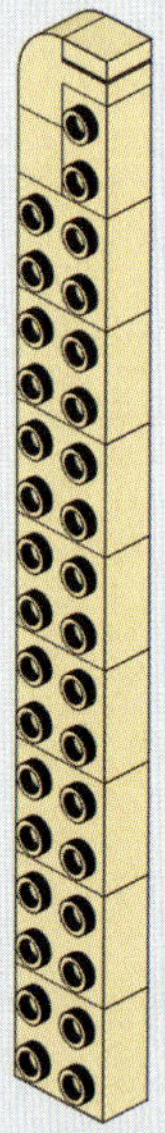

16

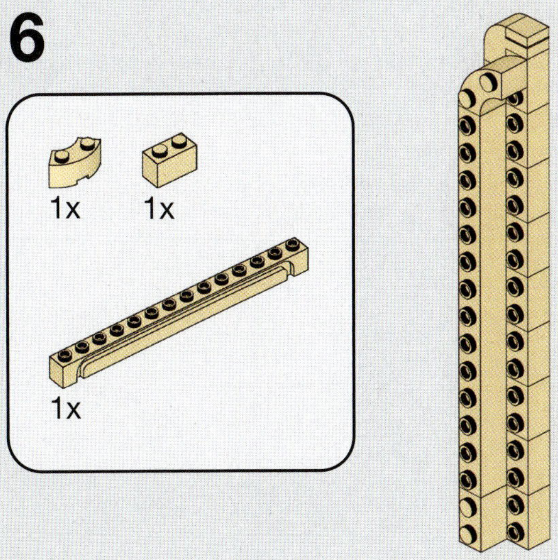

17

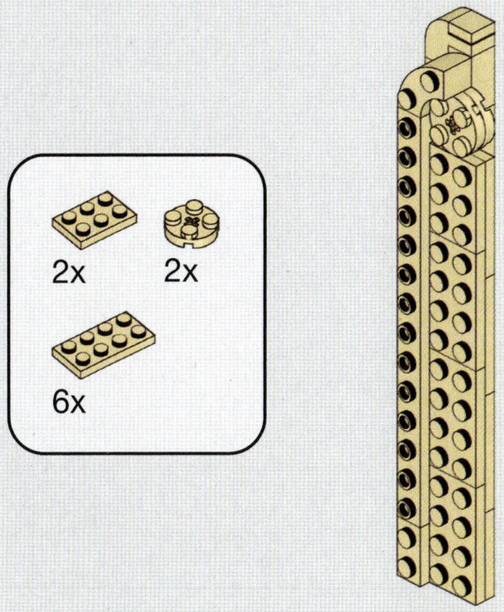

18

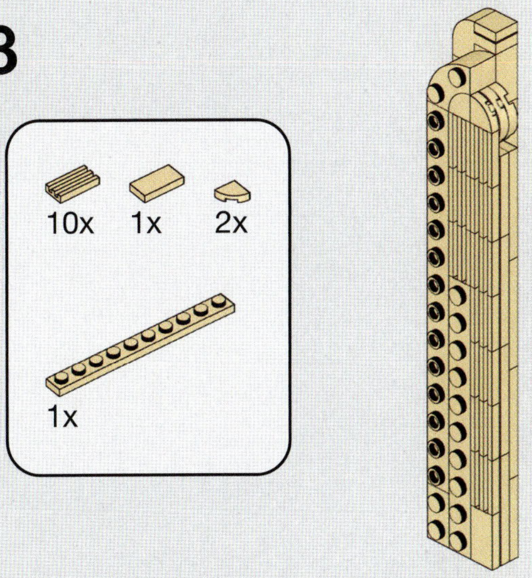

19

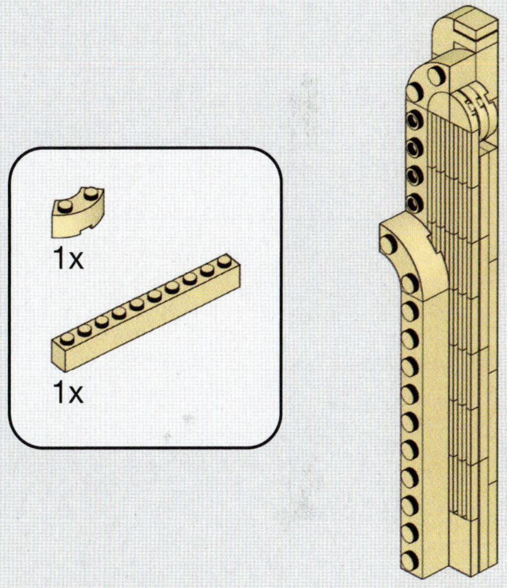

20

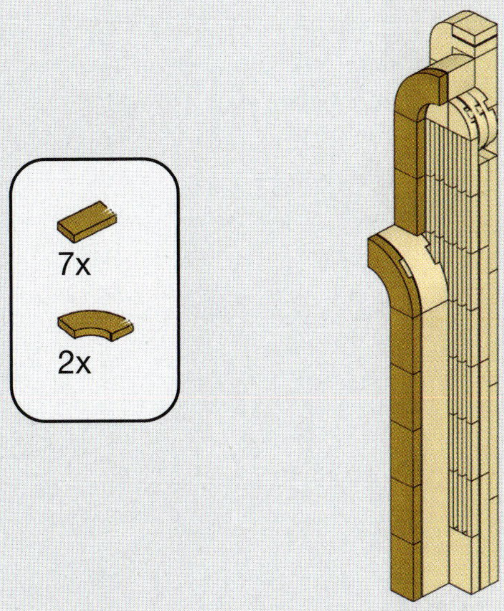

21

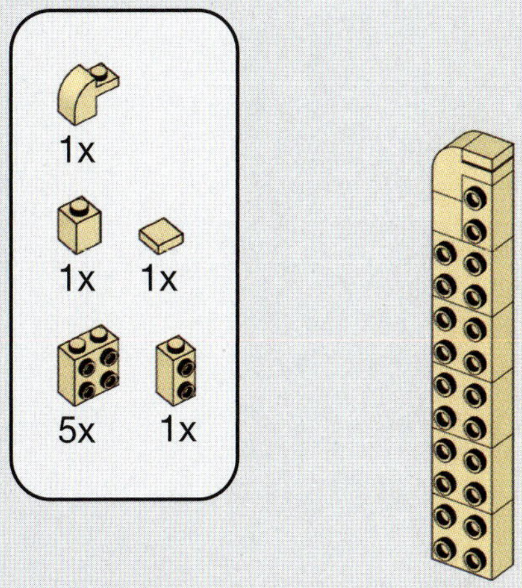

22

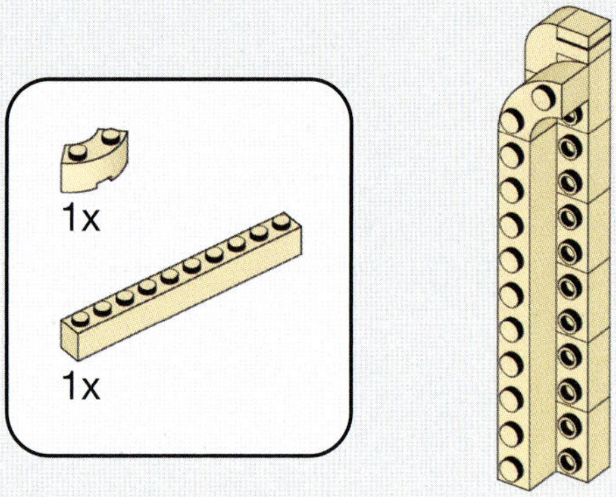

23

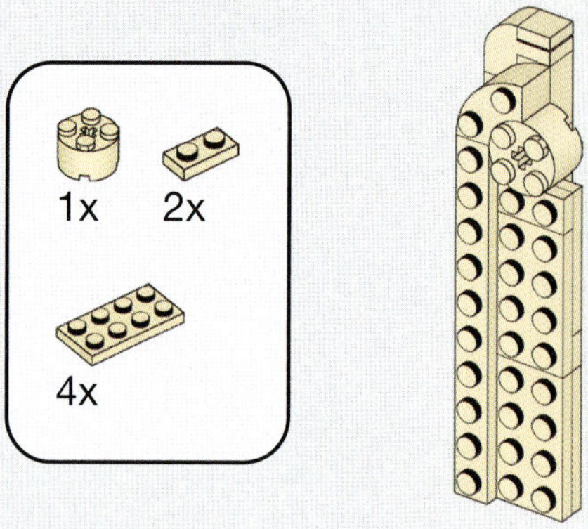

24

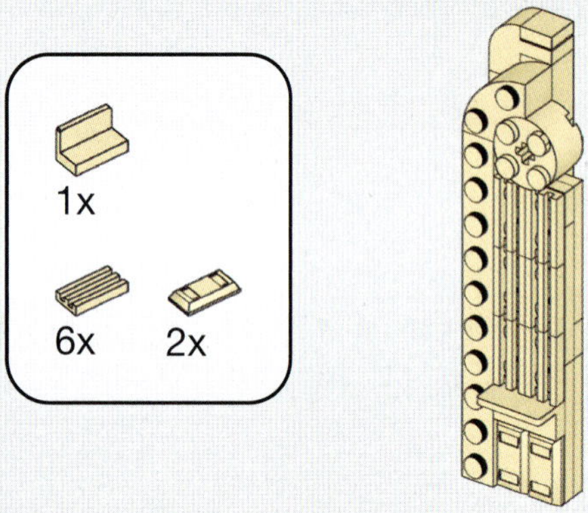

25

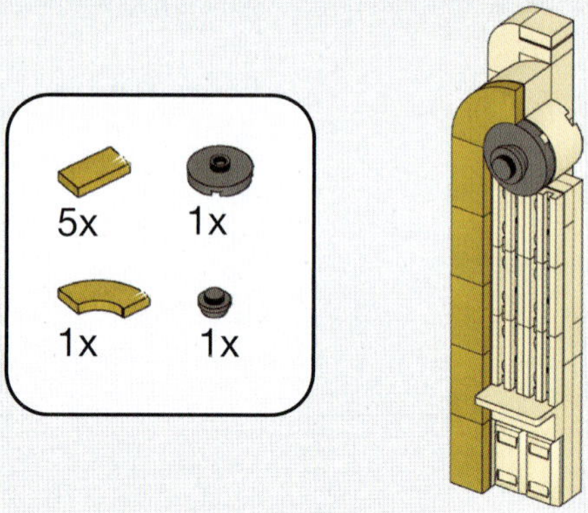

26

Attach the assemblies as shown.

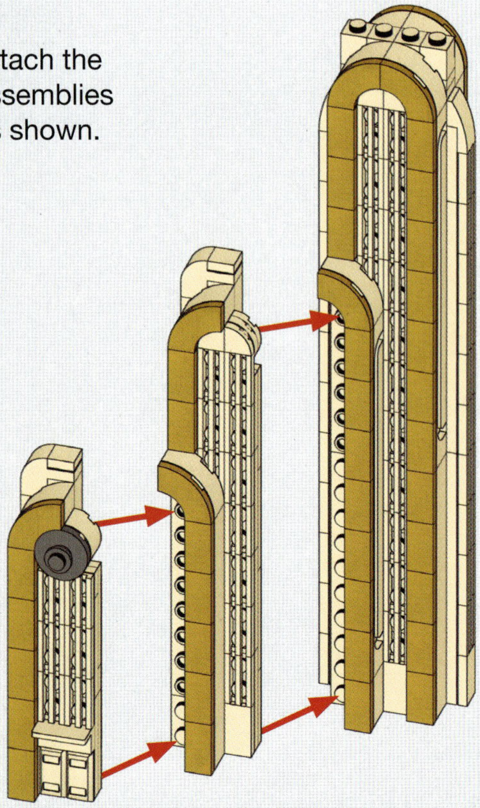

27

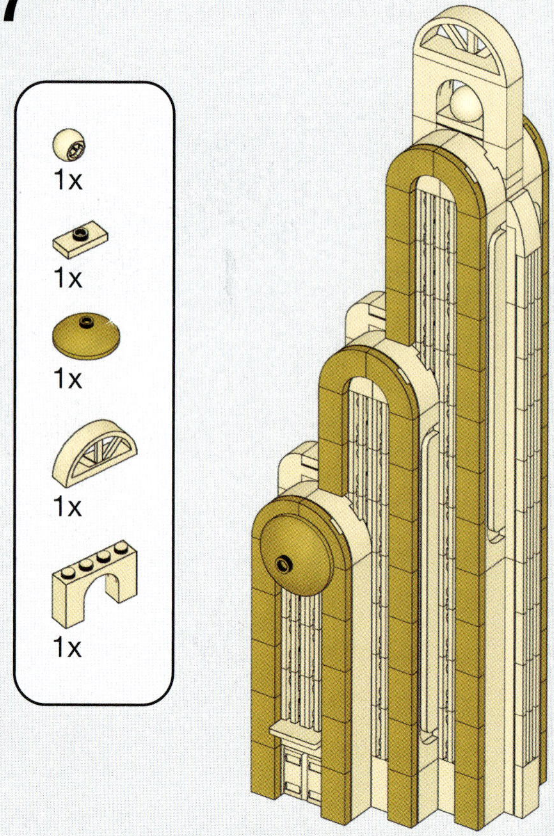

MAKE IT YOUR OWN

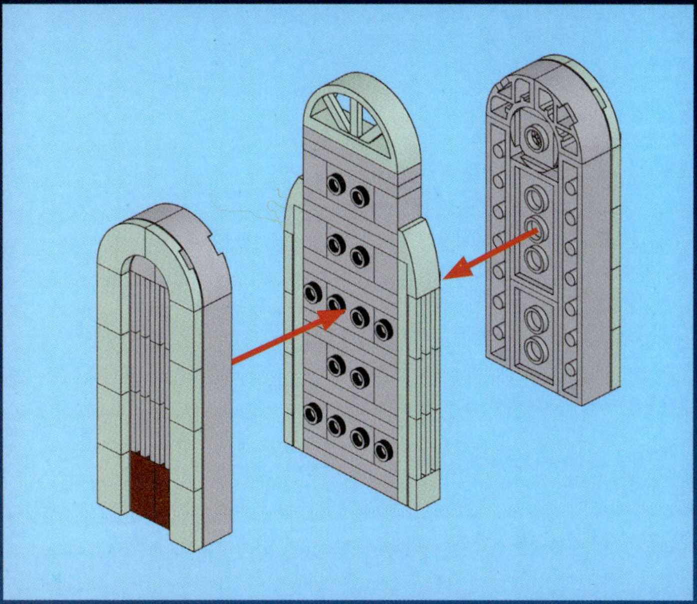

SCALE DOWN

You're forgiven for thinking the cost of LEGO metallic gold elements tracks with real gold bars. (LEGO gold may be the better investment, but this book claims no expertise in financial matters.) With that in mind, there's no aesthetic penalty for using non-metallic tile elements for trim. You can also scale the building down to a single-arched structure, as shown on the right.

SCALE UP

Of course, anything that can be scaled down can also be scaled up. If you're feeling ambitious, continue adding arched sections to the Sunburst at varying heights. The result is a sculptural statement on the skyline.

Each new section creates a rhythm of curves, echoing natural forms like hills or waves. Experimenting within the constraints of clean lines and modular repetition is a hallmark of Art Deco design.

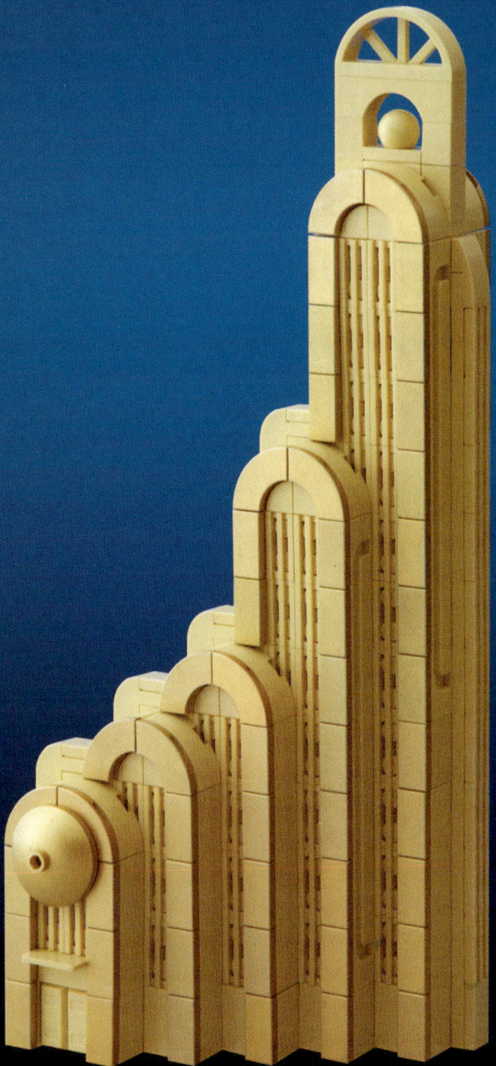

STEAMPUNK

Steampunk worlds imagine an alternate reality where steam power remains the driving engine of progress. Its appeal lies in its contradictions: It's gritty and refined, industrial and ornate, fantastical yet grounded in real machinery, with nary a circuit board in sight.

Steampunk architecture often draws from Victorian England, embellished with a maze of pipes and machinery. It's the kind of place where chimney sweeps get lost for days.

LEGO Technic elements, usually found in detailed vehicle models, take on new life as architectural components. Gears, axles, and linkages add mechanical flair to buildings and help convey the feeling that the city itself is a living machine.

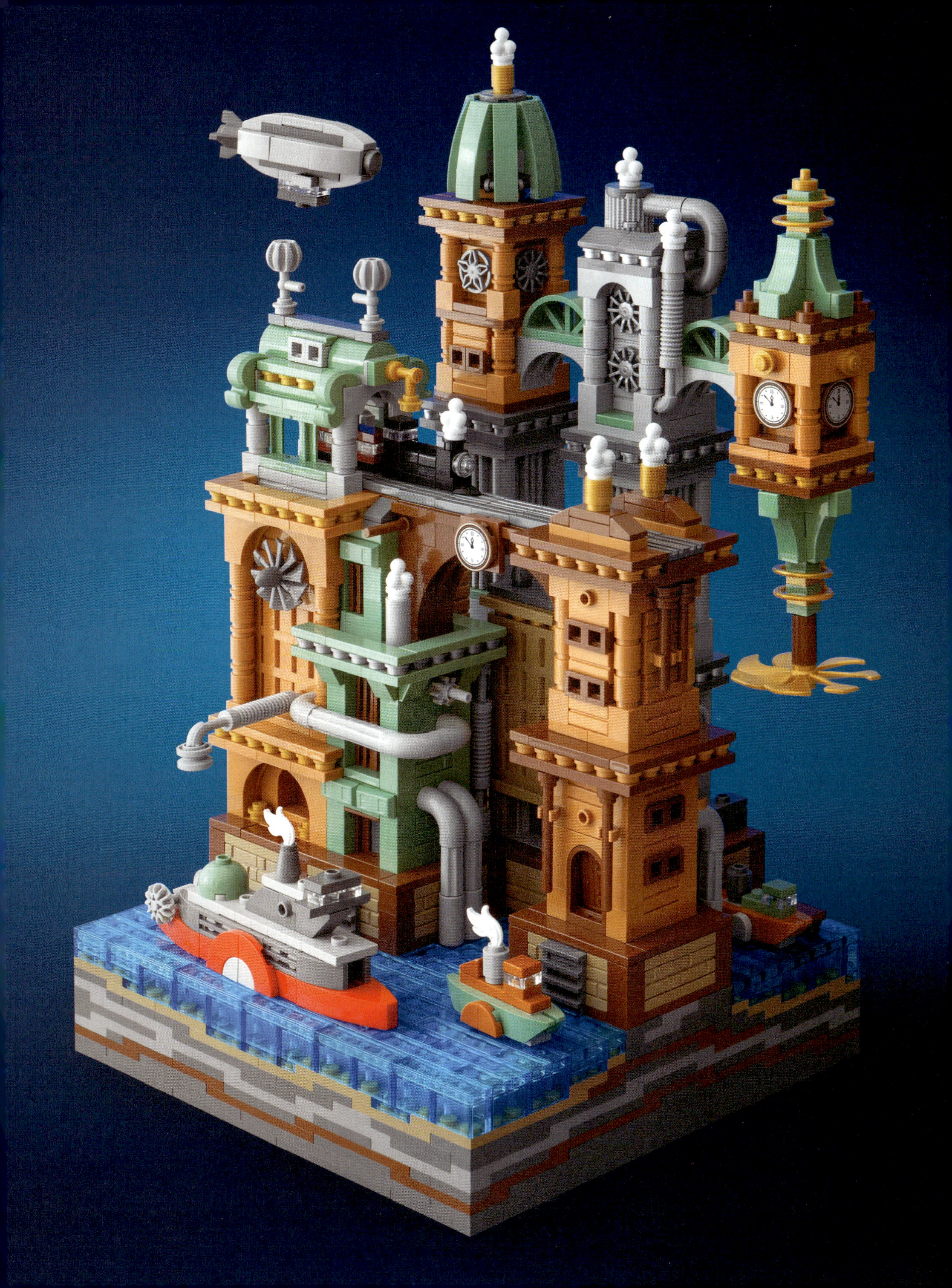

Clocks are important in a steampunk world, and this complex is dedicated to keeping accurate time. It's so important, in fact, that there's even a backup wind power system for the clock—clean energy that's considered sacrilege in a soot-spewing city.

This is the largest model in the book. It's actually made up of three buildings, two of which act as counterbalances for the cantilevered clock. The instructions are designed so each building is constructed separately. You can keep them separate, provided you create a base that allows the clock to stand on its own.

Even if you don't build this model, the roof techniques are worth studying and can be applied to other architectural styles.

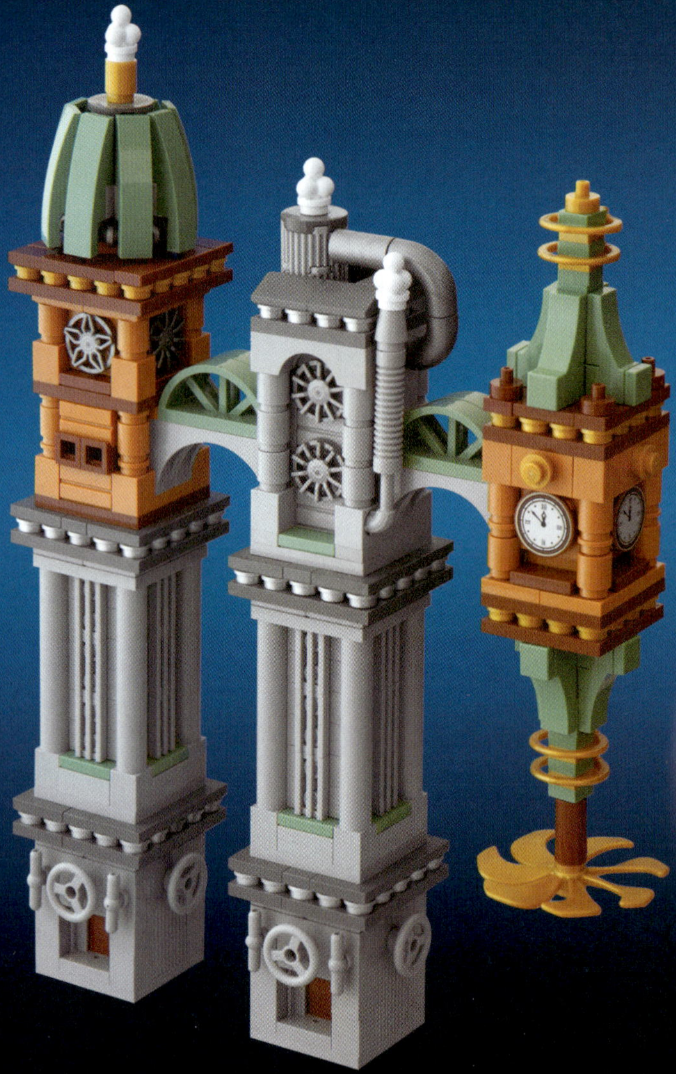

4x 18978b	**4x** 29117b	**4x** 61252	**8x** 61252	**8x** 3024	**14x** 3024	**4x** 3024	**8x** 3070	**4x** 20482	**1x** 20482	**74x** 4073	**12x** 4073	**44x** 4073
2x 4733	**8x** 87087	**1x** 6541	**19x** 3005	**12x** 3005	**2x** 3005	**2x** 26604	**2x** 87087	**4x** 4070	**12x** 3062	**1x** 4589b	**16x** 3062	**1x** 3062
8x 2877	**6x** 98283	**14x** 3700	**4x** 3004	**7x** 98283	**3x** 86876	**16x** 3023	**5x** 3023	**48x** 15573	**24x** 2412b	**5x** 85984	**8x** 30663	

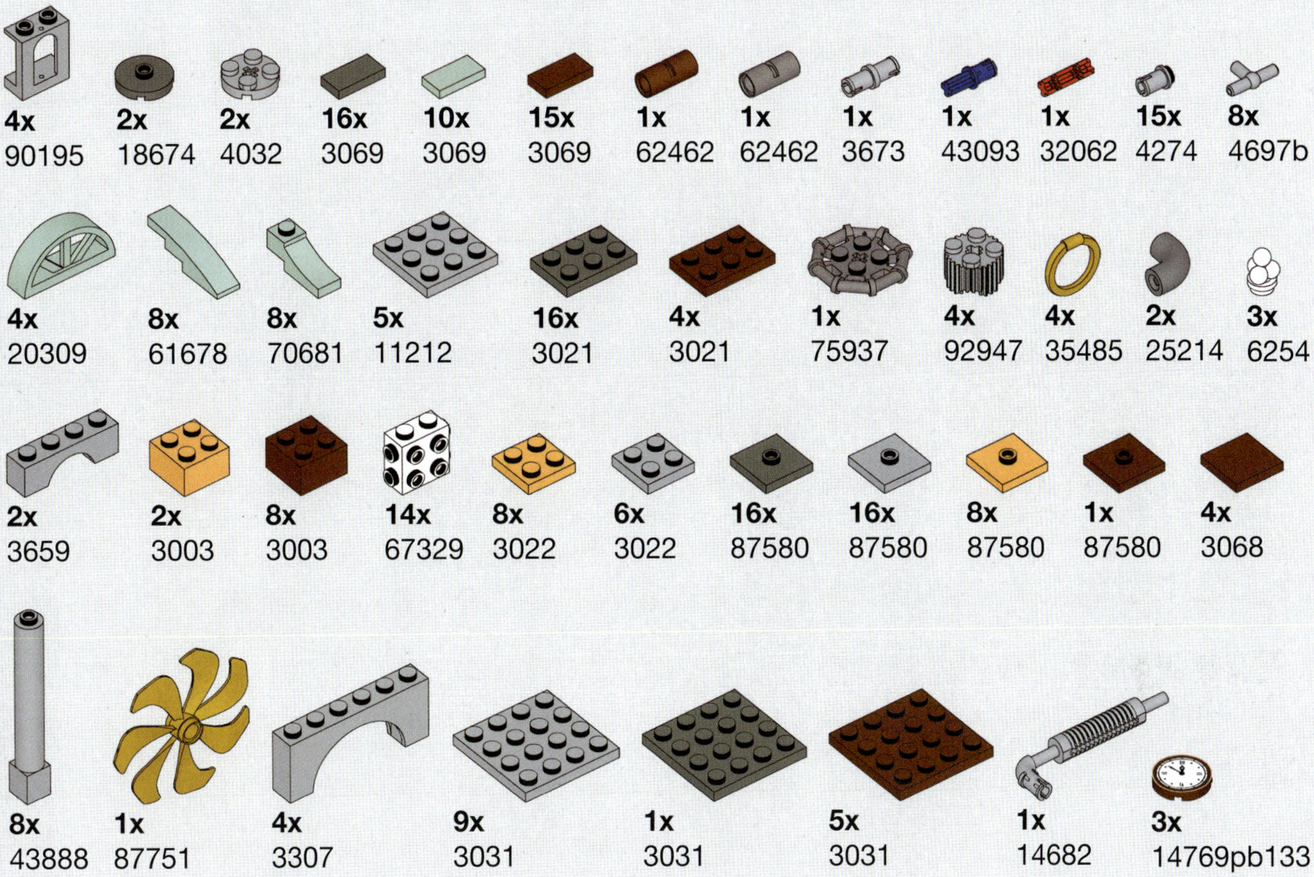
4x 90195
2x 18674
2x 4032
16x 3069
10x 3069
15x 3069
1x 62462
1x 62462
1x 3673
1x 43093
1x 32062
15x 4274
8x 4697b
4x 20309
8x 61678
8x 70681
5x 11212
16x 3021
4x 3021
1x 75937
4x 92947
4x 35485
2x 25214
3x 6254
2x 3659
2x 3003
8x 3003
14x 67329
8x 3022
6x 3022
16x 87580
16x 87580
8x 87580
1x 87580
4x 3068
8x 43888
1x 87751
4x 3307
9x 3031
1x 3031
5x 3031
1x 14682
3x 14769pb133

1

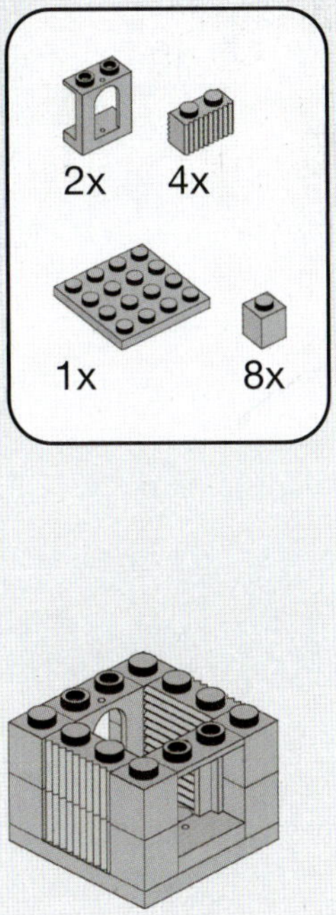
2x
4x
1x
8x

2

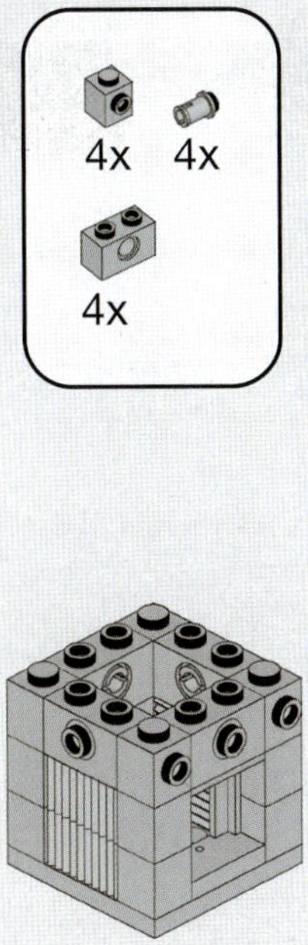
4x
4x
4x

3

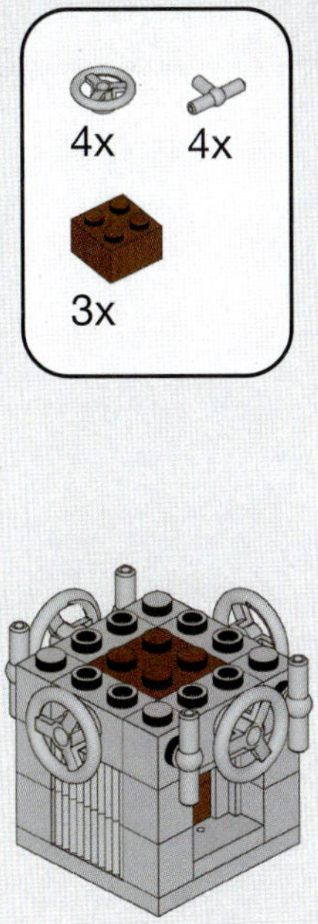
4x
4x
3x

4

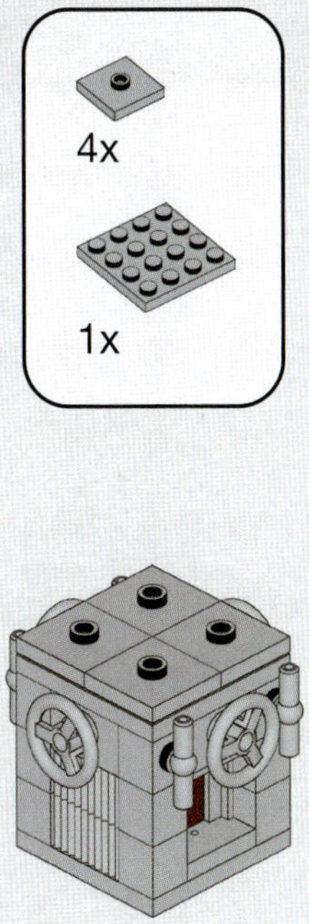
4x
1x

5

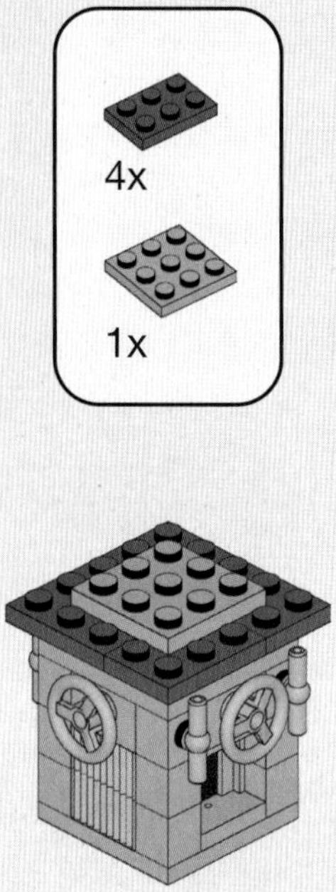

6

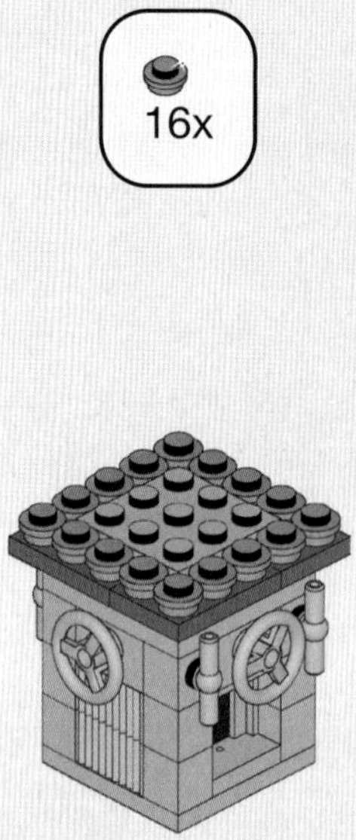

7

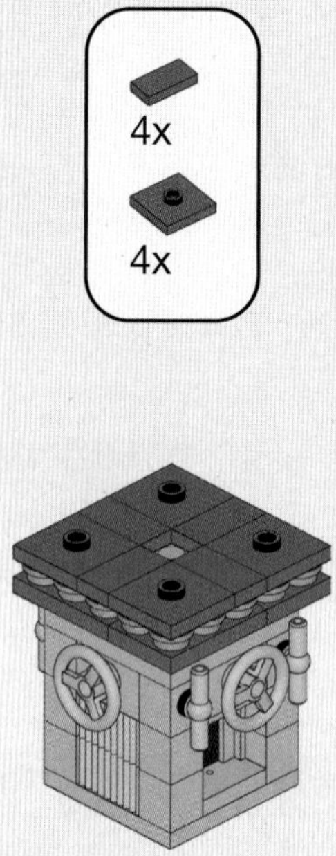

8

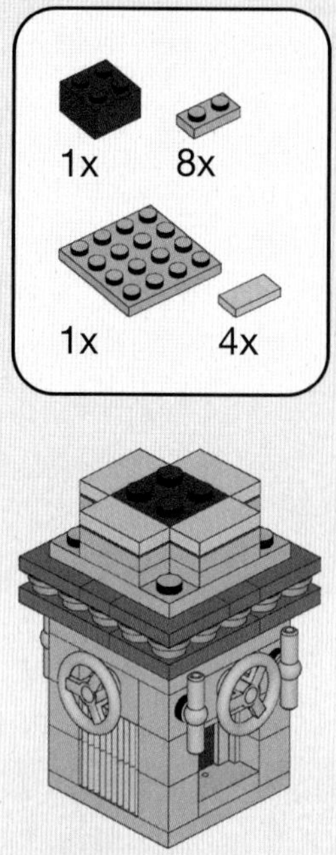

9

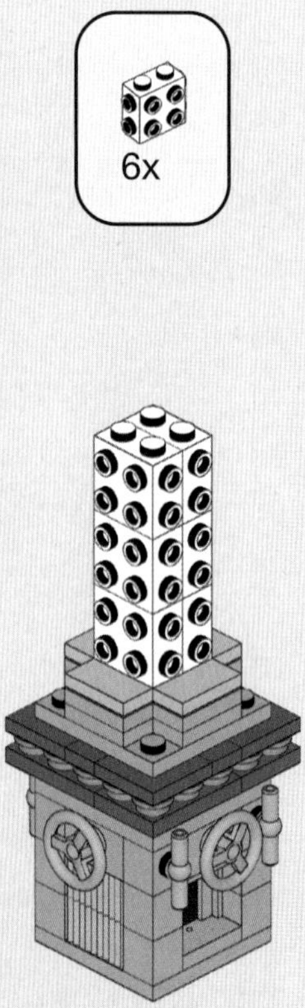

10

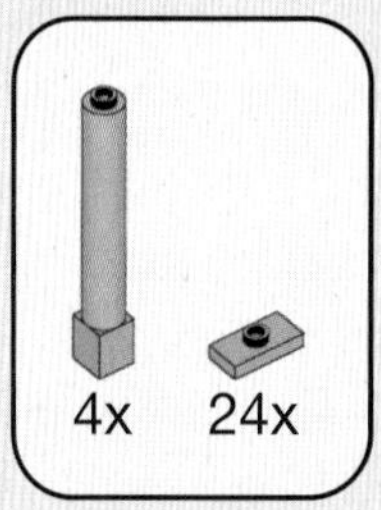

All sides are identical in this step.

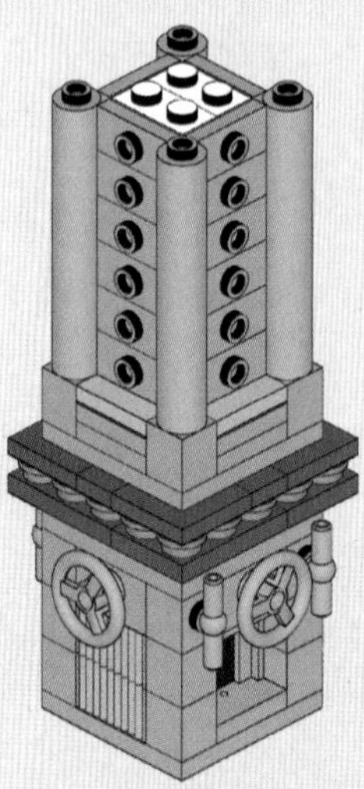

11

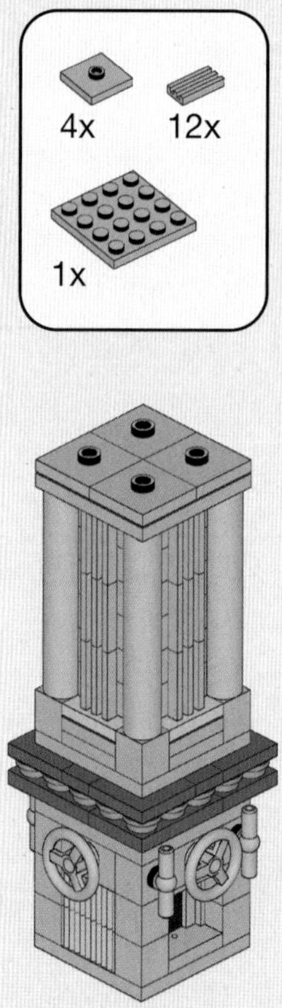

12

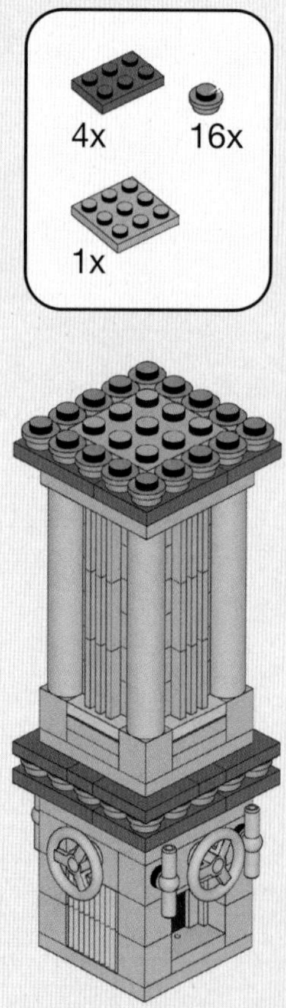

13

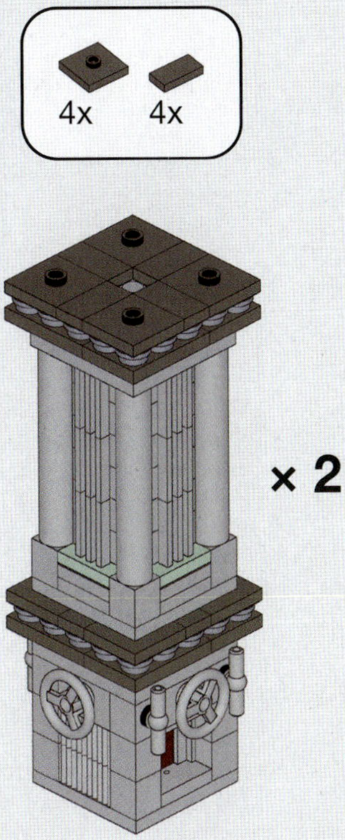

14

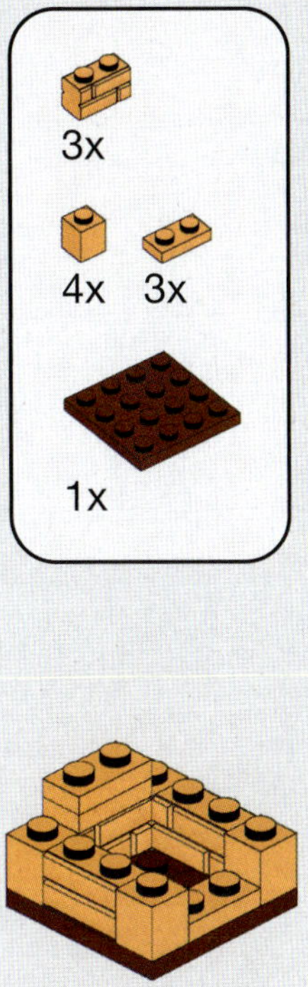

15

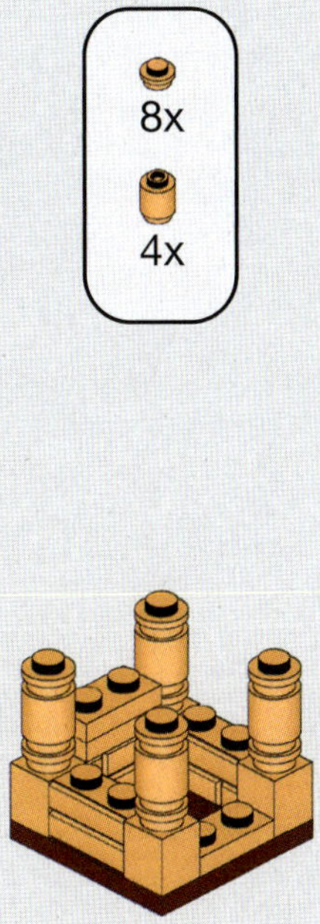

16

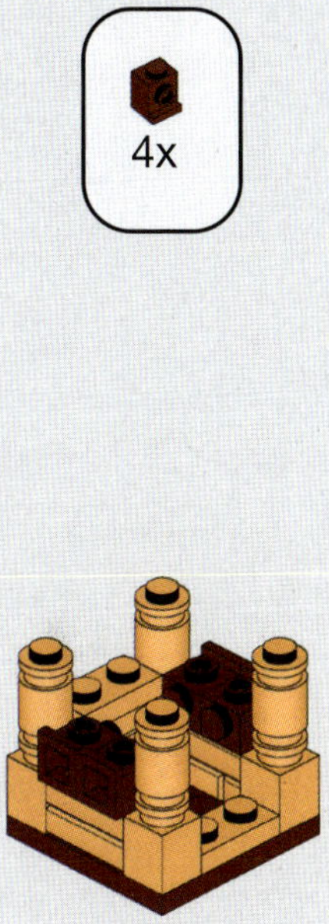

17

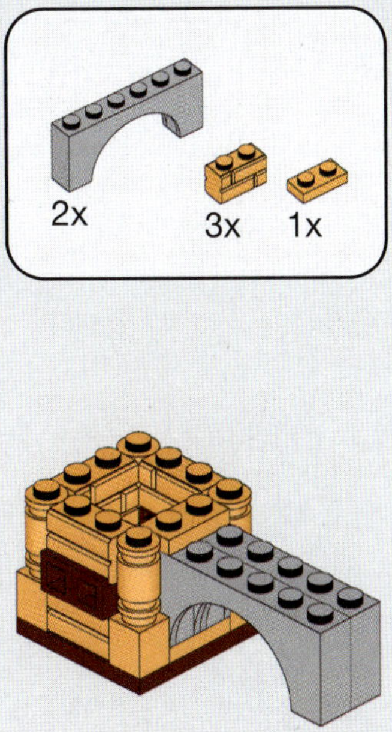

18

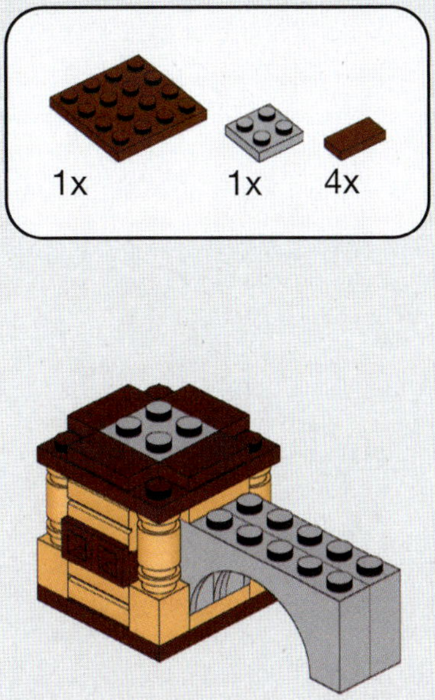

19

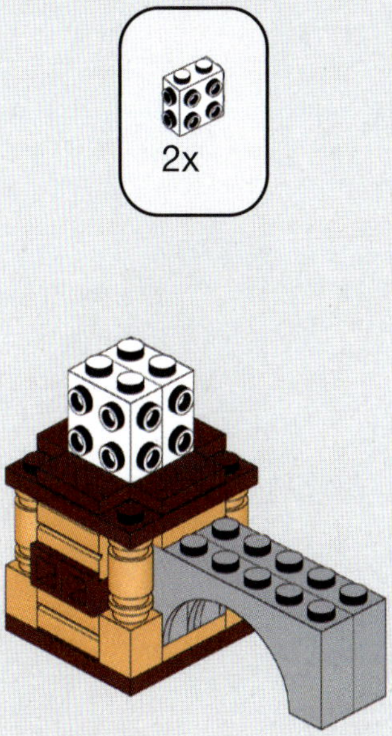

20

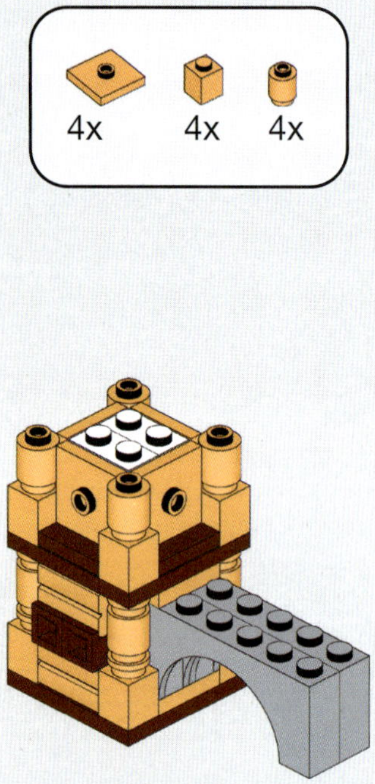

21

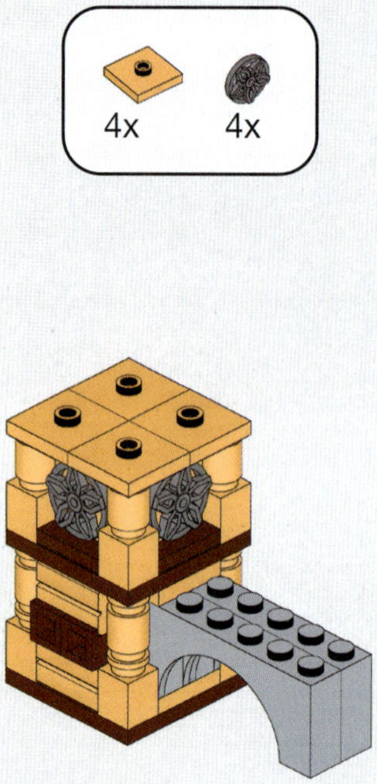

22

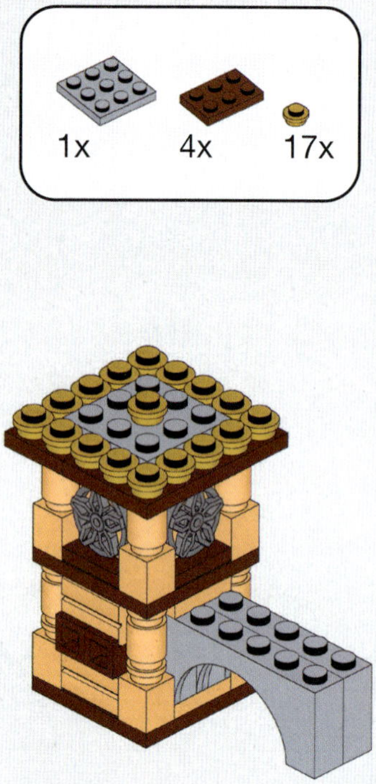

23

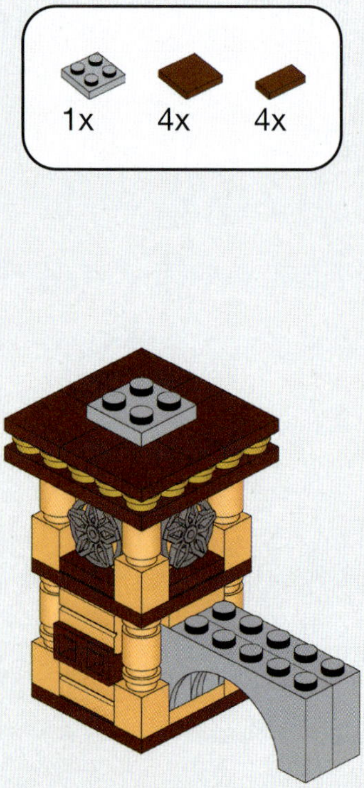

24

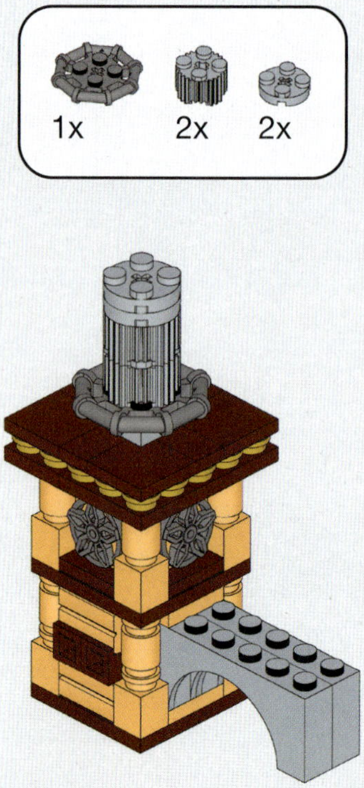

25

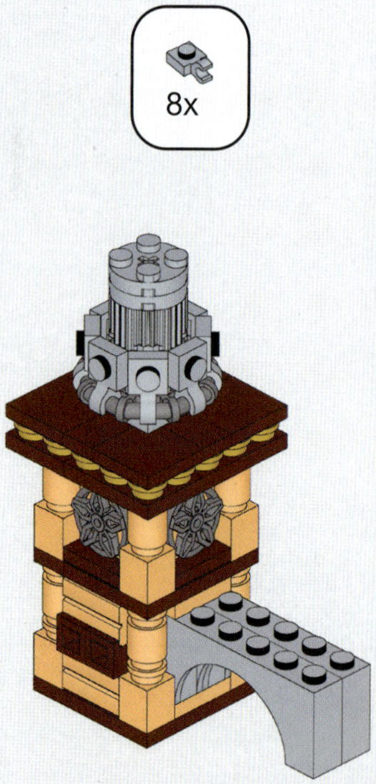

26

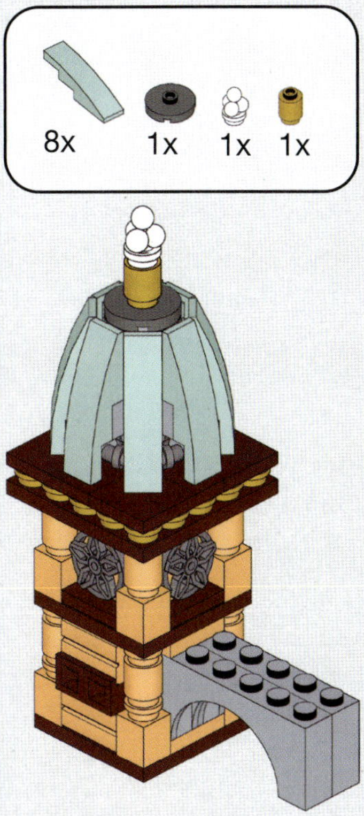

27

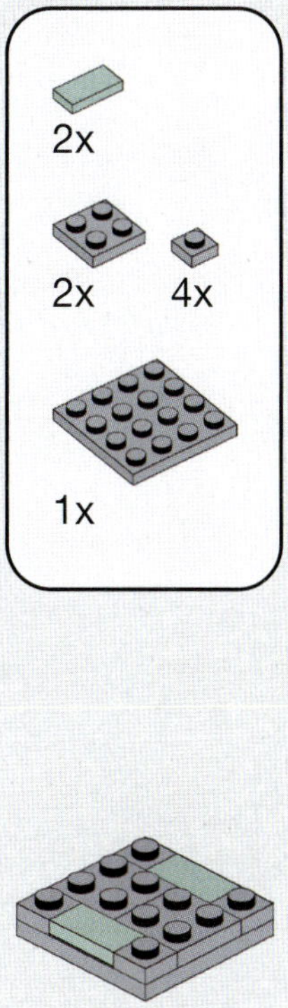

28

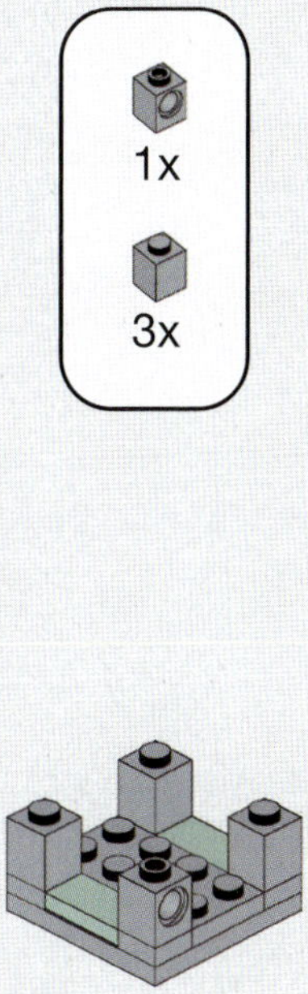

29

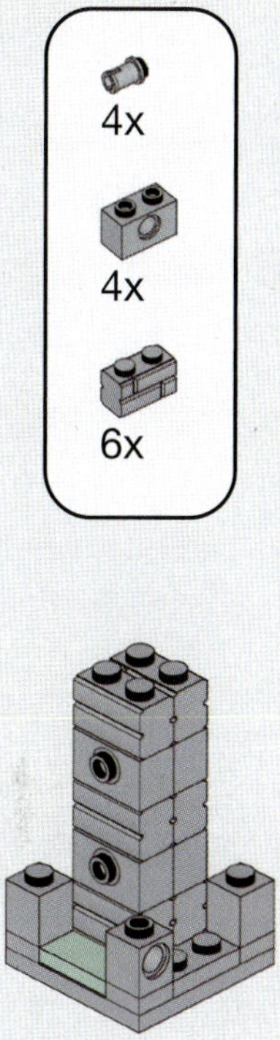

30

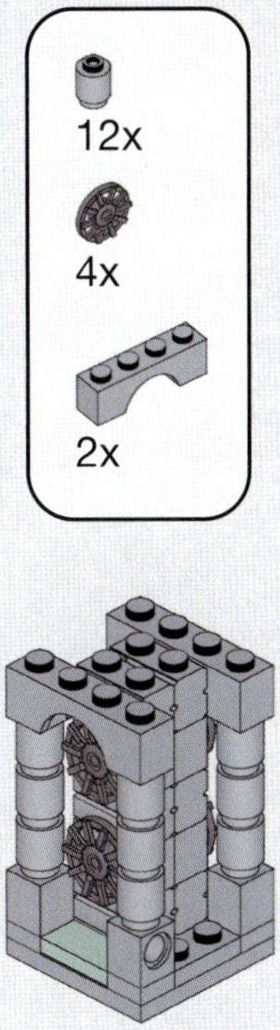

31

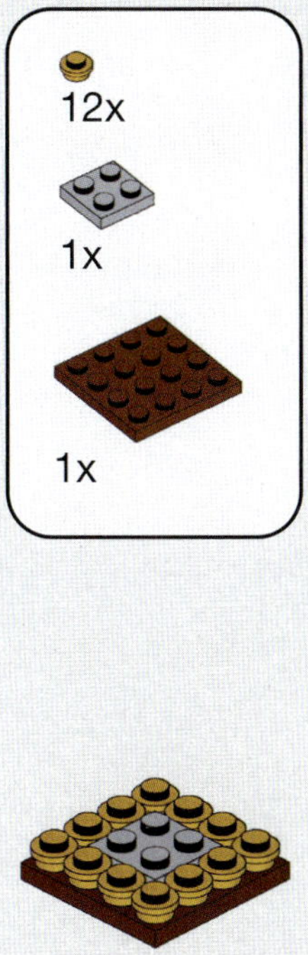

32

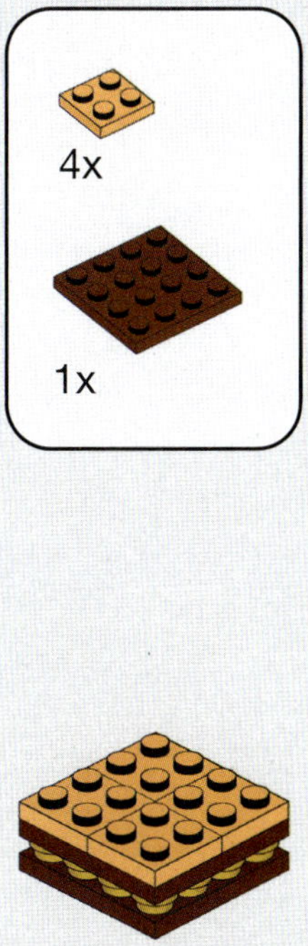

33

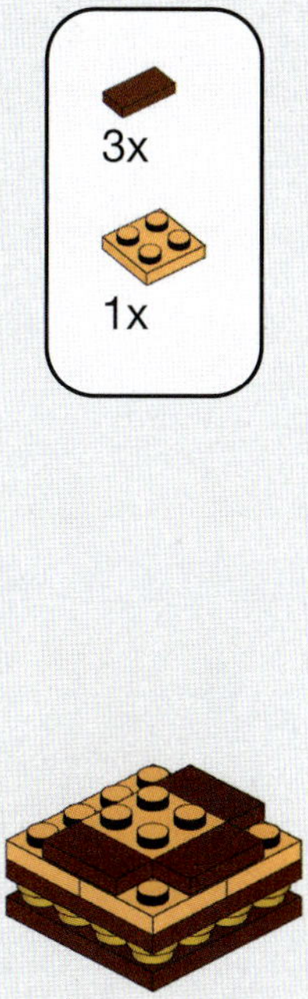

34

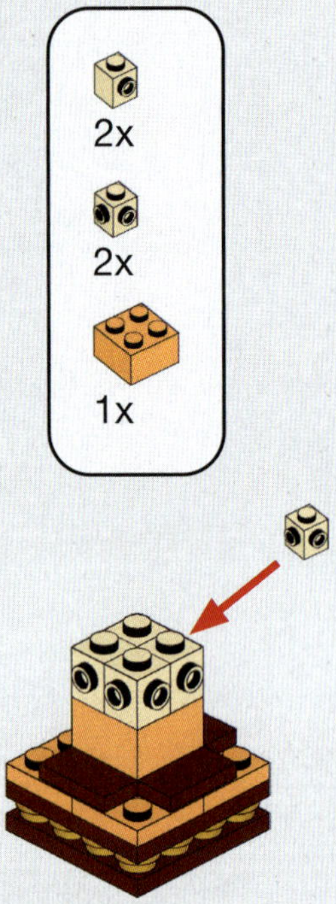

35

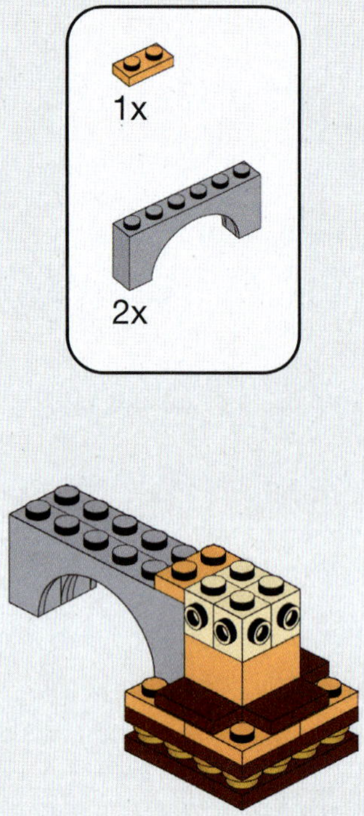

36

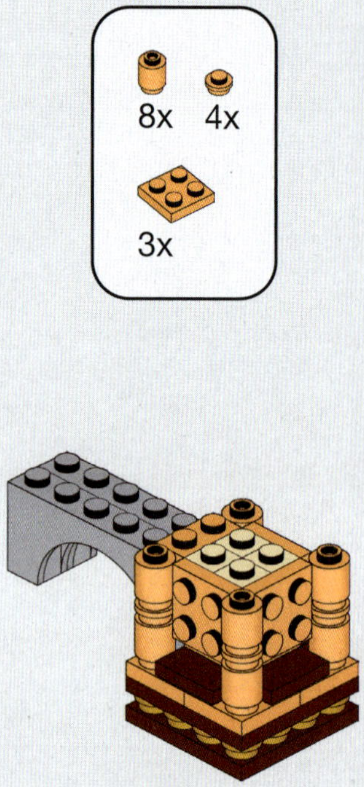

37

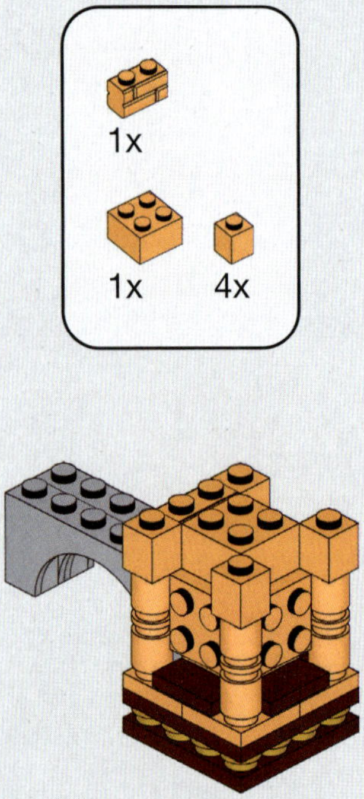

38

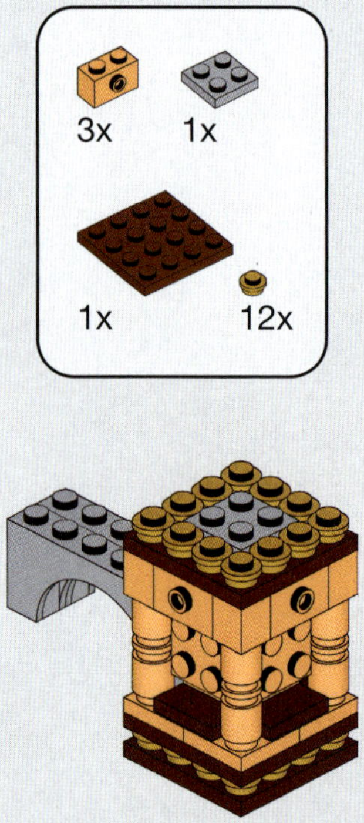

39

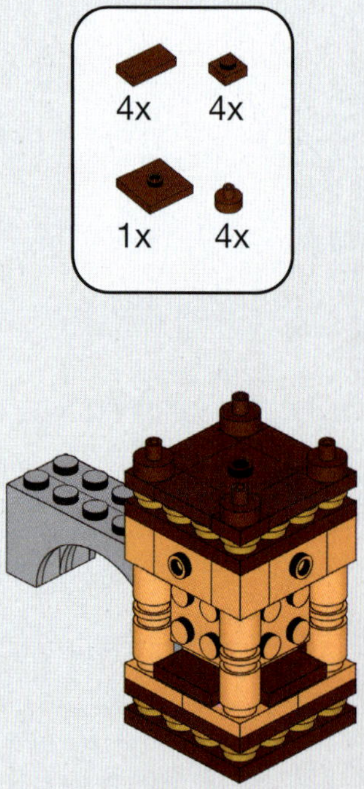

40

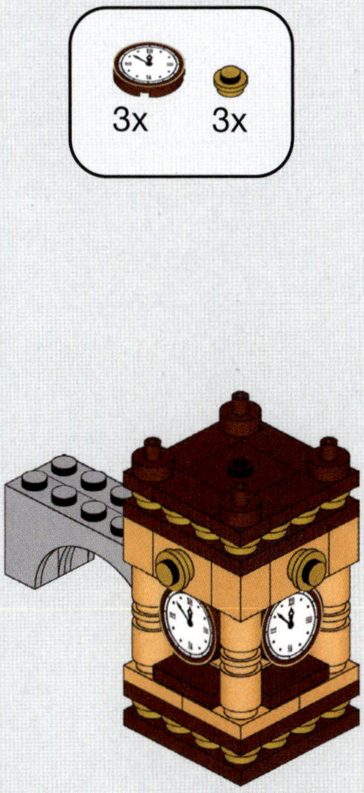

41

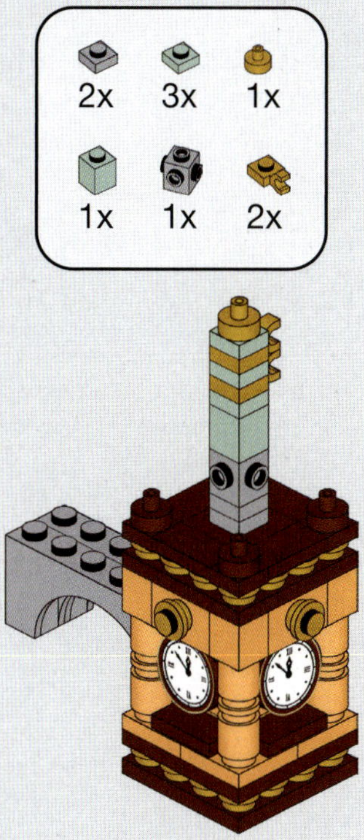

42

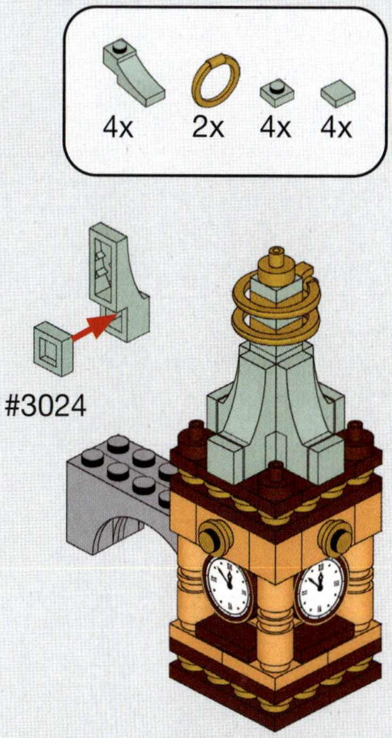

43

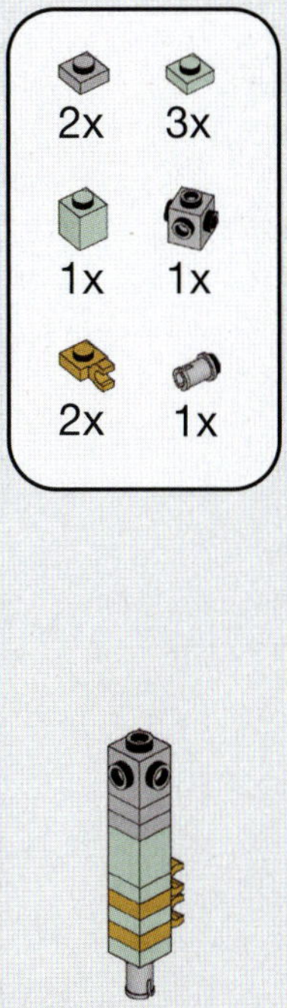

44

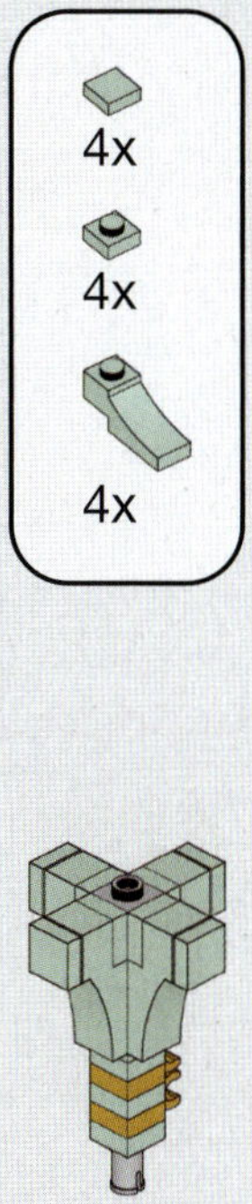

45

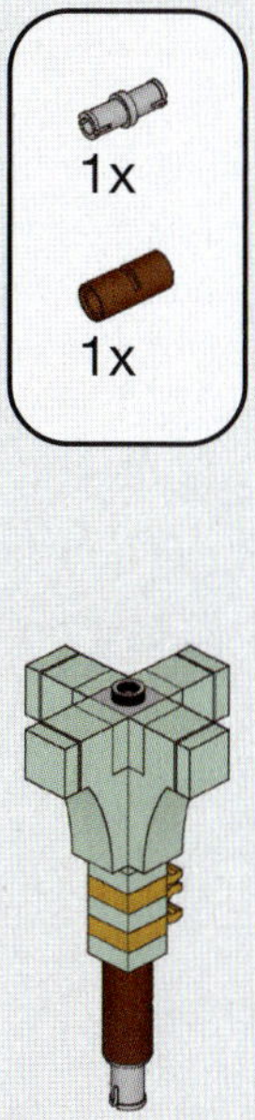

46

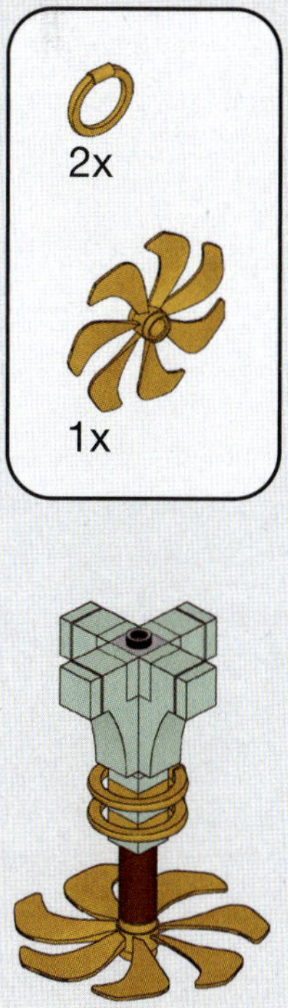

47

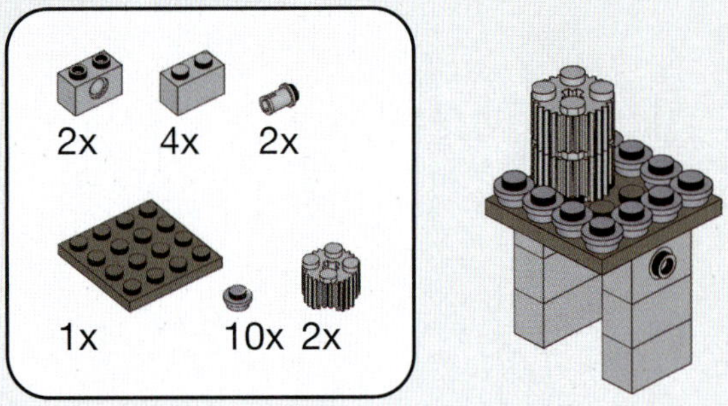

48

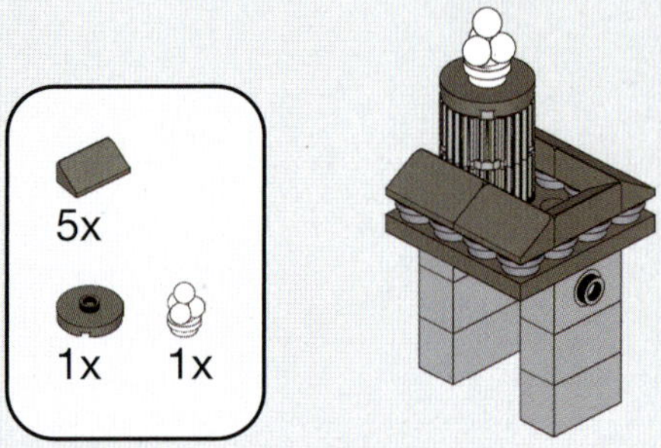

49

Attach the assemblies as shown. The cantilevered clock is secured in place using the step 48 assembly. It helps if you hold the clock module with one hand while attaching the step 48 assembly with the other.

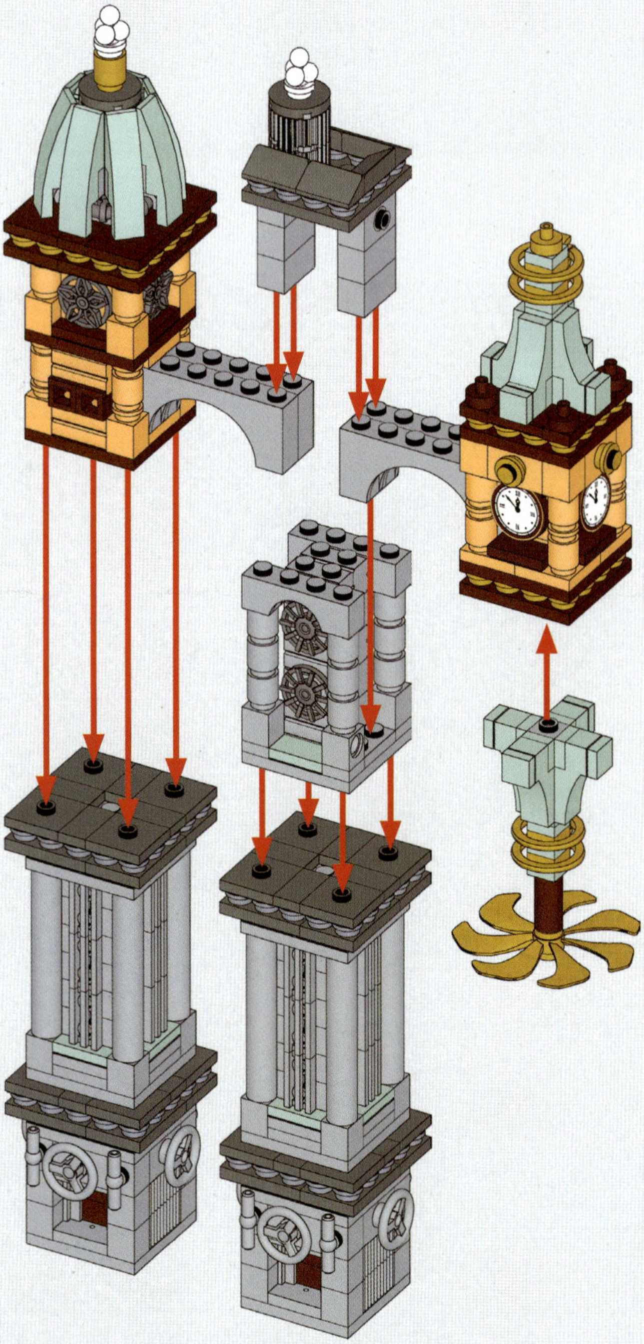

WHAT IS A CANTILEVER?

In architecture, a *cantilever* is a structural element that extends horizontally and is supported at only one end. The other end projects outward without any support underneath.

The cantilevered clock in this build would be too extreme to construct at full scale using real-world materials, but it works perfectly with LEGO!

50

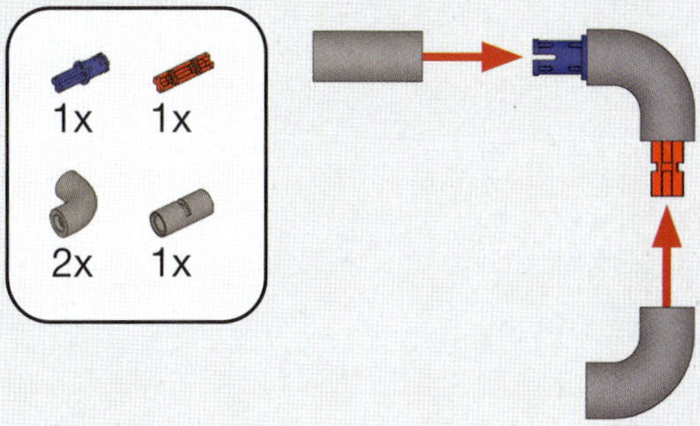

51

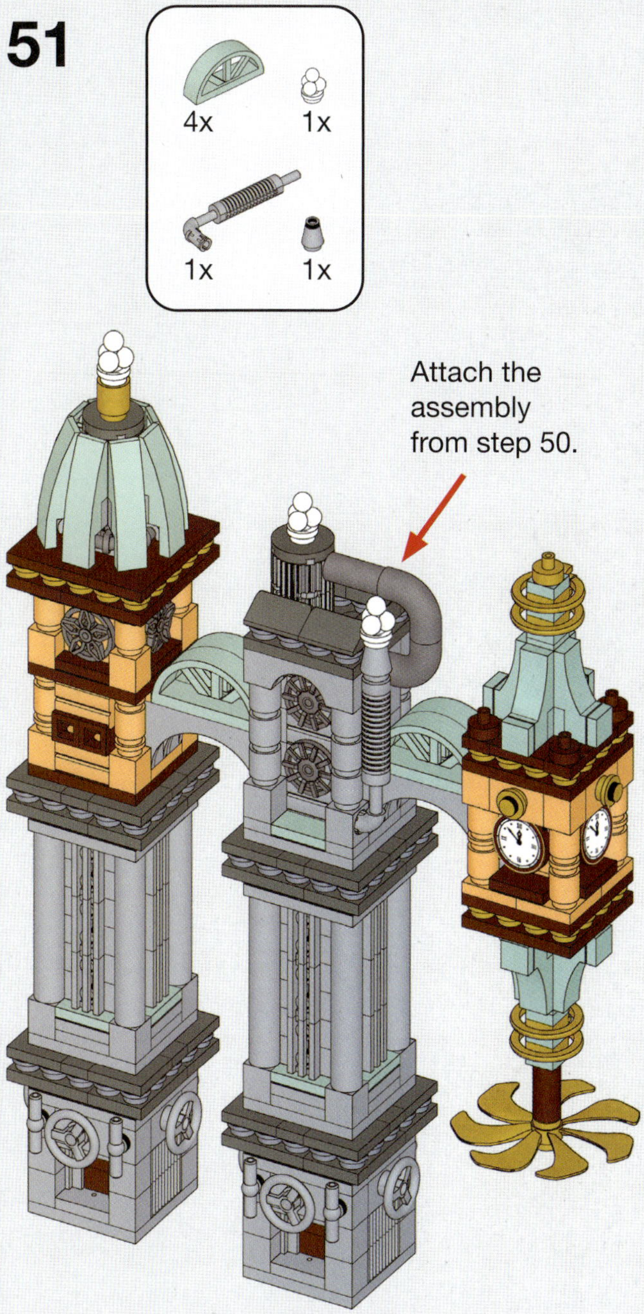

MAKE IT YOUR OWN

You can rearrange the clock to stand on its own support, with the roof now serving as the base as shown.

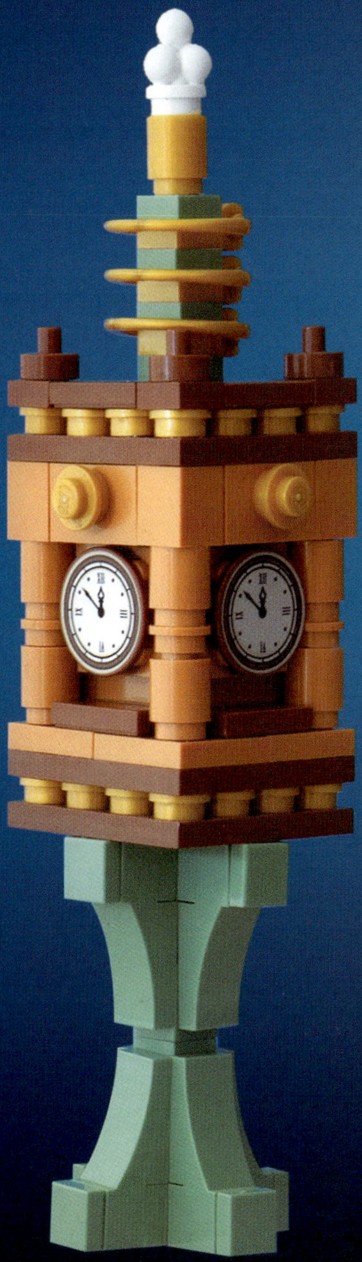

STEAM WHEELER

The Steam Wheeler is a river-faring steampunk vessel powered by side-mounted paddle wheels. It churns through murky water like a hungry goose.

Even if their purpose is vague, gears are valuable in steampunk design. They suggest mechanical complexity and the industrial ingenuity that defines the style.

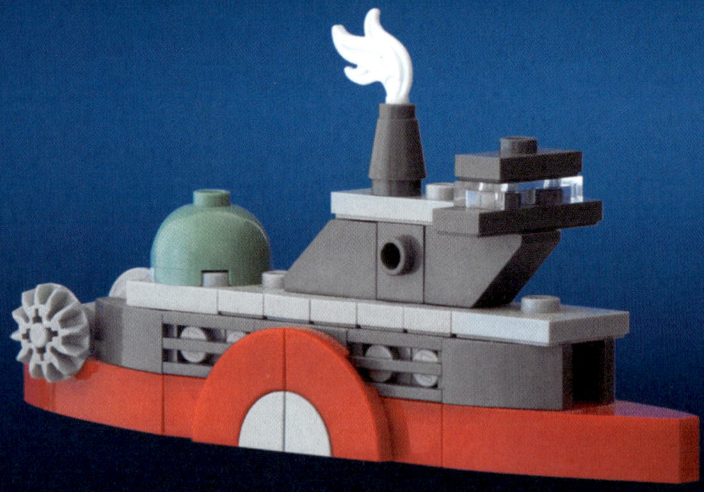

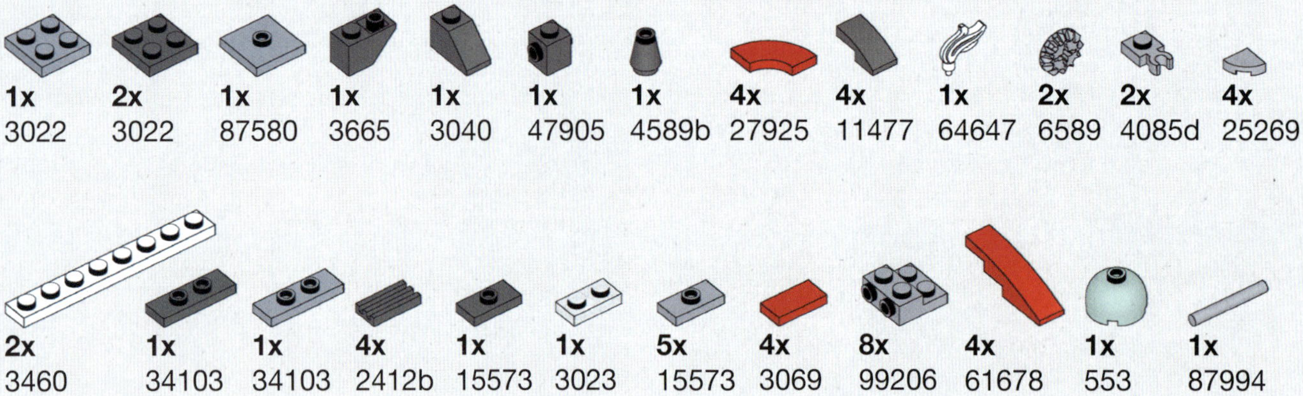

1

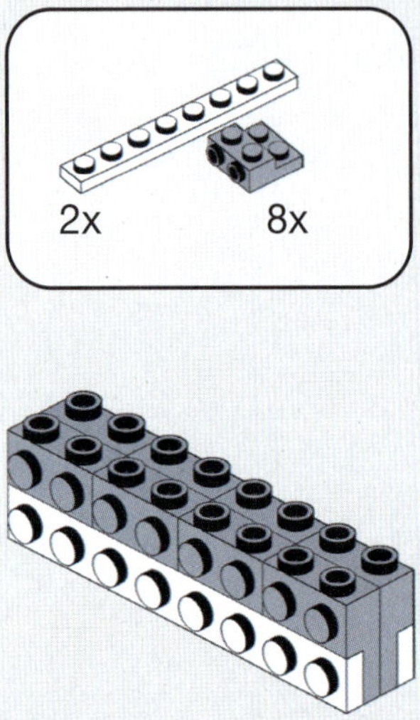

The ship's sides are identical.

2

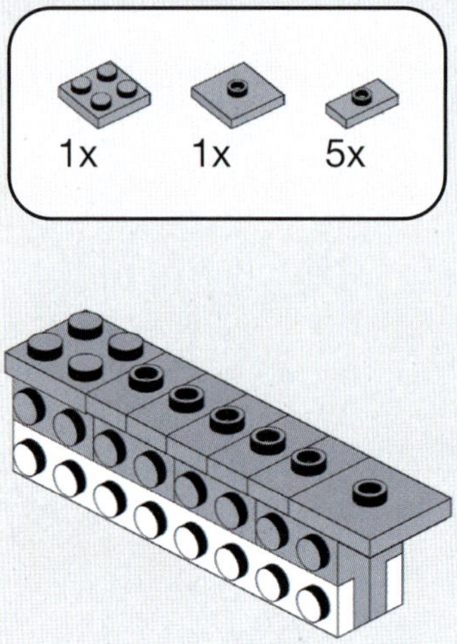

3

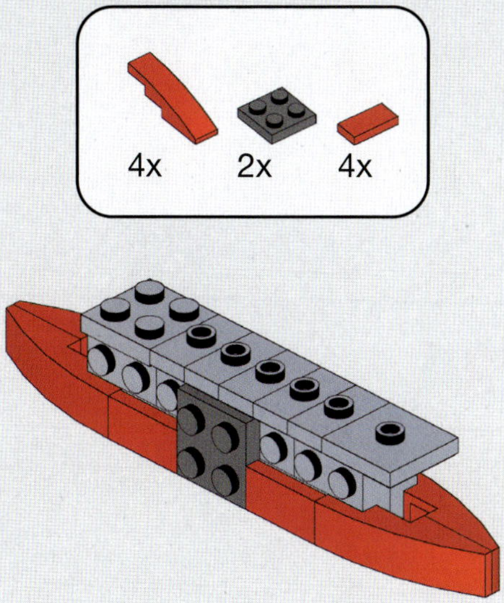

4

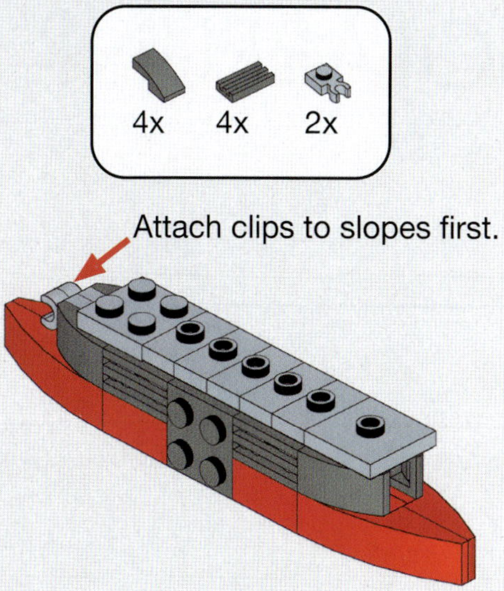

5

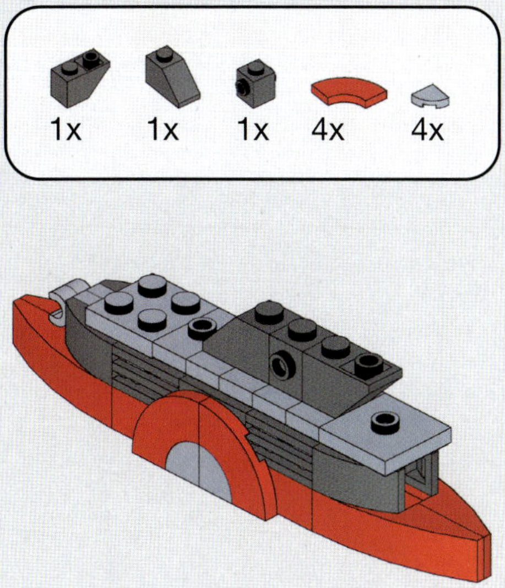

6

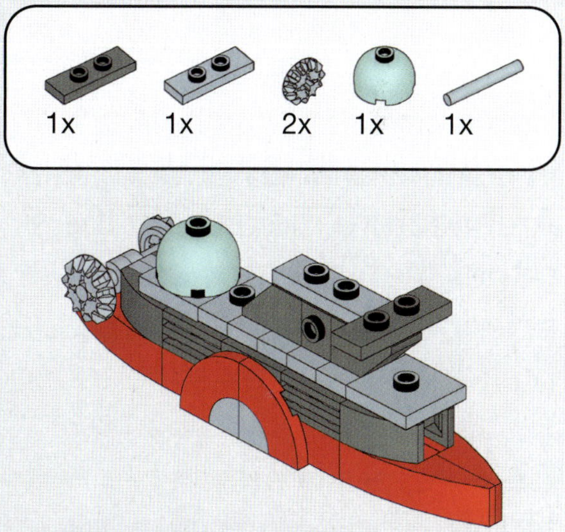

7

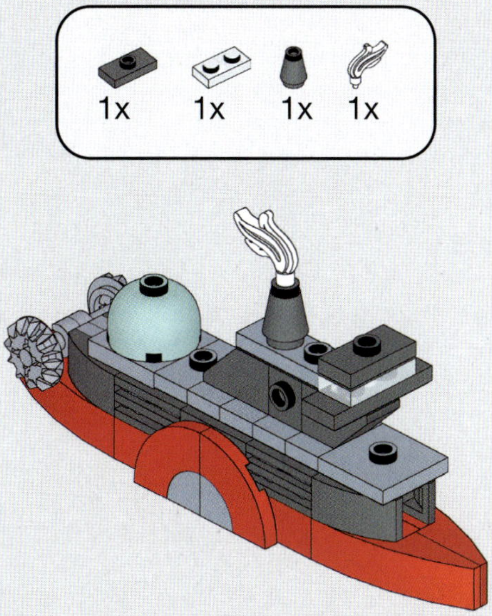

MAKE IT YOUR OWN

Add a turbo steam exhaust using an elbow macaroni brick (#71076), and replace the rear gears with pulleys (#4185) for bigger wheel spin.

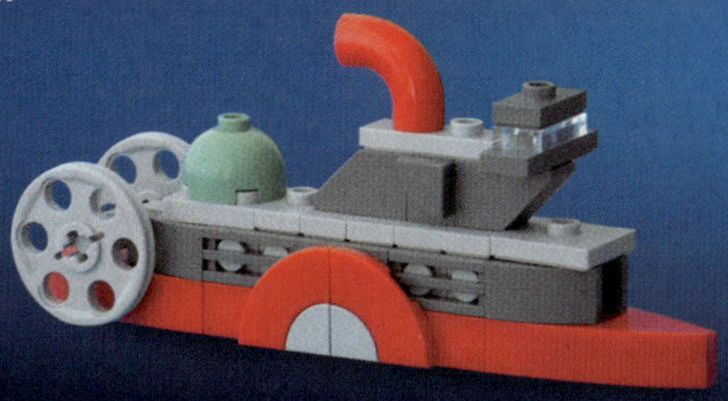

SOLARPUNK

Solarpunk is a vision of a world rooted in optimism and harmony with nature. Architecture melds with the environment rather than overpowering it. It looks like science fiction, but such a place can be built today with existing technology.

Can you really attach the "punk" suffix to this utopian paradise? Solarpunk isn't about loud rebellion or anarchy like some other "punk" styles. Its resistance lies in pushing back against dystopian futures and corporate control.

Curving forms can be challenging to create with LEGO, but by combining curved slopes with inverted arches, you can achieve elegant, flowing lines that capture the organic beauty of solarpunk architecture.

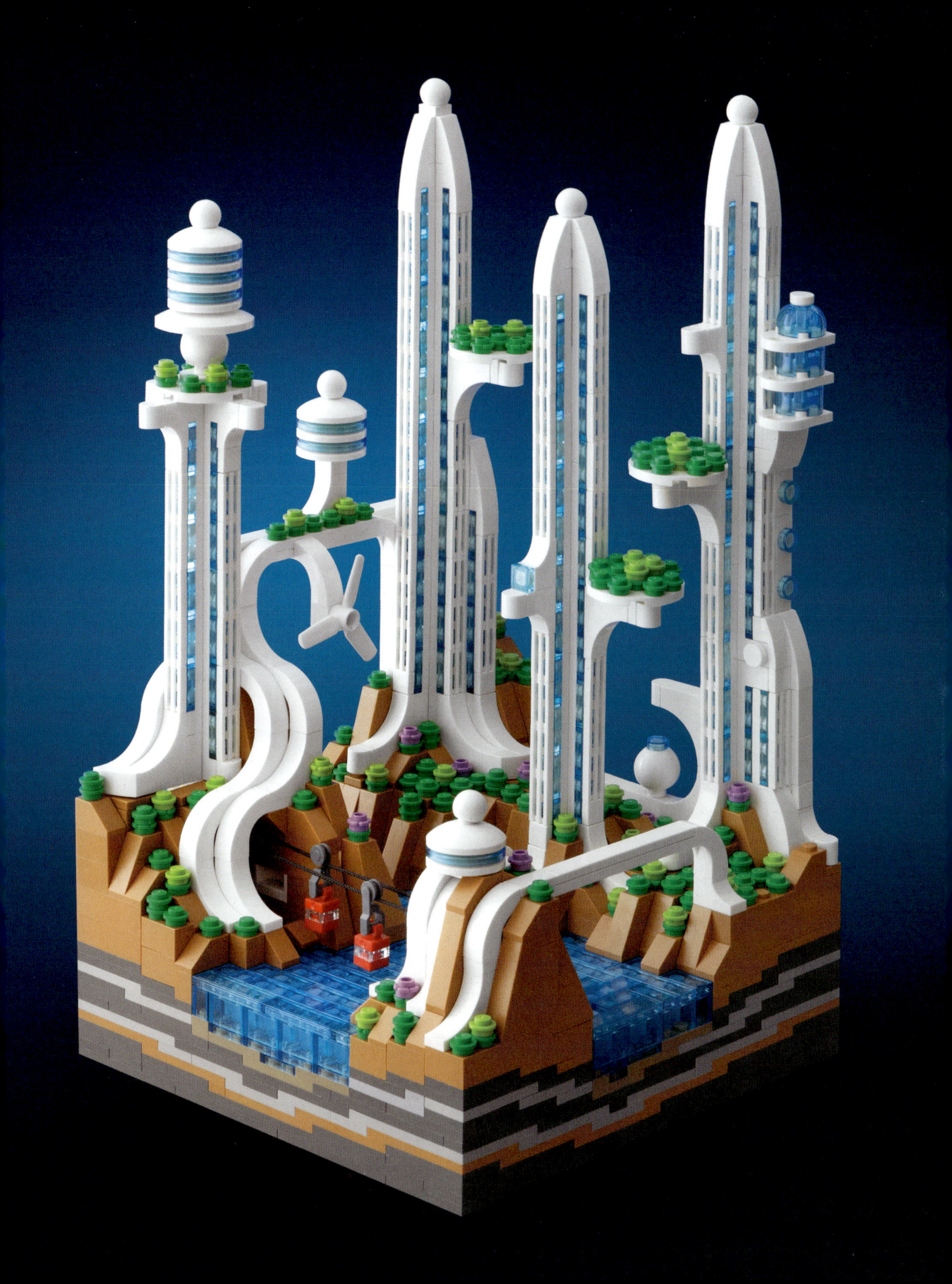

SOLSTICE SPIRE

Build a soaring sanctuary with a lush garden oasis perched high above the city.

Curves soften verticality, creating a flowing, graceful impression rather than rigid monumentality.

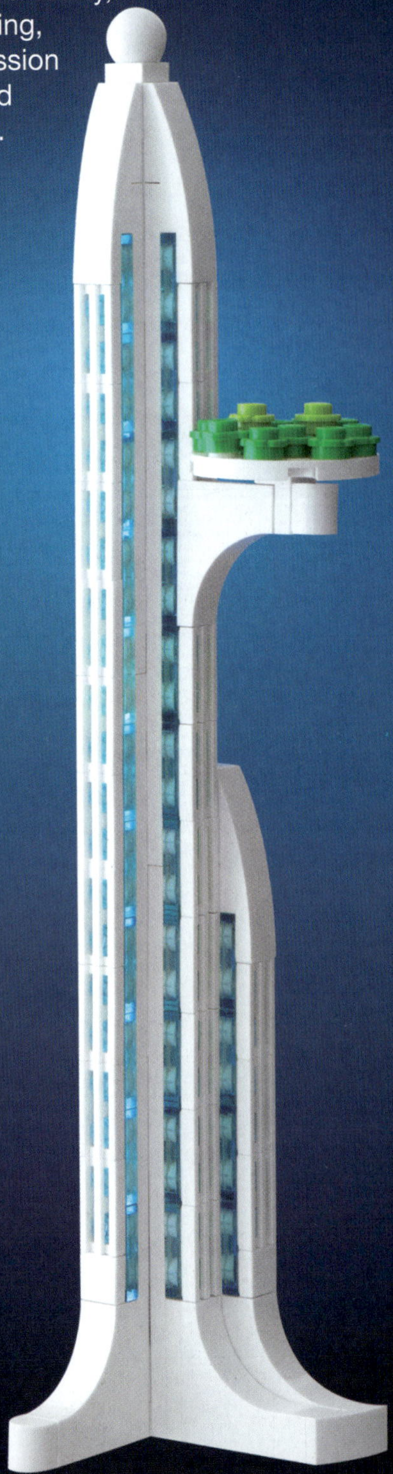

Quantity	Part
13x	4733
2x	3005
1x	36840
29x	3024
12x	4073
2x	4073
4x	3623
52x	3023
5x	3023
45x	2412b
3x	3069
7x	3070
7x	87079
1x	3068
1x	11477
1x	32474
2x	49307
2x	3035
4x	18653
1x	60474
7x	61678
2x	60479
1x	4477
5x	3460
1x	6112
2x	2445
3x	3666

1

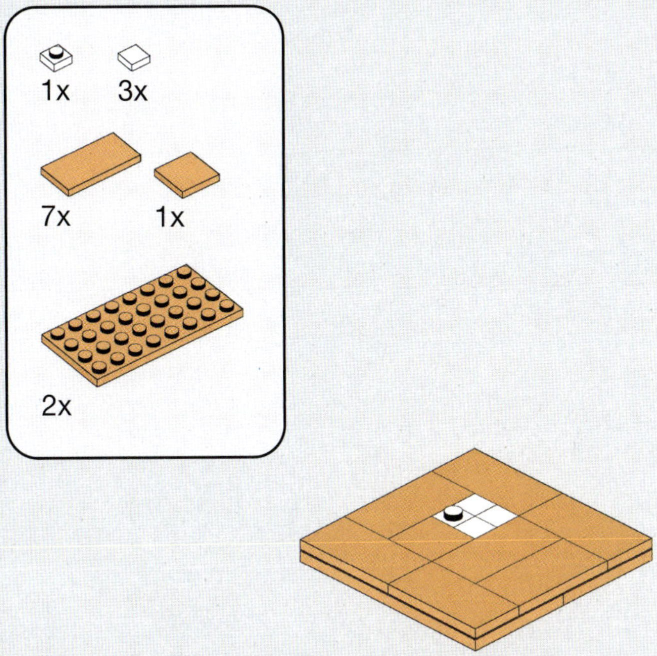

2

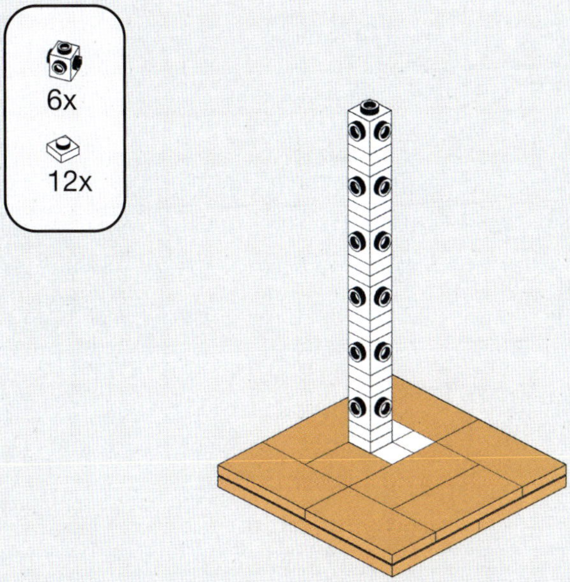

3

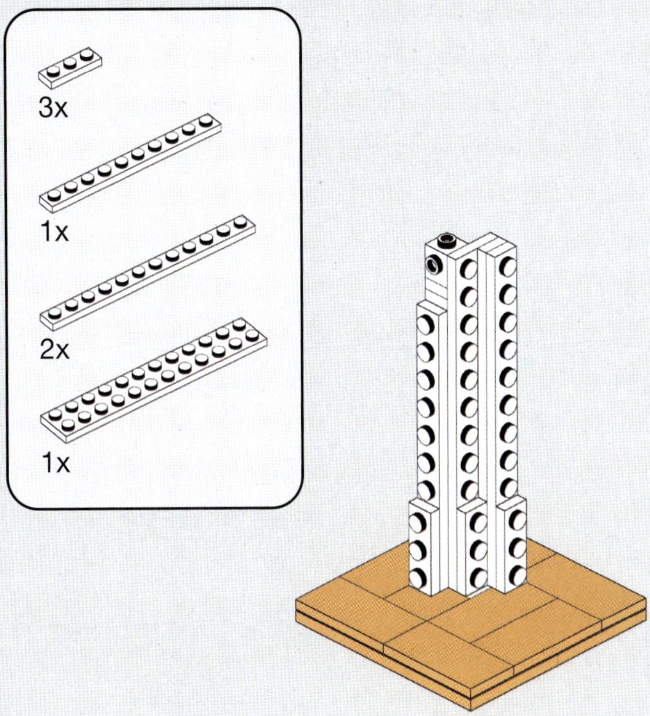

4

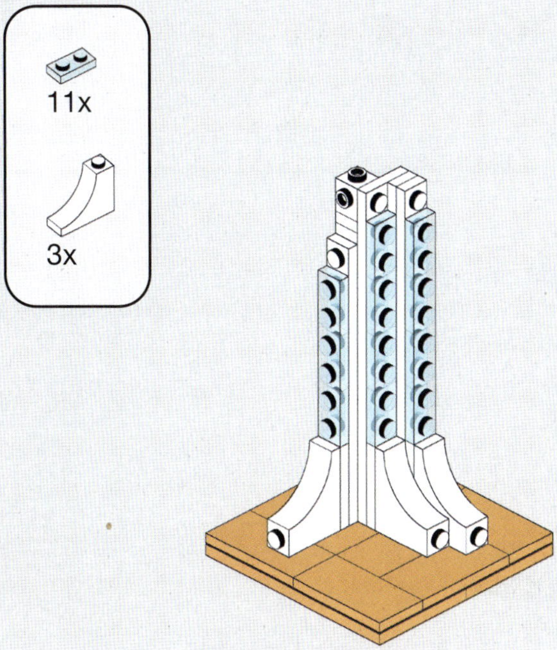

5

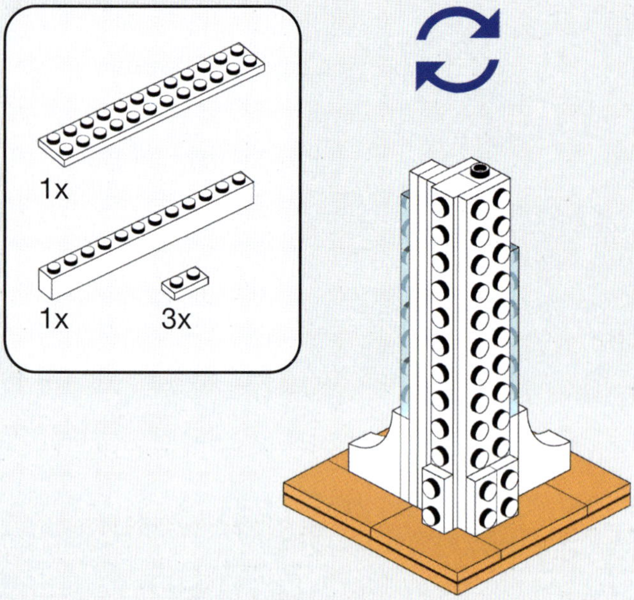

6

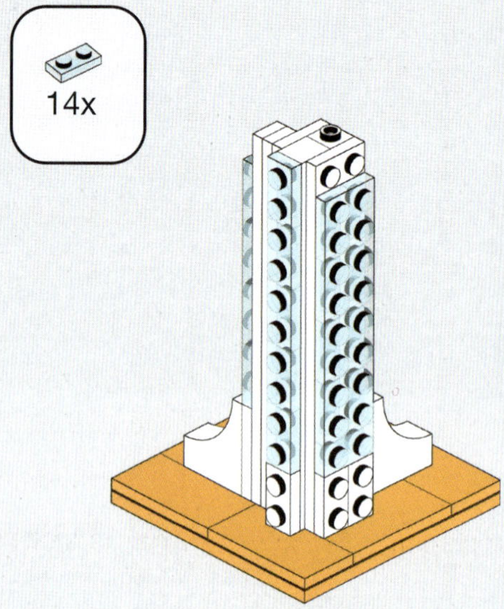

7

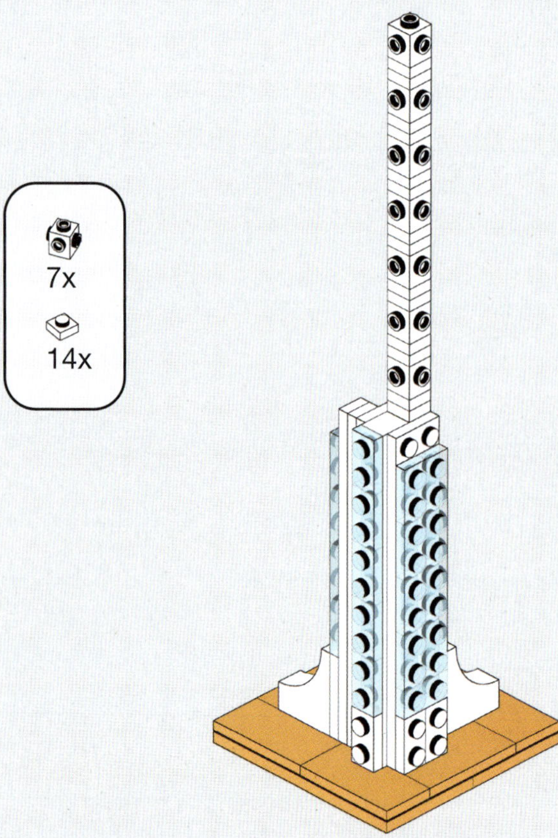

8

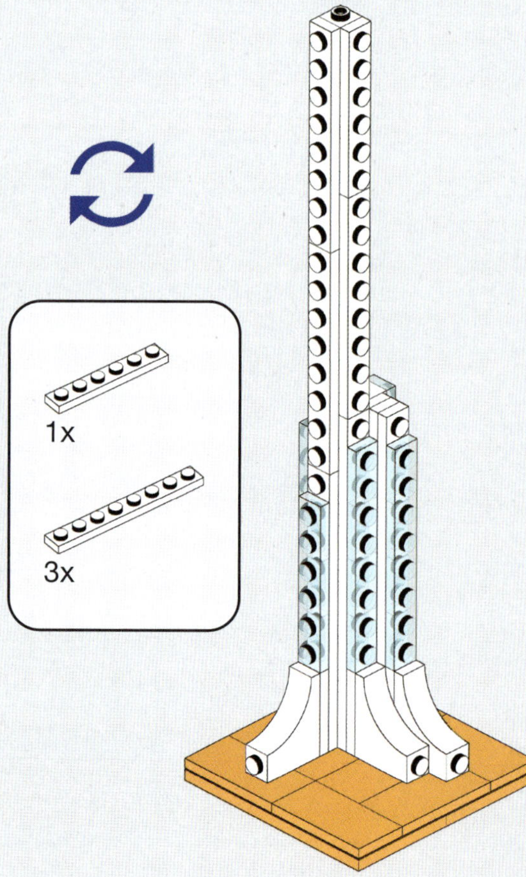

9

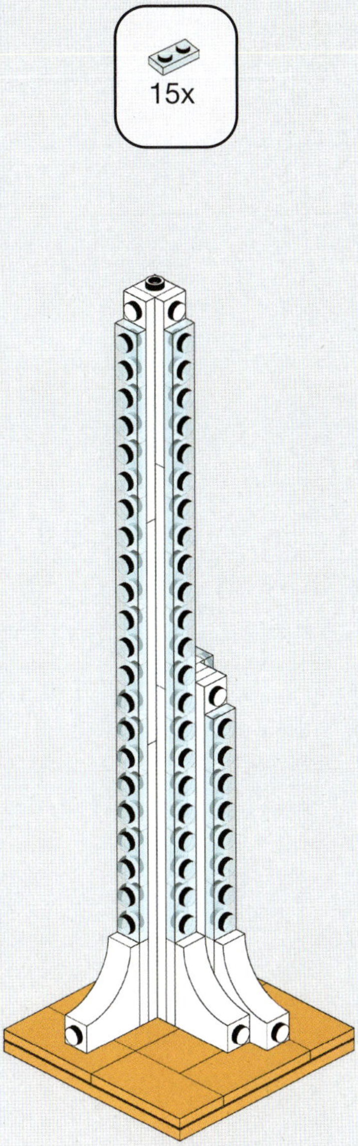

10

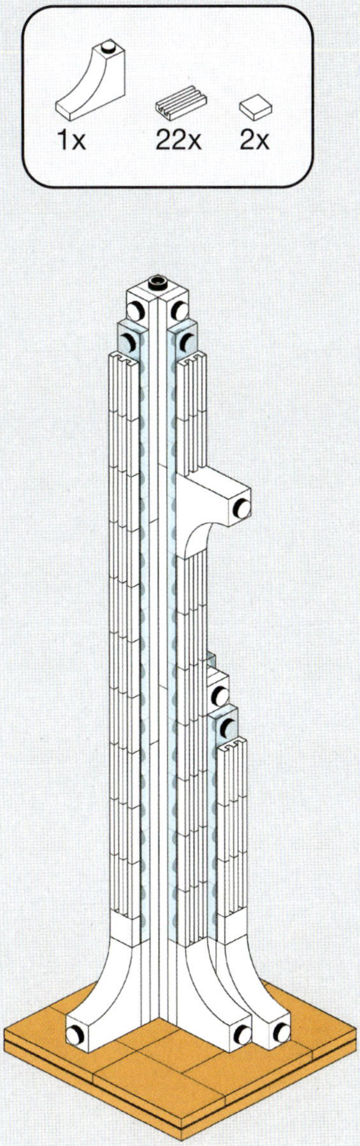

11

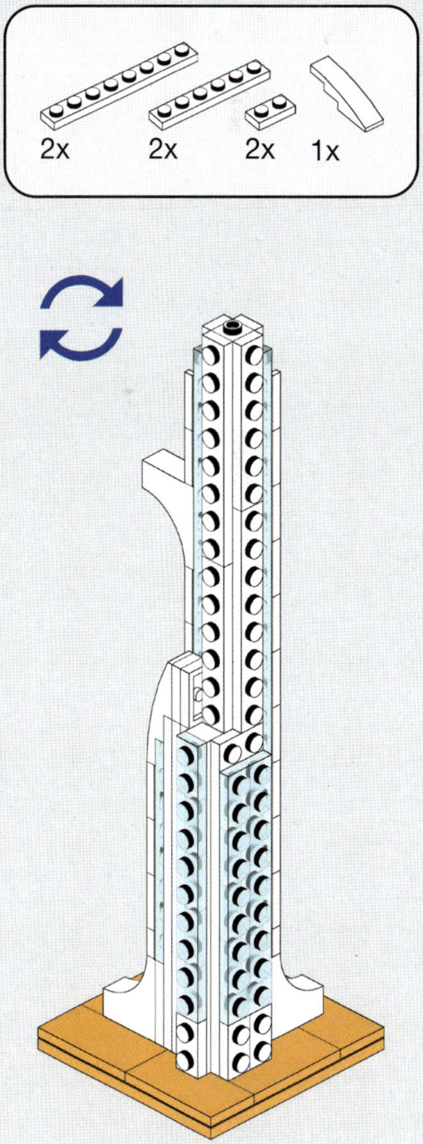

12

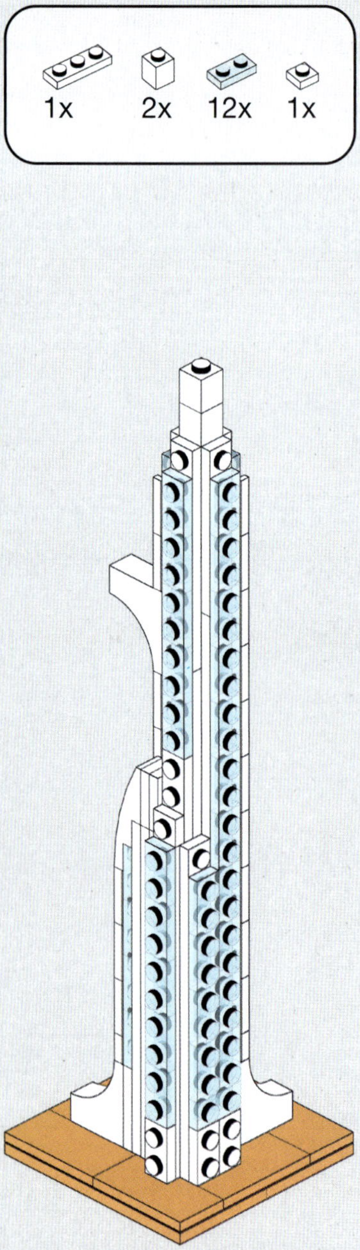

13

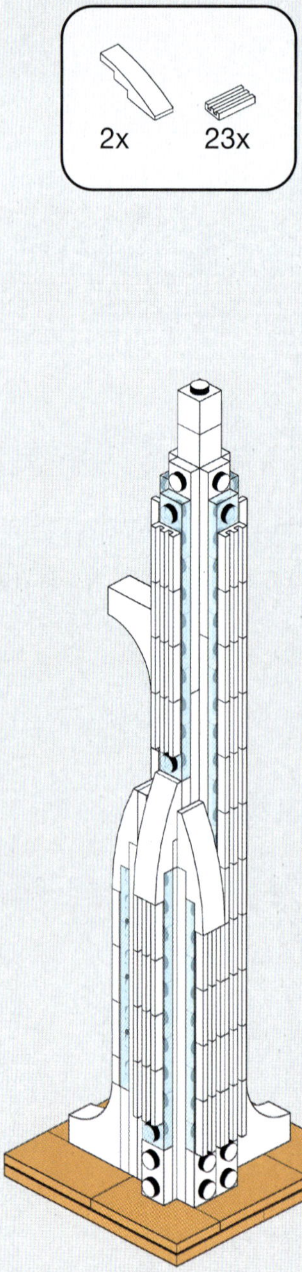

14

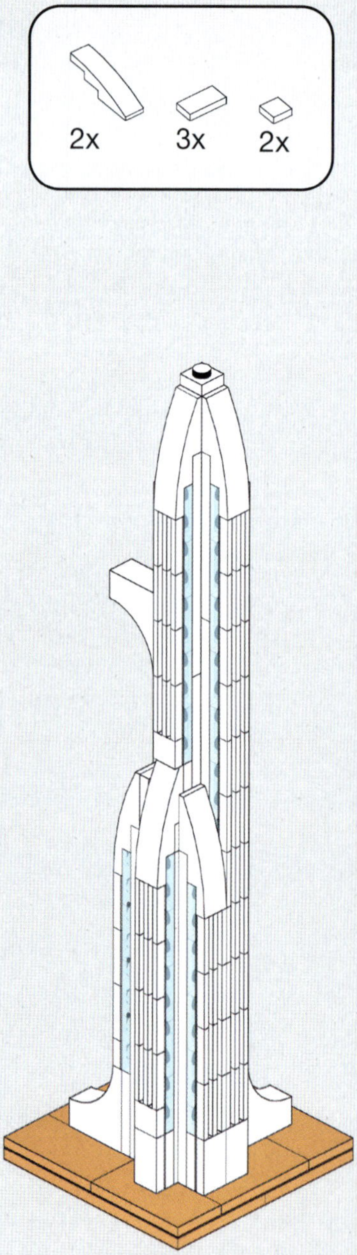

15

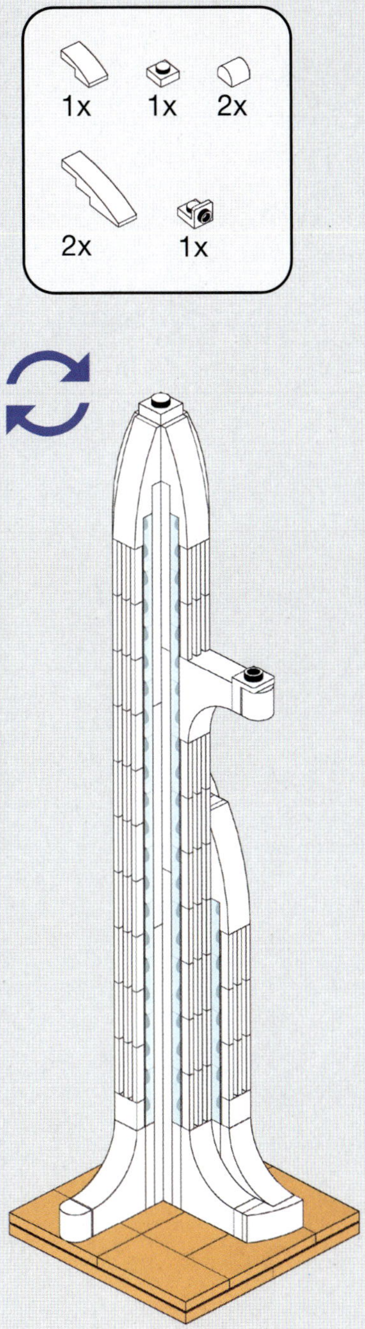

16

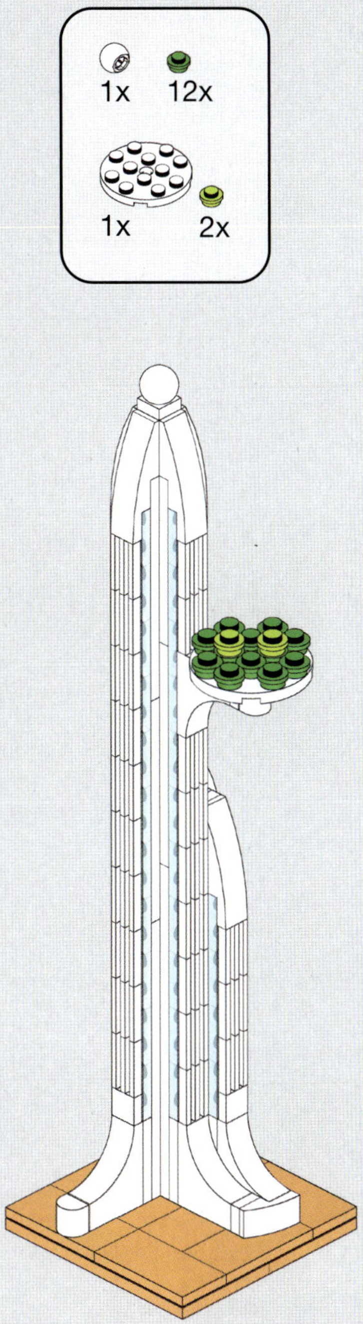

MAKE IT YOUR OWN

The Solstice Spire's cantilevered platform can serve as a landing pad or a rotating observation deck. You can also keep it as a garden and vary the plant life.

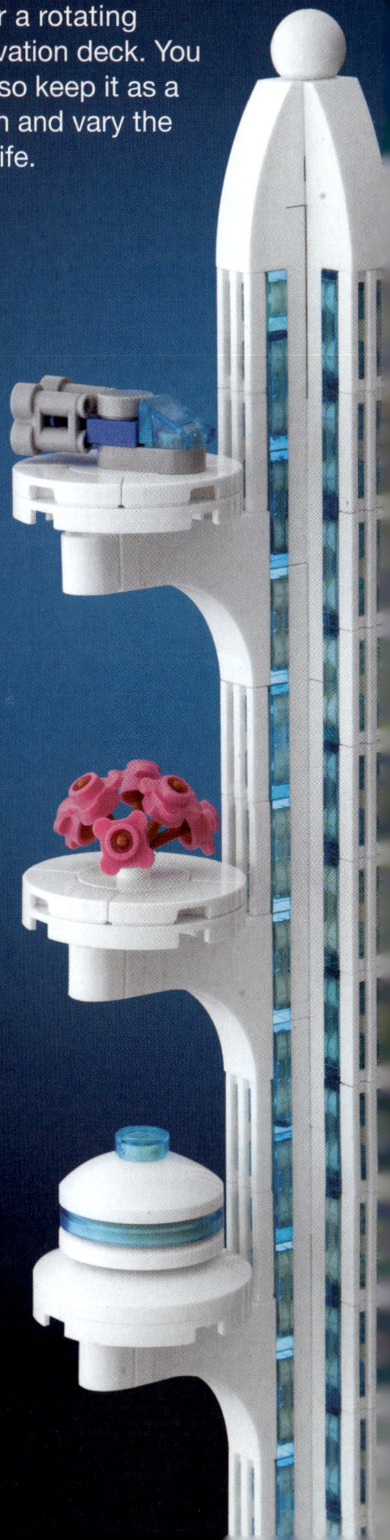

CLOUD GARDEN

Cloud Garden is a serene solarpunk skyscraper featuring a circular rooftop garden arranged around a sphere-shaped water reservoir. Its orb-like presence gives the building a sense of balance, as if the entire garden orbits a core of calm.

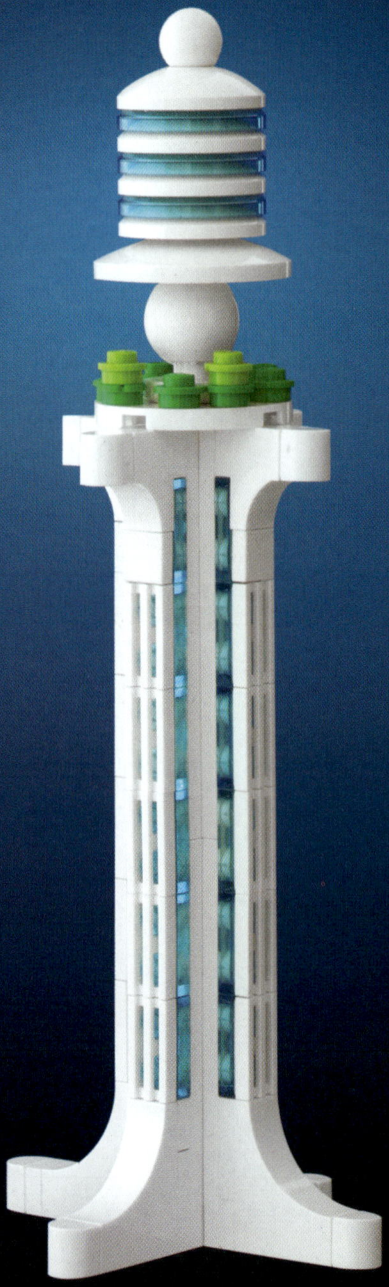

20x 3024	**4x** 3070	**9x** 4073	**4x** 4073		
4x 78666	**8x** 4733	**24x** 3023	**20x** 2412b	**1x** 32474	**8x** 49307
4x 43898	**3x** 43898	**1x** 20953	**4x** 3623	**1x** 18674	
8x 3460	**4x** 18653	**1x** 60474	**1x** 3960		

1

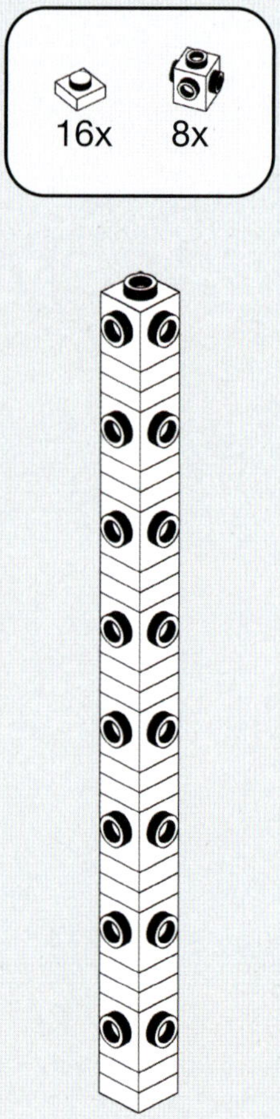

2

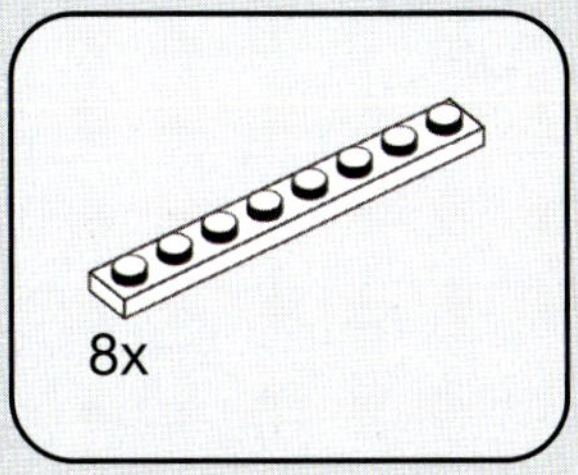

All four sides are identical.

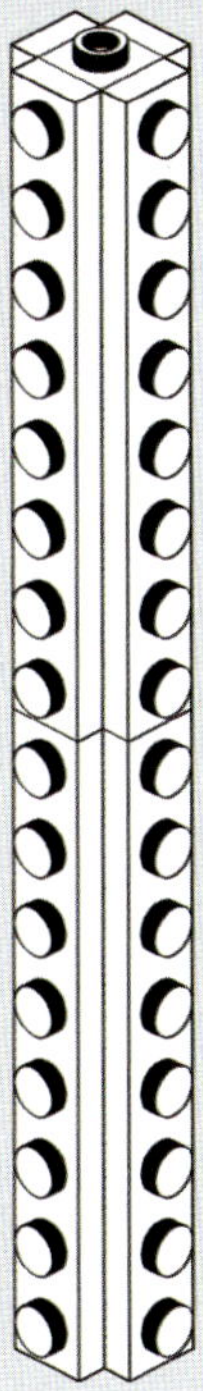

3

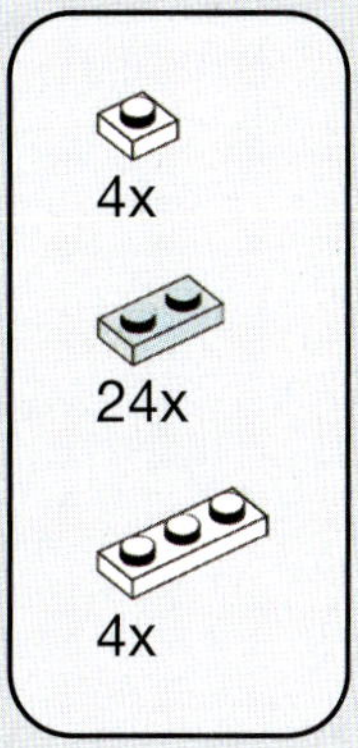

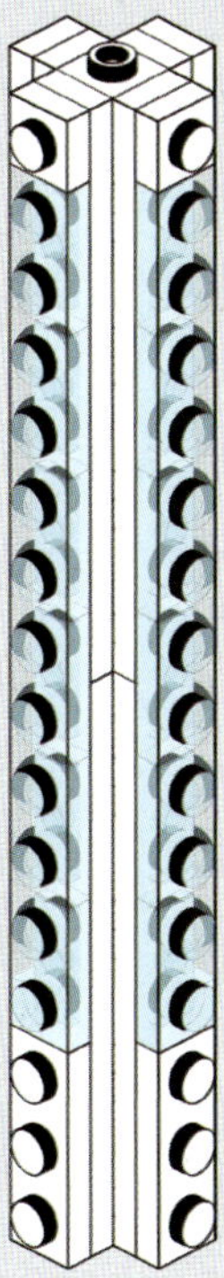

4

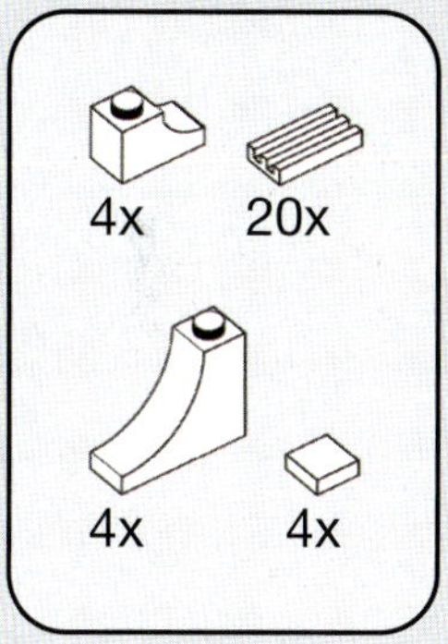

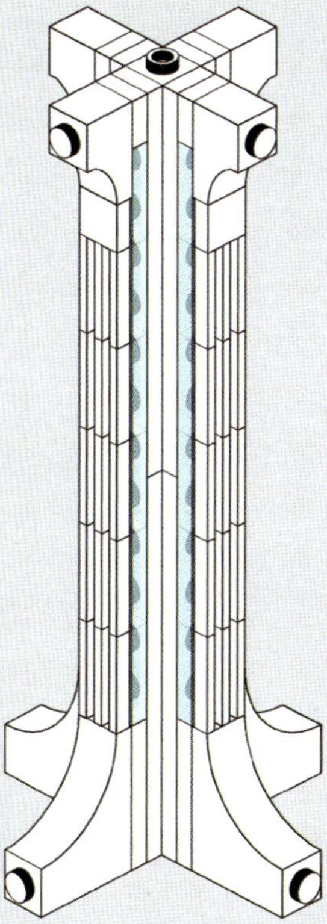

5

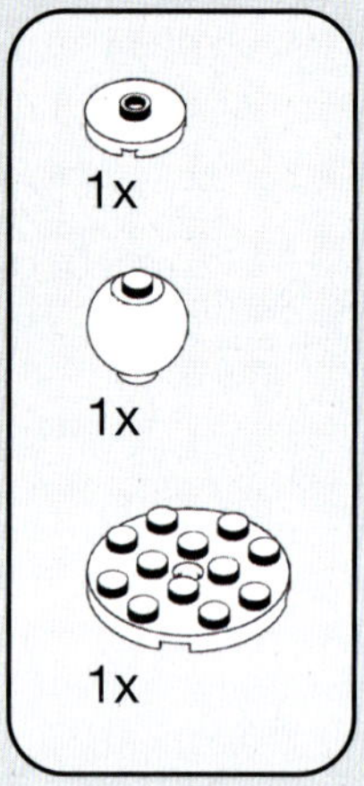

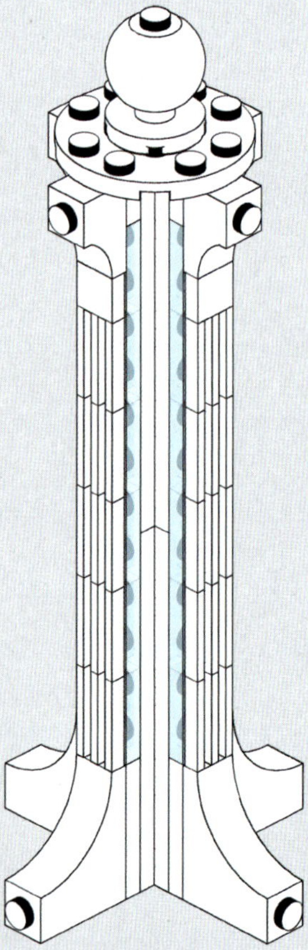

6

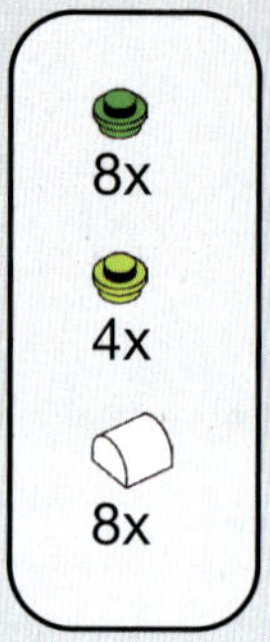

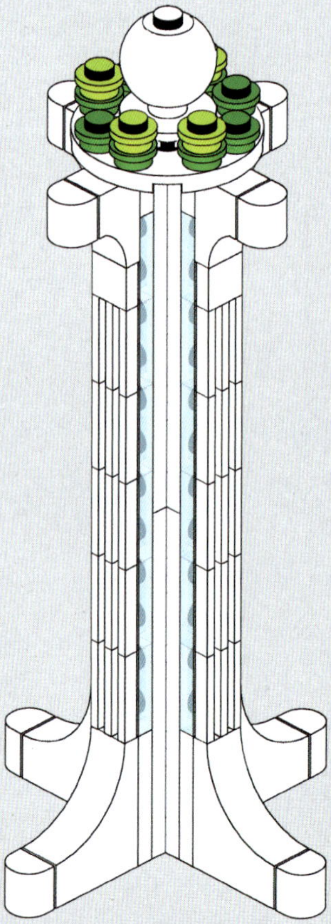

7

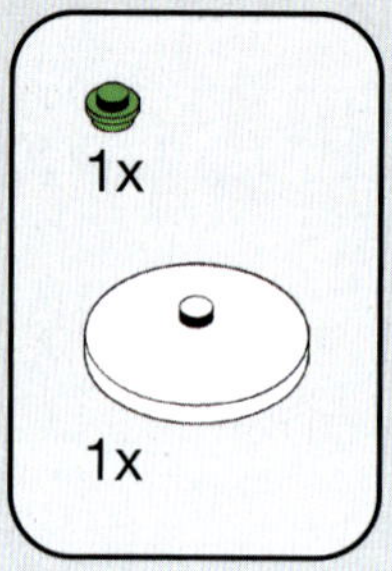

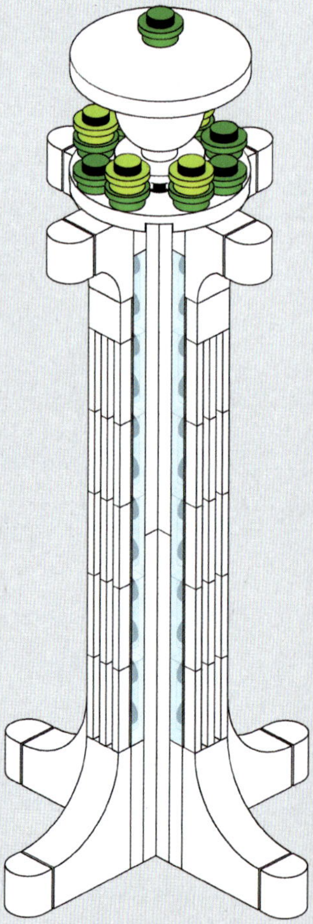

8

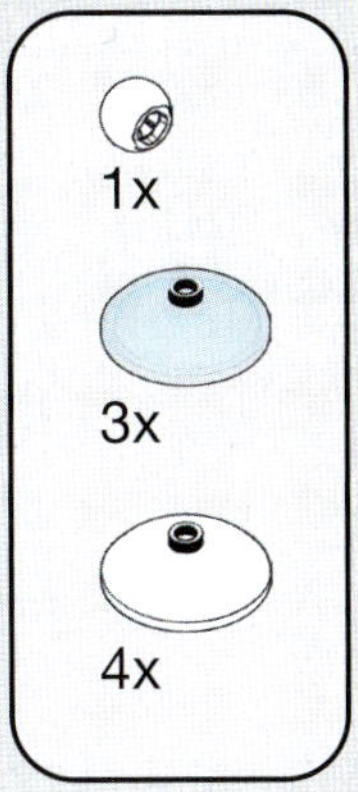

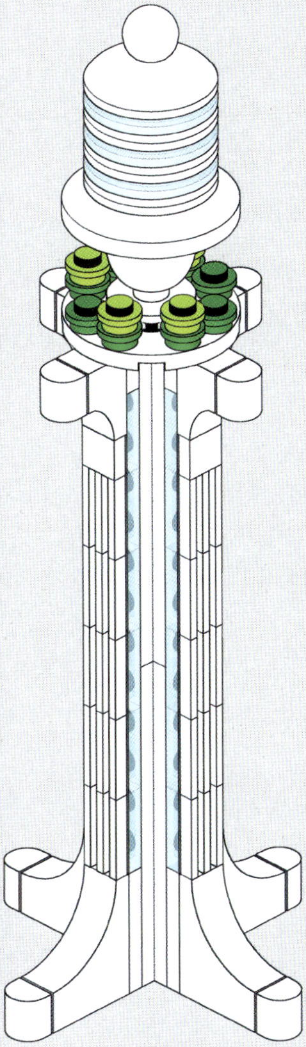

GONDOLA

A gondola offers an eco-friendly and scenic way to travel between neighborhoods.

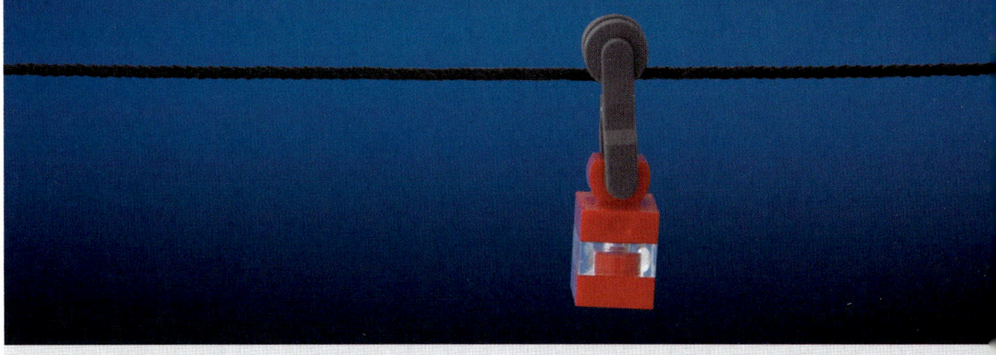

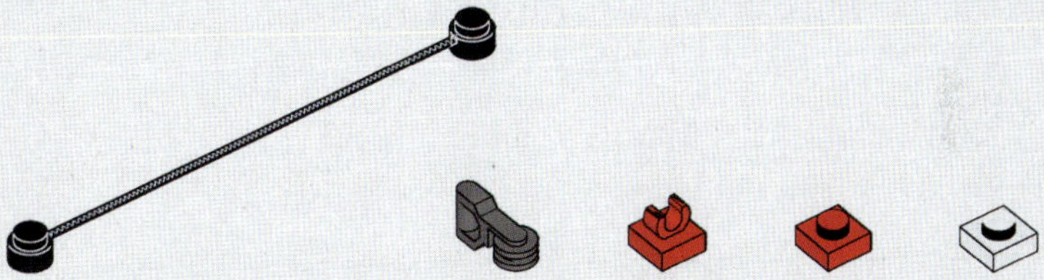

1x x127c20pb01 **1x** 30229 **1x** 15712 **1x** 3024 **1x** 3024

String elements, though uncommon, are available in several lengths.

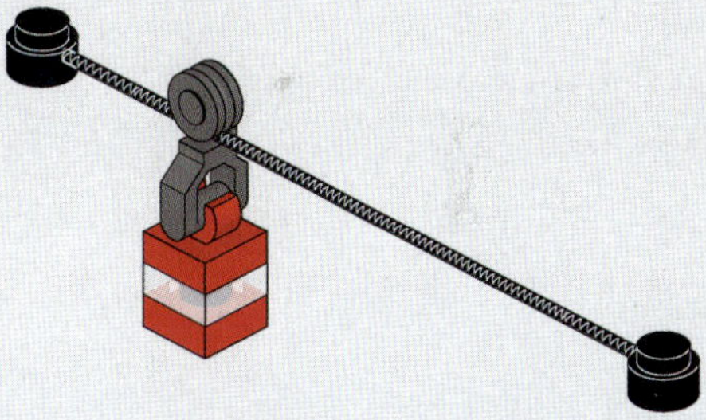

It's good practice to sandwich the string element's studs between two bricks to hold it securely in place.

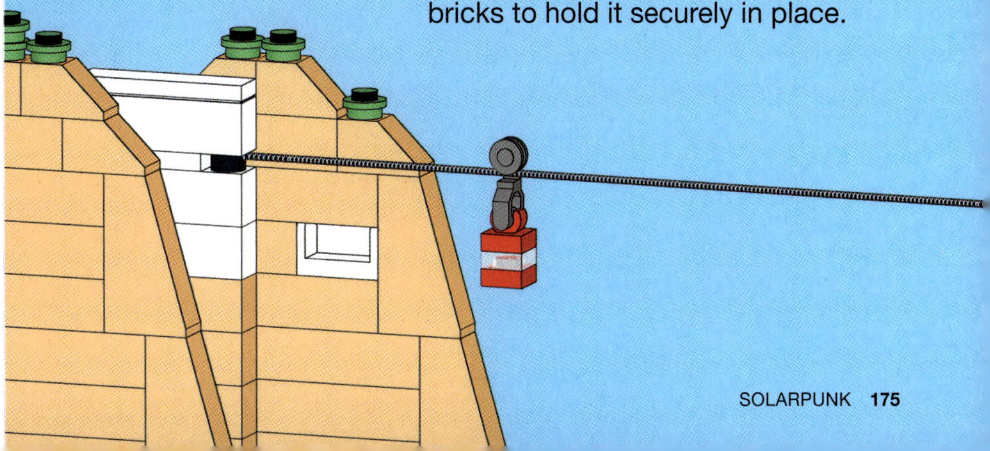

CYBERPUNK

Cyberpunk is a vision of the near future where advanced technology and urban decay collide. Corporations control this world, and digital advertisements flood the cityscape in a hailstorm of pixels.

Cyberpunk architecture is full of jarring contrasts: Gleaming skyscrapers loom over cramped streets tangled with makeshift structures. Concrete apartment blocks resemble massive wartime bunkers. Though oppressive, these worlds have lots of atmosphere and storytelling potential.

Translating cyberpunk into LEGO means embracing complexity and chaotic design. It's not a clean style, which can be liberating. You don't have to over-plan, as cyberpunk worlds themselves are a city-planning free-for-all. Experiment with printed tiles to capture the omnipresent advertisements.

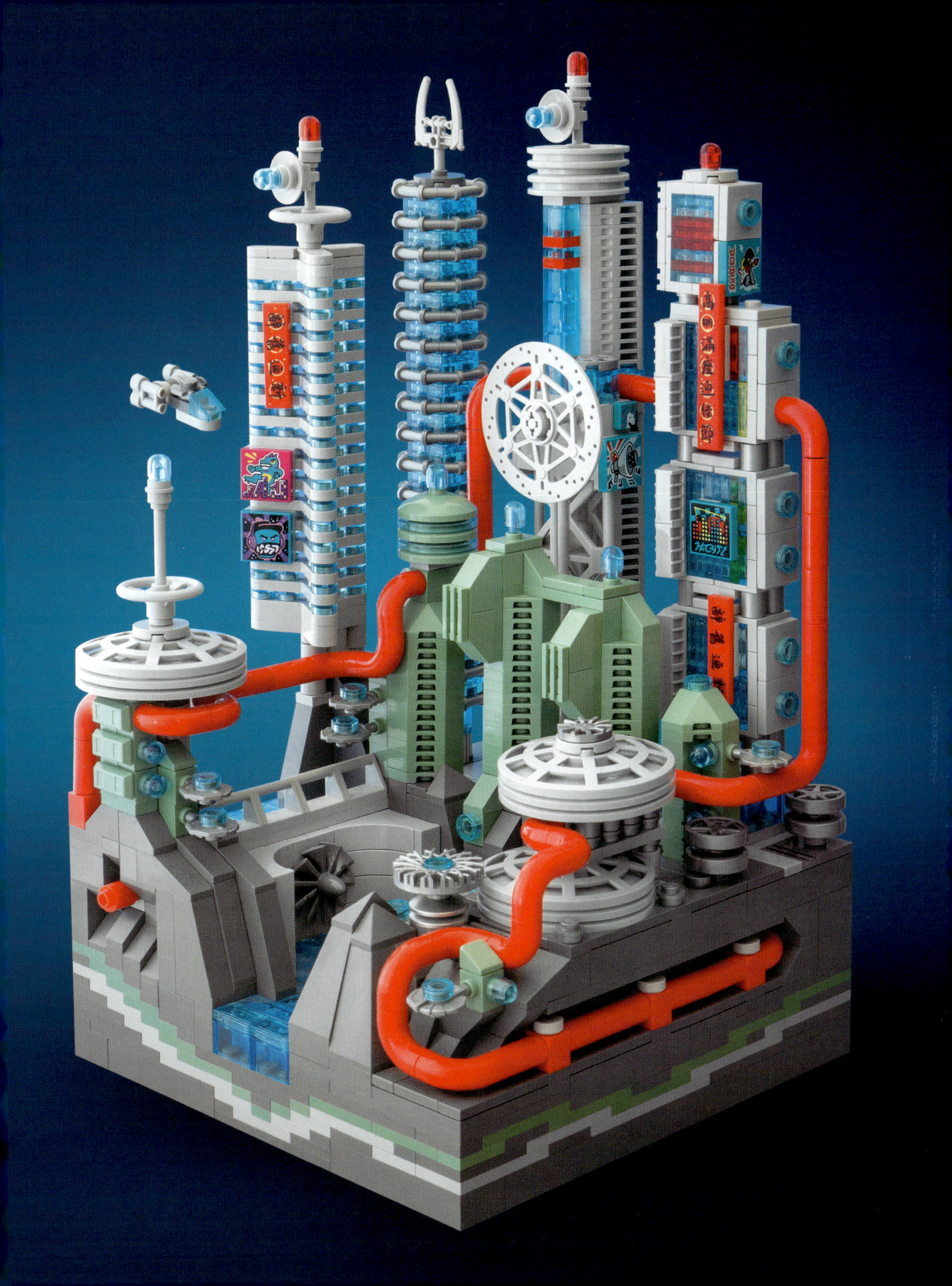

DATABUNKER

Brutalism is an architectural style defined by massive geometric forms, concrete construction, and an emphasis on functionality over ornamentation.

The Databunker is a towering Brutalist apartment megablock. Its concrete walls and bulky lines reflect a utilitarian design built to withstand acid rain, data jamming, and the general anarchy of a world on edge.

The elevators almost never work, so it's great for residents' health. They get plenty of exercise running from glitching androids in the stairwells.

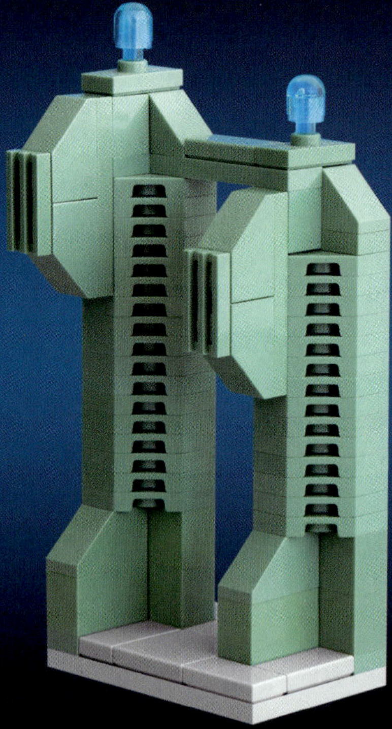

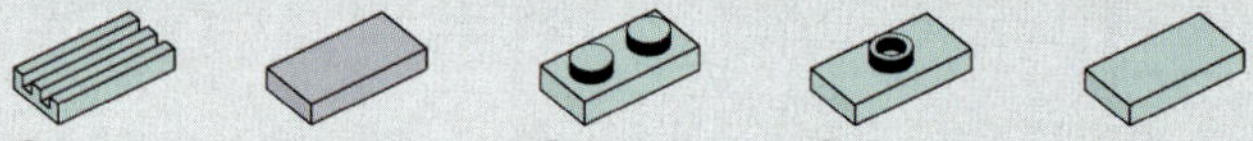

2x 2412b **4x** 3069 **6x** 3023 **2x** 15573 **1x** 3069

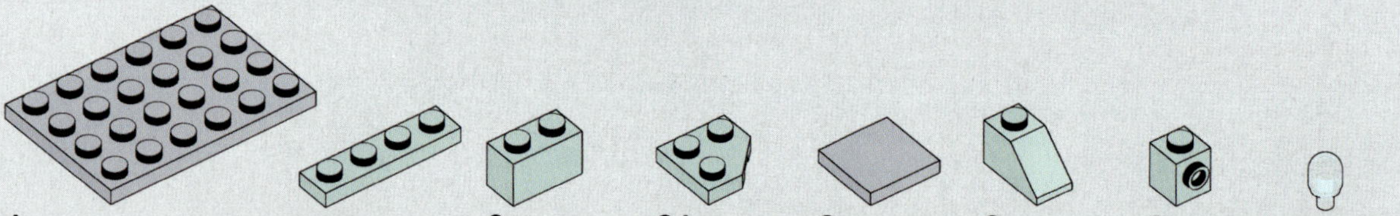

1x 3032 **3x** 3710 **6x** 3004 **31x** 26601 **2x** 3068 **8x** 3040 **2x** 87087 **2x** 58176

1

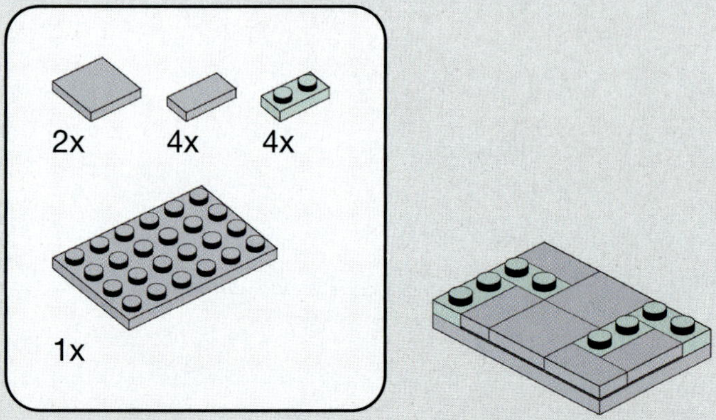

2

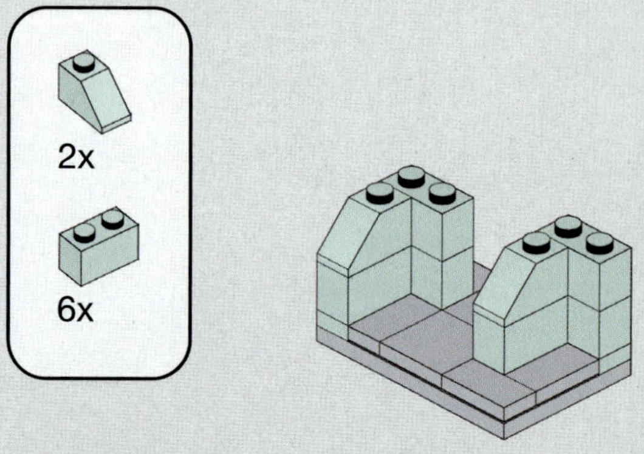

3

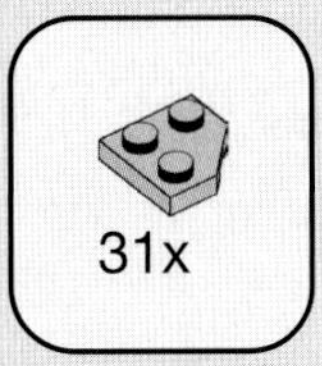

The left stack has 17 plates, and the right stack has 14 plates.

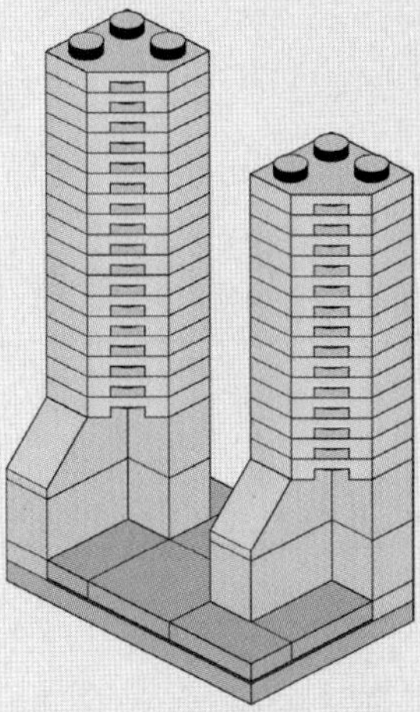

4

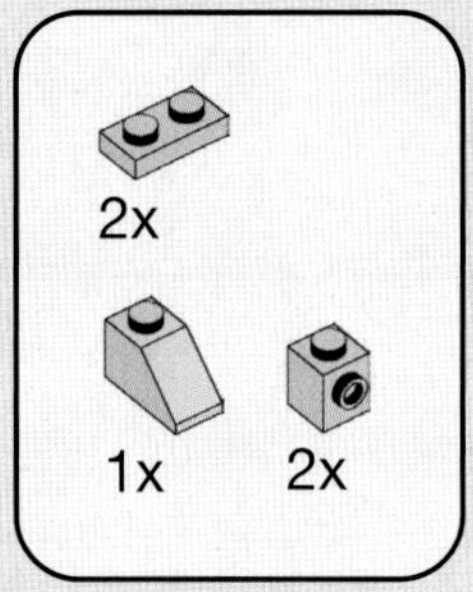

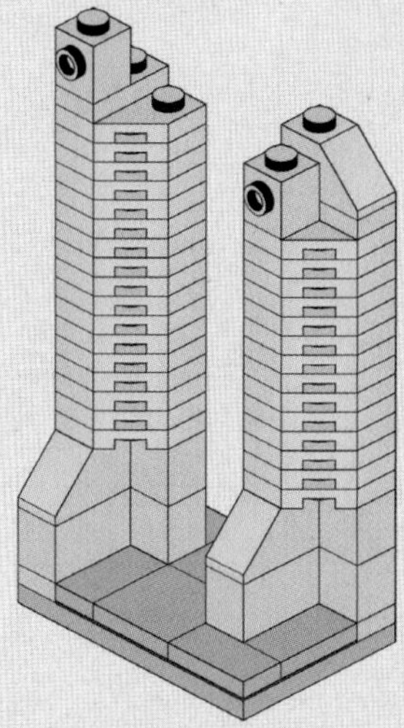

5

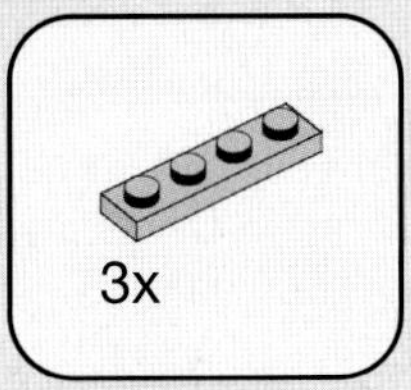

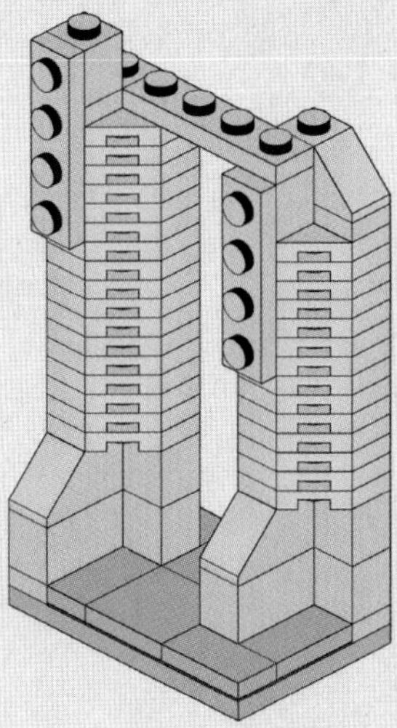

6

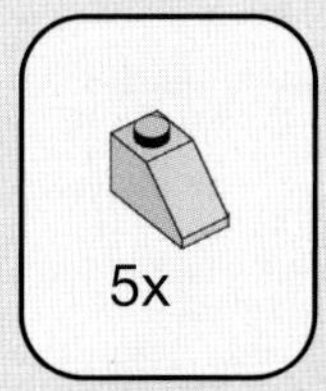

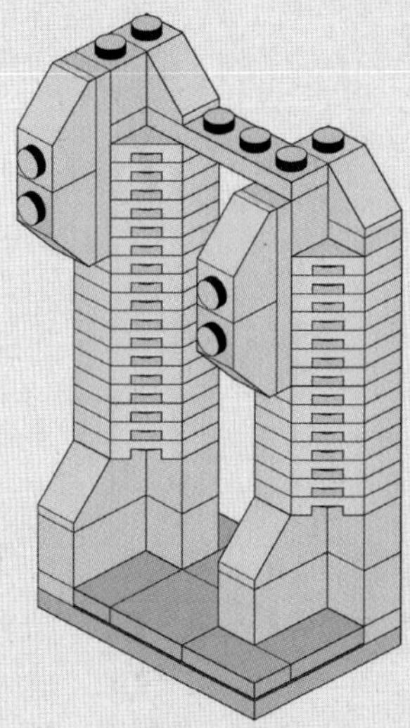

7

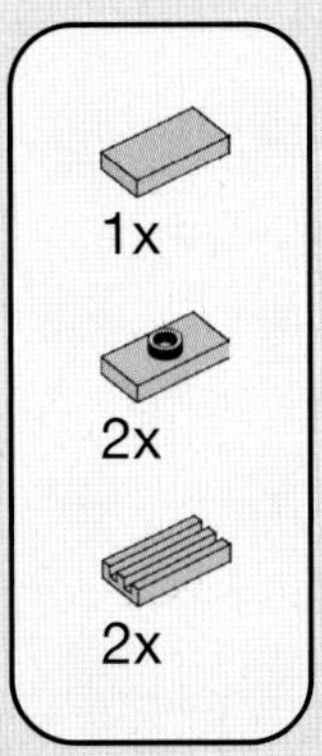

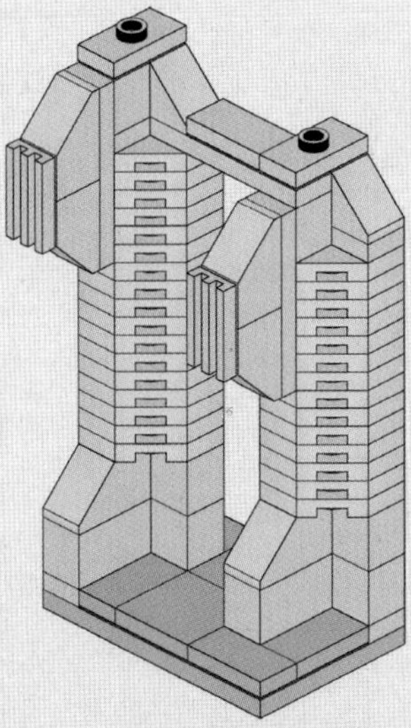

8

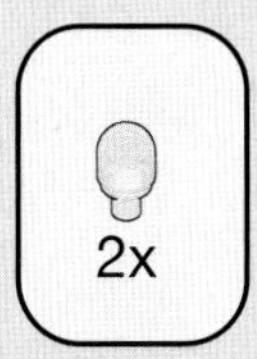

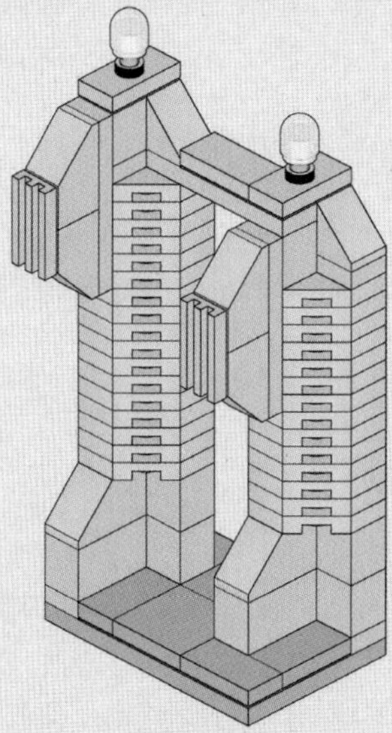

GLITCHTOWER

The Glitchtower is a vertical cyberware market covered in screens to attract the short attention spans of a society overloaded with information.

You'll notice that the printed tiles seen in the chapter's opening image have been replaced with plain ones in these building instructions. It's not a glitch, it's a feature.

LEGO offers an ever-growing selection of printed tiles. Which ones you use to decorate your Glitchtower depends on your parts inventory and your taste. This model provides the framework. You can keep it relatively calm by using the plain tiles shown here or bring the data flood with printed tiles.

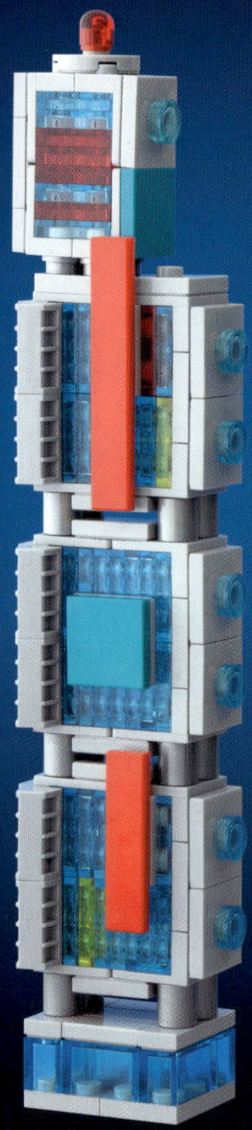

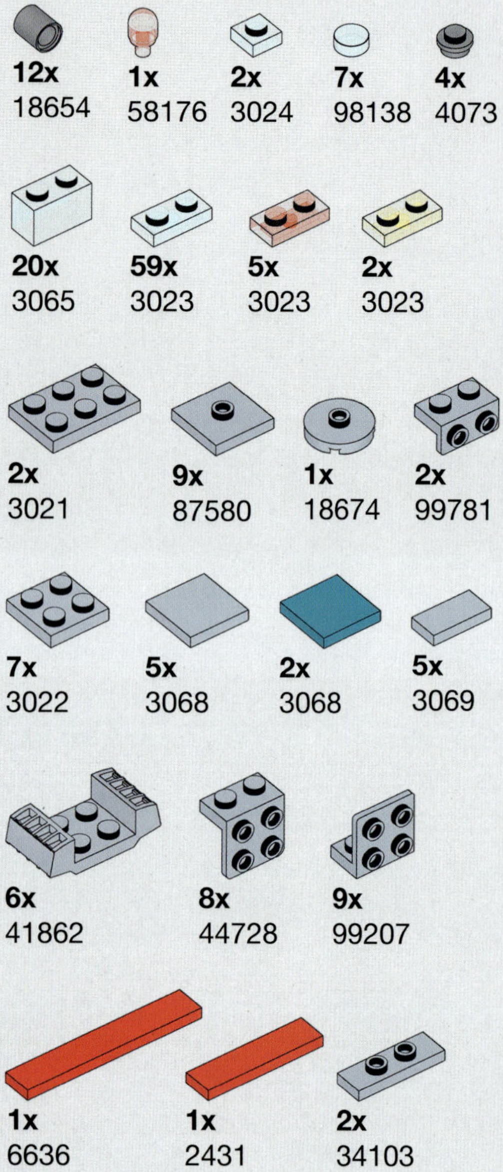

1

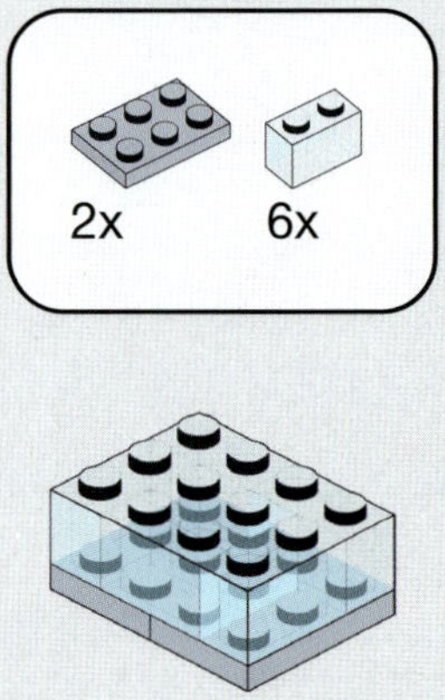

2

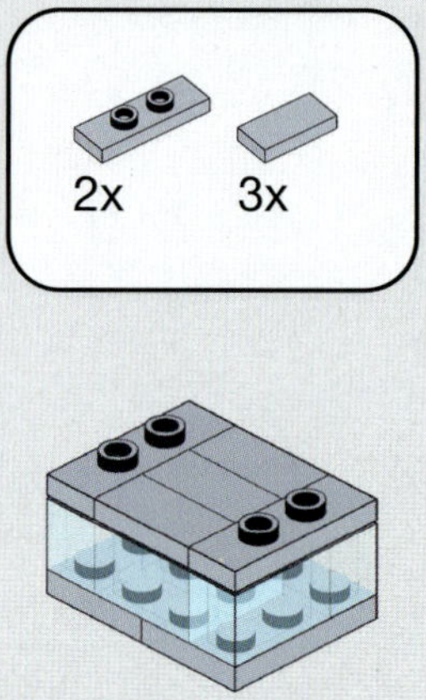

3

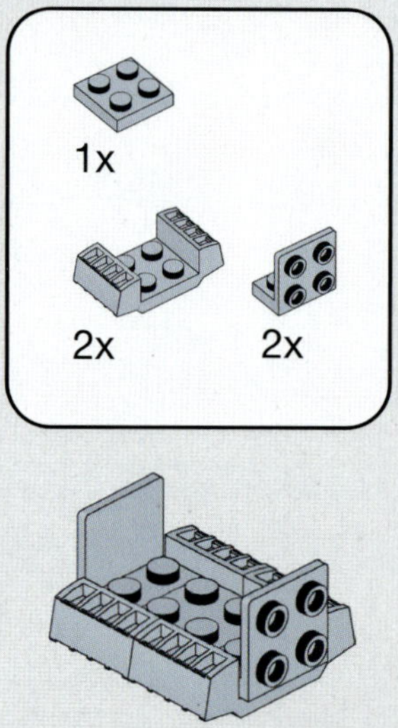

4

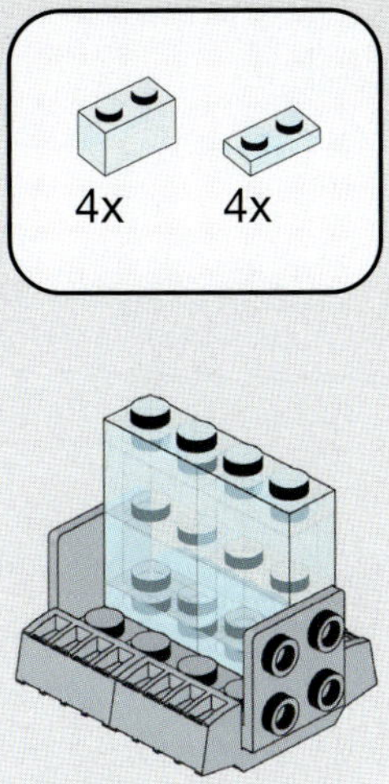

5

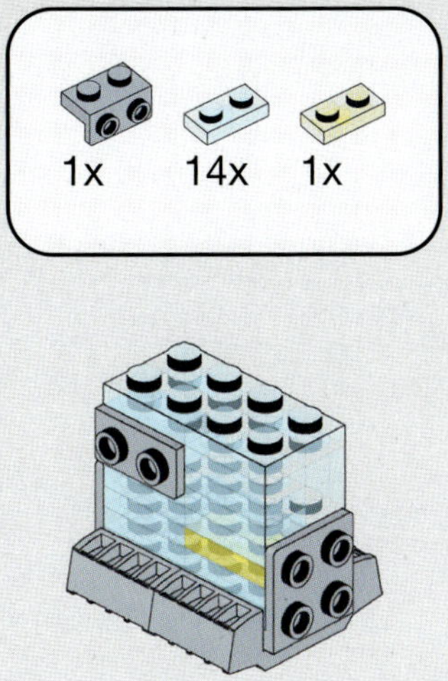

6

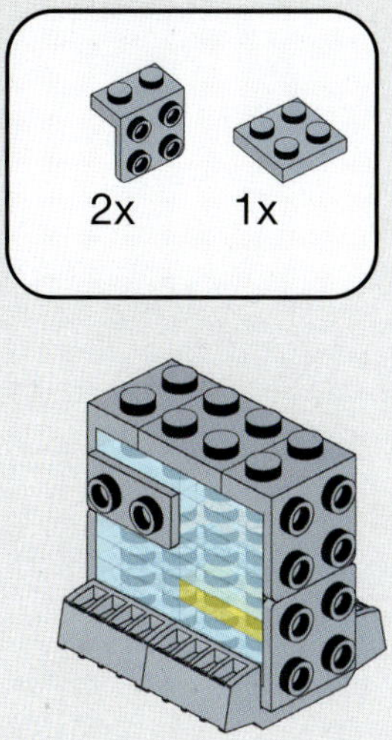

7

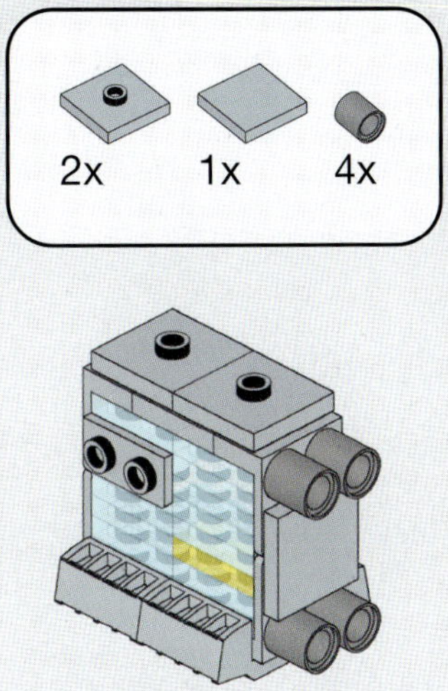

8

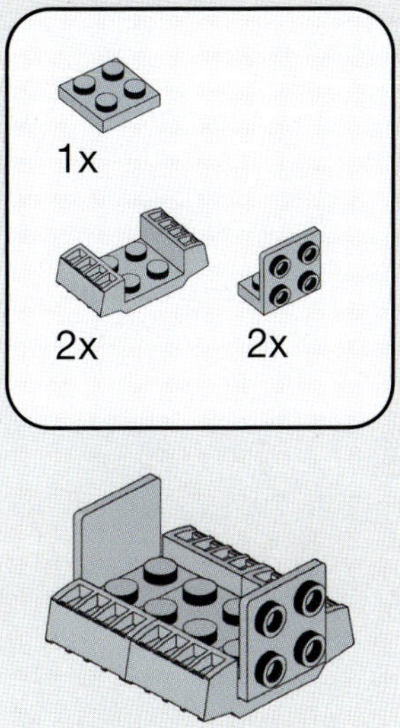

9

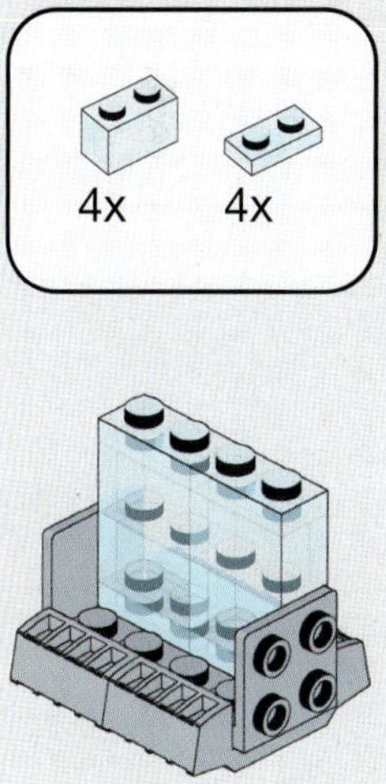

10

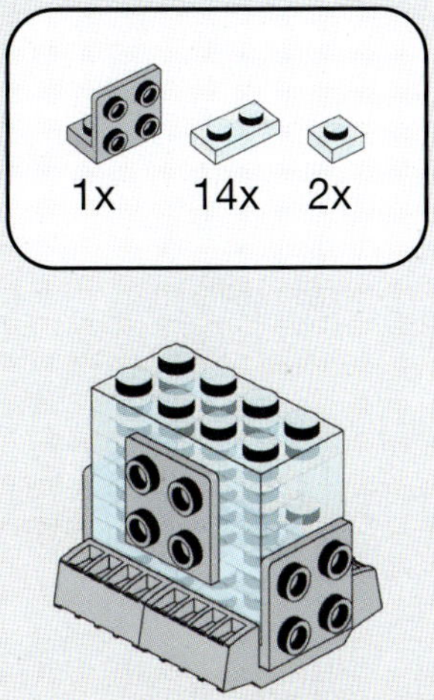

11

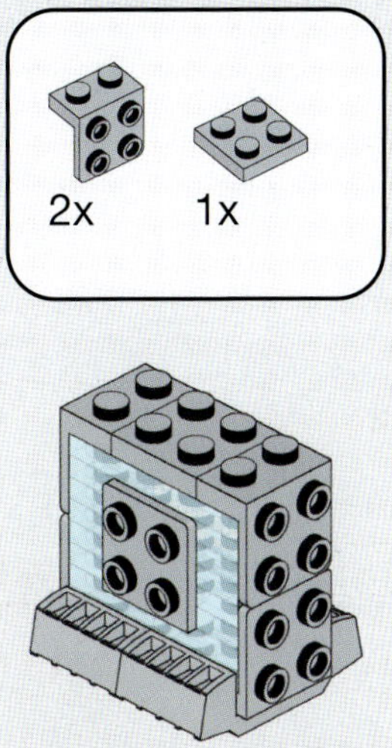

12

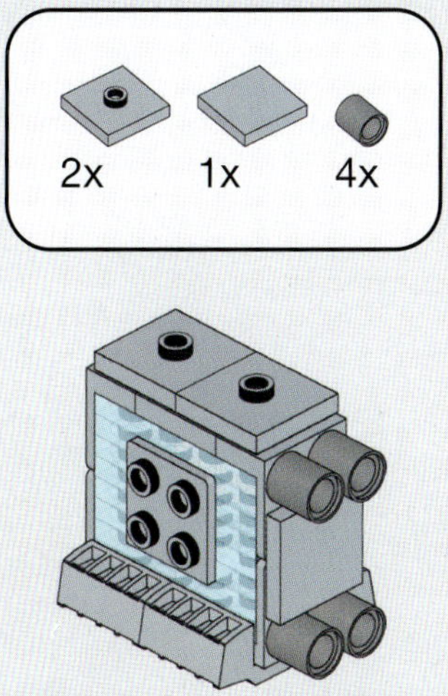

13

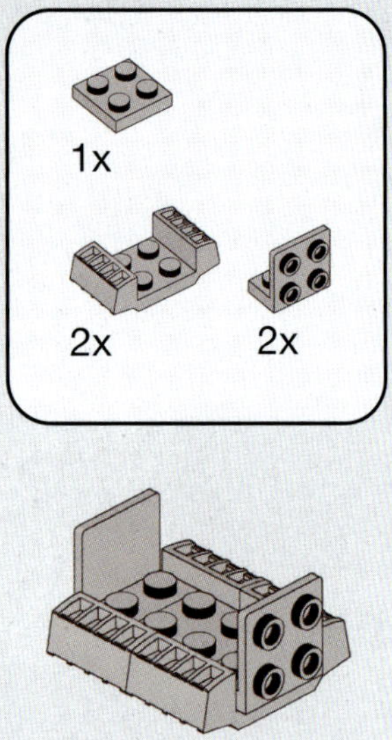

14

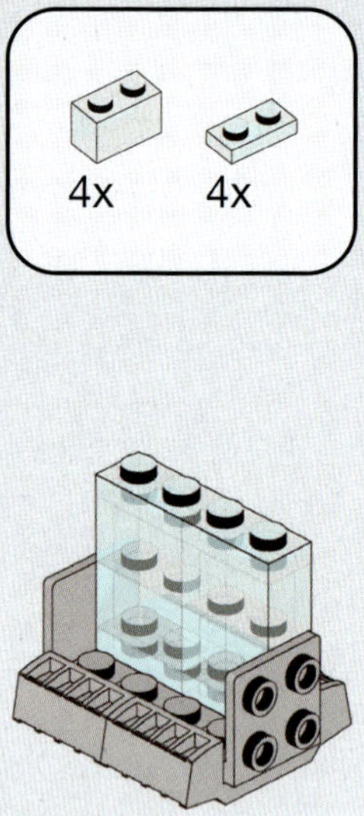

15

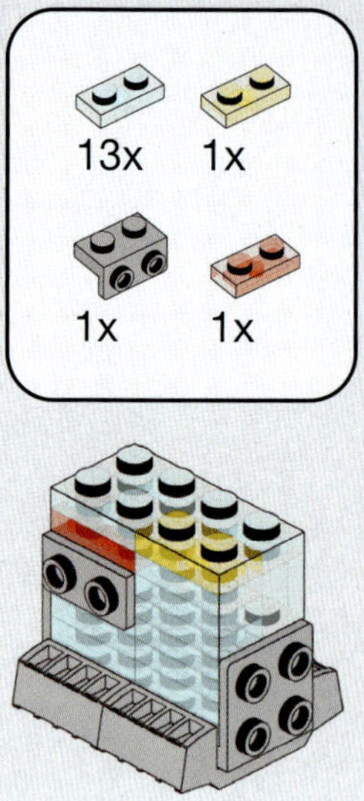

16

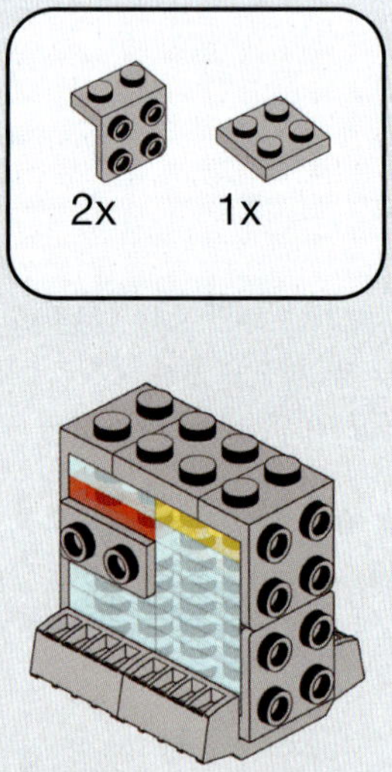

17

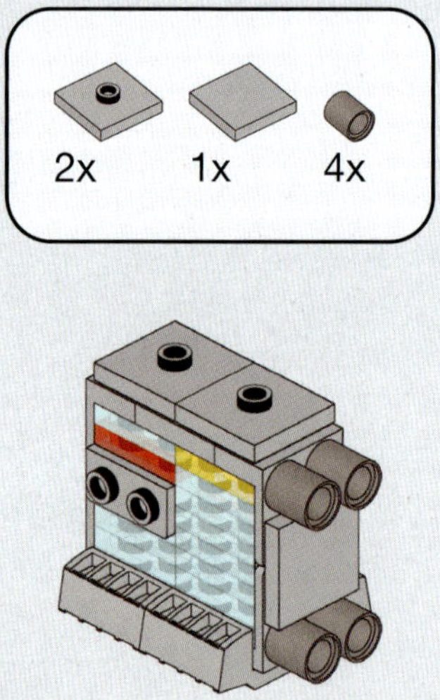

18

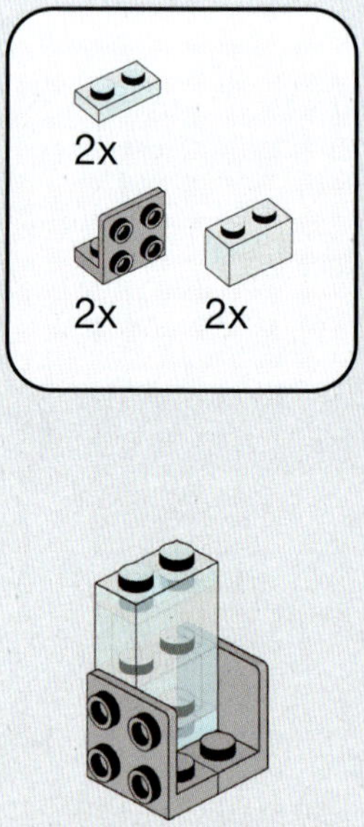

19

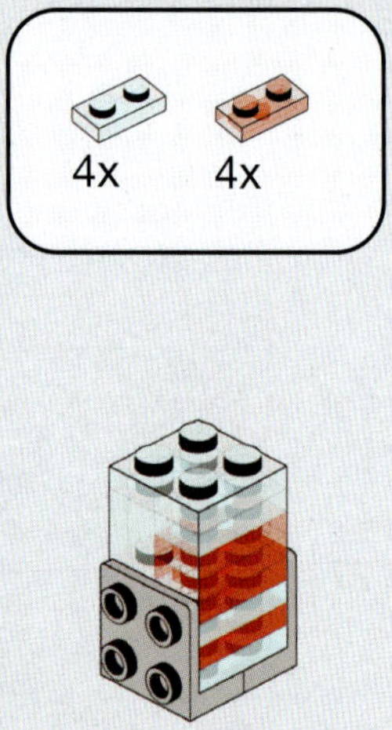

20

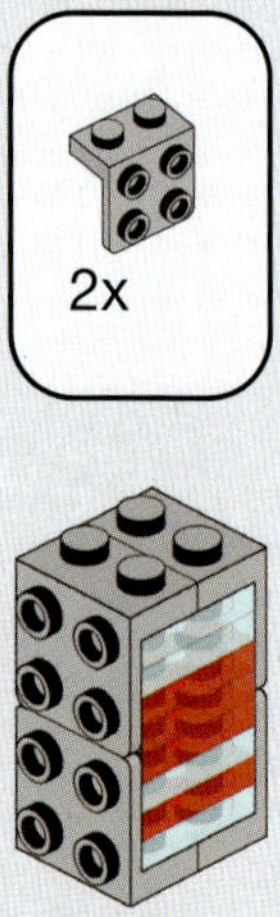

21

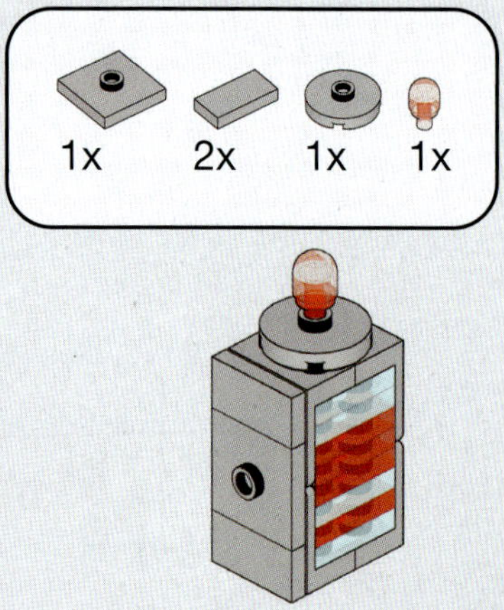

22

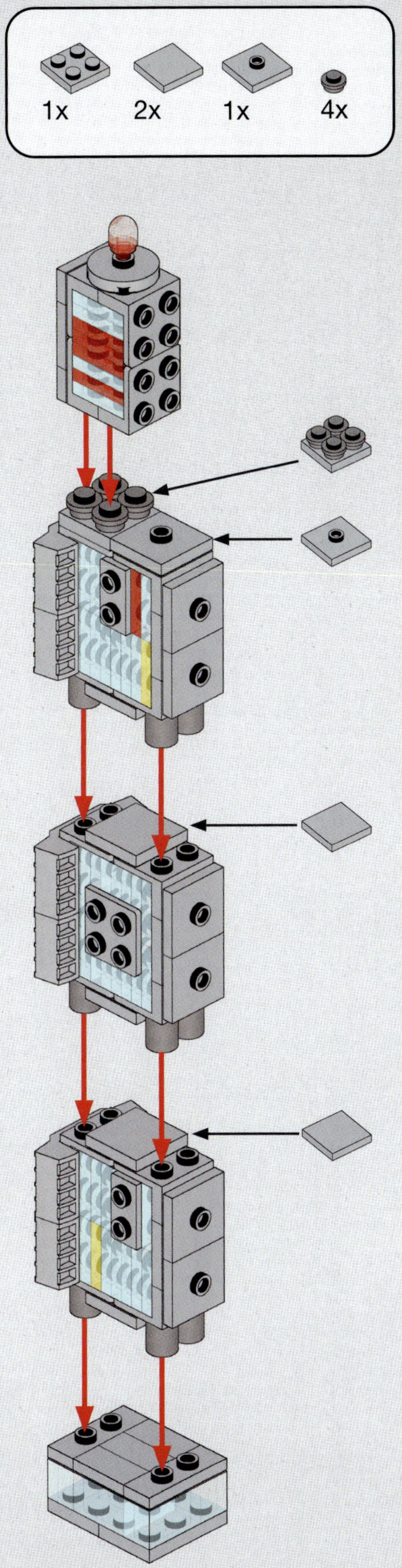

23

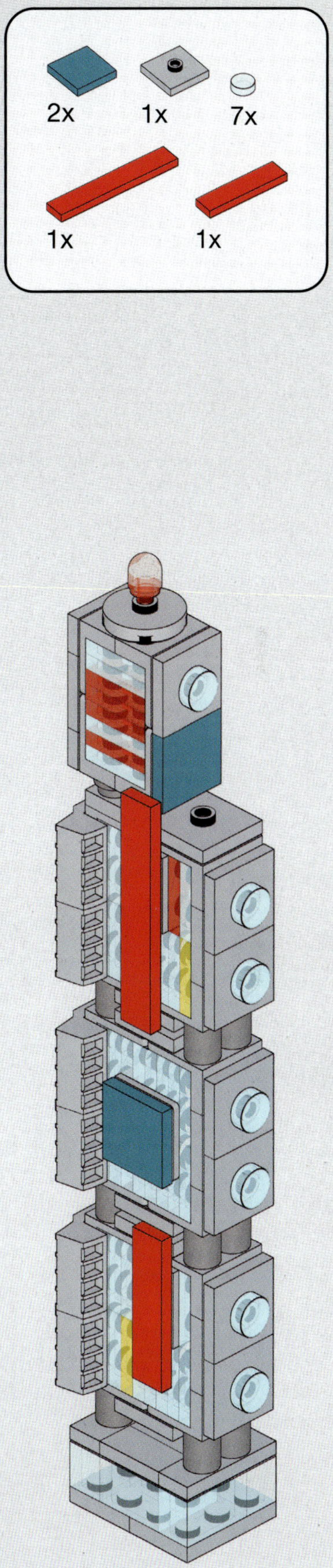

MAKE IT YOUR OWN

Not only can you replace the blank tiles with printed ones, but you can also swap out the 2×2 jumper plates or use 1×1 printed tiles in place of the round tiles used for windows, like the unicorn tile featured in the model on the immediate right.

A great source for printed tiles that work well in cyberpunk worlds is the collection of BeatBits from LEGO's Vidiyo line. Designed to resemble album covers, BeatBits add visual noise and color. Although the line is discontinued, the tiles are still widely available on BrickLink at reasonable prices.

You can also forgo tiles altogether and customize the building's three modules, as shown in the model on the far right. It features minifigure circular saws (#50018g) used as cantilevered apartments near the top and connects to a tube transportation network made with elbow macaroni bricks (#71076).

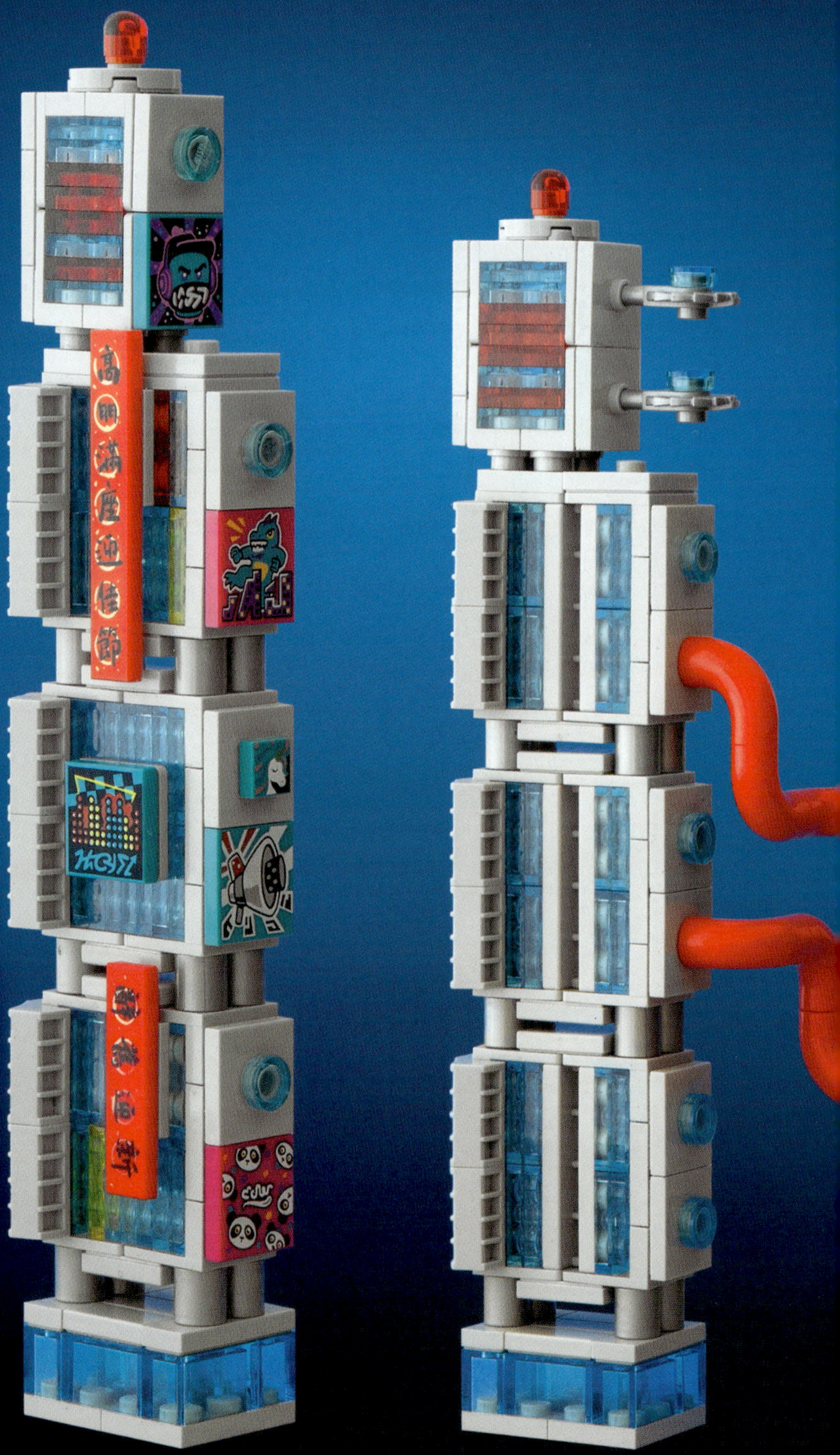

SIGNAL HALO

Stray signals flicker from the Signal Halo's abandoned concrete crown, though no one claims to control them. An armored glass elevator adds a touch of polish to the otherwise brutal exterior.

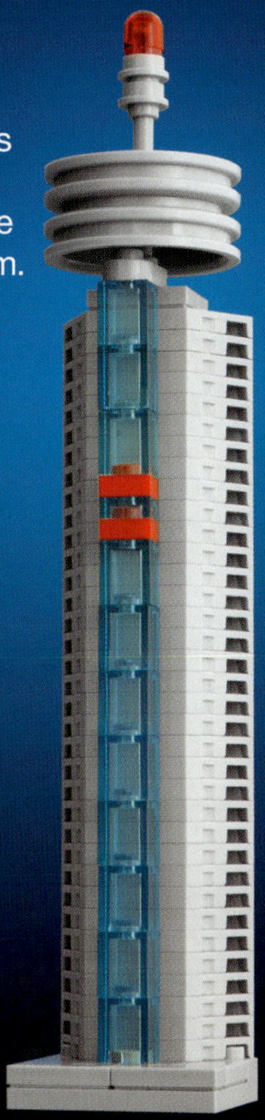

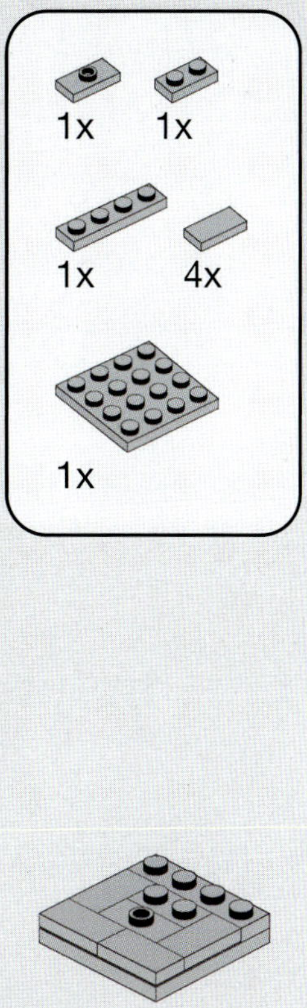

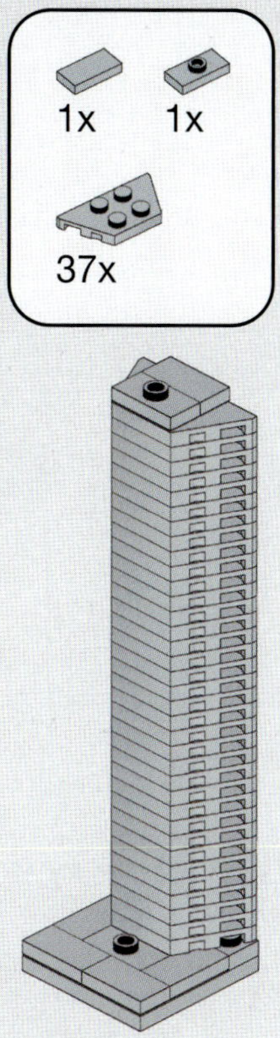

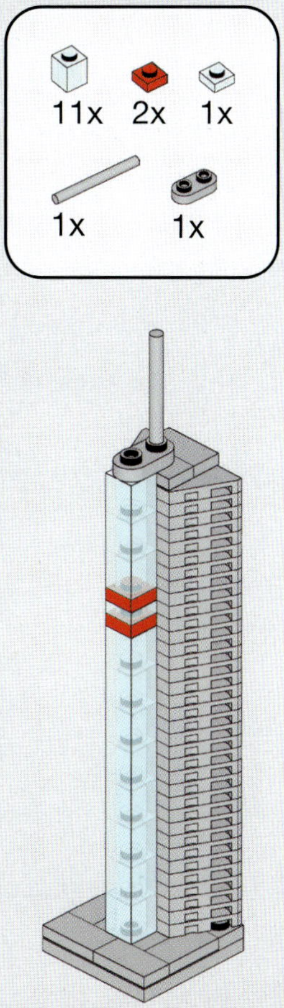

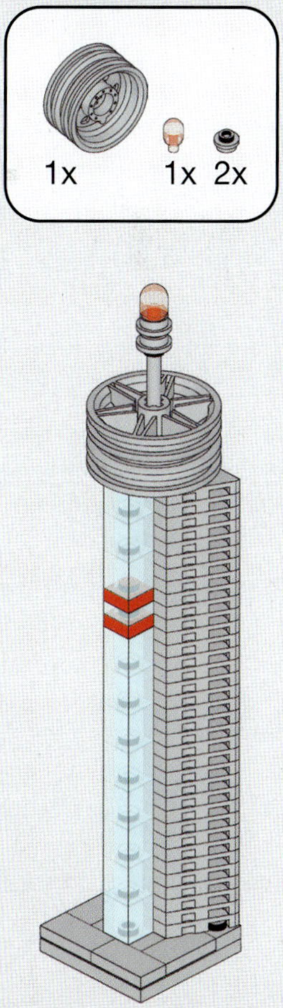

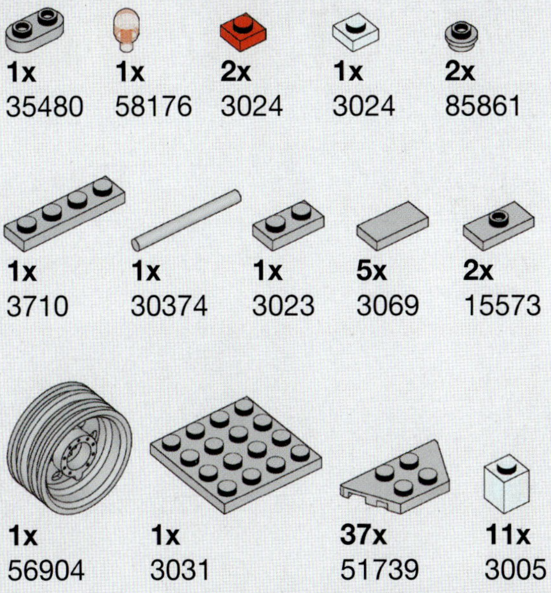

DATAFORGE DAM

This hydroelectric facility helps feed the insatiable power appetite of a cyberpunk city. It's currently locked in a quiet war against a rogue AI trying to take control of its systems.

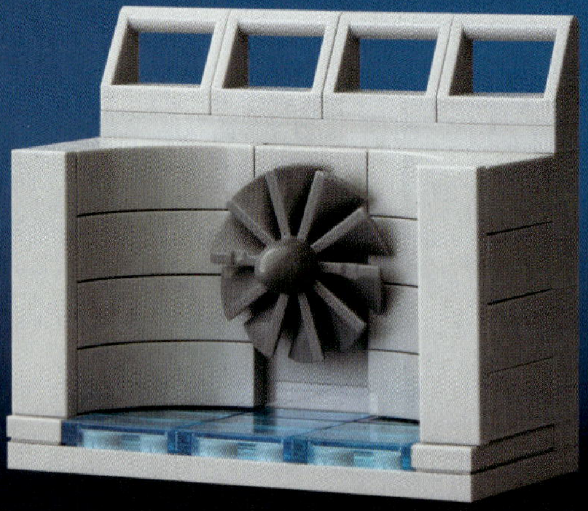

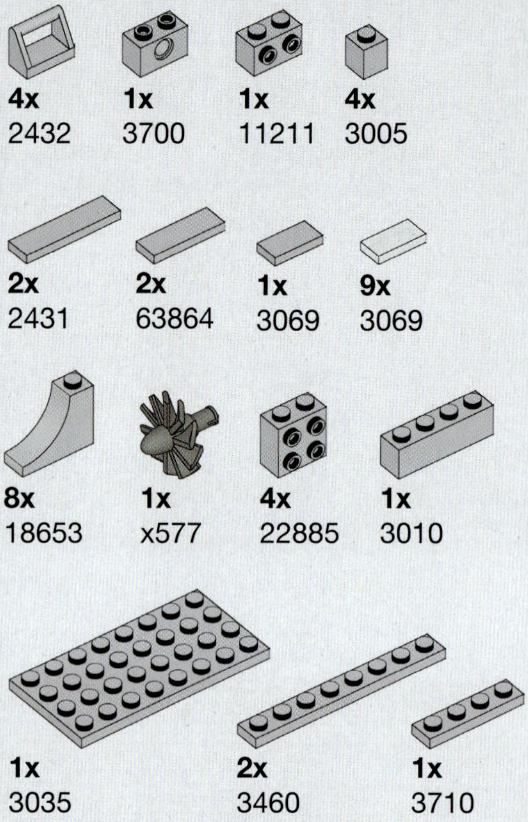

1

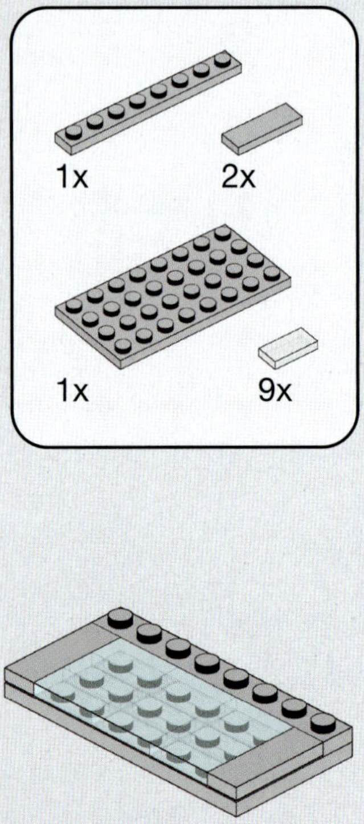

2

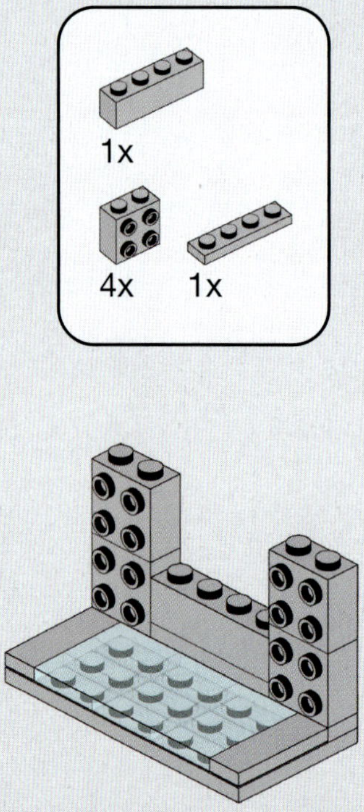

3

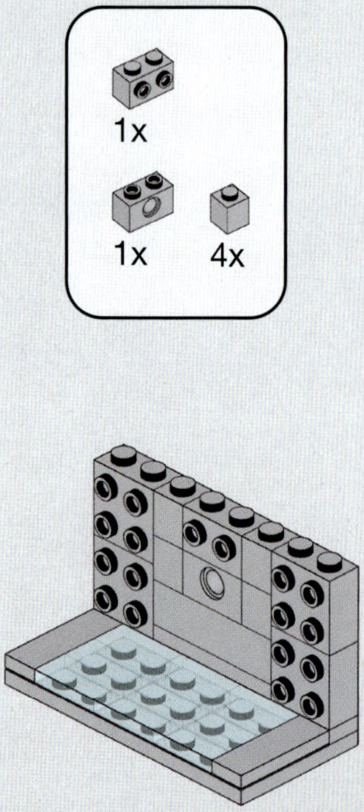

4

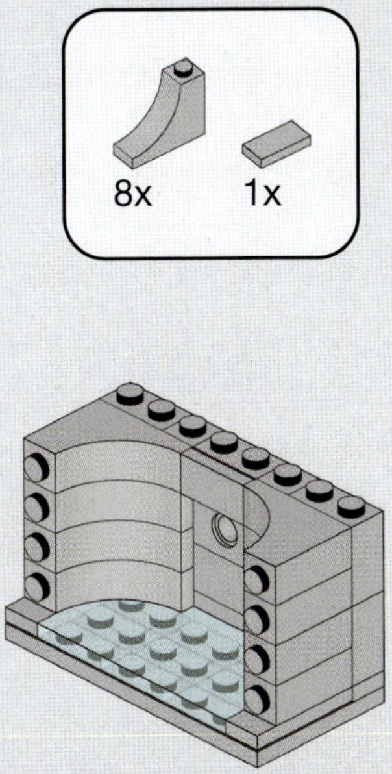

5

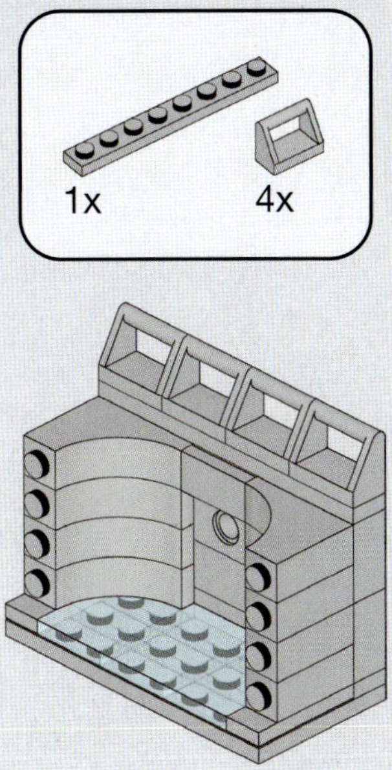

6

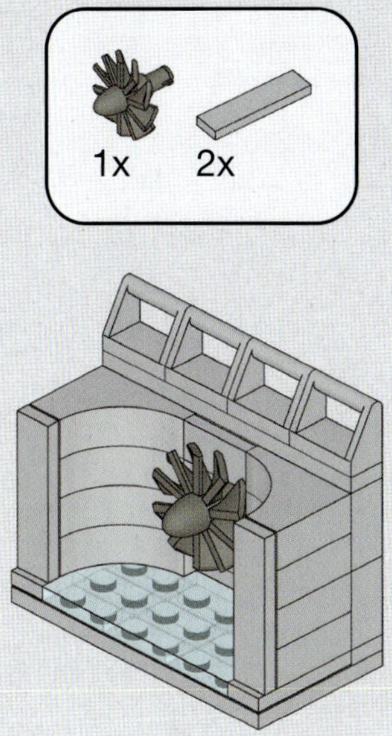

CRYSTAL CORE

The Crystal Core, a tower reserved for the corporate elite, rises like a shard of frozen light. Its residents enjoy floor-to-ceiling views of the chaotic streets below.

You can replace the antenna with a bar element, which is easier to find.

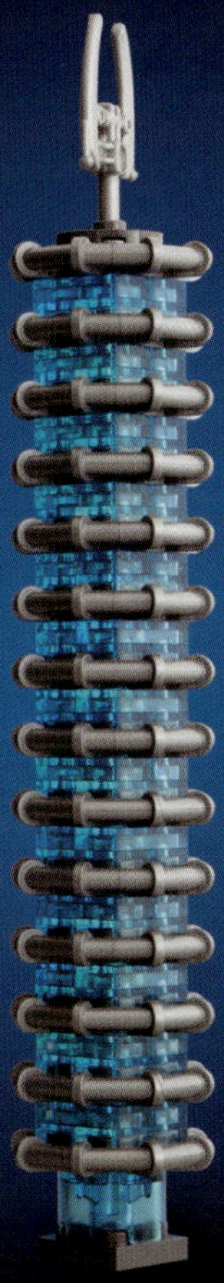

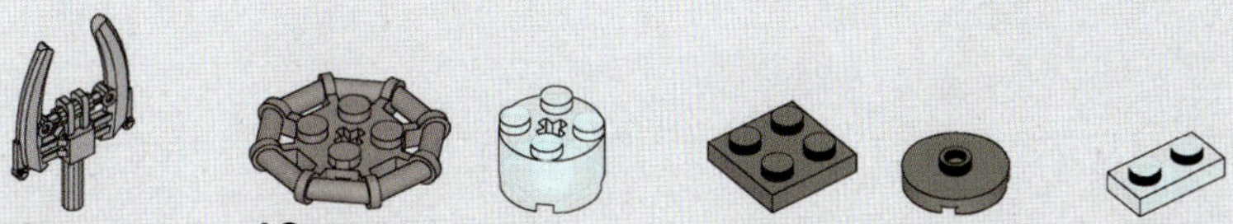

1x	**12x**	**1x**	**1x**	**1x**	**48x**
55237k	30033	3941	3022	18674	3023

1

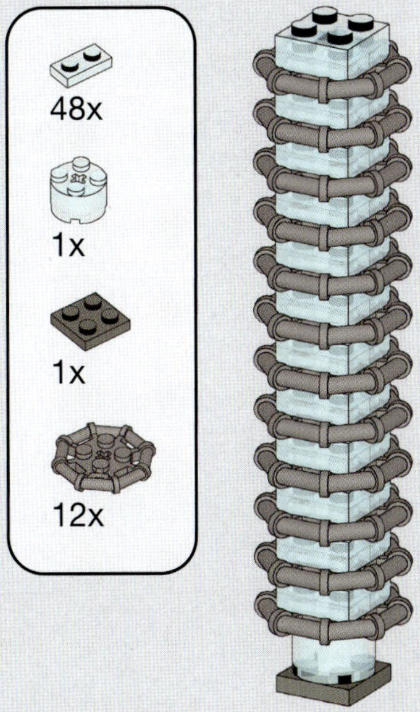

2

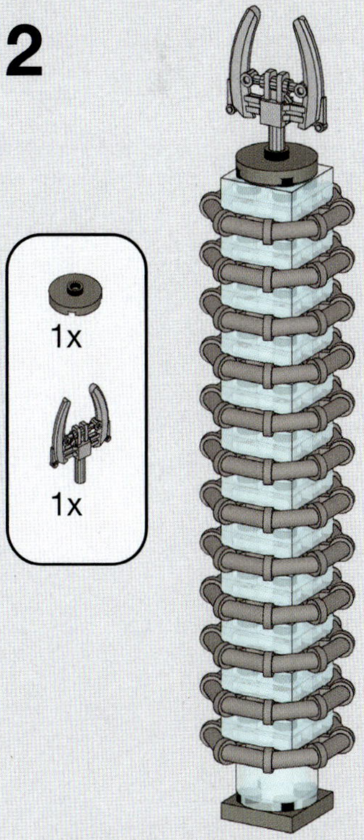

Printed in China

First printing

30 29 28 27 26   1 2 3 4 5

ISBN-13: 978-1-7185-0484-4 (print)
ISBN-13: 978-1-7185-0485-1 (ebook)

Published by No Starch Press®, Inc.
245 8th Street, San Francisco, CA 94103
phone: +1.415.863.9900
www.nostarch.com; info@nostarch.com

Publisher: William Pollock
Managing Editor: Jill Franklin
Production Manager: Sabrina Plomitallo-González
Production Editor: Sydney Cromwell
Developmental Editors: Nathan Heidelberger and Jill Franklin
Compositor: Jeff Friesen
Copyeditor: Tessa Carvalho
Proofreader: Michele Kessel

Library of Congress Control Number: 2025951235

For customer service inquiries, please contact info@nostarch.com. For information on distribution, bulk sales, corporate sales, or translations: sales@nostarch.com. For permission to translate this work: rights@nostarch.com. To report counterfeit copies or piracy: counterfeit@nostarch.com. The authorized representative in the EU for product safety and compliance is EU Compliance Partner, Pärnu mnt. 139b-14, 11317 Tallinn, Estonia, hello@eucompliancepartner.com, +3375690241.

[DC]

Building LEGO® Worlds is set in Helvetica Neue and Futura PT.

RESOURCES

Visit *https://nostarch.com/building-lego-worlds* for errata and more information.

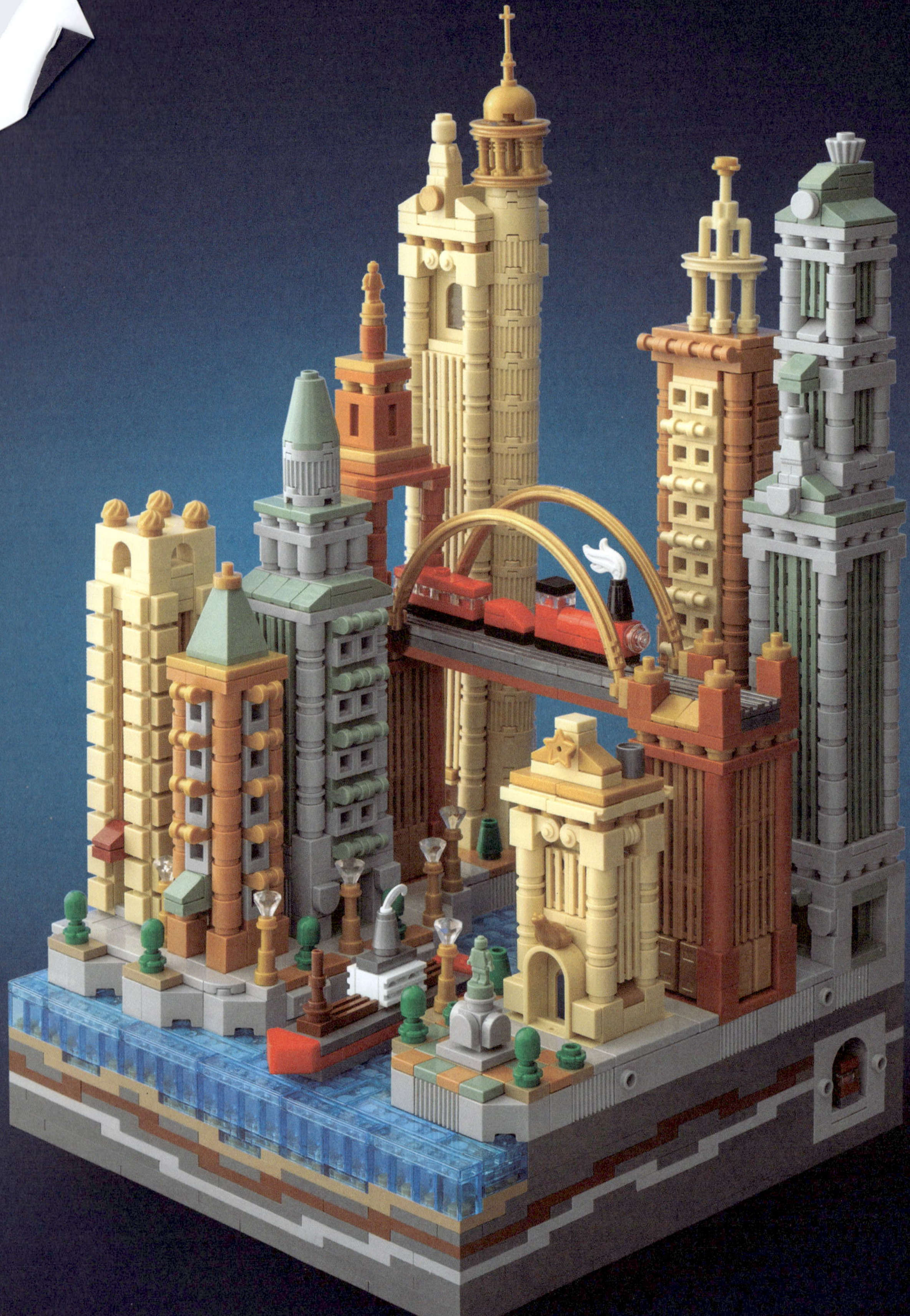